D0184136

International Human Resource Management

3rd Edition

Chris Brewster, Paul Sparrow, Guy Vernon and Elizabeth Houldsworth

Chris Brewster is Professor of International HRM at Henley Business School, University of Reading.

Paul Sparrow is Director of the Centre for Performance-Led HR and Professor of International HRM at Lancaster University Management School.

Guy Vernon is Lecturer in Human Resource Management at Southampton University.

Elizabeth Houldsworth is Lecturer in International HRM at Henley Business School, University of Reading.

The Chartered Institute of Personnel and Development is the leading publisher of books and reports for personnel and training professionals, students, and all those concerned with the effective management and development of people at work. For details of all our titles, please contact the publishing department:

tel: 020–8612 6204

email publish@cipd.co.uk

The catalogue of all CIPD titles can be viewed on the CIPD website:

www.cipd.co.uk/bookstore

International Human Resource Management

3rd Edition

Chris Brewster, Paul Sparrow, Guy Vernon and Elizabeth Houldsworth

Chartered Institute of Personnel and Development

Chartered Institute of Personnel and Development
Published by the Chartered Institute of Personnel and Development, CIPD House,
151 The Broadway, London, SW19 1JQ

First published 2011
Reprinted 2013

© Chartered Institute of Personnel and Development, 2011

All rights reserved. No part of this publication may be reproduced, stored in a retrieval system,
or transmitted, in any form or by any means, electronic, mechanical, photocopying, recording, or
otherwise, without the prior written permission of the publisher.

This publication may not be sold, lent, hired out or otherwise dealt with in the course of trade or
supplied in any form of binding or cover other than that in which it is published without the prior
written permission of the publisher.

No responsibility for loss occasioned to any person acting or refraining from action as a result of any
material in this publication can be accepted by the editor, authors or publisher.

Designed and typeset by Fakenham Prepress Solutions, Norfolk
Printed in Great Britain by Bell & Bain Ltd, Glasgow

British Library Cataloguing in Publication Data
A catalogue of this publication is available from the British Library

ISBN 978 1 84398 266 1

The views expressed in this publication are the authors' own and may not necessarily reflect those of
the CIPD.

The CIPD has made every effort to trace and acknowledge copyright holders. If any source has been
overlooked, CIPD Enterprises would be pleased to redress this in future editions.

University of
South Wales
Prifysgol
De Cymru

Library Services
13913409

Chartered Institute of Personnel and Development, CIPD House,
151 The Broadway, London, SW19 1JQ

Tel: 020 8612 6200
Email: cipd@cipd.co.uk
Website: www.cipd.co.uk
Incorporated by Royal Charter
Registered Charity No. 1079797

Contents

List of Tables

Chapter 15

List of Figures

Walkthrough of textbook features and online resources

LEARNING OUTCOMES

When they have read this chapter, students will:

● appreciate the growing internationalisation of the world in which HRM is conducted

● understand the additional complexity of HRM in an international context

● be able to describe the key features of the three main approaches to IHRM

● be able to identify some of the key HRM challenges facing organisations working internationally

● understand the format of the rest of the book.

LEARNING OUTCOMES

At the beginning of each chapter a bulleted set of learning outcomes summarises what you can expect to learn from the chapter, helping you to track your progress.

THEORY AND PRACTICE

KEY FRAMEWORK

The mechanisms through which culture shapes HRM

The literature indicates that cultural values shape the conduct of HRM through the following mechanisms (Sparrow and Hiltrop, 1997):

● attitudes held about, and definitions of, what makes an effective manager, and their implications for the qualities recruited, trained and developed

● the giving of face-to-face feedback, levels of power distance and uncertainty avoidance, and their implications for recruitment interview, communication, negotiation and participation processes

● expectations of the manager–subordinate relationship, and their implications for performance management and motivational processes

● differential concepts of distributive justice, socially healthy pay and the individualisation of rewards, and their implications for the design of pay systems

● the mindsets used to think about organisational structuring or strategic dynamics.

THEORY AND PRACTICE: KEY FRAMEWORKS

Key theoretical frameworks are highlighted throughout the text, helping you to get to grips with these important ideas and debates.

CASE STUDIES

TRANSFER OF MASS PRODUCTION ACTIVITIES TO CHINA

From the mid-1990s, and with gathering momentum, manufacturing companies in Japan and also South Korea have transferred substantial elements of their activities to China, sometimes to wholly owned facilities, but more often via joint ventures with local companies or via some form of close subcontracting arrangement. These developments are particularly apparent in clothing manufacture and in electronics, for example. Typically, the activity transferred has centred upon the more standardised element of the production operations, with more complex and higher value added activities, as well as most – if not all – research and development activity maintained in the home country. The organisation of work in the Chinese production operations was typically very much more Taylorist than that in the production operations in the home country, the tasks more finely broken down and the employees more closely monitored in China.

Source: Gamble *et al* (2004)

CASE STUDIES

A range of case studies from different countries illustrate how key ideas and theories are operating in practice around the globe, with accompanying questions or activities.

REFLECTIVE ACTIVITY

In considering work–life balance:

Might it be that an employee's total annual working time is of more significance than specific initiatives like flexi-time and compressed working weeks which re-order a given amount of working time?

If so, why is there so little discussion of total hours worked in many countries?

REFLECTIVE ACTIVITIES

In each chapter, a number of questions and activities will get you to reflect on what you have just read and encourage you to explore important concepts and issues in greater depth.

LEARNING QUESTIONS

1 We have limited evidence on how work is typically organised in the developing and newly industrialising worlds, but what would you expect to be typical?

2 Consider the basis of your view of the work organisation typical outside the established OECD or old industrialised world. Check that it is consistent with what we do know about the comparative organisation of work.

3 Why is Taylorism still influential in work organisation a century after its development?

4 Might the importance of overcoming the gulf between managerial and non-managerial employees be more important to organisational effectiveness in some countries than others?

5 Which are the best methods to facilitate upward and downward communication? Are they likely to vary with different cultures?

6 How should an MNC in, say, retail approach work organisation in the various countries in which it operates?

LEARNING QUESTIONS

Learning questions at the end of each chapter will test your understanding of the chapter and highlight any areas of development before you move on to the next chapter.

KEY LEARNING POINTS

- Although it is sometimes rather neglected in discussions of HRM, there are many indications that this is one of the vital arenas of HRM activity.

- Taylorism remains influential in contemplations of work organisation and in practice.

- Many organisations now seek to overcome the limitations of Taylorism with communication initiatives but also with a more radical and broader-based reform of work organisation.

- The balance of approaches to work organisation varies dramatically across countries, even within Europe.

- Sheer economic development, or GDP per capita, does not explain the cross-national comparative variations in work organisation.

- Cross-national comparative variation appears importantly driven by culture and most particularly by institutions.

- There are some indications of an international best practice in work organisation.

KEY LEARNING POINTS

At the end of each chapter, a bulleted list of the key learning points summarises the chapter and pulls out the most important points for you to remember.

EXPLORE FURTHER

Tregaskis, O. and Brewster, C. J. (2006) 'Converging or diverging?A comparative analysis of trends in contingent employment practice in Europe over a decade', *Journal of International Business Studies*, 37 (1): 111–126. The authors provide a detailed comparative analysis of the influences on flexibility practice.

Bloom, N., Kretschmer, T. and Van Reenan, J (2009) 'Work-life balance, management practices and productivity' in Freeman, R. B. and Shaw, K. L. (eds) International Differences in the Business Practices and Productivity of Firms. Chicago. University of Chicago Press. The authors provide a detailed

international analysis of the link between work–life balance practices and business performance.

Chandola, T., Martikainen, P., Bartley, M., Lahelma, E., Marmot, M., Nasermoaddeli, A. and Kagamimori, S. (2004) 'Does conflict between home and work explain the effect of multiple roles on mental health? A comparative study of Finland, Japan and the UK', *International Journal of Epidemiology*, 33 (4): 884–893. This article examines some of the health implications of the differing national practices in these arenas.

EXPLORE FURTHER

Explore further boxes contain suggestions for further reading and useful websites, encouraging you to delve further into areas of particular interest.

For Student and Tutor Online resources, visit www.cipd.co.uk/orl or scan the QR code on the back cover with your Smartphone.

ONLINE RESOURCES FOR STUDENTS

- Annotated web-links – access a wealth of useful sources of information in order to develop your understanding of the issues in the text.

- Multiple choice questions – to test your understanding.

ONLINE RESOURCES FOR TUTORS

- PowerPoint slides – design your programme around these ready made lectures.

- Lecturer's Guide – including guidance on the activities and questions in the text.

- Additional case studies – these can be used as a classroom activity, for personal reflection and individual learning, or as the basis for assignments.

CHAPTER 1

International Human Resource Management: An Introduction

LEARNING OUTCOMES

When they have read this chapter, students will:

- appreciate the growing internationalisation of the world in which HRM is conducted

- understand the additional complexity of HRM in an international context

- be able to describe the key features of the three main approaches to IHRM

- be able to identify some of the key HRM challenges facing organisations working internationally

- understand the format of the rest of the book.

INTRODUCTION

This chapter starts with a general introduction to the text – it outlines the dual objectives of the text:

- to give readers a better understanding of international HRM (IHRM) in a way that will help them as practitioners

- and, for those who are concerned, to help them get through the International Personnel and Development element of the CIPD Standards.

The first section explains what is new about this updated and enlarged latest edition of the book. The next section (*Key Trends*) considers the background of the growth of international business and the implications for HRM. The third section (*International HRM*) outlines the importance of countries and presents the three main approaches to IHRM: cultural, comparative and international. In so doing it explores the differences between domestic and international HRM for practitioners. The final section of this chapter (*An Outline of the Book*) provides a guide to the other chapters in the book.

WHAT IS NEW ABOUT THIS EDITION?

We have introduced a number of additional chapters from the previous edition. Notably, the textbook now gives more coverage to institutional influences on IHRM. We have strengthened the comparative sections of the book with a new chapter on the organisation of work and have redeveloped the material on flexible work. We have also introduced a new chapter on performance management. This new material enables lecturers to provide much broader functional coverage in a comparative setting. All the other chapters have been updated to pick up developments in both the literature and practice over the last four years.

The aim of this text, however, remains the same: to help you explore the meaning and implications of the concepts of cross-cultural, comparative and IHRM. We do not assume that there is only one way of defining or understanding the nature of HRM. On the contrary, we believe that HRM varies according to the country in which HRM is conducted: that provides the cultural and institutional environment for HRM. This text addresses directly the issues raised by the fact that HRM is different from country to country. One effect that this must have is on people like you, who are trying to gain an understanding of the full range of meanings of HRM. Another effect is on those, like some of you, trying to manage HRM in organisations whose reach crosses national boundaries. These issues are covered in this text.

A key task for organisations which operate across international boundaries is to manage the different stresses of the drive for integration (being coherent across the world) and differentiation (being adaptive to local environments). Reading this text will give you some flavour of the way that HRM – and particularly what is seen as 'good' HRM – is defined differently in different national cultures, and is presented and operates differently in different national institutional environments; some flavour, too, of the ways in which international organisations attempt to deal with the issues these differences create.

We believe that the text will be of value to anyone involved in, or interested in, comparative and IHRM. Whereas in the past the book has focused particularly on HRM specialists, for this edition we have sought to take a more general approach, acknowledging that for some readers they may only be studying IHRM as one component in a broader qualification programme. At the same time we have kept a close eye on the CIPD's International Personnel and Development Standards. If you are teaching a course, or studying for the CIPD qualification, this book will therefore form a comprehensive course text.

This book is unusual in that it provides evidence of cross-national variation in HRM policies and practices from the Cranet survey. Cranet is the largest ongoing academic survey in the world and has, over more than 20 years now, gathered comparative data from countries around the world. The survey database is broadly representative of the countries in which data is collected, matching the employment patterns of organisations (of more than 100 employees) in now more than 50 countries. The data is collected from the most senior person responsible for HRM in each organisation, and mainly only 'factual' questions (involving yes/no or numbers or percentages as responses) are asked. For consistency we have used the latest data from France, Germany, Japan, Spain, Sweden, the UK and the USA in each chapter, but we have also referred where appropriate to recent articles that cover a wider range of countries.

 REFLECTIVE ACTIVITY

- Why would a global approach to managing people be beneficial to an organisation?
- Why might it be harmful?

Provide examples for each perspective.

For many of you, these first paragraphs will already be raising some key questions. What is the culture of Spain, with its Castilians, Catalans, Andalucians, Basques, etc? What is the culture of Singapore, with its Malay, Indian and Chinese populations? What is the institutional and labour market position of the European Union, where many laws apply across national boundaries and there are few institutional limitations to cross-border labour markets? And, of course, basing the text on national differences inevitably blurs some of these important 'within-nation' and 'beyond-country' issues. These are critical matters – but outside the scope of this text. We have chosen here to concentrate upon the national differences partly because they are so powerful (employment laws, labour markets, trade unions, etc tend to operate at national level), and partly as an introduction to an often-neglected element of HRM – the fact that it does vary considerably around the world. Our consideration of these issues is focused on Europe, but we will take the opportunity to draw on examples from other continents whenever that is appropriate.

We have also taken the opportunity in the new edition not just to improve our coverage of this rapidly changing subject (see Sparrow *et al*, 2004) but also to extend both the number of chapters and the material covered within the chapters. It has been fascinating to note that the number of books and articles on international and comparative HRM has expanded almost exponentially even in the short time since the first edition of this text. Whereas in many organisations IHRM used to be the concern of a rather separate department arranging terms and conditions for expatriate employees, it is increasingly becoming a more and more significant part of organisations' attempts to manage their entire workforce across the world in the most cost-effective manner possible. As such, it is becoming a key contributor to organisational success. It is little wonder that it is beginning to attract the attention of more and more researchers, publishers and consultancies.

We note in the *Outline of the Book* the details of the new topics that we have addressed chapter by chapter. Here it suffices to say that we have responded to the book's users by adding specific chapters detailing comparative aspects of the organisation of work and of performance management, and have used the latest research to extend the material on the way that international organisations manage their workforces internationally.

It is a truism to point out that the world is becoming more international. This applies to our technology, our travel, our economies and our communications – if not always obviously to our understanding. The growth of global enterprises leads to increased permeability in the traditional business boundaries, which in turn leads to high rates of economic change, a growing number and diversity of participants, rising complexity and uncertainty.

Traditionally, much of our understanding about IHRM has been based on the study of multinational corporations (MNCs). A multinational corporation is defined as an enterprise that operates in several countries but is managed from one home country. In practice, once an enterprise derives more than one quarter of its revenues from outside its home country, it is considered an MNC. MNCs may take any of four forms: a decentralised corporation that has a strong home-country presence; a global and centralised corporation that can acquire a cost advantage through centralised production; an international company that builds on the parent company's technology or research and development; or a transnational enterprise that combines all three of these approaches. In general, an MNC may not have co-ordinated product offerings in each country, because it is more focused on adapting its products and service to each individual local market. Some people prefer to use the term 'multinational enterprise' (MNE) because the word 'corporation' implies business organisations, whereas many other forms of organisation – such as non-governmental bodies or charities – might be deemed to have multinational characteristics. The term 'transnational corporation' (TNC) is typically used to describe much more complex organisations that have invested in foreign operations, have a central corporate facility, but give decision-making, R&D and marketing powers to each individual foreign market. We shall generally use the abbreviation 'MNCs' throughout the textbook for the sake of convenience and simplicity.

MNCs are presented as being economically dominant: the world's 1,000 largest companies produce 80 per cent of the world's industrial output.

The United Nations Conference on Trade and Development (UNCTAD) was originally set up as an as an intergovernmental forum for North–South dialogue and negotiations on issues of interest to developing countries, including debates on the 'New International Economic Order'. Its *World Investment Report* focuses on trends in foreign direct investment (FDI) worldwide and at the regional and country levels. As of publication the latest data for non-financial organisations relates to 2008. Based on an average of three ratios (the ratio of foreign assets to total assets, foreign sales to total sales, and foreign employment to total employment) the Transnationality Index often paints a surprising picture. The most transnational firms from the transition economies, in order, are First Pacific Company Limited (Hong Kong, with an index of 99 per cent), China Merchants Holdings International (Hong Kong, 97 per cent), Guangdong Investment Limited (Hong Kong, 95 per cent), Road King Infrastructure Limited (Hong Kong, 90 per cent) and Li and Fung Limited (Hong Kong, 90 per cent). Acer of Taiwan would rate 12th, Tata Steel of India 18th, and Samsung 41st.

Using one of the three measures of geographic spread, some more familiar names appear in the list of all financial organisations. In terms of scale, the top five financial firms based on 2009 data were Citigroup (USA), BNP Paribas (France), Allianz SE (Germany), Generali Spa (Italy) and Société Générale (France). In the list of all non-financial TNCs, using 2008 data, by asset the top five largest firms are General Electric, Shell, Vodafone, BP and Toyota. On the TNI they are Xstrata (UK, Mining), ABB, Nokia, Pernod Ricard and WPP Group.

Across nations. the UNCTAD World Investment Report 2010 expected global inflows of foreign direct investment (FDI) to reach more than US $1.2 trillion in 2010, to rise further to US $1.3–1.5 trillion in 2011, and to head towards US $1.6–2 trillion in 2012. However, these FDI prospects were considered to be fraught with risks and uncertainties. These risk factors included the slow global economic recovery, investment protectionism, rising sovereign debt and continued volatility in the currency markets – all likely to slow down the pace of FDI across the globe in 2011. The United States, the epicentre of the global economic meltdown in 2008, gradually recovered from the crisis, with FDI flows increasing by 40 per cent in 2010 to US $186.1 billion from US $129.9 billion in 2009. Developing and transition economies attracted half of global FDI inflows, and invested one quarter of global FDI outflows. There was a sharp increase in global FDI flows to East and South-East Asian countries and Latin American nations in 2010. This marked the first time that developing countries outpaced rich nations in attracting foreign investments.

PROGRESS TOWARDS TRANSNATIONALISATION?

UNCTAD (2007) defines transnationalisation as the intensity of foreign activities in relation to domestic or global activities. Between 1990 and 2003, the values of assets of foreign affiliates of the world's TNCs have increased by a factor of five, and sales and employment have multiplied respectively by three and two. By the early 1990s there were an estimated 37,000 TNCs in the world, with 170,000 foreign affiliates. Of these, 33,500 were parent corporations based in developed countries. By 2006 there were an estimated 77,000 TNCs in the world, with more than 770,000 foreign affiliates. These affiliates generated an estimated US $4.5 trillion in value added, employed some 62 million workers, and exported goods and services valued at more than US $4 trillion. Around 60 per cent of international trade involves transactions between two related parts of a single MNC. This means that the *physical location of economic value* creation is now difficult to ascertain.

Continental shifts in economic activity continue at a pace. In 2003 economists at Goldman Sachs bracketed Brazil with Russia, India and China as the economies that would come to dominate the world. However, interpreting trends in international HRM that might result from shifts in economic power is never easy and complex factors are always at play.

We see a number of traditional regional strategies, often reflecting past cultural and institutional linkages. For example, while the Spanish economy was contracting in 2009, Spanish MNCs capitalised on their Latin American connections. Telefónica, the telecommunications company, was the biggest investor in the region, making 35 per cent of its profit there. Its US $100 billion of investments in Latin America represented about a third of the company's value (*Economist*, 2009a). Santander made 43 per cent of its profit there. Six Spanish MNCs accounted for 95 per cent of all the Spanish investment in Latin America. At the same time, however, Spanish MNCs made large acquisitions in Europe and the USA to balance their exposure to Latin America. MNCs hedge their bets across geographies.

They also create new patterns of mobility and trade. Chinese expansion into Latin America and Africa creates both a new geographical demography in terms of international mobility, and new patterns of comparative management. For example, in 2009 the China Development Bank and Sinopec lent US $10 billion to Brazil's state-controlled oil company Petrobras in return for 10 years' supply of 200,000 barrels of oil a day. As foreign direct investment has gone into Brazil, it has spawned a new set of Brazilian MNCs, such as Petrobas in oil, Vale – one of the world's largest mining companies – and Embraer, the world's third-largest maker of passenger jets, with steel-makers, bus-builders, food companies, textile and cosmetics firms soon expected to follow (*Economist*, 2009c). Out of a list of 100 companies from the emerging markets that are expected to evolve into MNCs, compiled by Boston Consulting Group, 14 are based in Brazil. Living in the shadows of this shift in economic power, UN data suggests that the informal economy still represents about 40 per cent of Brazilian GDP – it is only 13 per cent of GDP in China. China has now become Africa's largest trading partner and buys one-third of its oil from the continent. It exports US $60 billion to Africa, and imports a little more from Africa (*Economist*, 2011d). 14 per cent of Chinese overseas investment is in sub-Saharan Africa, with 19 per cent to Latin America, 17 per cent to the Middle East and North Africa, 17 per cent to other parts of Asia, 13 per cent to Europe, 11 per cent to Australia and only 9 per cent to the USA.

Much is spoken about relative levels of productivity around the world driving investment and growth. In fact, much of China and the USA's gains in productivity were due to capital investment rather than true improvements in efficiency. From 1990 to 2008, OECD data on a better measure of 'total factor productivity' – the percentage increase in output that is not accounted for by changes in inputs (ie the volume of work hours and capital investments) – showed that China still had an annual growth rate of 4 per cent in productivity. No other country in history has enjoyed such rapid productivity gains (*Economist*, 2009d). On the same measure and time period, productivity increases were 2.8 per cent in India, 2.3 per cent in Singapore, and 1.8 per cent in Thailand, falling to 1.2 per cent in Britain, 1.1 per cent in the USA, 0.3 per cent in Brazil and 0.2 per cent in Russia. The determinants of such long-term productivity are the rate of adopting existing technologies, the pace of domestic scientific innovation, and changes in organisation and production, which in turn depend on opennesss to foreign direct investment (FDI) and trade, education and the flexibility of labour markets. China's technology penetration and innovation is very high, so China's growth is twice as fast as seen in Japan and South Korea when they were at similar stages of development.

We also witness different responses internationally within the labour force. For example, within the rich Group of Seven economies, the USA has the lowest share of 'prime age' males aged between 25 and 54 in work (*Economist*, 2011e). The proportion has fallen from 95 per cent in the 1960s to 80 per cent today. The figure is still 96 per cent in Japan and 94 per cent in France. The main reason for the falls in economic participation in the USA, the UK and Canada are structural changes that have reduced demand for less-skilled workers. US university graduation rates have slipped in recent years from near the top of the world league table to the middle.

Another issue is labour arbitrage. Although taking advantage of lower wages abroad, especially in poor countries, has been important, in practice MNCs consider many factors when they think of locating activities offshore. A study by Boston Consulting Group in 2011 (*Economist*, 2011f) found that pay for factory workers in China increased by 69 per cent between 2005 and 2010. On current trends of annual wage growth of 17 per cent in China, modest appreciation in the value of Chinese currency and existing productivity growth rates, by 2015, they argue, manufacturers producing for consumption in America will be indifferent to locating in America or China on cost grounds. Factories take time to build. The behaviour of MNCs has therefore already started to factor in such trends. Caterpillar and NCR have already begun to move some manufacturing from abroad back to the USA. General Motors is investing US $2 billion and adding 4,000 jobs at 17 American plants. Complex supply chains at risk of disruption, energy prices, inventory costs associated with importing all require consideration.

These shifts are not always as easy or rapid as made out in the business press. For example, in the area of consumer electronics, when firms moved production to Asia they created a supplier base and infrastructure that would now be hard to reverse. Despite rapidly rising wages in India, productivity growth means that the software and back-office offshoring industry is similarly expected to retain cost advantage for the foreseeable future. Infosys, India's most celebrated IT company, earns only 1.2 per cent of its revenue in the Indian market, earning 375 per cent more from overseas exports than in domestic operations. So despite Infosys, Wipro and Tata Consultancy Services, it is the US firm IBM that is the leading provider of IT services to Indian companies (*Economist*, 2009a).

Whatever the driving factors, we are nonetheless witnessing the global transfer of work – either in terms of the creation of new jobs or through the global sourcing of certain parts of an individual's or unit's work. This is having a major impact on the type of organisations and nature of work that remain viable in different parts of the world. In the first wave of globalisation two decades ago, low-level manufacturing work began to transfer to low-cost locations. In the second wave, simple service work such as credit-card processing began to relocate. In the third wave, higher-skill white-collar work is being transferred.

WHAT IS INTERNATIONAL HUMAN RESOURCE MANAGEMENT?

In all these MNCs or MNEs, HRM is a key to success. For the vast majority of organisations, the cost of the people who do the work is the largest single item of operating costs. Increasingly, in the modern world, the capabilities and the knowledge incorporated in an organisation's human resources are the key to performance. So on both the cost and benefit sides of the equation, HRM is crucial to the survival, performance and success of the enterprise. For international organisations, the additional complications of dealing with multicultural assumptions about the way people should be managed and differing institutional constraints become important contributors to the chances of that success.

The need for human resource specialists to adopt an increasingly international orientation in their functional activities is widely acknowledged and becoming ever clearer. It is important not just to people working in the giant MNEs, but also to many in small to medium-size enterprises (SMEs). The freer economic environment of the twenty-first century, the reduction of restrictions on labour movement in areas such as the European Union, and the advent of new technology have combined to mean that many fledgling enterprises operate internationally almost as soon as they are established. It is also worth reminding ourselves that international organisations do not have to be in the private sector. Governments have staff working around the world. Many international organisations such as those in the UN family, the OECD, the regional trade bodies, etc have employees working across national borders. So do many charities and religious groups (Brewster and Lee, 2006).

Any review of world events over the last few years will emphasise the essentially unpredictable and rapidly changing nature of political, economic and social upheavals. Vaill (1989; p2) used the metaphor of 'permanent white water' to describe the nature of doing business in the latter part of the twentieth century:

> Most managers are taught to think of themselves as paddling their canoes on calm, still lakes . . . Sure, there will be temporary disruptions during changes of various sorts – periods when they will have to shoot the rapids in their canoes – but the disruptions will be temporary, and when things settle back down, they'll be back in a calm, still lake mode. But it has been my experience that you never get out of the rapids!

Managers working in an international environment are obviously more subject to the impact of multi-country, regional and global change and dynamism than managers in a single-country operation. And this applies to HR managers as much as any others (Stiles, 2006). Hardly surprisingly, choices in this context become complex and ambiguous.

HRM professionals who contemplate internationalisation typically need to address the following:

- Do we have a strategy for becoming an international firm?
- What type of managers will we need to be successful? And how do we find or develop them?

- How can I find out about the way that HRM is conducted in other countries: the laws, trade unions, labour market, expectations, etc?

- What will be the impact of local cultural norms on our home-based ways of working? Can we use all or any of them in other countries?

- How will we choose whether to send expatriates or use local employees?

- How do we manage international moves if we choose to send some people out from home?

- How do we manage knowledge across geographical and cultural distance?

The additional complexities of managing an international workforce in any of these organisations call for a different mindset and different skills for practitioners. A publication for the Chartered Institute of Personnel and Development (CIPD, 2002) argued that individuals working in an international context need to be competent in:

- interpersonal skills (especially cultural empathy)

- influencing and negotiating skills

- analytical and conceptual abilities

- strategic thinking

and that they will also need a broader base of knowledge in such areas as:

- international business

- international finance

- international labour legislation

- local labour markets

- cultural differences

- international compensation and benefits.

Furthermore, and to complete for a moment the list of complexities that internationalisation adds to the role of HR managers, they will have to manage a wider set of multiple relationships. HR managers in the European context, for instance, might find themselves having to deal with such groups as:

- headquarters, regional and subsidiary line managers

- headquarters and subsidiary employees

- national, European-level and international trade union bodies

- national and European-level legislative bodies

- local and regional communities.

From the mid-1980s to the turn of the 1990s the field of IHRM was considered to be in its 'infancy' (Laurent, 1986). Since its early beginnings, there has both an evolution of territory covered by the IHRM field as well as more critical discussion of whether this evolution has been towards an expanded field, or represents a process of fragmentation.

Scullion (2005) tracked the evolution of definitions of IHRM. He observed that although there has been little consensus, definitions have broadly concentrated on examining the HRM issues, problems, strategies, policies and practices which firms pursue in relation to the internationalisation of their business. Schuler *et al* (2009) similarly recently positioned the different views that have existed about the nature of IHRM.

DEFINITIONS OF IHRM

IHRM encompasses:

'. . . the worldwide management of people in the multinational enterprise' (Poole, 1990; p1)

'. . . human resource management in an international environment . . . problems created in an MNC performing business in more than one country, rather than those posed by working for a foreign firm at home or by employing foreign employees in the local firm' (Briscoe and Schuler, 2004; p1)

'. . .how MNCs manage their geographically dispersed workforce in order to leverage their HR resources for both local and global competitive advantage' (Scullion, 2005; p5)

'. . . a branch of management studies that investigates the design of and effects of organisational human resource practices in cross-cultural contexts' (Peltonen, 2006; p523)

'. . . all issues related to the management of people in an international context [including] human resource issues facing MNCs in different parts of their organisations [and] comparative analyses of HRM in different countries' (Stahl and Björkman, 2006; p1)

'. . . complex relationship between globalisation, national systems and companies [which provides us with] three distinct "levels of analysis" for interpreting and understanding HRM strategies and practices [the globalisation effect, the regional and national effect, and the organisation effect]' (Edwards and Rees, 2008; p22)

'. . . the subject matter of IHRM [must be] covered under three headings: cross-cultural management; comparative human resource management; and international human resource management' (Brewster *et al,* 2007, p5)

'. . . how MNCs manage the competing demands of ensuring that the organisation has an international coherence in and cost-effective approach to the way it manages its people in all the countries it covers, while also ensuring that it can be responsive to the differences in assumptions about what works from one location to another' (Dickmann *et al,* 2008; p7)

'. . . the ways in which the HRM function contributes to the process of globalisation within multinational firms' (Sparrow and Braun, 2008; p96)

'. . . the implications that the process of internationalisation has for the activities and policies of HRM' (Dowling *et al,* 2008; p293).

 REFLECTIVE ACTIVITY

Look at the sequence of definitions used above to define what IHRM is about. How do the definitions change over time? What do these changing definitions tell you about the sorts of knowledge – and the theoretical understanding – that might be important for the field and that should be incorporated into a textbook like this?

STRUCTURING THE FIELD INTO THREE COMPONENTS

How are we to start the process of understanding all this complexity? The first step is to be clear about different kinds of analysis. These are not always defined in the literature – partly perhaps because of a confusion in the USA, where 'international' is often applied to anything outside the USA. However, generally, the subject matter of IHRM is covered under three headings:

- cross-cultural management
- comparative HRM
- IHRM.

In broad terms, authors in the *cross-cultural* tradition argue that every nation has its own unique sets of deep-lying values and beliefs, and that these are reflected in the ways that societies operate, and in the ways that the economy operates and people work and are managed at work. The *comparative* HRM tradition focuses more specifically on the way that people work and explores the differences between nations in the way that they manage this process. In general, the comparative tradition makes more of the institutional differences than the cultural differences. *International* HRM (and its more recent 'strategic' derivative, SIHRM) examines the way organisations manage their human resources across these different national contexts.

CROSS-CULTURAL MANAGEMENT

A key factor in the increasing internationalisation of employment is that there are cultural differences between nations – differences in national values and attitudes. Many of us have stereotypes of taciturn Finns, ebullient Spaniards, work-obsessed Americans, polite Japanese, modest Malays, etc. These are stereotypes: even though the next Finn we meet may be loud and confident, the next Spaniard quiet and reserved, and so on, they indicate real, general, truths. There is now plenty of research evidence (see Chapter 2) that different nationalities do have different values and that these affect the way people organise, conduct and manage work. An awareness of cultural differences is therefore an essential part of an international HR manager's brief. The normal HRM activities such as recruitment and selection, training and development, reward and performance appraisal, may all be affected by cultural values and practices in the respective host countries. As a result, great care must be taken when deciding whether or not to adopt standardised HRM policies and practices throughout the world.

COMPARATIVE HUMAN RESOURCE MANAGEMENT

The distinction between comparative HRM and IHRM was clearly made by Boxall (1995). Comparative HRM (CHRM) explores the extent to which HRM differs between different countries – or occasionally between different areas within a country or different regions of the world, such as North America, the Pacific Rim states or Europe (Brewster and Larsen, 2000). We know that countries may be small or large, have more or fewer regional differences, include one or many language groups, and be more or less economically developed. More immediately we know that they may have different labour markets and education systems, different employment laws and trade unions, and the different cultural expectations that we have already noted. It should be no surprise, therefore, to find that employment systems differ noticeably between countries and that managing human resources has to vary from country to country.

As should already be clear, 'HRM' is a term with widely disputed definitions: many books and articles have attempted to pinpoint its meaning. One less often explored source of variation arises from national differences. The concept of HRM itself originates in and builds on a particular view of the world, a view initially from the USA. As Legge (1995; pxiv) put it in her typically trenchant way:

> Why the appeal of HRM's particular rhetoric? Because its language . . . celebrates a range of very WASP [White Anglo-Saxon Protestant] values (individualism, work ethic, those of the American Dream) while at the same time mediating the contradictions of capitalism.

Other countries have been more resistant to the notion of HRM, either taking it up as a concept much later or staying with the 'personnel management' label. It is notable, for example, that the European and the world professional bodies still call themselves, respectively, the European Association of Personnel Management and the World Federation of Personnel Management Associations. This is not a question of backwardness: the New Zealand association is one of the most modern, but still uses the Personnel Management title. In many cases, the 1990s and the first decade of the twenty-first century saw academics and consultants in a country taking up the term while practitioners in the same country remained stubbornly attached to 'personnel' as the title of their area of work.

Whereas some commentators look for universal issues, others are more concerned about understanding their local contingencies. Researchers in the USA typically assume that the focus of HRM is on the well-being of the organisation. On the other hand, in many other countries, commentators tend to be more critical and to take account of a number of stakeholders whose interests do not always overlap – and they are less than committed to the idea that the shareholders' interests are always paramount. This is summed up in a quotation (Storey, 1995; p23) about the way HRM is presented in US texts:

> I believe HRM to be amoral and anti-social, unprofessional, reactive, uneconomic and ecologically destructive.

Even when the terminology has been adopted, we should not assume that the subject matter is uniform across the world. When the multinational team involved in running the Cranet surveys on HRM policy and practice (Tregaskis *et al*, 2003) met to decide on the areas their survey would cover, there was far from total unanimity in understanding the nature of the topic. 'Where,' the Swedish colleagues wanted to know, 'are the questions about the relationship of the organisation to the natural environment?' They saw this as an element of the HRM role. German colleagues wanted more on the role of works councils,

French colleagues more on the social environment. When the Japanese joined the network, they felt that despite the importance of national comparisons they could not use all of the questions, some of which would be perceived as too intrusive.

Research in the CHRM field, then, which has generally but not exclusively been of more interest to European researchers, has typically incorporated a country comparison perspective.

TYPICAL QUESTIONS ASKED BY COMPARATIVE RESEARCHERS

How is HRM structured in individual countries?
What strategies are discussed?
What is actually put into practice?
What are the main differences and similarities between countries ?
To what extent are HRM policies influenced by national factors such as culture, government policy, and educational systems?

The bulk of work in the CHRM field has thus concentrated on the nature and impact of institutional differences between countries, the consideration of which HRM practices are more or less culturally sensitive, and an empirical examination of patterns of convergence or divergence in HRM practices across national borders. The CHRM field has covered comparisons of management practices across different cultures and nations and studies that look at management in specific (single) countries. It concentrates on how people are managed differently in different countries by analysing practices within firms of different national origin in the same country or comparing practices between different nations or regions.

INTERNATIONAL HUMAN RESOURCE MANAGEMENT

IHRM has traditionally examined the way in which international organisations manage their human resources across these different national contexts. Early research in the field of IHRM reflected that in the broader field of international management, and focused on the role of MNCs and MNEs. Research has since focused on understanding those HRM functions that had to change when firms went international. Finding and nurturing the people able to implement international strategy was seen as critical for such firms, and considerable attention was given to the management of expatriates.

The organisation that manages people in different institutional, legal, and cultural circumstances has to be aware not only of what is allowed and not allowed in the different nations and regions of the world, but also of what makes for cost-effective management practices. To take one often-quoted example: a performance appraisal system which depends upon US-style openness between manager and subordinate, each explaining plainly how they feel the other has done well or badly in their job, may work in some European countries. However, employer branding, e-enablement, outsourcing, global networks – now needing to find [more] voice within the literature.

The problem-solving perspective acknowledges that there is an increasingly complex set of contextual factors at play, but also considers that the IHRM field has expanded in parallel with – and has been driven by the drumbeat of – progressive problems of internationalisation. These problems have undoubtedly become more deeply embedded within organisations.

AN OUTLINE OF THE BOOK

Following this introductory chapter, the text is divided into the three areas of theory we have already identified, and a section examining new developments and the role of HRM.

Part One deals with **cross-cultural management**.

- *Chapter 2 The impact of national culture* defines the meaning of culture, outlines the literature on cultural differences, and explores the extent to which aspects of work practices are nationally or locally based. It uses some previously developed frameworks and applies these to the world of work.

- *Chapter 3 Culture and organisational life* continues this exploration, looking at the implications of operating across national cultures for concepts of business, management and HRM. It first examines the impact of culture on organisational behaviour and HRM. It then examines concepts of leadership. The extent to which national cultures have different styles of leadership are discussed, and whether organisations can create global leaders. Finally, it considers the debates about the nature of cultural intelligence.

Part Two addresses the issue of **comparative human resource management**. There is an overall theory chapter and then a series of chapters exploring the way that different aspects of HRM practices vary across national boundaries. It is important that readers understand that in these topics there is no longer a simple divide between comparative and international HRM modules. Many of the topics and issues covered under a comparative theme would find relevance on a course on international HRM. To provide an example: in the chapter on *Recruitment and selection*, the discussion of the impact of culture on practices is used to show how an in-country business partner of an MNE has to understand the local complexities of practice – a topic easily taught under an IHRM banner. Similarly, the coverage of new developments in global mobility and resourcing in that chapter could well be taught alongside traditional IHRM topics of expatriation. We have adopted this structure to best organise the material, but stress that the conceptual divide between Parts Two and Three – and the relative number of chapters in each Part – should not be seen as indicative of the best way to either teach or learn about these topics. In the world of actual HRM practice, the two perspectives are inherently interconnected. Part Two, therefore, concentrates principally on key HRM functions.

- *Chapter 4 Comparative HRM and institutional influences* identifies the differences between the universalist and the contextualist paradigm and explores the contextual determinants for differences in country-level HRM practices. Attention is paid to the different employment law and institutional contexts within which HRM specialists have to operate. This chapter also explores the attempts that have been made to 'group' countries in relation to similarities of HRM practices, explores whether HRM in different countries is converging as a result of globalisation and, given the origin of the notion of HRM in the USA, explores how far HRM prescriptions from the USA might apply in the rest of the world.

- *Chapter 5 Employee relations and communication* explores the range of structures of employee relations common in Europe and around the world. It examines the differences in the meaning and role of unions and other representative employee bodies. It draws attention to the role of history, national cultures and legal institutions in influencing these structures and bodies, and signals what this means for the managers of people.

- *Chapter 6 The organisation of work* is a new chapter that introduces the topic of work organisation and reviews international variation in practices of direct communication. It considers Taylorism and other broader-based alternatives. It examines how these alternatives are applied in different countries and explains the bases of cross-national comparative variation in work organisation.

- *Chapter 7 Flexibility and work–life balance* explores trends in the issue of flexible working practices and patterns. Flexible working practices include the development of such approaches as part-time employment, short-term employment and a host of other non-standard working forms. It explores the similarities and differences in the use and meaning of such practices across national boundaries and considers the impact of these practices at national, employer and individual levels, as well as the implications for HRM specialists. Finally, it looks at developments concerning work–life balance in an international context.

- *Chapter 8 Recruitment and selection* explores and compares some of the ways in which organisations across different countries act in order to obtain and retain the kinds of human resources they need. The chapter examines the resourcing process: making sure the organisation has people of the right quality. It therefore looks first at recruitment and selection and considers the ways in which culture can be seen to influence such local HRM practices. However, much international recruitment today is carried out in the context of global resourcing strategies and increasingly global labour markets. The chapter therefore also looks at global skill supply strategies and the role of recruitment in the internationalisation of the organisation. Finally, it introduces some of the questions that these developments raise about the recruitment of international employees.

- *Chapter 9 Performance management* is a new chapter which defines performance management and performance appraisal, and provides an overview of their Western origins. Typical approaches to performance management within MNCs are described with reference to the elements of planning, managing and reviewing. The chapter then considers the factors

EXPLORE FURTHER

The following websites provide useful information:

The United Nations Conference on Trade and Development (UNCTAD) website can provide updated information on transnational organisations:
http://www.unctad.org/

OECD guidelines for multinational enterprises:
http://www.oecd.org/department/0,3355,en_2649_34889_1_1_1_1_1,00.html

CIPD International Research:
http://www.cipd.co.uk/research/_inthrm.htm

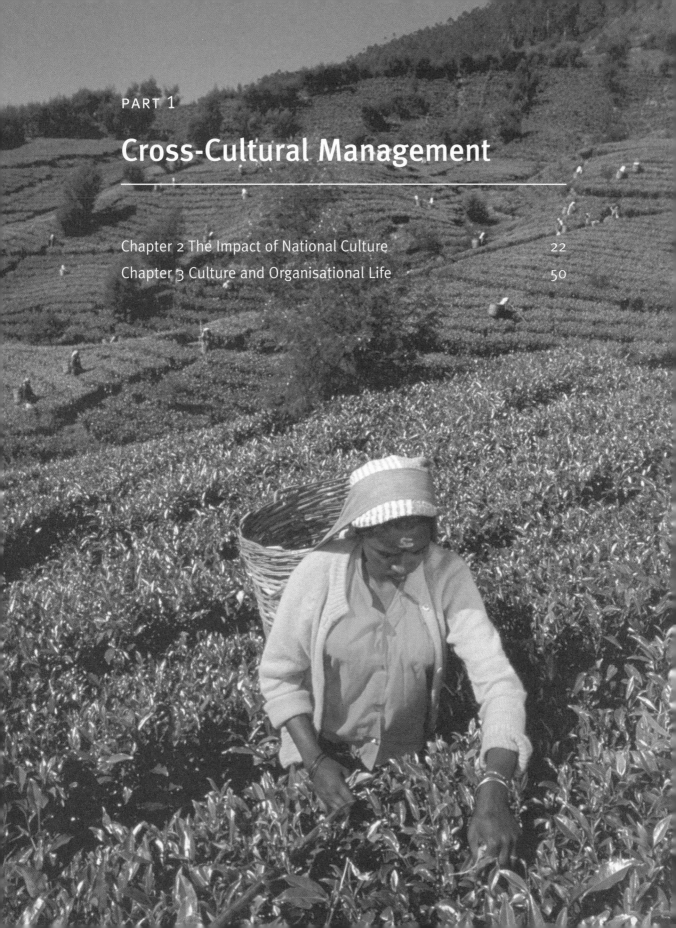

PART 1

Cross-Cultural Management

CHAPTER 2

The Impact of National Culture

LEARNING OUTCOMES

When they have read this chapter, students will:

- understand what culture is

- appreciate how national cultures differ

- be able to interpret the major cultural frameworks

- know how to use culture to define attitudes and behaviours at work

- be aware of the dangers of over-generalising from the study of culture.

INTRODUCTION

We begin here with the first of three theory chapters – each picking up the key disciplines within the field of cross-cultural management: this chapter, a chapter on comparative human resource management (see Chapter 4), and another on international human resource management as seen from an international business perspective (see Chapter 13). For those who want to understand 'the big picture' all at once, we would suggest reading these three chapters in succession. In particular, we would note that there can be some benefit in understanding the ideas in Chapter 13 fairly early in any course of study. However, there is also value in exploring the three disciplines in sequence. Here we begin, then, with cross-cultural management.

Differences in national cultures are apparent to any of us, even if we never step outside our own countries. The impact of information technology and global media has brought the world into our living rooms. We can experience many of the manifestations of different cultures through the films, soaps and documentaries that abound on our screens. Travelling to another country heightens this sense of difference: food, customs, language, transport, housing, entertainment – all these everyday things may have to be reconsidered and seen through other eyes.

At the same time as we are gaining more knowledge about different cultures, the increasing globalisation of markets, competition and organisations has led many people to believe that cultures are converging. Advances in telecommunications, information technology and global consumer products are thought of as leading to a 'global village' in which everyone will be wearing the same brand-name jeans and trainers while watching MTV on Japanese digital televisions, texting their friends with the latest mobile phone technology, and sharing what they perceive to be inner truths on social media websites. The rush to adopt 'world-class' manufacturing, logistics and marketing processes brings with it a belief in the convergence of management practice and the creation of a global corporate village. Under the convergence argument, management is management, consisting of a set of principles and techniques that can be universally applied.

In contrast, world events reflect a move towards divergence in cultures. For example, the tensions in world politics since 11 September 2001 have vividly illustrated the deep and enduring nature of differences between the values and beliefs of the Western (capitalist) world and those of many Muslim societies. Ethnic conflicts in Central Europe, Africa and South Asia in the last 20 years have revealed a desire to protect and reinforce cultural differences between groups.

In the management context, the need to take cultural differences into account is demonstrated in worldwide mergers and acquisitions. Studies by the major strategy firms such as KPMG and Mercer indicate high failure rates – an often-quoted KPMG study in 1999 based on interviews with over 100 senior executives involving some 700 deals over a two-year period revealed that the overwhelming cause for failure was the people and the cultural differences; 83 per cent of all mergers did not improve shareholder value, and only 25 per cent of the large-scale mergers succeeded. Reviews of the academic literature similarly suggest that the findings on post-merger success are fragmented across various disciplines, including strategic management, international business, and finance (Angwin and Vaara, 2005; Banal-Estañol and Seldeslachts, 2005, 2009; Cartwright, 2005). The practitioner press exhorts creating interculturally competent organisations as the way to success in global business. It also reports on many failures!

TRANS-CULTURAL BUSINESS FAILURES: USA AND GERMANY

CASE STUDIES

1) The Daimler-Chrysler mismatch

On 7 May 1998, the CEOs of Daimler-Benz AG and Chrysler publicly announced their merger. The intention was to create a trans-Atlantic powerhouse in the automobile sector. The combined company was a colossus, with $132 billion in annual revenues and the largest industrial merger the world had ever seen. At the time of the original deal, the two co-chairmen of the newly created company, Jurgen Schrempp and Bob Eaton, said it provided the platform to create the world's biggest car maker. The total value of DaimlerChrysler shares at the time of merger was $47 billion. In the short term, synergies of $1.4 billion were expected, and more than double that in the medium term. However, after five years the merger was seen as hugely problematic. There had been a $5.8 billion loss in 2001, the biggest loss in German business history. DaimlerChrysler ended 2003 with losses, wiping out the gains of 2002. By 2005 many were saying that the merger between Daimler and Chrysler was a failure (Banal-Estañol and Seldeslachts, 2005). A couple of years later it was! The merger was discontinued when DaimlerChrysler announced on 14 May 2007 that it would sell Chrysler to a private equity firm. Daimler sold its American luxury brand for just $7.4 billion. It was a remarkable admission of corporate failure. Since then, the two halves of the company have plunged from one crisis to another, axing tens of thousands of jobs. For the IBS Centre for Management Research, the different culture and management styles of the companies were primarily responsible for this failure. In their case study 'Daimler-Chrysler Merger: A Cultural Mismatch?' they argue that Daimler-Benz was characterised by methodical decision-making while Chrysler encouraged creativity. Chrysler was considered to be a symbol of American adaptability and resilience, valuing efficiency, empowerment, and egalitarian relations among staff. In contrast, Daimler-Benz was considered to value respect for authority, bureaucratic precision, and had a centralised decision-making style. These cultural differences became manifest in the daily activities of the company.

2) Did WalMart smile too much in Germany?

Similarly in 2006 Walmart ended its long battle to survive in Germany's $370 billion retail market. In the UK, WalMart purchased ASDA. It had entered the German market in 1997 when it took over the Wertkauf and Interspar supermarket chains. It was there at the outset of the upswing in discount retailers, taking over 95 stores and initiating a price war. Competitors, like the low-cost chains Aldi and Lidl, continued to grow and succeed in Germany. The WalMart retreat from Germany cost it about $863 million. What was behind WalMart's struggle in

Germany? Did the Germans' preference for shops run by local businessmen and stocked with organically grown food kill Walmart? The main factor cited by many analysts was a mismatch in the cultural philosophy. WalMart tried to relocate the American retail model. This model encountered cultural challenges in many ways. Trans-cultural business case studies point out that the first head of German operations was an expat from the USA – who did not understand Germany or its culture and insisted that all business operations be carried out in the English language. Top management refused to acknowledge the differences in customer behaviour in Germany compared to its US customers, and failed to listen to the feedback from its employees. WalMart stores were designed for customers who were willing to spend lot of time shopping. But in Germany, shopping hours were shorter and customers were not in the habit of spending lots of time in a store, wandering around for the things they needed. Coupled with this problem, German customers did not like to be assisted by WalMart's friendly store assistants. Germans prefer to do their own searching for bargains. WalMart got its store merchandising wrong. Germans like to see the advertised discount products upfront – without having to ask the store assistant. The service with a smile approach from the bag-packer, with employees chanting W-A-L-M-A-R-T to raise morale and an ethics code which included banning sexual relations between employees did not fare well. The attempt to introduce a telephone hotline for employees to inform on their colleagues was overturned in 2005 by the German courts. A Bloomberg Business Week analysis in 2006 noted that sales assistants ordered by supervisors to smile at customers were reported to have discovered their smiles were often interpreted as invitations to unwanted social interaction in a country where smiles are exchanged between friends but not between strangers! Also, of course, WalMart had industrial relations issues in its German operations (see Chapter 5).

This chapter and the next examine what is involved in such challenges – and why as in the examples cited here it is so easy for cultural issues to derail international management.

In this chapter we first explain the nature of national culture and the way in which it has been studied. In the next chapter we examine the ways in which culture affects organisational life and the ways in which organisations attempt to improve intercultural competence.

PUTTING THE STUDY OF CULTURE INTO CONTEXT

We introduced the field of cross-cultural management in Chapter 1. A number of academic professions have contributed to our understanding of how and why behaviour appears in specific cultural contexts – anthropologists, sociologists, cross-cultural psychologists, cultural psychologists, indigenous psychologists and psychological anthropologists – and most recently, international management researchers. This has led to a host of models, frameworks and theoretical propositions to explain the connection between national culture, ethnicity and human thought and behaviour, but a good deal of debate remains (Menon, 2004; p135):

> National culture has long been an elusive construct, seemingly offering a ready explanation for observed cross-national differences in values and behaviour, and yet very difficult to pin down in terms of definition, structure, or invariant processes that can yield infallible behavioural prescriptions.

It is important to realise that people who study culture have to make a number of tacit assumptions and each of these carries potential biases (Sackmann and Phillips, 2004). A 'framework' can be seen as a conceptual or real structure that can be used to help build or expand on an idea. The way in which we conceptualise culture tends to make it more or less legitimate to ask certain questions and identify different effects of culture. Using this, we can think about three approaches that have been used in cultural research:

THEORY AND PRACTICE

KEY FRAMEWORK

Three streams of CULTURAL research:

1 *Cross-national comparisons*: driven by a logic and assumption that 'culture equals nation'. This kind of research has been guided by a quest to identify universally applicable dimensions of national culture to help managers 'navigate' in different countries while doing their work. These dimensions of culture have generally been identified in large-scale quantitative studies. In this chapter we outline the best-known of these models.

2 *Study of intercultural interactions*: generally initiated once the competitive success of non-US management models was being questioned (such as the success of Japanese transplant factories in the USA and the growth of European and Asian multinational corporations). National culture is still seen as a fundamental source of individual identification, but within an organisational setting culture is considered to emerge as a result of a 'hidden negotiation' between interaction partners. More attention in this type of study is given to how

people interact across cultures and the characteristics and processes through which new cultures are formed.

3 *The multiple cultures perspective*: based on more recent conceptions of organisations operating in a multi-cultural context. Organisations are considered to be home to and carriers of several cultures at levels that include function, organisation and business unit, profession and occupational group, ethnic group, project-based network, regional institution, geographical and economic region, ideology and religion. Developments in information technology have enabled and accelerated the process of globalisation and new communication media have brought a wealth of real-time information from remote cultures, thereby changing patterns of problem-solving at work. This approach argues that individuals may identify with and hold simultaneous membership in several cultural groups.

The IHRM field has done much to bring the topic of national culture to the attention of researchers (Aycan *et al*, 2000) through the work successively of writers such as Hofstede, Trompenaars, Schwartz, Inglehart and the GLOBE team. Today we have therefore 'inherited' a number of dominant constructs from these early studies – and these will be covered in this chapter. But first it is important to note how we got to the understanding that we have today.

Much work in IHRM has been driven by assumptions of 'fit' – that certain HRM practices better fit into specific cultural contexts. Theories have examined national culture at different levels of analysis, ranging from behaviours and practices, through underlying values, down to underlying assumptions (Erez and Gati, 2004).

The field of cross-cultural HRM – the topic of this chapter – concerns the understanding, researching, applying and revising of our assumptions about the core values that differentiate culture, and then understanding their implications for behaviour at work.

KEY FRAMEWORK

Six implications of culture at work

Sparrow *et al* (2009) argue that cross-cultural HRM requires an understanding of:

- the ethnocentric management of what are called *theories of action* dominant in different countries

- the processes through which managers become *socialised* into these different theories of action

- the *ideological assumptions* that managers make through this socialisation

- comparisons of the *actual organisational behaviours* of people across countries and cultures

- the degree to which *cultural environments influence such behaviours*

THEORY AND PRACTICE

> • the way in which cross-cultural differences may be *linked to other domains of behaviour*, such as models of leadership, motivation, or human resource management.

To provide a balanced and contemporary understanding of the issues involved, we now go on to explain:

- key perspectives on the cross-cultural management field
- dimensions and models of culture
- methodological insights and more critical views of the evidence.

WHAT IS CULTURE?

The opening section has indicated the all-pervading influence of culture on our actions and values, and also the ongoing tensions between the forces of convergence of cultures and those of divergence. The concept of culture is deeply rooted in human history and its scope extends far beyond the boundaries of organisational activity. However, organisations are the product of the societies and times in which they exist, and as such are important manifestations of prevailing values and belief sets. But what *is* culture, exactly?

 ## REFLECTIVE ACTIVITY

Think about the differences between countries – and try to write a definition of 'culture'.

Attempting a definition of culture is difficult. At present there are estimated to be over 200 different definitions. The concept of culture is often seen as being vague and hard to grasp.

One of the core elements of culture is that it is a shaping process. For a culture to exist, members of a group or society share a distinct way of life with common values, attitudes and behaviours that are transmitted over time in a gradual, yet dynamic, process. Schein (1985; p9) defined culture as:

> A pattern of basic assumptions – invented, discovered, or developed by a given group as it learns to cope with its problems of external adaptation and internal integration – that has worked well enough to be considered valid and, therefore, to be taught to new members as the correct way to perceive, think, and feel in relation to those problems.

Although the problems that all human societies face are universal ('etic'), different groups will resolve them in different ways ('emic'). The resolutions are internalised and become taken for granted, but shape the way in which groups of people live and think. They represent the 'why' – *why* people behave the way they do, and *why* they hold the beliefs and values they espouse (Schneider and Barsoux, 1997).

Schein's (1985) model of organisational culture can also be applied to the broader concept of culture (see Figure 1). This model sees culture in terms of three levels, each distinguished by its visibility and accessibility to individuals.

Figure 1 Schein's three levels of culture

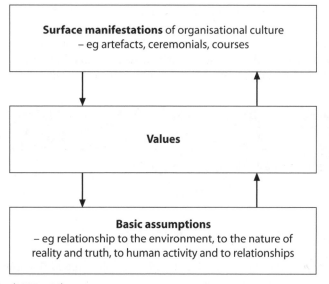

Source: Schein (1985; p14)

The *first level* consists of easily observed artefacts, rituals and behaviour. At this level culture is manifested in objects, customs, language and architecture. Within an organisational context we can observe many examples, such as differences in office space – ie preference for open or closed offices. In Japan, a highly collectivist country, large, open offices are the norm, whereas in Germany, a society where privacy is valued, separate offices are more likely. Where management fads impose practices that do not fit the culture of the society, we see adaptations such as the use of partition walls in open-plan offices by US and British workers, immortalised in the Dilbert cartoons. Dress codes, greetings rituals, the level of formality in addressing people – all these things and more make up the easily perceivable culture of the organisation (and likewise the nation).

The *second level* concerns values and beliefs. These are located below the surface manifestations and underpin them. Management scholars such as Hofstede, Trompenaars and Laurent (see below) have shown that employees and managers around the world differ widely in their values regarding work practices. Indeed, most work on national culture has concentrated on this level of analysis. Values, defined by Schwartz (1992, 1994, 1999) as cross-situational principles, lend themselves to easier measurement and can be linked to a lot of other work on individual psychology.

Finally, at the *third level* basic assumptions are the core of the culture. They include assumptions that individuals hold about societies and organisations and how they function. They relate to aspects of human behaviour, the nature of reality and the community's relationship to its environment. They are invisible, preconscious and 'taken for granted', and are therefore difficult to access.

Across these levels, cultural differences can be seen to lead to strongly contrasting ideas about what constitutes good management. In countries such as France, a leader has to stand apart and be the expert. In contrast, Scandinavian countries prefer a more democratic and participative style of leadership. These issues are explored in more detail later in this chapter and the following one.

 REFLECTIVE ACTIVITY

- What is the predominant style of leadership within your organisation?
- How does this reflect cultural influences?

ELEMENTS OF CULTURE

Triandis and Wasti (2008; p1) explain that Kluckhohn argued that culture is to society what memory is to individuals:

> It consists of what 'has worked' in the experience of a group of people so it was worth transmitting to peers and descendants.

The basic elements making up national-level cultures were seen by anthropologists Kluckhohn and Strodtbeck (1961) to lie in the responses that nations make in relation to six fundamental questions:

1 *Who are we?* How does a society conceive of people's qualities as individuals? If societies believe that people are basically good, they will try to exercise social control through praise and encouragement. If people are seen as fundamentally bad, control will be exercised via rules, laws and policing. If societies see people as capable of being changed, they will prefer reform to punishment. In management, this assumption can be seen in McGregor's (1960) Theory X and Theory Y. Under Theory X, workers are seen to be lazy and therefore to require as much direction and control as necessary. In contrast, under Theory Y, workers are seen as self-directed and responsible and requiring very little direct management.

2 *How do we relate to the world?* How important is nature and the environment in our thinking? And how do we conceive of nature? Some societies feel that

it is important to fit in with the world and accept it, as expressed in the Arabic 'insh'allah' or 'God willing'. In contrast, countries like the USA expect to overcome the constraints imposed by the environment. The American belief, continually voiced by celebrities such as Oprah Winfrey, that 'Anyone can be whatever they want' is exemplified in the Nike slogan 'Just do it!' This belief in individuals' ability to change strong environmental constraints is viewed by many in Europe and the East as naïve, where the influence of context in terms of societal norms and history is acknowledged.

3 *What do we do?* How do we think of ourselves and our situation? If you ask Britons 'What do you do?', they will tell you what profession they are in. If you ask the Japanese the same question, they will tell you who they work for. Are the most important things those you have done for yourself, or are they connected to your background and your group? Basically, status can be based either on what someone does, or on what someone is. In an ascriptive society, such as China or Venezuela, status is usually attributed to those who 'naturally' evoke admiration – for example, males and older people, or members of high-ranking families. In an achievement-based society, in contrast, a person gains status as a result of his or her own efforts and the climb up the organisational hierarchy.

4 *How do we relate to each other?* Do we think of ourselves as individuals or as members of a group? In many Western cultures we are happy to live far from members of our family and to have non-emotional links with the organisations we work for. In contrast, members of collectivist societies expect support from and loyalty to the extended family. In the business world, this aspect of culture affects the extent to which countries are happy with individual leadership and individual responsibility and target-setting, or the extent to which they prefer group-working and shared responsibility instead.

5 *How do we think about time?* In a cultural sense, time has two elements, locus and speed. In Western societies time moves in one direction, with the locus of attention on the future. In other societies – in much of the Asia-Pacific region, for example – all parts of time are connected. The past is as important as the present, with the future seen as less important. In a business context, Western societies see time as a commodity to be managed and used well. Other societies have a more relaxed approach to the timing of things, causing problems with perceptions of correct business conduct.

6 *How do we think about space?* The amount of space we feel we need varies around the world. In the northern hemisphere, the further west you go, the larger the rooms and offices tend to be. Physical space between people is also culturally determined. In Arab societies it is common to stand close to the person one is talking to; the British prefer to stand at about an arm's length away. The use of space in organisations gives clues as to the status of the person occupying the area, but these need to be interpreted from a cultural perspective.

These dimensions are amongst the most commonly used by management scholars, as shown in Figure 2. Note that after this original analysis, Hofstede

Figure 2 Key dimensions of culture

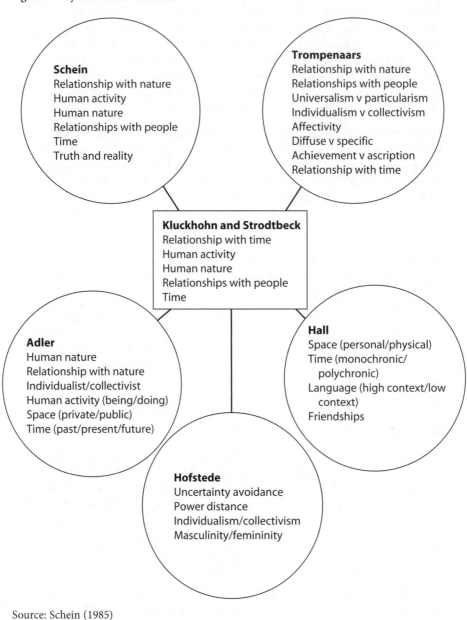

Source: Schein (1985)

added a fifth dimension to his work, and further work has been carried out under the GLOBE study on leadership (see the next chapter).

The increasing internationalisation of business has made the concept of culture and its impact for good or bad on organisations' operations a critical topic for study. An extensive literature has emerged in respect of both organisational culture and national cultural differences as they relate to work.

NATIONAL CULTURES AND ORGANISATION

Early research on the influence of cultural conditioning on collective human behaviours challenged the assumption of the universalism of management practices emanating from the USA (and, indeed, from other countries such as Japan). In an increasingly borderless world, managers need to know how national cultural differences might affect organisation structure and processes, notions of leadership, HRM practices, etc. Management scholars have consequently been inspired to translate the work of social anthropologists to the world of work. Three European researchers – André Laurent, Geert Hofstede and Fons Trompenaars – and a US anthropologist – Edward Hall – have been particularly influential in this respect.

HALL'S RESEARCH

Hall (1959, 1976, 2000) made a distinction between what he described as 'high-context' and 'low-context' cultures. This is a multi-faceted concept, but at its heart is the understanding that all cultures can be situated in relation to one another through the styles in which they communicate. In high-context cultures information is pre-programmed within the individual receiver of the message and the setting. Only minimal information is transmitted in the message. In a low-context culture the reverse is true. Context therefore refers to the framework, background and surrounding circumstances in which any communication or event takes place. Individuals from high- or low-context cultures have different ways of experiencing the world. Contexting allows individuals to screen data and avoid information overload, increasing their capacity to deal with higher amounts of complex information.

Individuals combine pre-programmed culture-specific context and information to create meaning, but the use of this context varies across cultures. Various country classifications have been created using Hall's concept, although there is debate about the strength of such categorisations (see Kittler *et al,* 2011 for a review). Examples of high-context societies include Japan, China, Korea, Taiwan, and Asian cultures in general, as well as native societies such as the Maoris in New Zealand. African, Middle Eastern, Latin American, Latin, Central and Slavic European cultures also fall in this category. So countries such as Argentina, Brazil, Colombia, Ecuador, Mexico, the Philippines, Hong Kong, Thailand, India, and Turkey are in this category. In high-context cultures there is a tendency to cater towards in-groups – groups that have similar expectations and experiences – and these groups can rely on their common background and on the context of the situation to explain what is really meant, rather than words. Much information is already internalised within groups. Discussions within in-groups can be wide-ranging and mutual expectations are generally accurate. Group members have their own private networks for information, which they keep to themselves. Many things can be left unsaid – the culture explains the meaning. Messages include other clues that enable you to understand the communication, such as body language and the use of silence. Understanding the role played by family status, age differences and social setting also help the receiver decode the real message. Messages can be implied and not uttered. The focus on in-groups means that relationships and group processes are important. High-context cultures are often more traditional and unchanging such that the context can remain stable over generations. Because of the importance of relationships, they tend to be deep and longer-lasting.

Examples of low-context societies include most of the English-speaking (interestingly, Britain is an exception to this rule) and Germanic-speaking countries, such as the USA, Canada, Australia, New Zealand, northern European countries such as Germany, Austria, Denmark, Sweden and Switzerland. In low-context cultures the situation has to be explained more explicitly because there are not common backgrounds. The boundaries between in-groups are much more fluid. Low-context cultures tend to be more changeable such that the context from one generation to another is very different. Mutual expectations are less accurate and communication is therefore more verbal, explicit, direct, linear and task-focused. Channels of communication are generally clear. Information is easy to obtain and is shared more overtly. Communication has an informational function and is a neutral tool to convey thoughts. Accuracy, directness and clarity in speech are therefore valued. Communications are more transactional and can end once completed. Familiarising yourself with the people before you communicate or conduct business is unnecessary. Hall also argued that time is not socially absolute and is similarly culturally programmed. He talked of low-context societies generally also being 'monochronic', by which he meant that time is sequential and highly scheduled – an endless ribbon of appointments and obligations – such that time can be 'wasted', 'killed', or 'saved'. Many high-context cultures are 'polychronic' (Japan is actually an exception). They have a more indulgent view of lateness. Time is like a balloon that swells and deflates dependent upon what is going on. The more people present, the larger the social network, the more useful the moment is. Meetings are just for giving general guidelines and may be cancelled or postponed if they are outside this moment.

Hall's ideas have been applied to the fields of international marketing, negotiation, conflict, communication (Kittler *et al*, 2011), with different studies classifying different combinations of countries as high- or low-context. Britain, France, Israel, Russia and Spain seem to create problems for researchers, having been classified as both high- and low-context.

 REFLECTIVE ACTIVITY

- Would you say that Britain is high or low context? Why?
- What aspects of international management might be more susceptible to differences between high- and low-context?

On balance, studies suggest that the UK should be considered to be a relatively high-context culture. Consider the following amusing examples in Table 1 that have been used to demonstrate to foreign managers the role that context can play in understanding what a British manager might really mean. The examples show that the individual must know what is meant at the covert or unexpressed level, and this knowledge enables them to react appropriately.

Table 1 Interpreting high-context communication

What the British say	What they really mean
Not bad	Good, or Very good
Quite good	A bit disappointing
Interesting	That *is* interesting, or It is interesting that you think it is interesting – it seems rather boring to me!
Oh, by the way . . .	I am about to get the primary purpose of our discussion
I was a bit disappointed that you . . .	I am most upset and cross
I hear what you say	I disagree and I do not wish to discuss it any further
With the greatest respect, . . .	I think that you are wrong (or a fool)
Perhaps we could consider some other options	I don't like your ideas

[handwritten margin note: Interpretations – different to what they mean]

The potential for miscommunication and misinterpretation of actions between high- and low-context cultures is clear from the example in Table 1. In general, differences in communication context have been shown to be important in relation to issues such as cross-cultural negotiations, mergers and acquisitions and, one could infer, performance management discussions.

There is some correlation between high-context cultures and cultures that value the group over the individual (collectivist societies) – but the correlation is limited. Similarly, not all high-context cultures are necessarily polychronic. Within a low-context culture, individuals can find themselves in high-context situations, and vice versa. So, for example, within a low-context American culture, communications among family members are generally high-context because of the high level of shared experience.

LAURENT'S RESEARCH

Laurent (1983, 1986) studied different conceptions of what an organisation is. He showed the importance of exploring national differences through the implicit management and organisational theories that managers carried in their heads (Laurent, 1986) – that is, that the best way to understand the role of culture is to ask managers questions and see how they solve the problem. Their solution will show how they think about the role of managers, hierarchies and power (as an example, see Figure 3). Analysis of the results showed that nationality had three times more influence on the shaping of managerial assumptions than any of the respondent's other characteristics such as age, education, function, type of company, etc.

Figure 3 The role of managers

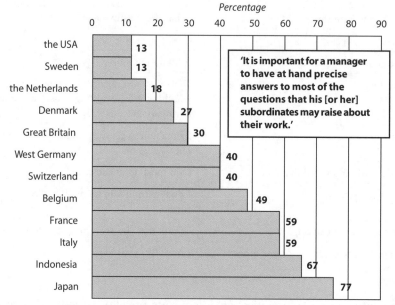

Source: adapted from Laurent (1986)

Whereas only a minority of North American and northern European managers agreed with this statement, a majority of southern Europeans and South-East Asians did. Laurent classified the nationalities concerned according to separate theories of organisations. Political systems epitomise organisations in which managers are seen to play a political role and negotiate. Obtaining power is seen as more important than achieving specific objectives. Latin European managers were more likely to adhere to this view than their Nordic and Anglo counterparts. Role-formalisation systems describe organisations where managers prefer detailed job descriptions and well-defined roles and functions. Germanic managers felt at ease in this type of system, whereas Nordic and Anglo managers felt that the world was too complex to be able clearly to define roles and functions. Finally, hierarchical systems reflect the differences in opinion mentioned above, where the boss is expected to be respected through the possession of expert knowledge.

Laurent (1986, p96) made it clear that 'the art of managing has no homeland'. He argued that HRM is itself a cultural artefact, that universalist management principles needed to be differentiated, and that examinations of culture internationally should focus more on understanding how behaviours might be adaptable to an organisational culture without being immersed in the 'deeper ideological textures' or 'fabrics of meaning' associated with national cultures (Laurent, 1986; p98), and that without understanding these different levels of culture, international organisations likely had illusions of control with regard to many of their international subsidiaries.

HOFSTEDE'S RESEARCH

One of the most influential pieces of research in relation to national cultures is the work of Hofstede (1980, 2001). Hofstede's framework is widely used by researchers and practitioners in the field of intercultural management – although, as we show later, the work has also been subject to more criticism as time has gone by. Hofstede found that the differences in responses could be explained by four main factors:

- power distance
- uncertainty avoidance
- individualism
- masculinity.

POWER DISTANCE

Power distance relates to the extent to which societies accept that power in institutions and organisations is and should be distributed unequally. In organisational terms, this relates to the centralisation of authority and the degree of autocratic leadership. Societies with 'high power distance' scores are reflected in hierarchical organisations where it is felt to be right that the superior is seen to be more powerful than subordinates. Examples of countries with high power distance scores are the Philippines, Singapore, France and Greece. In contrast, countries with lower power distance scores such as Britain, Sweden and New Zealand favour a more democratic style of management and flatter organisational structures (see Table 2).

UNCERTAINTY AVOIDANCE

Uncertainty avoidance refers to the degree to which societies feel threatened by ambiguous situations and the extent to which they try to avoid uncertain situations. In countries with high uncertainty avoidance, such as France, organisations adopt strong bureaucracies and career stability and generally discourage risk-taking activities. Countries such as Sweden, Britain and Norway which exhibit low uncertainty avoidance will adopt more flexible structures and encourage more diverse views (see Table 3).

INDIVIDUALISM

Individualism reflects the extent to which individuals are integrated into groups. Where individualism is high – for example, in the USA – people are expected

Table 2 Power distance index (PDI) rankings for Hofstede indices

Score/rank	Country	Score/rank	Country	Score/rank	Country
1	Malaysia	18/19	Turkey	37	Jamaica
2/3	Guatemala	20	Belgium	38	the USA
2/3	Panama	21/23	East Africa	39	Canada
4	the Philippines	21/23	Peru	40	the Netherlands
5/6	Mexico	21/23	Thailand	41	Australia
5/6	Venezuela	24/25	Chile	42/44	Costa Rica
7	Arab countries	24/25	Portugal	42/44	West Germany
8/9	Ecuador	26	Uruguay	42/44	Great Britain
8/9	Indonesia	27/28	Greece	45	Switzerland
10/11	India	27/28	South Korea	46	Finland
10/11	West Africa	29/30	Iran	47/48	Norway
12	Yugoslavia	29/30	Taiwan	47/48	Sweden
13	Singapore	31	Spain	49	Republic of Ireland
14	Brazil	32	Pakistan	50	New Zealand
15/16	France	33	Japan	51	Denmark
15/16	Hong Kong	34	Italy	52	Israel
17	Colombia	35/36	Argentina	53	Austria
18/19	El Salvador	35/36	South Africa		

Source: Hofstede (1991)

Table 3 Uncertainty avoidance index (UAI) rankings for Hofstede indices

Score/rank	Country	Score/rank	Country	Score/rank	Country
1	Greece	19	Israel	37	Australia
2	Portugal	20	Colombia	38	Norway
3	Guatemala	21/22	Venezuela	39/40	South Africa
4	Uruguay	21/22	Brazil	39/40	New Zealand
5/6	Belgium	23	Italy	41/42	Indonesia
5/6	El Salvador	24/25	Pakistan	41/42	Canada
7	Japan	24/25	Austria	43	the USA
8	Yugoslavia	26	Taiwan	44	the Philippines
9	Peru	27	Arab countries	45	India
10/15	France	28	Ecuador	46	Malaysia
10/15	Chile	29	West Germany	47/48	Great Britain
10/15	Spain	30	Thailand	47/48	Republic of Ireland
10/15	Costa Rica	31/32	Iran	49/50	Hong Kong
10/15	Panama	31/32	Finland	49/50	Sweden
10/15	Argentina	33	Switzerland	51	Denmark
16/17	Turkey	34	West Africa	52	Jamaica
16/17	South Korea	35	the Netherlands	53	Singapore
18	Mexico	36	East Africa		

Source: Hofstede (1991)

Table 4 Individualism index (IDV) rankings for Hofstede indices

Score/rank	Country	Score/rank	Country	Score/rank	Country
1	the USA	19	Israel	37	Hong Kong
2	Australia	20	Spain	38	Chile
3	Great Britain	21	India	39/41	West Africa
4/5	Canada	22/23	Japan	39/41	Singapore
4/5	the Netherlands	22/23	Argentina	39/41	Thailand
6	New Zealand	24	Iran	42	El Salvador
7	Italy	25	Jamaica	43	South Korea
8	Belgium	26/27	Brazil	44	Taiwan
9	Denmark	26/27	Arab countries	45	Peru
10/11	Sweden	28	Turkey	46	Costa Rica
10/11	France	29	Uruguay	47/48	Pakistan
12	Republic of Ireland	30	Greece	47/48	Indonesia
13	Norway	31	the Philippines	49	Colombia
14	Switzerland	32	Mexico	50	Venezuela
15	West Germany	33	East Africa	51	Panama
16	South Africa	34	Yugoslavia	52	Ecuador
17	Finland	35	Portugal	53	Guatemala
18	Austria	36	Malaysia		

Source: Hofstede (1991)

to take care of themselves and their immediate family only. In collectivist societies such as Japan, however, people are integrated into strong, cohesive groups which throughout people's lifetimes continue to protect them in exchange for unquestioning loyalty (see Table 4). Whereas in individualist societies the emphasis for individuals within organisations is to gain self-respect and personal achievement, in collectivist societies the focus is on fitting in harmoniously and face-saving.

Hofstede (1991) found a strong correlation between high power distance and collectivism and vice versa in the countries within the IBM sample. He explains this by stating that in cultures in which people are dependent on groups, the people are usually also dependent on power figures. The converse is true in individualist countries. Exceptions to this are countries such as France and Belgium, which combine high power distance with strong individualism. Crozier (1964) argues that a belief in an absolutist authority can be reconciled within a bureaucratic system where impersonal rules avoid the need for direct dependence relationships, a characteristic of collectivist societies.

MASCULINITY

Masculinity measures the extent to which the dominant values are (in Hofstede's terms) 'male' – values such as assertiveness, the acquisition of money and goods and not caring for others. Gender roles are more rigidly defined in masculine societies than in 'feminine' societies. The most masculine countries in Hofstede's framework are Japan and Austria, with the USA falling into this category. In contrast, the Scandinavian countries fall into the feminine category, with more emphasis on work–life balance.

Table 5 Masculinity index (MAS) rankings for Hofstede indices

Score/rank	Country	Score/rank	Country	Score/rank	Country
1	Japan	18/19	Hong Kong	37/38	Spain
2	Austria	20/21	Argentina	37/38	Peru
3	Venezuela	20/21	India	39	East Africa
4/5	Italy	22	Belgium	40	El Salvador
4/5	Switzerland	23	Arab countries	41	South Korea
6	Mexico	24	Canada	42	Uruguay
7/8	Republic of Ireland	25/26	Malaysia	43	Guatemala
7/8	Jamaica	25/26	Pakistan	44	Thailand
9/10	Great Britain	27	Brazil	45	Portugal
9/10	West Germany	28	Singapore	46	Chile
11/12	the Philippines	29	Israel	47	Finland
11/12	Colombia	30/31	Indonesia	48/49	Yugoslavia
13/14	South Africa	30/31	West Africa	48/49	Costa Rica
13/14	Ecuador	32/33	Turkey	50	Denmark
15	the USA	32/33	Taiwan	51	the Netherlands
16	Australia	34	Panama	52	Norway
17	New Zealand	35/36	Iran	53	Sweden
18/19	Greece	35/36	France		

Source: Hofstede (1991)

THE CHINESE VALUES SURVEY

Concerned about the Western bias amongst cross-cultural researchers, Bond – a Canadian who lives and works in Hong Kong – and a group of Chinese colleagues developed a questionnaire reflecting Chinese cultural values. Twenty of the countries were also in Hofstede's study. The results from the study revealed four dimensions of culture, three of which reflected Hofstede's dimensions of power distance, individualism/collectivism and masculinity/femininity. The fourth represented Chinese values related to Confucianism. Bond and his colleagues called this dimension 'Confucian work dynamism'. Hofstede relabelled it 'long-term versus short-term orientation'. In countries exhibiting a high Confucian work dynamism, or which are long-term-oriented, there is a focus on the future, and thrift (ie saving) and persistence are valued. Companies in Japan, which is an example of a long-term-oriented society, have traditionally taken a longer-term view of investments. In contrast to companies in Western economies, it is not necessary to show profits year by year, but rather progress towards a longer-term goal. Japan's continuing economic crisis may well force a fundamental change in perspective for its organisations. In contrast, countries low in Confucian work dynamism, or short-term-oriented, value the past and present. There is respect for tradition and fulfilling social obligations, but the present is the most important.

MANAGEMENT IMPLICATIONS OF POWER DISTANCE AND UNCERTAINTY AVOIDANCE

These dimensions can inform our understanding. For example, taking these two dimensions together reveals differences in the implicit model that people from different cultures may have about organisational structure and functioning (see Figure 4).

Employees in high power distance and low uncertainty avoidance societies such as Singapore, Hong Kong and Indonesia tend to think of their organisations as traditional families. The head of the family is expected to protect family members physically and economically in exchange for continued loyalty from family members. A key control and co-ordination mechanism for the family is a standardisation of work processes by specifying the contents of the work.

In societies where both power distance and uncertainty avoidance are high – such as France, Brazil and Mexico – organisations are viewed as pyramids. Reporting lines are clear. Management provides co-ordination and control by emphasising who has authority over whom, and in what way this authority can be exercised.

A combination of medium uncertainty avoidance and low power distance gives rise to organisations which are perceived as well-oiled machines. Roles and procedures are well defined and co-ordination and control are achieved through standardisation and certification of skills. Examples of countries in this quadrant are Israel, Austria, Germany and Switzerland.

Finally, in countries where there is low uncertainty avoidance and low power distance, a 'village market' model is apparent. This model includes countries such as the UK, the USA, Denmark and the Republic of Ireland. Here, control and co-ordination tends to take place through mutual adjustment of people through informal communication, and by specifying desired results.

 REFLECTIVE ACTIVITY

Using the Hofstede dimensions,

- What would be the key people management considerations for a UK-based organisation that wished to expand into France, Germany and Japan?

Figure 4 Power distance index and uncertainty avoidance index comparison

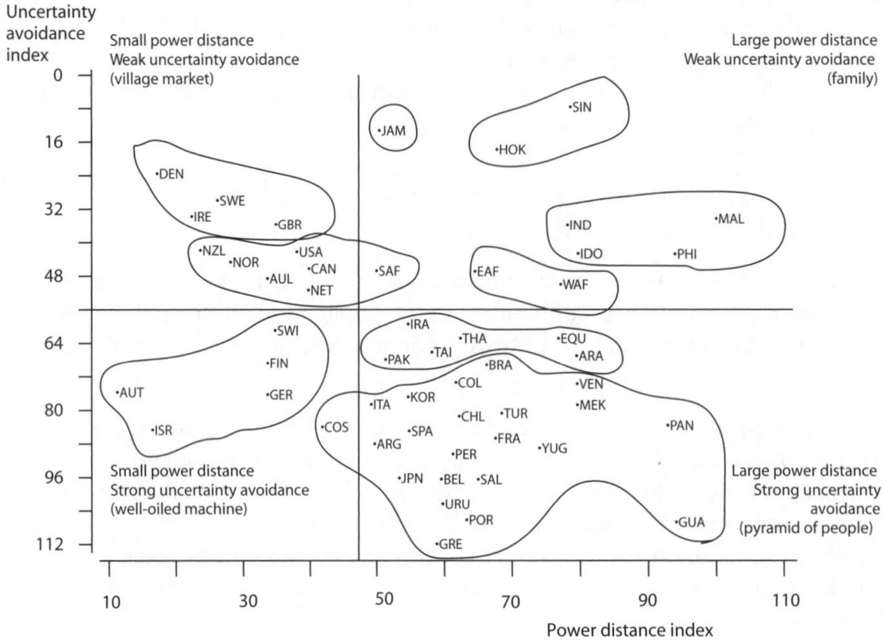

Uncertainty
avoidance
index

Small power distance
Weak uncertainty avoidance
(village market)

Large power distance
Weak uncertainty avoidance
(family)

Small power distance
Strong uncertainty avoidance
(well-oiled machine)

Large power distance
Strong uncertainty
avoidance
(pyramid of people)

Power distance index

Key							
ARA	Arab countries (Egypt, Lebanon, Libya, Kuwait, Iraq, Saudi Arabia, the UAE)	EAF	East Africa (Kenya, Ethiopia, Tanzania, Zambia)	IRE	Republic of Ireland	PHI	the Philippines
				ISR	Israel	POR	Portugal
				ITA	Italy	SAF	South Africa
		EQA	Ecuador	JAM	Jamaica	SAL	El Salvador
ARG	Argentina	FIN	Finland	JPN	Japan	SIN	Singapore
AUL	Australia	FRA	France	KOR	South Korea	SWE	Sweden
AUT	Austria	GBR	Great Britain	MAL	Malaysia	TAI	Taiwan
BEL	Belgium	GER	West Germany	MEX	Mexico	THA	Thailand
BRA	Brazil	GRE	Greece	NET	the Netherlands	TUR	Turkey
CAN	Canada	GUA	Guatemala	NOR	Norway	URU	Uruguay
CHL	Chile	HOK	Hong Kong	NZL	New Zealand	USA	the USA
COL	Colombia	IDO	Indonesia	PAK	Pakistan	VEN	Venezuela
COS	Costa Rica	IND	India	PAN	Panama	WAF	West Africa (Nigeria, Ghana, Sierra Leone)
DEN	Denmark	IRA	Iran	PER	Peru	YUG	Yugoslavia

Source: Hoecklin (1994; p34)

REFLECTIVE ACTIVITY

To highlight the complexity of culture, take the key cultural models that have just been explained and analyse the national culture of India. How would you handle the many regional (state) cultures in this analysis, or differences between the industrialising areas versus the others?

LIMITATIONS AND CULTURAL GENERALISATIONS OF WORK AT THE NATIONAL LEVEL

 CONFUCIANISM IN ASIA

CASE STUDIES

In Korea the role of national culture, including Confucianism, is still considered to have a powerful, multi-faceted and ingrained influence on HRM (Rowley and Bae, 2004). It is embedded however within the *chaebol* (meaning an octopus with many tentacles) – family-founded but large organisations owning and controlling large diversified business groups with a plethora of subsidiaries. These include such organisations as Samsung, LG, Hyundai Motors, and Hanwa. Rowley and Bae (2003) have laid out the 12 most dominant characteristics and paradoxes of culture and management in Korea based on three shaping factors of Confucianism (family), Japan and the military. For each influence they explain the concept, meaning, management behaviours and characteristics, and the paradoxes this creates. Six of the 12 influences are Confucian:

- *Inhwa* means harmony and solidarity (with company as a family-type community)

- *Yongo* concerns connections by blood, geography or education, and influences solidarity within inner circles, recruitment via common ties and relationships with owners

- *Chung* concerns loyalty and subordination to superiors, shaping a paternalistic approach to employee welfare

- *Un* concerns indebtedness to the organisation and members, impacting on respect, tolerance and patience towards organisational agendas

- *Uiri* concerns integrity towards others in everyday life, impacting on long-term relationships

- *Gocham* concerns seniority in service and being an old-timer, impacting on seniority-based rewards and promotions.

In Hong Kong – also considered a Confucianism culture – it is small, local Chinese family businesses that employ a significant number of employees. Their key decision-makers and managements have reached the third generation following on from founders at the beginning of the 1900s. HRM policies are different from the strategic HRM model. Chinese heads encapsulate ethnocentric values of Confucian paternalism, patriachy and personalism manifested in three key relationships: power connected to ownership, a benevolently autocratic leadership style and personal rather than neutral relationships. Decision-making is centralised and emphasises harmony and compliance, seniority, loyalty, mutual obligation and informal networking at the workplace. Consequently (Chan and Lui, 2004; pp82–83),

firms may recruit from a variety of sources but selection is pragmatically based on personal recommendations ... Remuneration reflects seniority and degree of loyalty rather than performance ... Firms can enjoy a strong internal labour market ... However, the HRM functions are still found to be separated from the decision and power core of the business and from other business operations [which] may pose problems as these companies expand overseas.

Question:

What is the more dominant influence on culture in Hong Kong and Korea here – Confucian values or the way these operate in their national context?

Lin and Ho (2009) explain how, after 50 years of political and economic separation, people in China, Taiwan, and Hong Kong vary in their adherence to Confucian values.

Although cultural frameworks are useful in explaining some of the key ways in which societies (within a work context) might differ, it is important to note some of their limitations. The topic of *national* culture is not without debate. Some people go so far as to say that we might even be asking the wrong questions. As the field has matured there has been some disquiet about many inherited research assumptions (Schwartz and Bardi, 2001; p268):

> Researchers, including ourselves, have focused almost exclusively on differences in value priorities. When we switch our focus to ask about similarities, we discover a striking degree of consensus across individuals and societies.

There has been a growing critique of work on national culture in the international management field. In attempting to categorise cultural groups, a lot of models have produced dichotomies – such as individualistic versus collectivistic cultures – that rely on what might be erroneous assumptions. By categorising cultures we might be tempted to view culture as being immutable, monolithic and able to be captured with scores on a limited set of cultural dimensions.

REFLECTIVE ACTIVITY

Hofstede's work – and also the GLOBE study on leadership discussed in the next chapter – have been very influential, but of course as time has gone by the evidence has come under greater critical scrutiny. Gerhart and Fang (2005) re-analysed the original data, and Gerhart (2008) has marshalled a number of criticisms of such work which tend to support the view that the evidence is strong enough to argue that effective organisations have to adapt foreign management to local cultures. Research on national culture assumes a number of things, such as that: between-country differences are substantially larger than within-country differences; country differences in culture are larger than differences due to other factors such as organisation; country effects can be equated with culture; a misfit between practice and culture produces inefficiency; management discretion is substantially lowered by culture; and that companies have no ability to shape the way they attract, recruit and hire and so reflect national patterns. He argues that Hofstede's evidence is inconsistent. When the effect size is calculated, and a standard is used to estimate the importance of this effect size, their re-analysis suggested that when looking at the individual level, country on average explained only 2.2 per cent of the variance in values. Looking at the GLOBE study, which analysed country differences in organisational culture, the researchers found that 23 per cent of differences in organisational culture (practices) could be explained by country (which means that national culture accounts for roughly one quarter of the total country effect, signalling the importance of institutional influences covered in the next chapter). When looking between countries, national culture only explained 6 per cent of differences in organisational culture.

● Does the management literature overstate the role of national culture versus organisational action?

The majority of the work undertaken in this area still has been carried out by Western, and in particular, European, researchers. Bond's work on Chinese values is an example of a move to address this problem. A study of global values carried out by the Dentsu Institute of Human Studies (2001), based in Japan, between 1996 and 2000 called into question several conventional Western perceptions of Asian cultural values and showed more similarities between Western and Asian respondents than is usually the case.

It is dangerous to over-generalise or stereotype on the basis of these descriptions of generalised characteristics of cultural values. Hofstede himself makes the point that these generalisations are valid only as statistical statements about large numbers of people. Value contrasts are not either/or dichotomies but rather descriptions of two cultures' overall tendencies to be nearer to or farther from a particular value orientation. For instance, when comparing two countries across the same value, it is important to note that the strength of the value in each country will have its own bell-shaped distribution curve. However, the norms between the two may be quite different. Understanding the relative distance between the norms allows people to generalise about the relative difficulty members of one culture may have in relating to members of the other culture along that dimension (see Figure 5). In addition, an awareness of the exceptions to the norms at the end of the curves and the possible overlap between the curves helps to avoid stereotyping (see Wederspahn, 2000).

Approaches that create categories of cultures have then been criticised for making a *homogeneity assumption*. This criticism argues that there are significant differences on most of these sorts of measures across groups within any single

Figure 5 Value contrast curves

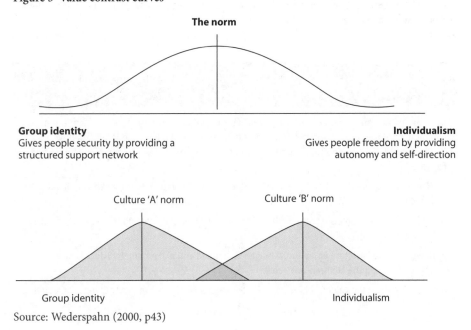

Source: Wederspahn (2000, p43)

country (Koslowsky *et al,* 2002). Not only huge countries – such as Russia, China, Indonesia and India – but also small countries – like Belgium and Switzerland – may contain distinctive multiple cultures within their national borders. For example, the individualistic cultures of the USA, Italy, Germany, France and Britain can still be differentiated and even within any one of them, multiple brands of individualism exist across ethnic groups. Regional differences have an impact. In the USA, for example, there are distinctive Northeast, Midwest, West and Deep South brands of individualism that can be identified. Similarly, the collectivistic systems of Confucianism, Buddhism and Marxism differ significantly from each other in particular values, meanings and customs. The homogeneity assumption rests on the ability to infer that there are commonalities of core beliefs and assumptions that cut across ethnic, linguistic and religious differences within any single country, and that these shared commonalities can still explain important work behaviours, despite the variety of espoused values and observed behaviours that evidently differ within a country (Menon, 2004).

WHICH CULTURE DO YOU BELONG TO?

Is it a fair or sensible question in today's world to ask people which country has their cultural allegiance? What sort of complex cultural identities do people have? How does this impact on organisational behaviour? Wibbeke (2009) talks about leaders having a 'tri-partite' culture: the culture you grew up in, the culture you live in, and the culture of your organisation. She notes that if you look at a company like Google, about 70 per cent of the people who work there were not born or raised in the USA. This is true of most high-tech companies in Silicon Valley. She says that if you look at somebody who was raised in China until the age of 15 then went to the USA to go to school in New York and now is working in California for Oracle and ask them: 'When you're making an important ethical decision, what do you go back to?' they always say, 'I go back to the ethics that my parents gave me. Those will help guide me.'

 REFLECTIVE ACTIVITY

Develop a short questionnaire drawing upon on the Hofstede (or Trompenaars) continua (see how hard it is to construct some questions that make sense at the individual level!). Use this instrument to determine where you and a group of other nationals fall against the constructs.

● Where do you feel you reflect a national culture – where do you believe that you are in some way different?

● Is there a considerable standard deviation around the averages that cultural researchers write about?

● How pervasive is culture at the individual level? Should you expect that individuals might or might not reflect the cultural constructs?

● Is culture about the values of individuals or the values of the institutions that they subscribe to?

Closely associated with this argument about within-societal variation, Gelfand *et al* (2006) have redrawn attention to the idea of 'cultural *tightness* or *looseness*', and developed a series of explanations for how this impacts on life in organisations. 'Tightness' reflects the strength of social norms (how clear or pervasive the norms are within any society) and the degree of sanctions (how much tolerance there is for deviation), both of which vary from one society to another. Loose and tight societies also differ in terms of the amount of accountability (Tetlock, 2002) and the degree to which there is 'felt accountability' amongst individuals (Frink and Klimoski, 1998). It is only where individuals have this 'felt sense of accountability' that external societal constraints get internalised into their own behaviour. It is a separate construct from individualism/collectivism. Anthropologists argue that countries such as Japan, Germany or Singapore, or certain ethnic groups such as Pueblo Indians, are tight societies, whereas for example in the USA, New Zealand, northern Finland or in Thailand, society is much looser (Pelto, 1968). The degree of tightness depends on things like the degree of population density, the economic system and the role of kinship. Individuals in 'tight' societies have a lower sense of separation of their own self from others' selves (called psychological differentiation). This idea has only sporadically been discussed by people studying national culture – in the work, for example, of Berry (1966), Triandis (1989) and Carpenter (2000). Gelfand *et al* (2007) point out that tightness/looseness varies within societies as well – between, for example, different domains of life, regions, and ethnic and religious groups.

 REFLECTIVE ACTIVITY

- To what extent would someone from the southern states of the USA share their values and beliefs with those of all North Americans?

- Would a person from Delhi share the values and beliefs of someone from Madras?

Finally, some important points have been made about how individuals will vary in how they exhibit a culturally related behaviour *depending on the situation*. Members of a collectivistic culture may be highly communal with ingroup members, but that does not mean they are communal with outgroup members. Members of individualistic cultures may actually be more communal with outgroup members than collectivists! Consider the hospitality that individualist Americans can show to strangers. The reference group is therefore very important (Freeman and Bordia, 2001). Single-dimension cultural factors rarely capture the complexity of such individual behaviour.

It is important to be aware, then, that the more popular culture has become as a means of explaining the way people behave the way they at work across countries, the more careful the global HRM practitioner has to be at taking findings at face value. There are good and bad studies of national culture, and there are good and bad measures of cultural values. Even when culture has been assessed in some direct way, or where cross-country differences are used as a proxy for culture, it is important to be aware of some of the main criticisms that have been made about cultural research.

A common feature of many studies has been to test the way that national contextual variables – such as individualism and collectivism – moderate the behaviour of individual workers. This is sometimes done by either taking a country-level measure (like the ones outlined in this chapter devised by people like Hofstede or Trompenaars) and then assigning each individual a score on the basis of the average score for the nation they come from. Or they might measure the individual using instruments that were really designed to assess national-level constructs. The first approach falls foul of the *ecological fallacy*, observed by Hofstede (1980), whereby national-level data is used to predict individual-level behaviour, which leads to incorrect estimations of the real effects of the contextual variables. This manifests itself in two ways. Firstly, cultural values which are known to be held by a group are projected onto an individual who is a member of the group. This is known as stereotyping. Stereotyping of itself is not necessarily a negative process, but rather a way for us to try to make sense of the world by categorising things and individuals. However, it can become problematic when it is inaccurate – if, for example, we assume that all Japanese are group-oriented and do not show emotion, or that all Swedish managers favour consensus-based, participative work practices. Stereotyping becomes dangerous when group-level data is used to categorise individuals, particularly in a negative and prejudicial manner. Secondly, an ecological fallacy can occur by projecting from individuals to groups.

 REFLECTIVE ACTIVITY

From our discussions of recent criticisms of research into cultural differences:

- Can we safely assume the existence of single national cultures?
- Is the influence of culture as an explanatory variable decreasing in the wake of continued globalisation?
- Are there conditions that elicit universal responses from employees regardless of culture?

- The study of national culture is still a topic of vigorous ongoing academic debate.

- The practitioner press greatly encourages the creation of interculturally competent organisations as the way to success in global business. It also reports on many failures.

- Evidence from both the research world and business events repeatedly emphasises the enormous impact of different cultural orientations (for good or bad) on our everyday lives.

- A number of academic professions have contributed to our understanding of how and why behaviour appears in specific cultural contexts – anthropologists, sociologists, cross-cultural psychologists, cultural psychologists, psychological anthropologists and, most recently, international management researchers.

- There have been three main streams of work: cross-national comparisons driven by a logic and assumption that 'culture equals nation'; the study of intercultural interactions and how people interact across cultures and the characteristics and processes through which new cultures are formed; and more recent conceptions of organisations operating in a multicultural context.

- Organisations are considered to be home to and carriers of several cultures at levels that include function, organisation and business unit, profession and occupational group, ethnic group, project-based network, regional institution, geographical and economic region, ideology and religion.

- Theories have examined national culture at different levels of analysis, ranging from behaviours and practices, through underlying values, down to underlying assumptions.

- A good deal of work in IHRM has been driven by assumptions of 'fit' – the idea that certain HRM practices better fit into specific cultural contexts.

- Our understanding of cultural differences relies mainly, however, on cross-cultural frameworks, working at a national level and derived from quantitative sampling techniques. National culture is also reflected at the individual level in terms of the value orientations that people hold.

- These frameworks provide practising managers with an initial map of the types of issues they may need to take into account when working in an intercultural context.

- But it is dangerous to overgeneralise or stereotype on the basis of these descriptions of generalised characteristics of cultural values. Such generalisations are valid only as statistical statements about large numbers of people.

- By keeping these as helpful indicators, and understanding the limitations of some of our evidence and the assumptions that we make when we try to study culture, managers can avoid the tendency to stereotype, but can also experiment with appropriate behaviours and processes that will hopefully lead to better intercultural ability.

- Although the impact of cultural differences is important at an individual level, it is more important to understand what effect they can have at the team and organisational level.

LEARNING QUESTIONS

1 How well do the indices and measures here reflect your own country? Give reasons for your answer.

2 Are national cultural differences likely to be more, or less, strong than organisational or gender differences in culture? Explain your views.

3 How might cultural differences make it difficult for a UK visitor to Japan to do business?

4 Choose an aspect of HRM such as selection, appraisals, training or industrial relations, and explain how cultural differences might affect it.

5 Argue that an organisation should have clear rules about the management of people that cover operations in all its different countries. Argue that such rules should be varied for the different national cultures represented within the organisation. Can the two views be reconciled?

6 What does the study of how managers actually spend their time and their decision-making powers in like-for-like organisations really tell us? What are the messages for key areas of HRM policy?

EXPLORE FURTHER

Sackmann, S. A. and Phillips, M. E. (2004) 'Contextual influences on culture research: shifting assumptions for new workplace realities', *International Journal of Cross Cultural Management*, 4 (3): 370–390. This article explains the ways in which researchers conceptualise culture, the research questions they consider it legitimate to ask, and their attempts to identify its effects. It lays out the assumptions that underpin three different approaches within the field: cross-national studies, studies of intercultural interactions, and the multiple cultures perspective. In explaining the research discourse in recent years, the article also highlights the increasing criticism of the cross-national comparison research stream, and argues that we now must examine more than just bicultural contexts.

Aycan, Z., Kanungo, R. N., Mendonca, M., Yu, K., Deller, J., Stahl, G. and Khursid, A. (2000) 'Impact of culture on human resource management practices: a 10 country comparison', *Applied Psychology: An International Review*, 49 (1): 192–221.

Gelfand, M. J., Nishii, L. H. and Raver, J. L. (2006) 'On the nature and importance of cultural tightness-looseness', *Journal of Applied Psychology*, 91 (6): 1225–1244.

Kittler, M. G., Rygl, D., Mackinnon, A. (2011) 'Beyond culture or beyond control? Reviewing the use of Hall's high-/low-context concept', *International Journal of Cross Cultural Management*, 11 (1): 63–82.

CHAPTER 3

Culture and Organisational Life

LEARNING OUTCOMES

When they have read this chapter, students will:

- be aware of the impact of culture on organisational behaviour and HRM practices

- appreciate the impact of culture on leadership styles

- be aware of the role of individual factors such as global leadership and cultural intelligence in helping organisations to internationalise.

INTRODUCTION

In the previous chapter we examined the notion of national culture. We argued that even though we need to avoid falling into the trap of cultural stereotyping, culture can have some surprisingly deep and complex impacts on organisational behaviour. In this chapter we explore just what these may be. However, the world is changing rapidly and it is sensible to ask if all of the messages from international management research always translate to the new global contexts. We began the last chapter with the example of some transcultural failures faced by some US-German organisational combinations. Will MNCs from the emerging economies face the same cultural constraints?

CASE STUDIES

THE INDIAN QUESTION

In 2003 the Indian government allowed companies with proven track records to make investments in non-related areas. Data from finance advisers revealed that in 2002, 28 foreign companies were acquired by Indian companies. The figure climbed to 49 in 2003, 60 in 2004 and 100 in 2005. By 2006 the business press began to ask what the experience of globalising Indian MNCs would be in the field of international mergers. India was reaching the point where Indian companies would be acquiring more overseas than international companies would be acquiring in India. India moved to fifth place among outwardinvesting emerging markets. Only Hong Kong (China), China, Brazil and Russia had higher outflows in the year 2006. That year the Sakhalin-I oil project in Russia, Betapharm Arneimittel GmbH, a generic drug company in Germany, Thomson SA, a plastic tubes company in Italy, and Comicrom, a Chile-based IT company were all acquired either fully or partly by Indian companies. The Tata group also acquired a 30 per cent stake in Energy Brands Inc, a speciality mineral-water and energy drink company in the USA. India's top 24 MNCs by foreign assets that year had US $15.3 billion in assets abroad, nearly US $13 billion in foreign sales, and employed 60,000 persons abroad. 2007 then saw the Tata Steel acquisition of Corus Group in the UK for about US $12.7 billion, while GAIL – formerly the Gas Authority of India Limited – invested US $4.2

billion in petrochemicals in Saudi Arabia. The scale of the outward foreign direct investment (OFDI) from emerging markets was estimated at US $332 billion in 2008 – six times as much as the total world flows of US $56 billion 25 years earlier.

The 2009 Ernst & Young *Global Megatrends Report* noted that the financial crisis that erupted in the United States in 2008 and the global economic crisis in 2009, with falling or negative growth, falling exports and investment, and tightening credit markets, would dent progress for a while, but that we are witnessing a new dynamic. MNCs from emerging markets are positioned across a range of sectors, with radically different governance structures from each other and from Western MNCs, ranging from family-owned conglomerates to narrowly focused corporations, and they approach expansion in different ways.

Questions:

- Are MNCs from emerging countries globalising in the same way as those from developed countries did?

- Will their acquisitions face the same sorts of cultural challenges as documented in the Western literature?

- Using the cultural frameworks from the previous chapter, what specific cultural differences might hamper Indian MNCs?

THE IMPACT OF CULTURE ON ORGANISATIONAL BEHAVIOUR AND HRM

Cultural assumptions answer questions for group members. They suggest the types of interactions and behaviours which should lead to effectiveness. They determine the information that managers will notice, interpret and retain. They lead to different ways of seeing the same event and therefore different problem-resolution strategies. A vast body of literature exists which reports empirical evidence suggesting that employees and managers from different cultures are different from each other in the processes, behaviours and values that come into play in a decision-making situation. Cultural assumptions are therefore linked to a wide range of organisational behaviours (Tayeb, 1996).

REFLECTIVE ACTIVITY

Draw upon some of the evidence in this chapter to argue, in any one national setting, how culture could be considered to impact on each of the following:

- power and authority relationships
- coping with uncertainty and risk-taking
- interpersonal trust
- loyalty and commitment
- motivation
- control and discipline
- co-ordination and integration
- communication
- consultation
- participation.

To what extent are these organisational behaviours also determined by an individual's psychology (itself a product of various cultural, social, political and personal influences), his or her life-stage, and his or her generational subculture?

One way in which academics attempt to show the impact of national culture is to compare managers who work in similar organisations across societies. For example, Tayeb (1988) found that matched-pair Indian and English organisations were similar on such universal dimensions as specialisation and centralisation but were considerably different from one another on the amount of consultation and delegation of authority that took place. English managers consulted their subordinates more widely before they made a decision and delegated authority farther down the hierarchy than did their Indian counterparts. Also, English employees communicated with each other to a far greater extent than did the Indian employees. The differences between the two samples were consistent with the cultural differences between Indian and English peoples as a whole (Tayeb, 1988; p91).

A comparative study of Chinese and British manufacturing firms showed that decisions which were broadly within the competence of supervisors in the British organisations were within the gift only of senior managers in China (Easterby-Smith *et al*, 1995). Observational studies also showed that whereas party and ideological work only took up 1 per cent of a Chinese manager's time now, the manager spent nearly a quarter of the time servicing a series of 'father- and mother-in-law' relationships. Chinese managers spent the same amount of time looking down the pyramid as their Western counterparts, but four times as much looking up, and half the time looking outward (Boisot and Xing, 1991).

CASE STUDIES

ENTENTE CORDIALE

De Vries and Florent-Treacy (2002; p301) recounted the case of Groupe Danone's acquisition of a company in Moscow. They noted that the Russian and French employees of the factory managed to overcome the mindset still often found in Russia based on the Soviet legacy of a centrally planned, production-oriented economy. The new CEO, sent in by Danone to lead the transformation process, had gone about his task in an unexpected way. By virtue of his own French-Russian bicultural background, he understood that the Russian employees were not yet ready for empowerment or participatory management as practised in Western countries. Accustomed to job security at any cost, their primary concern was for stability, and they looked to strong leadership to protect them from the turbulence in Russia. Thus, the CEO's first actions were designed to reassure his subordinates. Very significantly, he assured workers that

Danone headquarters had a long-term vision for the factory and would support it through temporary market downturns. He directed the factory's HR department to do everything possible to help employees who had been laid off to find new jobs, a policy nearly unheard of in Russia. At the same time, he kept relatively tight control over decision-making and information flow, knowing that paternalistic, autocratic leadership is still seen by Russians as a guarantee against anarchy. The authors commented that although employees at Danone were in no way 'empowered' according to Western standards, the CEO's actions helped establish a reassuring sense of community. Even at the shop-floor level, employees said that their new leader was a man they respected and trusted, and that they were proud to be a part of a French global organisation. They were also motivated and positive about the future, a state of mind still rare in Russia.

The experience of this manager illustrates how important it is to understand the way differences in national cultures can affect attitudes and behaviours in the work environment. These attitudes and behaviours in turn become embedded in organisational cultures and systems. The need to study the impact of national cultures on organisational life should therefore be a given in this global world. However, many management texts (primarily US and Western) still adopt a universalist approach, focusing on 'best practice', often without any acknowledgment of how transferable these practices might be in different societal contexts. This chapter looks at the ways in which national culture impinges on organisational life, in particular with respect to HRM policies and practices, managerial values, leadership styles, teams and the development of cultural intelligence.

REFLECTIVE ACTIVITY

Identify some of the ways in which we might examine how culture influences organisational life.

- How might you try to design such a study, and what sort of things should you look at?

The last chapter showed that the work of cross-cultural researchers such as Hofstede and Trompenaars argues that organisations are 'culture-bound' and that management practices are heavily influenced by collectively shared values and belief systems. Laurent (1986; p97) also warned against assuming that management approaches developed in one particular culture can be deemed to be valid for any other culture:

> If we accept the view that HRM approaches are cultural artefacts reflecting the basic assumptions and values of the national culture in which organisations are embedded, international HRM becomes one of the most challenging corporate tasks in multinational organisations.

He observed that in order to build, maintain and develop their corporate identity, multinational organisations need to strive for consistency in their ways of managing people on a worldwide basis. At the same time, in order to be effective locally, they also need to adapt those ways to the specific cultural requirements of different societies. Laurent inserts a note of caution into attempts by international organisations to create a 'supra-national' corporate culture. He argues that the concept of organisational culture should be restricted to the more superficial layers of implicit and explicit systems of norms, expectations and historically based preferences, constantly reinforced by their behavioural manifestations and assigned meanings. Using this reasoning, organisations could expect their employees to display appropriate behaviours to match the corporate culture, but could not demand any further immersion in corporate ideology.

KEY FRAMEWORK

THEORY AND PRACTICE

The mechanisms through which culture shapes HRM

The literature indicates that cultural values shape the conduct of HRM through the following mechanisms (Sparrow and Hiltrop, 1997):

- attitudes held about, and definitions of, what makes an effective manager, and their implications for the qualities recruited, trained and developed

- the giving of face-to-face feedback, levels of power distance and uncertainty avoidance, and their implications for recruitment interview, communication, negotiation and participation processes

- expectations of the manager–subordinate relationship, and their implications for performance management and motivational processes

- differential concepts of distributive justice, socially healthy pay and the individualisation of rewards, and their implications for the design of pay systems

- the mindsets used to think about organisational structuring or strategic dynamics.

THE ROLE OF THE MANAGER, LEADERSHIP AND MANAGEMENT STYLES

Another important linking mechanism is the role of managers, and in particular their leadership style. Leadership styles are a key determinant of the organisational context in which HRM policies and practices are developed. Another way of understanding how culture shapes organisations, therefore, is to examine the way that people *lead* in different countries. Leadership involves being able to set a vision, communicate it, and motivate people to follow. In essence, every manager should be a leader . . . but that does not always come to pass.

CASE STUDIES

GLOBAL LEADERSHIP DEVELOPMENT AT INFOSYS

Infosys Technologies Ltd was set up by seven people in India in 1981 with an investment of US $250. It now considers itself to be a global leader in next-generation IT and consulting solutions, with revenues of over US $4.18 billion in 2008 and year-over-year growth of 35 per cent. Infosys employs 91,187 people and has offers out for an additional 18,000. It is known for its emphasis on talent management. In the opening section of its 2007–08 Annual Report its Chairman stated that 'Our core assets walk out every evening. It is our duty to make sure these assets return the next morning, mentally and physically enthusiastic and energetic.' The report was entitled *The Power of Talent*, and detailed initiatives undertaken by the Infosys Leadership Institute (ILI) to develop global leaders. In 2007–08 ILI provided

180,019 training days on behavioural and leadership skills and personal development for leadership (Smith, 2010).

Infosys splits its leaders into three tiers (*Workforce Management*, 2008). Tier 1 leaders are the top 50 people in the organisation, including the heads of the business units, who have an average of 20 years of experience. Board members mentor these 50 leaders. Tier 2 consists of 180 leaders with an average of 15 years of experience. They are mentored by Tier 1. Tier 3 represents 550 people who average 10 years of experience and are mentored by Tier 2.

In 2010 ILI published its first book – *Leadership @ Infosys*, produced by Penguin Books India – which explained Infosys' 'continued success as a corporation ahead of the curve'.

However, is being a good leader the same thing in India or China as it is in the USA? We have already seen the different levels of decision-making discretion and the different ways in which managers prioritise their time. One look at the shelves of leadership texts written by management gurus in airport bookshops might well lead us to believe that there is one recipe for successful leadership and that this emanates from the USA.

Cross-cultural studies generally indicate a strong connection between culture and leadership styles. Specific cultural traditions, values, ideologies and norms are 'bound to differentiate as much or even more than structural factors between societies' (Lammers and Hickson, 1979; p10). The cross-cultural frameworks presented in the last chapter provide evidence of distinct national differences in working values and behaviours, and Laurent's (1986) work suggests significant differences in managerial values across nations.

This work has been carried on in more recent projects. A key example is the GLOBE Project (House *et al*, 2002). The GLOBE project findings on leadership show a picture of subtle, but meaningful, variations in scores around leadership dimensions, but also demonstrate that charismatic, team-oriented and participative styles are the most effective leadership styles. House *et al* (2002) stress that although the dimension 'charismatic' (which consists of such attributes as visionary, inspirational, self-sacrificial, of notable integrity, decisive, and performance-oriented) appears to be universally rated as the most important leadership style, the interpretation of 'charisma' in different societal settings may differ. Likewise, the dimension 'team-oriented' has to be interpreted differently in individualistic cultures as opposed to family- or group-oriented cultures. The GLOBE project introduces a new cross-cultural framework and positioning of societies into clusters which provides a link between cultural background and preferred leadership styles. Overall, the research supports the argument that leadership is culturally contingent, although the key dimensions of effective leadership are consistent across societal clusters.

THE GLOBE PROJECT

CASE STUDIES

The GLOBE (Global Leadership and Organizational Behavior Effectiveness) Project is a multi-phase, multi-method project in which investigators spanning the world are examining the inter-relationships between societal culture, organisational culture and organisational leadership. The Project involves 150 social scientists and management scholars from 61 cultures (the findings are detailed by Ashkanasy *et al*, 2002; House *et al*, 2002; and House *et al*, 2004). The meta-goal of GLOBE is to develop an empirically based theory to describe, understand, and predict the impact of specific cultural variables on leadership and organisational processes, and the effectiveness of these processes. Four of the fundamental questions which the Project is trying to address include:

- Are there leader behaviours, attributes and organisational practices that are accepted and effective across cultures?

- Are there leader behaviours, attributes and organisational practices that are accepted and effective only in some cultures?

- How do attributes of societal and organisational cultures affect the kinds of leader behaviours and organisational practices that are accepted and effective?

- Can the universal and culture-specific aspects of leader behaviours, attributes and organisational practices be explained in terms of an underlying theory that accounts for systematic differences across cultures?

Questionnaires were distributed to middle managers in 62 national cultures. These measured aspired values (asked in terms of 'what should be') but also asked what values were reflected in behaviours and practices (asked in terms of 'what is'). Ten distinct national clusters emerged within the overall sample in terms of preferred leadership styles, based on nine dimensions of national culture. Many of the nine cultural dimensions were already in the literature and have been discussed in the previous chapter, such as Hofstede's uncertainty avoidance and power distance. His masculinity dimension was also reflected in what the GLOBE Project called 'gender egalitarianism and assertiveness', and long-termism was reflected in a 'future orientation'. However, because data was analysed at the organisational level, two additional dimensions of 'performance orientation' (the extent to which an organisation or society encouraged and rewarded group members for performance improvement and excellence), and 'humane orientation' (the degree to which individuals in organisations or societies encouraged and rewarded individuals for being fair, altruistic, friendly, generous, caring and kind to others) were identified. The findings also differentiated between 'societal collectivism', which reflected the degree to which organisational and societal institutional practices encouraged and rewarded collective distribution of resources and collective action, and 'in-group collectivism', which reflected the degree to which individuals express pride, loyalty and cohesiveness in their organisations or families.

A total of 23 different leadership styles were deemed to be effective in one or more of the different societal cultures of the world (each leadership style was considered to represent a *culturally endorsed implicit leadership theory* or CELT). There were six underlying dimensions or styles of an effective global leadership style. The results showed a picture of subtle but meaningful variations in scores around leadership dimensions, but also demonstrated that the charismatic, team-oriented and participative styles were the most effective leadership styles across cultures. The charismatic dimension appeared to be universally rated as the most important leadership style, but the interpretation of charisma in different societal settings was considered to vary. There was high within-culture agreement with respect to leader attributes and behaviours, and two out of six leader behaviour dimensions were viewed universally as contributors to effective leadership. One was viewed nearly universally as an impediment to leadership, and one as nearly universally a contributor. The endorsement of the remaining two varied by culture. In short, there were 21 specific behaviours that were universal, eight impediment behaviours, and 35 behaviours that depended upon the cultural context. Overall, the research supported the argument that leadership is culturally contingent, although the key dimensions of effective leadership are consistent across societal clusters.

CULTURE AND THE INDIVIDUAL

In the last chapter we could see that objections to the validity of studying national cultural differences are put forward by those who resist the notion that culture is a significant influence on behaviour, or a necessary constraint on management. Another line of argument is that individual differences, not cultural ones, explain why people act the way they do. A key problem that can occur when working in intercultural situations is the tendency to confuse personality and culture. Culture is, by definition, a group-based concept, whereas personality is an individual-based concept. Psychologists have started to find ways of looking at how important cultural values might be reflected at the individual level. It has become known as the *new cultural paradigm research tradition*. They have used scales that can treat cultural dimensions as quasi-individual difference characteristics. Earley and Mosakowski (2002) argued that although people from a particular culture can on average share or endorse a given cultural value or belief, and it is only the level of the country that is the single most important determinant of these scores, when values are measured at the individual level there is still enough distribution of scores across a cultural scale between members from within any single country for their scores on the value orientation to be treated as an important individual difference. Where such measurement of culture is also based on values that are known to operate at the individual level (rather than, for example, just using scales that were designed to reflect nationally-derived cultural dimensions), this approach can be helpful to global HRM practitioners.

One question that has been pursued by these researchers has been to investigate individual preferences for HRM practices and then find out which preferences are values-free, and which can be predicted at the individual level by knowing that person's value orientations (Sparrow, 2006a). Put practically, this question concerns the room for manoeuvre that there might be for international HR directors in transferring practices abroad. If the *values* of an organisation's workforce significantly predict their preference for the nature of HRM practices, then the organisation will have a harder job in transferring them successfully. The organisation can change employee attitudes and mindsets to specific practices by communication and educational processes, but employee values tend to be more resistant to change. Preliminary evidence suggests that the answer to this question might be sobering for international HRM directors. In a study of over 400 Taiwanese employees at firms such as Tatung, Mitac and Acer, Sparrow and Wu (1998) found that 75 per cent of the 'menu' of various HRM practices (for example, choices like 'Should the performance appraisal scheme measure what you achieve (objectives) or how you achieve it (competencies)?') could be predicted by individual-level cultural values. A similar impact was also found in a later study of Kenyan employees (Nyambegera *et al,* 2000).

Clearly, in some countries cultural values, as reflected at the individual level, will help explain whether people find the HRM practices they are subjected to desirable, sensible, appropriate, or not. An HRM professional might, however, also ask *how* important is culture, especially in relation to other factors that might explain how desirable an individual finds any particular HRM practice? There are lots of other individual factors that might shape the extent to which employees will find a specific HRM practices desirable or not. By looking at various demographic factors, such as age, service, gender, and grade, an individual's cultural values by themselves explain from 10 to 16 per cent of the attractiveness (or not) of various HRM practices to them (Sparrow, 2006a). Cultural values are important and worth knowing about, but they are of course just one of many factors that explain differences in work behaviour across countries. Attention is also being given to other factors, and a broader set of explanations of cultural behaviour at the individual level is being explored. As Earley and Mosakowski (2002, p316) noted:

> Now is an opportune time for researchers to move away from the tried and true friends of cultural values as the sole indicators of cultural differences.

CAN WE DEVELOP GLOBAL LEADER COMPETENCIES?

We have looked at the way that culture shapes HRM practices and pointed out that a key challenge is for managers to understand the role of culture and then incorporate this learning from the globalisation process into their solutions. We have also shown that fundamental managerial behaviours such as values, decision-making latitude, use of time, and leadership style are all affected by national culture. We now take a brief look at different sets of competencies that can assist individuals and organisations in coping with these cultural differences.

Some attempts have been made to develop a global leadership model including the studies by Adler and Bartholomew (1992), which link different types of global strategy with different types of leader competencies. A key study in this area was carried out by Black *et al* (1999). An important finding from their research was that about two-thirds of the characteristics of effective global leaders are generalisable, with the other one-third idiosyncratic or context-specific. Four major context-specific factors were perceived to affect idiosyncratic characteristics: company affiliation; managerial position; country affiliation; and functional responsibility.

Researchers have learned about these competencies by attempting to understand three important aspects of organisational life:

● how managers demonstrate global leadership behaviours

● what being a successful member of a multicultural team involves

● what it takes to demonstrate 'cultural intelligence'.

Confirmation of differing leadership styles around the world poses a critical question for all organisations operating across borders: is there such a thing as a global leadership model? After all, Morrison (2000; p19) has stated that:

> As companies rely more and more on global strategies, they require more and more global leaders. This tie between strategy and leadership is essentially a two-way street: the more companies pursue global strategies, the more global leaders they need; and the more global leaders companies have, the more they pursue global strategies.

In thinking about this issue, a distinction is typically made between:

● expatriate (or international) managers: executives in leadership positions that involve international assignments across countries and cultures, with skills defined by the location of the assignment, and

● global (or transnational) managers: executives assigned to positions with cross-border responsibilities, who have a hands-on understanding of international business, with competencies defined more by their frame of mind.

We deal with the knowledge, skills and abilities that become important for international managers and expatriates in Chapter 14 on *Managing Expatriation*. However, we concentrate here on the issue of global leadership, which involves a different set of capabiltities. Pucik (1998; p41) points out that:

Some global managers may be expatriates; many, if not most, have been expatriates at some point in their career, but probably only few expatriates are global managers.

The earliest debates on international management strategy argued that strategic capability is ultimately dependent on the 'cognitive processes' of global managers and the ability of firms to create a 'matrix in the minds of managers' or a 'transnational mentality' (Bartlett and Ghoshal, 1989; p195). There have only been a few studies that have looked at global leaders in detail, and the evidence still tends to be more anecdotal. For example, from a practitioner perspective, the Chief Executives of HSBC, Schering-Plough, General Electric, Flextronics and Egon Zehnder have given their response to the pioneering work of Bartlett and Ghoshal to explain their view of what global leadership involves (*Harvard Business Review*, 2003).

Academics have focused more on how organisations can help 'build' global leadership skills in managers. They have looked at the role played by both the social networks and also at what distinguishes effective global leaders. Rather than just focusing on a particular set of skills or range of competencies that are important for effective international management, there are two important additional aspects or components to this 'global mentality':

- attitudes and values
- mindset (cognitive structures).

The first aspect – attitudes and values – has been called an *international orientation*. This attitude is assumed to correlate with both the extent and the quality of international experience. Researchers have attempted to develop measures that correspond to the core dimensions of a manager's thinking about international strategy and international organisation, and have then shown how this mindset changes over time. For example, Murtha *et al* (1998) looked at the type of cognitive change towards a more global mindset in managers over a three-year period within a single multinational organisation, identifying a core value-set or logic that is associated with global operations.

Global managers also need to have a 'good' *mental model of how knowledge and information is shared* across the people with whom they need to interact if they are to help their organisation deliver an important global business process, product or service. Recent work has looked at the role of international managers as important brokers of knowledge, arguing that they help to diffuse practices across borders. Global managers also need to understand how tacit knowledge spreads within top management teams. What are the 'advice networks' that exist inside the organisation? International managers often build up a lot of 'social capital' because they have 'boundary-spanning roles' and this puts them in touch with lots of different networks inside the organisation. They also develop important insights into the organisation through their interpersonal cross-border relationships. All of these factors help global managers build superior mental models of the organisation, and enable them to become more effective (Sparrow, 2006a).

Organisations like Shell International argue that global leadership in a mature multinational organisation depends on creating face-to-face cross-cultural leadership at all levels (Steel, 1997). Graen and Hui (1999), coming from an industrial and organisational psychology perspective, argue that in order for cross-national differences to be managed effectively, organisations need to develop global leadership by enhancing the level of 'transcultural skills' and using these to help resolve the complexity of cross-cultural management (see Table 6).

Table 6 Progressive stages of transcultural competence

Progressive stage	Characteristics distinguishing transculturals from non-transculturals
Adventurer	*Stereotypes held from an ethnocentric perspective:* Development of an adventurer's mentality towards cultures other than one's own
Sensitiser	*An outsider's view of norms:* Attunement of behaviours and attitudes to a culture other than one's own; has learned to read and conform to new cultural norms
Insider	*Knows what one doesn't know:* Has developed a knowledge base rich enough to behave and display feelings inside another culture vastly different from one's own; has sufficient insight to understand the value of what is not known
Judge	*Makes valid generalisations about attributes:* In the eyes of observers is considered to be able to conceptualise useful differences and similarities between cultures for purpose of comparison; has developed behaviours, feelings and knowledge to conduct cross-cultural negotiations
Synthesiser	*Can discover functional equivalences:* Has been socialised into the culture of interest and can synthesise both the home and host culture; can identify constructs of functional equivalence between cultures or develop a third culture of relevance to both cultures

Source: adapted from Graen and Hui (1999)

 REFLECTIVE ACTIVITY

Debate the following:

Graen and his colleagues argue that even the most adept global leader has only learned how to operate through insight into approaches that can serve an equivalent function in a new culture, rather than truly being of that culture.

- Do you agree with this, and if so, what are the implications for multinational organisations?

DEVELOPING CULTURAL INTELLIGENCE

In the final section of this chapter we pull together much of the material covered in the book so far by asking the question 'Can organisations develop cultural intelligence amongst their employees?' We have seen that a familiarity with cultural differences is an important part of global leadership skills and that it also is important for the effective functioning of international management teams. A book by Earley and Ang (2003) and a subsequent article by Earley and Mosakowski (2004) has moved the debate on and has sparked off an important exchange of views between cross-cultural researchers. In the article, the authors introduced a concept that they termed 'cultural intelligence' (CQ). This is an attitude and skill that enables individuals to adapt effectively across cultures. In practical terms, it enables an individual to interpret unfamiliar and ambiguous gestures in ways as accurately as a national resident could. Understanding the nature of CQ has important applications for individuals, teams and organisational functioning. Earley and Mosakowski (2004, p140) argue that managers with global responsibilities can be socially intelligent in their own settings, but ineffective in novel cultures, yet:

> A person with high cultural intelligence can somehow tease out of a person's or group's behaviour those features that would be true of all people and all groups, those peculiar to this person or this group, and those that are neither universal or idiosyncratic. The vast realm that lies between those two poles is culture.

As we have seen, research on intercultural competence has a long tradition and it shows that a range of factors can predict effectiveness in this area, including previous experience, personality factors, cross-cultural attitudes and communication behaviours, and situational factors such as cultural training or the 'distance' between two cultures. Cultural intelligence is an individual difference, but unlike personality, which is relatively enduring, it is considered to be something that can be developed and enhanced through interventions that organisations can make.

THEORY AND PRACTICE

KEY FRAMEWORK

The four components of cultural intelligence:

- Mind (meta-cognitions): learning strategies, whereby people can acquire and develop coping strategies. We need to identify a 'point of entry' into a foreign culture – for example, a form of behaviour or a context that can be used to subsequently interpret different patterns of behaviour

- Knowledge about different cultures (cognition)

- Heart (emotional/motivational): people must have the desire to persevere in the face of challenge when adapting to a new culture, and a belief in their own ability to master a situation (called self-efficacy)

- Body (physical behaviour): people need to develop a repertoire of culturally-appropriate behaviours. This centres around the ability to mirror customs and gestures, and adopt habits and mannerisms, in order to enter the world of a foreign culture and enable the development of trust.

Rather than the progressive stages of transcultural competence suggested by Graen and Hui (1999) that were discussed earlier in relation to the debate about global leadership, for Earley and Ang (2003) an individual may be strong in some of these areas, weaker in others. Based on survey data from 2,000 managers from 60 cultures, six typical combinations were identified (categorised as provincial, analyst, mimic, natural, ambassador and chameleon), with the ultimate being a chameleon, who has strengths in all areas.

They argued that CQ shares some common features with another 'brand' of intelligence – emotional intelligence – but also has unique features. It shares the propensity to suspend judgement and to think before acting, because in order to avoid the hazards of stereotyping, managers have to gather information about all of the personalities that are interacting before them and discern how they are different from those in the home culture yet similar to each other. However, emotional intelligence is developed within the confines of a single culture, whereas cultural intelligence requires that people develop understanding across cultures. Although some aspects of cultural intelligence are considered to be innate, Earley and Mosarkowski (2004, p140) argue that:

> Anyone reasonably alert, motivated and poised can attain an acceptable level of cultural intelligence.

There are commonplace training strategies that can be designed to build capability in each of the four elements noted above.

 REFLECTIVE ACTIVITY

Debate the following:

Hampden-Turner and Trompenaars (2006) point out that supporters of the concept of CQ have to contend with and come up with convincing answers to three critical views:

- Cultures are entirely relative in their values. There is no 'best way' of understanding culture as an issue in organisational life, or understanding other cultures (this is the cultural relativism argument). We cannot judge values or use values – we can merely ask questions that help us understand how values fit the environment that any particular society finds itself in.

- Cultural studies are a backward step, leading to grand theories. We need to have multiple theories and perspectives, all of which can be partially legitimate. Given that everything just represents a point of view, there cannot be an objective thing called cultural intelligence (this is the postmodernist argument).

- All attempts to categorise cultures are crude stereotypes inferred from superficial features of culture, and they miss deeper and subtler realities and meanings (this is the latent argument). All that cross-cultural research does is tell us what we already know – for example, that Japanese are impassive and French excitable. It all depends really on circumstances.

- Do you think that the evidence for CQ can answer these criticisms or not?

The briefing-style case study below helps to bring together the discussion of different taxonomies of culture covered earlier in the chapter with the range of work on transcultural competence discussed above. The latest thinking shows increasing consensus amongst experts. It is important that global HRM practitioners understand these viewpoints because they guide most of the currently available cultural awareness and training products and processes.

Thomas *et al* (2008) note that a range of cultural studies have alluded to the idea that certain attributes possessed by some individuals can make them more effective in things such as cross-cultural communication. They argue that the construct of cultural intelligence has enormous potential in explaining effectiveness in cross-cultural communications, interactions, or indeed success in overseas assignments. However, a host of associated terms have made their way into the international management literature – such as 'intercultural competency', 'global mindset' and 'social intelligence'. The current focus has been to think instead about such effectiveness as a form of intelligence rather than as a general competency – as a set of abilities necessary to adapt to, select, and shape the environmental context. In reviewing the literature, they tease out the following key definitions:

- a person's capability to adapt effectively to new cultural contexts
- an ability to interpret unfamiliar gestures in the same way a national resident would, and to mirror them
- an understanding of the fundamentals of intercultural interactions
- a mindful approach to such interactions
- an ability to build a repertoire of adaptive skills and behaviour
- a capability to gather, interpret, and act upon radically different cues.

CASE STUDIES

IS CULTURAL INTELLIGENCE JUST ANOTHER TRENDY CONCEPT OR HAS IT GOT SUBSTANCE? WHAT THE EXPERTS SAY

Work by Chris Earley and colleagues (Earley and Ang, 2003; Ng and Earley, 2006) has been used to argue that in order to understand the impact of culture on organisational life, we have to think about the evidence both of the effect of intelligence in the workplace and of the effect of the workplace on intelligence.

There is pervasive evidence that people in different cultures think and act differently and that what is considered intelligent differs from one place to the next (Sternberg and Grigorenko, 2006). People's implicit theories of social intelligence go beyond what is typically measured in psychometric instruments, which concentrate on cognitive

intelligence. Successful intelligence (understanding how to adapt, shape or select out and achieve goals) requires a combination of analytical, creative and practical abilities, and these tend to apply within a single culture. It is the tacit knowledge that these abilities assess that is the most predictive of managerial performance and certainly leadership effectiveness. This tacit knowledge does not correlate with more traditional cognitive measures of intelligence. CQ, as articulated by Earley and Ang (2003), is a form of social intelligence that is relevant across cultures and helps us understand intelligence in a broader way.

Cross-cultural experts such as Brislin, Trompenaars, Hampden-Turner, Thomas and Triandis have all helped explain the sorts of learning strategies and 'meta-cognitions' that become important. The term 'meta-cognition' is used by psychologists to refer to knowledge of and control over one's thinking and learning. Possessing such an ability enables the deliberate, planful, goal-directed and intentional application of a set of knowledge and mental skills to produce behaviour that others define as intelligent. The individual has to be able to monitor, control, regulate and orchestrate these behaviours for it to be intelligence.

These are some of the most important ways in which these work.

- CQ revolves around the ability to suspend judgement until further relevant information has been understood. The culturally intelligent person looks for current behaviour in different situations to identify the impact that personality might have on another's behaviour. A culturally intelligent individual has the ability to identify what is important information on which to base an assessment. To make a person culturally intelligent requires extensive training. Cognitive, emotional and behavioural training are all necessary to help people integrate a lot of information, learn how to use multiple cues, and suspend judgements. Only then can we limit our natural tendency to assume that 'normal' is what happens in our own culture. This is the view taken by Triandis (2006).

- A culturally intelligent person has to possess three capabilities in order to see beyond differences in values across cultures: the ability to see the synergies that exist between the contrasting values in any culture and understand how people reconcile them; the ability to treat these opposing values as complementary rather than contradictory

and understand how people move between each value; and the ability to understand how dominant and more hidden values interact with each other and how people express the less dominant values in any culture. This is the view taken by Hampden-Turner and Trompenaars (2006).

- Culturally intelligent people are skillful at recognising behaviours that are influenced by culture and do this in four ways: observing behaviours in different cultures, developing reasons that explain these differences, considering the emotional implications and associations that arise from these behaviours, and then transferring this new knowledge into novel situations. In order to do this, people need to be able to anticipate and to accept confusion, but also to make a distinction between competitive encounters, where their cultural exploration might be exploited, and collaborative encounters, where it will be accepted. This is the view taken by Brislin *et al* (2006).

- CQ has three components: knowledge of culture and fundamental principles of cross-cultural interactions; a heightened awareness of, and enhanced attention to, current experience, such as a new cultural environment (this is called 'mindfulness'); and behavioural ability to become competent across a wide range of cultural situations. Of these three, it is the mental skill of 'mindfulness' that is perhaps the most important. People make the link between having knowledge about other cultures and developing the ability to behave appropriately through this 'mindfulness'. It allows us to concentrate on new strategies rather than falling back upon tried and tested ways of behaving, which is what we all do unless we focus our mind. This is the view taken by Thomas (2006).

However, Thomas *et al* (2008) note that although cultural intelligence may have much utility for organisations as they internationalise, 'it awaits the development of a valid measure' (p138).

KEY LEARNING POINTS

- National culture has a powerful on key organisational processes and practices – including HRM practices, leadership, and international management teams.

- Despite movements towards global convergence, there are still consistent national cultural differences that affect approaches to broad organisational and HRM policies and practices and leadership.

- The influence of culture can be seen through power and authority relationships, coping with uncertainty and risk-taking, interpersonal trust, loyalty and commitment, motivation, control and discipline, co-ordination and integration, communication, consultation and participation.

- These organisational behaviours are a result of an individual's psychology (itself a product of various cultural, social, political and personal influences), their life stage and their generational subculture.

- In order to build, maintain and develop their corporate identity, MNCs need to strive for consistency in their management of people on a worldwide basis, but in order to be effective locally, they also need to adapt this management to the specific cultural requirements of different societies.

- International HR practitioners must develop the ability to blend the best of the many different approaches that societies adopt when they manage and motivate different workforces.

- The role of managers, and in particular their leadership style, becomes an important linking mechanism in achieving this balance.

- Cross-cultural studies generally indicate a strong connection between culture and leadership styles. Being a good leader is not the same thing in India or China as it is in the USA.

- Researchers have identified global leadership competencies by attempting to understand three important aspects of organisational life: how managers demonstrate global leadership behaviours; what being a successful member of a multicultural team involves; and what it takes to demonstrate 'cultural intelligence'.

- So, if we ask how important is culture in relation to other factors that also explain how desirable an individual finds any particular HRM practice, it is clear that culture is a significant factor, but there are many other individual factors (and institutional factors) that also shape the extent to which employees will find specific HRM practices desirable or not.

LEARNING QUESTIONS

1 Can HR managers rise to Pucik's challenge of not standing in the way of globalisation while also remaining the guardians of national culture in an organisation?

2 Can leadership be considered to be more than just a product of national culture? What do leaders have to do to transcend national borders?

3 Is global leadership something that can be readily developed in managers, or do you think that it would be better to recruit a handful of ready-made international managers?

4 In what ways are the skills needed by international management teams any different from the traditional team-building skills needed to cope with heterogeneous groups from within a single culture?

5 Is there such a thing as CQ, and if there is, can we now specify what it involves? What, then, does it involve?

EXPLORE FURTHER

House, R. J., Javidan, M., Hanges, P. and Dorfman, P. (2002) 'Understanding cultures and implicit leadership theories across the globe: an introduction to project GLOBE', *Journal of World Business*, 37: 3–10. This article focuses on the linkage between models of culture and the impact that differences in culture had on organisational practices and leadership attributes. By the beginning of this decade, cross-cultural research had shifted away from just explaining differences, or even searching for underlying theories, towards the challenge of applying cross-cultural research to specific management issues. The GLOBE study helped advance research methods, making a number of important contributions to method as well as applied knowledge. The importance of measuring values in terms of the 'what should be' as well as the 'what is' context proved an enduring contribution, and the nine cultural dimensions studied – which represented an amalgam of previous cross-cultural research to that time – have provided an alternative framework to Hofstede's work. The article also shows the importance of being able to integrate theories of cross-cultural values with theories relevant to other domains of HRM such as implicit theories about leadership, motivation, and organisational form.

An understanding of the challenges of global leadership and of cultural intelligence can be gleaned from the following two books:

Earley, P. C. and Ang, S. (2003) *Cultural Intelligence: Individual interactions across cultures*, Stanford, CA, Stanford University Press.

Black, J. S., Morrison, A. and Gregersen, H. (1999) *Global Explorers: The next generation of leaders*, New York, Routledge.

PART TWO

Comparative Human Resource Management

CHAPTER 4

Comparative HRM and Institutional Influences

LEARNING OUTCOMES

When they have read this chapter, students will:

- be able to describe the strengths and weaknesses of the universalist and contextual paradigms
- understand the cultural and institutional bases for differences between countries in the way they manage their HRM
- appreciate the arguments concerning convergence and divergence
- be able to identify some key areas of similarity and difference in HRM practice between countries.

INTRODUCTION

This chapter explores why we should be considering the comparative dimensions of HRM. After all, every organisation has to recruit workers, deploy them, pay them, motivate them and eventually arrange for their departure. Indeed, many texts are written as if their messages are universal. However, there is little doubt that things are done differently in different countries: not only do they have different cultures (as discussed in Chapter 2), but they also operate in different institutional environments – with differently educated and skilled workforces, in different economic situations, with different labour laws, trade union arrangements, government support or control, and so on. It is hardly surprising, therefore, that research shows not only that HRM varies between countries in the way that it is conducted, but that how it is defined and what is regarded as constituting good practice are also very distinct.

REFLECTIVE ACTIVITY

Examine your existing HRM practices.

● Which of them are the product of your country's legal, economic, political or social institutions?

Provide explanations for your answer.

Fundamentally, there are two approaches to exploring HRM: the universalist and the contextual (Brewster, 1999) – or, in the terms of this chapter, the comparative. These two approaches are reflected in two further dichotomies: the debate about the causes of differences in HRM between the cultural and the institutional schools, and the debate between the two schools of thought that contest the notion of convergence. Some argue that even where there are differences, they are diminishing as globalisation becomes more entrenched and societies become more alike – including more alike in the way they manage their human resources (see below and, for example, Lammers and Hickson, 1979; Child, 1981; Miles and Snow, 1986). Others argue that there is little evidence of such a moving together and that, in fact, societies remain steadfastly different and even unique (see below and, for example, Maurice *et al*, 1986; Poole, 1986).

This chapter explores these conceptual differences as an introduction to the subsequent chapters in Part Two, which examine evidence about CHRM policies and practices. It outlines the notions of universalism and contextual HRM; it examines the cultural and institutional explanations of difference; it explores concepts of convergence and divergence and, within that, explores the impact and relevance of US versions of HRM.

UNIVERSALIST VERSUS CONTEXTUAL HRM

Universalism and contextualism are paradigms – that is, they are taken-for-granted truths that the proponents of each simply assume must be correct. The fact that there are people who hold fast to each paradigm indicates that they are intellectual constructs capable of being challenged, but for the proponents of each one, they are 'obviously' correct and 'the only' way to think about management science and HRM.

UNIVERSALIST HRM

The universalist paradigm is dominant in the USA but is widely used elsewhere. This paradigm assumes that the purpose of the study of HRM, and in particular strategic human resource management (SHRM – see for example Tichy *et al*, 1982; Fombrun *et al*, 1984; Ulrich, 1987; Wright and Snell, 1991; Wright and McMahan, 1992), is to improve the way that human resources are managed strategically within organisations. The ultimate aim of this work is to improve organisational performance, as judged by its impact on the organisation's declared corporate strategy (Tichy *et al*, 1982; Huselid, 1995), the customers (Ulrich, 1989) or shareholders (Huselid, 1995; Becker and Gerhart, 1996; Becker *et al*, 1997). It is implicit in these writings that this objective will apply in all cases. Thus the widely cited definition by Wright and McMahan (1992; p298) states that SHRM is:

> the pattern of planned human resource deployments and activities intended to enable a firm to achieve its goals.

Arguably, there is a degree of coherence in the USA around what constitutes 'good' HRM, and views tend to coalesce around the concept of 'high-performance work systems'. These were characterised by the US Department of Labor (1993) as having certain characteristics:

- careful and extensive systems for recruitment, selection and training
- formal systems for sharing information with the individuals who work in the organisation
- clear job design
- local-level participation procedures
- monitoring of attitudes
- performance appraisals
- properly functioning grievance procedures
- promotion and compensation schemes that provide for the recognition and financial rewarding of high-performing members of the workforce.

It would appear that although there have been many other attempts to develop such lists (see, for example, from the UK, Storey, 1992, 2007), and they all differ to some degree, the Department of Labor list can be taken as an exemplar of the universalist paradigm. Few researchers in HRM in the USA would find very much to argue with in this list, although they are likely to label their studies as SHRM. Both researchers and practitioners in other countries, however, find such a list contrary to experience and even to what they would conceive of as good practice. So they might argue for sharing information with representative bodies such as trade unions or works councils, for flexible work boundaries, for group reward systems. And they might argue that attitude monitoring, appraisal systems, etc are evidence of low trust and thus culturally inappropriate.

Writings by the universalists are often produced in one country and are based on a small number of by now well-known cases. As long as they are read by specialists in the relevant country, with interests in these kinds of organisations, this may not be too much of a problem. But the world, and especially the academic world in HRM, is becoming ever more international. This is a major problem in relation to the US literature. The cultural hegemony of US teaching, publishing, websites and the US journals means that these texts are often utilised by other readers. US-based literature searches – now all done on computer, of course – generally fail to note any writing outside the universalist tradition. For analysts and practitioners elsewhere, and with interests in different countries, many of these descriptions and prescriptions fail to meet their reality.

CONTEXTUAL HRM

In contrast, the contextual or comparative paradigm searches for an overall understanding of what is contextually unique, and why. In our topic area, it is focused on understanding what is different between and within HRM in various contexts, and what the antecedents of those differences are. The policies and practices of the 'leading-edge' companies (something of a value-laden term in itself), which are the focus of much HRM research and literature in the USA, are of less interest to contextualists than identifying the way labour markets work and what the more typical organisations are doing.

Among most researchers working in this paradigm, it is the explanations that matter – any link to organisational performance is secondary. It is assumed that HRM can apply to societies, governments or regions as well as to firms. At the level of the organisation (not just the 'firm', for public-sector and not-for-profit organisations are also included), the organisation's objectives and strategy are not necessarily assumed to be 'good' either for the organisation or for society. There are plenty of examples, particularly in the last few years, where this is clearly not the case. Nor, in this paradigm, is there any assumption that the interests of everyone in the organisation will be the same; nor any expectation that an organisation will have a strategy that people within the organisation will support.

The assumption is that not only will the employees and the unions have a different perspective from that of the management team (Kochan *et al*, 1986; Barbash, 1987; Keenoy, 1990; Storey, 1992; Purcell and Ahlstrand, 1994; Turner and Morley, 1995), and different groups of employees within the organisation will have different needs and requirements (Lepak and Snell, 1999), but that even within the management team there may be different interests and views (Kochan *et al*, 1986; Koch and McGrath, 1996; Hyman, 1987). These, and the resultant impact on HRM, are issues for empirical study. Contextualist researchers explore the importance of such factors as culture, ownership structures, labour markets, the role of the state and trade union organisation as aspects of the subject rather than as external influences upon it. The scope of HRM goes beyond the organisation to reflect the reality of the role of many HRM departments: for example, in lobbying about and adjusting to government actions, in dealing with such issues as equal opportunities legislation or with trade unions and tripartite institutions.

REFLECTIVE ACTIVITY

Take a moment to think through the follwoing questions:

- What are the advantages and disadvantages of each paradigm (you might think about theoretical and practical implications)?

- Which stance does the management of your organisation take? (Do they talk more about 'spreading best practice' than about 'adapting to local environments', for example?)

- Which approach are you more comfortable with?

THE VALUE OF THE DIFFERENT PARADIGMS

Many management researchers find that the universalist paradigm, ironically, excludes much of the work of HRM specialists in such areas as compliance, equal opportunities, trade union relationships and dealing with local government and the environment. In addition, the universalist paradigm only operates at the level of the organisation, ignoring policy at the national or international level. This is not helpful in regions like Europe, where much employment contract bargaining is still above the organisational level and significant HRM legislation and policy (eg freedom of movement, employment and remuneration, equal treatment) is enacted at European Union level as well as at the level of particular countries or sectors (Sparrow and Hiltrop, 1994; Brewster *et al*, 2004; Brewster, 2004). The contextual paradigm provides better insights into these issues.

Nevertheless, the universalist paradigm exists because it has strengths – a simple, clear focus, a rigorous methodology, and clear relationships with the needs of industry. Neither paradigm is right or wrong. Both these approaches, and the others that exist in other parts of the world, have a contribution to make. The difficulty comes when writers are unaware of the paradigm within which they are working.

It is to some degree the difference between these paradigms, lack of awareness of them, and the tendency for commentators to drift from one to another that has led to the confusion about the very nature of HRM as a field of study pointed out by many of its original leading figures (eg Conrad and Pieper, 1990; Guest, 1992; Singh, 1992; Storey, 1992, 1995; Boxall, 1993; Dyer and Kochan, 1995). In practice, these are often debates between the different paradigms used to understand the nature of HRM.

INSTITUTIONAL THEORY

Before discussing institutional influences on HRM we need to explain the nature of another theoretical perspective: institutional theory.

Institutional theory focuses on the 'taken-for-granted' character of social institutions such as religion, work, family, politics (Berger and Luckman,

1967) and explains how these realities are created and then institutionalised. In the management sphere, structures, for example, are not determined by an organisation's work activities and the demands made by competition and the needs for efficiency as much as we might believe (DiMaggio and Powell, 1983). Rather, they arise as a reflection of rules that become rationalised in the search for legitimacy and recognition. From the perspective of institutional theory, organisational decision-making is not an outcome just of strategic choice but also of powerful social forces within and outside organisations. External 'institutional agencies' can create a drive for similarity in unrelated forms (called 'isomorphic processes') within any particular organisational field (which is defined as an aggregate set of organisations that constitute a recognised area of institutional life).

KEY FRAMEWORK

Isomorphic pulls

There are three isomorphic pulls (DiMaggio and Powell, 1983):

- *coercive* – eg pulls resulting from the pressures of external institutions such as the state, the legal environment, cultural expectations of societies

- *mimetic* – eg where organisations model themselves on other organisations in their 'field' as a standard response to uncertainty (triggered, for example, through attempts at benchmarking, global performance metrics, employee transfers or through agencies such as consultancies)

- *normative* – eg pulls that result from the professionalisation of functions and individuals, such as through educational institutions or through practice dissemination by professional networks.

THEORY AND PRACTICE

Institutional theory also focuses on the role of agencies from *within* an organisation. The environment is considered to 'enter' the organisation through processes of 'imposition', 'acquisition' and 'authorisation'. There is also a series of 'pulls' exerted by the internal agents from within an organisation (Scott, 1987; Westney, 1993). These include:

- 'inducement' of organisational structure (eg where an organisation that lacks power to impose patterns on other organisations instead offers inducements such as funding or certification)

- 'incorporation' (eg where organisations come to replicate salient aspects of differentiation that can be found in their environment within their own structures)

- 'bypassing' (eg where shared values are so institutionalised they can substitute for any formal structure)

- 'imprinting' (eg where an organisational form retains some of the patterns that were institutionalised at the time its industry was founded).

Institutional theory has been mostly used to examine sectoral or occupational variations, but the theory has left a strong mark on conceptual work in the area of SIHRM (Amable, 2003; Hall and Soskice, 2001; Westney, 1993; Whitley, 1999) and increasingly on empirical work in which institutional theory has been used to:

- examine the HRM practices found in foreign-owned subsidiaries of multinationals in terms of the degree of global 'integration' or 'standardisation' versus local 'responsiveness' or 'local adaptation' (Rosenzweig and Nohria, 1994; Björkman and Lu, 2001; Rosenzweig, 2005)

- attempt to identify how differently foreign MNCs manage their people compared to indigenous MNCs (Ferner and Qunitanilla, 1998; Wood *et al*, 2009)

- compare HRM practices across countries (Brewster *et al*, 2008; Gooderham *et al*, 1999; Tregaskis and Brewster, 2006).

Rosenzweig and Nohria (1994), using institutional theory, argued that, of all functions, HRM tends to most closely adhere to local practices, in that they are often mandated by local regulation and shaped by strong local conventions. Within HRM they see the order in which six key practices most closely resemble local practices as: time off, benefits, gender composition, training, executive bonus and participation. Where there are well-defined local norms for the HRM practices, and they affect the employees of the affiliate organisation, practices are likely to conform to practices of local competitors.

 REFLECTIVE ACTIVITY

Think of three or four other HRM practices.

- In what order would they fit onto this list, in terms of their likely alignment with local practices?

INSTITUTIONAL APPROACHES TO COMPARATIVE HRM

The cultural differences explained in Chapter 2 are not the only explanations for comparative differences between nations. Some people argue that it is unnecessary to look into issues that are so amorphous and difficult to explore as 'culture' because there are very obvious and visible institutional differences which explain most of the variation. In HRM terms, for example, it is not likely that the same approach to recruitment would be as cost-effective in an African country, with only 20 per cent of the population in a formal job and few people with good education, as in a Scandinavian country where almost everyone already has a job and all are well educated. Multinational corporations do not pay people in Samoa the same rates that they pay in Canada. Consulting with the workforce in a fully unionised country is not the same as consulting with one in a country where trade unions are illegal. Non-discrimination policies in Malaysia, where the law gives a privileged position to native Malays, is not the same as it is in the Netherlands where discrimination on the grounds of race is unlawful. Gender equality looks different in the USA, where quotas are allowed, from in the European Union, where quotas are unlawful, and different again in Saudi Arabia. The examples could be multiplied.

Organisations operate within a specific political, economic, social and technological environment largely determined by history. In order to be effective in that environment these organisations need to manage in ways that recognise the local circumstances and create and sustain legitimacy with key stakeholders. This view is drawn from socio-economics and is known as institutional theory. We will draw out the HRM implications of such an approach.

The socio-economic school developed largely in opposition to the rational hierarchical view common to modern economics that sees human beings, and the organisations they control, as making logical decisions, based on strong property rights for owners, that are designed to maximise their own self-interest (Powell and DiMaggio, 1991; Shleifer and Vishny, 1997; North, 1990). It has been argued that the socio-economic literature can be divided into three main schools or traditions: the 'varieties of capitalism' literature, business systems theory, and 'regulationist' thinking (Wood *et al*, 2011). For all these schools the central notion is that an organisation is embedded in the society in which it operates, and although that provides a series of supportive complementarities (one part of the system ensures the success of other parts), it also provides a series of constraints on how it can behave. A problem that the socio-economic theories are now struggling with is, if societies are embedded and complementary, then how does the change that we see going on around us occur?

The relevance of such theories to HRM is not just apparent, but the different forms of society that are produced have been divided by these researchers according to relationships *between* organisations (such as between different companies, between companies and the state, etc), and *within* organisations – between the owners, managers and employees and other workers. Hence, institutional theories may go much wider than HRM but they have an obvious relevance for it.

In each society there is of course room for variation – the telescope analogy (Brewster, 1995) applies. But also, according to institutional theory, each society tends to have a common paradigm about 'appropriate' or even 'effective' ways to do things. Most organisations within a society operate in broadly the same way, because there are a range of pressures on them to do so (DiMaggio and Powell, 1983; Meyer and Rowan, 1977; Strauss and Hanson, 1997). Organisations that step too far out of line – break the law, for instance – get pressures that do not apply to those who conform. So firms operating in the same environment tend to adopt similar HRM practices – referred to as 'isomorphism' (Kostova and Roth, 2002).

This suggests that at the level of organisation, industry or society, there are internal and external pressures that can be violated or ignored, but only at a cost, most prominently a loss of the 'legitimacy' which organisations need in order to operate successfully. As a result, most people or most organisations do not choose to challenge the status quo in such a way (Brewster and Mayrhofer, 2009). An example here would be the issue of pay compression, which is the multiple between the pay of the most senior managers and that of the lowest-paid employees within an organisation. In the USA it is not uncommon for the multiple to be 400–500 times, whereas in Sweden pay compression has traditionally been maintained at a multiple of 40–50 times, as a result of a co-ordination of the labour movement via a confederation of unions representing both high- and low-paid employees.

REFLECTIVE ACTIVITY

If you wish to learn more about it, follow this link, which explores whether such an approach could ever work in a different context:

http://www.devoutreach.com/february06/SpecialReport/tabid/567/Default.aspx

Interestingly, when these theories have been tested against HRM practice (Goergen *et al*, 2009a, 2009b; Wood, 2009), it seems that the political theories explain almost nothing and the legal theories only a little and then not quite as those authors expected.

VARIETIES OF CAPITALISM

Institutions do not exist in a vacuum. They evolve with history and practice (Hall and Soskice, 2001; Boyer, 2006). The fall of the Berlin Wall and 'market' reforms in China led to a reduced focus on the capitalism/communism divide and increased attention to the different forms that capitalism takes. Why did the more regulated economies in continental Western Europe and Japan outperform more 'archetypal' capitalist economies such as Britain and the USA through much of the 1980s? Why did the latter outperform the former in the 1990s and early 2000s, and why has the pattern reversed again in the recent past? (As Wood *et al*, 2010, point out, the even better performance of the more regulated Scandinavian countries was largely ignored.)

In *Capitalisme contre Capitalisme* (1991), Michel Albert, a former director of the French Planning Agency, distinguished an 'Anglo-Saxon' capitalism (principally the USA, but also the UK) from a continental, West European type of capitalism which he labelled the 'Rhineland' model. The former is a 'shareholder economy' under which private enterprise is about maximising short-term profits for investors rather than any broader harmony of interests. In contrast, the 'Rhineland' model may be seen as a regulated market economy with a comprehensive system of social security. Government, employers' organisations and labour unions consult each other about economic goals in order to try to achieve a harmony of interests (Bolkestein, 1999). In short the Rhineland model is a 'stakeholder economy' in which competition and confrontation are avoided in the belief that they undermine sustainable, stable economic growth. Patrolling this economy is the state, which variously acts as a referee, guarantor, employer and owner.

The 'varieties of capitalism' literature (see for example Dore, 2000; Hall and Soskice, 2001; Lincoln and Kalleberg, 1990), also termed the comparative capitalism literature (Jackson and Deeg, 2008), followed this analysis. It saw societies as webs of relationships that were interdependent.

THEORY AND PRACTICE

KEY FRAMEWORK

Two types of market economy

These earlier accounts drew a dichotomous distinction between the Anglo-Saxon, liberal market economies (LMEs) and the collaborative market economies (CMEs) of continental north-western Europe (particularly Germany) and Japan. In the LMEs, shareholders are more powerful and the system largely works to maintain their freedom to pursue their rational hierarchical interests. Within the latter other stakeholders, such as governments, local governments, trade unions and consumer groups, share power (Dore, 2000). Unlike previous approaches, these authors argued that both systems were self-reinforcing and both could be successful in terms of organisational and societal performance.

The differences between the two systems are reflected in HRM institutions and this is referred to in more detail in Chapter 11 on *Training and Development*. For instance, in LMEs, trade unions have fewer members and are weak, external labour markets (with as few limitations on hire-and-fire as possible) predominate, individuals have fewer rights at work, much of education, training and welfare relies on the private sector or is absent and employment legislation puts few constraints on the kinds of contracts that can be applied in the workplace. In CMEs unions often are well supported and have influence through legal and industrial muscle, internal labour markets are preferred where people stay with the same employer, the state supports education and training and provides welfare provisions (so that, for example, employees who have lost their jobs can be paid while they retrain for another one) and employment legislation determines important elements of the employment contract – working hours, holidays, non-discrimination, communication rights, and security of tenure.

The 'varieties of capitalism' literature has been criticised for assuming that all complementarities are positive (Crouch, 2005; Deeg, 2005; Streeck, 2005); for ignoring substantial differences within nation states (Hollingsworth, 2006; Whitley, 1999); and for not being able to explain change (Boyer, 2005; Hollingsworth, 2006). The dichotomous approach has been critiqued as being too simplistic, and Hall and Thelen (2006) proposed a third set, 'mixed market economies' found in France and southern Europe. Despite this, however, survey evidence does point to the persistence of widespread packages of practices in LMEs and CMEs such that the dichotomy can provide a theoretical basis for comparison (Brewster *et al*, 2007a, 2007b; Richbell *et al*, 2011). There is a practical example of the way the theory can be used in Chapter 11 on *Training and Development*.

BUSINESS SYSTEMS THEORY

The business systems literature attempts to overcome some of the limitations of the 'varieties of capitalism' theories. As the name implies, the business systems approach is also rooted in the embeddedness of organisations within a network of complementary relationships, but argues that these are constantly under pressure from firms innovating and experimenting in order to gain competitive advantage (Morgan, 2007; p136).

THEORY AND PRACTICE

KEY FRAMEWORK

Comparative characteristics of business

The nature of the firm

- the degree to which private managerial hierarchies co-ordinate economic activities
- the degree of managerial discretion from owners
- the specialisation of managerial capabilities and activities within authority hierarchies
- the degree to which growth is discontinuous and involves radical changes in skills and activities
- the extent to which risks are managed through mutual dependence with business patterns and employees

Market organisation

- the extent of long-term co-operative relations between firms within and between sectors
- the significance of intermediaries in the co-ordination of market transactions
- stability, integration and scope of business groups
- dependence of co-operative relations on personal ties and trust

Authoritative co-ordination and control systems

- integration and interdependence of economic activities
- impersonality of authority and subordination relations
- task, skill and role specialisation and individualisation
- differentiation of authority roles and expertise

- decentralisation of operational control and level of work group autonomy
- distance and superiority of managers
- extent of employer–employee commitment and organisation-based employment system.

Source: Whitley (1992)

Table 7 National business system archetypes

Type Form	Fragmented	Co-ord. industrial district	Compartmentalised	State organised	Collaborative	Highly co-ordinated
Examples	Hong Kong	Italy	USA, UK, NZ, Australia	post-war South Korea	Sweden, Austria, Norway	Japan
Ownership co-ordination						
– owner control	direct	direct	market	direct	alliance	alliance
– ownership integration of production chains/ sectors	low	low	high	some to high	high/ limited	some/ limited
Non-ownership co-ordination						
– alliance co-ord. of production chains/ sectors	low	limited/ low	low	low	limited/low	high/some
– collaboration between competing firms	low	some	low	low	high	high
Work and employment relations						
– delegation to employees	low	some	low	low	some	high
– interdependence between managers and workers	low	some	low	low	high	considerable

Source: Brookes *et al* (2005), based on Whitley (1999; pp41–44)

In business systems theory relationships within the organisation are a central feature (alongside the links between organisations), and the link to HRM is even clearer. Whitley (1999) defines the links in terms of the degree of employer–employee interdependence and the degree of delegation to employees. The former includes the extent of security of tenure and the extent to which each side has committed resources to continuing the relationship: spending on training by the employer and the development by the employee of capability specific to that firm. Delegation might include the extent of collective bargaining, works councils, consultation, teamworking, suggestion schemes and quality circles. Brewster *et al* (2008) found a strong relationship between variations in delegation and interdependence and country context.

On this basis, the business systems literature has identified a more complex range of model variations. Whitley (1999) identified six archetypical business systems – see Table 7.

Wood and Frynas (2006) identify a seventh business system archetype – the segmented business system found in tropical Africa, where a large proportion of jobs are in the informal sector and a tradition of patriarchal management means delegation is unlikely. Jobs tend in the main to be short-term, poorly paid and insecure (Brewster *et al*, 2006).

Amable (2003) identifies five systems: the Anglo-Saxon market (LME) model, a Continental European (CME) model, Asian capitalism, social democratic (Nordic-style) economies and a Mediterranean model. These categories seem to work well against large-scale HRM survey data (Goergen *et al*, 2009a). Indeed, the question has been asked: how many varieties of capitalism or business systems are there (Jackson and Deeg, 2006)? We as yet know very little about the business systems of Latin America, or the Indian subcontinent, or many other parts of the world.

REGULATIONISM

Regulation theory provides a somewhat different perspective on national differences, arguing that the key is the way that national regulation provides sets of rules (both formal and informal) that control the innovation and experimentation of firms (Jessop, 2001). The social processes through which institutions develop such regulations form a central concern of these theorists. Hence, unlike the varieties of capitalism or the business systems theorists, regulationists assume that change is endemic and every situation is open to dynamic forces that may lead to change (Jessop, 2001; Hollingsworth, 2006). And regulations may be found at every level – supra-national (European Union rules or United Nations goals, for example), national, regional, sectoral, etc (Boyer and Hollingsworth, 1997; Hudson, 2006).

Regulationist thinking tends to be in the critical tradition and argues that the elitist short-termism of the shareholder model is dysfunctional for society as a whole and that, despite the pressures of globalisation, regulation to control owner power and to develop work and employment relations that entrench worker rights and promote dignity will also lead to economic success and long-term growth. The global financial crisis that began in 2008 provided a significant challenge to the LME-style shareholder-value-oriented model; an excessive concentration on short-term shareholder value led to uncontrollable speculation and a lack of attention to developing sustainable methods of wealth creation. It seems that many of the export-reliant CME economies, though initially hit by reduced opportunities to sell their product to the USA and the UK for example, have proved better at coping with the economic stresses and have come through the crisis in better shape.

WHAT DO THESE THEORIES MEAN FOR HUMAN RESOURCE MANAGEMENT?

The link between these institutional theories and HRM is clear. Like the cultural theories they imply that it is unlikely that HRM practices will work the same way in all contexts. Institutionalism reminds us that some practices that are seen as standard in some countries will even be seen as unusual or even unlawful in others (Brewster and Mayrhofer, 2011). Even where they are not, if they cut too radically across the local norms they will risk employee or trade union or pressure group reaction. Either way, imposing such practices may be dysfunctional for internationally operating organisations (Stavrou *et al*, 2010). The debate between the desire of many organisational leaders to standardise their policies and practices and the need to be conscious of and adapt to local institutional requirements (and cultural differences) is addressed in detail in Chapter 2.

Katz and Darbishire (2000) identified what they term 'converging divergences'. Looking at the USA, Australia, Germany, Italy, Japan, Sweden and the UK they argued that they had found not one universal type of employment system but many – the CMEs are breaking down to develop more varied systems, like the LMEs. They suggested that although globalisation and internationalisation might be argued to foster a general converging trend in employment systems, such an analysis does not allow for managerial agency – managers can do different things. As a result, they argue that all societies will gradually develop a range of work practices. However, the literature on convergence shows that national differences remain.

What about the homogenising tendencies of MNCs? It is often felt that they bring new practices into their host countries and so lead to change and convergence. It is true that they do behave differently in HRM from local companies – but not *so* differently (Brewster *et al*, 2008; Farndale *et al*, 2008). And even here the different business systems of the host countries influence and constrain the business strategies and managerial practices of the subsidiary, despite headquarter pressures (Lane, 1998). We explore this issue further in Chapter 12.

THE USA AND THE REST OF THE WORLD

So if there are these differences, what does that imply for our understanding of HRM? The concept of HRM was developed first in the USA and it is still the American specialists and the US-based journals that drive the subject. Our critique of the universalist paradigm, however, indicates that US conceptions of HRM may not apply around the world. Although there is much to be learned from the USA, and the policies and practices of US multinational corporations and the academic conferences and journals remain the touchstone for thinking about HRM, it is also important to understand what and why things are done differently elsewhere.

Brewster (1994) has pointed out that a core assumption of North American HRM is that the employing organisation has a considerable degree of latitude in regard to taking decisions on the management of personnel, including *inter alia* the freedom to operate contingent pay policies, the option of an absence of or at least a minimal influence from trade unions, and an assumption that the organisation has sole responsibility for training and development. In other words, central to the notion of North American HRM is an assumption of considerable organisational independence and autonomy. This assumption is reasonable for companies in the USA, given the weakness of the trade union movement there and the comparatively low levels of state subsidy, support and control. It also fits comfortably with the notion that the state should interfere in business as little as possible and that it is the right of individuals to do the best for themselves that they can without external interference (Guest, 1990). The question is: how viable are such critical assumptions elsewhere in the world?

In this section, we look critically at a number of issues that make the USA, as one cultural authority put it, 'quite untypical of the world as a whole' (Trompenaars, 1993). Many of our examples are taken from the European context but, we argue, also apply elsewhere around the world.

FOUR FACTORS THAT MAKE HRM UNTYPICAL

- the role of the state
- the role of legislation
- the role of the unions
- the role of ownership patterns.

THE ROLE OF THE STATE

The legislation that determines the firm–employee relationship is a product of a wider, normative conception of what role the state should play within the economic arena. In Europe it is typical for governments to be major employers in their own right, since the public sector forms a substantial proportion of the total economy (as much as half, in Norway, for example). In addition, these governments subsidise jobs extensively. At the end of the twentieth century nearly a quarter of the French labour force, at least in the formal sector, relied on government support, whether in the form of unemployment benefit or subsidised jobs (Pedder, 1999; p11). In other countries – particularly, for example, in Africa – these figures may be much higher.

On becoming unemployed, workers in the USA initially receive a level of benefit of about two-thirds their income – not far below levels in much of Europe. But those benefit levels reduce very quickly. In many European countries, in contrast, benefits are either not time-limited or actually increase the longer that people are out of work. It has been argued that this minimal margin between benefits and wages for the low-skilled unemployed represents a serious disincentive to seek new jobs: a French study reported by Pedder (1999) showed that people at work in France are five times less likely to lose their jobs than those in the USA, but that the unemployed in France take five times as long to find a new job.

THE ROLE OF LEGISLATION

We can distinguish three aspects of the legal influence on HRM:

- employment protection
- legislative requirements on pay and hours of work
- legislation on forms of employment contract.

In regard to the first of these, Blanchard (1999) attempted to quantify differences in employment protection within Europe and the USA. The argument is that employment protection has three main dimensions:

- the length of the notice period
- the amount of severance pay
- the nature and complexity of the legal process involved in laying off workers.

Blanchard finds that the USA is significantly different from Europe in general, and Italy, Spain and Portugal in particular. There is less protection in the USA. Of course, in many countries around the world, employment protection does not exist at all.

In relation to the legislative requirements on pay and work there are also marked differences. For example, International Labour Organisation figures show that in the United States almost 80 per cent of male workers and 65 per cent of working women now work more than 40 hours in a typical week. By contrast, in France the working week is by law limited to 35 hours, with overtime limited to 130 hours a year. This policy even extends to making unpaid overtime by senior employees a penal offence.

Finally, legislation on employment contracts exists everywhere but the legislation varies country by country. In Europe, again, employment contracts are the subject of European-level legislation. Legislation in Europe goes beyond anything found in the USA, limiting the ways people can be recruited, the documentation necessary when they start work, how much they can be paid, how management must consult with them, and a host of other matters. One German authority (Pieper, 1990; p82) pointed out that:

> The major difference between HRM in the USA and in Western Europe is the degree to which [HRM] is influenced and determined by state regulations. Companies have a narrower scope of choice in regard to personnel management than in the USA.

This statement could be applied to many other countries outside Europe – but there are also countries where state regulation of employment is effectively zero.

THE ROLE OF THE UNIONS

Another core feature of the USA is the limited role for trade unions. Most workplaces in the USA are not unionised. In many other countries the situation is exactly the same but in others the opposite is true. In European states, legislative status and influence is accorded to unions. Most European countries are more heavily unionised in terms of union membership than the USA (see Chapter 5) and employers are more likely to deal with a trade union in a collective bargaining relationship which sets terms and conditions for all or most of the employees (Morley *et al*, 2000a). Chapter 5 explores this issue in more detail. Closely related to the issue of trade union recognition is the European practice of employee involvement.

THE ROLE OF OWNERSHIP PATTERNS

Patterns of ownership also differ in different countries. Public ownership has decreased to some extent in many countries in recent years, but it is still far more widespread elsewhere than it is in the USA. In some African states and in China, for example, most employment is in the public sector. And private-sector ownership may not mean the same thing. In many countries, ownership of even major companies remains in the hands of single families rather than in the hands of shareholders. By contrast, in Germany a tight network of a small number of substantial banks owns a disproportionate number of companies. Their interlocking shareholdings and close involvement in the management of these corporations mean less pressure to produce short-term profits and a positive disincentive to drive competitors out of the marketplace (Randlesome, 1993).

CONVERGENCE AND DIVERGENCE IN HRM

CONVERGENCE IN HRM

A third, and linked, significant debate is between those who believe in globalisation – arguing that all aspects of management, including HRM, are becoming more alike – and those who believe that each country continues to have its own approach to management in general and HRM in particular. For Pudelko and Harzing (2007), at the country level the debate has always been about convergence or divergence of HRM practice whereas at the organisational level it has been about standardisation versus localisation of practice, with standardisation (at least theoretically) being based on either a country-of-origin effect or a dominance effect (Smith and Meiksins, 1995).

Pudelko and Harzing's (2007) survey data from 849 HRM managers in nine groups of companies headquartered in, and with matched subsidiaries in, the USA, Japan and Germany, found that sudsidiaries in the three different countries acted differently. US multinationals were localising practices to a degree in Japanese subsidiaries, and significantly in Germany. Motivations for localisation also differed: Japanese subsidiaries in the USA localised for dominance reasons but localised in Germany for local institutional reasons. The subsidiary's strategic role has great importance.

There is more than one version of the convergence concept. Comparative HRM researchers have analysed changes in the adoption of a range of specific tools and practices across countries. In examining changes over time in HRM practice between European countries, and attempting to link the pattern of these changes to competing theoretical explanations of what is happening, Mayrhofer *et al* (2004; p421) noted that 'It is by no means clear what is meant by *convergence*. Although the general meaning, intuitively, is clear, it becomes more complex at a closer look.' We therefore need a 'more nuanced picture of convergence' (p434).

THEORY AND PRACTICE

KEY FRAMEWORK

What is meant by HRM practice convergence or divergence?

Mayrhofer *et al* (2004) differentiated between a number of forms of change:

- *Directional convergence*: When comparing changes in HRM practices between two countries, directional convergence exists when the trend (developmental tendency) goes in the same direction. Each country might start with a different proportion of organisations using a specific practice, and over time the difference in the proportion of organisations using that particular practice in the two countries might actually have grown larger. However, in both cases, a greater proportion of organisations now use the practice, there is convergence in direction – in this case going up. Similarly the opposite might apply, with change in a negative direction.

- *Final convergence*: When changes in the use of an HRM practice in two different countries mean that the two countries' practices get more similar (the differences in use of the practice between the countries decreases in magnitude over time), there is convergence to some final point. This might imply that the country with less uses increases faster, or that one country increases a usage while another one decreases it – as long as they get closer together there may be said to be final convergence.

- *Stasis*: When there is no change over time in the proportion of organisations using an HRM practice and a state of stability thus exists.

- *Divergence*: When the changes in use of an HRM practice in two different countries are progressing in truly different directions, one increasing and the other decreasing.

In addition, we might note that HRM might not be uniform. For example, some practices may converge while others diverge, or there may be convergence at the policy level but not at the operational level.

Some see this as a market-based issue. They argue, using a kind of Darwinian 'survival of the fittest' analogy, that the logic of technology and its increasing diffusion mean that eventually, in order to compete, everyone will have to move to adopt the most efficient management and HRM practices (Kidger, 1991). The underlying assumption here is that the predominant model will be the US universalist model (Smith and Meiskins, 1995). There is also an institutional perspective, which argues that although institutional differences in legal, trade union and labour market conditions can create differences in HRM, this might, where similar legislation covers a number of countries, as in the EU, lead to a diminution in the differences between the ways in which countries handle their HRM. The EU is passing legislation for all the member states, including social and employment legislation. There is a free labour market in the EU and some companies now try to operate as if the EU was one country. A developing European model of HRM would reinforce the idea of a move towards convergence – but not in the form of regional convergence, rather global convergence.

DIVERGENCE IN HRM

Opposed to the idea of convergence there is the concepts of cultural differences outlined in Chapter 2 and the institutional theories outlined above. Proponents of the various versions of each of these two main streams of explanation are unlikely to accept that there is any point at which the same practices will be utilised to the same degree and would have the same effect irrespective of country or location. This book is firmly based on such a notion. This, of course, gives IHRM practitioners a key paradox. For a number of good reasons, internationally operating organisations want to standardise practices wherever possible. But in many areas of management, and particularly HRM, they also have to be aware of and respond to or even utilise national differences. This is a central issue in IHRM and one that, once we have explored and understood the national variations found in HRM approaches, policies and practices around the world, we explore in the third section of the book.

Table 8 Summary of convergence *v* divergence

Convergence	Divergence
The world is becoming increasingly global and all aspects of management, including HRM, are becoming more alike.	Each country continues to have its own approach to management and HRM in particular.
In order to compete everyone will have to adopt the most efficient management and HRM practices.	It is the USA which is 'untypical of the world as a whole' due to its autonomy and independence in terms of people management. Elsewhere there is the greater influence of:
The predominant model of thinking is universalist.	• the state • legislation (eg EU) • the unions • ownership patterns.
	The predominant model of thinking is contextualist.

THE EVIDENCE

There is little empirical data on the issue of convergence versus divergence, and that is largely the result of the difficulties of researching the issue. A number of articles which claim to have researched convergence of HRM practices either use case studies, which are inappropriate for identifying whether national practices are becoming more alike, or use convergence to apply only to directional convergence – they find the same trends in different countries but can say nothing about whether they are becoming more alike. Others use single-point-in-time data to explore issues of convergence towards assumed best practices. Obviously, researching convergence seriously would require a longitudinal comparative research programme – but these are expensive and rare. And even they would not resolve the problem entirely. Which issues are we researching? Are we to research institutional arrangements or how they operate? Are we to research at a national level, an organisational level, or a workplace level? Whose opinions are we to canvass?

We have a limited understanding of how MNC headquarters export and diffuse HRM policies and practices out to subsidiaries. Less has been written about reverse diffusion processes (Edwards and Ferner, 2004), whereby advances in subsidiaries influence other parts of the MNC operation, but it appears to be minimal. Bouquet and Birkinshaw (2008) note that the attention of executives at corporate headquarters is scarce and ask how do subsidiaries gain attention? They found that the key attributes to do so were weight (the structural position that a subsidiary occupies within the corporate system), voice (the strategies used to gain attention), the success of the subsidiary, geographical distance and competence (with manufacturing, R&D, strategic support services or centres of excellence with knowledge that can be leveraged into other markets having a greater input).

Dickmann and Müller-Camen (2006) argue for a process perspective (focusing on broad processes such as innovation or lateral co-ordination) as a way of understanding patterns of IHRM. Similarly, Farndale and Paauwe (2007) call for a deeper examination of how multinationals balance the dualities between producing similarities or maintaining differences in global HRM practices, and how both sets of practices respond to either competitive or institutional pressures. Like us, they argue for a more contextual understanding of the competing drivers for change in HRM. The not unexpected conclusion of the research was that (Farndale and Paauwe, 2007; p371):

> Given the multitude of contextual factors and strategic choice opportunities, it is not surprising that the HR practices across these high-performing firms were found both to be similar in some respects and to vary in others at the global and the national level.

So, MNCs from different countries still differ systematically in their overseas operations (Björkman, 2006). The current consensus is that organisations are not as global or international as is often assumed. A country-of-origin effect is still clearly evident. US MNCs, for example, tend to be more centralised and formalised than others in their management of HRM issues, ranging from pay systems through to collective bargaining and union recognition. They tend to innovate more and import leading-edge practices from other nation states. Japanese MNCs on the other hand have been at the forefront of work organisation innovations through lean production, but expect their subsidiaries abroad to fit in with this approach. Even though standard worldwide policies and formal systems are not as apparent as in US MNCs, there is stronger centralised direction and ethnocentric attitudes. In short (Ferner and Quintanilla, 1998; p710):

> MNCs, far from being stateless organisations operating independent of national borders in some purified realm of global economic competition, continue to have their assets, sales, work-force ownership and control highly concentrated in the country where their corporate headquarters are located.

From the perspective of institutional theory, three factors are identified as being important in determining the extent to which an organisation adopts standard practices worldwide or adapts them to suit local conditions:

- the degree to which an affiliate is embedded in the local environment – through its method of founding and its age, as well as its size, its dependence on local inputs and the degree of influence exerted on it from local institutions

- the strength of flow of resources such as capital, information and people between the parent and the affiliate – the stronger and more important the flow, the more there is a need for global co-ordination

- the characteristics of the parent – for example, the degree of uncertainty avoidance (see Chapter 2) of the home country will affect the freedom of subsidiaries. Equally, if the culture of the home country is perceived to be very different from the culture of the subsidiary country, more cultural control will tend to be exercised by headquarters (ie an ethnocentric approach) in order to achieve internal consistency.

REFLECTIVE ACTIVITY

Each of these theoretical perspectives has value, but assume for a moment that you were asked to choose between them.

● What order would you put them into, based on their value in explaining SIHRM?

Some of the best available evidence on country-level convergence is from the Cranet data. Mayrhofer *et al* (2010; p60) carry out careful and detailed statistical analysis of the data over 15 years and summarise its findings on convergence and divergence as follows:

> Empirically, the results support the notion that converging and non-converging developments occur simultaneously. While no final convergence can be observed for HRM in Europe … directional similarity is visible in a majority of the areas of HRM analysed. The results also show the effects of the embeddedness of HRM in national institutional contexts and the interplay between supra-national drivers and national institutional forces.

In other words, there are common trends, but no evidence that countries even in Europe are becoming more alike in the way that they manage their human resources. Undoubtedly, if it were possible to extend the analysis beyond Europe, even greater differences would be found.

ORGANISATION AND MANAGEMENT IN AN ANGLO-FRENCH CONSORTIUM: TRANSMANCHE LINK

CASE STUDIES

The Channel Tunnel proved to be an adventurous project, technologically unique and built under enormous pressure and conflict between partners. It was also the subject of international comparative organisational and cultural research to explore the behaviour of British and French managers under a common structure (Winch *et al*, 2000). A series of organisational and behavioural variables was measured across more than 200 managers. The French managers reported higher unit cohesion based on competition between units. They had significantly more work and decision-making autonomy and were less procedurally oriented than the British, but provided less feedback and opportunity for

mutual adjustment. While both nationalities had high personal accountability and followed the procedures that existed, the French had more control of their work by knowing more about it in advance. Power emanated more from the personal responsibility of the senior managers than from the position and control systems. The French were more action-oriented (*fonceur*) and the British more procedural. There were no differences between the two in terms of job satisfaction or motivation from pay and promotion. However, the British were far more motivated through the use of feedback (praise and encouragement from others). This was unimportant to French managers. The British were also more directly job-involved, in that they expressed unhappiness when performing badly on the job. The boundary between work and home life was more porous for the British, and reported stress was lower. The French managers were by contrast more distant from colleagues and shouldered more personal responsibility, and therefore carried more stress.

Source: Winch *et al,* (2000)

Questions:

Thinking about the TransManche Link case, what elements of the chapter to this point can you see reflected in the example? How would you summarise the different approaches theoretically? How and why do you think the project was a success even despite these differences?

What does all this mean for international HRM practitioners? It implies that – despite the work outlined in Chapter 2 – they cannot just simply measure cultural values across their operations and predict the behaviours that are related to such values. Instead, the development and success of any specific managerial structures and practice (such as HRM) can only be explained by giving due cognisance to the various institutional contexts. Not all management methods are transferable, even where employee values have converged. The effectiveness therefore of any universal conceptualisation of HRM will very probably be constrained by the different institutional contexts. This is a powerful argument in favour of the need for local responsiveness.

 REFLECTIVE ACTIVITY

Take a few minutes to think about the options.

- Is the way organisations have to go through the processes of recruiting, inducting, developing, paying and working with staff so similar in every country that general points about how human resources are managed (or perhaps should be managed) are valid?

- Or is it the case that things are done so differently in different countries that we have to be very aware of the location in which human resources are being managed before we can understand them?

- Or can we combine these two accounts? And if so, how?

 REFLECTIVE ACTIVITY

Fortunately, perhaps, the field is still open. We can each have our views and our different interests. Before going further it may be worth asking yourself:

- Where do I stand on the universalist/contextual axis?

- What are my views about the dominance of the US approaches to HRM?

- And what are the implications of my views for my interests in and study of HRM?

- Any analysis of HRM must be clear about the *level* of analysis.

- There will be some aspects of HRM which may be applicable in any country and any circumstances: every organisation in every country has to conduct basic HRM practices such as recruitment, payment, etc.

- There will also be many aspects of HRM which cannot be understood at that level and which must be explored at different levels: workplace, sector, national or regional. A focus on any one of these areas will, like focusing a camera, clarify some areas but blur others. It does not make either view true or false – they are merely different perspectives.

- The national level of analysis is particularly informative, but it is often given less priority than it should be. We provide evidence on these issues in the following chapters.

- At the national level, as we show in the following chapter, HRM can be very different. This is because of cultural and institutional differences between countries.

- This means that universal 'best practice' approaches to HRM – often originating in the USA (or for multinational organisations, at headquarters) – should always be considered critically: are they appropriate for other environments?

- There are signs that these national differences are decreasing, but the best evidence we have implies that they remain critical. Although globalisation seems to be creating some common trends in HRM, it is not reducing the difference between countries in the way HRM is managed and conducted.

LEARNING QUESTIONS

1 Argue for or against the statement that we are seeing an increasing convergence of HRM practice within Europe.

2 In the light of the arguments produced in this chapter, is the concept of 'best practice' not applicable in the context of HRM?

3 Do you see the state as having any role in determining HRM policy and practice in an increasingly global world?

EXPLORE FURTHER

Brewster C. and Mayrhofer, W. (2011) *A Handbook of Comparative HRM*, Edward Elgar, Cheltenham. This new book explores these issues in depth, looking at concepts, specific comparative aspects of HRM policies and practices, and the different ways that HRM is conceived of and carried out in the different regions of the world.

The CIA *World Factbook* (www.cia.gov/library/publications/the-world-factbook) is an excellent source of information about countries and their institutions.

CHAPTER 5

Employee Relations and Collective Communication

When they have read this chapter, students will:

- understand the range of structures of employee relations common in Europe and around the world

- be aware of the differences in meaning and role of unions and other representative employee bodies

- be able to assess how such bodies may influence management communication with workforces

- understand the role of history, national cultures and legal institutions in influencing these structures and bodies

- be aware of cross-national variation in the nature and relevance of labour law as awell as union representation

- have an appreciation of the immediate implications for managers of people.

INTRODUCTION

Employee relations concerns matters of overarching employment or collective workforce policy, particularly where it concerns broad matters of bargaining (the traditional focus of industrial relations), the governance of the employment relationship by social actors (ie actors outside the management hierarchy/ conventional director structure) and arrangements for the distillation and expression of the collective voice of employees. Typically the workplace, enterprise or company-level approach in this arena is profoundly affected by the prevailing national system of employee relations, and in particular by the social regulation of work by unions and national or regional governments.

In most – if not all – nations now, employee relations is often considered a less glamorous aspect of people management. In the realm of people management, the strategic integration of HRM practice or HRM functions, and more broadly management activity, entrepreneurialism and intra-preneurship, are generally considered rather more significant than the matters encompassed by employee relations. This is particularly true within Britain, the USA and the larger Anglo-Saxon world and in developing and newly industrialising countries. Yet governance by social actors, collective voice, and the joint regulation of the employment relationship may have stabilising and beneficial implications in terms of consistency and order in, and legitimation of, the relationship between employer and employee, as many managers in the Nordic countries in particular recognise.

The focus of the present chapter is very much upon the institutions and processes of governance, leaving many matters of effect to be taken up in other chapters. The discussion centres on the joint regulation of work by independent bodies such as unions and works councils, with some attention also to board-level employee representation. There is some attention also to the direct statutory regulation of the employment relationship.

The social regulation of work, whether by unions or governments, is rarely initiated with the promotion of economic or business performance as the central objective. Nonetheless, the social regulation of work impacts not only on the management process but typically also on performance in these respects. It is noteworthy that this impact need not be negative. In light of the extent of general debate and the availability of general evidence, there is some attention here to the broad matter of the business performance implications of unions and joint regulation or collective bargaining specifically (see later).

REFLECTIVE ACTIVITY

Consider the national framework of employee relations in a country with which you are familiar. What is the balance between the governance of the employment relationship by unions, works councils based on statute, and direct statutory regulation?

WHAT ARE TRADE UNIONS?

Unions are central to employee relations, and to the governance of the employment relationship by actors external to the management hierarchy. Unions are enduring collective organisations of employees with the broad aim of ensuring that the interests of employees are respected and furthered. Typically, they are organisations quite independent of management, although perhaps rather less so in Japan than in European nations or North America (eg Vernon, 2006b). Typically, too, they are quite independent of national governments. This is so even in modern Russia, for example, although unions there are rather uncommon in most sectors, and have in very many cases struggled to find an identity in post-socialist times (eg Clarke, 2005).

Whereas unions' independence is a pretty general characteristic, unions' traditions and ideologies differ significantly across countries. Hyman (2001) locates the identities of national union movements in a triangle which identifies the extent to which they embody in their discourse and activities an emphasis on the three attractors of 'class', 'society' and 'market'. Movements such as the French (or Italian), with its traditional emphasis on the rhetoric of class conflict and, indeed, revolution and its preference for public displays of resistance coupled to arms'-length sectoral bargaining (or stalemate) have been between 'class' and 'society', with the 'market' orientation much less significant. Movements such as the German (or Dutch), with its more conciliatory efforts to integrate unions into detailed policy discussion, its preparedness to engage in partnership with employers, and its combination of sectoral bargaining activity with informal bargaining activity at company and enterprise level (even if this is via works councils formally independent of unions), have traditionally been located between 'society' and 'market', with the discourse of 'class' being of more marginal relevance. Movements like the British (or, indeed, to a perhaps surprising extent, the US) have been much influenced by notions of 'class' and class conflict in some of their rhetoric, but other facets of their discourse and their predominant practice is a rather practical economic, or 'bread-and-butter', bargaining approach centred at the workplace or enterprise level. This has traditionally located them between 'class' and 'market', with less emphasis on the integration of unions into the daily life of civil society. Hyman (2001) detects some signs of convergence in the approaches of union movements since the 1990s, but stresses that national union identities display considerable continuity.

Other distinctions are useful within the established industrialised world. Mediterranean or southern European union movements (eg France, Italy, Spain, Greece) are not only more political in their orientation but also more politically divided, featuring various different unions associated with different (predominantly but not exclusively left-of-centre) political parties. This contrasts with union movements in the UK, USA and the rest of the Anglo-Saxon world, where any such political splintering is generally transient. Meanwhile, union movements in continental northern Europe (eg Germany, Austria, the Netherlands, Norway, Sweden, Finland) feature neither overt political divisions nor the fragmentation of union organisation by an occupational (eg craft and general) basis and/or by an emphasis on enterprise or workplace activity generally found in the Anglo-Saxon world, vertically organised unions representing all employees regardless of skill or grade, at least amongst blue-collar employees, and in the case of Austria regardless too of the blue-collar/white-collar divide.

In terms of the unionism which managers face in the workplace, it is perhaps the principle of union organisation or the structure of unions in terms of occupational membership which is most important. Where unions are organised on the basis of occupations, such that even manual employees with different skills or qualifications join different unions (the 'craft and general' structure), there is not only more of an emphasis on occupational division within workplace union activity, but more of a tradition of assertive and sometimes adversarial union workplace activity largely autonomous of the policies and priorities of the larger unions represented. Despite union mergers in the UK, this tradition still influences union activity in the UK. It is also influential in the Republic of Ireland, Australia and New Zealand, but most visibly in Denmark – due to the strength of unions there (see the case study on Danish 'flexi-curity' later in the chapter).

Where the company or facility (enterprise) is the key locus of union activity, such that employees of different grades band together in what are effectively company or business unions with little or no life beyond organisational boundaries, conflict may more easily be kept off the shop floor. This is the case most clearly in Japan, but also in the USA and in Canada. Where unions are organised along industrial lines, one union in each sector taking in at least all interested blue-collar employees regardless of their skill or qualifications, much of the locus of union activity is outside the workplace – and indeed, company – in industrial negotiations. Whilst this very clearly displaces workplace conflict, this implies a need to observe systems of job classification and job evaluation, and an expectation of career ladders or internal labour markets (see the chapter on *Comparative HRM: Reward* here). This external structuring of posts tends to be more significant and detailed in principle and application where industrial unions are stronger in terms of membership, so that although some element of this structuring is present in France, it is much more elaborate in Belgium and Norway and most particularly Sweden and Finland. Lazear and Shaw (2008) provide a detailed overview.

In many developing and newly industrialising countries unions represent an elite of employees and have a very close if not clientilist relationship with ruling parties. Thus in many African countries, unions often serve to protect the privilege of elite groups of employees, and their leaderships have complex and often intimate relationships with national governments (see Wood and Brewster, 2007) – the closest European parallel is perhaps Greece. In India, unions hardly exist outside the rather small formal sector of the economy, and even within this are concentrated very much in the public sector or in large public enterprises, so that in practice they too serve a relative elite.

CASE STUDIES

UNIONS IN CHINA

In the period of Chinese central planning, when state-owned enterprises (SOEs) almost completely dominated industry, unions functioned as a transmission belt for the ruling Communist Party, charged with the pursuit of social and political peace and stability. Now, though, the state accounts for only a third of GDP, and where unions have developed in the newly dominant private sector they have a rather conflicted identity, combining their traditional task of pursuing social harmony with a countervailing role, defending employee interests vis-à-vis private entrepreneurs and employers. Although Chinese unions are still distinct from those typical in the established or old industrialised world, their new aspirations are driving practical effects. A recent survey suggests that unions are present in more than half of the larger private sector enterprises, including many foreign MNCs. Moreover, although they do not have a discernible impact on the pay of the employees they represent, they do have impact. They have developed their traditional welfare role, focused on organising parties or purchasing presents for deserving or departing staff, such that they now have a substantial impact on the enterprise-level provision of employee benefits such as pensions, medical insurance and unemployment insurance (Metcalf and Li, 2006; Lu *et al*, 2009). They thus appear a variant of business or enterprise unions in some respects.

Sources: Clarke, 2005; Lu *et al*, 2009; Metcalf and Li, 2006; Ng and Warner, 1998.

REFLECTIVE ACTIVITY

Consider the character of unions in a country with which you are familiar. How is this of relevance to managers at organisation or workplace level?

COMPARATIVE STRUCTURES OF GOVERNANCE

MULTI-EMPLOYER BARGAINING: PREVALENCE AND NATURE

Even within the established advanced industrialised world there is dramatic comparative variation in the coverage of collective bargaining. In the USA it now languishes at not much above 10 per cent of the workforce, and a little more in Japan, but in Canada and most particularly the EU it is typically much higher. In many European countries trade union recognition for collective bargaining is required by law, and collective agreements that are reached through negotiations with trade unions are spread, by law in most cases, to other employees, ensuring a much wider coverage of collective bargaining than trade union membership figures alone would suggest.

Even within the expanded EU, though, there is considerable variation around the average. Generally, coverage rates have shown a gradual decline over the last few decades. However, in many cases these declines have been slight, and some countries – eg Slovenia and Denmark – have seen increases in collective bargaining coverage in recent years. Economy-wide bargaining coverage remains very high in all the countries of continental northern Europe: 85–100 per cent in Denmark, Sweden, Finland and Germany, 80 per cent in the Netherlands, around 75 per cent of the working population in Norway, compared to only around 50 per cent in the UK (just as in OECD, 1996). Figure 6 shows Cranet 2010 data on coverage or recognition of collective bargaining in a representative range of countries of the old industrialised world. Cranet excludes small and some medium-sized organizations, focusing on larger organisations which tend to be covered; this is particularly evident for the USA and Japan. No data is included for Sweden because coverage there is so comprehensive that organisations cannot sensibly be questioned about it.

Figure 6 Coverage of collective bargaining/union recognition by organisations

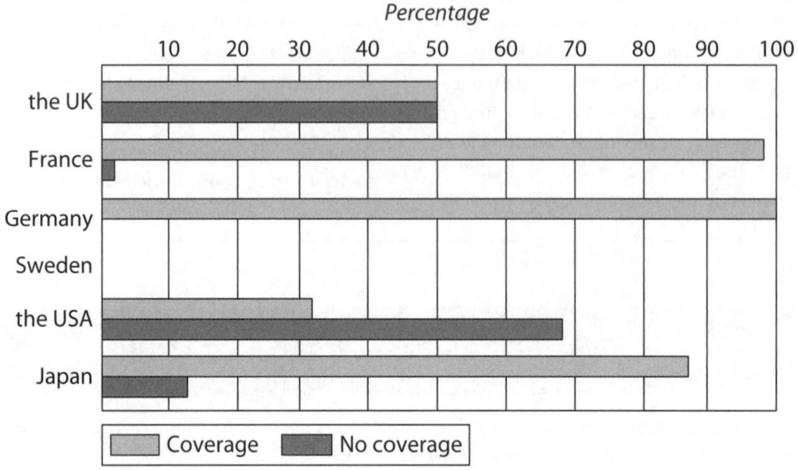

Percentage

	10	20	30	40	50	60	70	80	90	100

the UK

France

Germany

Sweden

the USA

Japan

☐ Coverage   ■ No coverage

Source: Cranet (2010)

High levels of collective bargaining coverage are secured principally not by establishment- or company-level agreements but by multi-employer bargaining and agreements (eg Vernon, 2006a). Multi-employer bargaining may occur at various levels, according to the centralisation of bargaining (sectoral, multi-sectoral), and may be more or less closely co-ordinated across sectors and subject to extension beyond the employers who pay their dues to employers' associations. Where such multi-employer bargaining and agreements do not generally prevail – as for example in the USA, Japan and, indeed, China – coverage is much more limited.

COMPANY AND ENTERPRISE JOINT REGULATION

Company- and enterprise-level employee relations or joint regulation concern local collective bargaining, governance procedures and company- or enterprise-level collective voice. Such company- or enterprise-level arrangements are often part of a multi-level structure of collective bargaining and joint regulation, particularly within Europe. This multi-level structure maybe more or less vertically co-ordinated or articulated (eg Stokke, 2008). In northern Europe there is often a formal hierarchy of collective bargaining or joint regulation, with collective agreements at multi-sector and/or sectoral level explicitly defining the role of collective bargaining or joint regulation at the lower, company or enterprise, level. In the Nordic countries, and particularly Sweden, Finland and Norway, such tiered bargaining is perhaps most intricately structured, and transparently involves unions at all levels. In Germany and Austria there is formal derogation of responsibility, particularly regarding arrangement of working hours, from sectoral bargaining involving unions to company- or enterprise-level works councils formally independent of them (although see later regarding works councils in practice).

Union recognition in the sense of an acceptance of bargaining outcomes either within the workplace or at higher levels is near universal in some countries – as would be expected from collective bargaining coverage rates. Yet even in countries where coverage is high and recognition a matter of course, unionisation rates at enterprise level may vary starkly. Figure 7 indicates not just the stark differences in average unionisation rates across countries but also the stark differences in the extent of enterprise-level variation in unionisation. In most countries, unionisation is either typically high or typically low. However, in some countries there is a striking bifurcation of unionisation rates, with density low in a high proportion of enterprises but also high in a high proportion of enterprises; Japan provides an example.

Figure 7 Unionisation rates or density of union membership across organisations

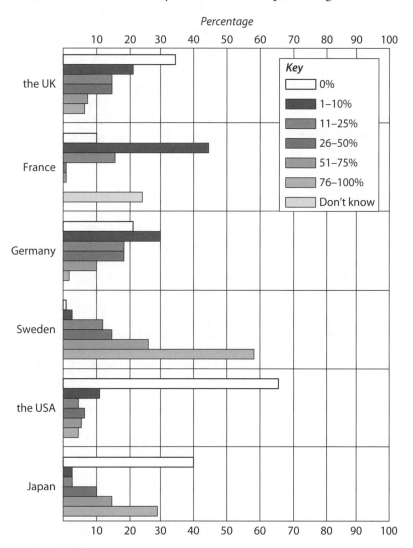

Source: Cranet (2010)

The union movements of many countries have lost members over the last decades in many countries, and in some countries the union movement is struggling to come to terms with the modern economy (Rigby *et al*, 2004). The decline of the traditional areas of union strength in primary industries and giant manufacturing plants, the unions' failure to deal effectively with internationalisation and with the developments in flexible working (Croucher and Brewster, 1998), and government and employer strategies have all led to reductions in union membership and influence. In the hostile environment of recent years, unions have suffered at least some membership loss and some level of loss of influence even in the northern European countries (Morley *et al*, 2000b). Although membership is declining slowly, there is a remarkable level of stability. Even in the UK, where there was a sustained governmental attack throughout the 1980s and much of the 1990s on the unions, trade union membership levels amongst organisations with over 200 employees remained remarkably stable (Morley *et al*, 1996) and have declined only very steadily since.

In some countries where sectoral bargaining predominates, it is nonetheless the case that many of the largest employers effectively opt of sectoral agreements and negotiate separate company agreements with their local unions. Often, in the Netherlands for example, these are the companies with the greatest union density, and the sectoral agreements serve in practice as a minimum benchmark for negotiations in most – if not all – regards.

CAN COMPANIES ESCAPE GENERALISED STRUCTURES OF COLLECTIVE BARGAINING OR JOINT REGULATION?

Some employers may be tempted to try to avoid the restrictions implied by the joint regulation of the employment relationship by unions or works councils (while not seeing any countervailing benefits of such joint regulation). However, employers face real difficulties in escaping arrangements which are generalised within a country, or within the particular industry within which an organisation operates in that country. Employee expectations of employer behaviour are in such countries importantly formed by such structures. Ultimately, employers may exert considerable effort to escape and find that they have to introduce parallel company arrangements which may require very substantial and sustained investment if they are to have the legitimacy of independent arrangements. Moreover, of course, it is difficult to escape employees' expectations of the substantive concomitants of independent governance in terms, for example, of salaries or benefits. This has been the experience in the Netherlands (eg Paauwe, 2004; Visser and Hemerijck, 1997).

Of course, organisations may simply avoid operating altogether in countries in which unions exercise much power in joint regulation – but this is a very extreme response.

WORKS COUNCILS

Although the term is sometimes used rather loosely, particularly in the Anglo-Saxon world, in a strict sense works councils are representative bodies of employees which have a statutory basis rather than staff councils or joint consultative committees set up autonomously by employers. These independent employee bodies, which may exist at several levels of the organisation (eg plant or enterprise level, central level) have certain rights mandated by law, rather than roles prescribed by employers. As is the case in the Nordic countries, works councils or workplace clubs are often formally and explicitly for the local representatives of unions only (Berggren, 1994). Sometimes, however, they exist alongside and are formally independent from union channels, as is the case in Germany, for example – but even here they have in practice a very close relationship with local union representatives and broader union structures (eg Streeck, 1992).

Figure 8 shows the incidence of works councils, or in the case of the Anglo-Saxon and some other countries, the joint consultative committees which are the closest parallel to them, amongst the medium and large-sized companies covered by Cranet (2010). Where there is statutory provision for works councils, such institutions are found in the clear majority of these organisations (eg France, Germany and Sweden). Where there is no statutory provision for works councils, as in the Anglo-Saxon countries, the employer-established joint consultative committee (JCC) is found in fewer organisations – this is particularly extreme in the case of the USA. JCCs have less certain roles than do statutory works councils, but may have a very significant role in some organisations.

Figure 8 The incidence of works councils/joint consultative committees across organisations

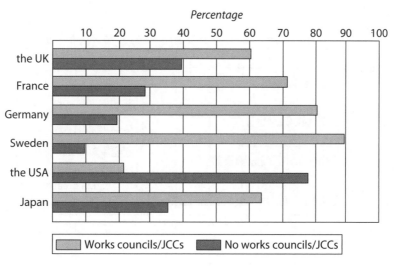

Source: Cranet (2010)

Typically more significant than joint consultative committees, the roles and functions which statute provides for works councils nonetheless vary from country to country. In France, although near universal, the works council (*conseil du travail*) has rights to consultation on a range of matters, but little right to negotiation or joint decision-making. In the case of Germany, however, works councils not only have specific negotiation rights, requiring employers to follow certain procedures in a number of areas, but also have a right to joint decision-making or co-determination in some areas. Thus, employers in Germany must secure the agreements of the works council in order to change pay systems – the works council holds a right to veto in this area (Streeck, 1992). Similarly, in Sweden the works council, or 'workplace club', may veto the outsourcing of some of the companies' activities (Kjellberg, 1998). Works councils may use their legal rights as a basis for more or less formal bargaining activity. In Germany, for example, although formally works councils may not bargain over pay rates (despite their co-determination rights regarding systems), it is clear that in practice there has been informal negotiation in these matters (eg Marsden, 1995).

What use have employers made of such institutions for communicating with employees? In Europe, works councils based in statute are the predominant form of representative staff body used for collective communications. Organisations usage, and changing usage, of such channels of collective communication is of considerable interest (Mayrhofer *et al*, 2000). Figure 9 shows that at least in the medium- and larger-sized organisations covered by Cranet (2010), works councils remain for many an important channel of communication in Europe, and that the closest equivalent employee representative bodies in Japan also have great significance.

Figure 9 The extent to which managers communicate with employees via the works council/joint consultative committee

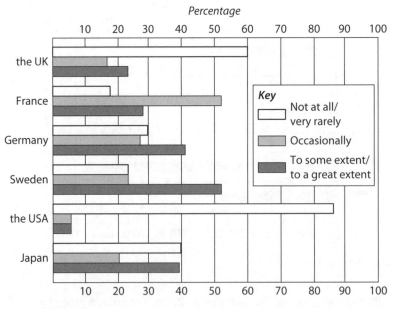

Source: Cranet (2010)

BOARD-LEVEL EMPLOYEE REPRESENTATION

Some public sector organisations in most countries feature employee directors on their main boards. A degree of employee board representation also occurs, however, in the private sector in northern Europe, and most strikingly in the Nordic countries (eg Jackson, 2005a). Where present, statutory provision for employee representation on boards usually provides that between one-third and a half of the board are to be employee representatives, depending on country, sector, and size of company. Employee board representation is less frequent in smaller organisations, and indeed the smallest – of fewer than, say, 25 to 50 employees – are often excluded under the terms of the legislation. However, although small organisations and their medium-sized counterparts together constitute the vast bulk of companies (indeed, if SMEs are defined as companies of fewer than 250 employees, they typically constitute 97–99 per cent of all a nation's companies), they almost always employ a minority of employees. Board-level employee representation is near ubiquitous in the larger organisations of Sweden, Norway and Finland, and more than this is in place in the organisations employing the vast bulk of employees in these countries (Hagen, 2010, IIRA European Congress, June 2010). Such worker-directors have the same rights to information and to scrutiny of the executive as other board members.

Germany's two-tiered board structure has the main board overseen by a supervisory board which features representatives of creditors but also, under the terms of co-determination legislation, often representatives of employees. These employee supervisory board representatives are present in almost all the largest companies, and still cover around half of all employees in Germany as a whole. Such worker-directors are elected in a system that is formally independent of union representation but, as with works councils, that is in practice closely related (eg Streeck, 1992). The situation is almost identical in Austria, and rather similar in the Netherlands.

Employee representation on boards can give considerable (legally backed) power to the employee representatives and tend to supplement rather than supplant the union position. In relatively highly unionised countries it is unsurprising that many of the representatives of the workforce are, in practice, trade union officials. In most countries, the majority of them are union representatives. Whatever the precise arrangements, board-level employee representatives constitute part of the matrix of union governance of organisations, and part also of unions' and employees' means of accessing corporate information and coming to bargaining judgements.

EMPTY NATIONAL STRUCTURES OF JOINT REGULATION?

Structures of joint regulation are rather empty in some countries. France provides a prominent example, where there is very high collective bargaining coverage but where the multi-employer agreements feature rather little content. In other countries, however, the arrangements are very clearly significant in practice. Typically, as Vernon (2006a) shows, the higher are national unionisation rates, the more significant and substantial is collective bargaining – ie the weightier is joint regulation. Of course, national or aggregate unionisation rates can only provide an indication of the general situation in a country – there is typically significant variation in the significance of joint regulation across sectors. However, in some European countries – eg Sweden, Finland, Norway, Denmark, Belgium and Slovenia – it is difficult to find a sector where joint regulation is not a significant consideration for managers of people. Such cross-national variation is indicated by people management specialists' views about the influence of unions in their organisation in Figure 10. Later comparative chapters here elaborate in detail on some of the implications of national arrangements of joint regulation for other arenas of people management.

Figure 10 Personnel/HRM directors' views of the extent to which unions influence their organisations

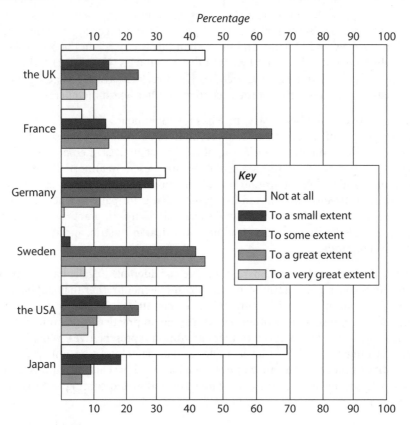

Source: Cranet (2010)

DANISH FLEXI-CURITY

Within the EU, the Danish approach to governance of the labour market and of employment relationships is the subject of much discussion. The European Commission has suggested that the Danish system of 'flexi-curity' provides a model of balancing the flexibility employers favour and the security desired by employees which is potentially applicable to the rest of Europe. Security is imparted in large part by the national government's commitment to an active labour market policy, by retraining the unemployed, and also by comparatively generous short-term welfare provision aiding/supporting the incomes of those without work in transition to new jobs. Although much of the flexibility of the system is imparted by the very limited direct statutory regulation of the employment relationship – most particularly in terms of job protection legislation – the character of union activity in Denmark is important to this model (Andersen and Mailand, 2005). Denmark's unions – now more than those of even the UK, for example – are marked by the tradition of craft and general unionism, and by the focus on enterprise and most especially workplace activity associated with this. Sectoral bargaining in Denmark results in sectoral agreements which set substantial minimum rates of pay for the very lowest grades of employees, but have little further content. At workplace level, it is now estimated conservatively that 80 per cent of all employees in Denmark are covered by a shop steward (Ilsøe et al, 2007). There is single-channel employee/interest representation in Denmark, in contrast, for example, to Germany and Austria with their works council arrangements. Yet although Danish workplace representatives are thus always formally representative of a union, the shop stewards under the predominance of craft and general are not only typically coloured by its occupational basis, but are influenced by a tradition of workplace- or company-level independence which renders them in practice largely independent of the broader union structures. Indeed, to the extent that these structures are of relevance to their activity, the most important influence is typically a more or less loose network of shop stewards. Ilsøe et al (2007) stress the 'widespread presence of shop stewards who (unlike the German works councils) have substantial bargaining rights' (p218), and that these stewards exercise 'comprehensive bargaining rights at company level' (p207). This implies flexibility in the sense that managers deal with union representatives at workplace level to find compromises which work in the particular enterprise context, rather than being restricted by the terms of sectoral agreements.

CASE STUDIES

REFLECTIVE ACTIVITY

What might be the advantages to management of more centralised bargaining arrangements (ie multi-employer bargaining at sectoral or even multi-sectoral level)?

What might be the advantages to management of decentralised arrangements (ie single employer or workplace bargaining)?

DIRECT STATUTORY REGULATION OF THE EMPLOYMENT RELATIONSHIP

Employee relations also concerns a response to or, at minimum, compliance with direct statutory regulation of the employment relationship by national or sometimes regional governments. Some national governments are reluctant to use the law to intervene directly in employment relationships beyond some rather minimal contract law and certain provisions over health and safety. In many nations, particularly in Europe, there is considerable regulation of dismissals by what is called 'employment protection legislation'. There is an increasing tendency for countries to introduce some forms of direct statutory regulation of minimum pay levels, sometimes differentiated by region – the spread of such regulation is, interestingly, particularly evident in the 'transition' countries of central and eastern Europe. The practical significance of such comprehensive statutory floors to employees' pay varies markedly in practice. Given cross-national differences not only in the cost of living but in typical pay levels, the 'bite' of such statutory minima is best expressed by the ratio of the minimum to average (median) pay – see Figure 11.

Figure 11 The 'bite' of legal pay minima

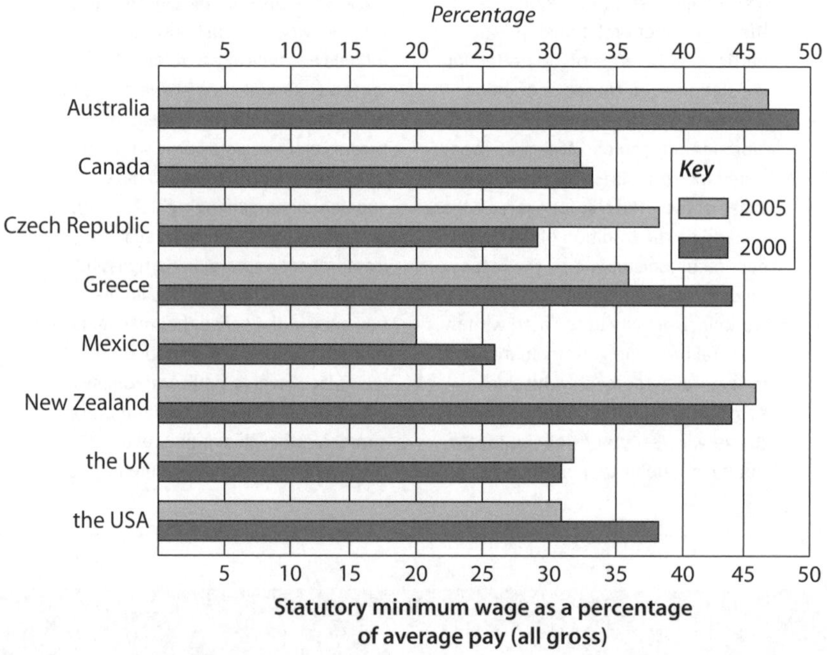

Source: Immervoll (2007, Tables 2 and A1)

Another aspect of the employee relations framework of a nation is the extent of the legal protection afforded regular ('permanent') employees threatened with dismissal or redundancy.

THEORY AND PRACTICE

KEY FRAMEWORK

Four ways in which statutory protections vary

- Procedural barriers to an employer's terminating the employee's employment (requirements of oral or written notification to employees, notification to a representative body or relevant authority, or beyond this, authorisation of body required and the delay typically involved)

- The difficulty of an employer's justification of the dismissal in law (justification merely in terms of redundancy of post or worker capability, or with consideration of age or tenure, or subject to failed attempt at transfer or retraining)

- Notice period and severance pay requirements for no-fault dismissal (extent of notice period, extent of severance pay)

- Other statutory constraints regarding maximum length of trial period, strictness of definition of unfair dismissal and compensation involved.

Sources: Bassanini *et al* (2008, Table 1); Andersen and Mailand (2005)

Indices of individual protection across these four different aspects:

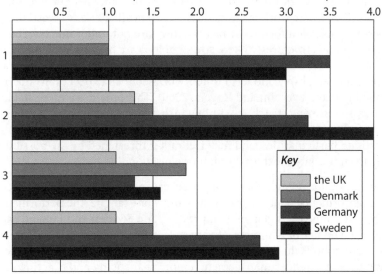

Source: OECD (2004a), cited in Andersen and Mailand (2005, Table 3)

REFLECTIVE ACTIVITY

Consider whether managers might find it easier to deal with social regulation of the employment relationship by law rather than by unions. To what extent does this depend on the character of the law and of the unions?

UNIONS, MANAGEMENT AND BUSINESS PERFORMANCE

Strong unions, and strong works councils supported by intensive local union membership and the larger union structure, pose challenges for managers. Quite generally, managers operating under significant joint regulation face substantial restrictions on their decision-making and may have a sense not only of decisions being slowed or delayed but of an affront to presumed managerial prerogatives. This is the real meaning of external governance for managers.

Where strong unions are organised on a craft and general basis, conditions may seem particularly challenging, with managers confronted by work groups bargaining opportunistically to extract whatever they can where new technology is introduced or where work is reorganised (eg Metcalf, 2004). At least, though, managers may take comfort in the fact that they are not under much scrutiny from larger union structures. Where strong unions are organised on an industrial basis, managers often confront quite elaborate systems of job classification and evaluation, and employee and local union/works council expectations that they are applied in detail (Vernon and Rogers, 2009). This provides a more stable and perhaps reassuring structure within which managers can work, although they may feel constrained by external agents with limited understanding of their organisations' particularities, and may feel rather threatened by the possibility of scrutiny from this larger external union organisation.

More generally, it is notable that stronger governance is associated with better business performance on a range of indicators. For example, the performance of the Nordic countries is generally impressive, and Sweden and Finland each constitute the homes of a number of very successful companies. It is clear that powerful unions do not typically undermine productivity performance – although they may render management a more challenging and exacting activity, and circumscribe quicker and easier (or dirtier) routes to profitability.

Vernon and Rogers (2009) show that labour productivity growth is faster in countries with stronger unions, as long as those unions are organised along industrial (as opposed to company/enterprise or craft and general) lines. Industrial unions are characteristic of most of continental Europe, with Denmark an interesting exception. However, where unions are organised along craft and general lines, as in the UK and in Denmark, stronger unions slow productivity growth. Unions in Japan but also the USA, which tend to be centred very much on particular companies, appear neutral in their effect.

WHAT INFLUENCES COMPARATIVE PATTERNS OF EMPLOYEE RELATIONS STRUCTURES?

Some commentators suggest that long-standing, deeply embedded differences in national cultures underpin differences in structures of employee relations. There is certainly some general tendency for countries with stronger unions to be countries of low power distance and low masculinity on Hofstede's dimensions. However, there are some countries low on power distance which have rather weak unions – the UK now being the most striking example. Moreover, there are some countries which rate low on both power distance and masculinity which now have rather weak unions – the Netherlands is the clearest example here – while countries high on collectivism are rarely countries with high unionisation.

The comparison of Sweden and the UK is particularly intriguing in that during the 1930s these countries appeared rather similar in many respects, but they now appear very different in matters of employee relations. Sweden has extensive and multi-levelled joint regulation, whereas the UK features generally low and fragmented coverage. One obvious recourse in explanation is to party politics, the Swedish Social Democrats offering more consistent support than the much less electorally successful British Labour Party has been able to offer. More deep-seated explanations are possible. Fulcher (1991) suggests that it is the differing nature and ambitions of the union movements in the two countries which explain this difference, the British movement always more fragmented, conservative, and concerned merely to keep the state out of its affairs, and the Swedish movement much more influenced in its crucial early stages by an integrative socialist ideology and pursuing a more ambitious transformative project – aided by the Social Democratic Party constituting the political wing of the Swedish labour movement.

Some recent literature has suggested the possibility that patterns of labour law may have an impact on patterns of joint regulation. The notion of functional equivalence suggests that countries will be very similar in their sum totals of social regulation, but with differing balances of statutory regulation on the one hand and regulation by unions on the other. Indeed, the Danish case of 'flexi-curity', with its relatively limited labour law and intensive collective bargaining and joint regulation at the level of enterprises and companies might be taken to support this notion.

However, even within the advanced or old industrialised world, there are clear differences in the sum total of the social regulation of work. Thus, for example, the Nordic countries generally have not only powerful unions and joint regulation but also very significant direct statutory regulation of work, whereas the USA lies at the other pole, with generally very weak joint regulation beyond certain sectors or occupations (eg education, firefighting) and very weak direct statutory regulation of the employment relationship. Indeed, although labour law is seen as limited in Denmark (see the case study on 'flexi-curity'), it is so only relative to joint regulation there – in comparison with labour law in the USA it looks comparatively extensive.

These examples are expressive of a more general truth that law and unions are not alternatives – indeed, to the extent that they bear any relation, they appear complementary. That is to say, there is a rather loose tendency for countries with more significant joint regulation by unions also to be more strongly shaped by labour law. This is apparent, for example, in the findings of Jackson (2005) on the influences which have given rise to statutory employee board representation in many European countries. He finds that, broadly speaking, countries with such statutory arrangements are co-ordinated market economies rather than liberal market economies, and in particular that alongside consensual politics and concentrated ownership patterns, strong co-ordinated collective bargaining is a key influence on this statutory right. It is also apparent in Brewster *et al* (2007) who note that, internationally, works councils (and also joint consultative committees) are more often found in organisations with union presence.

BEST PRACTICE IN EMPLOYEE RELATIONS

It is difficult to imagine that there is a generalised best practice with regard to employee relations, given the very different national legal frameworks which prevail, the still more dramatic variation in the established practices of collective bargaining and joint regulation, and the apparently very variable business performance implications of joint regulation. To some extent at least, companies must respond to the employee relations context they find, whether this is of a generalised form or highly differentiated in a way which implies a make-or-buy decision (see the box below) and whatever the business performance implications of joint regulation in the country concerned.

The recent purchase of the Volvo Car Corporation by China's Geely provides a fascinating example of the need to respond to local (ie national) context. Although Geely executives may find the difference between Swedish and Chinese unions bewildering, car production in Sweden requires that they need to come to terms with – or at least accept – Swedish bargaining arrangements and established practice. Intriguingly, in this case, given the strength of the industrial unions in Sweden, and especially in car assembly, it is likely that their acceptance of the structures of multi-employer bargaining will imply business performance benefits.

EXERCISING CHOICE: 'MAKE-OR-BUY' COLLECTIVE VOICE AND GOVERNANCE

In some countries, organisations often face a fairly stark 'make-or-buy' decision (Willman and Bryson, 2003) with regard to many of the matters of collective voice and governance in employee relations. In the UK, for example, in many sectors the 'make-or-buy' decision is particularly pertinent. It is neither generally the case that unions are absent, nor that they are present – although absence rather than presence is the norm within the private sector, there is considerable variation in the role and significance of unions even here. Employers may facilitate or encourage union membership and seek to promote such independent employee representation, or they may seek to discourage it, and establish in its place some form of works or staff committee through which employee ideas and discontentments may be aired, and which might also in principle be linked to governance via the involvement of representatives in grievance and disciplinary proceedings, or even in the formation of rules structuring those proceedings. The 'make' decision implies difficulty in establishing the legitimacy of the management established body. There is of course a danger that senior management considers such arrangements for governance and collective employee voice – and even more the involvement of employee representatives in governance – unnecessary and/or inconvenient, and so a decision is made to neither buy nor make. This may then pose very real difficulties for the line manager in treating staff consistently and fairly, and in seeking to be seen as acting legitimately, in the absence of a clear and transparent procedure.

KEY LEARNING POINTS

- There is enormous cross-national comparative variation in national systems of employee relations, even within the established OECD (or old industrialised world).

- Unions and collective bargaining or joint regulation are declining – although often very gradually – in many countries in the established OECD.

- Unions and collective bargaining remains widespread and important amongst larger employers and across the public sector in Europe in particular.

- Although unions are generally weaker in the developing and newly industrialised world, they are showing signs of growth and development there.

- Often allied to unions are other forms of independent employee representation such as works councils or employee representatives on boards, carrying statutory rights.

- Works councils are often – and, in many countries, increasingly – used by employers for collective communication with employees.

- Direct statutory regulation of the employment relationship, most particularly in the form of legislation on job protection and on pay minima, is significant in many countries within and beyond the established OECD.

- Although to many managers, unions and works councils – and, indeed, board-level employee representation – may appear challenging or even threatening, they often improve business performance.

- The governance that unions and works councils provide can be a valuable resource.

LEARNING QUESTIONS

1 What might explain the fact that trade union membership is higher in some countries than in others?

2 Are trade unions a positive or negative in organisational communications? Is the answer dependent upon or independent of country? Give reasons for your answers.

3 Consider the supports and challenges to managements pursuing business performance which joint regulation offers. Do you feel that strong unions make people management more challenging for managers? Do you feel that strong unions promote organisational and business performance? Do these questions amount to the same thing?

4 Consultation with representative bodies is now required for all organisations over a certain size by the European Union. What reasoning might have led the EU to take such a step?

EXPLORE FURTHER

Vernon (2006a) 'Does density matter? The significance of comparative historical variation in uniuonisation', *European Journal of Industrial Relations*, 12 (2); 189–209. This article provides a detailed assessment of the significance of unions and collective bargaining (or joint regulation) across the established OECD.

Andersen and Mailand (2005) 'The Danish Flexicurity Model', Faos Working Paper, Copenhagen. Here the authors overview the Danish 'flexi-curity' model which has been influential in EU-level discussions of employee relations.

Lu, Tao and Wang. (2009). Union effects on performance and employment relations: evidence from China. Mimeo, University of Hong Kong, August. The authors provide a fascinating assessment of the significance of union activity in China.

CHAPTER 6

The Organisation of Work

LEARNING OUTCOMES

When they have read this chapter, students will:

- appreciate the continued relevance of Taylorism in discussions of work organisation

- appreciate the international variation in practices of direct communication, but also the ultimately limited significance of communication *per se*

- understand that there are broader-based alternatives to Taylorism

- appreciate that these alternatives are applied variably in different countries

- understand the bases of cross-national comparative variation in work organisation

- acknowledge the evidence that there is an international best practice in work organisation.

INTRODUCTION

There is a good deal of managerial discussion of matters of skills, human capital and, indeed, talent, in which the individual capabilities or capacities of employees are stressed. This presents a danger of some neglect of how front-line employees are managed and their skills combined, drawn out or allowed to emerge. Yet these issues of the organisation of work, of the engagement between management and non-managerial employees, functional flexibility, employee involvement, 'empowerment', autonomy in work built in by job design, and of meaningful 'teamwork' (and 'groupwork'), may be crucial for development as well as for the realised performance of the individual and the wider organisation. Indeed, it would be surprising if they were not central to encouraging front-line employees to go the extra mile, displaying commitment, discretionary effort or organisational commitment behaviour.

The organisation of work is a matter of particular resonance in comparative context because, as we shall see, there are enormous variations in the organisation of work across national boundaries, even within the established nations of the OECD, or indeed within old Europe – and these variations cannot be explained by differences in sectoral or occupational composition.

TAYLORISM AND FORDISM AS A SOLUTION ... AND A PROBLEM

Frederick Taylor's early twentieth-century prescriptions for the effective organisation of work in industrial production remain an invaluable benchmark in considering the character of current organisational approaches – not, it should be clear, as a 'best practice' ideal at which organisations should aim but in the location of the approaches actually deployed by organisations, for better or for worse. Taylorism, or 'scientific management', is a useful benchmark because it constitutes such an extreme form, but simultaneously, as we shall see, remains a powerful influence on the organisation of work in many countries (see Figure 12).

Figure 12 An overview of Taylorism

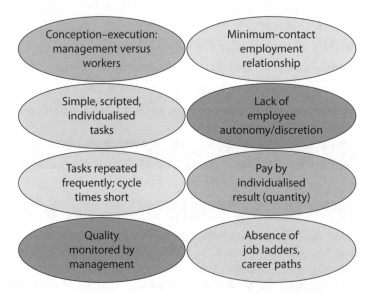

Source: adapted and developed from Warner (1994); Callaghan and Thompson (2001); Taylor *et al* (2002); Berggren (1994); Vernon (2006b)

The separation of the management group and its activity from the employee group and its activity lies at the foundation of Taylorism, with many if not all of its other features flowing from this separation. A Taylorist organisation of work charges management with all the conceptual or 'think' work, with front-line employees then charged with the execution of management's orders. Front-line employees thus operate within very narrow confines, performing individualised and simplified tasks with little or no opportunity for individual judgement or discretion. The echoes of Taylorism in the Fordist manufacturing operation parodied by Charlie Chaplin's *Modern Times* are obvious; indeed in many respects Fordism is simply Taylorism plus a moving assembly line.

REFLECTIVE ACTIVITY

Many authors on HRM suggest that organisations should seek to avoid or move away from a Taylorist organisation of work. Why should Taylorism be seen as undesirable?

Whether it is seen as outmoded, inappropriate, unethical or ineffective or not, it is clear that Taylorism still exerts a powerful influence on the organisation of work experienced by front-line employees in many organisations in many countries. Although systematic cross-national comparative study is limited, it does seem that manufacturing in the developing and newly industrialising world is more often of a Taylorist character, and perhaps most particularly in recent years in China (see eg Warner, 1994; Gamble *et al*, 2004). Yet Taylorism remains influential in the early twenty-first century in the established countries of the OECD, and not just in manufacturing but also in fast food and in clerical or white-collar work in call centres (EFILWC, 2009; Callaghan and Thompson, 2001; Taylor *et al*, 2002; Doellgast, 2010; Mayhew and Quinlan, 2002). This underscores its continued usefulness as a benchmark in considering matters of the organisation of work.

DIRECT COMMUNICATION: INITIATIVES AND THEIR COMPARATIVE COVERAGE

In the 1970s, and with increasing force in the 1980s, there was a mounting sense in many organisations that the character of communication within organisations – and in particular that between managerial and non-managerial employees – was inadequate. This impression was nurtured in large part by the emergence of Japan as an industrial power. Japanese continuous improvement activity, or *kaizen*, involved a very deliberate effort at communication between first- or front-line management and employees. Such matters of communication were seen as a crucial – perhaps *the* crucial – defining factor of Japanese people management, which was itself viewed as central to what was seen as superior Japanese business performance.

Thus it became increasingly common amongst managers in Europe, the USA and elsewhere in the countries of the advanced industrialised world, or OECD, to refer to the knowledge held by those actually doing the job (front-line employees) and to the need for management to garner or capture this knowledge to improve business performance. Relatedly, many organisations tried to extend but also move beyond traditional efforts at management–employee engagement such as suggestion schemes, taking initiatives also in terms of quality circles or quality control circles (QCs/QCCs) which were in large part centred on improved commnunication between front-line employees and first-line management. These initiatives were efforts to overcome the divisions wrought by the division of labour within organisations, and specifically the divide between management and employees implied by the predominant Taylorist or Fordist approaches to the organisation of work.

In the modern organisation, the importance of effective communication is emphasised by the notion that it is only through exploiting employees' ideas and talents that organisations will be able to compete and survive. This suggests a need to convince employees that working for the organisation is something that they should be committed to and to which they should devote their ideas, their energy and their creativity.

It is argued that effective communication can:

- increase job satisfaction (Miles *et al*, 1996)
- foster greater commitment (Dutton *et al*, 1994; Kane, 1996; Lippit, 1997)
- act as a conduit for the promotion and development of collaboration between organisational stakeholders (Folger and Poole, 1984; Monge and Eisenberg, 1987; Bolton and Dewatripont, 1994; Mintzberg *et al*, 1996)
- facilitate the diffusion of teamwork (Mulder, 1960; Barnes and Todd, 1977; Daft and Macintosh, 1981; Lawson and Bourner, 1997; Pettit, 1997)
- improve internal control and facilitate strategy development (Baird *et al*, 1983; Fiol, 1995; Smyth, 1995; Steinberg, 1998).

This implies a need to focus upon communication between managerial and non-managerial employees. A useful distinction has been made between two types of consultation and communication, variously called 'collective', 'indirect' or 'representative' to represent one type, and 'individual' or 'direct' for the other (Gold and Hall, 1990). For each form, the influence of employees on decision-making within the organisation may be greater or less. A useful categorisation of subjects for communication has been made (Knudsen, 1995) which divides managerial decisions into strategic, tactical, operational, and welfare. In general, the representative form has tended to address the wider strategic and tactical issues (such as investments, mergers, labour issues and pay systems), whereas the direct forms have tended to concentrate on operational workplace and working practice issues. The focus here is on the latter, individual or direct form, whereas indirect or collective communication involving employee representatives was considered in Chapter 5.

It is noteworthy that an exclusive focus on such direct communication with the individual employee implies a unitarist philosophy founded upon a notion of a simple common interest between managers and the managed, an interest supposedly centred solely on the organisation's success in the marketplace (Blyton and Turnbull, 1992; Storey and Sisson, 1993). Some consultation mechanisms are designed principally to integrate employees into the organisation, but also apparently to ensure that there is no challenge to the basic authority structure of the enterprise (Marchington *et al*, 1992; Blyton and Turnbull, 1992).

As organisations become increasingly knowledge-intensive, and indeed knowledge-dependent (Conner and Prahalad, 1996; Doz *et al*, 2001; Grant, 1996; Mowery *et al*, 1996), so it becomes ever clearer that the crucial knowledge in the organisation rests not with the senior management but with those who make up the organisation and contribute to its work. A key management task becomes understanding the people within the organisation, appreciating their talents and abilities, and being able to motivate and commit them to the organisation so that it can draw on this reservoir of skills and understanding in the most effective way. However, as Morley *et al* (2000b) point out, this is a difficult area for organisations, and the literature abounds with reports of obfuscation in corporate communications (Filipczak, 1995), information distortion (Gill, 1996; Janis, 1982; Larson and King, 1996), miscommunication and problematic talk (Coupland *et al*, 1991).

 REFLECTIVE ACTIVITY

In your organisation, or one that you know of, what forms of up and down direct communication are used? Elaborate on as many as you can.

Below, we analyse successively developments in both downward and upward direct communication; and then we outline lateral communication.

DIRECT DOWNWARD COMMUNICATION

Downward communication is the flow of information from management to the employees. With regard to the information channel used, the use of direct ways of communications has increased. Across Europe, direct verbal communication is increasing in a majority of organisations. A tiny minority of organisations across Europe report using less direct verbal communication. A similar picture arises from the evidence on direct written communication to employees. Of course, with computerisation, human resources information systems and mail-merge techniques it becomes much easier for managers to write 'individually' to all staff involved in a particular change – and the opportunity is being taken. Around half of European organisations have increased their use of direct written communication, a similar proportion have increased their use of team briefings, and over a third have increased their use of electronic communication with employees. In all these cases, almost no organisations have decreased their use of communication mechanisms.

Regular meetings of the workforce are another way in which management is able to talk directly with all employees. Again, and following a by now expected pattern, increases in the use of such mechanisms outweigh the decreases by a considerable margin in nearly all European countries.

The writers on HRM who are advising employers that individual communication with their employees is vital to the future success of the organisation can take comfort from these figures. Of course, when the question is asked of senior personnel practitioners (as it was in this survey), it is possible that they are exaggerating the extent of the improvement in communication: there may be an element of wishful thinking here. However, the figures are so large and so consistent that it seems likely that they reflect some kind of reality. We are encouraged in this view by the fact that in other respects the same data does indicate that respondents are likely to report that their organisations are not following the received wisdom. Furthermore, these figures reflect similar findings in the European Foundation's EPOC survey (Sisson, 1997). It would seem that organisations are indeed communicating more with their employees.

With regard to what is communicated through these channels, this varies from case to case. Two areas of central interest for management and employees are information on:

- organisational strategy
- organisational finances.

In Europe, at least nine out of every ten organisations formally brief their managers about the organisation's strategy and financial results. However, there is a marked 'slope' in the provision of information below the managerial level. The further down the organisation one goes, the less likely employees are to be given this information. There is great variation in the proportions of organisations providing information about strategy to manual employees. Generally, the figures are not high, even allowing for an expected differential between the information that would be given to managers and to manual workers. Organisations become increasingly dependent on employees' knowing the corporate strategy, understanding how their own performance contributes to the implementation of the strategy, wanting to contribute in this way, and being able to communicate this strategy to co-workers and external parties (customers, suppliers, public agencies, etc). The more the organisation is providing services, know-how or other types of immaterial 'products', the more an understanding of – and acceptance of – the overall corporate strategy is a prerequisite for competent performance. This is not the case to the same extent when the job involves the manipulation of physical production processes.

A similar reasoning applies to the communication of financial information about the organisation, although here the slope indicating the difference in providing information for different groups of employees is not so steep. The financial performance of the organisation is made known to employees to a greater extent than is the case in the area of strategy. In nearly two-thirds of the countries, 50 per cent or more of the organisations also brief manual workers, the least informed group within the organisation, about financial performance. Figure 13 shows the briefing patterns for various employee groups in three European countries in the area of strategy and financial performance. What is noticeable is that the 'slope' of information reduces from management to manual worker grades, and that the 'slope' varies in each country – so that manual workers in

Sweden are considerably more likely to get such information and manual workers in Germany much less.

Figure 13 Strategic and financial briefing of different groups of employees in Sweden, the UK and Germany

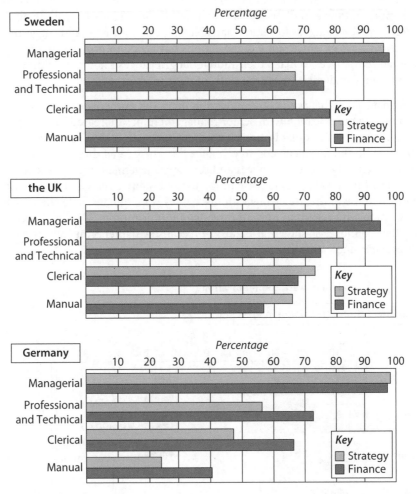

Source: Cranet (2010)

Northern European countries generally present their non-managerial employees with more data on these matters than countries elsewhere in Europe (Morley *et al*, 2000b). In many Pacific countries information on these issues is generally only given to senior managers (Zanko, 2002). It seems that there is a widespread assumption that those lower down the organisation simply do not need to know what the organisation is trying to do, or the value or constraints imposed on the organisation by the extent to which it is succeeding in reaching those objectives.

UPWARD DIRECT COMMUNICATION

Upward communication is the other key issue in terms of management/ non-management communication – the feeding of information, concerns or ideas from the employees to the management.

Communication to an employee's immediate superior is, perhaps inevitably, the most important form of direct upward communication. However, we can also include here direct access to senior management, quality circles and suggestion schemes as ways in which some organisations have tried to provide channels to encourage employees to make their individual grievances known or to draw on the innovative and entrepreneurial skills of their workforce.

Cranet data show that both communication up to the immediate superior and direct communication with senior management has increased. In Europe, a quarter to a third of organisations have increased such communication, depending on the European country involved. In the case of direct communication between employees and senior management, the figures are generally a little lower. The increase in the use of quality circles is still less, and the net increase in the use of suggestion schemes is marginal. These changes left the situation with regard to upward direct communication in 2010 in European and other countries as shown in Figure 14 (see also Chapter 5 on collective or indirect communication).

Figure 14 Channels of upward communication

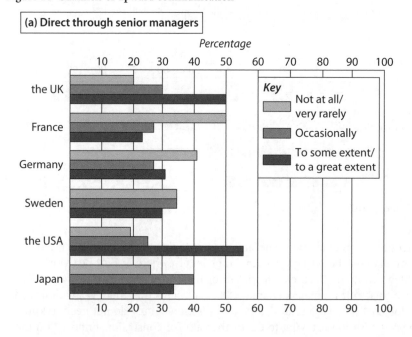

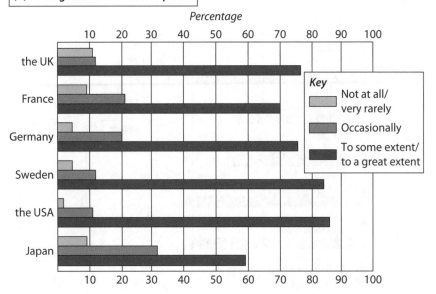

(b) Through the immediate superior

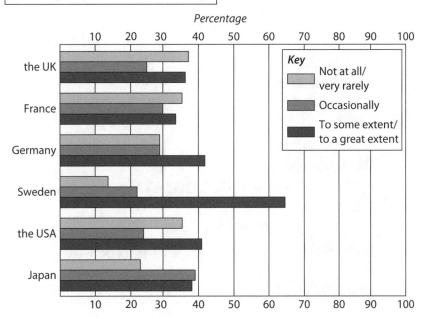

(c) Through regular workforce meetings

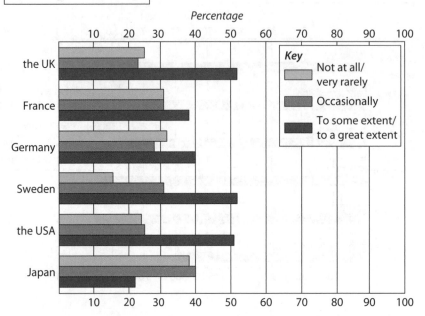

(d) Through team briefings

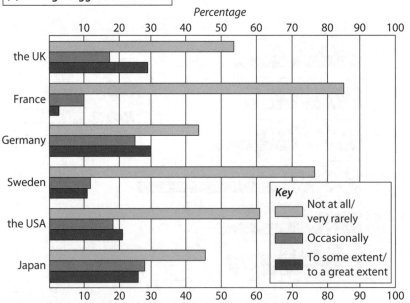

(e) Through suggestion schemes

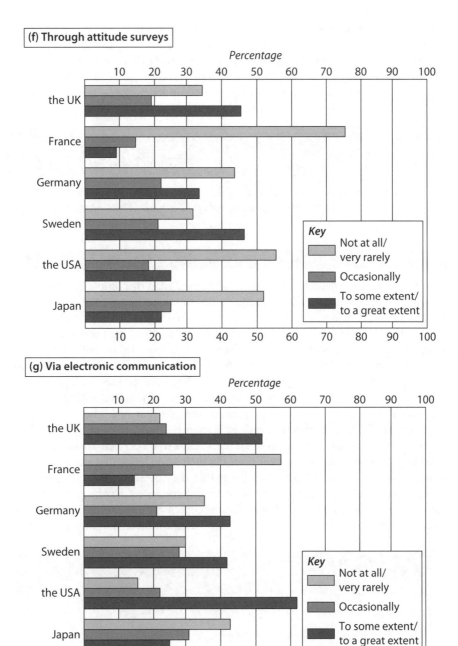

(f) Through attitude surveys

(g) Via electronic communication

Source: Cranet (2010)

What of the *relative growth* in *upward* as opposed to *downward* communication? As we have seen earlier, Cranet evidence on HR specialists' perceptions of recent change suggests a very strong and universal reported increase in direct downward communication, and this is so whether in terms of verbal, written, or specifically email communication. As we have seen in this section, Cranet suggests strong and pretty universal increases in proportions of organisations reporting increases in upward communication via line managers, and rather less strong but still general increases in upward communication through quality circles or direct to senior management. There thus seems a general trend in direct communication in both directions between managers and front-line employees – but a clearer trend in downward more than in upward communication.

REFLECTIVE ACTIVITY

Why should the tendency towards greater downward direct communication be stronger and more consistent across countries than the tendency towards greater upward direct communication?

LATERAL COMMUNICATION

In recent years, considerable attention has been devoted by companies and researchers to the notions of knowledge management and knowledge flows within employing organisations. It has, indeed, been argued (Kostova and Roth, 2003; Nahapiet and Ghoshal, 1998; Tsai and Ghoshal, 1998) that this may be the factor that distinguishes the successful from the unsuccessful organisation. A company's strategic advantage is usually found in its specific knowledge (Penrose, 1959; Caves, 1982), and this specific knowledge (eg advanced technological expertise or specific marketing knowledge) can only be acquired within the company. It is obviously in the organisation's interests that such knowledge is shared internally. Yet this is not as easy as it sounds. The kind of knowledge that can be shared through computerised systems tends to be explicit knowledge – and that is often much less potent than the tacit knowledge that people hold in their heads, sometimes without realising that they do. Thus, for example, knowing how to deal with key clients in different countries may be something that an individual has only developed through extensive experience, and it is not always straightforward to pass what has become an intuitive skill on to others.

REFLECTIVE ACTIVITY

What might create difficulties in the transfer of information and knowledge between individuals within an organisation?

Amongst the factors that might create 'stickiness' in the passing of information are lack of understanding, or even antipathy, between different functions within the organisation; a feeling that information is power, so that those with it want to hang on to it; strong notions of hierarchy; a desire not to pass on anything that is not polished and complete; and personal predilections to share. It should be obvious by now that many of these will be influenced by the culture of the country in which the individuals operate – high power distance and strong uncertainty avoidance may make knowledge sharing less likely.

Given the differences we have identified in communication practices between countries, it is no surprise to find that cross-national communication is particularly problematic. The cultural dimensions discussed in Chapters 2 and 3 will have an impact here: clearly where, for example, hierarchies are seen as very important (power distance is high), the flow of information between different levels of the hierarchy may be more difficult – and probably so too will be the flow of information between departments. The assumption will be that this should be passed up the management chain until more senior figures can relate to each other: passing information to another department rather than to the boss may not be seen as appropriate. The consensus now seems to be (Foss and Pedersen, 2002; Riusula and Smale, 2007; Szulanski, 1996; Zander and Kogut, 1995) that there are various factors that make knowledge 'sticky' – ie immobile – around organisations, and especially across national boundaries. Establishing systems that allow the information to be transferred more readily becomes a key task – often one of the reasons for using expatriates. For example, in an analysis of knowledge management and expatriation within professional legal service firms (Beaverstock, 2004), it was shown that expatriation was not homogeneous for every region of the world. In some areas, expatriation followed a one-way knowledge diffusion from headquarters. In these cases, expatriates represented the traditional managerial role. In contrast, expatriates from HQs in other regions worked with locally qualified employees and expatriates of other nationalities in an environment where these different groups of people joined partnerships and led teams. The type of learning and its impact on careers will probably be quite different in these two cases.

REFORM BEYOND COMMUNICATION: EMPLOYEE DISCRETION AND AUTONOMY

Despite the particular and increasing focus on communication in many organisations, many authors suggest that initiatives in this arena are too narrowly focused. In both Europe and North America there are traditions of theorising and of practice which challenge Taylorist and Fordist approaches on a much broader front and/or more fundamentally. Hackman *et al*'s (1982) job characteristics model emphasises the nature or character of the daily work activities performed, or faced by, employees. In particular, this analytical approach suggests, the job satisfaction and commitment of employees hinges upon the scope they have to exercise discretion and autonomy. The tempering of Taylorist or Fordist approaches by direct communication initiatives is in this light seen as an inadequate and ineffective 'sticking plaster' response. In a similar vein, Emery and Thorsrud (1969), Karasek and Theorell (1990) shaped a 'socio-technical' approach to work organisation departing fundamentally from Taylorism and its variants, emphasising job enrichment and the delegation to non-managerial employees of managerial tasks or prerogatives. To such authors, Taylorism is antithetical to the 'good work' to which organisations should aspire (see Berggren, 1994). These ideas have been particularly influential in shaping discussions of the organisation of work in the countries of Northern Europe.

ALL TEAMS AGAINST TAYLORISM?

It is sometimes suggested that teamwork is central to the organisation of work – indeed, that the crucial issue in work organisation is whether front-line employees engage in teamwork or not. Evidently, though, the formal designation of teams by managers is insufficient of itself to imply that front-line employees engage in teamwork on any meaningful definition of the term, any more than the absence of formally designated teams for front-line employees necessarily implies that there is no meaningful teamwork. Moreover, in practice, although if it is to have any meaning at all then teamwork must necessarily involve a collective output, teamwork may still be of very different complexions (see Table 9).

Table 9 All teams against Taylorism?

	Lean/Japanese-style 'teams'	Groupwork/Nordic socio-technical 'teams'
Individual work pace	Dictated by management	Employees may vary work pace through the shift
Enlargement/enrichment of work	Employees rotate tasks, each of little complexity	Increased work content with responsibility for managerial tasks
Authority/co-ordination	Dense authority structure; foreman or supervisor is key	Delegation of co-ordination to the group
Administrative control	Team leader selected by management	Group leader elected by the group
Performance demands	Imposed by management: no absolute upper bounds	Agreed between group and management
Production arrangement in the manufacturing context	Traditional production lines, with just-in-time	Line buffers or assembly in stationary 'docks'

Source: adapted from Berggren (1993), Rehder (1994) and Vernon (2003, 2006b)

The contrast between lean teams and socio-technical or Nordic teams was elaborated in studies comparing the organisation of work in car and more general automotive vehicle production, reaching its pinnacle in comparisons of approaches to assembly at Japan's Toyota and Sweden's Volvo in the 1980s and 1990s (especially by Berggren, 1994), but is of more enduring and general relevance in locating and analysing the organisation of work. The central contrast between these forms of teamwork is in the extent to which front-line employees, both collectively in their teams and individually in their own contributions, enjoy discretion and autonomy and engage in conceptual and co-ordinating work. In other words, these models of teamwork differ in the extent to which they imply a departure from the division, simplification and fragmentation of Taylorist work organisation.

CROSS-NATIONAL COMPARATIVE WORK ORGANISATION

The evidence on cross-national comparative variation in work organisation is less thorough and systematic than that available for some other aspects of people management. Even within the nations of the established OECD or old industrialised world an overview must draw on a variety of differing sources.

One approach to getting a grip on comparative variation deploys data on occupational compositions from national censuses and labour force surveys (eg Gordon, 1996). These can be used to construct aggregate measures of the span of control of those in managerial positions. One might expect that where the span of control is smaller, or as Gordon (1996) puts it 'supervisory intensity' is greater, non-managerial or front-line employees have less autonomy or discretion in their work (see also Maurice *et al*, 1986). Conversely, a greater span of control might be expected to indicate greater non-managerial autonomy. Yet profound difficulties are implied by international variation in the use of the label 'manager', employees in some countries much more likely to be so labelled than in others, despite doing identical work. Ultimately, the only cross-national comparative differences in authority structures clear from such evidence are those between North America and the Nordic countries (Vernon, 2003). Although in the USA and Canada organisations (and official statisticians) are much freer with the term 'manager' than those in Sweden and Norway, it is also very clearly the case that very many more employees have meaningful authority over others in North America than in the Nordic countries. The aggregate span of control is much greater in the Nordic countries, the intensity of supervision much lower, than in North America, providing an indication at least of much greater employee autonomy in the Nordic countries (Vernon, 2003).

Figure 15 A categorisation of models of the organisation of work

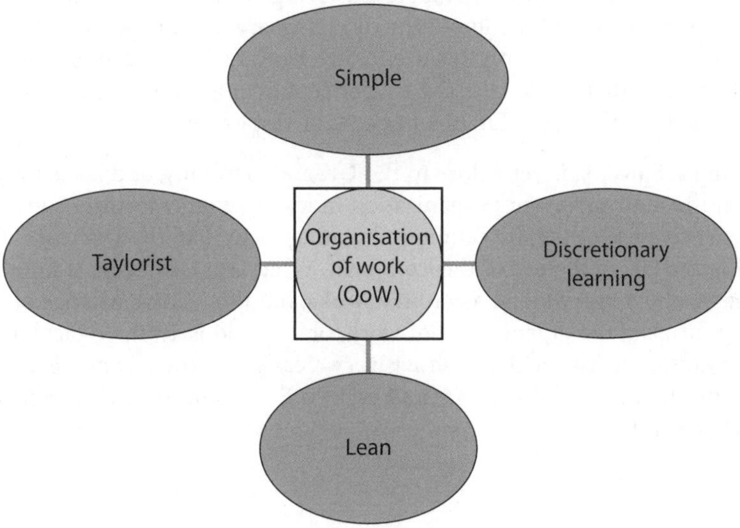

Source: European Foundation for the Improvement of Living and Working Conditions (EFILWC, 2009)

What of more direct forms of evidence? Case studies of particular companies (eg Berggren, 1994) offer depth and richness but can provide no indication of what is typical in a country, nor locate the typical approach in one country compared to another. Yet systematic survey evidence is now at least available across the EU. EPOC and ESWC studies have culminated in the recent EWCS report (EFILWC, 2009) which offers an overview of the use of forms of work organisation in Europe in 2005. This work deploys a fourfold categorisation of models of the organisation of work (OoW): see Figure 15.

The EFILWC (2009) 'simple' approach is essentially a residual category featuring the informal work organisation typical in many or perhaps all countries in cafés or small retailing businesses. The 'Taylorist' approach is very much as described above. The lean model is characterised by teamwork, task rotation in the form of multi-skilling, self-assessment of work quality informed by relatively strong quality norms, some limited autonomy but with various constraints on the pace of work. The discretionary learning form has many of the features of Scandinavian socio-technical work, characterised by employee autonomy in work, task complexity, learning and problem-solving, self-assessment of work quality and autonomous teamwork (if any). Examples of each of the various forms distinguished under various categorisations may probably be found in all the countries of the world, and certainly within the EU. What, though, of the relative preponderance of different forms of the organisation of work and the balance of use of the different models in each country?

The EFILWC (2009) report has assembled an index by country of 'innovative work organisation' which summarises the extent of departure from 'simple' and 'Taylorist' models. Comparatively across the EU27 on the innovative work organisation index (2009, Fig.2) the Nordic members (Sweden, Denmark, Finland) are at the top, with the UK and Germany in the middle, and the new central and eastern European members clustering at the bottom. National rankings on the extent of the use of the discretionary learning form specifically is similar (2009, Table 7), with this use in Sweden (at 67.5 per cent of employees) more than twice that in the UK (at 31.7 per cent of employees) and more than three times that in Bulgaria (at 20.6 per cent of employees).

Interestingly, Slovenia is very close to the UK and Germany, and leads Italy and Spain on the innovative work organisation index; it actually features substantially more extensive use of the discretionary learning form than the UK while also matching the UK in the use of the lean form. What is at issue here is not the manner in which everyone in a country works, but the relative balance of differing forms of the organisation of work, or, more loosely, the typical means of work organisation. The evidence shows very clearly that there is no necessity that the organisation of work in central and eastern Europe need be cruder than that in western Europe.

REFLECTIVE ACTIVITY

There is no comparable study to that on the organisation of work in the EU for North America. How would you imagine that the use of the four different models of work organisation in the USA and Canada would compare with European countries if there were such comparable evidence?

There is rather little systematic comparative analysis of the character of the organisation of work in newly industrialising and developing countries compared to that in the old industrialised world. What analysis there is supports anecdotal evidence that Taylorism is of greater purchase in the developing and newly industrialising countries (see the case study *Transfer of mass production activities to China*). Although this may change as development proceeds, the generality and speed of such change remains uncertain and should not be presumed.

CASE STUDIES

TRANSFER OF MASS PRODUCTION ACTIVITIES TO CHINA

From the mid-1990s, and with gathering momentum, manufacturing companies in Japan and also South Korea have transferred substantial elements of their activities to China, sometimes to wholly owned facilities, but more often via joint ventures with local companies or via some form of close subcontracting arrangement. These developments are particularly apparent in clothing manufacture and in electronics, for example. Typically, the activity transferred has centred upon the more standardised element of the production operations, with more complex and higher value added activities, as well as most – if not all – research and development activity maintained in the home country. The organisation of work in the Chinese production operations was typically very much more Taylorist than that in the production operations in the home country, the tasks more finely broken down and the employees more closely monitored in China.

Source: Gamble *et al* (2004)

INFLUENCES ON COMPARATIVE PATTERNS OF THE ORGANISATION OF WORK

There are some indications that national culture plays some limited role in shaping the extent to which organisations seek to develop communication between managerial and non-managerial employees beyond the crude, primitive form it takes in the Taylorist or Fordist models (Papalexandris and Panayotopoulou, 2004, Table V). In particular, the cross-national comparative pattern of organisational practices revealed by Cranet is linked in some respects to the cultural profile of nations in terms of Hofstede. Cultures exhibiting greater power distance generally feature more limited/less communication via some though not all channels, both downward and upward, and also more limited use of some of the briefings discussed above. More consistently, though, the findings show that greater uncertainty avoidance is associated with a greater effort at communication between managerial and non-managerial employees. To some extent, then, management activity is shaped by managers' or by employees' notions of reasonable or legitimate communication across the divide.

What, though, of the grounds for broader-based departures from Taylorism? Stage of industrial development is an obvious influence on the organisation of work. Generally, there appears an inverse relationship between the use of Taylorist or Fordist systems and GDP per capita or labour costs per hour worked. It is noteworthy that this is not merely – nor perhaps even mainly – a matter of the extent of manufacturing or broader industrial sectors. Even within manufacturing, for example, there seems a tendency for Taylorist or Fordist approaches to predominate in developing or newly industrialising countries much more clearly than in the established OECD. However, this relationship is ultimately rather loose. As we have seen, amongst the countries of the established OECD for which there is better evidence it is clear that there are very substantial differences in the organisation of work.

The contrast in the forms of team and group work which have taken hold in Sweden and Japan are intriguing. Given the successes of the Japanese educational system, it would be difficult to argue that the greater autonomy of the Swedish employee is a result of their greater human capital – their greater skill or education. Of course, the apparent tendency for employee autonomy to be less developed even in newly industrialised countries with very good educational achievement, such as South Korea, also suggests the limited purchase of human capital.

However, as we have seen, the best available evidence on comparative organisation of work is from Europe (see above on the EFILWC report, 2009). This data also allows assessment of the importance of industrial composition. It is very clear that the economic structure of countries in terms of their composition by broad industrial sectors, company sizes, occupational structure and demographic characteristics generally plays a small part in cross-national comparative variations. The Netherlands is exceptional precisely because the preponderance of the discretionary learning form *is* significantly linked to such structural features (EFILWC, 2009; p23). Rather than being mere incidental composition effects, the comparative variations generally express enduring characteristics of the context of employment and work.

The typically more innovative approaches to work organisation in the Nordic countries compared to others in Europe suggests that the exceptional union strength in these countries has wrought a distinct approach. Given the remarkably innovative approach to work organisation in Slovenia, distinguishing it from its central and eastern European neighbours, the unusual strength of unions there underscores the suggestion that union strength is the overwhelming influence on the autonomy of employees and complexity of work. Over time, it seems, countries find their place in the international division of labour in a manner which is influenced powerfully by the strength of their unions. Within western Europe, the relatively favourable positions of France and the Netherlands in rating close to the Nordic countries on the innovative work organisation index, and in terms of the use of discretionary learning approaches in particular, suggest that the broader density of institutionalisation of the labour market by labour law and welfare states is also of relevance. The limited comparable data available on occupational classifications shows a very marked contrast between North America and the Nordic countries, which also suggests that the social regulation of work across these contexts may be significant.

Cross-national comparative differences in the organisation of work might be read as expressive of differences in culture, with these then thought to give rise to the institutional differences that are associated with, or in turn shape, the organisation of work. However, it is often difficult to see links between cultural features and the cross-national pattern of departure from Taylorism, and in any event, as is noted in Chapter 5 (*Comparative HRM: Employee Relations*), the available evidence seems to suggest that at the level of countries, institutions (shaped by politics and thus perhaps particular subcultures within policy elites) drive generally prevailing culture rather more than being driven by it.

It is clear that within the countries of the established industrialised world there is considerable internal variation in the organisation of work, so this is not of course to say that examples of autonomous employees, socio-technical work or discretionary learning may not be found in the USA or Japan. There are also of course instances of this approach – though perhaps still less numerous – in the developing or newly industrialising world.

ONE BEST WAY INTERNATIONALLY IN THE ORGANISATION OF WORK?

Reviews by Boselie *et al* (2005), Wall and Wood (2003) and Paauwe (2004), and most recently Heffernan *et al* (2011), indicate the accumulating evidence of a tendency for high-involvement work systems (HIWS) or high-commitment management (HCM) to be associated with better organisational and specifically business performance regardless of national boundaries.

THE BEST PRACTICE OF HCM/HIWS

- Selection: screening and expectation-setting
- Training: off-job time and money
- *Teamwork*: problem-solving/cross-function
- *Job design*: complexity and autonomy
- *Communication*: information and consultation
- *Appraisal*: regular, multi-sourced, behaviour-centred
- Pay: pay for performance principally on a team, group or departmental basis.

This best practice bundle centres upon matters of the organisation of work (*in italics* above), and is to a great extent defined in contradistinction to Taylorism, but also carries distinct echoes of socio-technical semi-autonomous 'group' work in the Nordic tradition.
Source: developed from Wall and Wood (2003)

This evidence is consistent with findings that the delegation of management tasks to semi-autonomous groups of employees has a greater effect on business performance where organisations simultaneously deploy group incentives (Antoni *et al*, 2005). Meaningful team or group work, coupled to team or group reward, seems to deliver results. Indeed, there are indications that this combination has the capacity to make up for weak product development/ innovation by management (see Antoni *et al*, 2005).

Of course, ideas such as these provide only a broad-brush guide to evidence-based best practice in the organisation of work, and there is considerable space for these principles to be adjusted to specific national environments. The implicit warning – that Taylorism is generally not the most effective form of work organisation, even if managers can get away with it – is, however, highly significant.

KEY LEARNING POINTS

- Although it is sometimes rather neglected in discussions of HRM, there are many indications that this is one of the vital arenas of HRM activity.

- Taylorism remains influential in contemplations of work organisation and in practice.

- Many organisations now seek to overcome the limitations of Taylorism with communication initiatives but also with a more radical and broader-based reform of work organisation.

- The balance of approaches to work organisation varies dramatically across countries, even within Europe.

- Sheer economic development, or GDP per capita, does not explain the cross-national comparative variations in work organisation.

- Cross-national comparative variation appears importantly driven by culture and most particularly by institutions.

- There are some indications of an international best practice in work organisation.

LEARNING QUESTIONS

1 We have limited evidence on how work is typically organised in the developing and newly industrialising worlds, but what would you expect to be typical?

2 Consider the basis of your view of the work organisation typical outside the established OECD or old industrialised world. Check that it is consistent with what we do know about the comparative organisation of work.

3 Why is Taylorism still influential in work organisation a century after its development?

4 Might the importance of overcoming the gulf between managerial and non-managerial employees be more important to organisational effectiveness in some countries than others?

5 Which are the best methods to facilitate upward and downward communication? Are they likely to vary with different cultures?

6 How should an MNC in, say, retail approach work organisation in the various countries in which it operates?

7 To what extent do you think companies are constrained in their approaches to work organisation by what their managers, and perhaps in particular their line managers, are comfortable or confident with?

8 May 'best practice' in work organisation be inoperable some contexts? Is this always because it wouldn't improve productivity performance?

EXPLORE FURTHER

Doellgast, V. (2010) 'Collective voice under decentralized bargaining: a comparative study of work reorganization in US and German call centres', *British Journal of Industrial Relations*, 48 (2): 375–399. This article identifies Taylorism amongst white-collar employees within the established OECD.

The European Foundation for the Improvement of Living and Working Conditions (EFILWC). (2009) Working Conditions in the European Union: Work Organisation. EFILWC. Dublin. This provides a detailed examination of the cross-national comparative variation in the organisation of work across the countries of the EU.

Gamble, J., Morris, J. and Wilkinson, B. (2004) 'Mass production is alive and well: the future of work and organization in East Asia', *Journal of Human Resource Management*, 15 (2): 397–409. These authors consider the relevance of Taylorism in the developing and newly industrialising world.

CHAPTER 7

Flexibility and Work–Life Balance

LEARNING OUTCOMES

When they have read this chapter, students will:

- be familiar with the concepts of non-traditional or flexible work patterns and work–life balance, and the relationship between them

- be aware of developments in working-time flexibility, non-permanent forms of employment and work–life balance

- be able to identify similarities and differences at country level, in relation to flexibility and work–life balance

- understand the principal factors underlying cross-national comparative differences in practice in these arenas

- be able to draw conclusions about managing flexible working and work–life balance across country borders.

INTRODUCTION

Discussions of flexibility begin with the employer or manager, and his or her notion of what is required for effective operations, to meet fluctuations in throughput or demand, and sometimes to take advantage of the structure of taxation on employment and employers' social insurance contributions. Necessarily, though, managers must take account of the possibilities that the labour market presents of pursuing a certain policy focused upon effective resource planning to meet operational need. In many respects, flexibility and work–life balance are flip sides of the same coin. Discussions of work–life balance begin with the employee, as employers and managers seek to interpret and accommodate employees' needs and situations. Of course, here too there must ultimately be reference to organisational objectives. Yet a focus on the newer agenda of work–life balance implies a rather softer approach to HRM than does a focus on the older agenda of flexibility.

With regard to the older flexibility, or non-traditional working, agenda there are distinct terminological problems. 'Flexibility', which is the term used here, is the most common term in Europe, even though it has certain linguistic connotations that may be inaccurate. Even in Europe some commentators prefer the phrase 'the peripheral workforce' (Atkinson, 1984) or the (equally inaccurate) term 'atypical working'. Others have referred to the 'just-in-time workforce' (Plews, 1988). Some trade unionists talk about 'vulnerable work'.

A broad definition of 'atypical' employment is that adopted by Delsen (1991; p123), who describes it as deviating 'from full-time open-ended work employment: part-time work, ... seasonal work...'. In the USA the most common term which largely overlaps what is referred to in Europe as flexible working patterns is 'contingent work' (Freedman, 1986), although some consultants have tried to foster the term 'complementary working'. Polivk and Nardone (1989; p10) define contingent employment as 'any arrangement that differs from full-time, permanent, wage and salary employment'. Morishima and Feuille (2000) note that contingent employment can include a wide variety of workers. They conclude that:

> The common themes that unite the individuals in these diverse categories are that they receive few or no fringe benefits, they have little or no expectation of long-term employment with the firm on whose premises they work at any given time, and they occupy a secondary position to the regular, full-time (or core) employees in the firm's status hierarchy.

Although an accurate account of the situation for most flexible workers in the USA and Japan, within the European context such distinctions do not hold true. Apart from the fact that in many European countries local employment protection helps guard against discrimination, the EU has passed legislation guaranteeing the rights of part-time and temporary workers, which apply across the EU. Furthermore, there will be a minority, but an important minority, of highly in-demand and successful people on flexible work contracts to whom none of these factors applies.

 REFLECTIVE ACTIVITY

What implications might be inherent in these different terminologies?

The concept of 'labour flexibility' remains, both in theoretical and practical terms, highly problematic. In the literature, the term 'flexibility' is applied to a series of quite distinct (if related) theories and practices. The concept that some kinds of work are peripheral or atypical carries with it the idea that they are in some way less significant or worthy than other, more standard, kinds of work. Thinking about this kind of work as 'contingent', 'just in time' or 'disposable' is clearly looking at such work from an employer's perspective, focusing on the positive side from that position, so that the individuals concerned are almost defined out of existence as real people. By contrast, 'vulnerable' work implies thinking from the employees' point of view – and, moreover, from that viewpoint is focused on the downside.

The labour that an organisation employs is, in most cases, the most expensive item of its operating costs. There is increasing pressure on operating costs. In the private sector, competition – particularly international competition – is getting tougher. In the public sector, ever-tightening public-sector financial constraints mean that organisations here too are having to use their expensive labour resource in ever more cost-effective ways. Standard *employment* has built-in inefficiencies unless *work* comes in exactly the standard employment patterns. That is rarely the case now, and many organisations have attempted to match their employment patterns more closely to the work (Brewster and Larsen, 2000).

These changes and the development of a more flexible labour market have been controversial. There are those who see the development of the flexible workforce as a long-overdue move away from rigid forms of employment towards forms that can be more responsive to the needs of employees, or can be 'family-friendly'. There are many who would argue that part-time, shift- or home-working allows them to spend more time with their children or elderly or disabled family members (Bevan, 1996). However, the growth in flexibility at the end of the last century and the beginning of this one has been driven by employer demands. In a comparative study of German, French and UK industries, Lane (1989) found that each country responded differently to the same economic pressures for flexibility. She argued that whereas German industry embraced flexible specialisation, British industry tended to adopt a combination of Fordist and contractual flexibility principles of management. Lane's (1989) interpretation of the German experience highlights a further meaning of flexibility – ie *functional* flexibility, concerning matters of work organisation, and in particular, job design, which is dealt with in a separate chapter here.

THE IMPLICATIONS OF FLEXIBILITY

 ### REFLECTIVE ACTIVITY

What might some of the implications of the development of flexible working patterns and work–life balance policies be for employers, individuals, and the state?

For employers, flexibility offers significant advantages. They are able to develop ways of employing people, or even getting the work done without employing people, that more closely match the need for the work. Organisations need flexibility, and in particular time and contractual flexibility, in order to ensure the most economic use of labour. But increased flexibility is not without its problems for organisations. Less training of flexible workers means lower skill levels in a society. Other problems centre round the difficulty of establishing policies, administering the system, communication and commitment. There are obviously benefits for employers in matching better the work they pay for and the work they get done. Arguably, however, the major benefit of the use of flexibility for organisations lies in the transfer of cost and risk from the organisation to individuals and to the state, or to society as a whole (Brewster, 1998; Sparrow and Cooper, 2003).

For individuals, flexible working patterns can provide additional opportunities to work, can enable family incomes to be supplemented, and can allow work to be fitted in with family responsibilities. However, the transfer of the costs means that flexible work is often low-paid. It is the individual and the family who bear the cost of not working standard hours and contractual arrangements. In addition, workers may well be expected to arrange for and to pay for their own training and skill updating. The transfer of risks means that many individuals and the families that they support cannot be sure of employment much beyond the immediate future. This becomes more than just an immediate financial problem for the families involved; it has a major effect on the rest of their lives, because so much of our society is built on the assumption that most people have standard employment. Thus the ability to purchase goods on credit, to have bank loans, to arrange housing and to provide pension arrangements are still sensitive to some degree in every European country on individuals having a full-time, long-term job.

Governments also have to address these changes in labour markets more directly. One important implication concerns the effect on government finances. Even if it reduces unemployment, flexible working tends to increase the number of those in employment who, because they do not work enough hours a week, or enough weeks in the year, end up paying no taxes.

For society in general the costs have been transferred directly, because the state supplements low earnings and provides support for the unemployed. The costs have also been transferred indirectly in that the requirements for training, for health and safety and for the provision of other relevant benefits have to be borne by the state. The transfer of risk means that during periods of unemployment – between short-term contracts, for example – the state is again expected to provide support. And there are arguably many indirect aspects of this transfer in terms of the effects of insecurity and stress on health levels, in terms of pension arrangements and in terms of housing support.

It appears, for instance, that part-time jobs are likely to be replacing full-time jobs on a one-for-one basis, rather than that full-time jobs are being replaced by two part-time jobs to cover the same number of hours. Even if two people were getting work rather than one, though, the overall benefit might be extremely limited if one or both remain on income support, do not pay tax (or even in many cases National Insurance) and have little extra money to spend in the economy. The increased flexibility in Europe means that risks and costs have been transferred from employers to individuals and to the state. This may make the employing organisations more efficient, but not necessarily make the country more competitive.

CONTRACTUAL FLEXIBILITY: 'NON-PERMANENT' EMPLOYMENT

Many of the developments in flexibility relate to contractual flexibility. There is a range of methods by which organisations can get work done. In some cases these involve contracts of employment which are quite distinct from 'typical' contracts in more significant ways than just a change to the time at which the employee works – they may involve short-term or even casual employment, for example. Or they may involve getting the work done through a non-employment option.

SHORT-TERM EMPLOYMENT

This is a phrase used to cover any form of employment other than permanent open-ended contracts. To some extent 'temporary', 'fixed-term' and 'casual' contracts are substitutes, and which is used most heavily in a country depends largely on legal and quasi-legal regulations and national expectations. Temporary contracts are those that can be terminated with just the appropriate notice and are recognised by both parties as not intending to lead to permanent employment commitments. They can range from a few weeks' work (for example, on building sites) to as many as three years', although typically they are at the lower end of such a distribution. Fixed-term contracts, in contrast, are those which the parties agree will end on a certain date, often after 12 or 24 months. By law, the terminations of these contracts are not treated as terminations of employment *per se* since the contracts have simply been completed, not broken. Temporary and fixed-term contracts tend to overlap, but often appear to substitute for each other depending on local legislation. Temporary contracts tend to be set with lower-skilled workers, whereas fixed-term contracts tend to be set with higher-skilled employees. Employers avoid expectations that either type of contract will lead to permanent employment and, consequently, avoid some of the legal obligations, as well as trade union reactions, that the termination of employment might otherwise prompt. Casual contracts occur when both employer and employee accept that the employment will be on an 'as necessary' basis. Thus students working in certain occupations over the Christmas and New Year sales period, or catering staff called in to a restaurant just to cover children's parties, would be examples of casual work. Similar examples can be found in many industries.

REFLECTIVE ACTIVITY

When and why might an employer prefer to offer a short-term contract rather than a permanent one?

In general, it seems that employers are likely to offer short-term contracts in three broad sets of circumstances: when, for one reason or another they are not sure whether or how long a job will last (for example, in the construction industry or when government funding for a charity project might be of limited duration); when they seek to avoid the commitments to employees that come with permanent work (employment rights, pensions, etc); and when they are uncertain that they have chosen the right person. In practice, the first reason has always existed and probably has not changed much, and the capacity to avoid obligations has been much reduced in places such as the countries of the EU by legislation. The third reason seems to be growing. Many employees are now appointed on short-term contracts while the employer checks whether they will be good employees (see Chapter 8).

Using detailed evidence from Cranet 2004 data, Brewster *et al* (2007) noted that at the time the use of fixed-term contracts remained generally limited, but there was considerable variability across countries. Despite their reputations as nations displaying great flexibility in the character of their employment relationships, the Anglo-Saxon nations clustered towards the bottom end in terms of organisational use of these sorts of contracts. The Netherlands was a striking exception to this general tendency of limited use of fixed-term contracts. Although second to Finland at the time, on the basis of a threshold of 5 per cent of employees on fixed-term contracts, many more Dutch organisations reported very heavy or intensive use of fixed-term contracts.

Figure 16 shows the data for 2010 in six countries. Again, it is Swedish, German and French organisations that are more likely to use fixed-term contracts (also Japan), only 26 per cent of British organisations and 11 per cent of US organisations using them.

Figure 16 Organisations with more than 5 per cent of employees on fixed-term contracts

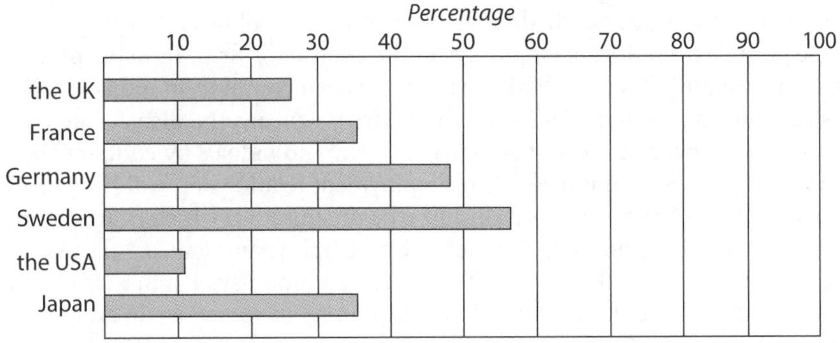

Source: Cranet (2010)

Generally, the extent of organisations' use of temporary and casual employees also remains limited, but as with their use of fixed-term contracts, there are some marked variations across countries. Again, in 2004 data showed that the UK, the USA and New Zealand, but most of all Australia and Canada feature quite prominently in using these contracts (Brewster *et al,* 2007). Some continental European nations, specifically France, Spain and the Netherlands, figured more prominently, while most of continental Europe features more limited use.

Figure 17 shows the situation using 2010 Cranet data. Sweden, France and the UK have between 25 per cent and 45 per cent of organisations that use these contracts. German organisations are less inclined to use them, and in the USA and Japan they are now relatively infrequent. The shift in use in the USA is a rather unexpected finding, but might in fact be indicative of a general collapse of external recruitment at the time of writing.

Figure 17   Organisations in which more than 5 per cent of employees are temporary or casual

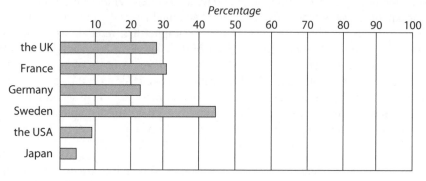

Source: Cranet (2010)

SUBCONTRACTING

Subcontracting is 'the displacement of an employment contract by a commercial one as a means of getting a job done' (Atkinson and Meager, 1986). For some employees this will make little difference in terms of flexibility: they might well be permanent full-time employees in the contractor firm. In many other cases, however, this system – which has always been common in industries like construction, and in countries in Asia and Africa – means the displacement of more traditional contracts of employment with individuals by contracts for services with other organisations. The employment relationship will have been superseded by a commercial relationship. The organisation which is giving out the contract will have no further concern with employment issues – these will have been passed on to the contractor. This is a common system in many of the poorer countries around the world, but is beginning to spread again amongst the richer countries due to cost concerns and a move towards outsourcing.

WORKING TIME FLEXIBILITY

PART-TIME WORK

The degree of flexibility in part-time work has been debated. The argument is that if someone is doing regular part-time work, and has other commitments which cannot be moved, then he or she is not individually very flexible. However, from the viewpoint of management, part-time employment – which in some cases can in practice be readily reduced, extended or moved to a different place in the day – is more flexible than standard full-time work.

REFLECTIVE ACTIVITY

What advantages might accrue to employers and to employees from employing people on a part-time basis?

Part-time work helps managers to match the labour available to peaks and troughs in demand during the working day and week. Recruiting a few part-time workers to cover particularly busy periods, for example, may mean that other employees can work more standardised hours and the total full-time equivalent headcount can be kept down. It is also argued that judicious use of part-time employment allows employers to pay only for the most productive hours of an employee's time (the longer one works the less productive per hour one becomes). On the other hand, such arrangements can be beneficial for those with, for example, family care responsibilities who find that longer working hours exclude them from participating in the labour market. Approximately 85 per cent of part-time workers in Europe, it might be noted, are female.

Part-time employment varies around the world. Since a substantial majority of part-time workers are female, it is no surprise to find that there is also a correlation with female participation in the labour force (Rubery and Fagan, 1993; Rubery et al, 1996) and, indeed, with childcare arrangements (Rees and Brewster, 1995). It is much used in northern Europe (over one-third of the workforce in the Netherlands, a quarter of all employment in the UK and Sweden) and common in northern America, but much less common in other parts of the world.

Part-time work is an example of flexible working which provides something for the employee, involving lower pay for fewer hours, but allowing the employee time outside work for caring for children, relatives and friends, charitable work or self-actualising or emancipatory activities of their choosing. Most employees with part-time contracts express satisfaction with working less than full-time, given their other commitments, responsibilities and interests.

Definitions across national boundaries can be complex. Part-time work, for example, will apply to any work hours short of the normal working week for each country, which vary across the globe. Thus, in France and Belgium, part-time work is defined as four-fifths or less of the collectively agreed working time; in the Netherlands and the USA as less than 35 hours per week; in the UK as less than 30 hours, with lower thresholds in relation to social security contributions. Elsewhere, the norm is concentrated around 25–30 hours per week (see Bolle, 1997, or Brewster et al, 1996, for more complete listings).

The evidence offered by Cranet 2004 data showed marked comparative variation in the use of what employers themselves regard as part-time employees (Brewster et al, 2007). The Anglo-Saxon nations were quite heavy users, comparatively speaking. However, the heaviest users were amongst the smaller nations of continental Europe.

Figure 18 Organisations in which more than 10 per cent of employees work part-time

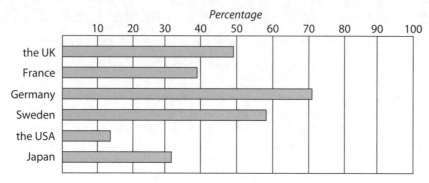

Source: Cranet (2010)

Figure 18 shows the situation based on the 2010 data. Once more, practice in the USA seems to have been impacted significantly, but the UK remains a high user of part-time contracts, although this form of working is still more prevalent in continental European countries such as Germany and Sweden. In Japan and France only between 30 per cent and 40 per cent of organisations have more than 10 per cent of employees working part-time.

In some respects, job-sharing represents a development of the established idea of part-time work. It remains rather uncommon. The Cranet 2004 data showed only 5–10 per cent of organisations in the vast bulk of nations reporting that more than 5 per cent of their employees job-share. However, as usual there were some exceptions to the general tendency. More than two-fifths (42.4 per cent) of Slovakian organisations reported that over 5 per cent of their employees job-share. In Turkey, the proportion was more than a quarter (27.6 per cent). These comparatively very high incidences were perhaps the flipside of the very limited use of part-time employment in these two countries.

OTHER FORMS OF WORKING TIME FLEXIBILITY

Annual hours contracts typically offer full-time employment without necessarily offering consistency in hours week-to-week. From the employer's point of view, they offer a means of adapting to variations in the amount of work to be done. From the employees' point of view, though, they can be very disruptive. Although annualised hours contracts have been becoming increasingly common, their incidence across nations varies markedly. It is in France that they figure most prominently – both in 2004 and now again in 2010 (see Figure 19), some 30 per cent of organisations reporting that more than half of their employees are on annual hours contracts. In principle, it might seem that annualised hours offer the possibility that parents might be able to work longer weeks in school terms in order to be able to take the entirety of school vacations with their children, although it is not at all clear that this is common in practice in most countries. This is an indication of a more general principle – that annualised hours tend to imply flexibility from the point of view of the employer.

Figure 19 Organisations with more than half of their employees on annual hours contracts

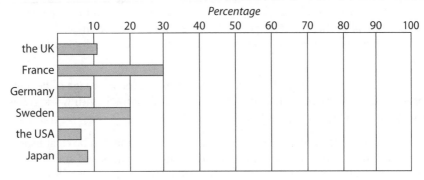

Source: Cranet (2010)

There is a wide variety of other flexible working time patterns available – some of them very new – but in general they are less widespread. They include such approaches as shift-working, weekend working and term-time working, networking, working as consultants or government-sponsored trainees, and tele-working. All are much smaller in extent, but all are growing.

THE RATIONALES FOR FLEXIBILITY

Working patterns and contracts are established according to a complex set of factors – employers' needs, competition, the sales market, the availability of particular skills, the bargaining power of trade unions, managerial understanding, tradition, and employment legislation. The use of these various practices varies considerably by country. And so do the implications. Being on a short-term contract in a country with generous social security provision has a completely different connotation from being on such a contract in a country where such provision is very limited.

In some versions of HRM, particularly those that deal with the soft, friendly face of HRM, concentrating on 'high commitment', 'high performance', 'competence' and 'human resource development', the evidence in this chapter is particularly challenging. How are organisations to develop highly committed, energised and enthusiastic contributors to managerial objectives when the organisations' commitment to the employees is severely limited? Why should organisations train and develop people when the costs of doing so are the same as the costs for the long-term full-time employees, but the pay-off is obviously limited to the proportion of time the employee is at work or the length of his or her association with that organisation? It is no surprise to find that, in practice, employers provide much less training or development for atypical workers (Brewster *et al*, 1996).

WORK–LIFE BALANCE

Debate around work–life balance arises in the context of the changing future of work, flexible working patterns, a feminisation of the labour force in many countries, and, increasingly and perhaps relatedly, a reassessment by many employees of the priorities in their lives. Organisational initiatives may range from symbolic devices to counteract poor publicity, through efforts to deal with an immediate problem of recruitment or retention, to efforts to foster a new atmosphere and perhaps greater personal integrity and a more sincere workplace. Currently, rhetoric about a new balancing often exceeds the reality in many workplaces.

To some extent the language of 'work–life balance', like the language of flexibility, is problematic. In practice, life and work overlap and interact, with work giving substantial meaning to peoples' lives (Taylor, 2002):

> In the experience of most people no clear-cut distinction can be established between the world of work and the world of family, friends and social networks and community. In practice, over the length of our lives it is impossible to establish neatly constructed demarcation lines. Moreover, the word – balance – implies the existence of a settled equilibrium that can be achievable between paid employment and a life outside the job. This is highly questionable.

In this context, terms such as 'reconciliation' or 'synergy' may be more appropriate to the discussion, crystallising better the issues at stake (Taylor, 2002). The terms 'work-family conflict' and 'family-work conflict' capture the agenda in a more striking way. Whatever the terminology, the work–life balance agenda implies a questioning of the effectiveness of the rigidity of many of the established dimensions of paid work, around the regularity of hours, work location, and indeed the effectiveness of long hours where employees feel torn, feel resentful, or experience self-loathing as a result of their time commitment to work. Initiatives in work–life balance offer the employee more autonomy in seeking to reconcile his or her differing roles, allowing him or her to reorder the boundaries between work and non-work.

Very often, discussion of work–life balance revolves around a need for 'family-friendly' policies, in recognition of the very severe difficulties which work can pose for family roles, and of the significance of those roles to so many employees, most obviously in terms of parenting but also in terms of caring for older relatives or friends. Of course, the work–life balance agenda can also encompass consideration of the implications of employees' commitments to voluntary work, or any activity that in some respects competes for attention with paid work roles.

 REFLECTIVE ACTIVITY

What advantages might accrue to an organisation from the introduction of 'family-friendly' policies?

Employers rarely introduce policies that make for a better work/non-work balance because they feel altruistic. Those in the private sector need to make money and those in the public sector need to provide cost-effective services. But there are arguments that employers can gain considerable benefits from such policies: more motivated and committed staff, less absenteeism, less turnover, etc (see the case study below for an example from BT).

CASE STUDIES

FAMILY-FRIENDLY POLICIES IN THE UK AND WORK–LIFE BALANCE AT BT

Bond *et al* (2002) found that in the UK organisations adopting family-friendly policies did so to retain staff. They also found, though, that often arrangements were not formalised and considerable discretion was left to line managers. Moreover, their work suggested that where unions were present, family-friendly provision was more widespread. The latest Workplace Employment Relations Survey of the UK showed that family-friendly practices were spreading rapidly, but also that companies increasingly felt that it was the employees', not employers', responsibility to balance life and work. In part this may be a reaction to a series of policy initiatives by the UK government aimed at improving the position of working parents.

British Telecom's Work–Life Balance project evolved over two decades of continual development and experimentation, and is remarkable in the UK context. In 1998 the results of a staff survey revealed that 62 per cent of its managers felt that their lives were too skewed towards work and 33 per cent said they were not prepared to accept promotion or greater responsibilities because of the effect on their domestic life. In response, BT committed to substantial investment in pursuing a flexible employment strategy. The HRM team piloted a 'Freedom to Work' programme, offering staff the chance of arranging their own work hours and patterns, subject to the achievement of business objectives, though usually these hours were organised around a total 41-hour working week. BT extended the initiative to 8,000 employees. The key reference is the psychological contract between employer and employee, and the need for people to feel that they are valued. There is evidence of an improvement in productivity within teams, a reduction in absenteeism, and, most strikingly, a continued improvement in the return rate after maternity leave, which now stands at 96 per cent. A number of key roles support the development and extension of such policies – the Director of Employment Policy, the Social Policy Finance Manager and the Manager of Employment Philosophy – and a senior executive forum also helps to develop the strategy. The BT intranet is used to promote and enable the Work–Life Balance programme.

Source: Seneviratna and Turton (2001); Higginbottom (2001)

FLEXI-TIME

In some respects flexi-time offers something similar to annual hours contracts, although it tends to be led by the employee rather than the employer. Flexi-time is now quite common in many countries but the comparative variation in incidence is still enormous. Flexi-time is very common in the Nordic nations, approximately 35 per cent of all organisations in 2004 reporting its use for more than half of their employees (Brewster *et al*, 2007). High incidence was also apparent in other continental northern European countries: Austria, Switzerland and Belgium. There was comparatively little flexi-time in the Anglo-Saxon world. Figure 20 shows the situation by 2010. There has been massive use of flexi-time in Germany, compared to very little use in France. In the UK, the USA and Japan around 15 per cent of organisations have gone down this route.

Figure 20 Organisations with more than half of their employees on flexi-time

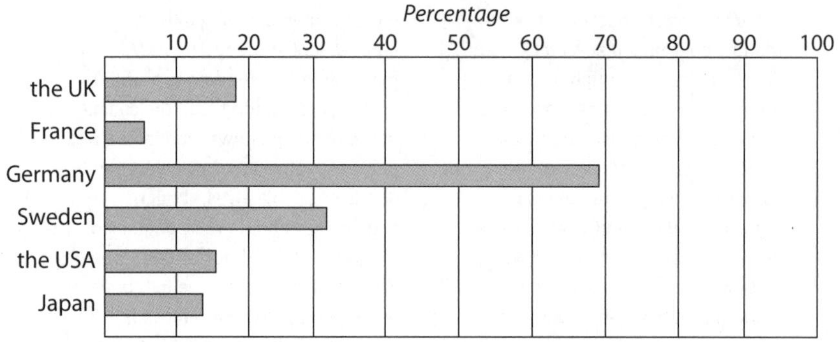

Source: Cranet (2010)

COMPRESSED WORKING WEEKS

Compressed working weeks offer an alternative means of balancing commitments to and outside work, and are often used by parents of pre-school children. The very limited use of compressed working weeks in any country deserves stressing. However, cross-national comparative variation in organisational use was quite marked in 2004. North America and the UK featured comparatively extensive use of this relatively new practice, around 10–20 per cent of organisations having five per cent or more employees on compressed working weeks. The extent of use in the UK and the USA has remained fairly stable, but once more there has been a widespread adoption of the practice in Germany, with Sweden also going down this route. There are real differences in the extent to which the organisations of different nations have begun to operationalise forms of working which accommodate work–life conflicts more readily.

TOTAL WORKING HOURS

Much of the debate around work–life balance centres on the manner in which working time is structured, in particular with regard to the rigidity of the commitment which employees must make. Yet total working time is of obvious relevance to work–life balance. The comparative differences are immense. Within the EU, the number of public holidays per year ranges from eight to 14, with the UK at the bottom and Portugal at the top. This is just the beginning of differences even in holidays, however. The average number of vacation days (including public holidays) taken by employees around the world varies enormously, from 13 days in the USA, to 28 days in the UK and 42 days in Italy (ONS, 1999).

Weekly working hours in the UK are famously long compared to other European countries, such that the EU's *Employment in Europe* survey reported that almost half of the seven million male workers working over 48 hours a week in the EU were employed in Britain. Much of this overtime is not specifically rewarded. The 1999 Social Trends survey reported that 42 per cent of UK employees reported that they always or often left work in a state of exhaustion. The Working Time Regulations have had little effect on reducing these extreme working weeks. Working hours seem to be longer in the USA and very long indeed in Japan, with the accompanying problems manifest in those countries too.

Unsurprisingly in this context, 'working sick' is a common experience for British employees, and appears shared with employees in the USA and Japan. Indeed, increasingly in the UK, as in Japan, a small but growing minority of employees are expected to take days off as part of their holiday entitlement rather than to take them as 'off sick' not only when their children are sick but when they themselves are so sick that they cannot work. This sort of situation is much rarer in the bulk of the advanced industrialised world.

Differences in vacation time, in the normal working week, in overtime, and in sickness absence, but also in study leave, result in striking differences in average annual hours actually worked across countries. Aside from a lengthening of typical German working hours, there has been little comparative change in this regard since the mid-1990s, for which Vernon (2000, Table 20) provides comparative data centring on the manufacturing sector. The very long hours worked in the UK are exceeded by those in the USA and Canada, and, despite

Table 10 Average annual working time (hours), in manufacturing

Country	Annual hours
USA	1,980
Japan	1,978
Canada	1,902
UK	1,839
Italy	1,741
Austria	1,668
Norway	1,659
Sweden	1,646
Finland	1,633
France	1,610
Germany	1,521

Source: Vernon (2000)

the falling hours consequent on slump, also in Japan. Hours in emerging and developing nations are, as far as we can tell, generally much longer than the longest reported here for the established advanced industrialised world. Vernon (2000) shows that within the advanced industrialised world annual hours are strongly related to the significance of collective bargaining – this would of course also account for the very long hours of work in developing and newly industrialising countries, where collective bargaining is generally weak. See Table 10.

It is clear that there are associations between total working hours and health. Sparks *et al* (1997) established correlations between work hours and poorer physiological health, gauged by indicators including headaches, work accidents, coronary heart disease and general health symptoms. Long hours also showed a stronger correlation with psychological health, gauged by, for example, irritability/tension, problems with relationships, lack of concentration, tiredness, role strain, anxiety, frustration, insomnia, depression, and general mental stress.

REFLECTIVE ACTIVITY

In considering work–life balance:

Might it be that an employee's total annual working time is of more significance than specific initiatives like flexi-time and compressed working weeks which re-order a given amount of working time?

If so, why is there so little discussion of total hours worked in many countries?

FACTORS UNDERLYING COMPARATIVE VARIATION IN FLEXIBILITY AND WORK–LIFE BALANCE

Generally, there is little evidence that national culture – conceived in the manner of Hofstede, for example – influences patterns of flexibility and work–life balance. Brewster and Tregaskis's (2002) analysis showed that sector of operation accounts for 17 per cent of variance in the levels of uptake of flexibility. MNC status accounts for very little variance – a mere one per cent. However, their analysis also shows that the country of operation has the largest effect, accounting for 25 per cent of the variance. The importance of something around nation of operation is clear, even if the relevance of culture is dubious.

Tregaskis and Brewster's (2006) study of five European countries shows the importance of the advantages offered to employers by fixed-term contracts over permanent or open-ended contracts for the extent of fixed-term work. Where labour law, or employment protection legislation, places relatively more restrictions on dismissal or redundancy for employees on permanent contracts, fixed-term use tends to be higher. Thus in the Netherlands, employment protection legislation places exacting requirements on employers wanting to terminate the contract of a permanent employee, whereas there is little restriction on the use of fixed-term contracts, encouraging fixed-term contracting. In contrast, in the UK the balance of labour law is such that the employment of permanent employees imposes relatively little restriction on employers beyond that involved in the use of fixed-term contracts. Use is thus much lower in the Netherlands than in the UK (Tregaskis and Brewster, 2006). Similarly, the 'fire at will' reality of even permanent employment relationships in the USA means that fixed-term contracts are little used there. The exceptionally low use of fixed-term contracts in Denmark within the Nordic group underscores the power of this explanation, because employment protection legislation for permanent employees is much more limited in Denmark than in the other Nordic countries (see eg Andersen and Mailand, 2005). As Tregaskis and Brewster (2006) note, there is also some suggestion that patterns of skill formation interplay with labour law in shaping the use of fixed-term contracts, such contracting being rarer where there is more emphasis on firm-specific rather than transferable (or generic) skills.

Although generally, at least within the established OECD, the industrial composition of countries seems of very limited relevance to their organisations' use of contractual flexibility, it seems that in some countries this is of particular importance. Tregaskis and Brewster (2006) suggest that the importance of agriculture and tourism in Spain help to account for the comparatively heavy use of temporary labour there. A similar argument, perhaps focused in particular on agriculture, might be made for France or even Australia. Certainly, though, there is more to the use of temporary staff than industrial structure.

Although to some extent there is a tendency that fixed-term contracts are used for employees who are more skilled and/or better qualified whereas temporary or casual work is used for employees who are less skilled and/or less qualified, to some extent, temporary work and fixed-term work seem to substitute for each other. Organisations in the Anglo-Saxon nations tend to secure numerical flexibility via the use of temporary and casual employees, rather than through fixed-term contracts. As we have suggested, fixed-term contracts often offer little advantage to Anglo-Saxon employers over permanent contracts, but temporary or casual work, often via agencies, offers much more. It seems that the willingness of Anglo-Saxon employers to deploy temporary or casual staff is also expressive of a comparatively weak emphasis on firm-specific skill in people management, with skills regarded as transferable, or perhaps even relatively unimportant (see Tregaskis and Brewster, 2006). Thus the low value placed on educational qualifications in the UK context, in combination with the lower level of vocational training, encourages poaching and reliance on external labour markets. This places more of a premium on contractual flexibility.

Fixed-term contracts in occupations that are in high demand and low in supply, such as software designers, can prove quite advantageous for individuals in terms of reward packages and opportunities for skill enhancement. Yet generally, the evidence is that most employees with a temporary or fixed-term contract would prefer a permanent one. Often, though, part-time employment allows those with other responsibilities (young children, elderly relatives, etc) to be away from work when they need to be. Across Europe, EU surveys show that most people on part-time employment tend to prefer those kinds of contracts. They tend to be less common in the southern European countries where pay levels are lower (part-time work = part-time pay, and if the pay is low anyway, that may not be attractive) and where family support for working mothers is higher. The use of part-time (as well as fixed-term and temporary work) in the Netherlands is particularly great even for comparatively high-wage northern Europe, reflecting to a great extent the efforts made by the Dutch government to reduce unemployment in the 1990s (Visser and Hemerijck, 1997).

What of other forms of working time flexibility? The exceptional use of annual hours contracts in France is in large part a response to the French '35-hour week' legislation of the 1990s, which actually implied not that employees must work 35 or fewer hours in any particular week but rather that annual working time should be such that the average working week is 35 hours. Employers and employees have often come to the view that the mutually beneficial way of handling this working time reduction was that employees would work more variable hours across the weeks of the year. Many, although not all, of the countries where annual hours contracts are more common are countries where unions are particularly strong and/or labour costs particularly high, suggesting that employers seek them as a means of maintaining competitiveness, and employees and their representatives accept them as a means of maintaining comparatively high levels of pay.

There is currently little cross-national comparative research on the drivers of work–life balance. Wood's (1999) research on the UK suggested that the work–life balance agenda may be more prominent in the public sector (due to political accountability), in larger private sector companies (due to visibility but also due to the greater influence of unions), in organisations taking a broader performance informed approach to HRM, and in organisations with a higher percentage of women employees. This rather understates the importance of the labour market to the differential development of work–life balance policies for different grades or job families. Often, attention is focused on a particular segment of the workforce regarded as particularly valuable or likely to leave, so that the scope of discussion of work–life balance is heavily conditioned by the labour market situation and its perceived implications for organisational performance.

In the Nordic countries, particularly Sweden, incidence of flexi-time is heavy, and we might reckon its incidence to be expressive of the extent of the feminisation of the labour force, particularly as this extends to full-time work, given the high figures for female participation in the Nordic countries. But flexi-time is common in northern continental Europe more generally, with its strong unions generally rendering collective bargaining weightier, and its industrial relations generally more heavily subject to legislation. In these circumstances it seems that employees often expect, and employers often grant, the daily personal flexibility which flexi-time gives. As we have seen, there is much less use of compressed working weeks generally, and to an extent where this is used it seems used as an alternative to flexi-time, perhaps where the social regulation of work is lighter, and total working time longer.

What, then, of total working time, regardless of how it is arranged? Vernon (2000) shows for the established industrialised world that the strength of unions in collective bargaining, and indeed the extent of the role of national governments in shaping and regulating the employment relationship, are central influences on the average annual hours of work of employees. The very long working hours typical in developing and newly industrialised countries, which typically feature less social regulation of work by unions and governments, and in which employees also typically have fewer financial resources on which to fall back, underscore the importance of the collective and individual resources held by employees for the containment of their total working time.

 REFLECTIVE ACTIVITY

Currently we have little but anecdotal evidence on work–life balance in developing and newly industrialising countries. What do you think the general situation in, say, India or China might be? Why?

INTERNATIONAL BEST PRACTICE IN FLEXIBILITY AND WORK–LIFE BALANCE

We might expect that in this area organisations necessarily must respond to their contexts, adapting their approach in a considered way to the requirements of their industry and niche, and indeed to the national context of their operations. It seems particularly implausible that there might be a best practice in terms of the older agenda of contractual or working time flexibility, given that of its essence this agenda concerns an organisational effort to match employees to work or product demand. Yet might there be an approach to flexibility and/or work–life balance which at least generally or typically delivers better organisational and business performance across countries?

Perhaps in part due to the implausibility of any generic notion of best practice in this dimension of people management, there is rather little research evidence on which to draw. Yet with regard to work–life balance there is one crucial recent study. Bloom *et al* (2009) examine the business performance impact of work–life balance initiatives in hundreds of medium-sized manufacturing companies in the USA, the UK, France and Germany. They find that there is an association between work–life balance, gauged in terms of practices and employee perceptions, on the one hand and (better) productivity performance on the other. Yet they show that this is entirely due to a coincidence between organisations' deployment of work–life balance initiatives and the use of management practices concerning work organisation and performance management which constitute the 'good management' approach they identify as doing the work in improving productivity performance.

This careful study thus suggests that there is no productivity *benefit* of work–life balance *per se*. Yet it simultaneously shows that there is no productivity *cost* of work–life balance initiatives. Thus, it seems, in the realm of work–life balance, although organisations should not generally hope to find a means to boost productivity, they can find a means of rendering work and working lives more pleasant and manageable for employees without impeding productivity. One implication of this, as Bloom et al (2009) themselves suggest, is that the tendency to emphasise work–life balance in Europe, as compared not only to North America but other regions of the world, does not generally imply a productivity cost.

The 'encompassing' service-intensive welfare states of the Nordic countries feature more or less universal childcare provision, the bulk of which is orchestrated by national or regional government (Esping-Andersen, 1999). Although less comprehensive, France has extensive provision by the state, particularly for children aged three and over. To a significant extent, the work–life balance agenda in the Nordic countries in particular has, through childcare initiatives and other support for parents, been taken out of the hands of employers. The quality of working life agenda pursued systematically by the Nordic trade unions has also sought to reduce working time and to allow employees more easily to balance home and work responsibilities. Employers have often responded creatively to the pressure applied by unions in negotiations at multiple levels, bringing, as we have seen, more flexible working in the Nordic nations, and productivity and competitiveness has been combined to a remarkable extent with improvements in the quality of working life (see Gallie, 2003).

Chandola *et al*'s (2004) comparison of the UK with Japan and Finland show that it is in the latter that employees have the best mental health, and in which work–family and family–work conflicts have the least severe impacts on mental health. This is most particularly the case for those employees who are single parents. Japanese employees experience the poorest mental health, with their work–family and family–work conflicts showing the most severe impact. Where employers act with less institutional encouragement and support for the work–life balance agenda than experienced in Finland, or the Nordic countries more generally, the development of an informed and sophisticated approach is more problematic in important respects. Increasingly, though, organisation or workplace level initiatives can draw on wider debate and experience.

REFLECTIVE ACTIVITY

Why might we expect practices with regard to flexibility and work–life balance to affect employees' health?

KEY LEARNING POINTS

- The traditional flexibility and newer work–life balance agendas have very different emphases.

- There are some general trends in flexibility which seem to be happening in many countries: there is a widespread move to increase the extent of flexibility within the workforce.

- There are, however, sustained national idiosyncrasies in the nature and extent of the flexibility practised.

- Despite the general currency of the new work–life balance discourse, the nature, extent and implications of work–life balance initiatives also vary markedly between countries.

- Companies are constrained or influenced in their flexibility and work–life balance practices by culture, financial and corporate governance arrangements, legislation, training provision, multi-employer agreements and trade union involvement and consultative arrangements.

LEARNING QUESTIONS

1 Do the differences in flexible and work–life balance practices discussed in this chapter constitute a barrier to MNCs' transferring personnel policies and practices across borders?

2 Why do countries respond differently in terms of flexibility and work–life balance to what seem similar economic pressures?

3 What country factors does an HR manager need insight into in order to understand the flexibility and work–life balance trade-offs that are preferred in any particular country?

4 Given the imperatives of modern capitalism, should we expect convergence across countries, or at least convergence across the national operations of MNCs?

EXPLORE FURTHER

Tregaskis, O. and Brewster, C. J. (2006) 'Converging or diverging?A comparative analysis of trends in contingent employment practice in Europe over a decade', *Journal of International Business Studies*, 37 (1): 111–126. The authors provide a detailed comparative analysis of the influences on flexibility practice.

Bloom, N., Kretschmer, T. and Van Reenan, J (2009) 'Work–life balance, management practices and productivity' in Freeman, R. B. and Shaw, K. L. (eds) *International Differences in the Business Practices and Productivity of Firms*. Chicago, University of Chicago Press. The authors provide a detailed international analysis of the link between work–life balance practices and business performance.

Chandola, T., Martikainen, P., Bartley, M., Lahelma, E., Marmot, M., Nasermoaddeli, A. and Kagamimori, S. (2004) 'Does conflict between home and work explain the effect of multiple roles on mental health? A comparative study of Finland, Japan and the UK', *International Journal of Epidemiology*, 33 (4): 884–893. This article examines some of the health implications of the differing national practices in these arenas.

CHAPTER 8

Recruitment and Selection

LEARNING OUTCOMES

When they have read this chapter, students will:

- understand the different purposes of recruitment and selection systems
- be able to identify the ways in which recruitment practice can be affected by national legislation
- appreciate some of the most marked differences between countries in recruitment and selection practice in cultural and institutional terms
- understand the dominant regional issues in the area of recruitment and selection.

INTRODUCTION

Good recruitment is essential to effective HRM. The effectiveness of many other human resource activities, such as selection and training, depends largely on the quality of new employees attracted through the recruitment process.

There is usually a flow of linked activities inside organisations from job analysis, recruitment, initial screening, selection, placement through to training. By 'linked' we mean that any practices in one part of the chain can only be understood when they are placed in the context of the practices earlier or later in the chain. Organisations might choose to invest more in one part of the chain. For example, if little can be done to deal with recruitment challenges, then more money might be spent on selection to make up for shortcomings. Or an organisation might prefer to invest more in training to make up for a lack of influence over the quality of the labour market. These differences might form a pattern at national level.

In this chapter we concentrate on two key parts of this resourcing chain – first recruitment, and then selection.

KEY FRAMEWORK

The purposes of recruitment

- to determine present and future staffing needs in conjunction with job analysis and human resource planning

- to increase the pool of applicants at minimum cost

- to increase the success rate of the (subsequent) selection process: fewer will turn out to be over- or under-qualified

- to increase the probability of subsequent retention

- to encourage self-selection by means of a realistic job preview

- to meet responsibilities, and legal and social obligations

- to increase organisational and individual effectiveness

- to evaluate the effectiveness of different labour pools.

Selection – a linked but separate practice after recruitment – then involves the identification of the most suitable person from a pool of applicants.

KEY FRAMEWORK

The purposes of selection

- to obtain appropriate information about jobs, individuals and organisations in order to enable high-quality decisions

- to transform information into a prediction about future behaviour

- to contribute to the bottom line through the most efficient and effective way to produce service/production

- to ensure cost-benefit for the financial investment made in an employee

- to evaluate, hire and place job applicants in the best interests of organisation and individual.

As will become evident later in the chapter, even this specification of purposes is itself extremely culturally embedded. Not surprisingly, both recruitment and selection practices differ depending on the type and level of employee required – but they also differ between countries. The breadth of potential legislation that affects recruitment is considerable.

The employment relationship is typically governed by the combination of three sets of factors (Snape, 1999):

- a complex mix of individual and collective agreements

- the rights and obligations enshrined in legal statutes

- the implicit and explicit understandings of such rights and obligations.

These rights and obligations – codified or implied – are in turn embedded in highly nationalistic legal systems and frameworks. The International Classification of Status in Employment (ICSE), used by the ILO, considers that employment contracts are best categorised in terms both of the *type of economic risk* carried by an employee, and of the *authority that is involved* in the job – defined as the set of tasks and duties that are to be performed by one person.

Sparrow (2011) has recently analysed the employment contract from a comparative context. The employment contract is a *contract of service* (or apprenticeship) between an employer and an employee, rather than a *contract for services*. Under the law the contract may be expressed or implied, and if it is expressed, it may still have standing whether it is oral or in writing. As an agreement between an employer and an employee, it sets out an individual's employment rights, responsibilities and duties. However:

- Without understanding the workings of the surrounding legal system, any examination of even codified rights becomes almost meaningless.

- Without insight into the cultural embeddedness of these terms, interpretation of the codified artefacts of the employment contract, and the legislation that might go along with recruitment to this contract, can be very misleading.

 REFLECTIVE ACTIVITY

Consider the issue of equality legislation.

- Identify two countries where such legislation exists, and two where it does not.

- How is the issue of equality dealt with – informally and informally – in each instance?

- What does this tell you about the implementation and effectiveness – or ineffectiveness – of this legislation? Even when legislation exists, that does not imply that it works!

RECRUITMENT

In light of the fact that even what is implied by an employment contract is culturally embedded, you can imagine the depth of knowledge that is needed to establish an appropriate recruitment policy towards that job, or to apply a recruitment practice. Local HRM practitioners, whether operating in a domestic or an international organisation, have to understand the law as it affects:

- the use of employment exchanges and job centres

- outplacement

- temporary work

- fixed-term contracts

- hours of work
- time off work
- termination of employment
- unfair dismissal
- redundancy
- maternity leave
- discrimination and equal opportunities
- health and safety
- recruitment codes of practice
- the use of psychological testing, and
- the disclosure of information.

A core part of the role is of course that specialists also have to understand the nature or source of the law in any particular country, which ranges from codified legislation, constitutional rights, national or sectoral collective agreements, to codes of best practice that have set precedents in labour courts.

REFLECTIVE ACTIVITY

Even the wording above implies that there is legal coverage of all these issues around the world, which is not the case everywhere.

- Are these terms especially meaningful to all international managers?
- If they are meaningful in your context but not in someone else's, how would you try to broach the issues with that someone else?

Sparrow (2007) pointed out that the challenges for HRM business partners (another concept that can mean different things from one country to another!) in handling recruitment for an international organisation vary in each country, but a common need is the question of how to ensure rigour and consistency across operations in very different cultures, business markets and labour markets. The whole HRM team has to devise frameworks that can be applied in the countries in which the organisation already has a presence, but also has to be aware of the countries into which the organisation *may* enter. The business model often makes it easier to be forewarned about this.

Recruitment is more complex as organisations internationalise.

THEORY AND PRACTICE

KEY FRAMEWORK

The recruitment challenge in setting up new international operations

Typically, in establishing new country operations the organisation has to:

- set up the legal entities to transfer employees
- decide what is the best mix of local recruitment
- investigate how local job centres should be used and local networks be built
- assess what regionalised funding might be available from governments
- understand the implications and ramifications of general employment law
- understand specific legal frameworks (as they apply to issues such as payroll details, salary and reward factors such as contractual benefits or the value of extra work hours, contractual agreement compliance, disciplinary arrangements) both in the country and in the operation of specific sectors in that country.

REFLECTIVE ACTIVITY

Select a country of your choice and investigate the main elements of employment law in that country in terms of how they affect recruitment.

- Which aspects of legislation do you find most surprising or might be seen as challenging to your organisation?

There are four specific areas of country difference that international HR managers must be aware of:

- the type of *labour legislation* – which varies from one country to another in terms of scope, whether it conveys an employer or employee bias, and the recency of codification, and attention therefore to particular areas of deficiency in the behaviour of individuals, organisations and institutions
- the type of *labour market* – which may be internal or external, formal or informal, linked to levels of education or not
- the *recruitment sources* usually tapped to attract people
- the *recruitment methods* in practice, such as whether pay is mentioned (eg in France and Japan the public sector is number one choice).

THE SCOPE OF LABOUR LEGISLATION

Governments are involved in the recruitment process, both through the provision of recruitment services and through legislation – mainly concerned with discrimination. In Europe, at least, discrimination against job-seekers for reasons of race, gender, age or legal history, or because they belong to disadvantaged groups in society, is seen as undesirable from a moral, legal and, sometimes, organisational point of view. Other countries may be different. India, for example, has laws to privilege its lower castes; some Arab and Asian states have rules to privilege locals over migrants. In Europe, though, monitoring staffing practices and outcomes to avoid discrimination is crucial for many HR managers.

The scope of labour legislation and associated collective agreements or custom and practice varies markedly. For example, some constitutions convey rights in relation to appointment. In Norway the Employment Act of 1947 specifies that every citizen has the right to make a living. Article 1 of the Italian Constitution defines the country as a democratic republic based on labour in which the employer is the provider of work and the employee the lender of labour.

In France a range of collective agreements at national or industry level shape recruitment practice. For example, in the chemicals sector rehire arrangements give priority to candidates who were ex-employees in the previous six months. The motive is to stop companies rationalising and then rehiring under new terms and conditions. In Germany works councils have to agree to the use of personnel questionnaires, can see personal information on all shortlisted candidates, and can veto an appointment within one week of offer. The motive is to ensure fairness and an absence of nepotism. In Spain high salary indemnity rates have been associated with a shift by organisations towards temporary employment.

CASE STUDIES

THE ROLE OF COLLECTIVE AGREEMENTS IN FRANCE IN SHAPING THE TREATMENT OF OLDER WORKERS IN RECRUITMENT

The European Industrial Relations Observatory reports that the employment rate in France for people aged 55 to 64 years was only 38.9 per cent in 2009 compared with the EU target of 50 per cent for this age group by the end of 2010. New legislation requires all companies employing more than 50 people to be covered by a collective agreement signed by the social partners to boost the employment of older workers, or face a fine. Larger companies (more than 300 employees) have the option of producing an action plan.

Employee rights in France are contained in legislation, conventions and collective agreements. In most EU member states collective agreements are defined in legislation as formal written agreements that regulate working conditions for individual employees. They outline the minimum protections that an employer owes to its employees. Some collective agreements negotiated at national level are automatically applicable to certain commercial and industrial sectors. In other sectors, such agreements are only applicable when agreed to by the employer. Collective agreements cover all workers, whether or not unionised.

The Ministry for Employment and Vocational Training (*Direction générale à l'emploi et à la formation professionnelle*) carried out an initial appraisal of the extent to which collective agreements dealt with the employment of older workers. Faced with a choice between hiring new workers or maintaining the employment of those already in the workforce, companies preferred to keep existing staff. It found that 75 professional sectors have set an overall objective of maintaining the employment rate of older workers – in response to potential increases in the average age of retirement (currently 55 years). Agreements can cover issues such as the development of skills, transmission of knowledge and skills, anticipation of career development, improvement of working conditions and prevention of arduous work, transition between work and retirement, and recruitment of older workers. For example, the ArcelorMittal agreement seeks to ensure that at least 2 per cent of workers are aged 50 years and over and the GDF Suez agreement sets a target for an employment rate of older workers of 12 per cent of the total workforce by 2012.

INTERNAL AND EXTERNAL LABOUR MARKETS

There are also marked differences across countries in terms of labour markets. Germany, Japan, France and Switzerland are noted for a more widespread use of internal labour markets where recruitment tends to be focused on specialised entry points at low levels of the hierarchy, and where promotion is through internal assessment. Internal labour markets are considered to have such benefits as improved morale, commitment and security among employees, more opportunity to assess (and more accurate assessment of) competencies and accrued knowledge, more control over salary levels given lower exposure to market forces, and more specialised HRM skills around dedicated entry points (such as graduate recruitment). The downside, however, can be high levels of political behaviour associated with advancement, informal 'glass ceilings' that go unchallenged, complacency, and structural shocks when major market and technological changes force change in the whole vocational educational and training system and require a significant overhaul of the whole HRM system. The advantages of external labour markets can be the opportunity to bring in new blood as part of culture-change processes, insights into competitor capabilities, and the ability to respond to equal opportunities issues more visibly.

Job mobility is then a complex phenomenon, involving movements between employers (job-to-job mobility), between occupations and steps on the career ladder (occupational mobility), between different types of contracts, and in and out of employment (employment mobility) (Centre for Policy and Business Analysis, 2008). The 2005 Eurobarometer Survey, using a simple measure of current job-to-job mobility (the share of employed persons who have experienced a job change within a certain time-frame) found that the share of employed persons who experienced a change of job during the year 2005 was 8.8 per cent on average in the EU. This was exceeded considerably in the UK, where 22.9 per cent of the employed experienced a change of job during 2005. The shares were also relatively high in Denmark (11.5 per cent), Hungary (11.5 per cent), and Spain (10.6 per cent), and lowest in Cyprus (5.8 per cent), Finland (5.7 per cent), and Greece (5.6 per cent). The share of the respondents who changed employers during the previous 10-year period varied from approximately 34 per cent in Malta to 65 per cent in the UK.

Average job tenure – the amount of time a worker has spent working for the current employer, even if the job within the firm has changed – is another indicator of the stability of employment relationships. There is an inverse relation between average tenure and current mobility. Countries with high levels of current job mobility (eg Denmark, the UK and the Baltic states) tend to be characterised by low average tenure (less than eight years) whereas those with low levels of current mobility such as Greece, Portugal, and Slovenia also have high average job tenure (exceeding 12 years).

The extent and character of job mobility using all three measures of job-to-job, occupational and employment mobility in Europe highlights that levels of job mobility continue to vary significantly between the EU member states (Centre for Policy and Business Analysis, 2008).

RECRUITMENT METHODS

In 2004 Cranet data showed that recruitment agencies were most popular in the UK, Australia and New Zealand, but distinctly unpopular in Germany, Norway, Sweden, and Greece, for example (Brewster *et al,* 2007). Word of mouth, by contrast, was very common in Turkey, Greece and to some extent France, but not a preferred practice in the UK, Germany or the Netherlands. Recruiting direct from chosen educational institutions was more common in countries like Italy and Spain than elsewhere.

The Cranet data for 2010 (see Figure 21) show that an internal labour market is still very dominant in Japan and, perhaps surprisingly, in the USA and the UK. In the latter two countries, traditionally there has been a strong external labour market. The 2010 findings are probably indicative of the recession and the near-collapse in external recruitment in these two labour markets. In Sweden in particular, an external labour market is still fairly much in evidence. As these data show, countries might revert to more traditional patterns once immediate economic factors dissipate, and similarly, new methods may move into common practice. As a reflection of this, note that the use of recruitment agencies remains traditionally high in the UK and the USA, but has now entered the German labour market. They are still uncommon in Japan. The use of company websites is also much higher in the traditionally external labour market countries of the USA and the UK, but are nowhere near as important in Japan. Direct targeting of chosen educational institutions has grown in importance in some countries. In 2004 fewer than one per cent of UK organisations reported using this method, but by 2010 the proportion had grown to 20 per cent.

Recruitment occurs through both informal and formal methods. Informal methods rely on the contacts of existing employees or on people just applying. Because they risk being discriminatory, word-of-mouth recruitment is rarely acceptable in the public sector. In contrast, in the business services sector, word-of-mouth recruitment is common, particularly in those societies rated more collectivist by writers such as Geert Hofstede and Robert House (see

Figure 21 Recruitment practices for managers in six countries

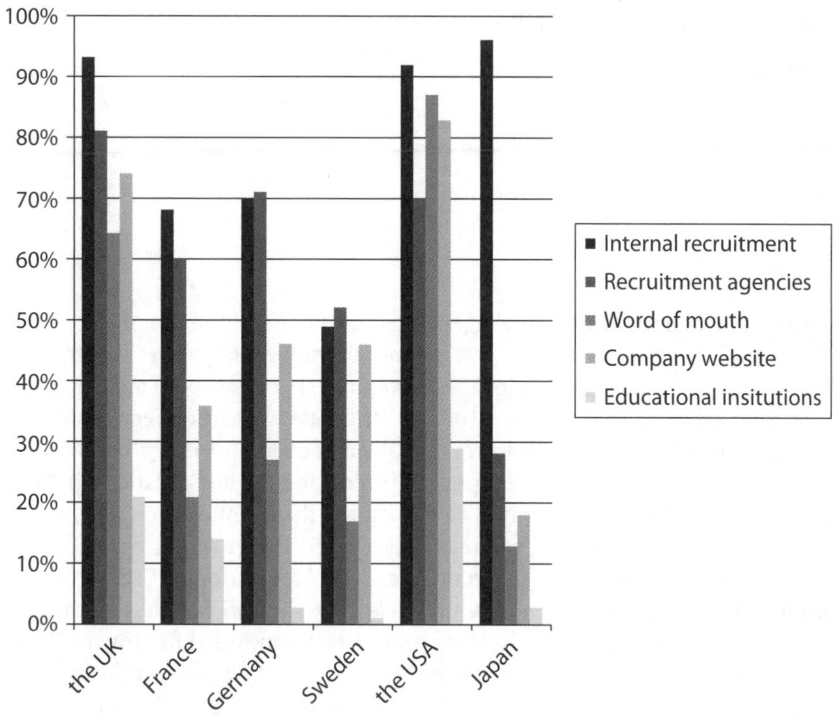

Legend:
- ■ Internal recruitment
- ■ Recruitment agencies
- ■ Word of mouth
- ■ Company website
- ■ Educational insitutions

Source: Cranet (2010)

Chapters 2 and 3). International differences in the use of informal recruitment are substantial but it is widespread throughout the world, especially in poorer countries. Many specialists would defend it. Recruitment of 'family and friends' is very cheap, it aids a sense of community in the workplace, and it provides at least the option of informal control ('If you behave like that, you will embarrass your uncles who got you the job...').

CASE STUDIES

HIDDEN DISCRIMINATION? WHAT SURVEY EVIDENCE CAN HIDE

In spite of the fact that there is relatively strict anti-discrimination legislation in the Czech Republic, in order to avoid the legislation many organisations – and reportedly many international organisations – adopt novel practices to work around the issue (Koubek, 2009). It is forbidden to mention any age limits in advertisements, but adverts might be written saying 'The organisation offers interesting work in a young dynamic collective.' A well-known international organisation was found to be selecting 80 per cent of male candidates despite a majority female candidate pool. Another asked candidates about potential membership in a trade union, and another asked women about their family plans stating that the question was linked to their interest in planning for a maternity career programme. Koubek (2009, p149) warns: 'It is necessary to consider all the facts when looking at the survey data. The data alone cannot display fully the reality of recruitment and selection in Czech organisations.'

Formal methods are invariably more expensive than informal ones. We make specific mention here of four methods of recruitment that take on more significance for international HR managers:

- headhunting
- cross-national advertising
- the Internet
- international graduate programmes.

HEADHUNTING

The developed countries are where agency recruitment and the use of 'headhunters' for managerial positions are most common. Executive search is defined as the recruitment of senior executives and specialists with an average annual compensation level of over $100,000. The total worldwide recruitment market (employment services industry) is valued at over US $420 billion and has grown at an average 12 per cent per annum during the last decade. The US recruitment industry derives around 81 per cent of its revenues from placing temporary/contract employees, whereas only around 19 per cent is derived from search and placement recruitment companies. The Association of Executive Search Consultants' (AESC) 2009 Member Outlook Survey showed that despite the economic recession, executive jobs in several sectors continued to grow in 2009, namely in healthcare, government, natural resources and pharmaceuticals/biotech. China had the greatest need for talent in 2009, based on the global average vote (66 per cent), and India was expected to see the second greatest demand for top executives (43 per cent), with eastern Europe set to be the third most talent-hungry market in 2009. Anecdotal evidence indicates that up to 50 per cent of executive searches are now cross-border. The cross-border capability and geographical spread of individual search firms has therefore become critical (Sparrow, 2006c).

CROSS-NATIONAL ADVERTISING

Organisations are looking to Europe and beyond to attract professionals to work in the UK, or to work in locations around the globe. If the costs of getting a recruitment campaign wrong are high in the domestic market, then the potential costs of errors in global campaigns are very high. Trends in advertising vary across sectors. There is a shift away from press advertising into creative alternatives, such as targeted outdoor poster sites – airport lounges, airline magazines, and journey-to-work routes. Many recruitment advertising service providers now operate as part of global networks in order to deliver targeted pan-European or global campaigns (Sparrow, 2006c). Advertising agencies gather a broad spectrum of international intelligence which focuses on the location of the target audience, the kind of market they operate in, sample salaries, recruitment competitors, and whether the job-seeking audience is passive or active. Knowledge of the best recruitment media and national custom and practice are important in order to ensure the 'cultural appropriateness' of a campaign.

CROSS-CULTURAL DIFFERENCES IN JOB ADVERTISING

From an advertising perspective, the most important cross-cultural differences concern:

- the role qualities associated with jobs
- the desired company qualities
- softer cultural issues, such as what ideal brochures should look like and the wording of adverts, whether salaries are mentioned, etc.

National differences in the use of advertising are large. More use is made of newspapers, specialist journals and Internet recruiting in the developed countries; less in the Third World.

INTERNET RECRUITMENT

The Internet offers considerable potential as a source of recruitment for internationally mobile managers, small firms seeking specialist skills, or larger firms wishing to demonstrate their presence. The online recruitment market size is estimated to be US $3 billion globally. It is proving most useful for international graduate recruitment, attracting MBAs and PhD-level candidates, and for specific roles such as marketing and IT staff. A series of electronic recruiting products and services is reshaping the job-finding process. E-recruitment (electronic recruitment) has the potential to reduce the barriers to employment on a global scale. The technology – which might include organisation websites, job-boards and online newspaper job pages or the use of social networking sites – can be used to:

- deal with the applications – email enquiries, emailed application forms/CVs, online completion of application forms
- select candidates – online testing, information-gathering
- enhance an employer brand
- create a personal relationship with the talent pool.

THE ADVANTAGES OF USING THE INTERNET

It allows firms to:

- speed up the recruitment cycle and streamline administration
- make use of IT systems to manage vacancies more effectively and co-ordinate recruitment processes
- help handle high-volume job applications in a consistent way
- widen recruitment sourcing and reduce recruitment costs
- reach a wide pool of applicants by advertising vacancies – on your organisation's website, on job sites, or on social networking sites

- reach a niche pool of applicants and attract applicants on a more specialised skills match (by encouraging applicants to use personal search agent facilities)

- improve on traditional advertising approaches by targeting particular lifestyle or culture-fit groups (such as expatriates or people who consume services similar to the those provided by the host firm)

- make internal vacancies widely known across multiple sites and separate divisions

- provide a brand image of the organisation, reinforcing employer branding and giving an indication of organisation culture

- offer access to vacancies 24 hours a day, seven days a week, thereby reaching a global audience

- provide a cost-effective way to build a talent bank for future vacancies

- provide more tailored information to the post and organisation – eg case histories of the 'day in the life' or a self-assessment questionnaire or quiz to assess fit with the role.

Using the Internet for international recruitment has received a mixed reaction but is slowly emerging as a useful process. Firms have faced a number of problems with web recruitment: many existing service providers do not yet have truly global coverage, and the web is currently not appropriate for all countries. The main impact can be to increase the volume of applicants, and in a time of tight resources within HRM this is not always good news. There are then also problems with using e-recruitment methods:

- Targeting particular populations becomes difficult. For example, in running web pages in Singapore, applications are likely to be received from places such as Malaysia.

- Generating a larger number of applicants from more diverse social groups may lead to a need for extensive screening activities.

- Company image or brand may not be well known in untried markets (see Chapter 16).

- Quality becomes more variable and needs managing.

- It can move firms away from relying on targeted universities.

- Equal opportunities issues might exist, in that most applicants still tend to be male and from a small range of countries.

Nonetheless, the Internet has become the primary port of call for a good proportion of international talent, and so developing this as a viable recruitment channel is important. It is one of the fastest-growing methods of recruitment – especially for senior professionals, technical specialists and managers. Obviously, its use is restricted to those countries and organisations where the Internet is widely used. Indeed, there are some important differences in privacy attitudes related to the use of the web in recruitment across cultures (Harris *et al*, 2003).

INTERNATIONAL GRADUATE PROGRAMMES

Another form of international sourcing is the external recruitment of graduates into international roles. Organisations that have initiated international graduate recruitment programmes tend not to replicate the competencies that they use for experienced managers in these programmes. Instead, they have attempted to understand and manage graduates through the process of developing an international management career. A number of significant problems with international graduate programmes must be planned for:

- It only has a slow impact on the level of internationalisation, acting as a slow-burning fuse.

- Retention rates may be low.

- It can be difficult to encourage receiving units to prepare themselves to be able to manage the new international recruits accordingly.

- Visa issues mean that the cadres have to be managed for a significant period of time.

- Many organisations note that graduates (as is also the case for established managers) are becoming more reluctant to move.

- This reluctance to be mobile is also changing attitudes to compensation, forcing organisations to be more responsive to individual circumstances.

CASE STUDIES

THE RECRUITMENT CHALLENGE AT INTERCONTINENTAL HOTELS CHINA

In recent years InterContinental Hotels, with its many associated brand names such as Crowne Plaza and Holiday Inn, has been expanding rapidly, with a plan to open a new hotel every day from 2009 to 2014. It owns, manages, leases or franchises, through various subsidiaries, almost 4,000 hotels and more than 585,000 rooms in 100 countries and territories (Pollitt, 2009). In China, the InterContinental Hotels workforce is expected to more than double from 26,000 in 2009 to 60,000 people in 2014 as 107 new hotels open in the country. Only half of recent graduates from hotel-related courses in China have moved on to work in hotels and there is a high turnover among new graduates. The company responded in 2006 by launching the InterContinental Hotels Academy, in which it teams up with academic institutions to offer tailored education and on-the-job training. The academy has established 12 centres in six Chinese cities. Each year, around 2,000 people graduate from the academy, all of whom are guaranteed employment at an InterContinental hotel. The company also awards scholarships in the Asia-Pacific region for a master's degree in hospitality management at Comell-Nanyang University.

SELECTION

Organisations can choose from a wide range of selection methods, including references, interviews and tests. Many organisations use not just one but a combination of selection practices.

Figure 22 Selection practices for managers in six countries

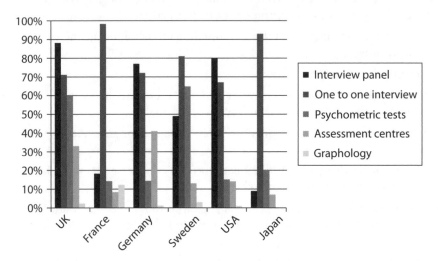

If there is one area in HRM where national differences are very apparent, it is in the area of selection. For example, in 2004 Cranet data showed that the proportion of organisations using assessment centres was 6.4 per cent in the UK, 5.5 per cent in Germany, 3 per cent in the Netherlands, and 2.1 per cent in France. Perhaps reflecting the type of organisations more likely to take part in the international survey, the figures for Italy and Greece were 12.8 per cent and 11.7 per cent respectively. Psychometric tests for clerical positions were very popular in Spain, Italy, Denmark and Finland, but distinctly unpopular in Germany, the Netherlands and Norway (Brewster *et al*, 2007). Data gathered for the Cranet project from 2010 for six key countries are shown in Figure 22. Some key differences in practice can be observed. Interview panels are particularly popular in the UK, the USA and Germany, but are only infrequently used in France and Japan. One-to-one interviews are by far the most frequent practice in those two countries. Psychometric testing is relatively widespread amongst UK and Swedish organisations, but in the USA, France and Japan only between 10 per cent and 20 per cent of organisations use this method. Some selection methods are then common in some countries but may not be used at all in others. Reflecting a long-standing finding, graphology – reading character through handwriting – features as a method only really in France (even here it is only used in around 12 per cent of organisations).

FRENCH VERSUS BRITISH ASSUMPTIONS ABOUT SELECTION

Such variations reflect different assumptions about the nature of selection. In the UK, for example, an empirical predictive model is the norm. Here the assumption is that selection is about the conversion of good-quality information into accurate, reliable and valid prediction of important outcomes. If a selection method has low validity or reliability, it is considered inappropriate. In France, by contrast, selection systems work on a principle of clinical assessment. It is considered that accurate prediction of career success and performance at

the point of entry is either unnecessary (educational achievement at *grandes écoles* might suffice) or improbable. Rather, selection systems should be designed to take out unnecessary risk. An overall clinical assessment of match is possible, but no finite prediction. And so although graphology has almost zero predictive validity, it is considered a cheap source of additional information that just might detect extreme risks. Judging selection systems based on the models implicit within one's own system can be misleading

The most common selection method is through interviews. But other methods have recently begun to attract more attention, such as assessment centres and psychological testing.

INTERVIEWS

In theory interviews should follow a structured format so that each applicant is asked the same questions. Often this is not the case, even though unstructured interviews have low predictive validity (Cook, 1999). There are also national differences in the number of people involved in the interviews and who they are. Thus an HRM specialist would often be one of the interviewers in northern Europe; less commonly so elsewhere. There can be important cross-cultural differences (Sparrow, 2006c). For example, one US MNC, when recruiting managers in Korea, found that interviewers had to be trained in cross-cultural awareness. It is the cultural norm in Korea, when asked a 'good' question, to keep silent as a sign of respect. The better the question, the longer the period of silence the candidate maintains. In US culture, if you ask a good question and are met with silence, you do not attribute the behaviour to respect but to ignorance. Face-to-face interviews can create quite distorted judgements.

ASSESSMENT CENTRES

Because assessment centres are regarded as one of the most robust and valid selection techniques in general, it should be expected that they would be used to assess competence for international managers. We focus on international diffusion of the assessment as a rigorous recruitment, selection and personnel evaluation process, for as Delmestri and Walgenbach (2009) note, it can be considered as belonging to the package of 'high-performance' HRM practices. However, they are not common.

Thornton and Krause (2009) noted that the early adopters of assessment centres were predominantly in North America and the UK, but soon thereafter applications appeared in German-speaking countries, Japan, and South Africa. Practices were extremely mixed, and although national patterns were not analysed, the study showed the increased localisation of assessment centre design. Data on the percentage of national firms adopting the practice may therefore hide many differences. The assessment centre method is seen as highly 'plastic' – ie it can be moulded and shaped in different ways, with such variations in the method as the dimensions specified (job requirements), types of exercises, numbers and types of assessors, methods of observing and recording observations, methods of integration of evaluations across assessors, dimensions, and exercises, and methods of feedback. Assessment centres may also be used for selection or promotion (evaluation, judgement or prediction), or mainly for developmental purposes (diagnosis, development or training).

Delmestri and Walgenbach's (2009) study demonstrates this opportunity for high or low local embeddedness of this selection technique. They examined the adoption of assessment centres in 161 MNCs from five countries – France, Germany, Italy, the UK and the USA – both in their HQ and in their Italian subsidiaries. Their study showed that diffusion of assessment centres followed a similar pattern at HQ level in all national contexts. This demonstrated the importance of transnational institutions of Anglo-American origin for MNCs of any nationality. However, there was considerable local variation in the degree of institutionalisation of assessment centres. This ranged from fully fledged support in culture and the professions being assessed in Germany, the UK and the USA, to weak or negative backing in France and Italy. The adoption of the technique in their subsidiaries in Italy was explained by different characteristics of the corporate field of firms with headquarters in different countries, as well as organisational size and labour market conditions.

Even where assessment centres are used to select managers in international settings, the key to cross-cultural assessment centres clearly seems to be to design the assessment process so that it is very adaptable to the local environment in which it will be operated (Sparrow, 2006c). For example, differences in the labour market often mean that the assumptions made about candidate behaviour in the UK do not translate well abroad. The need for adaptability argues against having overly structured exercises, and most structured tools (such as situational interviews and work simulations) have to be modified. Interviews are easy to adapt, but assessors also have to build as many anchors into the local marketplace as possible in order to give the assessment process meaning. This involves a series of steps, from the simple renaming of case studies and scenarios through to the adoption of local norms for psychometric instruments, and beyond.

PSYCHOLOGICAL TESTING

The validity of some psychometric testing methods is also disputed. Psychologists claim that the variability of validity across settings for the same type of job and across different kinds of jobs is small (Schmidt and Hunter, 1998). Nevertheless, some variation is observed, and in particular there are concerns for organisations operating internationally about the cross-cultural transferability of many psychometric tests. Of course, only a small minority of organisations in any country use psychometric testing, and the proportion of organisations that use assessment centres is even smaller. International HR managers are increasingly becoming aware of cross-cultural assessment issues (Van de Vijver, 2002; p545):

> Psychological assessment increasingly involves the application of tests in different cultural contexts, either in a single country (involving migrants) or in different countries … In the near future the demand for cross-cultural assessment will increase, due to the growing internationalisation of business and the increasing need of migrant groups for culture-informed psychological services.

Developing culture-free, culture-fair and more recently culture-reduced instruments has long been a goal for psychologists. Where it is accepted that existing instruments are invalid, unreliable or do not cover the construct they are intended for when used in a different cultural setting, developing culture-specific variations becomes an alternative. This can be costly – so is it necessary, and is it cost-effective? Does adaptation add sufficient incremental value to the bad but common practice of straightforward applications of existing tests and their norms? The answer to the first part of this question involves more than immediate concerns about fairness and discrimination.

 REFLECTIVE ACTIVITY

Sparrow (2006c) raises the following questions. In the light of increases in the use of assessment:

- Can organisations use psychological tests fairly in multi-cultural settings?
- Do the psychometric properties of tests translate to different cultural groups?
- Can 'culture-free', 'culture-fair' or 'culture-reduced' tests be developed?
- Or if tests do not translate from one culture to another, can new instruments be developed?

The use of psychological tests has become an increasing problem in the international selection field. In the pursuit of the global manager, organisations have to look outside their normal recruitment territory in order to benchmark interview candidates. Because they are aware that interviews or behaviour-based work simulations are subject to culturally different behaviours, from both the candidates and the assessor, international HR managers might be tempted to use more testing. On the surface, psychological tests may be seen as a way of avoiding the subjective bias of other options. Indeed, greater international mobility of candidates has increased the demand for tests to be used on job applicants from a number of different countries, and most test producers now sell their products internationally.

The costs of cultural bias in psychological tests do not lie in reduced performance of the candidates. They lie in the perceived stupidity of the assessment process and the impact on motivation (Sparrow, 2006c). There is also the problem of fairness. Candidates to whom inappropriate testing has been applied can find that they do not progress as well through internal selection systems. Such discrimination is equally inappropriate. Countries also differ greatly in terms of the practices related to user qualification, legal and statutory constraints on test use and the consequences for those tested, and controls exercised over the use of tests.

REFLECTIVE ACTIVITY

There are no simple answers to the issues posed by the use of testing cross-national samples. International HR managers face several practical dilemmas. How should the following questions be considered in an organisation?

- If a French manager is coming to work in the UK, is it appropriate to test the manager against the French or the UK test norm group?
- If you test the manager in the English language, is he or she disadvantaged?
- If international HR managers insist on using standardised tools such as psychological tests, does the degree of confidence in their accuracy have to be tempered?
- Can HR managers make up for this by putting more emphasis on the feedback process?

PUTTING RECRUITMENT AND SELECTION INTO CULTURAL CONTEXT

In this section we explain the ways in which culture weaves its influence on recruitment and selection practices. We devote considerable attention to culture here, therefore, but point out that these principles can be applied to the other functional areas covered in the book such as reward, training, rewards, flexibility and communication.

Interest in the role that culture plays in recruitment – and in people's attraction to and retention in organisations – traditionally stemmed from two territories: the existence of a growing number of multinational corporations headquartered in a wider range of geographies, and the internationalisation, or ethnic diversification, of many domestic workforces. For example, US Census Bureau data shows that over 33 per cent of the US population is made of minority group members, with the majority of both future population growth and immigration coming from non-European countries (Stone *et al*, 2008).

Generic recruitment models (Rynes, 1991) assume that a number of factors affect an applicant's motivation to apply for jobs and their subsequent job choice –

including recruiters, recruitment sources, and administrative or HRM practices. Based on assumptions from expectancy theory, these factors influence:

- the belief that action will lead to a successful outcome (expectancy)
- the belief that success will bring rewards (instrumentality), and
- the desirability of these rewards (valence).

These three elements of attitude affect pre-hire outcomes – such as the attractiveness of the job or organisation, the choice intentions, the attractiveness of the recruiter and the level of job pursuit. They also affect post-hire outcomes such as levels of satisfaction, commitment, and turnover.

The theory of planned behaviour (Ajzen, 1985) argues that the most important antecedents of the behaviour of job applicants are their intentions to apply for a job, and these in turn are a function of: the attitudes they hold toward jobs, the norms or beliefs of the people they refer to, and the control or otherwise they perceive that they have over the application process.

It immediately becomes clear how either cultural or institutional factors shape both individual behaviour and the (potential) effectiveness of otherwise of specific HRM practices in the area of recruitment. A number of studies have looked at international differences in selection practices and the role of national culture in explaining such differences in desirability and usage (Ryan *et al*, 2003). Huo *et al* (2002) examined data from 13 countries to establish if significant differences existed between nations in terms of commonly-used hiring practices. Ryan *et al* (1999) surveyed 959 organisations from 20 countries to assess whether differences in staffing practices are due to international differences in some of the institutional factors (for example, legislation, labour market factors) or to national cultural values. They found that 11 per cent of variation in the number of verification methods could be linked to scores on uncertainty avoidance and five per cent to scores on power distance. They concluded (Ryan *et al*, 1999; p385) that:

> National differences accounted for considerable variance in selection practices. This suggests that those attempting to implement standardised worldwide selection practices may face difficulties beyond the known problems of establishing translation equivalence of test and interview materials … The identification of staffing practices that 'travel well' is needed … Practices with universal appeal may be easier starting points for those pursuing global selection strategies, but these may not be the 'best practices'. We need to enhance our understanding of the many practical issues associated with global selection systems.

Differences across cultures in terms of factors such as perceptions of fairness (procedural justice) have been linked to the attractiveness or not of specific features of selection systems (Steiner and Gilliland, 2001).

In general, most selection systems give attention to the technical requirements of the job, the person's potential to do a good job and interpersonal qualities. However, the belief that there is a clear link between recruitment practices and organisational effectiveness clearly differs across countries when recruitment cultures are analysed. Within Europe, the Anglo-Saxon tradition is based on concepts of predictive validity, underpinned by the belief that variance in employee performance is sufficiently explainable by individual factors (knowledge, skills, abilities and other factors) to enable a cost-benefit and utility analysis of investments in sophisticated HRM process on the one hand, and returns through employee performance (on the basis of person-job or person-organisation fit) on the other. For Australian organisations, attention is given to the fit between the person and the organisation's values and ways of doing things. This is an assumption common to most Anglo-Saxon countries, and if assessments of competency are made, it is considered legitimate to ask about a person's values (Patrickson and Sutiyono, 2006). Anglo-Saxon countries – and their MNCs – might consider that an individual's alignment to the organisation's values (rather than their qualifications or technical capability) is an important part of the selection mix. The management competency approach has been popular in Anglo-Saxon countries, and the behavioural event investigation techniques that it relies upon identify skills, traits, attitudes and values, knowledge and social roles, motivations and management style as potential competency criteria. Many organisations use the expression 'Live the values.'

Yet in contrast, French traditions mean that an examination of an individual's personal values are not considered appropriate to a selection context. You want to know what *my* [private and in personal space] values are? What are my values to do with *you* [my employer, for whom I provide labour and appropriate service]? In any event, apart from showing me that if *I* share *your* values so that it will make life *easier* for you as my manager, what is your evidence that shared values produce *superior performance* (considered long-term, across complex changes in business models and environments)? Difficult questions for an HRM business partner to answer! French attitudes towards selection, then, are driven by the view that the prediction of performance is not really sufficiently achievable; others factors intervene over a career and therefore decisions must be influenced by robust processes that enable an assessment of risk rather than processes built on assumptions of predicted outcomes – hence the tendency towards (Sparrow and Hiltrop, 1994; p353):

> A more intuitive, interpretative and clinical model [that encourages] wider use of personality questionnaires, multiple one-to-one interviews and graphology. [However,] if the international mobility of managers does increase, then the 'cultural fingerprint' of national selection systems will be more widely felt.

There has been a pan-European trend towards the 'democratisation' of recruitment and selection common to countries such as the UK, Netherlands, Sweden and Germany, with greater emphasis on the perceptions, attitudes, reactions and rights of the applicant, and common emphasis on the introduction of more interactive procedures, constructive feedback, self-selection and realistic job previews. In some cases (in universities, for instance) this now extends to the involvement of potential workmates in the selection decision. For example, in the UK, recent legislation on freedom of information means that candidates can apply to see the written notes made about individuals by the interview panel, or the references provided in a promotion process. The attention to due diligence in recruitment processes and shifts in recruitment culture from this are clear to see. There has also been convergence in social legislation around forms of discrimination and employment rights which has created new influences on the nature of recruitment and selection. Nonetheless, the 'cultural fingerprint' was evident in the direct impact of certain cultural values on the preference for specific tools and techniques. Uncertainty avoidance has been linked to the use of the number of interviews involved in a process.

Values have a deeper relationship than this, though. For example, in Latin America, US principles of recruitment based on objective merit, qualification and equality cannot be applied to the way that employees might evaluate a recruitment and selection process. In countries such as Mexico or Peru, the notion of all men being equal does not hold and reality is not based on perceptions of objectivity but also 'interpersonality', for want of a better word. What is important is *who* the person is, and that perception of who they are is not just job-related but also reflective of social class and family ties. These values influence the way that managers think about justice and the impact they perceive justice has on employee commitment (Gomez and Sanchez, 2005; p67):

> In the United States, ensuring that fair procedures are in place is essential to gain employee commitment; in Mexico, it is more important to ensure that the treatment of the employee is of a 'high-contact', personalised nature.

Having the right personal connections at the top is an important factor in hiring (Huo *et al*, 2002), but while an MNC's strategic mandate might include objective mechanisms for assessing candidate qualifications (Gomez and Sanchez, 2005; pp68–69):

> Current employees may, through their relationships, provide a more culturally adept assessment of the true qualifications of an applicant ... US MNCs should consider potential candidates who enjoy 'in-group' ties, albeit indirect ones, with current employees. Such ties would help build social capital, but additionally, considering these candidates shows that the MNC looks after the employee's in-group, which hopefully will be expanded to include the organisation in its entirety.

Most selection research fundamentally concerns the question of person-environment (P-E) fit.

THEORY AND PRACTICE

KEY FRAMEWORK

Institutional arrangements that surround recruitment and selection

The institutional arrangements surrounding recruitment and selection practice can seek to create two sorts of fit:

- *Supplementary fit*: when an individual possesses characteristics that are similar to other individuals in the environment, and so embellishes the fit.

- *Complementary fit*: when a person's characteristics add what is lacking in an environment, or make it whole – either the individual supplies things that are in demand, or the environment supplies things that the individual needs.

The fit might just be perceived, or may be actual, as shown by some hard evidence. Based on theories of attraction–selection–attrition, the assumption is that a high level of fit leads to more positive individual and organisational outcomes. However, the fit might operate at different levels, notably person-organisation (P-O) fit, person-group (P-G) fit, person-job (P-J) fit in terms of knowledge, skills and abilties, person-vocation (P-V) fit or person-person (P-P) fit (Van Vianen, 2000).

REGIONAL CHALLENGES

In addition to cultural and institutional factors, each major region of the world may be considered to have specific challenges and issues with regard to recruitment and selection. For example, in Central and Eastern Europe (CEE) three major regional challenges are: the level of investment in human resources (which as a line management decision is generally lower in CEE than in Western Europe); higher levels of job insecurity; and the retention of young skilled employees in whom investments have been made (there are high levels of job-hopping within the high-potential population). A number of companies also find that there are 'very few people in CEE with the potential to become executives in other world markets … since both their talent and potential for growth may be below those of their Western European counterparts' (Vaiman and Holden, 2011; p188) – even in 'a huge company with highly standardised HRM procedures from recruitment to personnel development', local candidates are often not as rigorously screened and TM policies can be based on 'the immediate business needs'.

The recruitment and retention of talent in India has received much popular attention (Doh *et al*, 2008; Grant, 2008). The number of employees working in the Indian software industry increased from 242,000 to 697,000 between 2002 and 2004 alone – making staffing a very time-consuming process. On average, large companies recruit about 10,000 entry-level engineers annually, using several tests (assessing logical, analytical, and communication skills), with interviews before the final applicants are chosen, around 80 per cent of the time of an Indian HRM professional being spent on recruitment and selection (Ghosh and Geetika, 2007).

CASE STUDIES

RECRUITMENT IN THE INDIAN SOFTWARE INDUSTRY

Organisations rely on the judgements of line managers to predict future staffing requirements. Entry-level employees need intense training or a 'finishing school' to integrate them into corporate life, with 12 weeks of work-related training offered. Because the Indian educational system is perceived not to prepare graduates for business skills sufficiently, organisations have to provide a 'surrogate educational' system (Wadhwa, 2008). Job-hopping is very common, and in good economic times potential applicants usually have two to three job offers. Indian employees are also very brand-conscious and prefer to work for organisations that are well-known, so employer branding becomes an integral part of the recruitment strategy. In a study of recruitment of IT specialists in India, Rao (2010) found that employee referrals, succession

planning and internal recruitment were the predominant internal recruitment methods used. Applicants that are referred by current employees demonstrate a better person-organisation and person-job fit largely because current employees provide realistic job previews. The US-owned Indian firms also used e-recruitment and professional search agencies to identify senior and middle-management talent, but the Indian software companies did not rely on these external methods. Personality tests, behavioural interviews, and résumés were some of the predominant external hiring methods. Local staffing practices such as succession planning, employee referrals and internal recruitment of the software firms were attributed to the high-collectivist orientation of the Indian national culture.

In an Asia-Pacific context, institutional arrangements reflecting the relationship between the state and organisations becomes more important. For the *chaebols* in South Korea, seen as prestige employers, the culture is one of mass recruitment of graduates. Recruitment takes place biannually with a preference given to management trainee candidates from the elite universities (Rowley and Bae, 2004). Assessment is thus really made at point of entry into the education system rather than at point of entry into the organisation (which is not unlike the situation in France). However, after the Asian crisis of the late 1990s and the rationalisation and recruitment freezes, slowly there has been a move to more recruitment-on-demand practices and more flexible adjustments to labour demands.

In China, deregulation has led to a shift away from the practice of assigning employees to employers, and a greater reliance on the external labour market. Mass rural migration, the downsizing of state-owned enterprises and unemployment have helped fuel negative attitudes to the employment of women, who used to represent 40 per cent of the workforce. New regulations in recruitment are therefore aimed at removing gender discrimination (Cooke, 2001). As noted earlier in the chapter, it is still common practice for job adverts to specify gender and to place age limits, making both direct and indirect discrimination likely (Woodhams *et al,* 2009). However, in China, the greatest concern is not the potential for discrimination but the sheer scale of the talent management challenge.

 CHINESE TALENT MANAGEMENT CHALLENGE

CASE STUDIES

In 2009 China attracted US $108 billion of foreign direct investment. After several years of investment, more than 60 MNCs had relocated or established their Asia-Pacific regional headquarters in China, moving high value-added business activities such as global or regional R&D and logistics to China alongside the traditional offshore manufacturing plants and local sales activities. At the same time local Chinese firms such as Lenovo, Haier, Huawei, ZTE and TCI are pursuing rapid growth in global markets and state-owned enterprises are being restructured (Hou, 2010).

The gap between the requirements of the Chinese education system and corporate requirements (and, one could argue, the attractiveness of high-growth local careers) had created a situation where only one in 10 Chinese university graduates was prepared to work for MNCs. China Europe International Business School surveys of the CEOs of foreign MNCs operating in China showed that talent management was a more significant challenge even than business model innovation, subsidiary-HQ relationships and supply chain management.

In other Asian contexts, such as Malaysia, ethnicity is important, with positive discrimination efforts to create a Malay business class and promote employment of *bumiputras* (ethnic Malays and other native races) in return for the maintenance of a market-based business system favoured by overseas Chinese employers (Mellahi and Wood, 2006). The Islamic work ethic also shapes the sorts of competencies considered important in Malaysia.

THREE TYPES OF LABOUR MARKET

In the Middle East, the World Bank classified labour markets into three categories (Ali, 2011) based on the degree of availability of natural resources (mainly oil) and labour abundance:

- *Resource-poor, labour-abundant*: Djibouti, Egypt, Jordan, Lebanon, Morocco. Tunisia, West Bank and Gaza. Egypt, Lebanon and West Bank have traditionally provided the Arab Gulf with its labour.

- *Resource-rich, labour-abundant*: Algeria, Iraq, Iran, Syria and Yemen. These act as a source of skilled labour.

- *Resource-rich, labour-importing*: Bahrain, Kuwait, Libya, Oman, Qatar, Saudi Arabia and the

UAE. These act as importers of labour ranging from house servants to engineers, with the percentage of expatriates ranging from 79 per cent to 90 per cent in the UAE.

Recruitment and hiring practices are also subject to religious and government guidelines. The moral drive in Islam is not to recruit on the basis of favouritism or nepotism (Ali, 1999) but rather on the basis of experience and decency. However, the way in which these latter two qualities may be judged is still, in Western-eyes, very socially dependent. In Kuwait, for example (Ali and Al-Kazemi, 2006; pp89–90):

> Most of the hiring and promotion ... especially in the government sector, is influenced highly by social connectivity, tribal identity, and political and sectarian allegiance ... Social dignitaries, influential individuals and politicians normally interfere in the recruitment, retention and promotion process ... Like in most societies in the Middle East, it is often difficult to get things done without *wasta* – personal intervention of influential people on behalf of a particular person.

These factors combine to limit the role, function and independence of the HRM function. There are social currents arguing for a greater influence of performance and positive participation surrounding recruitment processes (Al-Enzi, 2002). In Algeria, the process of recruitment and selection is a bureaucratic and administrative formality, and friendship and kinship can take precedence over qualifications. The use of *piston* to get jobs (enhanced social prestige and influence resulting from support of administrative personnel recruited from relatives and friends) is still evidenced (Branine, 2006).

CASE STUDIES

TALENT MANAGEMENT, LOCAL EMPLOYMENT SUPPORT MEASURES, NATIONALISATION, POSITIVE DISCRIMINATION OR QUOTAS?

Many Middle Eastern states have been heavily reliant on expatriate workers both for advanced technical and professional expertise and for manual labour. One of the main socio-economic issues in the region is the need to increase national employment in the private sector (Harry, 2007) and to attend to the development and fulfilment of local talent. Effective localisation has only occurred when a local national can fill a required job sufficiently competently to fulfil organisational needs.

In 2000, Dubai, and the United Arab Emirates (UAE), attempted to increase the participation of locals in the workforce under a policy known as 'Emiratisation'. It was aimed at creating job opportunities for the UAE national workforce, reducing the unemployment ratio, and enhancing the skills and productivity of the national workforce (Al-Ali, 2008). Similar policies elsewhere in the Middle East have included Omanisation (Al-Hamadi *et al*, 2007; Aycan *et al*, 2007) and Saudisation, (Mashood *et al*, 2009).

The UAE government has constantly updated its Emiratisation policies (Rees *et al*, 2007). Pressure grew for co-ordination with local governments to step up measures to deny firms not complying with the prescribed Emiratisation quotas the right to obtain work permits and entry visas for foreign labour. In September 2007, the government 'stepped up the enforcement of existing rules, cutting fees for companies that complied and freezing all relations with the Labour Ministry with those that did not' – a painful deterrent, since it is illegal to bring new expatriate workers into the country without government approval. One of the key policies in Emiratisation is the quota system. Under a change in the labour law in 2007, the Labour Department had the right and duty to check quotas when conducting inspections of workplaces. Companies with more than 100 employees were told that they should employ only Emiratis in their human resource department, and move towards implementing the same rule for secretarial roles. At the same time a YouGov Siraj study of UAE residents monitoring the schemes found that 46 per cent reported that there were not enough trained or skilled Emiratis

to hire. Over 50 per cent did not believe that Emiratis' education levels prepared them well for employment, while 33 per cent said they viewed Emirati job applicants as either 'slightly below average' or 'well below average' compared to other nationalities. In addition it was believed that amongst Emirati employees there is an unwillingness to work long hours and a reluctance to engage with the team.

By 2009 the abundance of cheap expatriates from other emerging economies was making nationalisation schemes uneconomical. The national employment scheme was perceived as a burden that MNCs had to put up with – a hidden tax – rather than as a way of building up their host countries. Many companies often ended up hiring 'ghost employees' whose actual job was completed by a foreign worker. Yet by 2011, after the experience of the global economic downturn triggered by the credit crunch, a shift was again taking place, towards offering subsidies to companies to encourage them to hire Emiratis and to help private companies hire, train and retain Emirati staff.

REFLECTIVE ACTIVITY

Do such initiatives represent sensible strategic talent management and local employment support measures, nationalisation, attempts at positive discrimination ... or misguided management by quotas?

GLOBAL PRESSURES ON DOMESTIC RECRUITMENT

REFLECTIVE ACTIVITY

The previous section has noted some of the national practice and current developments in recruitment and hiring. However, does this matter for MNCs operating in those labour markets? Construct two arguments. First, list the arguments and suggest the ways in which local labour market practice will influence a local recruitment process conducted by an MNC. Second, outline the ways in which an MNC might be able to bypass some of these influences while still seeking local talent. Then, imagine you are an in-country HRM business partner and write a memo to your HRM director explaining your chosen strategy, mixing and matching your reasoning on both sides of the argument if necessary!

We have focused throughout this chapter on the comparative examination of recruitment and selection practices, later on noting some of the most notable regional challenges that are discussed. However, the recruitment and selection function inside many organisations has experienced particularly rapid global exposure. The need to recruit internationally develops very rapidly, but once established, the operations associated with new international recruitment channels can be very volatile and may be scaled down again, restructured or even disposed of within a fairly short period of time (Sparrow, 2007).

 REFLECTIVE ACTIVITY

In what ways might the following developments change the task faced by an international recruitment function?

● Global business process redesign and the global redistribution and relocation of work

● The merging of existing operations on a global scale and attempts to develop and harmonise core HRM processes within these merged businesses

● The rapid start-up of international operations and the need to manage the development of these operations as they mature through different stages of the business life cycle.

Organisations have to understand the labour markets, local, national or international, within which they recruit. Planning in tight labour markets, where there may be a shortage of key skills, is a different proposition from planning in markets where appropriately skilled labour is abundant. Shedding staff in countries such as many of those in Europe, where labour laws make that more expensive, is different from reducing numbers in some of the poorer countries of the world or in the USA, where there are few associated costs.

Labour costs in some countries are significantly higher than those in others, opening up the option of MNCs moving their production or, increasingly, their provision of services to the cheaper country. This is what has been called the international division of labour. This works where the costs of transporting goods back to the markets does not overwhelm the savings made by relocation, or where the service (telephone-answering or IT-working, to take common examples) can be provided from anywhere. It remains highly contentious.

For example, there have been long-standing concerns, generally expressed by unions, that jobs are being exported to cheap-labour countries. An associated concern is that employees are 'injecting' short-term skills into UK operations by hiring cheaper immigrants. Employers argue that ensuring sufficient skills levels and capability in a domestic market facilitates growth in that market, producing local benefits. This also serves their internal motivations, usually driven by a combination of the need for revenue growth and the need to reduce internal costs. Employers argue that barriers to the movement of expertise need to be removed so that they can access and deploy skills more flexibly across internal, but also international, labour markets. They have many strategies at their disposal that can address skills shortages in any one national labour market, including the use of technology to assist remote working, alterations to business process and work standardisation, the development of centres of excellence that can then be used to disseminate organisational learning throughout operations, and offshore outsourcing. There are also institutional pressures supporting flexible skills migration with, for example, the General Agreement on Trade in Services Mode 4 encouraging governments to liberalise the supply of services via temporary movement of people across borders.

KEY LEARNING POINTS

- Many differences in recruitment and selection systems occur within countries and a key to these differences is national cultures and institutions.

- When organisations plan their staffing needs, they do so within the context of a particular labour market.

- What they spend on recruitment and selection is affected by national laws and tax regimes.

- Organisations employ people within particular cultures and under particular laws and institutional arrangements.

- In addition to cultural and institutional factors, each major region of the world may be considered to have specific challenges and issues with regard to recruitment and selection.

- Organisations have to remain aware of these differences when they determine their HRM policies and practices.

- Notions of good practice in HRM differ from country to country.

- As organisations internationalise, it is often their recruitment and selection systems that are the first to have to cope with this new context.

- In some sectors, the labour markets themselves are becoming more global, and this is creating both new resourcing strategies and also a need for many domestic organisations to become skilled in overseas recruitment.

- International graduate programmes are no 'quick fix' for organisations that need to increase their supply of international recruits.

- In order to be successful, cross-national advertising requires an awareness of the cultural appropriateness of the techniques and media used.

- The e-enablement of recruitment is altering the economics of the international selection process.

- Assessment centres can prove an effective tool for international resourcing, but they require careful modification for an international setting.

- There has been an increase in cross-cultural assessment based on psychological testing.

LEARNING QUESTIONS

1 What are the main cross-national differences in the nature of recruitment and selection systems?

2 How would you characterise the underlying philosophy that British HR professionals have towards selection compared with French HR professionals? Is this evidenced in a different take-up of particular selection tools and techniques?

3 What are the main technical challenges faced by firms that wish to internationalise their selection and assessment approaches?

4 What are the main issues facing organisations as labour markets become more global?

5 What are the different resourcing strategies open to organisations as they operate in these global labour markets?

EXPLORE FURTHER

Sparrow, P. R. (2006) *International Recruitment, Selection And Assessment,* London, Chartered Institute of Personnel and Development. This research report for the CIPD explores the literature and examples of practice in the area of international recruitment, selection and assessment.

Ryan, A. M., McFarland, L., Baron, H. and Page, R. (1999) 'An international look at selection practices: nation and culture as explanations for variability in practice', *Personnel Psychology*, 52: 359–391.

Sparrow, P. R. (2007) 'Globalisation of HR at function level: four case studies of the international recruitment,

selection and assessment process', *International Journal of Human Resource Management,* 18 (5): 144–166.

Steiner, D. D. and Gilliland, S. W. (2001) 'Procedural justice in personnel selection: international and cross-cultural perspectives', *International Journal of Selection and Assessment*, 9 (1/2): 124–137.

Thornton, G. C. and Krause, D. E. (2009) 'Selection versus development assessment centers: an international survey of design, execution, and evaluation', *International Journal of Human Resource Management,* 20 (2): 478–498.

CHAPTER 9

Performance Management

LEARNING OUTCOMES

When they have read this chapter, students will:

- understand the background to performance management and its Western origins

- appreciate the component elements of performance management systems typically found within organisations

- be aware of the impact of culture and context on performance management

- be able to explain the links between performance management and other elements of the HRM architecture within an organisation

- be able to advise on the possible pitfalls of seeking to apply a 'one size fits all' approach to performance management without due regard for context and culture.

INTRODUCTION

Although commentators such as Smith and Goddard (2002) and Thorpe and Holloway (2008) have emphasised the multi-disciplinary nature of the emerging field of managing performance, in this chapter we are concerned with the processes that would be recognised by most larger Western HRM departments as the (usually yearly) cycle that has its origins in performance appraisal mechanisms, but is now often depicted as having 'grown up' beyond that to become performance management (Smith and Goddard, 2002; p253):

> The literature on performance management is eclectic, diffuse and confused. The definitive 'general theory' of performance management remains elusive, and is unlikely ever to emerge. Important contributions can be found in fields as diverse as strategy, organisational behaviour, operations management, industrial economics and accountancy.

Sparrow and Hiltrop (1994) suggest that performance management is one of the key areas of HRM policy and practice necessary to implement successful global HRM, because it is the HRM sub-system that links corporate goals with rewards, improvement of performance and employee development.

Within a book on IHRM, performance management is particularly worthy of consideration given its US origins and often contentious nature. As Heskett (2006) notes:

> It's the season for many employee performance reviews. Why do they seem to rank alongside root canal dental work on our list of things we look forward to as managers and employees? And what are we doing about it?

Even in the USA, the country where performance management has its origins and may be expected to have the best 'cultural fit', a consulting firm survey suggests that most employees do not believe their company's performance management programme actually improves performance.

WIDESPREAD BUT NOT TRUSTED?

Approximately 90 per cent of the surveyed employees reported being involved in a performance management program, but only 30 per cent of employees are convinced that the process helped them improve their performance. Less than 40 per cent of employees say the system establishes clear performance goals, generates honest feedback or capitalises on technology to streamline performance management processes. And only 39 per cent understand how their job fits in with the company's overall goals.

Source: WorkUSA®, 2004

Researchers have developed various perspectives for studying performance. These include the individual differences perspective (cognitive ability, motivation and personality, etc) and the situational perspective, which focuses on facilitators and impediments for performance and might include extrinsic rewards. The third perspective has been identified as the performance regulation one, which deals with the performance process (Sonnentag and Frese, 2002).

In order to present a comparative account of the performance management process, this chapter begins with definitions of appraisal and performance management and a brief account of its history and origins. It then describes how performance management is typically 'manifested' and the composite elements of planning performance, managing performance and reviewing performance that make up the performance cycle within organisations. Although it is difficult to avoid making reference to rewarding performance, the main reward discussion can be found in the following chapter. Having discussed definitions and background, the chapter then considers performance management in the light of the comparative literature in order to highlight the challenges of managing performance in different contexts and, in particular, the impact of national culture on shaping practice. Recent Cranet data is used to illustrate how practice and level of adoption varies across countries.

As Chapter 4 on institutions suggests, there is evidence of isomorphism, especially perhaps mimetic isomorphism (DiMaggio and Powell, 1983), with respect to the adoption of performance management systems as organisations have copied the practices of others in pursuit of what they hope will be 'best practice'. Large MNCs in Europe particularly seem to be taking the example of the Anglo-Saxon world (Barzantny and Festing, 2008). However, as Fletcher (2001) has stated, the context is important in order to understand performance management in different environments. This chapter seeks both to describe the common 'core' that sits at the heart of 'typical' performance management practice, and also to provide illustrations showing where the implementation of 'typical' approaches is likely to be problematic. Wherever possible the chapter seeks to link more theoretical content to practical examples and reflective activities.

REFLECTIVE ACTIVITY

Spend a few moments reflecting on what performance management means to you – jot down your thoughts.

- What are the organisational practices you associate with it?

- If you have work experience, how have you seen it being carried out?

- What is your emotional reaction to the term 'performance management'?

Consider your thoughts as you read through the following section of this chapter.

DEFINITIONS, AND THE BACKGROUND TO PERFORMANCE MANAGEMENT

Despite the increase in interest, research into performance management has revealed inconsistent results concerning its effectivness (Biron *et al*, 2011). However, as Bach (2000) points out, *performance management* and *performance appraisal* have long been confused, the terms often being used interchangeably, and this may in part account for some of the inconsistency over findings. In this chapter in general we use the term 'performance management' as wider than, but including, the process of 'performance appraisal'.

Performance appraisal, according to Erdogan (2002) and Fletcher (2001) is the basic process involving a line manager's completing an annual report on a subordinate's performance and discussing it with the employee in an appraisal interview. It has its origins in the first formal monitoring systems drawing on the work of Frederick Taylor and others who emphasised the importance of defining standards for performance. Such approaches were pioneered in the USA, and thus the origins of performance management should be recognised as culturally embedded in the strongly individualist nature of the US culture (Pulakos *et al*, 2008).

The early approaches were known as 'merit-rating' systems and were pioneered by Scott and others during World War I, focusing on officer ability. According to Muchinsky (1997), these early efforts led to the acceptance of performance management systems in government and industry and marked the first large-scale use of judgemental assessment. However, merit-rating systems were criticised for being subjective systems of assessment, because they were often based on 'personality'. The approach developed into standardised measures of performance, Patterson's Graphic Rating Scale providing a metric on which to rate a trait or factor, so supposedly obviating the need to make purely qualitative judgements. Commonly used factors for rating referred to the extent to which individuals were conscientious, imaginative, self-sufficient, co-operative or possessed qualities of judgement, initiative or original thinking (Armstrong and Baron, 1998).

In the 1990s and into the 2000s, multi-source feedback and the incorporation of behavioural competencies have become more common. As a result, a large range of methods and techniques now exist for performance appraisal. The main appraisal methods are work standards, comment boxes, checklists, ranking, forced distribution, rating scales, critical incidents, management by objectives (MBO), behaviourally anchored rating scales (BARS), behavioural observation scales (BOS), 360-degree appraisal, and self-appraisal, among others. For a summary of the many different forms of performance appraisal (rating, ranking, objective-oriented, critical incident, self-assessment, etc), with their relevant strengths and weaknesses, see Gunnigle *et al* (2006).

So, what about performance management? Writing in 1992, Bretz *et al* reported a major focus in the rhetoric of the practitioner literature of the day on transforming performance appraisal from an event to a process. Advice for how to do this, they say, is 'typically discussed under the rubric of "performance management"'(p329). Performance management has been defined as a variety of HRM activities through which organisations seek to assess and develop their total competence, enhance organisational performance and distribute rewards (Armstrong and Baron, 2004; DeNisi, 2000; Fletcher, 2001). It is, presented, in theory at least, as a strategic and integrated process, incorporating goal-setting, performance appraisal and development into a unified and coherent framework with the specific aim of aligning individual and group performance goals with the organisation's wider objectives (Armstrong and Baron, 1998; DiNisi, 2000; Den Hartog *et al*, 2004; Williams, 2002). Boselie *et al* (2011) suggest that an ideal performance management approach is akin to a form of 'mini' high-performance work system, focused on goal-setting, monitoring and appraising, developing and rewarding employees in order to increase employee performance and to achieve organisational goals. Relevant to such an outcome-based approach is the extent to which employees give 'extra' in the form of discretionary effort, which would not otherwise have been forthcoming. In such a form performance management has been 'sold' to employees in terms of its ability to serve their individual needs for development and self-actualisation (Festing *et al*, 2010), as well as delivering the organisational requirements which Claus and Briscoe (2009; p176) describe as being organisational competitiveness and control.

In summary, compared with performance appraisal, performance management is usually seen as the larger, more holistic and integrated approach. As Boselie *et al* (2011) point out, it

> is linked to or embedded in relevant areas of practice, including (1) culture management, (2) talent management, (3) leadership development (succession planning), (4) competency management, and (5) new technology.

As discussed earlier in Chapter 4 (on CHRM), the universalist paradigm with its dominance in the USA and widespread adoption throughout the world is particularly relevant to an understanding of performance management policy and practice. Indeed, performance management remains very much a Western construct, in line with what Rose (1991) describes as 'false universalism' as international organisations strive to 'mimic' Western best practice. Certainly, from its US origins performance management appears to have been embraced by large MNCs to become a common element of HRM practice. Even in countries as different as the USA and Japan, performance appraisals involve similar ideas of developing social and performance norms, monitoring the actions of employees in relation to the norms, assigning responsibility for the actions, and then ultimately providing rewards or punishment based on performance towards those norms (Sullivan *et al*, 1986).

As Brewster (1995) observed, it seems that a kind of assumed 'best practice' system has emerged – and before considering the comparative performance management literature and some examples of practice, we shall first outline what typical practice might involve.

TYPICAL PERFORMANCE MANAGEMENT PROCESS

What follows is an account of the 'typical approach to performance management' as commonly espoused by Western organisations and MNCs. The description makes reference to the main elements of performance management, usually described as planning, managing, and reviewing, and summarised in Figure 23.

The first of the elements of performance management is *planning/objective-setting*, typically linked to some sort of cascaded strategy or business plan, and concerned with setting individual or sometimes team objectives for the year ahead in line with corporate goals. This planning phase of performance management has its theoretical underpinning in goal-setting theory (Locke and Latham, 1990), with the belief that individuals are more likely to achieve something if they have an explicitly declared goal to work towards. It also links with expectancy theory (Vroom, 1964; Porter and Lawler, 1965) in terms of what the employee is expecting in return for his or her achievement of the targets set.

Objectives are intended to take into account current corporate objectives and be relevant to the job-holder's role. In some cases, to clarify or support the communication of the business planning process, organisations have sought to use devices such as the European Foundation for Quality Management (EFQM)

Figure 23 An overview of the performance management process

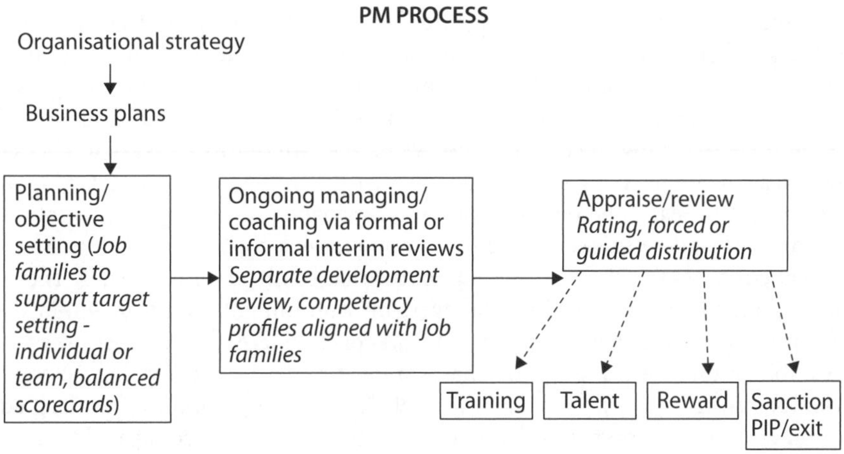

PM PROCESS

Organisational strategy

↓

Business plans

↓

| Planning/objective setting (*Job families to support target setting - individual or team, balanced scorecards*) | → | Ongoing managing/coaching via formal or informal interim reviews *Separate development review, competency profiles aligned with job families* | → | Appraise/review *Rating, forced or guided distribution* |

| Training | Talent | Reward | Sanction PIP/exit |

or a balanced scorecard. Conceived of by Eccles (1991) and popularised by Kaplan and Norton (1996) as a means of overcoming the short-termist and narrow focus of management accountancy, the balanced scorecard provides a framework that promises to enable organisations to measure both the hard tangible and soft intangible drivers of performance. Although organisations (often steered by consultancy firms) have sometimes tailored the perspectives that they track within their balanced scorecard, the rationale remains one of striving to identify a set of 'rounded' performance measures that go beyond only the financial.

The original four perspectives as outlined by Kaplan and Norton (1996) and some of the areas that are typically measured are shown in Figure 24.

Figure 24 Balanced scorecard perspectives and typical measures

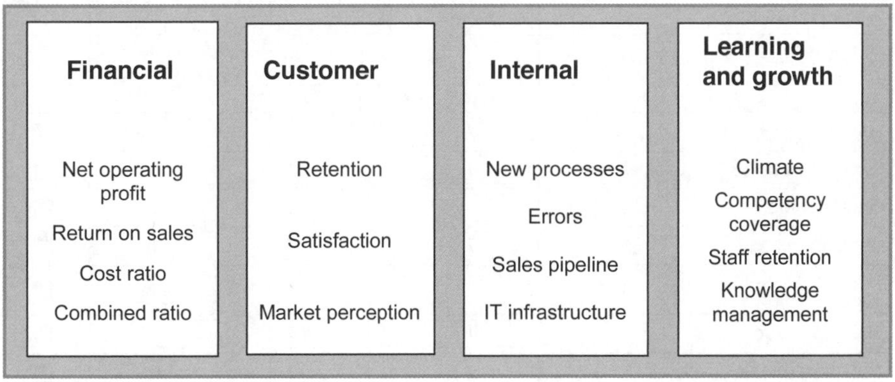

Financial	**Customer**	**Internal**	**Learning and growth**
Net operating profit	Retention	New processes	Climate
Return on sales	Satisfaction	Errors	Competency coverage
Cost ratio		Sales pipeline	Staff retention
Combined ratio	Market perception	IT infrastructure	Knowledge management

The second element of the performance management process in Figure 23 is that of the *managing/coaching* of performance. This is the phase of performance management which is about making sure that the individual is on track during the course of the year and that there are 'no surprises' in the final end-of-year review. In some organisations there is simply encouragement to line managers to provide regular informal coaching. In others there are suggested or mandated interim reviews during the course of the year. The aim of this phase is to check progress against objectives and also to consider the individual's long-term development needs. If the planning phase of performance management relates to theories of goal-setting, then the managing phase is concerned with the role of the line manager in the the ongoing motivation of the employee. There is of course a role to play here for line managers in continuing to motivate employees towards the goals that have been agreed, and coaching and development may play a role in this. One popular mechanism for it is via the use of a competency review, focusing on key behaviours for a role. Once an organisation has decided the contents of its competency framework, roles may be profiled against them. Individuals may then during the course of a development review, or even a performance review, receive feedback on how well they are meeting the behavioural or competency requirements of their role.

For example: in Figure 25, the competency profile for the current role of an individual in job band S2ii has been set in the first two columns. Next to it, the job-holder is able to see how this would change to become more challenging for the next level in that job family. The column entitled 'personal' aims to capture

Figure 25 Example of competency feedback in the performance management process

Incorporating competency feedback in performance management

1. Employee details	3. Results objectives	5. Personal objectives	7. Personal development plan
2. Vision 2003 business goals	4. Competencies review	6. Training and development	

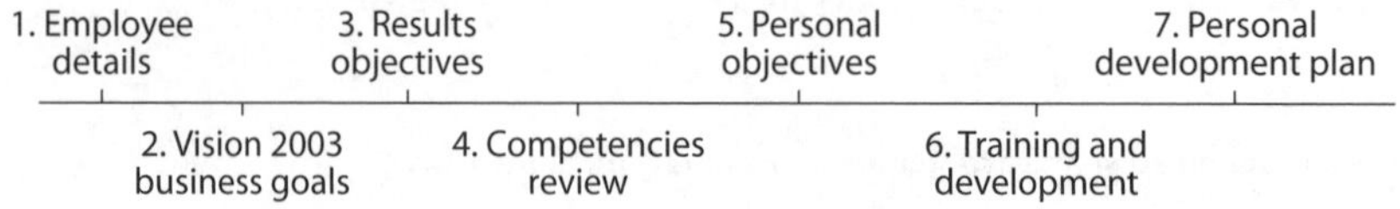

Job designation	Job band:	S2ii ▾			
Competencies	Job profile			Potential/ development gap	Critical
	Current	Next	Personal		
Specialist expertise	2	3	2	0	☐
Communication & persuasiveness	1	2	1	0	☐
Customer focus	3	3	2	−1	☑
Decision-making	2	2	1	−1	☐
Business & communication understanding	2	2	1	−1	☑
Building relationships	1	3	2	1	☐
Analytical thinking	2	2	2	0	☐
Being resourceful	2	1	2	0	☐
Quality	1	2	1	0	☐

the job-holder's current level of display for each of the competencies required for that role. It is thus possible to see (presented in the fourth column) the areas in which the job-holder has strengths that are not being utilised or development needs. Such information could be used for succession planning, or information about development needs might be linked to training plans.

EXAMPLE OF A DEVELOPMENT-ORIENTED APPROACH TO PERFORMANCE MANAGEMENT

CASE STUDIES

Sunrise Enterprise Agency supports new businesses in the south-east of England and has sought to inspire an entrepreneurial culture. From its small-scale origins (with 10 staff initially) it has now grown in size to 200 employees. A high proportion of the staff within the organisation are young and for many this is their first job. They report informally that the culture is one of 'blame' and 'name and shame'. Staff turnover is surprisingly high for the local area and exit interviews suggest lack of development and support from managers as key reasons for leaving.

Against this backdrop the organisation decided to professionalise its approach to performance management. In future the performance management approach would not contain an overall rating of performance, although managers were all to be asked every six months for their current assessment of potential amongst all their direct reports. The organisation did not have a highly geared performance-related pay system, but a link did exist at a subtle level between the performance discussions and resultant salary increases.

In order to emphasise development, the Sunrise management team decided to include a compulsory objective for all people managers around conducting timely performance reviews, quarterly reviews and the production of development plans for their direct reports, thus highlighting the importance of staff development. At the same time, the HR manager persuaded the executive board to look at culture within the organisation – where were they looking to get to in the light of their increasingly commercial imperatives? This work led to the creation of an eight-strong competency model, linked to the new values of 'succeeding together', 'serving the locality', 'honesty and integrity', and 'delivery focus'. Not only were these competencies incorporated in the development and performance review sessions, but at the same time a 360-degree feedback tool was piloted with the executive. It produced interesting results. Most of the executive received feedback which did not surprise them – with the exception of the CEO. His feedback pointed to a strongly autocratic and 'controlling' style – one likely to engender a climate of fear. The new HR manager feared that his job might be at risk, but upon reflection the CEO began to recognise elements of such behaviour and to discuss ways of better managing and masking these. He took the surprising decision of finding a personal counsellor/coach, and worked with her to complete a further range of diagnostics and (for the first time ever) a development plan.

Eighteen months later, the HR manager was happy still to be in post and was able to report on progress. Staff turnover had decreased, and staff feedback suggested that although there was still work to do, it was perceived to be a more motivating place to work.

Questions

In the case of Sunrise Enterprise Agency,

- What was the overall purpose of the performance management process?

- Was it primarily about the achievement of targets?

- Or was it about development and motivation?

- Can these two approaches be reconciled, in your view?

- Which do you think is the more important?

Phase three of the performance management process is concerned with *the appraisal and review* of performance and the aspects of HRM within an organisation which are linked to the outcome of this review. The review element involves the annual appraisal meeting with the individual and their line manager considering the extent to which the objectives have or have not been achieved. Not all performance management processes give rise to a rating. Where there is a rating scheme it typically contains three, four, or most commonly five levels of rating from 'not effective' to 'outstanding'. Recent years have seen an increase in the use of 'guided or forced distribution' approaches to reviewing performance, whereby managers have to allocate prescribed numbers of their direct reports into certain 'performance categories'. This compels managers to decide who their star performers are, and who is underperforming. One way to try to improve perceptions of fairness around rating – particularly where forced distribution is being used – is a technique referred to as 'calibration'. In such cases line managers produce an initial or tentative rating of performance, but it will not be shared with the direct report until after the calibration meeting. The calibration meeting, often facilitated by HRM specialists or a senior line manager, involves groups of line managers meeting together to review the performance and provisional performance ratings of members of their teams and comparing contribution and outcome ratings in an attempt to ensure compatible equivalence.

Once a performance rating has been produced, it may be used in support of a number of other elements of the HRM architecture, particularly reward and talent identification. Identifying talent may indeed rely on the performance rating alone, or it may seek to combine the performance rating with a potential rating, or possibly derive an amalgamation of the two. There is an example of this in the case study in the online supporting materials for this chapter concerning Intertel and its use of a nine-box grid.

In many organisations, reward is seen as inextricably linked to the performance review discussion. In such cases, once the performance conversations for the year have finished, there is a link between the outcome from performance management (typically the rating) to salary or bonus (or in some cases both). Significant problems arise when the outcome of the two systems is inconsistent: thus, a management consultancy may rate someone as underperforming because they have not, for example, developed their subordinates or contributed outside their immediate work role, but reward them at the top level because they have brought in significant new business.

As suggested in the earlier section on planning performance, expectancy theory is useful here (Vroom, 1964; Porter and Lawler, 1968) in terms of the effort an employee expends in relation to a goal, based on their assumptions on the probability of a reward being forthcoming. Equity theory (Adams, 1963) plays a key role here too. Based on exchange theory, it focuses on how fairly employees believe they have been treated in comparison with the treatment received by others. This is based on their expectations of an outcome (or reward) in exchange for certain contributions. Thus the review element sees the employee perhaps with expectations of 'reward' (whether as recognition or explicit reward or promotion). For more information on the challenges facing international organisations in terms of rewarding performance, see the next chapter.

The case study below illustrates how even efforts to balance the inputs to a performance management system can result in unexpected consequences.

CASE STUDIES

HOW PERFORMANCE METRICS CAN HAVE UNEXPECTED CONSEQUENCES

A computer manufacturer and retailer discovered it had a problem with its metrics around performance expectations. For its sales force it had sought to deploy what it believed to be a 'best practice' approach, which did not rely only on sales targets. The balanced scorecard approach also included measures relating to customer satisfaction, completion of internal processes and some ongoing personal development.

The customer satisfaction measure typically rewarded those staff who managed to achieve the highest levels of 9 or 10/10 in customer satisfaction surveys. Individuals who succeeded in achieving their sales targets and also achieved this high level of customer satisfaction would usually be in line for a performance rating of 'Exceeds Expectations' – triggering a high level of bonus. However, a review of sales profitability revealed a very different story. It transpired that the sales staff with the highest customer satisfaction scores were not working on the most profitable accounts, and indeed, the high customer satisfaction scores were misleading. The most profitable accounts were in fact those where customer satisfaction was rated at 6 or 7. An investigation revealed that in cases where the customer satisfaction score was higher, the sales staff were giving away considerable price discounts or 'incentives' to such an extent that the sales were scarcely profitable.

REFLECTIVE ACTIVITY

Reflect upon an appraisal you have experienced – this might, for example, be in relation to the assessment of a piece of work you have completed for your studies.

- What were the elements you were assessed or judged upon (written work, presentation, group work, class participation, etc)?

- How did you tackle the task – did you plan for success? – and what activities did you perform to help you meet your goal?

- What was the outcome for you following the assessment (perhaps you received feedback or were allocated a grade or mark)?

- As far as you are concerned, was the outcome in line with your inputs and contribution? Yes or no – and why was it or wasn't it?

COMPARATIVE LITERATURE ON PERFORMANCE MANAGEMENT

In reference to appraisal, Bai and Bennington (2005; p276) suggest that it remains one of the key tenets of performance management and organisational improvement in Western countries. However, they note that its emphasis may vary, although the purposes generally include individual development, legal risk management, compensation, promotion and two-way communication (see also Nakane, 1972; Ouchi, 1981; Staw, 1980). Moving beyond Western countries, Milliman *et al* (2002) acknowledge the influence of culture but suggest that there appears to be a convergence in this area, reporting that countries as diverse as the USA, Korea and Japan use performance appraisal. Festing *et al* (2010) suggest that in the case of global performance management many MNCs seek, to varying degrees, to standardise their systems. Authors such as Mäkelä *et al* (2009), Cascio (2006) and Festing and Barzantny (2008) have suggested how local customs and specifications concerning performance appraisal and performance management cannot be neglected.

Data from the Cranet survey tells us (Goergen *et al*, 2009a) that:

- Appraisal is widespread – even in this sample of larger firms (above 200 employees), however, the figure does not reach 100 per cent for managerial appraisal in any country.

- (Apart from Norway, Sweden, Finland and the Turkish Cypriot community) the majority of firms in most countries report that they appraise their employees. Apart from the category of manual employees, there is a (weak) inverse U-shaped relationship between the percentage of firms which monitor a given category of employees and trust.

- There is a weak positive linear relationship between the percentage of employees assessed and trust. Apart from the Turkish Cypriot community, the higher the levels of trust in a society, the lower the levels of appraisal.

- There is a negative linear relationship between trust and the proportion of firms that use the employee appraisal system to inform employees about the organisation of work. This may reflect the fact that in low-trust countries there is little communication between employees and their superiors, unless this communication is done via formal channels.

Figure 26 shows the comparative use of appraisal for manual and clerical employees in five countries.

Figure 26 Comparative use of appraisal for manual and clerical employees in five countries

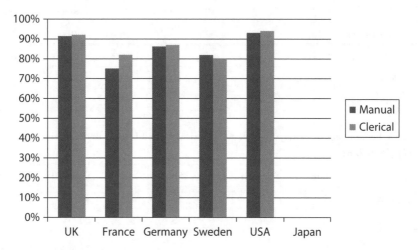

Source: Cranet (2010)

Previous Cranet data provide a more detailed understanding of comparative patterns (see Tables 11, 12 and 13).

Table 11 Percentages of firms with an appraisal system in operation for specified staff grades

		Denmark	France	Japan	Spain	Sweden	Switz'lnd	Neth'lnds	the UK
1995	Management	42	85	–	63	87	89	79	90
	Professional	41	77	–	77	83	94	82	87
	Clerical	39	61	–	64	83	89	79	76
	Manual	23	53	–	56	63	87	78	51
1999	Management	56	86	83	59	89	93	84	92
	Professional	48	84	82	66	84	95	82	90
	Clerical	47	5	79	46	95	92	82	85
	Manual	32	67	77	40	80	91	82	68

Table 12 Percentages of firms in which the specified people contribute formally to the appraisal process

		Denmark	France	Japan	Spain	Sweden	Switz'lnd	Neth'lnds	the UK
1995	Next levl mgr	21	47	–	44	–	44	63	65
	Self	34	67	–	22	–	76	75	86
	Subordinate	5	5	–	8	–	23	6	7
1999	Next levl mgr	31	39	82	47	23	46	67	61
	Self	73	73	10	61	90	85	88	94
	Subordinate	18	5	2	7	16	19	11	12
2004	Next levl mgr	59	–	–	–	68	68	63	80
	Self	98	–	–	–	88	88	83	99
	Subordinate	22	–	–	–	35	26	16	23

Table 13 Percentages of firms in which an appraisal system is used to determine the specified outcomes

		Denmark	France	Japan	Spain	Sweden	Switz'lnd	Neth'lnds	the UK
1995	Training	41	74	–	63	93	91	71	89
	Promotion	25	54	–	55	49	70	59	61
	Career	25	59	–	41	52	59	66	72
	PRP	16	53	–	52	35	53	52	40
1999	Training	82	95	29	77	98	98	83	98
	Promotion	49	74	85	63	48	74	69	62
	Career	52	74	37	50	54	55	80	77
	PRP	36	61	91	63	41	60	63	34
2004	Training	87	–	–	–	79	96	88	98
	Promotion	–	–	–	–	–	–	–	–
	Career	71	–	–	–	66	91	92	87
	PRP	66	–	–	–	86	76	75	54

Boselie *et al* (2011) present empirical data on performance management from the same Cranet survey and from their Global HR Research Alliance study of 16 firms. They find similar overall increases in the use of appraisal systems, in particular for clerical workers and manual workers. They also find few differences between regions in the case studies (probably because of their MNC nature), although there are differences between countries in their use of appraisal systems. There are, they say, some contextual differences that may affect performance management in different countries, mainly associated with variances in leadership, communication and self-evaluation. In other words, the leadership styles, the nature of communication and information sharing, and the role of the individual in the appraisal procedure differ between countries. They conclude that context matters in the optimal design of performance management systems.

CONTEXT AND PERFORMANCE MANAGEMENT

Figure 23 above showed the typical components of a performance management process. A comparative consideration requires us to locate this within the context of the country of operation. So what are the factors that shape how international organisations either standardise or adapt their performance management processes?

DeNisi and Pritchard (2006) have commended the trend in recent literature on appraisals, which has focused on the contextual factors. Claus and Briscoe (2009) have highlighted the fact that no one model provides an overall view of how the design, development and implementation of performance management across borders works in practice, whether from the perspective of an MNC or the application of the Western notion of performance management in a non-Western culture. Similarly, Varma *et al* (2008) highlight the lack of reliable literature detailing the kind of HRM and performance management systems relevant to firms operating in different national contexts. However, their book makes a particularly useful contribution, including a framework by Murphy and DeNisi (2008) which aims to capture the contextual factors that influence appraisal decisions at various levels of analysis as well as cognitive and motivational factors at individual level, which we will explain in more detail. They consider performance management in context by means of two models, one of which deals with the appraisal component and one with the performance component, which they see to 'fall out' of the outcome of the appraisal discussion. In Figure 27 we present an integrated model with seeks to simplify the main elements of their framework and is useful to underpin our consideration of comparative performance management practice.

Figure 27 suggests a number of *macro contextual factors*. These operate at the level of the nation or region but can still influence the appraisal process. They are best thought of as things that are fixed and so act as parameters for the actions an organisation might take. Examples include the legal framework of the country of operation: for instance, the degree of employment protection that is provided to employees is higher in western European countries than in the USA. Other nations have laws that allow discrimination against some groups but not others (on the grounds of race or gender). Finally, technology can influence the type of performance management information that is collected and how it is used. For example, the performance management system itself may be 'system'-generated and link an individual's role profile to their behavioural competency feedback (see Figure 25 above).

Organisational factors are akin to those described by Murphy and DeNisi (2008) as micro or proximal factors. They include the purpose of performance

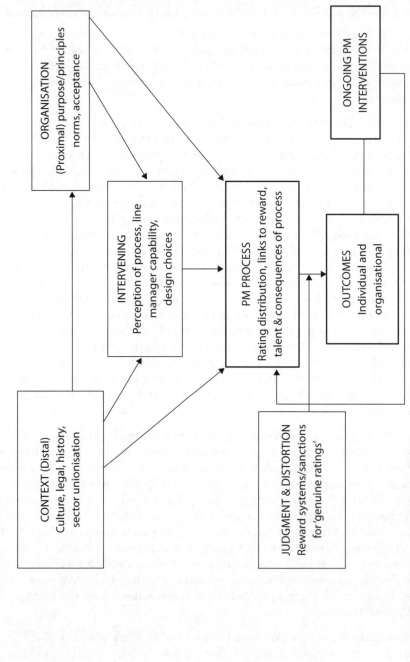

Figure 27 The performance management process in context

Source: adapted from Murphy and DeNisi (2008; pp82, 91)

management: is it primarily for decision-making (for example, to make reward decisions) or is it about development practices? Although some organisations claim to do both, according to Rotchford (2002) that is difficult to achieve in practice. Other organisational factors include norms of behaviour such as whether it is acceptable to rate anyone as 'not satisfactory' and the degree of acceptance of the appraisal process by both employees and line managers. According to Folger *et al* (1992), if employees do not accept the appraisal system as legitimate, they are less likely to see the ratings it generates as fair and rather than try to improve their performance will instead resent low ratings and reduce their efforts at work. Murphy and DeNisi (2008) suggest that the contextual and organisational factors impact on the performance management process via intervening variables which include line management capability and the perceptions of the performance management process.

Our version of the model then includes the *performance management process*, the detailed elements of which are presented in Figure 23.

Emerging from the performance management process are its *outcomes* at both individual and organisational levels of analysis. For the individual these might include the rating, reward, talent identification or sanctions for under-performance. They could also include both tangible business outcomes (although these are always difficult to attribute to the performance management process) as well as motivation and commitment.

In addition to showing the working constituents of performance management Figure 27 features three further elements.

Outcomes, we suggest, are possibly subject to *judgement and distortion factors* as described by Murphy and Cleveland (1995). These factors include what happens within the organisation in relation to subsequent rewards as a result of the performance management process, and whether this encourages the line manager to give a genuine rating of performance (in line with his or her true judgement) or not.

Finally, *performance initiatives* are the ongoing initiatives which may result from the monitoring of the performance management process. An example would be specific programmes to improve the performance of employees in the lower rating categories.

 REFLECTIVE ACTIVITY

Based on your reading so far, summarise the key factors to take into account when analysing the introduction of performance management processes into different operating countries.

Figure 27 provides us with a useful framework for considering the literature on comparative performance management. Sparrow (2008) reviewed practice in the UK (see Table 12). Barzantny and Festing (2008) do the same for France and Germany. Their chapter is particularly interesting because it considers two of the key economies within Europe while reinforcing the point that Europe does not present one cultural norm. The French legal system has been described as moderately regulated (Nikandrou *et al*, 2005) and as a result it is suggested that the legal environment has a minimal impact on performance management (Barzantny and Festing, 2008; p151). France is presented as having a culture which involves high individualism, high power distance and high uncertainty avoidance while also emerging with a 'feminine' attitude. What results therefore is a society which values hierarchy, and an 'elite' which still prevails in education, administration, the management of organisations and overall society (p152). This elite context impacts on the intervening factors in Murphy and DeNisi's model. For example, if an individual being appraised is from a more prestigious background, their appraisal will be more positive – making the process less objective than might be expected. According to Barzantny and Festing (2008), performance management in modern-day France appears to be linked to employee involvement and is described as being an important motivational instrument. However, according to Bourguignon (1998), appraisals are often used with the aim of confirming and justifying the impact on someone's remuneration. The presence of high power distance leads to low levels of openness and lack of transparency, employee–manager relations thus being typically characterised by a lack of trust. As a result, performance ratings emerge with rather average ratings for all employees in a department, firm or corporation, and therefore little discrimination between employees. In terms of distortion factors, in France appraisal appears to have a low impact on promotion and pay rises. The feminine nature of the culture means that well-being within the working environment is of importance along with personal relationships. This is a point of difference between France and Germany, where a more factual and task-focused orientation prevails. A final key point to make on context is that, as in most continental European countries, French employees value stability and longer-lasting, stable employment relationships. Here the French context is similar to that of Germany, although there are a number of other key differences.

Germany is perceived as a highly regulated legal environment with extensive labour market institutions of collective bargaining, co-determination and vocational training. In Germany, the most important industrial relations happen at the plant level. The social market economy is a key factor of the context, where the aim is high levels of staff security for staff members with an emphasis upon long-term career and succession planning (Barzantny and Festing, 2008). In terms of culture, Germany has been described as low power distance, high on masculinity, high on individualism and high on uncertainty avoidance. The high uncertainty avoidance is often associated with German expectations that a system should be precise and formalised, particularly in relation to defining goals and measurement methods, and the consequences of this (eg training or pay decisions). In terms of reviewing performance the tendency, as in France, is for the 'average' to be used for everyone, involving a preference for egalitarian approaches. The link to performance-based pay has increased in recent years in Germany but, according to Barzantny and Festing (2008), does not have the same meaning as in other countries – perhaps because of the need for approval by works councils – and as a result the practice has been implemented only to a modest extent. In summary, there is a high acceptance of performance management in Germany in terms of the link to career development, and given the masculine nature of the culture, status within society is valued and vertical careers are important.

COMPANY W PERFORMANCE VIGNETTE

CASE STUDIES

This large German organisation employees 260,000 individuals across 50 countries and is striving to produce a global approach to performance management. However, its Vice-President for Performance reports that there is much more freedom to do so beyond their home country. Within Germany there has been agreement between unions and works councils to introduce the approach beyond the managerial and supervisory level to those workers on collective pay agreements (*tarifs*). But in order to secure this concession it has been determined that the performance discussion between manager and employee must remain confidential, and only data relating to high potential may be shared by the line manager and linked to other elements of the HR architecture.

Table 14 presents selected comparative charactertistics of performance management for the UK, the USA, India and China.

Table 14 Cross-national performance management characteristics

Factor	the UK	the USA	India	China
Macro Norms, cultural and organisational	Low power distance, low uncertainty avoidance	Low power distance, low uncertainty avoidance, highly individualistic	Low individualism, high power distance, 'family culture'; organisational norms of job for life and unionisation	Collectivist culture and importance of harmony and 'face', behavioural norms of modesty and self-discipline; evidence of cultural shift towards individual performance-related reward schemes

Factor	the UK	the USA	India	China
Macro Strategy	Increasingly seen as component of strategic HRM	Strategic alignment sought in pursuit of business objectives; history of MBO approaches	Not really due to tendency for HR systems to focus more on maintenance rather than performance	Majority of organisations do not have strategic goals or a cascade
Macro Technology	Increased use	Increasingly technology-enhanced, using, eg, PeopleSoft, Oracle and SAP	Recent rapid increase	Lack of sufficient IT to support performance management
Organisational Purpose of performance management	Mixed: development and culture change programmes as well as PRP	To meet legal requirements, and as an administrative process for decision-making – on reward and promotion	Decision-making on promotions	Decision-making, narrow focus on reward
Organisational Acceptance of approach	Accepted, but largely ill-regarded	Accepted as necessary evil	Low level of acceptance – seen as time-wasting	Low level of acceptance; not taken seriously
Intervening factors Manager/ appraisee relationships	In the context of increased devolvement of HRM to line, still seen as a time burden; line managers are required to play the role of judge and/or coach	Manager predominantly as judge; both sides report dissatisfaction with processes	Subjectivity of managers in rating, particularly inflation of ratings for those they care about	Highly subjective manager evaluations; avoidance of criticising bad behaviour causes poor performance to be tolerated
Performance management process and practices	Use of competencies, 360-degree feedback; links to reward and high talent	Multi-source feedback, calibration of ratings, results focused on a combination of 'what' and 'how'	Some team-based appraisal and use of 360-degree feedback; paternalistic approach, top-down, and systems typically operated 'closed'	Effort traditionally more important than outcomes; self- and peer/ subordinate evaluations used

Factor	the UK	the USA	India	China
Outcomes	Reward (increased emphasis upon total reward) Use of 'corrective' performance approaches	Reward justifications	Promotion and possibly reward, less clear link to performance and productivity improvement	Reward
Adapted from Murphy and DeNisi (2008)	Drawn from Sparrow (2008)	Drawn from Pulakos *et al* (2008)	Drawn from Sharma *et al* (2008)	Drawn from Cooke (2008)

PERFORMANCE MANAGEMENT AND CULTURE

Culture appears as a distal or macro factor in the model of Murphy and DeNisi (2008). Indeed, culture appears to be the dominant factor in terms of shaping performance management practice both in terms of its adoption and in the way it is experienced on the ground in different locations, associated with a considerable body of literature which suggests that culture impacts on performance appraisal (Atwater *et al*, 2005; Aycan, 2005; Cascio, 2006; Dunnett, 1993; Ji and Karakowsky, 2001; Kostova 1999; Kostova and Roth, 2002; London and Smither, 1995; Mendonca and Kanungo, 1996; Shipper *et al*, 2004; Tornow, 1993).

REFLECTIVE ACTIVITY

Review what you know about culture from Chapter 2.

Which factors (using Hofstede's terminology) do you believe are likely to most impact on the success of performance management processes?

The picture that emerges from the literature is one in which collectivist cultures tend to reward such factors as group loyalty and conformity and the maintenance of harmonious relationships (Sinha, 1990; Tung, 1984); individualist cultures prefer objective and quantifiable criteria (Varma *et al*, 2008). Japanese and US performance appraisals tend to vary in terms of measures, time horizon, communication style and form and extent of praise (Cascio and Serapio, 1991). US managers are much more likely to reward 'lone wolf' (non-interactional) individuals (Sullivan *et al*, 1986). In China issues such as *mianzi* (face) and *guanxi* (connections) remain important in performance appraisal (Bai and Bennington, 2005; Björkman and Lu, 1999) and affect the way in which performance appraisal is conducted. Managers from the People's Republic of China, and probably many other unresearched nationalities, tend to base their appraisals upon personal attributions (Claus and Briscoe, 2009). UK managers include in their appraisal criteria minimum supervision required – Chinese managers include obedience (Hempel, 2001). A sample of US and Chinese Taiwanese nationals research showed that it was possible to use performance evaluation and rewards to shift behaviour away from collective interests but not to move behaviour from individualistic to collective (Awasthi *et al*, 2001). On upward evaluation, US and European ratings tend to be more positive than Brazilian and Asian ratings (Adsit *et al*, 1997).

Culture also seems to account for some of differences in how performance is attributed. It is argued that individualistic cultures tend to attribute performance to personal-internal factors (Staw, 1980; Landrine and Klonoff, 1992) and collectivistic cultures tend to attribute performance to situational-external factors (Markus and Kitayama, 1998; Matsumoto, 1994; Morris and Peng, 1994). Although it is a mistake to assume that all Asian countries are similar in their approach to performance appraisal (Paik *et al*, 2000), Asian countries do seem to adopt a different approach from Western countries, and are particularly wary of individualised assessments, managers from Thailand and the Philippines being least likely to use them (Easterby-Smith *et al*, 1995; Vallance, 1995). There is a strong association between managers' perceptions of motivation and their appraisals. However, the attitudes to motivation also vary by cultures – in the USA they are seen as extrinsic, in Latin America as intrinsic, and in Asia as a mix of both (Devoe and Iyengar, 2004).

Differences have also been found in the preferences of Chinese workers for a performance-related pay system (Bozionelos and Wang, 2007); the implementation of systems involving employee appraisal of their managers in Argentina, Australia, China, Slovakia, Spain and the UK (Brutus *et al*, 2006); perceptions of the causes of successful employee performance in Canada, China, Finland and the UK (Chiang and Birtch, 2007); and in appraisal systems generally in Hong Kong and the UK (Snape *et al*, 1998). In terms of criteria and goal-setting there is evidence that individualistic societies tend to emphasise personal achievement in the appraisal whereas collectivist cultures highlight group-based achievement (Miller *et al*, 2001); fatalistic cultures, in which individuals perceive work outcomes to be beyond their influence, tend to accept performance below expectations as long as the individual displays effort and willingness (Kovach, 1995); low power distance and universalistic cultures are also more likely to stress task-related competencies and outcomes (Aycan, 2005). Japanese performance appraisal criteria typically include process as well as results, whereas the only criterion for US appraisals is, at least according to proponents there, results (Eshigi, 1985). In countries with low power distance, such as Germany, the objective-setting process might be achieved by way of a negotiation between superior and employee. In France, on the other hand, its high power distance means that objectives are set by superiors (Barzantny and Festing, 2008).

The managing or developing phase of performance management relies on line managers having the capability of giving feedback and handling conversations on behaviours. There is evidence that feedback is particularly impacted by cultural effects: it impacts on subordinates' work much more in the USA than it does in the UK (Early and Stubbledine, 1989; Fletcher and Perry, 2001; London and Smither, 1995) – praise and criticism improved US workers' performance, but in the UK only praise increased subordinates' performance. It has been argued that giving objective 'Western-style' feedback may not be appropriate in all contexts. Brutus *et al* (2001) found that 360-degree feedback increased performance in Ireland but decreased it in Malaysia. For countries with high power distance, the notion of giving upward feedback to a manager/supervisor would be very counter-cultural, whereas in countries with lower power distance employees expect to provide comment on 'how well' their boss has done in terms of managing their performance. For example Barzantny and Festing (2008) describe France as a being a context in which open criticism of others, notably up the hierarchical line, is avoided. As a result, feedback is often only given when improvements and corrections are requested by a superior. In Germany, on the other hand, feedback seems to be part of an ongoing process of dialogue about many informal elements, and the feedback might actually include open confrontations – something that would never be acceptable in an Asian country.

In terms of reviewing or appraising performance, usually construed as the potentially most difficult element of the process, there is evidence that this too is sensitive to the impact of culture. For example, feedback quality and relationships between supervisor and subordinate tend to be higher for matched collectivist-collective and individualist-individual dyadic relationships than for mismatched dyads (Van de Vliert *et al,* 2004). Evaluation based on direct feedback is more prevalent in individualist cultures and in low-context cultures, whereas collectivist societies focus on indirect, subtle, relationship-oriented and personal forms of feedback (Hofstede, 1998; Milliman *et al*, 1998). Low power distance cultures are more likely to have participative and egalitarian discussions around performance; high power distance cultures are more likely to use autocratic assessment styles, where there is little expectation that subordinates will express their views openly (Snape *et al*, 1998). There are also some indications that the subjects discussed during the performance appraisal interview may vary across cultures. Reporting on appraisal in Hong Kong, Snape *et al* (1998) found that the content of performance appraisal was more strongly geared towards reward and punishment, and less towards training and development, compared to British firms. Milliman *et al* (1998) found that in individualistic cultures such as the UK there is an expectation that the discussion will place a stronger focus on discussing employees' results and potential for future promotion (Milliman *et al*, 1998).

Not only is feedback likely to be perceived differently in countries with higher power distance, but the cultural dimension may also be a factor at the rating stage of performance management. For countries with higher power distance it may be considered inappropriate for an employee to receive a higher performance rating than their manager, thus mitigating against effective 'real' differentiation in terms of performance – hence an enactment of what Murphy and DeNisi (2008) describe as rating (for cultural/political reasons) rather than for reasons based on judgement.

PERFORMANCE MANAGEMENT PRACTICES IN THE MIDDLE EAST

Performance management, particularly in the Gulf States, is synonymous with directive goal-setting against narrow financial targets. The environment is heavily influenced by paternalistic management structures, despite Western expatriates often representing the senior leadership of international companies operating out here. The day-to-day middle managers' performance management practices, however, are rooted in the local cultures (with high power distance) of their Arabian or Iranian descent or imported from the Indian subcontinent.

On the surface, contemporary performance management systems, such as balanced scorecards, may well be adopted as official process and formats. However, individual goals are typically set unilaterally without input or discussions among managers and subordinates. Similarly, the individual performance is not actively managed but rather expected against the constant, if unspoken, threat of dismissal. Given the direct link between employer-sponsored work and residence permits (necessary to stay in the country and have a local bank account to rent accommodation, own a car, etc.), the prospect of job loss due to disagreement about performance carries considerable weight here. People therefore endeavour to be seen as outperforming any expectations, those set and many additional unplanned or last-minute demands.

Another aspect of performance management practice in the Middle East is the difficulty in reviewing performance, either throughout the performance cycle or at the annual appraisal. Admittedly, in any setting, giving feedback constructively needs skill and talent to do it effectively. Appraising performance, however, is seen as critiquing, and that means on the Asian continent it is related to loss of face. This perception offers no acceptable way to frame the review as objective and non-personal.

Similarly, people locally measure their value and contribution to the business in terms of their personal network and its potential to offer ever negotiable, long-lasting relationship benefits. These contributions can rarely be accounted for or only insufficiently in the short-term quarterly business review or even annual appraisal.

In summary, what gets measured (via financial and other quantitative performance metrics) gets managed by autocratic leadership behaviours. But what employees actually daily manage (relationships) does not get measured.

Source: contributed by Sabine Bruggeman, HRM practitioner and consultant based in Dubai

This chapter has shown that best practice performance management does not exist independently of cultural context (von Glinow *et al*, 2002). Overall, Claus and Briscoe (2009) sum up the debate about comparative performance appraisal as follows: there is a relative immaturity of research in the topic (a lot of issues and countries are not researched or researched in only a limited way) but, on the basis of the evidence we have, although there are signs that practices 'may be converging, there is still a great deal of divergence' (Claus and Briscoe, 2009; p191).

Similarly Boselie *et al* (2011) argue that in order to understand performance management it is

> important to take into account international cultural differences (Brewster, Mayrhofer and Morley, 2004) that might affect the leadership style, the type of communication, the nature of rewards and the use of self-evaluation.

As DeNisi *et al* (2008; p260) note, 'Visitors to India will find that McDonalds doesn't sell hamburgers but sells vegetable burgers.' This 'Indianisation' of the hamburger seems to be exactly the approach we need in the area of performance management. As countries develop more sophisticated systems, they should learn from other countries – but also make sure that, where needed, they modify programmes to fit with local 'tastes'.

KEY LEARNING POINTS

- Brewster (1995) has observed that performance management is an area where an assumed 'best practice' has emerged around the 'typical process' which includes planning, managing and reviewing.

- Performance management has Western (US) origins and there are challenges to the implementaion of the 'typical process' in non-Western contexts.

- Performance appraisal is a key component of performance management, but performance management is a more recent and more holistic construct, which aims to incorporate both target-setting and reviewing performance along with development and motivation of employees.

- Competencies or behaviours are a common element of both performance plan and performance review discussions – as with assessment centres, the use of these may be problemmatic if not adapted to suit different contexts.

- Cranet data informs us that appraisal is widespread, with similar overall increases in the use of appraisal systems for clerical workers and manual workers.

- Differences still exist between countries in their use of appraisal systems, the role of culture and institutions remaining a particular challenge for MNCs which are seeking to standardise global processes.

LEARNING QUESTIONS

1 What are the differences between performance appraisal and performance management?

2 What does a performance management process typically comprise in terms of its component elements?

3 Where do the origins of performance management and performance appraisal lie?

4 What are the major challenges to the implementation of 'global' performance management practices?

5 Provide some examples of how culture impacts on performance management.

EXPLORE FURTHER

Varma, A., Budhwar, P. S. and DeNisi, A. (2008) *Performance Management Systems: A global perspective*, Abingdon, Routledge. This book provides detailed coverage of performance management in a global context, with more comparative examples than could be contained in this one chapter.

Boselie, P., Farndale, E. and Paauwe, J. (2011, forthcoming) 'Performance management', in Brewster, C. and Mayrhofer, W. (eds) *Handbook of Research in Comparative Human Resource Management*, Cheltenham, Edward Elgar.

Biron, M., Farndale, E. and Paauwe, J. (2011) 'Performance management effectiveness: lessons from world-leading firms', *International Journal of Human Resource Management*, 22 (6): 1294–1311.

Claus, L. and Briscoe, D. (2009) 'Employee performance management across borders: a review of relevant academic literature,' *International Journal of Management Review*, 11 (2): 175–196.

CHAPTER 10

Rewards

LEARNING OUTCOMES

When they have read this chapter, students will:

- be able to describe cross-national variations in reward practice

- appreciate the extent to which the differences across countries in reward practice are linked to cross-national variation in the cultural and institutional context

- have a foundation for reflection on the complexity of international reward strategy in multinationals.

INTRODUCTION

Reward, and pay in particular, is often prominent in management discussions of people management. People are the largest single operating cost item of most businesses and there is also a need to motivate employees and/or engender their active commitment or engagement. Moreover, reward might appear a natural focus of activity for HRM departments, in light of the possibility of relatively direct leverage over pay practices. Yet the differing approaches to reward apparent in different countries – and the different contexts of reward in them – suggest that this is a particularly challenging area in the international and comparative context.

Pfeffer (1998) asserts that although people work for money, they also work to find meaning and a sense of identity, and Kohn (1998) goes further, to suggest that extrinsic reward erodes intrinsic interest. Yet a great deal of discussion in the realm of HRM now centres on pay, and pay systems often feature in broader discussions of the management of high commitment, involvement or performance. Certainly, although employees at all levels typically feel 'underpaid and overworked', the intensity of their dissatisfaction varies.

The influential expectancy theory suggests that motivation and performance are shaped by the links between effort and reward and by the significance or 'valence' of the reward to the person in question. This underpins Lawler's (1990) notion that 'line of sight' is the crucial issue in the design of reward packages. Accordingly, a good deal of thinking and discussion about reward now centres on motivation and, more specifically, on incentivisation. For senior managers and executives it has long been assumed that incentivisation through pay is necessary, and there has recently been a growing interest in extending incentivisation beyond these groups, and beyond managerial hierarchies, to the bulk of non-managerial employees, regardless of their prior exposure to such incentives. Yet the banking and financial crises of the last few years have led to some diminution in the faith of managements in immediate and short-term incentives.

This chapter briefly surveys the bases on which pay packages may be constructed. It goes on to consider in detail comparative variation in practice, with a focus on the situation regarding pay for post and then the various forms of pay for performance (PfP). The chapter then turns to outline approaches to understanding cross-national comparative variation in reward practice, focusing on the roles of culture and institutions. The emerging international evidence on best practice in reward is then considered. The chapter concludes by considering the 'strategic space' for reward (Vernon, 2005), and therefore the international management of reward, in MNCs. Throughout the chapter we consider comparative reward quite generally. Chapter 14 considers issues of expatriate compensation specifically.

REFLECTIVE ACTIVITY

How have management attitudes to the appropriate design of pay systems developed in the last few years? Does this change reflect properly the lessons of recent high-profile experiences?

REWARD AND BASES OF PAY

Discussions of 'total reward' seek to encompass the entirety of the offer to employees (Antoni *et al*, 2005), relating to some key aspects of the employers' side of the psychological contract. Notions of total reward thus extend beyond matters of pay, and indeed perquisites (perks) and benefits, to autonomy at work, learning and development opportunities, the quality of working life, and the rather more ephemeral issues of the nature of the company culture (see Armstrong, 2006). For the most part, however, discussion of reward in organisations tends to be more limited, focusing on matters of pay in cash and in kind.

Within this more limited sphere, a good deal of managerial discussion has traditionally focused on perks and benefits, which typically comprise around 20 per cent of the total labour cost. In some respects, though, this agenda seems on the wane. The validity of payment via company cars is increasingly questioned, as environmental issues and indeed concerns over the divisions wrought by such obvious status differentials come to the fore. Despite the erosion of the support and services provided by welfare states in many nations, and the concern of non-managerial employees about their plight in the event of severe sickness and upon retirement in particular, the weight of benefits in managerial discussions has also declined. The strategic use of pay is the new focus for debate. Pay is often seen as a sharper tool for directing and motivating employees than the range of options offered by benefits and perks.

ATTACHMENT TO BENEFITS?

CASE STUDIES

In China, pay is less important than the range of benefits (housing, food, childcare, etc) typically provided for employees (Verma and Zhiming, 1995). In China, as well as Japan and Korea, employees value benefits increases and bonuses above basic pay increases, partly because tax is levied on basic pay. Many benefits are not taxed in the USA either, and in the light of the paucity of national social provision, benefits increases are also popular there. We would expect in countries such as those in the Nordic zone, where childcare provision by the state is generous, not to see childcare as a significant part of an employee package. The Nordic countries and France, as examples, prefer to receive most of their pay and reward packages in cash and to be free to spend it as they wish. In Europe generally, benefit provision by employers is rather less important than elsewhere, reflecting the fact that many of the benefits offered elsewhere (such as healthcare packages) are, in Europe, provided by the state.

Some elements of pay packages are near-ubiquitous, regardless of occupation, industry or country. Almost always, there is a fixed or base element of pay. This base element generally reflects the grade and wider band (and often job family) of the job in question, sometimes determined on the basis of some formal job analysis, but also often reflects experience or seniority within the organisation or sometimes indeed simply age. It may also reflect the qualifications of the employee, even if these exceed the minimum job requirements, or perhaps the progression of the employee through some organisation-specific competence ladder. Although qualifications remain the subject of considerable discussion – for example, in considerations of human capital – and competence ladders remain the focus of some attention, the spotlight has fallen increasingly on pay beyond the base. Rightly or wrongly, the strategic use of pay has often become synonymous with an emphasis on incentivisation via pay for performance or variable pay.

Traditionally, individual performance was rewarded by promotion to a new job role or grade. In a sense, one might also suggest that some form of group performance has been implicit in organisation-specific upgradings of pay, but the solidity of this link between organisational performance and reward is rather uncertain. In any event, current discussions of pay for performance centre on reward which is separate from base pay, forming a distinct component of a pay package much more immediately related to the assessed performance of an individual or group. This appears attractive in the context of discussions of reward management linking immediately to the questions 'What do we value?' and 'What do we pay for?'

THEORY AND PRACTICE

KEY FRAMEWORK

Agency theory

Compensation for top management has been the subject of considerable discussion since the 1990s, and in relation to it agency theory became an influential perspective from which the issues could be considered (Barkema and Gomez-Mejia, 1998). The theory posits the existence of a 'principal' who employs an 'agent' to manage on his or her behalf, but accepts that this agent usually has a distinct set of interests, and that information asymmetries imply difficulties for the principal, or owner, in monitoring the agent, or manager, appointed. The problem is then conceived as one of the appropriate framework which can be introduced by the principal to ensure that the agent is working in the principal's best interest. The theory suggests that the principal's two recourses are investment in information-gathering systems which would reveal the manner in which the manager appointed was working, and an incentive system that would motivate the manager to work in the principal's best interest. Agency problems might be thought particularly severe in the context of MNCs, given the extent of information asymmetries, suggesting that the framework might be particularly valuable in this context (Björkman and Furu, 2000). However, the theory implies what is in some respects a rather crude representation of the problem of motivating top managers, or indeed other employees, and of the nature of their response. Ferner and Varul (2000) suggest the relevance of cross-national movements of personnel and international networks as informal means of monitoring and transferring practices across national borders. Moreover, the dangers of incentive systems which reward top managers for favourable movements in share prices have been increasingly obvious since the collapse of Enron and of WorldCom and more recently the banking crises in many countries.

Many of the contours of discussions of reward are shared across the nations of the advanced industrialised world and beyond. As we might expect, there are in practice some general international trends, but there remain very significant differences in the way that each country tends to compensate its workers for the time and commitment that they bring to work. As we shall see, in relation to non-managerial workforces and the external labour pool to which pay policies are applied, the evidence of convergence in rewards behaviour is less marked than in relation to top management or indeed to internationally mobile elites or expats.

LINKING PAY TO POST VIA JOB CLASSIFICATION AND EVALUATION: COMPARATIVE VARIATION

In traditional career structures, employees' job roles or categories imply a particular job class or job level, perhaps within a job grouping or job family. This is summarised by a system of job classification. The job classes or levels are then linked to pay grades – often via an elaborate system of job evaluation which scores employees' job roles on the responsibilities of the job, the skill or expertise required to do it, and perhaps also the physical challenge or social inconvenience involved. Particularly if they are accompanied by clear disciplinary and grievance procedures and elaborations of the training and or experience required for progression (eg Osterman, 1987), such job and pay hierarchies become meaningful job ladders or, as they are often termed in academic discussion, 'internal labour markets'. Although often regarded by managers (and some employees) as inflexible and outdated – particularly within the Anglo-Saxon world – such job and pay ladders still retain considerable significance in many countries, for example, within Europe.

PAY STRUCTURES IN A MANUFACTURING MULTINATIONAL: GERMAN *V* US OPERATIONS

CASE STUDIES

Grund (2005) compares the pay structures across the USA and German manufacturing facilities of a single multinational at the turn of the millennium. The plants feature near-identical technology and similar production processes. Both US and German plants exhibit convex pay profiles, with the absolute pay gap between levels or grades generally increasing through the jobs hierarchy. In both principle and practice pay for the higher blue-collar grades exceeds that for the lower clerical grades in Germany, whereas in the USA there is a continuous pay hierarchy from the lowest blue-collar to the highest white-collar grades. Overall pay inequality is much greater in the USA than in the German plant, with pay inequality across the grades similar in the two cases, but pay inequality at any particular grade much lower in Germany. In effect, the German firm features a traditional bureaucratic narrow-grading whereas the US firm features broad-banding. This US broad-banding is of an extraordinary degree with regard even to some non-managerial grades, the maximum of the (within non-managerial grade) pay range at well over 200 per cent of the minimum. In consequence, some 84 per cent of the overall pay inequality in the German operations is attributable to grade compared to only 60 per cent in the USA operations. The difference in the significance of grade for pay is not attributable to differences in workforce composition in terms of age, tenure, or even education in the USA versus the German operations. Rather, differential pay increases based on (apparently ad hoc and subjective) merit assessments have marked the USA operations. The author notes that promotions are much more common in the USA than in the German operations, particularly between the higher grades. However, the extent of within-grade pay inequality in the US operations implies of course that promotion is of much less relative consequence for pay.

In continental European countries, there is typically the quite generalised use of a national system of job classification, with organisational classifications elaborated from, or sometimes rather awkwardly superimposed on top of, them (eg Marsden, 1999; Antoni *et al*, 2007). In many – although not all – of these national cases there is evidence of the generalised use of a fairly standard system of job evaluation, linking job families and levels to pay (see eg Lazear and Shaw, 2008). Within organisational boundaries, at least, this implies a rather systematic tying of pay to post in countries such as Germany, Italy, Belgium, Sweden and Finland. Often, very substantial differences across organisations remain in pay for similar or even identical work, with organisations varying in their average pay and in the extent to which typical pay differs according to job family and level – ie in the profile of the job-pay ladders which their internal labour markets provide. Thus, for example, it is a commonplace that larger organisations tend to pay more on average, particularly within manufacturing (eg Streeck, 1997).

However, in some northern European countries a generalised system of linking job families and levels to pay levels is applied nearly universally in at least the larger organisations, implying not just organisation-level job and pay ladders (firm-based internal labour markets) but that job-pay ladders are very similar across organisations within the same sector. So, for example, Lazear and Oyer's (2004) analysis of white-collar employees in the 100 largest Swedish firms in the 1980s shows that the vast bulk of the overall pay variation between employees is attributable to job family-job level combinations – that wage levels 'are in large part dictated by occupation' (pp547–548). There is thus not only an intra-organisational but an inter-organisational attachment of pay to jobs within job ladders, by a close confinement of pay for jobs, skill and responsibility in the external labour market. The individual characteristics, social or negotiating skills of employees and the features and, indeed, munificence (ability to pay) of the organisations they work for are of comparatively little import to pay.

 REFLECTIVE ACTIVITY

Why might the close tying of pay to post be seen as outdated? Does this view necessarily reflect the impact of such pay systems for business performance?

THE INCIDENCE OF PAY FOR PERFORMANCE

As we have seen, organisations may seek to reward performance on a number of bases. Payment may be made on the basis of some assessment of individual performance, of team or group performance, of departmental performance, of the performance of a subsidiary or group or the whole organisation. The targets or criteria for reward may take an almost unlimited variety of forms. Sometimes some or all of these bases are used together to create a multifaceted or multi-layered bonus.

Good comparative data on the use of different forms of PfP is limited, but the large-scale Cranet survey has over the years afforded particular attention to this form of pay system. Cranet demonstrates the variation in the proportion of organisations in a variety of countries that make use of different forms of PfP for different groups of employees. Cranet provides the best available indication of the extent of organisations' use of different forms of PfP across different groups of the workforce. There are dramatic cross-national comparative differences in the use of PfP.

Figure 28 The use of individualised PfP (PRP) for manual employees in six countries

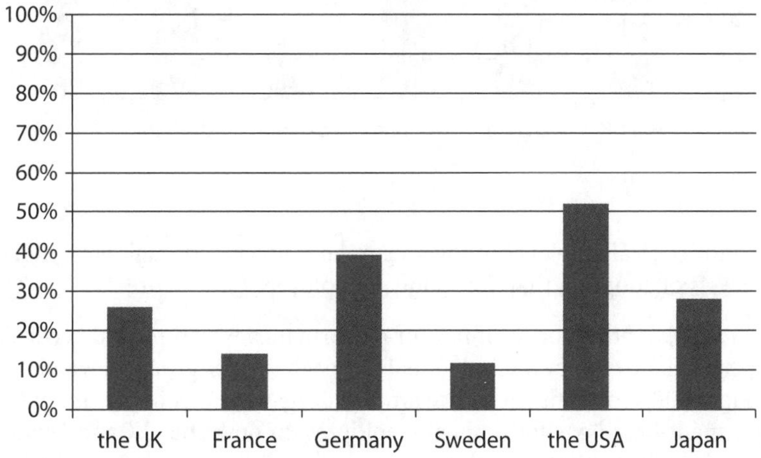

Source: Cranet (2010)

The situation with regard to organisations' use of individualised PfP – sometimes termed performance-related pay (PRP) – in the packages of manual employees provides an interesting starting point (see Figure 28). The variation in the use of individualised PfP is intriguing and in many ways surprising. The use of such PfP is quite extensive in the USA, often taken to be the leader in such practice, but in some countries in continental Europe, such as Germany, a significant proportion of organisations also make considerable use of such individualised PRP. The UK is similar to Japan in terms of level of adoption, while France and Sweden avoid the use of PfP for manual employees. Even the highest proportion of adoption across all countries does not exceed half of organisations.

Figure 29 The use of individualised PfP (PRP) for clerical employees in six countries

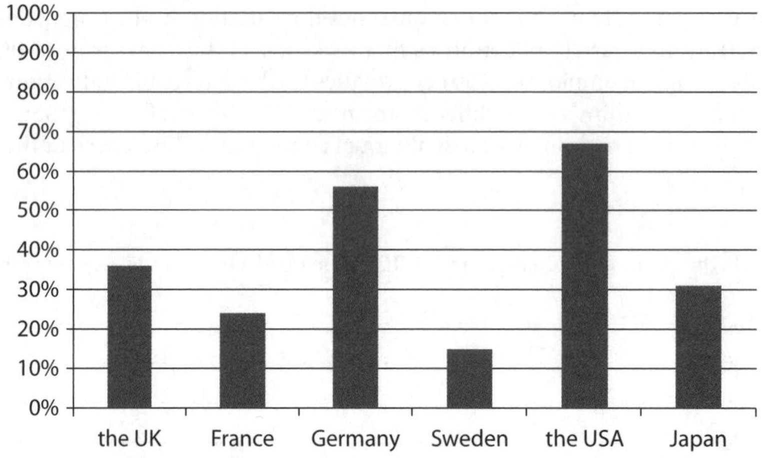

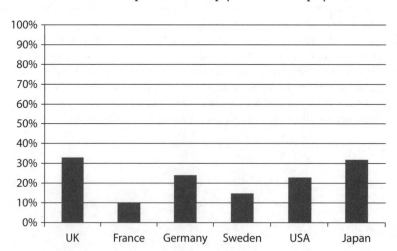

Source: Cranet (2010)

The data for clerical employees shows a similar pattern, although with slightly higher levels of adoption than for manual employees (see Figure 29).

What, though, of other forms of pay for performance which reward according to the performance not of the individual but of the wider group in which they work? Figure 30 shows the incidence amongst organisations of the use of team- or department-based pay for manual employees. In both the UK and Japan just under a third of organisations adopt this practice, followed in popularity in Germany and the USA – but only 10 per cent of French organisations have gone down this route.

Figure 30 The use of team- or department-based pay for manual employees in six countries

Source: Cranet (2010)

Of course, the unit at which performance is assessed may range more broadly, to encompass the organisation as a whole. Employees may be rewarded on the basis of the performance of the entire organisation of which they are a part via share ownership, stock options or profit-sharing (Pendleton *et al*, 2001, 2002). Such schemes can be either narrow, applied to managers in an attempt to overcome the 'agency' problem – to get them to act in the interests of the shareholders rather than themselves; or broad, applied to most or all people in the firm in an attempt to get them committed to boosting the share price (Pendleton *et al*, 2001).

Figure 31 The use of employee share ownership schemes for manual employees in six countries

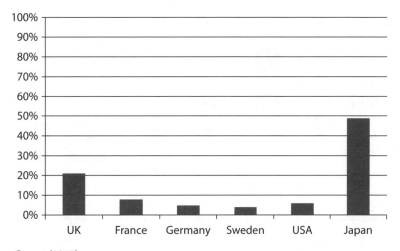

Source: Cranet (2010)

Employee share ownership schemes (ESOPs), in particular, were the subject of intense discussion in the UK during the 1980s. Figure 31 shows the dramatic comparative variation in the extent of the use of such schemes for manual employees (we use manual employees rather than managers to exemplify how shared or not across the hierarchy this approach to rewards is). We would expect share schemes to be more widely used in those countries with well-developed stock markets like the USA, the UK, France and the Netherlands. Brewster *et al* (2007) reported the situation using the 2004 Cranet data, which showed a comparatively high incidence of such schemes in the UK but this level being surpassed in France and Denmark, with all these countries surpassing adoption levels in the USA by a significant margin. The latest 2010 data show some patterns of continuity and some of change. Adoption levels in the USA remain lower than in the UK and France. However, it is in Japan that the use of this practice is significantly different – almost half of organisations using the practice.

Figure 32 shows that for France, Germany, and even the USA, the use of profit-sharing rather than share ownership schemes is the preferred option. In general, however, adoption levels are lower than might be expected from some management discussions. The comparative pattern for clerical employees (not shown here) is very similar, although quite generally the use of profit-sharing tends to be a little more extensive amongst this group than amongst manual employees.

Figure 32 The use of profit-sharing for manual employees in six countries

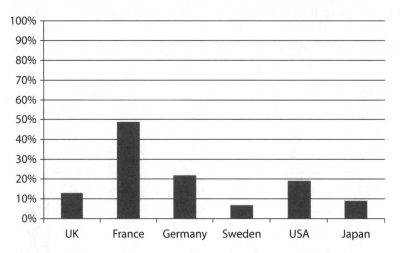

Source: Cranet (2010)

SEDUCTIVE STOCK OPTIONS

CASE STUDIES

Taking lessons from the high-technology start-ups of the US West Coast, larger US corporations began making extensive use of stock options in the 1990s. Stock options afforded those they were offered to the right to buy stock at below-market prices. Stock options were seen as a solution to the principal agent problem introduced by the separation of ownership and control – they could align the interests of managers and shareholders. Moreover, the expense of stock options did not have to be acknowledged until they were exercised. This had huge implications for balance sheets. Perhaps the most striking is the case of Microsoft, at which the cash realisation of stock options would have reduced 2001 profits of US $7.3 billion by a third.

When they were finally exercised, the extent of the implications for the surplus remaining for shareholders and reinvestment was often unclear, particularly in the context of an enduring stock market boom (Stiglitz, 2003). Recent developments in the banking sectors of many countries have deepened the concerns of commentators about the wisdom of certain forms of stock option.

We must expect some aspects of incentivising reward in which the USA would lead the world in terms of incidence across organisations. Cranet data suggest that the USA does still lead in terms of stock options, at least with regard to the management group (see Figure 33). The use of stock options for management is more extensive in the USA than in any of the other five countries shown. However, Germany and the UK are only marginally behind. In Sweden and France this is not a popular HRM practice.

Figure 33 The use of stock options for managerial employees in six countries

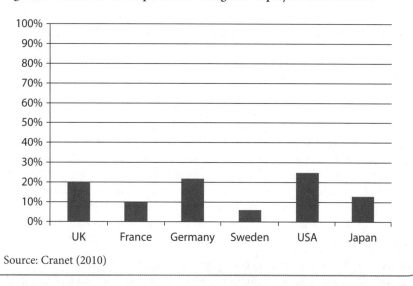

Source: Cranet (2010)

REFLECTIVE ACTIVITY

What rewards practices are indicative of the different pay for performance contexts in the USA, Germany, France, the UK, Sweden and Japan?

Which PfP practices do you think would be the easiest to converge?

VARIABLE PAY IN GERMAN MNCS

CASE STUDIES

Kurdelbusch (2002) explored the emergence of modern forms of variable pay, beyond piecework, in Germany in the 1990s, affording particular attention to the non-managerial employees of large and MNCs. There is a very powerful relationship between the extent of internationalisation of German MNCs, measured by the share of employees employed abroad and in particular by the share of foreign sales in total sales, and the use of incentive-based payment. Interestingly, though, German MNCs did not seem to be adopting practices in their foreign subsidiaries via a process of reverse diffusion. Sheer exposure to an international market appears to encourage the use of variable pay, although it remains unclear whether this is a rational response to a differing competitive context. Independently of the extent of this engagement in international markets, a shareholder value-orientation expressed in the remuneration of top executives, the existence of targets for annual rates of return and the quality of investor relations, also tended to promote variable pay for non-managerial employees.

THE SIGNIFICANCE TO EMPLOYEES OF PAY FOR PERFORMANCE

As Armstrong (2006; p35) notes, even where a great deal of information and data on PfP is available, there is a danger that consideration of it rather neglects the position and views of employees. Antoni *et al* (2005) summarise data available from the European Survey of Working Conditions of 2000, showing employees' perceptions of the incidence of all forms of PfP. In the UK, 11 per cent of employees reported that they are subject to PfP. This is above the proportion in Belgium, at nine per cent, but below that in most European nations. The proportion of employees in the Netherlands reporting their exposure to some form of PfP is the same as that in the UK, and short of the proportions of employees in Germany (12 per cent) and Sweden (14 per cent). According to employees, though, the incidence of PfP is by far the greatest in Finland, where 23 per cent are subject to some form. The survey thus confirms the inadequacy of the notion that weightier collective bargaining implies a lower incidence of PfP. Moreover, the proportions are generally rather lower than we would expect in the light of the Cranet results on the use of PfP by organisations, particularly in that Cranet targets larger organisations. To an extent it seems that managers and employees take different views over whether PfP is in place or not.

There is little data on the proportion of pay packages constituted by PfP, but some data is available for some nations, which is at least indicative. Even in the private sector, despite fairly extensive coverage, PfP of all types accounted for less than 10 per cent of the base pay of Italian employees in 2001. It seems that in Belgium it is of still less importance in terms of the financial reward package as a whole. Perhaps more significantly, evidence from case studies (see Vernon *et al*, 2007) suggests that in practice there is an extremely tight bunching of the actual payouts from PfP. In sum, the proportion of income which an employee experiences as at risk under PfP typically tends to be low in principle, and still lower in practice. This may of course mean that some employees formally subject to PfP are not even aware of this component of their pay package.

CULTURE AND DISTINCTIVE NATIONAL REWARD SYSTEMS

Unraveling the complex set of influences that culture can have on rewards behaviour has become a focus of recent research. Much of the literature on comparative and international HRM stresses the relevance of national cultures to reward, a lot of the discussion building on the work of Hofstede (1980) (see Chapter 2 for the strengths and limitations of Hofstede's original work).

THEORY AND PRACTICE

KEY FRAMEWORK

Cultural dualities in relation to reward

Bento and Ferreira (1992) distilled earlier work to offer a series of dualities in culture, together taken as a 'cultural lens' through which to view the underlying attitudes or assumptions of workforces regarding reward:

- equality – inequality
- certainty – uncertainty
- controllability – uncontrollability
- individualism – collectivism
- materialist foregrounding – personal foregrounding.

The debt to Hofstede (1980) is considerable, although there are differences beyond the terminological. These dimensions and their supposed bearing on reward practices are now outlined in turn.

Equality – inequality

Relating to Hofstede's (1980) notion of power distance, this concerns the national acceptance or toleration of rigid hierarchies featuring levels across which status and reward differ markedly. In the sphere of reward, the key contrast is between a focus on the incentives offered by high pay differentials and a focus on the benefit of low, 'socially healthy' differentials. It also involves elements of perceived fairness, or justice, within HRM systems.

Certainty – uncertainty

Related to Hostede's (1980) uncertainty avoidance, this duality generally concerns attitudes to uncertainty or ambiguity in the context or environment of the employment relationship. Where certainty is valued, employees seek rules, standards and clear procedures, and are uneasy about the returns from work being subject to risk, most especially where the basis of the variability of reward is not explicitly detailed. Conversely, where uncertainty is tolerated or, indeed, welcomed, employees do not expect that the employment relationship be so structured, and are more open to the possibility that work will deliver uncertain returns, even if the manner in which rewards will ultimately be determined is implicit and ambiguous.

Controllability – uncontrollability

This dimension, also covered in part by Hofstede's (1980) uncertainty avoidance index, concerns the attribution of responsibility for the uncertainty faced by an employee. In high-controllability cultures, the organisation is perceived as having

University of
South Wales

the potential to significantly shape or create the organisational context, and so is seen as largely responsible for the situation faced by employees. Where there is high uncontrollability, the organisational context is regarded as predominantly autonomous, beyond the control of actors at organisational level. In many respects, then, employees see the organisation as unavoidably transmitting unpredictability located beyond organisational borders. Where uncertainty is regarded with unease, high controllability implies that key organisational actors will be held responsible for an undesirable unpredictability of reward. Conversely, where uncertainty is tolerated or welcomed, low controllability may lead employees to assign the credit for a favoured variability in reward to the environment, not to their organisation.

Individualism – collectivism

This duality, present in Hofstede (1980), is of relevance to the motivation of employees, and to their assignment of responsibility for good or bad outcomes to an individual or to a larger grouping. Individualistic cultures favour individuals striking independent poses coming together in loose groupings. With individual approach and action critical, individualistic cultures hold that individuals should be rewarded for their contribution to the success of the wider organisation. Conversely, collectivist cultures favour tightly-knit cohesive groups. Rewards are most appropriately shared within the group, and a failure to distribute rewards in this way is disorienting for all and isolating for those seen to be rewarded relatively poorly.

Materialist foregrounding – personal foregrounding

In many respects this facet of attitudes echoes Hofstede's (1980) distinction between masculine and feminine cultures, but with an updating of the terminology. It relates to the relative emphasis placed upon action and achievement as opposed to relationships and empathy. Where the culture is one of materialist foregrounding, symbols of action and success are important, whereas under personal foregrounding, engagement between individuals, nurturing and development are valued in their own right.

NATIONAL CULTURE AND REWARD PRACTICE

Schuler and Rogovsky (1998) present an intriguing quantitative effort to systematically explore the link between national culture and indicators of national prevalence of pay systems across a dozen nations from across and even beyond the advanced industrialised world. They identify many relationships that can be made sense of through the use of the cultural lens.

They found that nations characterised by greater uncertainty avoidance – most commonly the Latin nations – tended to feature pay systems in which seniority and some notion of skill weighed heavily. These nations also put less focus on individual PfP. Conversely, nations with lower uncertainty avoidance – Protestant nations, but most of all, Anglo-Saxon nations – tended to feature less focus on seniority or skill, and more on specifically individual PRP.

They also found that nations characterised by greater individualism – most strikingly the Anglo-Saxon nations – tended to feature a greater focus on PfP generally, and still more strongly a focus on individual PfP. In contrast, nations with less individualism – most prominently Spanish- or Portugese-speaking countries – tended to feature less of such a focus, generally lying at the opposite end of the spectrum. The findings for the focus on share ownership or options are similar.

Nations which rely on a more materialist foregrounding, or greater 'masculinity' in Hofstede's terms, tended to feature more of a focus on individual bonuses. Thus, the Anglo-Saxon area but also Germany and to a remarkable extent Japan generally tended to feature more individual PRP amongst professional and technical staff, amongst clerical staff and amongst manual employees. The contrast here is with the general situation in nations that rely more on personal foregrounding, such as the Scandinavian nations, and indeed the Netherlands, which tended to feature a lesser focus on such payments for these non-managerial employees. Interestingly, there was no significant difference in the focus on individual bonuses for managers specifically between these groups of nations.

SHIFTING PERCEPTIONS OF DISTRIBUTIVE JUSTICE

Studies of distributive justice concern themselves with the rules and standards by which decisions about the allocation of resources (financial or non-financial) are both made and perceived to be fair (Meindl *et al*,1990). Exploring the nature of these decisions and the motives that surround them is perceived as one way

THEORY AND PRACTICE

KEY FRAMEWORK

Rules of fairness in reward

When there is a pot of 'reward' to be shared out, what is the fairest way to do it? Several rule sets have been identified. The two most potent rule sets distinguish between principles of meritocracy and egalitarianism. They are based on principles of:

- 'equity' – whereby entitlements are based on relative contributions, and differential reward is legitimate as long as it is based on an equitable way of differentiating performance. These are felt to be dominant in the USA and related national cultures, such as those of the UK, Australia, and Canada

- 'parity' or 'equality' – in which allocation solutions are insensitive to input differences and call for resources to be distributed equally to all regardless of relative productivity. These are felt to be applicable in collectivist cultures such as those of China and Japan. The decision rule is clearly bounded, in that collectivists make a clear distinction between in-group and out-group members and do not apply equality rules to out-group members. Where teams operate as in-groups, incentives and bonuses should only be given to the group, not to individuals.

in which researchers can gain insight into the social systems that surround rewards behaviour. Allocation problems are resolved by resorting to a series of decision rules that determine the entitlement of recipients. In practice, these rules reflect the familiar, normative rules of a society that concern issues of social and industrial justice. They are also seen to embody decision logics and the value position of individuals and their motives. These logics and value positions are linked to national culture (Meindl *et al*, 1990; p224).

There is evidence, however, especially in the special economic zones of China, that a radically altered institutional and social environment can change previously deep-seated psychological determinants of rewards behaviour, such as distributive justice. The 'new glorious rich' in China's free market challenge the underlying value of equality-based rather than equity-based justice.

Morris and Leung (2000) have provided a review of cross-cultural work on various forms of justice and concluded that different forms of justice – particularly, for example, assessments of distributive justice – can be linked to cultural factors, and a number of studies have examined the impact of distributive justice on important performance-related attitudes. Giacobbe-Miller *et al* (2003) have looked at the adaptation to foreign workplace ideologies of Chinese, Russian and US managers working in joint ventures, and Tata *et al*, (2003) have looked at the link between perceptions of fairness and cultural values of US and Chinese service employees working in foreign-owned enterprises and state-owned enterprises. Murphy-Berman and Berman (2002) examined perceptions of distributive justice amongst managers in Hong Kong and Indonesia, presenting distributive justice dilemmas in the form of vignettes and then attributing justice scores to the actions taken by actors within these scenarios. Although both Indonesia and Hong Kong are collectivist cultures, the value scores differed significantly between the two. Differences in justice assessments were found, and it was argued that culture influenced not only the criteria used to evaluate what was fair but also the degree to which what was seen as fair was additionally judged as good or bad. Lam *et al* (2002) examined the relationship between individual-level measures of individualism and power distance and perceived justice, job satisfaction, perceived competence and absenteeism amongst Hong Kong Chinese and US tellers in a bank. Justice perceptions were related to job satisfaction, performance and absenteeism in both cultures, and the effects were of a stronger magnitude among low power distance individuals. However, once cultural measures were applied at the individual level, country effects disappeared.

REFLECTIVE ACTIVITY

Do you think that differences in reward practices across countries reflect differences in national cultures or other influences?

IS CULTURAL EXPLANATION OF REWARD ENOUGH?

Culture is assumed to have relevance for reward practice via its influence on attitudes to pay. The typical presumption is that it is the attitudes or preferences of employees which are crucial, with employers and managers responding to these employee attitudes or preferences in shaping pay arrangements. Chiang and Birstch (2007) seek to gauge the reward preferences of banking employees in four countries (Canada, the UK, Hong Kong-China and Finland) directly, and then examine the extent to which culture – conceived in the terms of Hofstede – influences these preferences. They find that whereas cross-national variation in culture can account for some of the variation in employees' preferences for types of reward, it has distinct limits as an explanator.

Firstly, the authors show that across all four countries employees tend to value intrinsic more than extrinsic reward, but also that they are quite generally keen that performance be the key criterion or basis for reward – particularly if this is individual performance. Secondly, though, there are distinct limits to which culture can account for the cross-national comparative differences in employees' attitudes to reward which they identify. Indeed, it is not merely that culture conceptualised in the manner of Hofstede cannot fully account for these differences in employee preferences over reward, but that some of these differences appear quite inconsistent with the cultural profiles of countries.

CASE STUDIES

FINNISH EMPLOYEES' REWARD PREFERENCES

The success of Nokia prompts considerable interest in Finnish business and employment relationships more generally. Chiang and Birtch's (2007) findings on the reward preferences of Finnish employees stand out in a number of ways. Finnish employees accord even more importance to intrinsic reward than those in the other countries of their sample, but also value the working environment and work flexibility more than employees in other countries while valuing reward based on individual performance rather less. Most strikingly, however, although valuing reward systems structured around performance almost as much as employees in other countries, employees in Finland value even more (and much more than employees in other countries) reward systems structured around skill and competence. Correspondingly,

they prefer that reward be based predominantly on what Chiang and Birtch (2007) (rather confusingly) term 'human capital', but which the questions on which the authors base their analysis reveal relate to job ladders, career structures and internal labour markets. This is further underscored by Finns' particular preference for job security and basic salary as facets of reward.

These findings for Finland are intriguing because they can be linked to culture only to a very limited extent. Employee expectations and preferences appear driven by other influences. In particular, it is striking that Finnish employees display such attachment to the internal labour market structures which strong industrial unions such as those in Finland tend to create (see eg Pekkarinen and Vartiainen, 2006; Lazear and Shaw, 2008). Moreover, they show a marked valuation of the intrinsic rewards which Nordic unions have long made a focus of their activity (eg Kjellberg, 1992; 1998) – see also the chapter on the organisation of work here.

The findings thus provide a powerful indication of the relevance of unions and collective bargaining in shaping employees' reward preferences.

Although there are substantial indications of the usefulness of a consideration of national culture to an understanding of differences in pay practice, a focus in discussions of reward on such dimensions of national context also has its disadvantages (Vernon, 2005). Firstly, the evidence that these dimensions are enlightening in capturing and explaining either the basis for the incidence of different approaches to reward in different countries, or the typical reactions of a nation's employees to attempts to apply a single system universally, is still a little patchy. Moreover, in practice, nations display certain tendencies in these respects, but also display a great deal of individual difference in attitudes around the typical. More than this, individuals may display multiple or contradictory identities in these cultural respects, making such dimensions a shaky foundation for thinking about appropriate reward, or even for understanding the current basis of cross-national variability.

A related problem of a focus on national culture in thinking about comparative reward is that it disregards the autonomous influence of social actors and of institutions on pay structures and practices. These may act to shape cultures, cut across a dominant culture, or – perhaps most likely – channel cultural influences in a particular way. An alternative strand of research examines the role of social institutions on pay practices, with particular reference to the role of collective bargaining – the joint regulation of the employment relationship by unions and employers/managers.

THE ROLE OF UNIONS, EMPLOYERS' ASSOCIATIONS AND COLLECTIVE BARGAINING

Statutory pay minimums have been established in some central and eastern European nations, and are now a common feature of Anglo-Saxon nations, in force in the USA, Canada, New Zealand, and the UK (see Chapter 5). However, it is in those few nations of continental western Europe featuring such statutory pay minimums that they are set at the highest levels – the minimum rates in the Netherlands and France the very highest by any criterion (OECD, 1998). Yet even these French and Dutch statutory minimums are set at levels too low to be of direct significance to the pay arrangements of most larger, or multinational, employers (Vernon, 2005). That is to say, the statutory regulation of the level of pay is generally of very limited significance for large companies. Indeed, although there are particular exceptions, the same may be said for other forms of statutory regulation of pay arrangements. Meanwhile, in the sphere of collective bargaining and joint regulation, employers' associations now quite generally favour a derogation of detailed pay arrangements to individual companies (Vernon *et al*, 2007). It is unions and works councillors who, through collective bargaining and joint regulation, are the crucial social actors in shaping pay arrangements (Vernon *et al*, 2007).

Unions have traditionally tended to favour pay structures in which pay depends predominantly on the job role, qualifications, certificated competences, seniority/age or documented experience. Moreover, they have generally sought to contain pay differentials within their bargaining arena.

CASE STUDIES

SOCIALLY HEALTHY PAY VERSUS INCREASING PAY DIFFERENTIALS

Some recent discussion has centred on the concept of 'socially healthy pay'. Within societies there are boundaries placed around the range of pay differentials or multiples deemed to be legitimate. These are generally measured by metrics such as the ratio between the highest- and average-, or the highest- and lowest-paid. In the USA high multiples are both legitimate and expected. In continental Europe much narrower multiples are felt to be appropriate. If differentials move beyond accepted limits, social reaction can be marked. Thus, the influential Swedish confederation of manual unions, LO, has expressed considerable unease about the recent increase in the gap between the remuneration of workers and that of the most senior managers in organisations, such executives in large private sector Swedish companies now often paid 40 to 50 times as much as front-line employees. Yet in the USA, the multiple is now 400 to 500 – ie the multiple itself is ten times larger – and yet there is little public comment.

Certainly – as, for example, Marsden (1999) and Lazear and Shaw (2008) suggest – unions and collective bargaining have a very substantial role in shaping internal labour markets, whatever the balance may be between the direct impact of unions and their joint regulation of the employment relationship with employers on the one hand and their impact via the expectations of employees or indeed managers on the other (see also the case study on *Finnish employees' reward preferences* above). Unions organised on an industrial basis – at least, manual employees joining the same union regardless of skill or qualification – promote more unified career structures, and do so all the more strongly the more powerful are the unions concerned. Such internal labour markets are most widely and strongly structured in Finland and Sweden (see Chapter 5). The strength of unions in collective bargaining or the joint regulation of the employment relationship has an enormous influence on overall pay inequality, the stronger unions very substantially compressing pay distributions and differentials (Vernon, 2011).

Instinctively, unions have generally regarded PfP with some suspicion. Nonetheless, pressed by employers and indeed by employees, unions which sense some opportunity to shape developments now generally accept the principle of PfP, regarding the devil as in the detail (Vernon *et al*, 2007). Unions are often keen that no groups should be excluded from PfP where it is introduced for some, but simultaneously pursue the containment of any performance-related element of the overall pay package. Typically, unions regard PfP formally comprising 10 per cent of total remuneration as going quite far enough. They are often keen also to compress the variation of such payments in practice, such that the actual spread in the performance-related sums paid out is much more limited. In these respects union concerns with solidarity and the exposure of employees to risk survive.

With regard to pay systems, multi-employer agreements at the level of industries, for example, tend not to be directly restrictive of PfP (Vernon *et al*, 2007). Yet their specification of minimum pay rates or increases implies that payment for performance must be made on top of such agreed pay. Moreover, where there is established local union representation and/or a works council with statutory rights to negotiation or, indeed, co-determination over pay systems, such local employee representatives negotiate over the design and operation of all forms of reward, including PfP.

What more, though, of law and statutory regulation? Generally, signs of its impact are hard to identify. With regard to profit-sharing, the situation in France demonstrates the role which law can play in driving a wedge in practice between different nations, even in spheres such as this where there is cross-border management sympathy towards the broad desirability of a practice. In France profit-sharing is now mandatory in private sector organisations with a workforce of over 50 (van het Kaar and Grünell, 2001). The case of Finland shows something quite different – that profit-sharing can be quite consistent with powerful unions and significant collective bargaining.

Very clearly, the incidence of PfP is far from always being what we would expect on the basis of simple cultural characterisations of societies. Moreover, the findings belie ordinary presumptions about the implications of collective bargaining or joint regulation for pay systems. Whereas it is absolutely clear that more significant collective bargaining diffuses and strengthens internal labour markets and compresses overall pay inequality, it has no such clearly demonstrable effect on PfP arrangements.

CASE STUDIES

PERFORMANCE-RELATED PAY IN THE UK AND FINLAND

Large-scale national surveys of employees in the UK and Finland offer provocative findings (Vernon, 2005). Surveys of the UK show that across the economy as a whole, including the public sector, 25 per cent of employees are subject to individual PfP of one sort or another. In Finland, across the economy as a whole, 23 per cent of manual employees are subject to merit pay specifically. Among lower-level clerical employees the proportion is 40 per cent, and it is still higher among upper clerical employees and managers. Merit pay is the predominant form of individual PfP in Finland, but other forms are present. Conservatively, then, at least a third of Finnish employees are subject to some form of individualised PfP. Clearly, PfP is more common in Finland than in the UK. This strikingly contradicts any notion that individualised PfP occurs where unions and collective bargaining are weaker.

MANAGING PAY FOR PERFORMANCE: PROCEDURAL ISSUES

Experience within the UK demonstrates the complexity of the management of PfP in practice. Individual PfP is attractive to UK managers because it not only signals management's interest in performance (Kessler, 2007) but emphasises the role of the individual and also in principle meets the 'line of sight' criterion – the demands are manifold. Communicating the nature and purpose of initiatives, achieving meaningful objective-setting, eliciting employee acceptance of the legitimacy of the criteria and of the eventual distribution of reward, and avoiding the obscuring of developmental facets of performance management in review meetings have all proved particularly difficult for UK managers (Armstrong, 2006; pp276–277). More generally, in organisations that have tried it there is often a view that the proper management of PfP is tremendously costly in terms of management training and time (see eg Armstrong, 2006). The limitations of attempts at evaluating PfP schemes also often leave those more intimately involved in managing them unconvinced of their benefits.

As we have already seen, unions across the advanced industrialised world have rather common concerns about PfP. Beyond the containment of the practical effect of PfP on employees' take-home pay already discussed, unions are typically concerned to pursue procedural issues (Vernon *et al*, 2007). Unions' and works councillors' concerns tend to reflect those of employees who have been subject to the reality of PfP. The process of joint regulation in the development and application of PfP may well complicate the enactment of management initiatives in the arena of pay, but may well also contribute to the effective functioning of PfP as it unfolds. Marsden (2005), following his study of performance pay for teachers in the UK, suggests that unions can have just this role.

REFLECTIVE ACTIVITY

There are extensive discussions in the literature about the influence of national institutions, laws and culture on HRM issues such as rewarding staff. Obviously, there are a range of different practices even within the various national boundaries. Are these boundaries the best level of analysis?

In what respects might unions present problems to managements introducing PfP? In what respects might their input be valuable?

INTERNATIONAL EVIDENCE ON BEST PRACTICE IN REWARD

Despite the enormously varied practice of organisations, particularly internationally:

- Might there exist some generalisable or universal international best practice in reward, at least for front-line employees?
- What of the evidence on the relationship between pay systems and performance?

- Can we arrive at an evidence-based notion of best practice in the field of PfP?

The popularity of individualised incentives amongst many general managers and some personnel/HRM professionals makes PfP an obvious candidate. Yet the evidence that individualised incentives deliver better business performance is remarkably limited. Cases that they do rest remarkably heavily on Lazear's (2000) study, which shows that the mid-1990s introduction of a piece-rate pay system (with some minimum hourly guarantee) at Safelite – an autoglass installer in the USA – was associated with a 44 per cent increase in the number of units installed per person per day. Yet the study leaves a good deal unclear, arousing the suspicion that the productivity boom could have been generated by other initiatives. Moreover, the appropriateness of this very narrow performance measure, and so the significance of this performance achievement, even in this particular case remains rather debatable, and the potential of such an approach in other more complex work contexts highly dubious.

What, then, of the evidence for financial participation as a generalised best practice? This might appear a more attractive candidate in international context as it might be thought to meet fewer cultural barriers than does individual incentivisation. Kruse (1993) famously argued that profit-sharing could act via employee attitudes and motivation to improve financial performance, and presented some evidence on the link to the bottom line. Coyle-Shapiro *et al*'s (2002) longitudinal study of the implications of profit-sharing for attitudes and behaviours in a British organisation suggests that the (effective) organisational commitment of employees is promoted by their perceptions of the appropriateness and legitimacy of the profit-sharing scheme implemented. Kuvaas' (2003) study of a Norwegian organisation features very similar findings despite the very different context, suggesting that there may be general international lessons here. This, though, is no international evidence of the generalised business performance impact of any particular form of financial participation.

Kalmi *et al*'s (2005) study of larger listed organisations in four European countries offers some evidence based upon managers' perceptions of the outcomes of financial participation where schemes are in place. It is the non-findings which are striking. Whereas almost 90 per cent of managers regard improved productivity as a relevant aim for financial participation in principle, there is no relationship between managers' reports of the impact of financial participation on productivity and the extent of employee coverage of either profit-sharing or equity schemes. D'Art and Turner (2004) deploy Cranet data to analyse the relationship between profit-sharing for front-line staff and managerial ratings of business performance across 10 European countries. They uncover a powerful link between profit-sharing and respondents' ratings of recent profitability, and some rather weaker links to respondents' assessments of the relative productivity and service quality of the organisation. Yet there are fragilities in this evidence and profound doubts about the appropriate interpretation of this evidence – most particularly since profitability likely promotes profit-sharing rather than profit-sharing improving profitability (see Vernon, 2010).

Antoni *et al* (2005) consider the performance improvements from empowerment initiatives involving the delegation of management tasks to groups of non-managerial employees in 1,300 organisations in 10 EU countries, focusing in particular on the effects on the success of such delegation of the use of collective PfP (whether team/department performance, profit-sharing schemes or ESOPs). Companies with such collective PfP report significantly better outcomes from group delegation initiatives, with greater reductions in management and increases in output. Moreover, where delegation is carried furthest, such collective pay is also associated with reductions in costs and in throughput times. Yet of course this evidence does not imply that collective reward *per se* is evidence-based best practice – even across these European countries.

With little indication of any evidence-based best practice in PfP, might there be generalised promise in less celebrated facets of pay packages? Kessler (2007) stresses the continuing relevance of linking pay to post in legitimating pay structures. We would note that:

● Employees' notions of a good job often have at their core the structures and securities of the internal labour market (Jacoby, 1997).

● Internal labour markets are crucial to the active co-operation of employees which employers in a wide range of contexts require (Williamson *et al*, 1975).

● In this context it may be that more substantial steps in pay through a clearly elaborated job and pay hierarchy, or internal labour market, improve firm performance.

The evidence on the last of these observations is only now starting to emerge, and is currently rather contradictory. Certainly, though, internationally, a recent survey of more than 100,000 employees of a multinational hotel chain showed that elements of an internal labour market (job security, training opportunities and promotion opportunities) are critical to front-line employees' job satisfaction and organisational commitment (McPhail and Fisher, 2008). It would be surprising if this did not have implications for productivity performance.

In summary, the current research evidence cautions against a presumption that individualised incentives offer a universal best practice in reward. Collective PfP including but not limited to financial participation and/or an emphasis on internal labour markets appear more likely candidates. Still, it seems most likely that despite the focus on reward and most specifically pay amongst many managers, best practice cannot reside in isolation in this arena, but will rather take in a combination of practices across a number of arenas of people management including, for example, the organisation of work.

SPACE FOR STRATEGY

Although the implications of national culture and systems of joint regulation are not always what we might imagine, it is clear that they have an important effect on pay arrangements.

CASE STUDIES

COMPENSATION PRACTICE IN MCDONALD'S ACROSS EUROPE

Perhaps unsurprisingly, McDonald's has sought to export an approach to compensation from their domestic operations across their outlets, regardless of national location. This involves avoidance of and resistance to meaningful collective bargaining over pay, and a focus on containing wage costs. With regard to German operations it is also a matter of an ongoing struggle to prevent the formation at its restaurants of works councils which would have the right to co-determine pay systems (Royle, 2000; 2004). Nonetheless, the real pay levels of McDonald's counter staff, adjusted for the purchasing power of currencies, shows marked variation within Europe. For example, real pay is typically more than 50 per cent greater in the Nordic countries than in the UK (Royle, 2000). Whatever its corporate stance, McDonald's must both attract staff and offer them a reward package that they consider legitimate, necessitating adjustment not only to legal regulation but to the societal norms and generally prevailing pay practices which legal and bargaining institutions have served to shape.

This is not to say that organisations must simply take up what is existing typical practice with regard to reward. There is variability within nations in the cultures and expectations of employees, as well as in the bargaining institutions with which employers engage. Bloom *et al* (2003) stress the variability within nations in the pay practices to which employees are used, a variability present too within particular industries and occupational groups.

Moreover, Lowe *et al* (2002) indicates that the prevalence of a system is no necessary guide to its cultural fit. Examining the attitudes of managers and engineers towards pay systems, the research finds that PfP at this level is quite evenly spread across the 10 nations spanned by the study, even across the divide between the established advanced industrialised nations and the newly industrialised countries. Yet employees on the North American continent particularly would like to see more. Also, although variable pay tends to be contingent on group performance rather more in Asian nations than in North America, employees across the world are equally keen on such a basis. Perhaps most interestingly, whereas Anglo-Saxon nations displayed less emphasis on long-term performance in their pay systems, employees across the world valued such a long-term emphasis similarly.

Clearly, there are culturally permitted alternatives which, for some reason, are not reflected in pay practice. It might be added that the space allowed for innovation in reward by unions and collective bargaining is much greater than is often thought (see earlier discussion here and Vernon *et al* (2007). Managers must of course reflect carefully before positioning their pay practice at the extreme of any existing range of practices, and even greater care is required if this positioning is to be beyond the range of the normal (Vernon, 2005; 2010). Yet they are less constrained than they may sometimes feel.

KEY LEARNING POINTS

- Reward practices, and notions of good reward practice, vary considerably across countries, despite increasing commonalities in the language with which debates are conducted.

- National cultures, laws and institutional arrangements are important influences on reward practice.

- Organisations have to remain aware of these differences when they determine their policies and practices in reward as in other areas.

- Different logics in different nations mean that the 'political' messages that must be communicated in order to 'sell' a policy objective soon become immersed in national culture or expectations.

- Still, the 'strategic space' (Vernon, 2005, 2010) for innovation in pay practices is greater than is sometimes suggested.

- Indications of an international best practice in reward are only now starting to emerge – and they are *not* consistent with simple ideas about incentivisation.

LEARNING QUESTIONS

1 What are the main cross-national differences in the nature of pay systems and practices?

2 How would you characterise the underlying philosophy that British HR professionals have towards reward, compared with French HR professionals?

3 What are the main ways in which national culture influences rewards behaviour?

4 Is there a danger of focusing too much on national culture as a driver of pay practice?

EXPLORE FURTHER

Vernon, G. (2010) 'International pay and reward', in P. Edwards and C. Rees (eds) *International Human Resource Management*, 2nd edition, London, FT/Prentice Hall. The chapter provides an alternative and complementary overview of international reward.

Kessler, I. (2007) 'Reward Choices: Strategy and Equity', in Storey, J. (ed) *Human Resource Management: A Critical Text* (3rd Edition) London: Thomson. This chapter overviews the advantages of traditional pay structures linking pay to post.

Lazear, E. and Shaw, K. (2008) *The Structure of Wages: An international comparison*, Chicago, NBER. This constitutes a book-length treatment of cross-national comparative differences in reward structures within the established OECD.

D'Art, D. and Turner, T. (2004) 'Profit-sharing, firm performance and union influence in selected European countries', *Personnel Review*, 33 (3): 335–350. The authors provide an international analysis of financial participation and performance.

CHAPTER 11

Training and Development

LEARNING OUTCOMES

When they have read this chapter, students will:

- be able to provide a definition of training and development, and understand the range of underpinning institutional and cultural factors that go to make up a comparative knowledge of training and development

- be aware of the drivers for continued education within organisations, and the differing relative levels of this across regional/national groupings

- appreciate the reasons behind the rising levels of interest in management development and the different emphasis this interest may have in different contexts

- be able to integrate the themes contained within the chapter in order to articulate the implications and challenges for internationally-operating organisations.

INTRODUCTION

Training and development has long been seen as one of the key issues for management. In the light of the vast amount that has been written about training, learning and development and the variety of terms that are used, this chapter starts with some definitions. After the definitions the chapter then sets the scene for understanding comparative training and development by describing cross-national variations in systems of initial vocational education and training (VET) and considering them in relation to comparative national levels of attainment. It challenges the reader to consider the implication of these for organisations as they make decisions concerning the location of new enterprises or factories. Having considered both VET and typical attainment levels post-education, the chapter then moves on to consider the training and development investment that occurs within the workplace. Cranet data is used to illustrate the relative amount of time devoted by organisations and also the typical level of investment found in different contexts. Once the comparative training and development perspectives have been introduced, the chapter focuses specifically upon management development – a subject that has increased in its perceived importance.

We begin by providing some important definitions. According to Armstrong (1999), training is the planned and systematic modification of behaviour through learning events, programmes and instruction which enable individuals to achieve the levels of knowledge, skill and competence to carry out their work effectively, whereas development is the growth or realisation of a person's ability and potential through the provision of learning and educational experiences. Dowling and Welch (2004) suggest that whereas training aims to improve employees' current work skills and behaviour, development may be differentiated as being aimed at increasing ability in relation to some future position or role.

Although these definitions take an individual perspective, the OECD acknowledges human capital as a major factor driving economic growth, both in the world's most advanced economies and those experiencing rapid development. Tregaskis and Heraty (2011) report how the level of interest in training and development has spawned a growing literature on 'organisational learning' and 'human capital'. The terminological shift has seen a broadening of the agenda, which now extends well beyond the conventional territory of training interventions, and its integration with the business plan, to take in many aspects of work and corporate organisation (Reid *et al*, 2004). Such discussions are usually linked to those around high-performance work systems or high-performance practices for non-managerial employees (eg Appelbaum *et al*, 2000; Ashton and Felstead, 2001). At the same time there is a growing emphasis upon management development, much of which now occurs in the context of organisations that are international and wish to develop an international management cadre (eg Woodall, 2005; Mabey and Ramirez, 2004, 2011). However, most commentaries have tended to focus on a one-nation discussion, often based on US or UK companies. What tends to be lacking from such discussions is the contextual background necessary to understand the different manifestations of training and development in different environments. Contextual factors such as typical levels of educational attainment across the population of a country or nation and state/government influences that shape the vocational educational system provide the background to understanding comparative training and development. These contextual factors are particularly important for an understanding of the challenges facing organisations as they strive to operate, recruit, rotate and manage staff internationally. At a macro level a key contextual factor must be the state of the global economy, with the recent global financial crisis of 2008 having changed things, not least employment prospects, particularly amongst those with lower education levels (according to European Commission figures, 2009).

TRAINING AND DEVELOPMENT IN CONTEXT

A wide variety of authors have sought to identify the factors, external and internal to the firm, which shape HRM policies and practices (Harzing and Ruysseveldt, 1995; De Cieri and Dowling, 1999; Schuler *et al*, 2002). In order therefore to understand the factors which shape training and development provision in different contexts we must reconsider a number of the factors outlined earlier in Chapters 2 and 3 (on culture) and 4 (on CHRM and institutional theory). In particular, Chapter 4 contains some of the most relevant theories including the literature on varieties of capitalism, as well as more micro-level factors relating to the firm such as the nature of ownership (Jackson and Schuler, 1995).

Figure 34 seeks to map out the factors that shape the level and type of training and/or development delivered/required by organisations within a given context. The figure suggests that there are pre-existing factors or conditions that influence the type and nature of training and development practices in the workplace. These conditions include:

- culture
- ownership structures
- the role of the state and political and other forces which in turn shape:
  - the levels of workforce achievement, particularly literacy and numeracy which emerge as a result of the compulsory schooling system
  - educational and labour market norms
  - the national system of vocational educational training which sits 'on top of' the compulsory schooling system and which reflects the economic, political and cultural institutional forces at play within a country.

We will say a little about the first two of these before dealing in more detail with those that relate to the role of the state.

The tools of cultural analysis outlined in Chapter 2 are relevant here in terms of understanding how firms in different contexts might approach training and development – but the role of institutions is key too (see Chapter 4). Aycan (2005) notes that in cultures where there is a heavy emphasis upon performance excellence and quality there is a large budgetary allocation to the widespread application of training and developing, as an example citing work in China (Tsang, 1994) and in the United Arab Emirates (Wilkins, 2001). In collectivist cultures, rather than upon improving individual or team performance, the emphasis in training, according to Wong *et al* (2001) is more upon increasing loyalty to the organisation. Unsurprisingly perhaps in low power distance cultures, there is a discussion and joint decision-making on training needs which does not take place in more paternalistic, high power distance cultures (Wilkins, 2001). Similarly, in high power distance and collectivist contexts the selection of who receives training is more likely to be about in-group favouritism than about performance and actual training needs.

Figure 34 The impact of national and organisational characteristics on training and development

The impact of national and organisational characteristics upon training and development

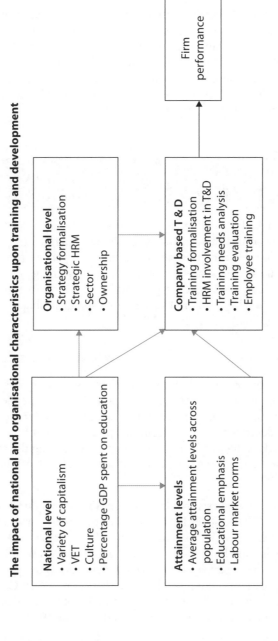

Source: adapted from Nikandrou *et al* (2008)

The question of ownership is likewise a key determiner in terms of shaping training and development strategy along with organisational size. Smaller organisations typically spend less on training than larger organisations (although they may do more coaching and mentoring) and this is likely to be compounded in locations where historically there has always been a preponderance of smaller firms. Earlier commentators such as Rosenzweig and Nohria (1994) have considered the influence of parent MNCs upon local subsidiaries, with training provision being one of these influential areas. As Mabey and Ramirez (2011) suggest, it has become a tendency of MNC subsidiaries to adopt parent or 'best-practice' norms particularly in the macro-HRD practices like training needs analysis, management development delivery and evaluation procedures, while allowing for the details of the delivery of local training to be determined by the subsidiary, as highlighted by Tregaskis *et al* (2001).

THE ROLE OF THE STATE NATIONAL SYSTEMS: VARIETIES OF CAPITALISM, EDUCATION, AND INITIAL VOCATIONAL EDUCATION AND TRAINING

Chapter 4 introduced the reader to institutional theory as it is relevant to an understanding of comparative HRM. It considered the role of the state and the related issue of the role and strength of the unions as well as differing ownership patterns. All of these help shape our understanding training and development, and we shall begin by considering typical attainment levels before moving on to describe how national systems and varieties of capitalism shape initial forms of vocational education and training (VET).

WORKFORCE ACHIEVEMENT: LITERACY AND NUMERACY

By way of definitions it is worth noting that 'lower secondary education' is defined as schooling between the ages of 11 and 13, and 'upper secondary' is the final element of secondary education, which differs in duration and different contexts and is described either as 'terminal' (ie preparing the student for entry directly into working life) and/or 'preparatory' (ie preparing the student for tertiary education). The term 'tertiary education' is defined as higher education (HE) (OECD, 2002).

Sahlberg (2007; p10) suggests that the average educational duration of the adult population in OECD countries is 11.9 years. In the 1960s a majority of adults in almost all societies had only basic education or less. For example, in Finland, the Netherlands, Spain and Italy 80–90 per cent of the adult population of 15 years or older had only basic education, and 10–20 per cent, some type of secondary education qualification. Changing labour markets in many OECD countries called for a better-educated labour force with different knowledge, skills and competencies compared with those educated before the 1970s.

According to Sahlberg (2007; p10) the proportion of individuals who have completed upper secondary education has been growing in nearly all OECD countries. Among 25- to 34-year-olds in most OECD countries the proportion currently ranges from 70 to 97 per cent. Many countries with traditionally low educational attainment levels are now rapidly catching up with more developed countries. The official target in the EU, for example, is to have at least 85 per cent of all young adults with at least an upper secondary education qualification.

However, developing countries generally have lower rates of adult literacy still, and are striving to achieve universal primary education in order to redress this situation. In many countries, low literacy undermines the competitiveness of cheap labour costs and a youthful population. The Asia-Pacific region has set the target of achieving universal primary education by 2015, although this might be a difficult task for countries such as India, Laos and Pakistan where teacher shortages are severe, enrolment rates are low, and nearly half of the adult population is illiterate. Until the late 1990s indications of the comparative capabilities of countries were weak and fragmented. The International Adult Literacy Survey (IALS) of the late 1990s offered a systematic assessment of literacy, broadly conceived, across 20 OECD nations (Crouch *et al*, 1999). The first IALS survey showed that the people of Sweden were the most literate and numerate. Sweden had the highest average scores on all three scales employed, ranking first on each of prose, document and quantitative literacy. The UK ranked 13th, 16th and 17th respectively on these scales, although it did better than the Republic of Ireland. The USA and other Anglo-Saxon nations did slightly better than the UK and the Irish Republic, but there was a clear gulf between the better-performing countries of continental Europe and those of the Anglo-Saxon world.

There was also a marked contrast in the extent of variation in achievement amongst the citizens of the different nations surveyed. Each of the Anglo-Saxon nations displayed very much greater variation in the literacy of its citizens than did the nations of continental Europe. Chile and Poland footed the rankings in terms of overall average, and also showed the greatest variation in their citizens' achievements. The IALS suggests very strongly that whatever its basis in cross-national comparative variation in education and training provision and development opportunities, there is great difference in the structure of achievement of the populations of the various countries of the established advanced industrialised world. We would expect that this difference between countries would be even greater if newly emerging nations were considered. Countries such as Finland, New Zealand, Korea and Japan scored consistently well across all areas. The UK and the Republic of Ireland were in the top 10 (out of 32). France was poor in two areas but came into the top 10 for maths. The USA scored only at average levels in all areas. Surprisingly, post-unification Germany scored between 20th and 22nd. Mexico and Brazil were in the two bottom places. The results show that basic skills acquired immediately post-school can be a good indicator of the subsequent load that is placed on VET systems.

The rationale behind such monitoring and the more recent updates including the Adult Literacy and Life Skills Survey (ALLS) and the Programme for the

International Assessment of Adult Competencies (PIAAC) is the belief that literacy skills (and basic cognitive skills more generally) are an important determinant of the life opportunities of individuals and of social and economic well-being at the level of nations. Schneider and Soskice (2009) state that representational systems and politics play a key role here, in that educational performance at the bottom end is strikingly better in the co-ordinated/proportional representative economies than in the liberal/majoritarian ones. Tessaring and Wannan (2004) estimated that by 2010 almost half of the net additional jobs would require people with tertiary-level qualifications; just under 40 per cent would require upper secondary level and only 15 per cent basic schooling. Thus they predicted a continuing major decline in job prospects for the low-skilled.

CASE STUDIES

CONTAINERS WORLDWIDE – THE CHALLENGE OF TRAINING AND DEVELOPMENT IN REMOTE LOCATIONS

Container terminals are almost always built in remote locations, away from cities and with a requirement for high-level operational structures and equipment, given that the task of handling around 1,000,000 containers a year is a complicated one.

HRM professionals face particular challenges when setting up such large infrastructure operations in highly remote locations where experience with highly modern operational equipment is far from the norm and the typical level of attainment might be low – which may also include 'employment skills' such as being able to drive. The apparent lack of existing qualified people in the workplace may be further compounded by an apparent lack of training infrastructure in the countries. Thus two major challenges centre on resourcing in time for the opening of the facility and the ongoing training required for continued competence of the workforce.

Containers Worldwide were developing a new Egyptian facility with a requirement for over 1,000 employees. The head of HR decided to start with the end goal in mind. He knew when the building works would be complete and when the equipment – such as gantry cranes, trucks, RTGs, straddle carriers, etc – would begin to arrive and, most importantly, when the first vessel would arrive.

The only really unknown variable in this start-up was the people. Here some innovative thinking was deployed in order to recruit individuals with even remotely appropriate skills. The approach adopted was to seek to recruit any local people who made a good first impression – ie taxi drivers, hotel employees, KFC and Pizza Hut service personnel – basically from anywhere. So, for example, taxi drivers should possess proven expertise in driving and could possibly be 'retrained' to operate a gantry train (not a simple task, but one that was trialled).

The training approach was to arrange the secondment of operators from other leading terminals in the global network to act as local trainers for a prolonged period. These individuals could both meet the immediate resourcing requirements to ensure that the facility was operational on time, and also could engage with the local recruits to develop them 'on the job'. In the case of their new Egyptian container port, Containers Worldwide was able to have the facility open for training purposes for approximately one month before the first ship arrived, thus allowing for simulation training before real 'on-the-the-job' training commenced.

Source: contributed by Tommy Olofsen, Henley MBA Programme 2010/11

REFLECTIVE ACTIVITY

Imagine you are the resourcing and training manager responsible for the establishment of a new operation. You have some influence in the selection of the location, but must meet both quality and budget requirements.

What factors would you take into account when evaluating the options?

GROWTH IN THE HIGHER EDUCATION MARKET

Education can, of course, continue beyond the normal school-leaving age on programmes that are not vocational in strict terms, being more theoretical or academic in emphasis. According to Hall and Soskice (2001), the proportion of those aged 25–34 who in the late 1990s held a university degree was estimated by the OECD to be in the range of 10 to 17 per cent for 15 nations. The exceptional nations were Austria and Italy, with outstandingly low proportions, and the USA, with a notably high proportion of 26 per cent. Beyond these exceptional nations, though, there was little difference between the proportion of the cohort who held degrees in continental European nations and in Anglo-Saxon nations.

RELATIVE ACHIEVEMENT?

CASE STUDIES

According to Cascio *et al* (2008), American teenagers perform considerably worse on international assessments of achievement than do teenagers in other high-income countries, a fact that may initially appear surprising. Cascio and Gordon (2008) used data from the first International Assessment of Adult Literacy (IALS) to find out if this skill gap remained once these teenagers became adults. They report that although US teenagers perform relatively poorly, ranking behind teenagers in the 12 other rich countries surveyed, this picture does not

continue. Indeed, by their late twenties, Americans have not just caught up but compare very favourably with those in other locations. What is the reason for this? Cascio and Gordon (2008) suggest that the 'catch up' in American literacy rates between teen years and late twenties is due to the fact that for most of the twentieth century the USA led the developed world in participation and completion of higher education. However, it will be interesting to see the picture emerging from future comparative studies as other countries expand access to university education.

The last decade has seen higher education (HE) continue to grow into a global business, with perhaps three million students studying outside their own countries, and billions of pounds, euros and dollars generated from tuition, living expenses, branch campuses, franchises and much else. The number of students in HE has increased substantially in developing countries in Asia and Latin America. China, in particular, saw the total number of students in HE increase from 3.6 million in 1900 to 30 million in 2006 – the highest total in the world. Many developing countries are also promoting HE as part of a strategy to achieve long-term sustainable economic growth. Malaysia and Tunisia are world leaders in education investment, and invest a substantial share of their wealth (around 8 per cent of GDP) in education.

CASE STUDIES

FOCUS ON EUROPE

A target has been established within Europe that 40 per cent of 30- to 34-year-olds should have tertiary education qualifications by 2020. Closely linked to this is the headline target that Europe should spend 3 per cent of GDP on research. Other EU-level objectives for higher education include the education benchmark for 2010 to increase the number of mathematics, science and technology graduates by at least 15 per cent over the 2000 level. To support the process in Europe, the 1999 Bologna Declaration set the European member states a list of specific tasks aiming at developing a common framework for HE.

According to Leney (2005):

The institutional settings of education and training sector are changing with national initiatives which include the permeability from VET to HE (eg Austria, Finland, Sweden, the UK), the increase of general education in vocational education (eg Belgium) or the creation of occupational-oriented study programmes at tertiary level (eg Bulgaria, Latvia, Germany, France).

VOCATIONAL EDUCATION AND TRAINING

What then, of education beyond school that does not result in a degree – the matter of intermediate skills?

Vocational education has been at the core of secondary education policies in OECD countries, and especially in the EU, for a decade. In most OECD countries vocational education is traditionally offered in schools, except in the UK where many vocational programmes are actually labelled as further education. In other countries, such as Austria, Iceland and the Czech Republic, however, about half of vocational and technical programmes are a combination of school- and work-based elements. In many countries new structures and alternative forms of vocational education have attracted more students to attend vocational programmes. In Finland, for example, a campaign to promote vocational education as an alternative to general education has led to a slow but sustainable increase of vocational education enrolments since the mid-1990s (Sahlberg, 2007; p7).

Given the possible benefits of VET, its form and extent have received particular attention (eg Crouch *et al*, 1999). As Chapter 4 illustrates, links have been made between varieties of capitalism and the nature and reach of VET. Hall and Soskice (2001) report a dichotomy between national systems in which the extensive provision of VET is co-ordinated by national governments or other societal actors to provide a broad skill base and those in which VET is more limited in its reach, and less co-ordinated, with greater polarisation in achievement. The co-ordinated market economies (CMEs: see Chapter 4) tend to have higher coverage of vocational educational training programme and a longer-term view (Hall and Soskice, 2001). At the other extreme, liberal market economies (LMEs: see Chapter 4) are likely to have a shorter-term focus. Broadly, extensive and co-ordinated provision of VET is characteristic of the nations of northern continental Europe, whereas VET is more limited and less co-ordinated in the Anglo-Saxon nations. Although the level of co-ordination of VET in Japan is questionable, it tends to be grouped together with the continental European nations in such analyses because it is often suggested that initial training, though grounded within organisations, is particularly sophisticated and broad-based.

Does it matter if VET systems differ in this way? Hall and Soskice (2001) would say that it does. They argue that the extensive and co-ordinated provision of high-quality VET facilitates certain production and product market strategies, in particular encouraging a focus on continuous improvement and incremental innovation in product strategies and production processes. They contrast this situation with that in which VET is limited and weakly co-ordinated, and where post-compulsory education and training is principally a matter of college and university education resulting in degrees. In these circumstances, evident in the Anglo-Saxon (LME) world, Hall and Soskice (2001) argue that radical innovation

Table 15 The form and reach of initial VET

Form of VET	Nation	Share of cohort in VET (per cent)
Dual apprenticeship	Austria	22
	Germany	34
	Switzerland	23
Vocational college	Sweden	36
	Norway	37
	Finland	32
Company-based	Japan	16*
	Italy	25
	France	38
Mixed	Belgium	53
	the Netherlands	43
	Denmark	31
Variable but weak	the USA	3
	the UK	11
	Canada	5
	Australia	9
	New Zealand	7

*Esteves-Abe *et al* suggest that this understates the extent of VET, particularly within large firms
Source: Esteves-Abe *et al* (2001)

in products and processes is encouraged. They suggest that this provides a partial explanation for the strength of Anglo-Saxon nations in sectors characterised by rapid change in fundamental technologies, such as IT, and the strength of continental Europe and Japan where gradual innovation within companies themselves is critical, as in mechanical engineering.

The differences in the reach of initial VET, beyond compulsory education, as shown in Table 15, are enormous. Rubery and Grimshaw (2003; p124) comment that there is a 'tendency for coverage of training programmes to be higher in consensus-led systems and lower in market-led systems'. Generally, despite the enthusiasm amongst many academics for dual apprenticeships combining workplace and off-the-job learning, it is the mixed regimes, featuring various forms of state and market-led VET, which reach the greatest number of the relevant age cohort. College-based regimes, characteristic of the Nordic countries, with the partial exception of Denmark, are also quite extensive in their reach. Regimes which rely on company training reach proportions of the relevant cohort similar to those that rely on apprenticeships. Finally, VET regimes that are of variable forms and are generally quite weak (perhaps undeserving of the term 'regime' at all) reach a very small proportion of the relevant cohorts.

CASE STUDIES

CO-ORDINATION OF VET POLICIES IN THE USA AND SWITZERLAND

UIS (2006) argues that in the USA vocational education has historically been the domain of states and local communities, with the federal government playing a lesser role. Traditionally, only a small proportion of total state expenditures in vocational education flows from the federal purse. Within this system, federal policy has primarily relied on inducements and capacity-building strategies to encourage states and local school agencies to shape vocational education in ways that it believes will lead to improved outcomes. Federal legislation provides guidance on programme improvements, requires states to address these in their state plans, and permits use of federal funds to develop them, with legislation in place to encourage greater compliance. States are required to develop and track four core performance indicators and negotiate with the federal government to establish benchmarks and targets for each. States exceeding targets are eligible for incentive bonuses, while those failing to reach targets may lose federal funds. In the absence of mandates or strong regulation, federal policy appear to have a relatively weak influence on vocational education delivery in the states. Federal policy is enacted consistent with state structures, policies and interests which emphasise improvements in general education, thus marginalising vocational education. The overall result has been to strengthen somewhat the academic rigour in vocational programmes, but at the expense of specific vocational and technical learning.

In Switzerland, where the cantons and social partners have a great deal of autonomy for VET, federal legislation on VET was recently reformed. The legislation declares that VET is the joint responsibility of the Confederation, the cantons, social partners and other organisations of 'working life', working collaboratively. The purposes of VET are identified in law: to enable individuals to find a place in society and at work, and to equip them with the flexibility to remain active; to contribute to the competitiveness of enterprises; to provide equal opportunities in access to training; to develop links between different pathways in education and training; and to establish a system that is transparent. The Confederation will take more responsibility for funding VET. These funds are to be distributed to cantons and 'working life' organisations – which hold major responsibilities – using mechanisms intended primarily to encourage initiatives and reform. The Confederation hopes to incentivise employers to be more active in initial and continuing VET and to encourage incremental reforms to both the school-based and dual systems. In each case, the Confederation intends to assume a more strategic lead.

The USA/Switzerland case study illustrates the differences in approach along the lines of the dichotomous view of Hall and Soskice (2001). Amable (2003) suggested more of a multi-level approach, and such an approach has been characterised in terms of training provision in five 'types' of capitalist environment, as summarised in Table 16.

Table 16 The likely impact of national/regional economy upon company training and development

Continental/ Rhineland economies (France, Germany, Austria, Belgium)	Highly standardised educational system, early selection into vocational training Training systems vocationally oriented, with state involvement Firms left to concentrate on 'topping up' firm-specific training Training spend low, jobs well protected and low staff turnover Unions and employer associations bargain on industry lines and have collaborative training schemes Industry-level wage-setting (quite high level) encourages individuals to acquire job-specific skills, poaching less of an issue Possible gap in general cross-functional skills for managerial and senior administrative roles than in LMEs
Social democratic co-ordinated market economies (Sweden, Finland)	Vocational training less effective, due to weakening industry links and increased theoretical focus Firms likely to have to provide more industry-relevant skills More emphasis (and investment) on training within organisations than in continental/Rhineland economies Gaps in vocational training mean that individuals are likely to take more responsibility for their own skill development
Liberal market economies (the USA, the UK, Republic of Ireland)	Variations in the quality and nature of school education and a large pool of poorly skilled job-seekers Low security of tenure May not equate with low training bills because the low entry requirements/high staff turnover contribute to high induction cost Good general university system provides pool of managerial potentials (may reduce training requirements in senior administration and management) Job-seekers are incentivised to acquire such skills and increase their employability and the likelihood of being retained Fierce competition in high-tech industries and in certain low-value-added areas of the service sector

Southern European (Mediterranean) economies (Italy, Spain, Portugal, Greece)	Education and training provision mixed due to weaknesses in both higher education and vocational systems Declining role of the state in promoting skills means that firms may have to make greater use of external training providers Skill gaps likely at both senior and junior levels Education system 'lags' having adapted to needs of low-technology industry in which a minor proportion of the workforce has secondary education
Transitional economies (Central and Eastern Europe)	Tradition of autocratic management, seen in high levels of managerial autonomy Increasing liberalisation coupled with a short-termist approach Pressure to converge with LME paradigm, but mitigated by the desire for incremental change and continuity (from the managerial population) Declining job security will discourage investment in people Mismatch between training needs and provision, due to gaps in the training infrastructure

Source: extrapolated from Goergen *et al* (2009a)

CASE STUDIES

CURRENT DEVELOPMENTS IN GERMAN APPRENTICESHIPS

Thelen (2007) argues that the German apprenticeship system has been regarded as the 'crown jewel' in the German political economy. This system combines school-based learning with practical firm-based training (with primacy traditionally given to the latter). The plant-based component is strongly 'collectivist' insofar as employers train not narrowly and for their own needs but broadly and to standards that are set nationally by committees composed of representatives of business and workers. The approach is characterised by:

- the participation of a wide range of firms in national skill formation (not just the largest enterprises)

- in-house training that is subject to monitoring and supervision, to maintain and enforce nationally defined standards in respect of the content and quality of skills

- state support but with a reliance on private sector sponsorship of training with apprentice training traditionally commencing when a firm hires an apprentice.

In terms of trends and threats, the past decade and a half has witnessed a decline in plant-based apprenticeships and the emergence of shortfalls in training opportunities for youth. The problem goes back in part to the changing skill needs of German employers (including new skills associated, often, with broader and more theoretical training) that increase the costs to firms of training and, in part, to longer-term structural trends associated with the decline of manufacturing and the transition to services, which has seen fewer apprenticeships being offered. Recent reforms point to incremental, though possibly transformative, changes in the system through the injection of new forms of flexibility in the structuring of apprenticeships and through a rebalancing between the school-based and the in-plant components of training, including legislation to benefit those who have attended full-time vocational schooling alternatives but whose practical plant-based experience is limited.

Thelen (2007) concludes that the changes are intended both to accommodate the altered skill needs of German employers and to attempt to relieve cost pressures on firms by shifting some of the financial burdens onto the state and onto trainees themselves.

REFLECTIVE ACTIVITY

What is VET?

What implications might the difference in initial training provision between the USA and Germany have for the organisation of work and the character of relationships between managers and non-managerial employees?

What are the institutional features required to support extensive initial VET, and what are the challenges involved in sustaining VET for the long term?.

CONTINUING TRAINING – THE ROLE OF THE EMPLOYER

Goergen *et al* (2009a; p462) highlight the relationship between dominant corporate governance regimes and the role of the state in ensuring the provision of education and training and the employment relationship. They suggest that the theories of corporate governance and links to VET are central to an understanding:

> of the nature and extent to which companies need to and are prepared to, and/or are encouraged to, invest in their people.

Thus, organisations find themselves with a skill/training gap which is to some considerable degree shaped by the context in which they find themselves (see Figure 34). However, irrespective of context, almost all organisations now have a written policy for training and development. Apart from pay and benefits, this is more common than any other HRM policy (Cranet data). Training provision (usually assessed by number of days training undergone annually by employees) is one of the very few indicators of the stance taken by an HRM department that can be related to organisational performance across the entire array of institutional and cultural context. Clearly, therefore, this is an area where HRM departments retain strong influence. However, the majority of continuing training tends to be concentrated on those relatively highly educated and trained already.

Discussion of company training may be seen in the light of 'high-performance work practices' (Appelbaum *et al*, 2000), in which training is seen as an element of an integrated approach to HRM, including work definition, appraisal and reward, and promotion. The extent of employee involvement is regarded as key here, along with team- and group-working and the scope of autonomy. It is argued that on-the-job development is more likely where responsibility rests with teams or groups, so that they take on many of the traditional functions of management – and so delegated responsibility is essential. Interestingly, despite the rhetoric, management delegation in the UK is very limited. Sweden stands out in terms of both delegation and participation, the Netherlands ranking as second. Similarly, despite their works councils, in terms of actual delegation Germany ranks lower than the UK. In the USA, despite enthusiasm for Appelbaum *et al*'s (2000) high-performance work systems ideas, delegation is not well spread. Similarly, in newly industrialised and developing nations, Zhang *et al* (2005) suggest that employee involvement and development is typically less advanced. Even in Japan, despite providing many of the leading examples from continued improvement movement, there may be less delegation and teamwork than suggested (Vernon, 2006b).

Firms that do not engage in training report that there has been no need for training. One in four surveyed said there was no time for training, and the same proportion said they recruit people with the necessary skills (Eurostat, 2002). Only three in 20 said that training was too expensive. In the newer EU member states the reasons given differed somewhat. Cost featured more saliently. There was also a view that initial training was sufficient. When this evidence is overlaid with a recognition that workers who are younger, have a higher level of education, work for larger firms and have a senior job have much higher chances of involvement in training, it can be seen that the opportunities for both older people and younger people with few qualifications fall away dramatically.

Despite these general truths and cross-national similarities, cross-national comparative training provision varies dramatically, as is clear in the data on the distribution of average training days for manual employees (see Figure 35). The latest 2010 Cranet data shows some marked differences. Note the remarkably high volume of training days in Japan at the moment. Germany and the USA outpace the UK and France on the volume of training for professional and technical grades; Germany stands out after Japan for management training. When it comes to training for manual staff, there is now little variation across European countries.

Comparison of previous Cranet data on training days with that for the early 1990s (Holden and Livian, 1993) reveals marked differences in national trends over the last decade or so. Provision for manual employees in Germany is very little changed, whereas that in France appears to have fallen off a little. In contrast, there has been a marked expansion in training provision in the cases of Sweden, Denmark and also the UK. Other countries have typically seen a more limited growth. There is thus little sign of convergence across national borders in training provision, despite the typical tendency for companies to set aside more days for the training of employees.

Figure 35 Comparative distribution of average training days for different categories of employees across six countries

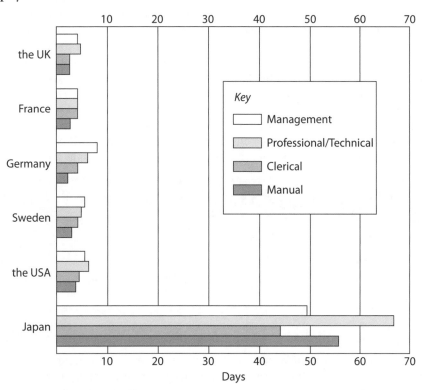

Source: Cranet (2010)

THE COSTS OF TRAINING

What of the extent of companies' commitment of financial resources to continuing training? Typically, organisations report that they spend less than 2 per cent of their total pay bill on training provision – a situation little changed from the early 1990s (Holden and Livian, 1993; Table 6.3).

France is exceptional, spending considerably above these levels, such that the bulk of companies spend more than 2 per cent of their payroll on training. Sweden ranks second in terms of such financial commitments to continuing training. Strikingly, however, it is not only that expenditure on training in France is comparatively great but that in France the training effort is particularly evenly spread across employees of all grades (Cranet, 2004). Uniquely in the advanced industrialised world, the number of days of training experienced by non-managerial employees in France is almost as great as that experienced by managerial employees. This egalitarianism in training provision contrasts even with the situation in Sweden and the other Nordic countries.

Much, but not all, of this French exceptionality is explained by law. French statute compels French employers of more than 10 employees to devote 1.5 per cent of their pay bill to continuing training. A substantial proportion of this total must be assigned specifically to the training of young employees, who tend to be on lower grades (IDS, 1993). However, it seems clear that training provision by French employers typically exceeds this statutory requirement. Some part of expenditures beyond the statutory minimum may be nurtured by the procedural requirements applying to those organisations subject to the terms of a collective agreement – the vast bulk in the French case (see Chapter 4). Such organisations must formally consider training requirements several times each year, in conjunction with works councils where appropriate, and establish an annual training plan. Statute and multi-employer agreements provide what amounts to a conceptual framework for the consideration of training needs (IDS, 1993). This both heightens awareness of training issues and eases their consideration.

REFLECTIVE ACTIVITY

Who gains from training and development?

Who is responsible for employees' training and development?

What role does context play in shaping the requirement for company training and development?

MANAGEMENT DEVELOPMENT

This section deals with management development, which in the light of its increasing emphasis within organisations is deemed to warrant separate consideration. Certainly, in many countries, particularly the USA, it is believed that senior managers are critical to organisational performance and therefore are worthy recipients of training and development investment. According to Mabey and Ramirez (2011), it might also be asserted that management development is central to an organisation's approach to HRM and a telling signal of the value it places upon its staff. Despite some doubts as to the logic and plausibility of the skills-performance link (eg Grugulis and Stoyanova, 2006), there is an ongoing preoccupation within governments, both national and international, with the calibre of their managers and leaders (Mabey and Ramirez, 2011). As a result of the level of interest, generic leadership competencies have emerged (eg risk-taking, initiative, analytical thinking) which have become the basis for leadership programmes for senior executives (Woodall, 2005). This has been accompanied by considerable energy devoted to understanding learning styles so as to facilitate the development of management better. There has also (particularly recently) been a focus on the development of high-flyers or high-potentials in the USA and across much of Europe. According to information from the Chartered Management Institute (2004), more than twice the amount of money is spent on management development per manager in Germany (€4,438) than in the UK (€1,625). However, it is not only the level of investment that varies but also the experience of management training that might be quite different depending on the location as well as the expectations of the managers themselves. This is linked to earlier work on career dynamics, as described by Schein (1978). He separates the concept of a career into two components: the 'internal career' (the individual involved in the pursuit of an occupation) and the 'external career' (the organisation attempting to establish appropriate developmental paths). The internal career has subjective elements, such as the person's perception of attributes and actions, while the external career is objective with its focus on status and office.

Sparrow and Hiltrop (1994) point out that in the light of the changes occurring in modern organisations, the external career is under considerable threat, and 'the "internal career" will begin to dominate managerial behaviour'. If this view is correct, managers are more likely to place greater emphasis on their own career than on loyalty to a particular organisation, a situation becoming more instrumental when making career decisions. Contextual factors, as discussed earlier in this chapter, are again influential here. For example, in certain contexts steady career progression is the norm within an organisation (the traditional continental European approach) versus the more *laissez-faire* approach of the Anglo nations in which it would be more usual to leave an organisation and join another (perhaps a competitor) in order to secure career progression.

Mabey and Ramirez (2011) have provided an outline of how different contexts place different expectations on managers and therefore recognise and serve different training needs. This is summarised in Table 17, and some of the key differences are highlighted in the following section.

In France, according to Lawrence (1993), being a manager is seen as more about identity than it is about activity, whereas in the UK, according to Sparrow (1996), the focus is upon getting things done through others. This is why interpersonal skills are so essential and have precipitated an increase in skill training and development to equip managers to lead and motivate a team. To address these different needs in the USA and increasingly in the UK, there tends to be an emphasis upon generalists, through general management programmes in business schools, versus rotation around functions which is more the norm in Japan and France.

The distinguishing feature of the French business system goes beyond education and is tied to the tiers of the so-called 'cadres' – which are unique to management in France (Mabey and Ramirez, 2011). Managers are highly respected but are divided up according to a series of formal titles. In France there is little inter-firm managerial mobility, particularly at lower levels. Woodall (2005) considers an attempt to forge an integrated organisation via management development following a hostile takeover of a French organisation by a UK company. The experience shows that different conceptions of the appropriate nature of such development activities still prevail. The elite cadres emerging from the *Grandes Écoles* to populate the higher reaches of management are rather wary of typical Anglo-Saxon attempts to identify high-potential individuals within what they consider to be an already demonstrably elite group. Moreover, French participants in executive education programmes seek more abstract discussion, broad principles and critical contemplation of complex situations. They are rather impatient with the pragmatic orientation and prescriptive direction that the British favour in their dash for practical application (Woodall, 2005).

Table 17 European management development systems

	Skills type	Career paths	Who pays for training?	Agents driving training and status of training institutions	Distinguishing national characteristics of managers
the UK	Managers can maintain skills when moving jobs (Buechtermann, 1998).	Less emphasis on firm-level career development (Bournois *et al*, 1994). Managers exposed to losing jobs in hostile takeovers	Growing general business education financed by employee (Bennett, 1997).	High status of chartered institutions. Low status of vocational training (Hall and Soskice, 2001).	High premium on the 'gifted amateur' (Bennett, 1997). Managers are 'specialist co-ordinators' (Lam, 1994).
Germany	VET for managers and employees technical/scientific skills prior to becoming managers (Streeck, 1993). Formal management education emphasises scientific, theoretical principles.	Strong emphasis on succession planning (Bournois *et al*, 1994). Low mobility between firms (Lane, 1989).	Hands-on managerial training funded by firms (Lane, 1989).	High status of VET for managers (Streeck, 1993). Formal management training roots lies in the *Diplom-Kaufmann* and BWL in the university system (Shenton, 1996). High-level CEOs would have PhDs.	Managers are subject to intense monitoring. Managers are 'players' (Lam, 1994). High consensus between managers and workers.
France	*Grandes Écoles* vocational origins and proximity to business world (Shenton, 1996).	More likely to lose skill status when moving jobs (Eyraud *et al*, 1990). Job hierarchies and seniority. Internal labour markets (Maurice *et al*, 1986). Promotion into *cadre* status is rare (Tregaskis, 1997).	Law requires firms to spend at least 1.5 per cent of wage bill on training (Thomson *et al*, 2001).	*Grandes Écoles* technocratic elite (Shenton, 1996). 75 per cent of senior execs in large firms have *Grandes Écoles* qualification (Bennett, 1997).	Managers are 'coordinators' (Lam, 1994). Comparatively weak retention and short-term training plans.

	Skills type	Career paths	Who pays for training?	Agents driving training and status of training institutions	Distinguishing national characteristics of managers
Spain	Traditional focus on internal training (Baruel, 1996).	Foreign assignments play an important role in career (Bournois et al, 1994). Careers paths offered to high proportion of managers.		Training and development concentrated within large firms (Paralleda et al, 2002). Successful MBAs because of traditional weakness of other management education (Shenton, 1996).	Few apprenticeships (Paralleda et al, 2002). Weak retention and comparatively short-term training plans.
Norway	Emphasis on company and VET training.	Strong long-term commitment, though increasing mobility.			Managerial autonomy, functional responsibilities and task variation enshrined in legislation.
Denmark	Combination of experiential firm-specific learning with formal education and VET.	Strong promotion and internal labour market opportunities.	State offers affordable postgraduate managerial training.	Combines VET and formal MBA education (Brewster, 1995). High degree of social capital. Co-operative and consensual system between state, employers, trade unions and individual managers.	Managers willing and encouraged to take risks supported by safety net (Hofstede, 1985).

Source: Mabey and Ramirez (2011)

In Spain a good deal of the literature focuses on the slowness of transition from the older structures of Franco. There are still hierarchical structures tied to job grades involving a pessimistic view of managerial retention, while MBA programmers have become popular through the weakness of firm-led management development.

Norway, by contrast, has been influenced by the traditions of the large countries and of its neighbours. During the interwar period this included North American ideologies of mass production. Whereas in the UK after World War II Taylorist principles of management prevailed, in Norway the emphasis was more upon egalitarian management systems with a focus on consensus and transparent forms of communication and a good quality of working life. Denmark is different again in being able to combine high manager retention, strong career structures and also strength in general vocational and internal firm-specific training for managers. Traditionally, the Danish institutional system has been considered egalitarian. What exists is a cohesive and consensual approach which is conducive to long-term investment in training and development.

Reliance in the UK has historically been upon unregulated external training providers rather than in-house, and this has been aligned with weak career structures and low levels of job security. Although in the UK the approach has traditionally been one of a lower level of qualifications for managers than in other European countries and the USA, there has been a recent and rapid increase and improvement in postgraduate qualification.

Germany, by contrast, has traditionally been considered an example of a highly integrated autonomous national training system. Shenton (1996) suggests that management training and education in Germany has evolved in quite a distinctive way that emphasises in-house training, a relatively long horizon for developing in-house skills and long tenure for managers (Ramirez and Mabey, 2005). Here the emphasis, according to Lawrence (1993) is all upon specialist knowledge. This knowledge is seen to have a technical nature and is all-important because, along with experience, it can only be learned on the job. Many high-level managers understand vocational education to consist of administrative and technical skills together with a recent expansion of formal management training, although, as with the rest of the university system, it steers away from direct contact with the business community, preferring to leave hands-on management to firm-specific on-the-job training. According to Franck and Opitz (2007), Germany is also an interesting case given the high number of its senior managers who hold a doctorate, signalling the importance of high levels of education as a likely prerequisite of leadership capability.

By contrast, a number of commentators have considered practice in Asia, where management development is seen as a science that can be taught and applied like any other systematic operation (eg Borgonjon and Vanhonacker, 1992).

Warner estimated in 1996 that around two-thirds of Chinese managers had no professional qualifications beyond high school. Branine (2005) reports that only since the mid-1980s onwards, once economic reform was under way, was it realised that the transfer of management knowledge and skills from Western countries was necessary in China. However, a challenge still remains as to how to achieve this. Branine (1996; p486) describes how the 'norms' of Western approaches to management development are unlikely to be appropriate in that the context is 'fundamentally different from the learner-centred approaches of Western countries'.

Branine (2005) also notes that Chinese managers see learning as a passive rather than an active process, that group discussions are regarded as 'a waste of time', and that although the learners want to be 'modernised' as Tung (1986; p23) described, they do not wish to be 'Westernised'. Berrell et al (2001) suggested using Chinese-based case studies to transfer management approaches, but these have traditionally been extremely difficult to source or create.

Where China is chosen as a low-cost location for manufacturing, a sophisticated approach to (non-managerial) employee development is often not a priority (Zhang et al, 2005). Generally, however, foreign MNCs have devoted considerable attention to management development (see below).

CASE STUDIES

MANAGEMENT DEVELOPMENT FOR LOCALISATION IN CHINA

European multinationals operating in China have shown an increasing interest in localising their Chinese operations – passing more and more responsibility for their running to Chinese-born managers. Meanwhile, Chinese employees have shown great interest in achieving management status in such foreign enterprises. European MNCs have generally regarded localisation in China as requiring a significant investment in promising individuals, yet have still on occasion underestimated the extent of the investment needed.

ABB achieved a substantial presence in China with a relatively few expatriate managers. Its formal planning of the localisation process was viewed as critical to the success of the company in China, in the light not only of their language skills but of their sensitivity to the cultural and political context, and to the conventions of business in China. Localisation was regarded as a business goal to stand alongside profit and market share. In recognition of the

importance of the goal – and of the dangers posed by expatriates' being asked to work to render themselves superfluous – expatriates were offered substantial bonuses tied to targets emerging from the localisation plan. This also helped to mitigate the danger that line managers would regard the immediate bottom line as the key objective. Interestingly, expatriate assignments were normally expected to be for two to three years, ABB stressing to assignees the significance of such international experience for them, and the importance for ABB of imparting ABB experience to the Chinese. They discouraged expatriates' attempts to learn Chinese, since they were only to be there for a short while. ABB moved from the identification of high-potential Chinese candidates for management through to their socialisation, making use also of local business schools.

Qualifications are important in China. Chinese managers often give preference to those with degrees, and also often expect to have their development certified. The action-learning-based programmes offered by the Siemens Management Institute to employees of Siemens and others suit Chinese managers well. Focused on the actual problems they face in their roles, and involving extensive group work, this sort of programme avoids the theoretical study that Chinese managers often find demotivating. From the organisation's point of view, the projects emerging result in initiatives with measurable economic impact.

As in other forms of management development, on-the-job training is critical. Indeed, given that authority structures tend to be centralised in China, it has a particular relevance because the absence of managers undergoing off-the-job training can have a severe impact on progress in their team. Sometimes, however, MNCs seeking localisation in China have deployed job rotation insufficiently, despite the willingness of local managers to be rotated. Job rotation can not only aid management development, but can form one element of a career and development path which encourages Chinese-born managers to remain with the organisation that has invested in their initial development. These development opportunities, alongside a good relationship with those to whom they report, are more important to the retention of the local managers than relative salaries (Worm, 2001).

For organisations operating internationally, they have of course to cope with these different contexts and operations. Mabey and Ramirez (2011) refer to the 'economies of scale' which permit MNCs access to a richer vein of resources for management development than is possible in many domestic companies.

The case study below provides an example of how an organisation sought to overcome regional differences to meet a business requirement for standardisation.

LEARNING FROM SPECIFIC COUNTRY INITIATIVES AT STEPSTONE

CASE STUDIES

Stepstone is an independent career and recruitment portal, founded in Oslo, Norway, in 1996, and has operations in 12 European countries. It is an integrated e-business. In 2001 it aspired to provide pan-European market reach via a consistent recruitment platform. However, it soon discovered that the intermediary relations it relied upon in the recruitment market were different from one country to another. For example, in Germany recruitment agents are virtually unknown, whereas in the UK they are commonplace. As a result, Stepstone chose a strategy of gradual integration through the use of pilot countries and then export of best practices across Europe. One such example was the Stepstone Academy established in Germany. Here the country manager (unsurprisingly, Germany was one of the most successful European operations) detected that a longer lifecycle of customer accounts was needed in order to change the attitude of the salesforce from hunter to farmer. He diagnosed that employees needed both to deepen their knowledge of Internet recruitment, and also develop their insight into the workings of the HRM function (as it operated in client organisations). The Stepstone Academy provided new models of team leadership training to provide this knowledge. In order to export the model more broadly it became apparent that a corporate training role was required with HR who could troubleshoot across country and also a new forum for country managers to share and problem-solve – which became known as country managers' meetings.

Source: Braun *et al* (2003)

KEY LEARNING POINTS

- There are differences in the national systems of VET, and these impact on the type and extent of in-work training and development that is required by organisations.

- The role of institutions is key here, with links to the literature on varieties of capitalism (VoC) as introduced in Chapter 4.

- Although the majority of OECD nations have educational systems involving compulsory secondary schooling, levels of attainment do differ across geographies, and this is a key factor for organisations to take into account when considering where to locate new plants or operations.

- Higher education has increased in terms of numbers of students: China now leads the world in total student numbers.

- Irrespective of context, almost all organisations now have a written policy for training and development, and apart from pay and benefits such a policy is more common than any other HRM policy (Cranet data).

- Training provision is usually assessed by number of days' training undergone annually by employees, and although there has been a general upward trend, there are no signs of convergence in terms of days of training or amount of investment.

- Latest (2010) Cranet data reveals a high level of training in Japan followed by Germany. Although Germany and the USA outpace the UK and France on the volume of training for professional and technical grades, when it comes to training for manual staff, there is now little variation across European countries.

- Management development has increased in terms of its perceived importance although challenges remain in tailoring approaches to fit with different cultural and institutional requirements.

LEARNING QUESTIONS

1 What are the implications for international HR departments of the range of levels of literacy and numeracy that they will encounter in different countries?

2 Describe the likely effects of the different concepts of management in, say, the USA and one other country on management development programmes.

3 What would be the implications for a training manager of moving from performing that role in Western Europe to performing that role in China?

4 For an internationally operating organisation, what aspects of training and development policies are best retained centrally, and what are best handled locally? Why?

EXPLORE FURTHER

Goergen, M., Brewster, C. and Wood, G. (2009a) 'Corporate governance and training', *Journal of Industrial Relations*, 51 (4): 461–489. This useful article contains more information and explanation on varieties of capitalism and the likely impact of these on education and training.

Mabey, C. and Ramirez, M. (2011) 'Comparing national approaches to management development', in C. Brewster and W. Mayrhofer (eds) *A Handbook of Comparative HRM*, Cheltenham, Edward Elgar.

There are many useful reports available from the OECD, such as 'Education at a glance': http://www.oecd.org/docum ent/52/0,3746,en_2649_39263238_ 45897844_1_1_1,00.html

Similarly, EU findings may be sourced from: ec.europa.eu/news/ culture/100908_en.htm

CHAPTER 12

The Role of the HRM Department

LEARNING OUTCOMES

When they have read this chapter, students will:

- understand that the term 'HRM' has different meanings for HRM departments in different countries

- understand that HRM departments variably meet the expectations which new ambitions place upon them

- be able to outline the differences between countries in the allocation or assignment of HRM tasks to line managers

- understand the potential effects of outsourcing, shared services and e-HRM on the role of the HRM function

- understand the cross-national differences in the place and/or role of HRM departments

- be able to evaluate the bases of cross-national comparative variation in the role of HRM departments.

INTRODUCTION

Chapters 5 to 11 have considered a range of specific arenas or realms of HRM – dealing with employee relations and communications, making decisions over the organisation of work, managing flexibility, dealing with recruitment and selection, performance management, rewards, and training and development. We have examined cross-national comparative variation in each arena of activity, and drawn attention to the relevance of cultural and institutional influences. This chapter departs from the focus of previous chapters on variation across different arenas in people management. Its focus is rather on cross-national comparative variation in the nature, status and role of specialist people management departments – ie of HRM departments or functions. By implication, this also involves consideration of the cross-national comparative variation in the relative roles of the specialist HRM function and of line managers in the task and activities of managing non-managerial or front-line employees.

The HRM literature accords considerable emphasis to the nature, status and role of the HRM function (eg Boxall and Purcell, 2011; Brandl and Pohler, 2010; Brewster *et al*, 2006b; Farndale, 2005; Mayrhofer *et al*, 2011a, 2011b). Although it is often not explicitly asserted, there is often a presumption that the HRM function – and its relationship to line managers – is of particular relevance to the manner in which front-line employees are managed. Cross-national comparative variations in the nature, status and role of HRM functions are thus of potential importance not only to specialist personnel but to line managers and the people they manage. These variations – and the bases of them – appear then of great potential importance.

If, as we argued in Chapter 1, the meaning of HRM is disputed, so too is the role of the department charged with managing human resources. This chapter is the last of those that take a comparative perspective, but it also serves as a bridge chapter to the topic of international HRM. We therefore begin by stepping back and discussing one of the better-known models that comes from a 'best practice' standpoint. When we compare the approaches that we see to structuring the HRM department across countries, this provides a useful reference point.

COMMON AMBITIONS FOR THE HRM DEPARTMENT?

There is a univeralist view about the ideal shape and role of HRM departments. The term 'organisational capability' was adopted by Ulrich (1987) for the HRM field. Ulrich and Lake (1990) then brought together perspectives from the fields of the management of change, organisational design and leadership, and argued that organisational capability was about competing from the inside out. Organisational capability focuses on the ability of a firm's internal processes, systems and management practices to meet customer needs and to direct both the skills and efforts of employees towards achieving the goals of the organisation. This perspective argues that HRM is an organisational capability, and that the structure of HRM departments should therefore reflect and develop this capability. It argues that trends of globalisation, market liberalisation, deregulation and technical evolution have both restructured global markets and have challenged the traditional approaches to gaining competitive advantage (Hamel, 2000). It is only the possession of specific capabilities and resources, the argument goes, that now enables firms to conceive and then implement strategies that can generate what the economists describe as above-average rates of return (Barney, 1997).

The idea also has its root in the resource-based view of the firm. This argues that in an environment characterised by the globalisation of markets, changing customer demands and increasing competition, it is the people and the way they are managed that are more significant than other sources of competitive advantage (Wright *et al*, 1994; Lado and Wilson, 1994). Competitive advantage is derived from both internal knowledge resources and the strategic resources or capabilities of the firm. It is 'bundles of resources' rather than any particular product-market strategy that provide an organisation with the capability to compete. These bundles of resources are generally considered to be complex, intangible and dynamic.

In addition to the management of people, developing organisational capability includes the means through which the organisation implements policies and procedures. These means are centred around – and require HR professionals to understand – economic and financial capability, strategic/marketing capability and technological capability. Strategic or marketing capability is based on offering uniqueness to customers. Perceived customer value is considered to result from responsiveness (meeting needs more quickly than competitors), the formation of endearing and enduring relationships, and the pursuit of service quality through guarantees.

The basic arguments that the Ulrich model – and a good deal of practitioner discussion in the USA and the UK – laid out is shown in Figure 36. These principles have now become a general mantra in these two countries, with increasing attention (though not actual practice) in other countries. The ideas have been developed over time, but began with the adoption of a 'three-box model' of HRM. It is necessary to outline the main implications that the model has:

- The first box represents the more transactional aspects of activity, which may be delivered from service centres or processing hubs, in multiple geographical locations, or outsourced to third party providers.

- The second box illustrates an embedded HRM business partner (HRBP) structure.

- The third box describes more added-value and specialist centres of excellence or functional support.

At the model's heart, then, lies a set of HRM professionals in the second box, embedded within line businesses and working on processes and outcomes central to competitive success. They are supported by both efficient processes to handle the more transactional aspects of HRM work. More strategically oriented expert HRM knowledge is handled by functional expertise or centre of excellence (COE) structures.

We shall see later in this chapter that the development of shared service models and the e-enablement of HRM systems are but two ways of delivering this organisational capability.

In order to make this diffuse concept of organisational capability more recognisable, over a decade ago Ulrich (2000) went on to describe the collection of attributes that it involves in terms of a series of important outcomes that result from their existence. The role of the HR professional is, it is argued, to help clarify these organisational capabilities and to craft the HR investments that are necessary to build them. The specification of the HRM department role is of course prescriptive – and, you might argue, very Western-centric.

Figure 36 The original Ulrich three-box model

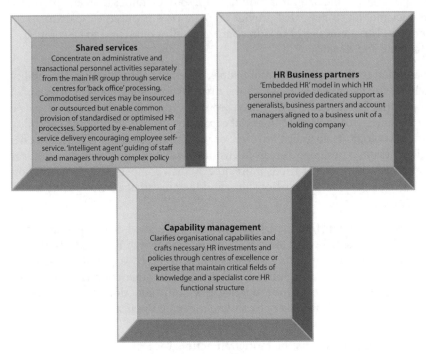

Source: Sparrow *et al* (2010) Leading HR. Basingstoke: Palgrave Macmillan.

THEORY AND PRACTICE

KEY FRAMEWORK

Rules of HRM engagement with the line?

For Ulrich the role of HRM departments should be:

- *to be able to move with speed and agility* into a new market in order to be the firm that sets the rules and then controls the future changes to these rules (in HRM terms, removing bureaucratic processes, establishing clarity of governance to enable rapid decision-making, building safeguarding disciplines into the organisational thought process, and removing vestiges of old ways of doing things)

- *to create a brand for the firm*, such that its reputation draws consumers, and the brand associated with the customer experience of the firm also becomes part of the experience or identity of the firm in the mind of all stakeholders (customers, employees, investors). Employee actions and HR policies should be aligned with this identity

- *a customer interface that captures and develops a more intimate relationship*, such that data on customers contains more insight into their actual behaviour and needs, business processes are built around these needs as a priority, and customers also have involvement in or can comment on the design and practice of internal systems (for example, providing feedback for performance management)

- *superior talent*, reflected in high levels of employee competence and commitment, such that there is an employee value proposition that makes the firm an attractive place to work, helps attract people into the right job, entices employees to give their discretionary energy to the firm, and orients them towards effective performance very quickly

- *leveraged innovation and learning*, reflected in new and faster-developed services and products, a culture of inquisitiveness and risk-taking, competencies of inventing and trying, and an ability and willingness to learn from mistakes

- *resources sourced across alliances*, whereby firms can work across boundaries, marshal connections, share information and develop a sense of mutual dependency between a network of partners, which means the best resources can be brought to bear on a situation, to everyone's benefit, without having to formally own or control them

- *assigned accountability*, such that standards exist for employees and that organisational decision-making (who makes them, how they are made and what processes are followed) is carried out with competence, authority and responsibility.

REFLECTIVE ACTIVITY

Consider some organisations from different countries:

- How does their HRM function measure up against these criteria?

- Do they do any of this in practice?

- Even if they do not, would HR aspire to organise itself in a set way to do this?

- Should it even aspire to doing this?

- Have HRM professionals from different countries got the same professional skills and career backgrounds to enable them to work effectively in such an HR structure?

Clearly, the answer to these questions could well differ depending on whether you were looking at a typical organisation operating in domestic markets in the country in question, or at an organisation that is an MNC or is globalising, or, indeed, if it was a subsidiary of an overseas MNC.

The HRM structure of an international firm within a country looks a bit different from one that is purely domestic. IHRM managers have to grasp the overall business-level and corporate-level capabilities that are relevant to a particular international strategy. Tallman and Fladmoe-Lindquist (2002) have summarised the key capabilities on three axes:

- strategies of international expansion or global integration
- the necessity to continue generating competitive advantage or to innovate through global learning
- skills and activities operating at the business level or corporate-level routines that integrate these skills across operations.

Yet some authors suggest that the HRM function should fulfil key roles regardless of context. Although seen as vague, overambitious or implausible by some, Ulrich's (1997) ideas have influenced the thinking of many HRM practitioners. Ulrich and Brockbank (2005) updated Ulrich's earlier work (1997) and identified five main roles for the HRM department:

- employee advocate
- human capital developer
- functional expert
- strategic partner
- HR leader.

In Ulrich and Brockbank's (2005) model, Ulrich's former (1997) category of 'employee champion' has been split into two:

- Employee advocate is a representational role, focused on the needs of today's employee, and
- Human capital developer is focused on developing and preparing employees to be successful in the future.

The model also features three further roles:

- *Functional expert*: holding that administrative practices are central to HRM value, the model suggests a more attractive heading than administration! Some HRM practices are delivered through administrative efficiency (such as technology or process redesign), and others through policy menus and interventions.

- *Strategic partner has multiple dimensions*: business expert, change agent, SHRM planner, knowledge manager, and consultant.

- *HRM leader*: this new emphasis in Ulrich and Brockbank (2005) is on leadership within the HR function but also in facing other functions and general management. It thus involves not only developing the other four roles but, for example, collaborating with other functions, setting and enhancing the standards for strategic thinking, and ensuring corporate governance.

The specification of roles continues to develop (see Ulrich *et al*, 2008). So too does work on the professional roles that HRM managers have to play in delivery models. For example, Evans *et al* (2010) draw upon recent academic work on 'HR delivery models' (see Lawler *et al*, 2006; Caldwell, 2008; Ulrich *et al*, 2008; Sparrow *et al*, 2010). They argue that research needs to catch up with developments in practice, and needs to differentiate between:

- the process and content development – ie how HRM policies, practices and processes are developed, who is responsible, who is involved, and in what capacity

- HRM service delivery – ie the solutions used to actually deliver HRM support to employees and internal customer units (such as the automation of transactions, use of self-service, the adoption of enterprise resource planning techniques to optimise HRM processes, and delivery through shared service centres)

- business support roles of the HRM function – ie the direct ways in which the HRM function works with line and top managers on HRM issues.

Friedman (2007) has examined these roles and linked them, conceptually, to the challenges created for each role in relation to Hofstede's five constructs of national culture.

 REFLECTIVE ACTIVITY

Research in *The HR Function: Structures, activities, resources and outcomes* by Björkman, Suutari and Sparrow asks a range of questions about delivery models in the international context. Discuss the following:

- As the boundaries of HRM work have expanded from the original personnel administration department into other more strategic areas, how has the definition of the structure and roles of the HRM function become increasingly blurred?

- What kinds of activities do HRM professionals engage in, why, and with what consequences?

- What kinds of *resources* do HRM specialists use in order to carry out their work, and with what results?

This provides an ambitious model for HRM departments and practitioners – and indeed for wider organisations looking to develop their people management. What, though, of actual practice internationally?

LIVING UP TO NEW AMBITIONS

There are three ways of answering the question about whether the typical background, education, skills and capabilities that HR professionals have equips them to work in the same HRM structures:

- to look at the professional standing and activities of the different national institutes that exist for them

- to look at the level of integration between the HRM function and the board

- to look at the involvement of the HRM function in strategic decision-making.

THE NATIONAL INSTITUTES

One way of answering the question about the typical background, education, skills and capabilities that HR professionals have is to look at the professional standing and activities of the different national institutes that exist for them. These personnel management institutes and associations vary considerably in their form and activity (Farndale and Brewster, 2005). The CIPD in the UK seeks to be an all-encompassing organisation, with well over 100,000 members, nearly all of whom have gone through a qualification process. On the other hand, the ANDCP in France is a resolutely elitist organisation covering the heads of HRM in the major organisations only. Most of the members of the DGFP in German are corporates. Spain has very strong regional associations, with a relatively weak centre. Sweden has a well-resourced central organisation. When these potential variations are extended to the rest of the world, with over 70 different national associations ranging from the giant, long-established Society of Human Resource Management in the USA to tiny, new associations in some of the developing countries of Africa and Asia or the transition countries of central and eastern Europe, the range becomes huge. Levels of entry qualifications, restrictions on membership, levels of education and the extent of training provided by the associations vary enormously (Farndale and Brewster, 1999, 2005).

The target group for membership of personnel management associations tends to expand, increasing the risk of competition with other professional associations. At the same time, more specialist organisations are established (for people management issues in the public sector, or for coaching specialists, for example). The role of these organisations is going to be increasingly important, and controversial, as the profession expands.

 REFLECTIVE ACTIVITY

How important is the professional HRM association in your country (or one you know)?

What might it do to achieve more influence?

MOVING AWAY FROM MERE 'PERSONNEL'?

For many countries, especially perhaps in what is often called the South – the less developed countries of the world – the department with responsibility for these areas is still most accurately entitled 'Personnel Administration'. That is what they do – and it is all that they do. The argument of the HRM gurus has long been that this misses the important and positive roles that Ulrich's other categories represent: HRM departments should be more strategic, aiming to create value within organisations (Beatty and Schneider, 1997; Bennett et al, 1998; Pfeffer, 1994). Further, many would go on to assert, most of these administrative tasks can now be done more effectively through the use of information technology or through outsourcing.

The diminution of the administrative roles will free up the department to concentrate upon the strategic partner and HRM leader roles. Studies in Sweden (Hedlund, 1990; Frank *et al*, 1990) 20 years ago had already identified a trend away from administrative, system-oriented HRM roles towards more strategy and consultancy work for the HRM professionals as the day-to-day HRM work became more integrated in line operations. Södergren (1992) defined changes in terms of the 'hardware' (formal structures) and the 'software' (working roles, competence, priorities and attitudes) of the decentralisation process. Her research convinced her that the software changes may be the more important. There is other evidence that HRM departments in some countries are moving from their traditional servicing and administrative role to a more developmental and strategic one. In Denmark, for example, personnel departments aim to contribute to the formation of corporate strategy by conducting opinion surveys and work environment surveys, and participating in industrial negotiations in close co-operation with the executive committee (Brewster and Mayne, 1995). And there does seem to be evidence in the UK, from the Workplace Employee Relations Survey, to show that HRM departments are becoming more strategic (Sisson, 2001).

Personnel or HRM specialists only rarely reach the very highest positions in employing organisations (Coulson Thomas, 1990; Coulson Thomas and Wakeham, 1991). In the UK, for example, an informed HRM input to top-level debates is most likely only where the head of the HRM function is a member of the key policy-making forum (Purcell, 1995; p78):

> There is clear, unambiguous evidence ... that the presence of a personnel director on the main board makes a considerable difference to the role played in corporate strategy.

Arguably, there are many organisations where the HRM people do not have the credibility to play a strategic role. There are others where the organisation's human resources will be taken into account anyway. Thus the position of employee representative required by law in many larger German organisations will encourage managers to do do just that – even if the head of the HRM function is not on the board. Little evidence is available about what we might call 'psychological' issues – whether the atmosphere and culture of the organisation means that people issues are intrinsically taken into account in all decisions. It is clearly possible to have an organisation with explicit policies and an HRM specialist on the board, nominally involved in the development of corporate strategy, and yet still to find, in Purcell's words (1995; p78), a 'relatively modest role for corporate personnel'.

INTEGRATION OF HRM HEADS INTO THE BOARD OF DIRECTORS

Figure 37 is taken from the Cranet 2010 data and shows the proportion of companies with an HRM presence at the level of the board (or equivalent – the data covers different countries with different legal governance arrangements and different sectors). There are significant differences. In 63 per cent of the organisations in the UK, the personnel manager is a member of top management, with a similar situation in the USA and Japan. In France and Sweden, on the other hand, around 90 per cent of organisations have an HRM representation on the main board. Note that the low figure for Germany is a reflection of other institutional arrangements (see later).

Other data in the research indicates that where there is no specialist presence at this level, the responsibility for HRM rests most frequently with the managing director or an administration manager. Of course, in such circumstances this could mean either that the topic is taken very seriously, being allocated specifically to the top person, or that it is not taken seriously at all, being dumped into the 'and everything else that goes on in the organisation' category and hence swept under the CEO's general responsibilities. In either case, it is not clear that the specialist input to decisions from the HRM angle is always going to be available.

Figure 37 The proportion of organisations with HR on the board in six countries in 2010

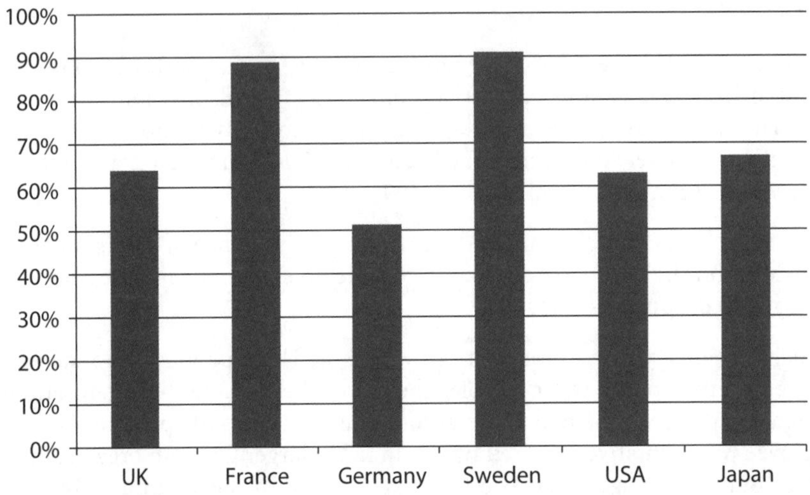

Source: Cranet (2010)

REFLECTIVE ACTIVITY

What are the advantages for the HRM department if its head is on the main board?

How might the cultural influences noted in previous chapters affect that?

THE INVOLVEMENT OF HRM IN STRATEGIC DECISION PROCESSES

Membership of the board certainly gives the head of the HRM function an opportunity to influence corporate strategy – but is it taken, and is it the only way to ensure that HRM is taken seriously in such decisions? Storey claimed back in 1992 that personnel directors were rarely involved in strategic policies as 'strategic changemakers', and Purcell (1995; p77) argued that both finance and personnel people believe that:

> It is in the implementation of decisions that the personnel function is most likely to be involved.

This too, however, seems to vary considerably by country. Other evidence from the Cranet study demonstrated at what point the personnel function is involved in the development of corporate strategy. It showed that on this key issue – using data collected, remember, from the senior HRM specialist in the organisation – that somewhere between a half and two-thirds of all organisations claim to be involved from the outset. In the UK, HRM influence from the outset of the development of corporate strategy approximately mirrors board-level involvement (see eg Farndale, 2005). In Sweden there are considerable numbers of HRM specialists with a place on the board who nevertheless, by their own admission, are not involved in the development of corporate strategy until a later stage. However, the data shows that in Germany human resource issues are taken into account from the outset in the development of corporate strategy by significantly more organisations than the number who have board-level representation for the HRM function: companies apparently consult with non-board HRM specialists at the earliest stage of formulating corporate strategy (Waechter and Muller-Camen, 2002).

IMPLICATIONS FOR THE CONCEPT OF STRATEGIC HRM

What are the implications of the above? In fact, the evidence is not only that the strategy process varies by country (Brewster and Larsen, 2000). It may involve different objectives (Brewster, 2006). In practice it may work in different ways and through different systems involving different people. Thus, the strategic implications of a management decision in Germany or Austria will be subject to the involvement or scrutiny of powerful works council representatives or the worker representatives on the supervisory board of the company (see Waechter and Muller-Camen, 2002, on Germany, and Brandl and Pohler, 2010, on Austria). Indeed, in most of these companies the knowledge that their decisions are subject to scrutiny – and can be reversed or varied – at that level means that managers tend to operate with HRM issues in mind. Inevitably, this means that the assumptions in the universalist paradigm that HRM strategies are 'downstream' of corporate strategies cannot be made: there is a more interactive process in which both sets of strategy potentially influence each other simultaneously. And assumptions that strategies are the preserve of senior managers (or even just managers) cannot be sustained either. Hence our finding that HRM is involved in the development of corporate strategy in, for example, Germany in more organisations than have allocated the HRM department head a place on the board.

Figure 38 HR involvement in the development of corporate strategy, in six countries

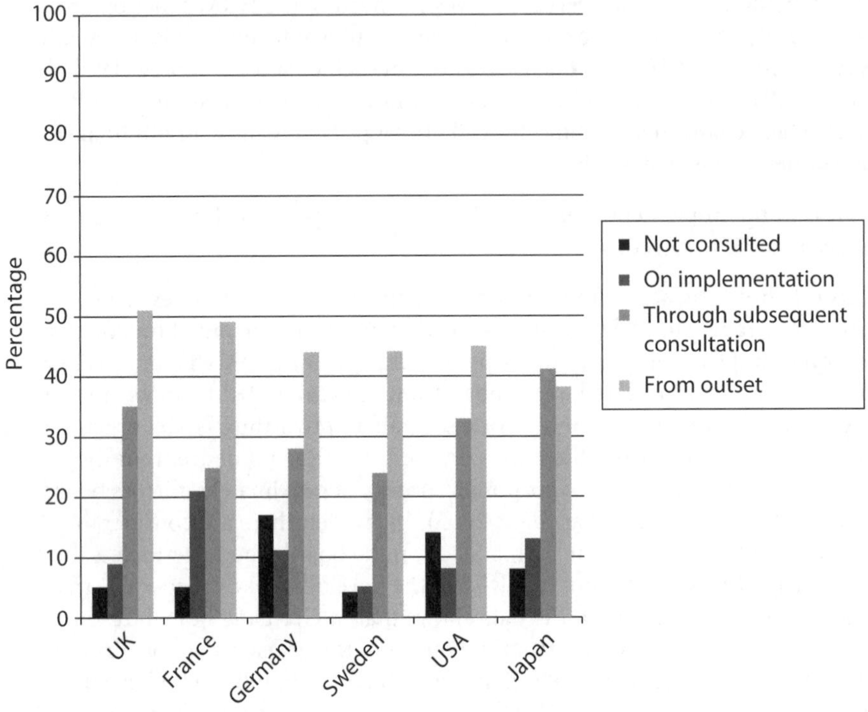

Percentage

Legend:
- Not consulted
- On implementation
- Through subsequent consultation
- From outset

UK · France · Germany · Sweden · USA · Japan

Source: Cranet (2010)

REFLECTIVE ACTIVITY

Identify the effect that worker-directors on the supervisory board and the existence of central (company-level) works councils might have on the role of the HRM department in Germany.

THE CHANGING NATURE OF THE HRM FUNCTION

Because it is a staff function, with costs but no profits, there is ever-greater pressure on the personnel or HRM department to prove its value. The evidence shows wide variations in the extent and kind of evaluation of the department used in European organisations. Evaluation of the effectiveness of HRM departments is not common – although the question is perhaps even less often asked of other support functions. In North America, studies have found that around one fifth of firms evaluate their HRM department (eg Cashman and McElroy, 1991).

The role of the HRM department in any country is ambiguous and dynamic (Stiles and Trevor, 2006). Like other functional specialists, HRM professionals are constantly challenged to meet three competing aims: to make themselves more cost-effective through reducing the costs of services and headcount (the operational driver), to improve their services to meet the increasing demands of line managers and employees (the relational driver), and to address the strategic objectives of organisations (the transformational driver) (Gueutal and Stone, 2005; Snell *et al*, 2001).

To meet these challenges, HRM departments, it was argued, needed to turn to changes in supply chain management and organisational restructuring policies, including (Cooke, 2006; CIPD, 2005a; Reddington *et al*, 2005):

- allocating more responsibility to line managers

- outsourcing transactional activities

- developing shared service models and greater use of electronic HRM

- downsizing the function.

In each case, it is worth pointing out that the rhetorical pressures might be greater than the extent of change in practice – and that these pressures will vary from country to country. The rest of this chapter addresses these issues in turn.

THE ROLE OF LINE MANAGEMENT IN HRM

One key issue in HRM – one that is said to differentiate it from 'personnel administration' (Freedman, 1991; Legge, 1989; Mackay and Torrington, 1986; Schuler, 1990; Weiss, 1988) – is the responsibility placed on line managers for the management of their people. This varies considerably around the world. What is the balance of responsibilities for the management of people between the specialists in the human resources department and the line managers who have day-to-day responsibilities for organising the work and the progress of their subordinates? This topic has preoccupied the attention of a number of authors for nearly two decades (see Brewster and Larsen, 1992, 2000a; Brewster, *et al*, 1997, 2000; Brewster and Soderstrom, 1994; Hoogendoorn and Brewster, 1992; Larson and Brewster, 2003; Mayrhofer *et al*, 2011a, 2011b).

Some have argued that because HRM is central to the well-being of an organisation and to its ability to perform effectively, the subject has to permeate the responsibilities of every single manager in an organisation. Guest (1987; p51) argued that:

> If HRM is to be taken seriously, personnel managers must give it away.

Alternatively, others have claimed that without a knowledgeable, experienced and influential human resources department specialising in the subject, the organisation will never give HRM the prominence that is needed, and will not have the necessary expertise in this crucial area. As a consequence, the organisation will be unable to take the most successful approach to the topic. Does the idea of sharing responsibilities mean that the specialists are in danger of not just giving HRM away but of giving it *up* (Blyton and Turnbull, 1992; p11)?

In historical perspective, it has been argued that, in relation to line management, developments have been almost tidal, ebbing and flowing as the HRM specialists move between opposition to the line, through the roles of power-holder, administrative centre, advocate for co-determination and change agent (Scott Myers, 1991). Here we outline the reasons that have been advanced for the growth in line management responsibility and consider some of the problems that it may involve; we examine the evidence for the trends, and particularly explore the differences between countries. Finally, we draw some conclusions about the implications for the HRM department and examine some of the dilemmas involved in the management of human resources within the organisation in the future.

It is argued that the line manager needs to be aware of the synergy between human, financial and physical resources. For line managers, allocating time, money and energy to the management and development of subordinate staff is not only an investment in enhanced effectiveness and future success but a necessary precondition for it. This responsibility cannot be undertaken by the human resource specialist. The HRM function is seen as playing the role of co-ordinator and catalyst for the activities of the line managers – a 'management team player ... working [jointly] with the line manager solving people-related business issues' (Schuler, 1990; p51).

To consider developments in the balance of responsibilities it is useful to use the term 'assignment' (Brewster *et al*, 1997) rather than 'devolution' or 'delegation'. 'Assignment' avoids any assumption of a particular direction of change in matters of the allocation of responsibility. The assignment of HRM issues to the line has become a major feature of HRM texts in the last few years (Brewster and Larsen, 2000b) because:

- there has been a trend towards managing organisations through the development of cost-centre- or profit-centre-based approaches – and labour costs are usually the major operating cost involved

- it is line managers, not the specialist staff in the HRM department, who are in frequent, often constant, contact with employees – allocating tasks, enthusing (or upsetting) them, monitoring performance: 'Line management is, and always has been, responsible for the performance of their subordinates' (Lowe, 1992)

- there is a growing influence of the service industries, with their focus on responsiveness to the customer

- staffing decisions are increasingly made in real time, and there has been a widespread movement towards reducing the numbers in 'overhead' departments, such as HRM. In such circumstances the role of line management in HRM can be seen as an alternative to outsourcing the function: the 'internalising' shift (Paauwe, 1995).

There is plenty of case-study evidence that responsibility for HRM is being increasingly allocated to line managers (Gennard and Kelly, 1997; Hutchinson and Brewster, 1995). And there was international survey evidence (Brewster and Larsen, 1992; Brewster *et al*, 1997; Brewster and Soderstrom, 1994; Holt Larsen and Brewster, 2003; Mayrhofer and Brewster, 2005) confirming this anecdotal data. The evidence showed that recruitment and selection, health and safety and the expansion and reduction of the workforce are more likely to have been assigned to the line, while industrial relations and training are more likely to stay with the HRM function. However, more recently, it appears that such trends have been reversed (Mayrhofer *et al*, 2011a, 2011b), highlighting the danger of assumptions that even well-documented trends will continue.

There are clear and consistent variations between countries in their overall assignment rankings, countries like Denmark and Switzerland consistently assigning most responsibility to line managers and countries like Italy, France, the UK and the Republic of Ireland retaining most responsibility for the HRM function. Not only are these figures consistent across subject and country, they are also consistent over time.

Of course, within each country there are considerable variations between organisations. It is important to emphasise that there are elements of choice here. Organisations can exercise their option differently from their neighbours. However, the effect of country differences is clear.

REASONS WHY THE ASSIGNMENT OF HRM RESPONSIBILITIES TO THE LINE HAS NOT GONE FURTHER

There are six reasons why this is the case:

- Line managers are often not enthusiastic about taking on responsibility for HRM for the people in their area.

- Line managers under pressure often give HRM responsibilities a low priority – they are often ignorant about legal requirements, trade union agreements or agreed practices.

- There is little evidence that organisations are providing any formal training to help their line managers to handle the human resource management tasks that are being allocated to them.

- They are not particularly interested in HRM issues and are unable to keep up to date with the latest HRM thinking.

- There will be, however devolved responsibility for HRM in the organisation has become, a need for co-ordination of HRM at some level (Paauwe, 1995).

- Perhaps most significantly, the devolvement of HRM responsibilities to the line will not achieve the objectives hoped for if it is done in a policy vacuum, as it often is, just as a means of cost-cutting.

REFLECTIVE ACTIVITY

Review:

● the reasons for the growth of allocation of HR responsibilities to line managers

● the reasons allocation has expanded no further.

What does this suggest for the future?

THE PRESSURE TO OUTSOURCE SOME TRANSACTIONAL ACTIVITIES

There are two strategies at play when organisations consider changing the way they locate their HRM activities):

● 'sourcing' (across organisational boundaries between a client entity and non-client entities such as vendors, suppliers and third parties), and

● 'shoring' (across either on-shore – same country – or wider geographical boundaries).

Sometimes offshoring may be further differentiated into near-shoring (shared borders or close institutional and cultural regulatory regimes) and offshoring (used specifically to refer to sourcing across a wide geographical and cultural distance).

THEORY AND PRACTICE

KEY FRAMEWORK

Four core strategies for HRM delivery models

Chakrabarty (2006) used a four-fold taxonomy to inform research on HRM sourcing and shoring. The core strategies that might be applied are:

● *In-country insourcing* – where the supplier–customer relationship is still formalised and contracted, and activities sent to an overseas location (generally for reasons of cost efficiency), *but* where the activities are still performed in-house, in one of the organisations' own subsidiaries or a service centre. The responsibility and delegation of tasks to the service provider means that they are still an internalised 'client-entity'.

● *Global insourcing* – where the redesign and reconfiguration of activities and processes to become more efficient and effective allows some geographical flexibility over the location of the activity. For economists, ownership of 10 per cent of offshore operations constitutes direct foreign investment between a parent operation and an affiliate.

● *Outsourcing* – when a third-party provider is used to carry out the activity, with the production of services purchased externally, but still within the same country. It is generally aimed at achieving higher profitability by using fewer in-house resources (Espino-Rodríguez and Padrón-Robaina, 2006). It involves a discontinuation of internal production (whether the production of goods or services) and an initiation of procurement from outside suppliers. Human resource outsourcing involves the purchasing by an organisation of ongoing HR services from a third-party provider that it would otherwise normally provide for itself.

- *Offshoring* – a particular type of specialisation in which the production of services or goods is moved overseas. Offshoring involves a broad range of tasks that are executed by a firm in another country, ranging from the establishment of a foreign subsidiary to a relatively arm's length relationship with another firm (Abramovsky *et al,* 2005). More arms'-length relationships tend to involve a more explicit practice of contracting with individuals or companies in foreign countries to perform work that might reasonably be conducted domestically. Offshore transactions also typically involve two parts: a transfer of *responsibility* for the operation and management of part of an organisation; and a *guaranteed provision of services* to the client organisation by the vendor for a time period. In the light of the distances involved in offshoring, the factors of production are rarely transferred to offshore sites, but the services, processes and decision rights are.

The four strategies listed in the *Key framework* above are part of a new rhetoric of HRM in many countries. However, many organisations also remain resistant to the notion – and there is a clear country effect, with outsourcers finding it very difficult to make any money in certain countries. Sparrow and Braun (2008) and Budhwar and Cooke (2009) have drawn attention to the persistence of wide international differences in the pursuit of HRM outsourcing, pointing to evidence that suggests that many non-US firms continue to favour captive (in-sourcing) arrangements rather than pure outsourcing scenarios. HRM directors in Europe still see an in-sourced shared services route as the best stepping stone to future HRM outsourcing.

Asian organisations are not adopting outsourcing to the same extent as found in US and European organisations (Budhwar and Cooke, 2009). They link the current (limited) use of outsourcing by indigenous MNCs or small firms to the size of domestic businesses, the sophistication of HRM functions, the extent to which there is a developed local HRM outsourcing market, cultural norms and other institutional factors. They examined the specific challenges associated with the offshoring of HRM work to India and China, noting that currently the motivation to offshore to each is different. They argue that, unlike IT outsourcing and offshoring, the same decisions in relation to HRM work tend to be tied far more closely to the internationalisation strategy of the firm, and driven by motivations to reduce levels of uncertainty and to gain insight into local market conditions.

Alewell *et al* (2009) examined the use and non-use of a broad spectrum of personnel services by German firms based on interviews with 1,021 chief executives and human resource managers. More than 40 per cent of the firms never even considered the external procurement of specific HR functions – even for well-known and comparatively often-used services such as temporary agency work, consulting and payroll accounting. For outplacement, interim management and the complete outsourcing of HR management, the respective proportions increased to more than 80 per cent of the firms. The triggers of explicit decisions on HR outsourcing were strongly related to organisational changes (such as restructuring decisions, in- and outsourcing decisions or innovations in processes and products).

Sparrow and Braun (2008) argue that IHRM functions clearly face complex decisions, and the outcome will continue to vary across national ownership. In a global context, local country managers argue that much of the corporate HR armoury requires deep tacit understanding of the national culture and therefore should not be a candidate either for operation through shared services or, indeed, for any subsequent outsourcing. Organisations must make sensible assessments of this tacit knowledge constraint. They also draw attention to other national factors which influence the effectiveness that might be achieved in outsourcing (and associated automation) of HR activity. Research looking at international differences in service perceptions draws attention to the role of ethics in explaining cultural differences in service perception, the way in which perceptions, attitudes and behaviours to the new organisational forms may differ internationally (Ruzic, 2006; p99):

> Within the e-business environment, while there is evidence that the processes of engineering and implementation of ... systems are being successfully exported ... as a consequence of globalisation, the adoption of Western social and ethical values ... is another matter.

Employee engagement with and use of e-enabled services is influenced by a series of ethical judgements made about the provision of such services, namely:

- perceived personal benefit
- social benefit
- societal consequences
- level of benevolence (help to those in need)
- paternalism (assistance to others to pursue their best interests when they cannot do it themselves)
- honesty (lack of deceit)
- lawfulness
- autonomy (freedom over action)
- justice (due process), and
- rights to information, privacy and free expression.

Such factors are likely to have some utility in explaining international differences in the attractiveness (or otherwise) of e-enabled HRM services that accompany outsourcing.

THE IMPACT OF SHARED SERVICES AND THE EFFECTS OF ELECTRONIC HRM

A newer development has been in shared services (Cooke, 2006). Shared services are created when the organisation chooses to concentrate its administrative personnel activities into a centralised 'back office' function. Administrative processing is carried out separately from the main HRM group. Although 'shared services' tend to denote centralised provision, a better term to use is 'common provision'. The relevance of this development to international HRM is considerable. Shared service thinking – and the associated technologies used to enhance delivery – represent a force for a fundamental realignment of the HRM function. It carries implications for the level of centralisation–decentralisation and devolvement evidenced across countries, regions and corporate headquarters. Moreover, it changes the economics of HRM service provision and introduces competing dynamics for not only the standardisation of HRM processes but also the potential for mass customisation. Several large organisations developed shared service models for their HRM. By the beginning of this decade, some MNCs believed that shared services would represent a fundamental change in HRM (Alf Turner, Director of HR Services, BOC, cited in Reilly, 2000; p2):

> Separation of strategy from service delivery and the creation of shared services is in that league of change with the switch from welfare to personnel in the 1930s and from personnel to human resources in the 1980s.

The sector that an organisation operates in, however, has a significant impact on the attractiveness of pursuing common technical platforms for the delivery of HRM services. For example, in the banking sector the employee cost base is variable across organisations and operations, but would be seen as low in comparison to other sectors – typically from 40 per cent to 60 per cent. Given a lower employee cost base, the pressure to reduce the costs of HRM service delivery are not as great as might be seen in other sectors. However, because the banking business model is itself technology-driven, there is an expectation that HRM functions should also be run off common technical platforms.

In theory, at least, solutions such as outsourcing or developing shared services would be combined with the extension of existing Information and Communications Technology (ICT) systems, and the implementation of new ones, to transform internal operations (CIPD, 2005b, 2002; Kettley and Reilly, 2003; Gueutal and Falbe, 2005). This process has become known as the e-enablement of HRM (e-HRM), which is qualitatively different from earlier applications of IT to the information function of HRM itself (known as HRIS): e-HRM (Bondarouk *et al,* 2009) refers to the application of ICT to HRM, in the process changing it from a solely face-to-face relationship to an increasingly virtual one. It is argued that it has the potential to fundamentally transform the nature of the HRM function as e-business has done in sectors such as financial services, retailing and knowledge management. Such transformation is already evident in translating individual e-learning into organisational learning and knowledge management, deep-web mining for talent, interactive self-selection and career management, real-time employee engagement surveys and other forms of interactive communications, creating virtual communities and teams, bringing customers/clients and employees into closer virtual relationships, and e-enabling home-working and other, more flexible, ways of working (Martin, 2005).

Currently, the application of ICT to HRM accounts for a substantial element of total technology-spend in organisations (according to some estimates, perhaps as much as 10 per cent of all ICT investment in British and American organisations). For example, in 2006 SAP claimed that 9,500 companies worldwide use their human capital management (HCM) application, a subset of e-HRM, to manage over 54 million employees, while Oracle claimed that 76 of the US top 100 Fortune 500 companies have adopted their software. However, little is known about the long-term cost-effectiveness of generic e-HRM systems, whether they promote offshoring and job losses in the UK (or whether this is offset by the creation of high-value jobs), or their overall contribution to organisational productivity and effectiveness. Also, despite the grandiose claims of their vendors it is not clear how generic systems enable companies to obtain a competitive advantage if they are operating similar business processes to their competitors (Lengnick-Hall and Lengnick-Hall, 2006).

Despite the ubiquity of e-HRM systems in large enterprises, at least, their implementation has been fraught with problems, in part because practitioners lack a sound body of theory and evidence on which to proceed (CIPD, 2005b), particularly in the area of innovation, absorptive capacity, technology acceptance and change management. HRM specialists cite lack of guidance as one of the most significant problems hindering the adoption of e-HRM systems (Martin, 2005). Few studies have systematically explored the nature of e-HRM technologies in use, the rationale for their adoption, problems influencing their implementation, technology acceptance and their broader organisational effects. Indeed, the consequences of ICT enablement for HRM specialists, line managers and other employees is not well understood, researchers highlighting both significant benefits and problems for these stakeholders (Florkowski and Olivas-Lujan, in press; Lawler and Mohrman, 2003; Shrivastava and Shaw, 2004).

Clearly, the dissemination of e-HRM technologies is uneven, reflecting the complex nature of inter- and intra- organisational relationships at regional and sectoral levels and between countries. This process is a relatively under-theorised one, although recent advances in institutional theory have focused on the causes and nature of such diversity in organisational practices, and differing degrees of receptiveness to new technologies (Streeck and Thelen, 2005; Brewster et al, 2006b).

REFLECTIVE ACTIVITY

Review

- the allocation of HRM responsibilities to line managers
- the pressure for outsourcing
- the impact of shared services
- the effects of electronic HRM.

If you can, compare these to the pressures on your own HRM department.

What would you expect to be happening to HRM departments in these circumstances? How would you assess the pressure from senior managers to reduce the size of the HRM function?

Some academics (Martin *et al*, 2008; Snell *et al*, 2001) have proposed that these developments may lead to the 'virtualisation' and/or significant 'leaning' of HRM by reducing substantially the numbers of HRM specialists required. However, although it has been argued that e-HRM simultaneously improves the quality of the services provided by the HR function by enabling them to play a more strategic role, a counter-argument is that e-enablement of HRM leads to routine administrative tasks simply being dumped onto already overloaded managers and employees or else eliminated. It can also have negative consequences on the expectations and benefits of face-to-face relationships between HRM staff and employees.

REFLECTIVE ACTIVITY

Discuss the following questions:

- Are shared service models going to represent a new force for convergence and standardisation of HR practices on a global basis, or will they result in more localised and customised policies and practices?
- How easy is it to develop shared service centres in different countries?
- Are there likely to be different attitudes to the attractiveness or otherwise of this way of operating?

THE INFLUENCES ON CROSS-NATIONAL COMPARATIVE VARIATION IN THE ROLE OF HRM DEPARTMENTS

The evidence about the (relative) size of the HRM department (numbers of HRM staff relative to total employees) shows unequivocally that although we imagine that there are universal performance and technological pressures on HRM functions, they are not everywhere equally large (Brewster *et al*, 2006b). Size varies considerably with the country in which the function is located as well as with the sector of the organisation and the overall size of the organisation, larger organisations having relatively smaller HRM functions. Interestingly, it is also clear that stronger unions are associated with relatively smaller HRM departments. Generally, countries with stronger unions feature smaller HRM departments, and moreover, even within national boundaries organisational-level variation in the strength of unions is negatively related to the size of HRM functions. It is also clear that despite the mooted changes in the nature of the function and the alternative ways in which people management can be carried out, the size of the function has changed very little over the last couple of decades (Mayrhofer *et al*, 2011a, 2011b). Whether this is because the changes have not been as dramatic as many people have claimed, or because the HR function is finding other roles to perform, is less clear.

It might be expected that culture and institutions might influence the role of HRM departments in practice. Thus, for example, policy formalisation may be more likely if an organisation operates in a country with comparatively low hierarchical structures, so that written policies that everyone can refer to may be viewed favourably. In other countries the senior specialists may prefer to leave themselves free to take decisions unencumbered by paperwork, knowing that their hierarchical position will give them the credibility they need for implementation. On the institutional side, the extensive legal and trade union constraints mean that there is inevitably more formalisation and a greater involvement of HRM in corporate strategy in order to make sure that the organisation does not fall foul of its obligations, with consequent disruption and cost.

Evidence on the forces shaping the extent of the strategic integration of HRM is now growing. There have been some suggestions, based on experiences in Germany and Austria, that the social regulation of work by employee representatives displaces HRM functions, inhibiting their strategic integration (eg Waechter and Muller-Camen, 2002, on Germany, and Brandl and Pohler, 2010, on Austria). Yet Farndale (2005) shows that the board representation of HRM grew very rapidly in the 1990s, converging on that in other countries. Moreover, recent international analysis (Vernon and Brewster, 2009) suggests that to the extent that statutory provision for employee representation in Germany and Austria still inhibits the strategic integration of HRM in these countries, this is a result of the very particular legal arrangements for representative employee participation in these countries. In general, internationally, the more prevalent are works councils and most particularly the stronger are unions, the *greater* is the strategic integration of HRM departments. Organisations with works councils and in particular stronger unions are more likely to have HRM represented on the board, viewing itself as centrally involved in strategic decision-making, and pursuing a greater formalisation of HRM strategy (Vernon and Brewster, 2009).

A glance at the cross-national comparative pattern of HRM board representation or early involvement in strategising apparent from Cranet data deployed earlier suggests also that the weightier labour law and more generous welfare states of, for example, France and the Netherlands may also promote the strategic integration of the HRM department, whereas the very limited social regulation of work in the USA inhibits it, whatever the ambitions of US HRM gurus may be. Overall, it seems that where employees have fewer resources on which to draw as individuals and as a group, organisational commitment to the strategic integration of the specialist people management function is less than where employees are well-protected and independently represented.

BEST PRACTICE IN THE ROLE OF HRM DEPARTMENTS

In the UK and some other countries, the traditional specialist people management function –'personnel' – acquired a rather bad name, and was regarded as something of a backwater, dealing with pedestrian or troublesome issues such as health and safety, grievances and disciplinary cases and payroll. Suggestions that HRM functions are – or should be – distinct from the personnel functions of old are common. The need for a strategically oriented HRM function rather than a reactive, 'firefighting' personnel department is often stressed (eg Boxall and Purcell, 2011; Brewster *et al*, 2006b). Yet the extent and nature of the departure from traditional emphases which is required or desirable remains contested.

Much of the discussion of the possibility of best practice relates to the relationship between the HRM function and line managers. Using Ulrich and Brockbank's (2005) five roles for the HRM department (see above) we can explore some of the implications of the allocation of HRM responsibilities to line managers. Sensibly, Ulrich argues that all the roles are still important and will still need to be handled effectively and with credibility. However, the roles have different implications for the relationship with the line manager. Those HRM specialists who act as human capital developer or functional expert may be thought of as a valuable source of advice and 'how to get it done' information by the line manager – or may be perceived as the worst kind of bureaucrat, insisting that the systems drive organisational behaviour. Those acting as employee advocate may well find themselves at odds with the line manager, in a kind of 'loyal opposition' role.

Nor are the strategic partner and HRM leader roles unequivocal. In theory, HRM specialists will have to be closely involved with their line management colleagues if they want to perform that role successfully. As partners, the theory is, they share totally in the creation of policy and also in its implementation. Of course, they expect to, and are expected to, contribute their specific expertise, knowledge and skill to the debate, and to argue their corner on the basis of that expertise. They will not be expected to agree with everything the line manager proposes, or expected to accept something when their professional expertise tells them that it is wrong to do so. To this extent, they will not be such comfortable colleagues as the much-touted 'internal consultants'. There is case study evidence that HRM specialists can, indeed, be influential 'strategic change-makers' (Gennard and Kelly, 1997; p35). On the other hand, it is clear that line managers as such are not a coherent group. Some senior executives may want their HRM departments to take a strategic role, but many line managers just want their HRM department to deal with the bureaucratic and sometimes difficult issues necessarily involved in managing people. They want a responsive operational partner, not a strategic one. It is a perhaps particular view of partnering which means that you ignore what your partner wants in order to do what you think is necessary.

The less exciting-sounding roles are still required. One implication of the devolvement of personnel work to line managers – the development of smart computer systems and the possibility of outsourcing standard tasks like payroll or training provision – may be that the department's 'administrative expert' work is sharply reduced. The theoretical dividing line the academics draw between policy and practice is not so obvious on the ground. However, there are differences: it is one thing to be charged with placing advertisements or conducting negotiations; quite another to be deciding whether to recruit people for the unit or for long-term careers with the overall organisation, or whether to recognise a union. The fact that this distinction may be less clear on the ground should make us wary of easy assumptions that the way forward would lie in splitting the roles so that specialist HRM directors set policy and line managers implement it. In practice, many of these less glamorous tasks still have to be accomplished, and there will in many cases be advantages in having them brought together under one specialist. Alternatively, with the spread of intelligent information and communications systems, much of this work will be available to the line manager without the intervention of an HRM specialist.

We discuss the challenges in making an Ulrich HR delivery model effective in the context of an MNC in Chapter 16.

However, the structure of the HRM department may have to change. One report (Hutchinson and Wood, 1995) argued that increasing devolution would have important implications for HRM departments: they would have more status, because those involved would have proved their worth (this, perhaps, requires more research than the first change). The departments would include more generalists able to turn their hand to any aspect of personnel work – and an associated change would see them developing greater skills and competences. Some researchers have found evidence of a move from departments consisting of fragmented specialist functions towards departments where most of the personnel staff undertake integrated generalist roles (Gennard and Kelly, 1997). But Adams (1991) argued the opposite – that there is now a need to be even more of a specialist, and Sisson (1995; p100) agreed:

> Personnel remains a highly fragmented occupational grouping; the image of the personnel manager as the general medical practitioner seems far removed from reality.

The balance of responsibilities for HRM between HRM functions and line managers varies cross-nationally and is continually shifting (Gennard and Kelly, 1997; Torrington, 1989; Tyson, 1995). Yet there is still, within organisations, a requirement for a focus on people management, for skills in people management, for an awareness of new developments and opportunities in this area, and for attention to be paid to the requirements and contribution of the people who make up the organisation. This requirement applies of course to the specialists in the HRM department, but it applies equally to line managers. We have little or no evidence to suggest that larger, smaller, more strategic or less strategic HRM departments promote better overall performance. It is likely that it is the manner of the integration of the specialist department and of line managers that is significant rather than that their independent characteristics are a central influence on organisational performance. That is a challenge for line managers and personnel specialists alike.

KEY LEARNING POINTS

- There are significant changes going on in HRM functions or departments: the strategic involvement of the head of the HRM department is changing; the role of line managers has more surely changed; the impact of outsourcing, downsizing, shared services and e-HRM are all being felt.

- New ambitions for HRM departments are common currency across and even beyond the countries of the established OECD or old industrialised world, yet there is marked cross-national comparative variation in developments in terms of the actual place and role of HRM departments.

- Even general trends cannot be assumed permanent, and countries start from quite different places, so that there is little evidence of convergence in the place or role of HRM departments.

- The influence on HRM departments of country, with its cultural and institutional environment, is strong.

- Any notion of international best practice in the place or role of HRM departments is a work in progress.

LEARNING QUESTIONS

1 Given that the notion of 'HRM' is seen in some countries to be more advanced than the idea of 'personnel management', why might the latter continue to be the preferred terminology in most of Europe?

2 Is a high level of assignment of HRM responsibilities to line managers a sign of HRM influence or of mistrust of HRM specialists? How might this vary by country?

3 What advantages and disadvantages might a line manager see in being asked to adopt greater HR responsibilities?

4 Choose three countries for which evidence is presented above. How far does the data presented in this chapter help you to identify the most significant roles in the Ulrich model for each country?

5 Consider three (other?) countries for which evidence features here. What are the key influences on cross-national comparative variation in the place and role of the HRM function?

6 Evidence on the role of HRM functions in developing and newly-industrialising countries is currently anecdotal at best. What role would you expect them to have? On what are you basing your conjectures?

EXPLORE FURTHER

Brewster, C. J., Wood, G., Brookes, M. and van Ommeren, J. (2006) 'What determines the size of the HR function? A cross-national analysis', *Human Resource Management*, 45 (1): 3–21. The authors analyse the basis of the marked cross-national comparative variation in the size of HRM departments.

Mayrhofer, W., Brewster, C. J., Morley, M. and Ledolter, J. (2011) 'Hearing a different drummer? Evidence of convergence in European HRM', *Human Resource Management Review*, 21 (1): 50–67. These authors show internationally that shifts in the balance of responsibilities between HRM departments and line management do not necessarily endure as we might assume.

Budhwar, P. S. and Cooke, F. L. (2009) 'HR offshoring and outsourcing: research issues for IHRM', in P. R. Sparrow (ed.) *Handbook of International HR Research: Integrating people, process and context*, Oxford, Blackwell, pp341–362. This chapter examines comparative developments in the outsourcing of the HRM department's activities.

International Human Resource Management

CHAPTER 13

International HRM:
Theory and Practice

LEARNING OUTCOMES

When they have read this chapter, students will:

- be able to link the choice of strategic IHRM approach with international business strategy approaches

- be able to identify the strengths and weaknesses of alternative theoretical perspectives on strategic IHRM

- be able to describe the components of IHRM.

INTRODUCTION

We have of course introduced some theory relevant to the study of IHRM in previous chapters. In Chapters 2 and 3 we looked at the ideas that have come from a cross-cultural management tradition. In Chapter 4 we looked at ideas from a comparative HRM and also institutional perspective. Having explored these comparative issues in detail, in this third section of the book we turn to the concept of IHRM, which can be traced back to the broader field of 'international management'. As explained in Chapter 1, IHRM examines the way in which international organisations manage their human resources in the different national contexts in which they operate. Usually, these are private sector international organisations, generally referred to in the literature as either multinational corporations (MNCs) or multinational enterprises (MNEs). We have already seen the extent and complexity of environmental factors such as different institutional, legal, and cultural circumstances. These affect what is allowed and not allowed in the different nations and regions of the world, but more significantly also create differences in what makes for cost-effective management practices. Organisations working across national boundaries, therefore, have to agree HRM policies and practices which maintain some coherence while still being sensitive to critical aspects of difference.

REFLECTIVE ACTIVITY

In each of the 'functional' chapters in the previous section of the book (Chapters 5 to 12) we have drawn attention to some particular regional challenges. Looking across each of the HRM functions outlined in these chapters – employee relations, organisation of work, recruitment and selection, performance management, rewards, and training and development – what do you think might be the unique influences on IHRM in each of the following geographies, and why are they important?

- western Europe
- transitional economies in Eastern Europe
- North America
- Latin America
- Africa
- Asia-Pacific
- the Middle East.

LOOKING TO THE FIELD OF INTERNATIONAL BUSINESS

The study of global strategy lies at the intersection of two academic fields: strategic management and international business. Peng and Pleggenkuhle-Miles (2009; p51) argue that global strategy has emerged as 'one of the frontier disciplines within business schools'. As IHRM researchers it is important when making observations on another field – that of international business – to avoid misrepresenting some of their debates or conclusions. However, it is worth signalling our understanding about some of their recent discussion.

International business researchers have always been concerned about context, culture and political risk. A framework can be seen as a conceptual or real structure that can be used to help build or expand on an idea. We present a number of such frameworks to help shape thinking about the link between theory and practice in this area.

THEORY AND PRACTICE

KEY FRAMEWORK

Three ways to view global strategy

- As one form of MNC strategy, whereby the organisation treats countries around the world as a common and global marketplace – the other strategies being international (export-driven), multidomestic or transnational. A number of writers argue that this type of global marketplace strategy is either: an ideal that hardly ever exists in practice (Rugman and Verbeke, 2004), or an experiment that can be disastrous (Ghemawat, 2007).

- As a form of international strategic management (Inkpen and Ramaswamy, 2006)

- The strategy of firms around the globe – ie their view of how they can compete successfully (Peng, 2006). This view of how to compete globally requires an understanding of both cross-border and domestic strategy.

International business researchers therefore do not always ask the same sorts of questions of people management in international organisations. They tend to have their own perspective on the world. So before we look at the sorts of theory that IHRM need to understand from this perspective, let us remind ourselves of what the international business field tends to focus on in the first place! There are four debates that currently lie at the heart of the international business field:

1 *Cultural versus institutional distance* – Between culture and institution, which is the more comprehensive construct? We raised this debate throughout Chapters 2, 3 and 4. Beginning with the work of Kogut and Singh (1988), this has also been a long-standing debate in international business research. Their debate, however, has been reignited by the recent resurgence of an institution-based view. This resurgence of an institutional view has not been seen just in the field of comparative HRM – as we explained in Chapter 4. It has also become important in the field of MNCs and of global strategy (Lee *et al*, 2008; Peng and Khory, 2008; Peng *et al*, 2008). This perspective argues that firms' strategies are enabled and constrained by the different rules of the game around the world.

2 *Global versus regional geographic diversification* – Determining the 'global-ness' of the firm also has a long history (Perlmutter, 1969). The recent consensus is that the majority of MNCs are actually organised more regionally. However, the evidence on this is debated between Rugman and Verbeke (2008) on the one hand and Osegowitsch and Sammartino (2008) on the other. This debate has raised the need to understand two things: the impact of *intra*-regional rather than inter-regional behaviour, on HRM activity; and the difficulty of managing internal international networks that cross between regions.

3 *Convergence versus divergence in corporate governance* – We also saw this debate in Chapter 4. Does ideology (and HRM *is* an ideology; market economics is another) or national culture drive societal values? Convergence protagonists argue that globalisation unleashes a 'survival of the fittest' process forcing adaptation to best practices. From the governance arrangements built into national business systems down to the structures and processes that manage human resources, economic or other performance evidence is used to argue best practice. Divergence protagonists argue that the informal norms, values and traditions that make any practice effective cannot be transplanted around the world, so some sort of cross-vergence of arrangements is best.

4 *Domestic versus corporate social responsibility* – Is it an obligation of organisations to maximise the wealth just of equity holders, or of the wider society whose resources they draw upon? Is social performance linked to financial performance? How can corporate social responsibility strategies be aligned with the conflicting demands of domestic and overseas markets, domestic and overseas employees and communities?

REFLECTIVE ACTIVITY

Looking at the sorts of issues above that those who study global strategy are interested in,

● How similar or different do you see the issues compared to those that were identified in Chapters 2, 3 and 4?

● What sorts of new insights would you hope that the study of global strategy should bring to the field of IHRM? What are the practical questions that you would hope that this chapter on theory should be able to answer?

● In Chapter 1 we outlined the evolution of definitions of IHRM, and the growth of more critical perspectives on IHRM. There are three criticisms of the existing literature that we would like to remind you of now. These criticisms should be noted and borne in mind throughout this chapter.

THEORY AND PRACTICE

KEY FRAMEWORK

Critical reflections on globalisation

● *There can be an over-statement of current levels of globalisation within multinationals* – Despite the sorts of statistics noted above in the UNCTAD reports, as was made clear in Chapter 4, researchers coming from an institutional perspective remind us still that in reality, stateless organisations operating independently of national borders under global rules of economic competition are few and far between (Ferner and Quintanilla, 1998; Edwards *et al*, 2005). The majority of multinationals continue to have assets, sales, ownership of workforces and control concentrated in home countries or regions.

● *The need for a broader geographical base to our understanding about IHRM* – Until recently, most of the writing in this area has reflected a predominantly US focus. There are now ever greater numbers of countries with substantial international organisations, and ever more internationally operating organisations that are *not* based in the USA. There are in practice US-global firms, European-global firms, Japanese-global firms, and others, each operating in distinctive national business systems with their own patterns of corporate governance and HRM (Sparrow *et al*, 2004). The strategies that they pursue towards the globalisation of HRM, and the associated shifts in centralisation and decentralisation, are therefore bounded by this inheritance. Strategic decision-making inside organisations has elements that are driven simultaneously by global, regional and national logics and these logics may not always be mutually supportive.

● *The need to study a wider and more diverse set of organisations, beyond just multinationals* – IHRM theory has tended to overlook important areas of internationalisation. Parker (1998) noted that a true understanding of global operation must also incorporate the learning from international family business units, overseas networks of entrepreneurs, and even illegal gangs, all of which have learned how to operate more globally. Inter-governmental international organisations, such as the United Nations, the EU and the regional banks, and internationally operating non-governmental organisations, such as charities and churches, employ increasing numbers of people around the world (Brewster and Lee, 2006).

We can also think of different levels of analysis that can be used to explore the consequences of globalisation.

KEY FRAMEWORK

THEORY AND PRACTICE

Different levels of globalisation

Sparrow and Brewster (2006) note that the main models and frameworks that have been used in the field concentrate on *four* different levels of analysis, each of which can present a different picture of the true extent of globalisation and the HRM issues that consequently need to be managed:

● *Globalisation of industries* – Global industries are ones in which a firm's competitive position in any particular country is dependent upon competition that might exist in other countries (Makhija *et al*, 1997). The level of international trade, intensity of international competition, worldwide product standardisation and presence of international competitors in all key international markets are all high and firms can only achieve efficiencies through global scale, local responsiveness and worldwide learning.

● *Relative levels of internationalisation of the firm* – Estimating the degree of internationalisation of the firm is still an arbitrary process and both the choice of constructs to evidence it and the actual measures used are contentious (Sullivan, 1994). The most popular single measures used are things like foreign subsidiaries' sales as a percentage of total sales; export sales as a percentage of total sales; foreign assets as a percentage of total assets, as an estimate of the material international character of an organisation; number of foreign subsidiaries, to distinguish the degree of foreign investment; tallying of the cumulative duration of top managers' international assignments; or the dispersion of subsidiaries across cultural groupings and zones in the world.

● *Progressive building of international capabilities within firms* – The concept of organisational capability focuses on the ability of a firm's internal processes, systems and management practices to meet customer needs and to direct both the skills and efforts of employees towards achieving the goals of the organisation. This level of analysis emphasises the way in which firms manage the resources that enable them to develop core competences and distinctive capabilities. International expansion is only possible when firms can transfer their distinctive knowledge-assets abroad into new international markets (Caves, 1996). Organisation structures have to respond to a series of strains faced by the process of globalisation (eg growth, increased geographical spread, and the need for improved control and co-ordination across business units) and organisations have to build capability in each stage sequentially in order to maintain integrated standards for some business lines but remain locally responsive in others (Hamel and Prahalad, 1985; Yip, 1992; Ashkenas *et al*, 1995).

- *Functional realignment within globalising organisations* – At this level of analysis it is argued that globalisation within organisations is driven by what happens within business functions as they seek to co-ordinate (develop links between geographically dispersed units of a function) and control (regulate functional activities to align them with the expectations set in targets) their activities across borders (Kim *et al*, 2003).

As the *Key framework* above shows, we need to understand how organisations enhance the ability of specific functions to perform globally.

 REFLECTIVE ACTIVITY

Debate the following.

Malbright (1995, p119) argues that true 'Globalisation occurs at the level of the function, rather than the firm.'

- Is this right? Using the *Key framework* above, what evidence would satisfy you that an organisation was becoming truly global?

Werner (2002) analysed research published in the field of international management in the top US journals – ie the discourse that is important within the US (and increasingly non-US) academic promotion system. Early international management research could broadly be divided into three categories:

- studies that looked at the management of firms in a multinational context – ie the international aspects of management that do not exist in domestic firms, such as the internationalisation process, entry-mode decisions, foreign subsidiary management and expatriate management

- comparisons of management practices across different cultures (cross-cultural studies) and nations (cross-national comparisons)

- studies that looked at management in specific (single) countries within the domain of international management. (in order to overcome the bias of early work that had a North American perspective).

THEORY AND PRACTICE

KEY FRAMEWORK

The 12 early domains of international management

Werner's (2002) analysis of published research broke the field down into 12 domains:

- *Global business environment:* threats and opportunities of global economy, global markets, political and regulatory environments and international risk
- *Internationalisation:* descriptions and measurement of internationalisation as a process, its antecedents and consequences
- *Entry-mode decisions*: predictors of entry-mode choices, equity ownership levels and consequences of entry-mode decisions
- *Foreign direct investment (FDI):* timing, motivation, location and firm and host-country consequences of FDI
- *International exchange*: international exchange, determinants of exporting, export intermediaries and consequences of exporting
- *International joint ventures (IJVs):* partner selection, partner relations and consequences of IJVs
- *Strategic alliances and networks:* alliance relationships, networks and outcomes of strategic alliances
- *Transfer of knowledge:* antecedents of knowledge transfer, processes and consequences of transfer
- *Multinational enterprises (MNEs)/multinational corporations (MNCs):* multinational enterprise strategies and policies, models of MNCs
- *Subsidiary-HQ relations*: subsidiary role, strategies and typologies, subsidiary control and performance
- *Subsidiary and multinational team management*: sudsidiary HRM practices, subsidiary behaviours, multinational negotiations and multinational team management
- *Expatriate management*: expatriate management, issues for expatriates, expatriate and repatriate reactions.

REFLECTIVE ACTIVITY

Look at the types of research literature in the *Key framework* above, and make a list of the strengths that this would give you (the sorts of phenomena that would be understood well by reading these sorts of studies). Then make a list of the sorts of phenomena that would be missed out – what these sorts of studies might ignore.

We noted the critical view on IHRM in Chapter 1. For De Cieri *et al* (2007) the term 'global' rather than 'international' used by many researchers reflects the view that IHRM has become a key aspect of MNC strategic planning and implementation – part of a bigger set of questions aimed at understanding what determines the international success and failure of firms. Big theory, they argue, does not assist us in answering such questions.

For many academics, the task of producing a grand theory that brings together the diverse perspectives inherent in these theories is neither feasible nor desirable – by their nature each theory sheds light on the many different processes and phenomena that come to the fore as HRM is managed in an international context.

What we have to do is link these theories to the sorts of organisational problems that they help solve in order to understand the value that each theory brings to the analysis of the problems of internationalisation.

The topic of IHRM or, more appropriately, strategic IHRM (SIHRM), has become a separate, and crucial, field of study in its own right. This chapter provides the theoretical underpinning of this section of the book. We explore IHRM in the following way:

- First, we explore a number of different lenses (life-cycle and organisational design models) through which we can examine the subject of IHRM.

- Then we consider the key issue of differentiation versus integration.

- Next we examine contingency approaches to strategic international HRM.

- We explore four key theoretical models that can be applied to the subject; and

- We present a model of 'global HRM'.

As the challenges of internationalisation have become more complex, there has been a 'transfusion' of ideas across these theories (Sparrow and Braun, 2008).

LIFE-CYCLE MODELS

Theoretical frameworks in SIHRM have been – and still are – influenced by three developments that emerged in broad historical sequence (Sparrow and Braun, 2007):

- early attention to life-cycle models based on the concept of 'fit' between HRM and the progressive stages of HQ management attitude to international operations: product life cycles, or organisational life cycles

- the subsequent development of ideas about organisational design and the process through which strategy and structure can be matched or ideal MNCs created

- the development of integrative 'contingency' frameworks premised on the need to both integrate and differentiate HRM policies.

At first, attention was given to a series of 'life-cycle models'. These models reflected the need for there to be strategic fit between HRM policies and practices and the international evolution of the firm. One of the earliest set of studies to leave a strong mark on future SIHRM frameworks was by Perlmutter (1969) and Heenan and Perlmutter (1979). These authors saw staffing decisions within MNCs as a consequence of attitudes of the management at headquarters. They identified four main approaches to describe how MNCs deal with the staffing and management of their subsidiaries.

THEORY AND PRACTICE

KEY FRAMEWORK

Attitudes to internationalisation

In *the ethnocentric approach*, few foreign subsidiaries have any autonomy; strategic decisions are made at headquarters. Key positions at the domestic and foreign operations are held by headquarters' management personnel. In other words, subsidiaries are managed by expatriates from the parent country (PCNs).

In *the polycentric approach*, the MNC treats each subsidiary as a distinct national entity with some decision-making autonomy. Subsidiaries are usually managed by local (host-country) nationals (HCNs) who are seldom promoted to positions at headquarters. Likewise, PCNs are rarely transferred to foreign subsidiary operations.

The *regiocentric approach* reflects the geographic strategy and structure of the multinational. Personnel may move outside their countries but generally only within a particular geographical region (eg Europe or Asia-Pacific). Regional managers may not be promoted to headquarters positions but enjoy a degree of regional autonomy in decision-making.

In *the geocentric approach*, the MNC takes a worldwide stance in respect of its operations, recognising that each part makes a unique contribution with its overall competence. It is accompanied by a worldwide integrated business, and nationality is ignored in favour of ability. PCNs, HCNs and third-country nationals (TCNs) can be found in key positions anywhere, including those at the senior management level at headquarters and on the board of directors.

REFLECTIVE ACTIVITY

Why do managers need to be able to understand the importance of attitudes to internationalisation?

How would you link them in with each of the areas of HRM explored in the previous 'functional' chapters on HRM? That is, how would you link them in with attitudes held towards the performance management system, to recruitment and selection, work organisation, and so forth?

What do you see as the practical implications of organisations (or key managers within the organisation) being positioned in each of the four internationalisation approaches? How would they manage each of the HR functions?

Adler and Ghadar (1990), in the early literature in this field, followed Perlmutter's approach but suggested that organisations will inevitably develop through certain stages – influenced very much by these different types of attitude – and will have to follow very different IHRM policies and practices according to the relevant stage of international corporate evolution, which they identify as:

- domestic
- international
- multinational
- global.

Proponents of life-cycle models argue that there is a link between the variation in an MNC's HRM policies and practices and either their product life cycle or organisational life cycle. Consequently, in all these models, human resource flexibility becomes central to effective internationalisation, and is dependent upon the capacity of HRM to facilitate the ability of the organisation to adapt to changing demands both from within the MNC or its context both effectively and in a timely manner.

However, there has been increasing discomfort with the view that firms have to follow a progressive stage model of globalisation. Malhotra and Hinings (2010) recently posed this question: why do we observe different processes of internationalisation, and consequently approaches to the commitment of resources to a foreign market, over time? They argue that there are some important characteristics of internationalising firms that determine the path they take. Many of our assumptions about the process of internationalisation stem from the original work, known as the Uppsala model (the 'U model') of Johanson and Vahlne (1977). This argued that internationalisation is an incremental process of building commitment in a host country. Market uncertainty is only reduced by the gradual acquisition, integration and then use of knowledge about the host context. Firms can only learn from these experiences by undergoing the experience.

 ONE SIZE DOES NOT FIT ALL

CASE STUDIES

Can firms be born global? The answer to this question depends on the type of organisation. Mass production organisations (whether product or service) tend to follow one of two paths, depending on the importance of the technical or relationship component needed as part of the physical presence in country. They either follow a 'slow and steady' path from exports or licensing – slowly moving to partnering arrangements then wholly owned ventures – or

a 'leapfrogger path'. Where an organisation has accumulated market experience because of the prior internationalisation of its other businesses in a host market, it might jump straight to a joint venture (experimenting with different depths of relationship) or advance rapidly from alliances to wholly owned subsidiaries. In service sectors where production can be broken up into several components – such as hotels, fast-food restaurants or car rental – then a 'contractual path' can be followed. The business performance tends to be more people-centric. To reduce market uncertainty, knowledge has to be codified and put into operating guidelines. There needs to be continual monitoring and scanning of for new local customer groups. Management service contracts, or franchise arrangements, can be renewed and engineered through successive or stepped-up levels of scope and control to create a consistent customer experience or brand. Finally, project-based organisations can follow a 'bounded commitment path'. They can ride on the coat-tails of a local partner or seek connections from one temporary project to another. Writing more than 30 years after their original piece, Johanson and Vahlne (2009) made clear that opportunities in international business are becoming less a matter of country specificity and more about relationship or network specificity. For project organisations, the mobile nature of the primary assets – people and project expertise – means that the depth of local resources and commitment can be switched on and off rapidly, either within a project, or between projects.

Over time, the debate ranged from whether incrementalism really existed, to which factors (or contingencies) moderated the relationship between market uncertainty and incremental behaviour, and how the process evolved through the strategic decisions that got made. Some studies demonstrated that there does indeed seem to be a series of stages – an incremental and successive establishment of operations in small steps, from exports through sales to manufacturing. Other studies suggested this view is too narrow and demonstrated systematic variations to this assumption (Malhotra and Hinings, 2010; p331):

> Since the Uppsala model was proposed, the landscape of internationalising organisations has changed significantly. A wider array of organisations are entering foreign markets. They include manufacturing firms; consumer services such as hotels, restaurants, leasing, car rentals and retailing; professional services such as accounting, engineering, architectural firms, management consulting, health and financial services; and other knowledge-based organisations providing software development and R&D services ... To understand why internationalisation processes proceed in a certain way we need to [pay] attention to what these organisations do to organise the creation and delivery of a product or service in a foreign market.

In practice, there are four conceptually distinct elements of an internationalisation process – four critical questions:

- Focus of entry: how does a firm enter a specific foreign market – by specific client or by market as a whole?

- Degree of presence: how does a firm sustain or enhance its commitment or continued presence in a market?

- Physical presence: to what extent and in what form does it need a physical presence in the market?

- Choice and path of international form: what international forms are adopted, and best reflect, a firm's evolving resource and institutional commitment to a host market?

CASE STUDIES

CAN YOU BE BORN GLOBAL?

eBay is often used as an example of rapid internationalisation. It was founded in California in 1995 and is now the largest platform for Internet auctions worldwide. Its first international operations were in the UK and Canada in 1998, with an adjusted Internet presence designed for local customers. By 1999 it had entered into a strategic partnership in Australia and expanded to Germany by acquisition. In 2000 it entered France and Japan, and Korea and Taiwan by 2001. By 2005, within ten years of its founding, it was present in 29 countries,

Hedlund and Kverneland (1985) talked about 'leapfrogging' to describe the situation when a firm jumps over stages in the classical stages of internationalisation model. Then the concept of 'born global' was first used in 1993 in a survey for *The Australian Manufacturing Council* by the consultants McKinsey (McKinsey and Co., 1993). The McKinsey report was interpreted by some as meaning that gradual internationalisation is dead. It was argued that even the smallest firm has access to information about the export markets and can begin to export from the birth of a new firm (Cavusgil, 1994; Knight and Cavusgil, 1996; Cavusgil and Knight, 2009).

Many – usually innovative – firms are also being described as 'born global'. Different yardsticks are used, but typically they are firms that have reached a share of foreign sales of at least 25 per cent within a time-frame of two to three years after their establishment. Post-recession, national governments are interested in understanding what can be done to help support such firms – asking what

the role of networks and ecosystems may be. These firms tend to be knowledge-intensive or knowledge-based firms, selling products that are so specialised that their market is global from an early stage. They therefore do not need to take the traditional route of developing a home market first and then expanding incrementally into a series of overseas markets. Firms that are international right from their birth are called a lot of things – 'international new ventures', 'global start-ups', and 'infant multinationals' (Rasmussen *et al*, 2001).

As time went by, people asked: can a firm really benefit from an accelerated process of internationalisation – where it can access competitive advantages across national borders, internationalising its value chain activities quickly? Research has gone on to examine what is really meant by becoming a 'born global' firm (Bell *et al*, 2003; Knight and Cavusgil, 2004; Gabrielsson *et al*, 2008; Weerawardena *et al*, 2007; Holtbrügge and Enßlinger, 2009).

Are there business models that allow such firms to be globally efficient, effective and competitive as possible right from the start? Both the entrepreneurship and international business literatures have shown that quick expansion, especially in foreign markets, can be very difficult to manage. A born global strategy can provide early advantages for firms; it can also introduce complexity that can destroy any potential benefits. Three criteria, – time, countries and ownership – have to be taken into account in order to differentiate early internationalising firms (EIFs) from born global firms (BGFs).

Questions

- Do BGFs create unique people management and organisational issues?
- What HR functions covered in Part Two of the book become most relevant for the management of such firms?

REFLECTIVE ACTIVITY

Think of a modern type of business.

- Does the argument hold true that it must work through successive stages of internationalisation before it can truly globalise?
- How might an organisation safely leapfrog some stages?
- What sorts of arrangements can be put in place to speed up the learning process?

ORGANISATIONAL DESIGN MODELS

INTERNATIONAL ORGANISATIONAL STRUCTURES

Another development was the advent of organisation design models. The challenge of considering *how* an MNC can best implement international policies and practices was taken up by giving attention to organisation design and the match between strategy and structure.

THEORY AND PRACTICE

KEY FRAMEWORK

Information processing theory

Many of the assumptions about organisation design in MNCs are driven by information processing theory. This makes a basic assumption that organisations are open social systems exposed to both external and internal sources of uncertainty (defined as the difference between information possessed and information required to complete a task). They have to develop information-processing mechanisms capable of dealing with this uncertainty (Tushman and Nadler, 1978; Egelhoff, 1991). Information processing in organisations includes the gathering of data, the processing and transformation of data into information, and the communication and storage of information in the organisation. Effective organisations create a 'fit' between their information-processing capacities and the information-processing requirements determined by such factors as their strategy, task characteristics, inter-unit interdependence and their organisational environment. MNCs are large and complex and have very high information-processing requirements because:

- a transnational strategy requires a reciprocal interdependence between affiliates and headquarters

- their focus on flexible, people-based co-ordination and control mechanisms requires high levels of informed action.

MNCs frequently reach the limits of their information-processing capacity and the competing demands of globalisation and localisation influence the choice of structure and management control processes within international organisations. A number of typologies of organisational forms have been developed. In general, these typologies denote a move away from hierarchical structures toward network or heterarchical structures.

THEORY AND PRACTICE

KEY FRAMEWORK

Different international forms

Hierarchy approaches – Under this form, control rests at the MNC's headquarters, with strong reporting and control systems for subsidiaries. Senior management is composed of parent-country nationals (PCNs). Birkinshaw and Morrison (1995) synthesise earlier work on hierarchical MNC structures to arrive at three basic assumptions underlying these configurations:

- Co-ordination costs are economised by grouping tasks according to the geographical or product markets on which they are focused.

- Critical resources (including management expertise) are held at the centre to ensure the most efficient use of scarce resources.

- The development of an appropriate system to monitor and control divisional managers ensures that the likelihood of opportunistic behaviour on their part is minimised.

Polycentric approaches – Organisations adopting this type of structure reflect less parent control and much greater autonomy of subsidiaries. The term 'multinational' is used by Bartlett and Ghoshal (1986) to define this type of organisation in that it operates in multiple geographical contexts, and functions may be duplicated internationally.

Network/heterarchy approaches – In this type of organisation the driving force is to capitalise on the advantages of global spread by having multiple centres. Subsidiary managers are responsible for their own strategy and the corporate-wide strategy. Co-ordination is needed across multiple dimensions (eg functions, products, and geography). Each subsidiary is aware of the role of the others; no subsidiary sees itself in isolation from the rest of the global organisation (Hedlund, 1986). This type of organisation has been called a transnational by Bartlett and Ghoshal (1987). Transnational organisations aim to develop a truly global culture and mindset amongst their employees.

REFLECTIVE ACTIVITY

Consider the *Key frameworks* presented so far.

● How might you combine the different forms of international operation and the different attitudes to globalisation?

● How might the different levels of globalisation impact on an organisation's forms and attitudes?

DIFFERENTIATION AND INTEGRATION

A unifying theme throughout all SIHRM studies is the tension between differentiation and integration – sometimes referred to as the 'global versus local' dilemma – as a defining characteristic of the international perspective on HRM (Ghoshal, 1987; Galbraith, 1987; Punnett and Ricks, 1992; Schuler *et al*, 1993; Evans *et al*, 2002). We return to a discussion of global integration versus local differentiation in Chapter 16.

REFLECTIVE ACTIVITY

Think about the answers to the following questions – questions that all international organisations face:

● What freedom does an international organisation have in regard to imposing its own approaches to HRM on its operations throughout the world?

● How can an international organisation, aware of the need to be sympathetic to local cultures, still ensure that it gains optimum value from its internationalism?

● What is the relationship between the strength of organisational culture and national cultures?

Evans *et al* (2002) see this tension as a critical component of duality theory. Proponents of this perspective argue that opposites and contradictions are not 'either/or' choices but 'both/and' dualities that must be reconciled. Fit or contingency theories are seen as too static for the fast-moving modern age and do not provide an adequate conceptual basis for understanding organisational dynamics. Explaining the nature of the local responsiveness/global integration duality, these authors (Evans *et al*, 2002; p83) write:

> All firms maintain corporate integration through rules, central procedures and planning, and hierarchy. But as the needs for integration grow, more rules, more control and more bosses at the center simply will not work, but instead will only kill local entrepreneurship and drive away good people. So these classic tools need to be complemented with more informal mechanisms for co-ordination: lateral relationships, best practice transfer, project management, leadership development, shared frameworks, and the socialisation of recruits into shared values. These tools of 'glue technology',

as we call them, are to a large degree the application of human resource management.

A key determinant of an organisation's eventual positioning on the integration-differentiation continuum is the nature of the international business strategic approach adopted.

REFLECTIVE ACTIVITY

Ask yourself:

- What range of options is open to international organisations carrying out operations across national boundaries?

- How might each of the 'glue technologies' discussed by Evans *et al* (2002) affect the strategic positioning of the IHRM function?

The ways in which MNCs organise their operations globally has been the subject of extensive research by international management scholars (leading names include Prahalad and Doz, 1987; Bartlett and Ghoshal, 1989; Porter, 1990). Recurrent themes in the literature are the link between the strategy-structure configuration in MNCs, and the competing demands for global integration and co-ordination versus local responsiveness. Where global integration and co-ordination are important, subsidiaries must be globally integrated with other parts of the organisation and/or strategically co-ordinated by the parent. In contrast, where local responsiveness is important, subsidiaries should have far greater autonomy and there is less need for integration.

Factors that influence the need for integration in global business strategy include:

- *Operational integration* – This might be the case in technology-intensive businesses such as chemicals and pharmaceuticals where a small number of manufacturing sites can serve wide geographical markets. Equally, universal products or markets, such as in the case of consumer electronics, lead to high demands for integration.

- *Strategic co-ordination* – Organisations can select specific areas where there is a need for centralised management of resources in line with strategy. For instance, significant resources such as research and development may be co-ordinated in terms of strategic direction, pricing and technology transfer, while other functions such as sales are not.

- *Multinational customers* – Global competition places greater demands on the co-ordination of resources, equipment, finance and people. For example, it is important to co-ordinate pricing, service and product support worldwide, because a multinational customer can compare prices in different regions.

Factors that influence the need for differentiation in global business strategy include:

- *Market demands* – Local responsiveness is more common where local competitors define the market competition. This is equally true where products have to be customised to local taste or regulations, such as in the case of processed foods or fashion.

- *Legislative demands* – Local legislation may prevent full standardisation of services across the globe, leading to a requirement for more tailored approaches.

- *Political demands* – Barriers to entry in some markets may require an organisation to set up a more autonomous subsidiary primarily staffed by host-country nationals (HCNs).

REFLECTIVE ACTIVITY

You are the HR manager of a UK-based small to medium-sized enterprise about to expand into several European countries. Based on your reading of the earlier chapters and this one so far, prepare:

- a brief report for the board outlining the key HRM issues you will face with internationalisation, and

- an initial project plan for the internationalisation activity.

STRATEGIC INTERNATIONAL HRM: CONTINGENCY APPROACHES

A full understanding of strategic IHRM in MNCs requires an integration of multiple disciplinary bases and theoretical perspectives (Sundaram and Black, 1992). Taylor *et al* (1996; p960) provide a definition of strategic IHRM derived from the strategic HRM literature:

> Strategic Human Resource Management (SHRM) ... is used to explicitly link HRM with the strategic management processes of the organisation and to emphasise co-ordination or congruence among the various human resource management practices. Thus, SIHRM (strategic international HRM) is used explicitly to link IHRM with the strategy of the MNC.

Schuler *et al* (1993) offer an integrative framework for the study and understanding of SIHRM which incorporates features unique to the international context (see Figure 39). They define SIHRM as (Schuler *et al*, 1993; p720):

> Human resource management issues, functions and policies and practices that result from the strategic activities of multinational enterprises and that impact on the international concerns and goals of those enterprises.

The breadth of issues is illustrated by their framework, which links SIHRM orientations and activities to the strategic components of the inter-unit linkages and internal operations of the MNCs. These authors again argue that the key determinant of effectiveness for MNCs is the extent to which their various operating units across the world are to be differentiated and at the same time integrated, controlled and co-ordinated. Evidence of different solutions adopted by MNCs to the tension between differentiation and integration are seen to result from the influence of a wide variety of external and internal factors.

External factors include:

- industry characteristics, such as type of business and technology available
- the nature of competitors
- the extent of change
- country/regional characteristics (political, economic and socio-cultural conditions and legal requirements).

Figure 39 The Schuler framework

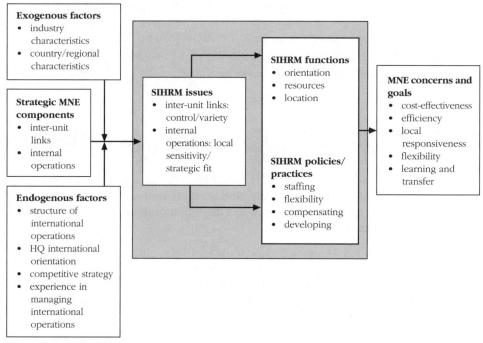

Source: Schuler *et al* (1993)

Internal factors include:

- the structure of international operations
- the international orientation of the organisation's headquarters
- the competitive strategy
- the MNC's experience in managing international operations.

So how does theory help international managers to make sense of these complex considerations? A recent overview of theoretical and empirical developments in the study of SHRM in MNCs identified five theoretical perspectives (Sparrow and Braun, 2007), which we now cover.

RESOURCE DEPENDENCY THEORY

The resource dependency perspective focuses predominantly on power relationships and resource exchanges between an organisation and its constituencies (Pfeffer and Salancik, 1978). In this respect, organisational decision-making is not seen as an outcome of strategic choice. Rather, the theory assumes that all organisations depend on a flow of valuable resources (eg money, technology, management expertise) into the organisation in order to continue functioning. MNC affiliates may have more or less dependence and power, as these resources are controlled by various actors, internal to the MNC (eg parent company or regional operations) or external to it (eg the stock market or government institutions). The higher the scarcity of the valued resource, the more the power of the entity that controls that resource increases. An example might be the lack of suitably qualified people in a certain country of operation, thus necessitating the costly transfer of personnel from other countries in the organisation's set-up. Equally, work permit restrictions in many countries limit the extent to which labour is completely mobile. If external parties control vital resources, an organisation is vulnerable and will strive to acquire control in order to minimise its dependence (De Cieri and Dowling, 1999). The resource dependency perspective highlights the important influence of external environmental conditions on the ability of an organisation to maximise the effectiveness of its human resources. It is one of the key building-blocks of the SIHRM frameworks discussed earlier (see Schuler *et al*, 1993; Taylor *et al*, 1996). It has been used to explain the findings of a number of studies that have looked at MNC HRM practices and HRM practices in joint ventures (Rosenzweig and Nohria, 1994; Hannon *et al*, 1995; and Lu and Björkman, 1997).

THE RESOURCE-BASED VIEW OF THE FIRM

The resource-based view (RBV) of the firm has become, perhaps, the most common theoretical perspective (Wright *et al*, 2001; Morris *et al*, 2005). This perspective sees the firm as a unique bundle of tangible and intangible resources (Wernerfelt, 1984). It stresses the inherent 'immobility' of valuable factors of production and the time and cost required to accumulate those resources. Firms accumulate different physical and intangible assets. It is only possible for others to imitate these assets if they have gone through the same process of investments and learning. This historical evolution of a firm constrains its strategic choice.

THEORY AND PRACTICE

KEY FRAMEWORK

Qualities needed for a resource to provide competitive advantage

Barney (1991) and Peteraf (1993) argue that in order for firm resources to hold the potential of sustained competitive advantage they must be:

- valuable – ie the resource exploits opportunities and/or neutralises threats in a firm's environment
- rare among a firm's current and potential competitors
- imperfectly imitable – ie other firms do not possess the same resources and cannot obtain them easily
- non-substitutable with strategically equivalent resources.

The RBV of the firm presents the clearest argument as to *why* firms must transfer capabilities globally. MNCs operate in multiple environments and so possess variations in both their people (reflecting the skill sets created by national business systems) and in their practices (which reflect local requirements, laws, and cultures). SIHRM practices allow a firm to capitalise on its superior skills and exploit the cultural synergies of a diverse workforce (Morris *et al*, 2005). Strategists argue that in a competitive marketplace the act of integrating disparate sources of knowledge within the organisation, utilising 'organisational capabilities' worldwide becomes a source of advantage (Ghoshal, 1987; Grant, 1996; Nohria and Ghoshal, 1997). In the HRM field the term 'organisational capability' was developed by Ulrich (1987). As a concept it combines ideas from the fields of management of change, organisational design and leadership. It concerns the ability of a firm's internal processes, systems and management practices to meet customer needs and to direct both the skills and efforts of employees towards achieving the goals of the organisation and is therefore about competing 'from the inside out'.

The RBV of the firm has been questioned recently. Although it discusses the importance of learning and knowledge transfer, it has tended to emphasise the role of the corporate centre in MNCs, which is generally assumed to be one of shaping the strategic direction of the organisation and designing the strategic change programmes pursued in the subsidiaries. Knowledge transfer processes inside MNCs are central to the global transfer of capabilities (Foss and Pedersen, 2004; Morris *et al*, 2005). Recently, more attention has been given to the mechanisms that explain why *mutual* transfer of capability (to and from the corporate HQ and subsidiaries) is beneficial to the organisation, and how this actually happens.

REFLECTIVE ACTIVITY

What does the pursuit of 'organisational capability' mean for the design of IHRM functions and for the role of HR business partners?

Why might the organisational capabilities associated with strategic goals such as 'meeting customer needs' be constituted in the same way in different international operations of the firm?

How would you use the resource-based view of the firm to explain how the following mechanisms can develop the business and technological skills needed to ensure the mutual transfer of capabilities?

- international diversification into multiple markets
- collaborating with organisations that have mutually complementary competences (for example through joint ventures)
- emphasising strategic leadership roles for national subsidiaries
- gaining access to foreign-based clusters of excellence
- building internal centres of excellence based on global best practice.

Although resources *can* provide a global advantage to the MNC as a whole, this is only *if* the knowledge, skills, and capabilities can be leveraged appropriately. We must draw upon organisational learning perspectives to understand how this can be done.

THE KNOWLEDGE-BASED VIEW OF THE FIRM AND ORGANISATIONAL LEARNING THEORY

Because of the increasing focus of attention that is given to knowledge transfer, knowledge-based views of the firm and theories of organisational learning have come to influence the field of SIHRM. We return to these issues in the next chapter, but at this stage outline some of the relevant theory. The knowledge-based view focuses explicitly on the role of tacit knowledge as a resource. There are two contrasting views that are taken (Tallman and Fladmoe-Lindquist, 2002):

- *Capability-recognising* – This strategy or perspective notes that although MNCs possess unique knowledge-based resources, these are typically treated as being home-country-based or belonging to central corporate functions and top teams. These capabilities are only disseminated to international operations on a 'need-to-know' basis.

- *Capability-driven* – This perspective (also called the 'dynamic capability' perspective in the strategy literature) is more proactive. It is concerned with a *wider process* of how firms build, protect and exploit *mutual* capabilities between, for example, corporate HQ and subsidiaries. In terms of international management, the world is not just a source of new markets but also an important source for new knowledge.

REFLECTIVE ACTIVITY

Debate the following in the light of the two different perspectives that dominate theories in this area, the capability-recognising and the capability-driven:

● What are the HRM implications for an organisation that pursues a capability-driven strategy rather than a capability-recognising strategy?

● How feasible is it for organisations to put this into practice?

● Will it matter to them if they cannot deliver this strategy? Why, or why not?

The organisational learning literature has had a major influence on the SIHRM frameworks discussed earlier in the chapter. These frameworks stress the effect that time and experience has on organisational learning. The capability-driven perspective has begun to dominate theory and research. It takes a very clear stance with regard to the question 'Should firms transfer HRM systems?' It argues that by deploying these resources and progressively integrating them into their most value-adding activities, organisations can build a series of important capabilities such as industry-specific skills, networks and relationships, and appropriate organisational knowledge and structures.

An important capability that must be developed has been called 'absorptive capacity' (Cohen and Levinthal, 1990) or 'knowledge transfer capacity' (Martin and Salomon, 2003). Prior related knowledge gives organisations the ability to recognise the value of new information, assimilate it, and then apply it to new ends. Organisations learn by 'encoding' inferences from history into their structures, designs, rules, and procedures. These routines also serve to help individuals learn because they socialise employees into desired ways of behaving, educate them about the business environment they face and ensure that practices imitate the assumed best ways of coping with this world. Knowledge transfer – and the integration of this knowledge into the routines of the organisation – is, however, only facilitated when the respective parties have the absorptive capacity or prior experience that is necessary to understand the new ideas (Szulanski, 1996; Tsai, 2002). Groups with large amounts of international experience, for example, are more likely to be able to integrate knowledge from other parts of the organisation than those that do not have such experience.

Globalisation is forcing organisations to improve their capability to transfer knowledge. If an organisation learns to do this well, than it can develop a superior 'knowledge transfer capacity'. This means that the organisation has to develop two mutually reinforcing capabilities (Martin and Salomon, 2003):

● the ability of the organisation (or business unit) to articulate the uses of its own knowledge, assess the needs and capabilities of the main recipients for that knowledge, and then transmit knowledge so it can be used in another location ('source transfer capacity')

● the ability of the transferee to assimilate and retain information from a willing source – ie evaluate external knowledge, take in all its detail, and modify or create organisational procedures to accommodate the new knowledge ('recipient transfer capacity').

REFLECTIVE ACTIVITY

Can organisations enhance their 'absorptive capacity'?

● If so, what managerial actions are the most important?

● What sort of organisational culture becomes important?

● What sorts of abilities and motivations do employees need?

● What does this mean for the design of IHRM policies and practices?

Source: Minbaeva *et al* (2003)

There have been some recent attempts to specify the contribution that HRM makes to global knowledge management processes. This topic is considered in more detail in Chapter 16.

RELATIONAL AND SOCIAL CAPITAL THEORY

The organisational learning theories discussed here have provided us with a much clearer focus on *how* organisations need to navigate their way through the internationalisation process. This focus on the need to better understand the 'how' has also been helped by work on relational and social capital theory (Buckley and Ghauri, 2004; p83):

> The process of globalisation is ... not only reorganising power at world level but also at national and subnational levels. As domestic firms move part of their production to other countries, technology, knowledge and capital become more important.

REFLECTIVE ACTIVITY

Think about the impact that e-commerce and more flexible networks of organisations has had on the way international business is conducted.

● How has it created new complexities in the relationships between organisations or new opportunities in the way they deal with each other?

One response to globalisation has been the development of complex cross-business networks. These networks might be built around groups of independent firms, or neighbouring firms within a regional industrial cluster or district that share a common need (Rugman *et al*, 1995). A number of changes inside organisations – such as more transparent internal transfer pricing arrangements or service level agreements – have brought internal prices more in line with external prices. This has sometimes allowed divisional managers to bypass what are considered to be weak or incompetent sections of their own organisation and develop supply or production arrangements that service all members of these broader cross-business networks. The literature on inter-organisational trust has considerable relevance to the study of global organisations. It gives attention to the role of what is termed 'relational capital' (Chen *et al*, 2004).

 REFLECTIVE ACTIVITY

Why is 'relational capital' important, and how does it help organisations build competitive advantage?

What links would you draw between national culture (see Chapters 2 and 3) and the importance of relational capital?

Relational capital is primarily concerned with business networks and the inter-firm relationships that exist within these networks. It concerns the sets of interdependent business relationships upon which repeated business transactions are based. This includes things like goodwill and trust that exists between a firm and its customers, suppliers, partners, government agencies, research institutions and so forth. Competitive advantage is assumed to result from this form of capital primarily for four reasons:

- Knowledge-sharing across these relational networks reduces the cost of transactions between network members, and thereby facilitates value creation and innovation.

- Organisations can access and deploy their existing capabilities within this network in ways that help them seek new markets, resources, efficiencies and assets.

- The social networks inherent in the relationships affect the rate of creation of new inter-firm links, and this improves the organisation's ability to align its structure and design with its global strategy.

- The ability of partners to absorb and learn from each other at more equal rates is facilitated, thereby extending the life cycle of arrangements such as joint ventures.

However, despite the growth of such cross-business networks, often made easier also by technology, face-to-face contacts with foreign partners are still crucial in cultivating trust, providing access to the flow of information within the network, and providing the opportunity for international managers to create new relationships. Many of these relationships can be captured in what is called an individual or group's 'social capital'. Bourdieu and Wacquant (1992; p119) defined it as:

The sum of the resources, actual or virtual, that accrue to an individual or group by virtue of possessing a durable network of more or less institutionalised relationships of mutual acceptance or recognition.

THEORY AND PRACTICE

KEY FRAMEWORK

Structural holes and social capital

International managers and expatriates often possess a lot of influence because their position in the organisation gives them 'brokerage' opportunities, in relation to their participation in, and control of, information diffusion across international operations. Central to this process of information diffusion is the concept of 'structural holes' (these are holes in the social structure within a network). The 'hole' might not reflect a total unawareness of the other parties, but it certainly reflects a lack of attention given to them (Burt, 2000). Structural holes are often implicit in the boundaries that exist between cohorts of employees, teams, divisions, subsidiaries and between firms. Individuals, units or organisations that have relationships that 'span' these holes or implicit boundaries can create a competitive advantage for themselves, depending on the nature of their 'brokerage'. Holes act as buffers, people on either side of the hole circulating in different flows of information. They therefore offer an opportunity to broker the flow of information between people and to control the projects that bring people together from opposite sides of the hole. Knowing the holes that exist inside the organisation and one's ability to broker across these boundaries can be of benefit both to an individual's career or, more altruistically, to the process of internationalisation. Would it help to know what relationships and social capital a candidate for an important international role has? Would these relationships be more or less important than their international skills? Across which holes inside your organisation would it be useful to force employees to work in order to foster their international mindset?

HRM's role in building social capital beyond organisational boundaries to encourage co-operation across the company and improve firm success has been recognised increasingly in the literature (Gratton, 2005; Lengnick-Hall and Lengnick-Hall, 2006; Mäkelä, 2007; Taylor, 2007).

Beware, though. Human and social capital – when applied to the practical realities of international managers and employees – is really a theoretical construct created originally by researchers in economics and sociology to interpret the relationships between individuals and the contexts they operate in. They are both 'capitals', in that they are considered resources accessible to all and destined for the realisation of individual objectives. Social capital can belong to individuals, but also to a community. It may be something that an international manager builds up after years of working as an expatriate or consultant, or it might be something that an important unit within the organisation develops because of the resources that it controls and influences. In the international context, it has been defined (Lengnick-Hall and Lengnick-Hall, 2005; p477) as:

the intangible resource of structural connections, interpersonal interactions, and cognitive understanding that enables a firm to (a) capitalise on diversity, and (b) reconcile differences.

Possessing the right relationships makes possible the achievement of certain ends that would not be attainable otherwise. The management of social capital has become viewed as a critical business competence. Whereas human capital theory assumes that people, groups or organisations do better (ie receive higher returns for their efforts) because of their personal traits and characteristics, social capital theory assumes that they do better because they are better 'connected' (Sparrow and Braun, 2006). This 'connection' might be realised in the form of trust, obligation or dependency. Certain network structures, or having a job or role that is located in a powerful place amongst this set of exchange relationships, become assets in their own right. The management literature has long pointed to the role of international managers and expatriates as 'information brokers' or 'transferers of knowledge' (Bonache and Brewster, 2001b).

For example, Mäkelä's (2007) study of expatriates showed how social capital becomes important for global talent – their relationships are richer, more trustful and longer-term than more arm's-length cross-border relationships, and these properties create more opportunities for knowledge-sharing, and have a multiplying effect by spreading ties more effectively across new units. Lengthened participation in the assignment unit typically leads to a higher level of shared cognitive ground, effectively facilitating knowledge. Taylor (2007; p337) argues that a pressing need now is:

> the identification, development and retention of managers, particularly those crossing geographic and cultural boundaries (high-value boundary spanners or HVBS), who can successfully develop social capital in multiple cultural settings.

She highlights the need for IHRM functions to manage both structural social capital (the configuration, density and strength of relationships between HVBSs) and cognitive social capital (shared goals and shared culture – ie language, codes and narratives). She notes that the competencies needed to do this are little understood.

Is it possible to ask the managers (or ask about the organisations that they work in) directly about their own human or social capital? Do you begin either from the responses an individual gives to other questions, or from their life or organisational story itself and then reinterpret the answers according to the definition of human and social capital we have chosen?

Sparrow et al (2009) note that recent empirical work has helped to explain the role of social networks in IHRM. A fair amount is now known about the extent to which networking is used by international organisations. Tregaskis et al (2005) described the function, structure and process typically associated with international HRM networks, which may be run through top-down or more collaborative remits and operate through leadership, project or special-event team structures. They can serve a range of functions including policy development and implementation, information capture, exploitation of knowledge, sharing of best practice, achieving political buy-in and socialisation of members. Face-to-face contact is also important in the process of relationship and reputation-building but is often supplemented by virtual working as a way of signalling more global cultures. The level of localisation is generally driven by the politics of acquisition, size, expertise and level of resistance in subsidiaries. HRM leadership through networks, it is argued, can facilitate more collaborative solutions, but this depends on the strength of international HRM networks.

REFLECTIVE ACTIVITY

In what ways, and through which structures, does greater social capital make international managers more effective?

Is social capital separate from human capital, or are there particular skills and competencies that help an international manager build social capital?

What other attributes must be combined with social capital in order to lead to the creation of a global mindset? (What, for example, is the role of cultural intelligence, discussed in Chapter 3?)

What is the role of HRM processes in building, protecting and capitalising on social capital?

Based on their study of a large international news and financial information organisation, Sparrow *et al* (2009) go on to identify learning points about the operation of social networks.

LEARNING POINTS ABOUT THE OPERATION OF SOCIAL NETWORKS IN ORGANISATIONS

1 In the continual duality between wanting global integration and being locally responsive, a key bridging mechanism for organisations involves networking.

2 The actual networks that are developed are dependent upon, but also help create, both social and political capital.

3 Understanding the shape of the networks offers powerful insights into organisation design questions within IHRM functions. By tracking the actual networks inside any multinational organisation, the validity of the existing structures, such as centres of excellence, regional hubs and strategic project groups can be assessed.

4 Delivering HRM leadership through networks can facilitate more collaborative solutions, but this depends on the strategic capability of the function, board-level support and the strength of IHRM networks.

5 Network and project-based structures have had – and will continue to have – an impact on the conduct and quality of international HRM interventions and the career trajectories of HRM professionals.

HOW COULD YOU MEASURE THE STRUCTURE OF THE NETWORK IN AN IHRM SETTING?

Sparrow *et al* (2009) developed a methodology that enables an IHRM function to analyse four 'positional attributes' of its networks:

- Who is particularly well-connected? What is the prominence or importance of an individual, as indicated by their centrality in the network? A high level of degree centrality indicates the presence of highly valued ties between an individual and their first-level connections. This is called 'centrality'.

- How 'near' is an individual (in terms of frequency of contact) to all the others in the network? This is called 'closeness'.

- How important an 'intermediary' is the individual? What is the position in the HRM-network and the extent to which an individual lies 'between' the various other important actors in the network? This is called 'betweenness'.

- Who are the most important brokers of exchange within this HRM network?

They designed an instrument that can be used to display how effective and complete the networks are inside an IHRM function. The exercise had two parts to it. In exercise one, respondents listed all the key people/units that formed part of their network. In exercise two, for each person or unit that they identified, respondents provided some key information (in the form of ratings) about the dyadic relationship. Respondents generated a list of (up to 10) people/units/stakeholders that they dealt with (each person/unit was called a *node*). They were asked the following questions:

1. In order to execute your HRM strategy, who is the target – ie who do you interact with?

2. Why do you interact with them?

3. How important is the relationship?

Respondents were then asked to select their top five interactions and answer the following 13 questions about each one, on a 1-to-5 scale:

1. How *frequently* do you interact with this node?

2. To what extent do you *transfer expert knowledge* to/from this node?

3. To what extent do you *broker information* to/from this node?

4. To what extent do you *provide consulting support* for this node?

5. To what extent do you *have to persuade* this node to do something?

6. How *deep* is the relationship?

7. How much *power* do you have in the relationship?

8. What would happen if interaction *never took place*? How serious would the consequence be for International HRM?

9. To what extent is *value added or created* for the HRM function from this relationship?

10. To what extent is *value protected* through this relationship (eg brand/reputation, corporate social responsibility, risks controlled)?

11. What is the *level of reciprocation* in this relationship?

12. Who *most influences what is delivered*?

13. How *central to (the organisation's) strategy* is the relationship?

A MODEL OF GLOBAL HRM

In a study of global HRM strategies in UK MNCs Brewster *et al* (2005; p950) found that there were five different strategic drivers (efficiency orientation, need for global provision, information exchange, core business processes and localisation of decision-making) but multiple ways in which the MNCs combined the drivers. They argued that we need now to challenge the view that single sequential paths to globalisation of structures and HRM make best sense:

> The field is changing rapidly and, arguably, theorising has not kept up with developments in practice ... To distinguish our analysis from those developed previously, we end the paper by using the term 'global HRM' (GHRM) rather than the more familiar terms 'international HRM' (IHRM) or 'strategic international HRM' (SIHRM). Our study set out to explore what is happening, at the beginning of a new century, to HRM in a global context.

They argue that there is a need for better understanding of these developments. The study used questionnaires and a longitudinal case-study design, involving organisations from both the private and public sector with a broad sectoral range of sizes and contexts. The authors note that extant models of the SIHRM process tend to be static and do not include many key drivers and enablers. Figure 40 provides a conceptual model of this process. These factors are creating a new set of pressures on HRM specialists.

Figure 40 Processes involved in globalising HRM

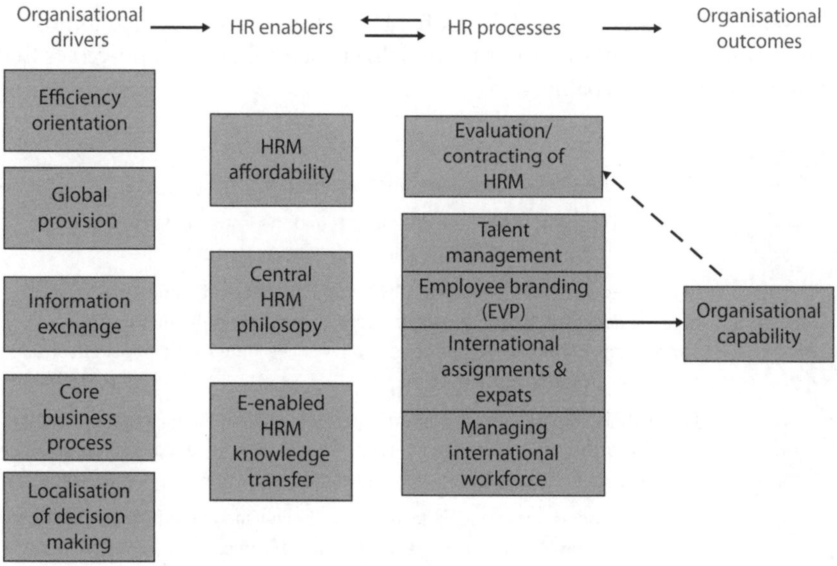

Source: Brewster *et al* (2005)

THEORY AND PRACTICE

KEY FRAMEWORK

Three enablers of high-performance international HRM are being developed for MNCs

As included in Figure 40:

- *HRM affordability*: the need to deliver global business strategies in the most cost-efficient manner possible. Both people and activities are now examined to identify their added value and organisations are devoting considerable attention to ensuring that people are operating where they can be most cost-effective and that central overheads are as low as possible.

- *Central HRM philosophy*: the need to ensure a common philosophy and coherent practice across disparate countries and workforces.

- *E-enabled HR knowledge transfer*: the use of networks and technology to assist organisational learning. In relation to this factor, Sparrow (2006b) has outlined five main forms of global knowledge management, or integration mechanisms that are currently dominating the actions of organisations, namely: organisational designs and the use of centres of excellence; managing systems and technology-driven approaches to global knowledge management systems; capitalising on expatriate advice networks; co-ordinating international management teams; developing communities of practice (COPs) or global expertise networks.

This research illustrates the need for global HRM functions to be able to position themselves in a range of ways in order to deliver the enablers and processes that lead to organisational capability.

KEY LEARNING POINTS

- HRM decisions in the international sphere are very complex.

- The broad scope of IHRM now goes far beyond the issue of expatriation to an overall concern for managing people effectively on a global scale.

- In adopting an SIHRM perspective, HRM practitioners in international organisations would be engaging in every aspect of international business strategy and adopting HRM policies and practices aimed at the most effective use of the human resources in the firm.

- Researchers coming from an institutional perspective remind us that in reality, stateless organisations operating independently of national borders under global rules of economic competition are still few and far between.

- The main models and frameworks that have been used in the field concentrate on *four* different levels of analysis, each of which can present a different picture of the true extent of globalisation and the HRM issues that consequently must be managed: globalisation of industries, relative levels of internationalisation of the firm, progressive building of international capabilities, and functional realignment.

- The task of producing a grand theory that brings together the diverse perspectives inherent in the range of IHRM theories is neither feasible nor desirable – by their nature each theory sheds light on the many different processes and phenomena that come to the fore as HRM is managed in the international context.

- Life-cycle models reflect the need for there to be strategic fit between HRM policies and practices and the international evolution of the firm.

- MNCs frequently reach the limits of their information-processing capacity and the competing demands of globalisation and localisation influence the choice of structure and management control processes within international organisations.

- A unifying theme throughout all SIHRM studies is the tension between differentiation and integration – sometimes referred to as the 'global versus local' dilemma.

- A key determinant of effectiveness for MNCs is the extent to which their various operating units across the world are to be differentiated and at the same time integrated, controlled and co-ordinated.

- Globalisation is forcing organisations to improve their capability to transfer knowledge. Attention has been given to the mechanisms that explain why *mutual* transfer of capability (to and from the corporate HQ and subsidiaries) is beneficial to the organisation.

- Despite the growth of such cross-business networks, often made easier also by technology, face-to-face contacts with foreign partners are still crucial in cultivating trust, providing access to the flow of information within the network, and providing the opportunity for international managers to create new relationships.

LEARNING QUESTIONS

1 Which of the theoretical approaches to SIHRM are the most useful in explaining *your organisation's* current IHRM policies and practices?

2 To what extent can there be such a thing as 'best practice' in IHRM?

3 Describe the key features of a typical HRM approach under each of Heenan and Perlmutter's (1979) orientations to internationalisation.

4 Plot your current organisational approach to HRM on the model of processes associated with the globalising HRM model in Figure 40.

EXPLORE FURTHER

Brewster, C. J., Sparrow, P. R. and Harris, H. (2005) 'Towards a new model of Globalizing HRM', *International Journal of Human Resource Management*, 16 (6): 953–974.

Kim, K., Park, J.-H. and Prescott, J. E. (2003) 'The global integration of business functions: a study of multinational businesses in integrated global industries', *Journal of International Business Studies,* 34: 327–344.

Schuler, R. S., Budhwar, P. S., and Florkowski, G. W. (2002) 'International human resource management: review and critique', *International Journal of Management Reviews*, 4 (1): 41.

Tallman, S. and Fladmoe-Lindquist, K. (2002) 'Internationalization, globalization and capability-based strategy', *California Management Review*, 45 (1): 116–135.

Taylor, S., Beechler, S. and Napier, N. (1996) 'Towards an integrative model of strategic international human resource management', *Academy of Management Review*, 21 (4): 959–965.

CHAPTER 14

Managing Expatriation

LEARNING OUTCOMES

When they have read this chapter, students will:

- understand how international assignments link to an organisation's international strategy

- be able to evaluate trends in the nature of expatriation

- recognise the critical components of the expatriate management cycle

- be able to critique theory versus practice in expatriate selection

- identify antecedents to adjustment in international assignments

- be able to design appropriate pre-departure preparation programmes for expatriates

- know how to compare ways of measuring the performance of expatriates

- be able to describe best practice in relation to repatriation.

INTRODUCTION

In this chapter we link international assignments with organisational strategy. A critical component of IHRM strategy is the management of internationally mobile staff. Traditionally, international organisations have deployed groups of managers and experts to disseminate corporate strategy and culture to local units and to transfer competence across borders. It seems that in newer affiliates there is a clear correlation between the use of expatriates and organisational success – and if it is a larger subsidiary, having more expatriates also correlates with success (Sekiguchi *et al*, 2011). In addition, high-potential managers from headquarters have been sent abroad as a developmental method prior to progression to senior management. Changes at both organisational and individual level are causing a fundamental rethink of international staffing policies. This chapter explores how international mobility fits within an organisation's overall strategic IHRM approach. It also examines critical components in the effective management of international assignees.

Aligning international assignments with organisational strategy can be thought of in relation to the dominant orientation of the international organisation. The generic patterns of expatriation associated with the four main modes of international orientation (ethnocentric, polycentric, regiocentric and geocentric) were outlined in Chapter 13.

The extremes are the ethnocentric approach, where expatriates are sent out from headquarters because they 'know better' (about organisational policy or specific skills or practices), and the geocentric orientation, where planning for international assignments is just one part of global HRM planning,. A trend towards a more global approach to international staffing would represent a significant move away from the traditional ethnocentric mode of international assignments. Mayrhofer and Brewster (1996), however, note that there has been no wholehearted rejection of an ethnocentric approach to international staffing, pointing out the numerous advantages, as well as the disadvantages, of such an approach (see Table 18). They point out that most MNCs are still fundamentally ethnocentric.

Table 18 The advantages and drawbacks of ethnocentric staffing

Advantages	Drawbacks
• efficient co-ordination • effective communication • direct control of foreign operations • diffusing central values, norms and beliefs throughout the organisation • broadening the view of expatriates and chance of growth for expatriates • rapid substitution of expatriates possible • no need for a well-developed international internal labour market • appropriate for entry into international business	• adaptation of expatriates uncertain • selection procedures prone to errors • high costs • complicated personnel planning procedures • private life of expatriates severely affected • difficulties in mentoring during stay abroad • reduced career opportunities for locals • potential failure rate can be higher • government restrictions

Source: Mayrhofer and Brewster (1996)

CASE STUDIES

HSBC: THE INTERNATIONAL MANAGER PROGRAMME

HSBC is a major financial services organisation that employs 284,000 employees worldwide and operates in over 80 countries. The bank has colonial roots and was originally based in Hong Kong. It was managed by international officers who were largely British expatriates. In the early 1990s, Midland Bank was acquired. Major acquisitions in North America have also made HSBC the largest foreign bank in Canada and the USA. The corporate centre is now in the UK. The bank's vigorous advertising campaign features the need to be sensitive to local culture and customs in order to succeed in business, proclaiming it to be 'the world's local bank'.

The expanding geographical reach of HSBC and its growth through acquisitions increased the need for the international deployment of people. It has operated a traditional elite expatriate model, virtually all senior managers being drawn from a tight-knit cadre of international managers (IMs) who were seen as 'the DNA of the organisation' (*Economist*, 2006; p99). This currently outweighs the decreasing need for expatriates in some of HSBC's earlier markets, where more highly skilled local people are now available. HSBC has retained a specific group of international managers. IMs are globally mobile, generalist commercial bankers who provide a pool of resources, often at short notice, to meet the group's needs. They are exposed to a wide range of commercial banking business areas across a range of geographical, operational, functional and cultural barriers. HSBC recruits and plans for IMs to stay with the group in the long term. Individuals are recruited direct into the International Manager Programme either from higher education or internally. The career deal for IMs is clear. They can be sent anywhere and at short notice, and so give high commitment to the organisation. In return, the individual has a good employment package, a wide range of challenging jobs and good career prospects leading to general management positions. Realistic job preview is an important feature of the recruitment process. Attention is drawn to the potential downsides such as not being able to choose where you work; being prepared to spend an entire career outside your native country; being trained as a generalist and not a specialist; being able to work and live amongst a range of cultures, customs, nationalities and languages; having an ever-changing circle of friends; and living in a world where partners and children must accept an IM lifestyle. Once the initial development programme has been completed after five years, the managers are deployed on new postings every two to three years on a rolling basis. Each move is planned to provide a steep learning curve. By their early forties successful managers become country managers or the chief executive of an operation. Development is measured against core skills throughout the process by means of a systematic Executive Performance Development Programme.

The scheme, which peaked with around 800 expatriates, has now been scaled back to 380 employees who come from 33 countries. Although it has been scaled back, there has been a large expansion in other types of foreign posting. In addition, there are 1,600 people working as secondees, contract executives and short-term assignees (mainly technical staff). Each group has its own compensation and benefits package.

TODAY'S CONTEXT FOR GLOBAL MOBILITY

CASE STUDIES

Consultants' surveys are usually done amongst their clients or potential clients for the purpose of selling their services and therefore have limited academic validity. But they are frequent and more up to date than academic texts and give us some indications of what is happening. Recent surveys (eg BGRS 2010, GMAC 2008) demonstrate that:

- Most organisations deploy 50 or fewer expatriates; much smaller numbers have up to 100 or even over 1,000 expatriates.

- More expatriates now are women (maybe as many as a quarter, amongst the larger companies) and most are aged between 20 and 45.

- Family concerns and spouse career issues continue to dominate reasons for refusal to accept an assignment and also assignment failure.

- Only a minority of employees in the surveyed organisations have international experience.

- The economic crisis starting in 2008 led many companies to reassess their use of these very expensive employees. But the latest figures show that increasing growth in the numbers has been re-established.

- Formal cross-cultural training is made available to only a minority of employees.

- Expatriate attrition rates are at least double those of other employees, around a third to a half of repatriates leaving their organisation within two years of return.

As the second case study shows, there have been major changes in terms of the profiles of individuals undertaking international assignments and their expectations. The traditional expatriate profile is changing. We are moving away from the standard career-expatriate model, usually filled by white middle-class male employees from headquarters.

Key features of the modern expatriate population include:

- There are more people from outside the headquarters country: 'third-country nationals' (not from the home or the host country) and inpatriates (ie people brought into headquarters) as part of a more geocentric staffing policy.

- There are more women. The numbers of women expatriates vary with country (Bonache *et al*, 2007), but early estimates range between 2 per cent and 15 per cent of the total expatriate population (Adler, 1986; Scullion, 1994; Harris, 1995; Caligiuri and Tung, 1998). The number of women expatriates is increasing, even though they continue to face numerous barriers to participation (see Chapter 15).

- The number of 'dual-career couples' has increased significantly. For them, an international assignment presents a series of challenges (Caligiuri and Tung, 1998; Harvey, 1997; Punnett *et al*, 1992; Reynolds and Bennett, 1991). There is little research on the expatriate family as opposed to research on partners and children as constraints on the expatriate (although see Andreason and Kinneer, 2005; Haslberger and Brewster, 2008). Fewer partners, male or female, are prepared to accept a 'trailing' role – not working, but being expected to act as support to their MNC-employed partner, and even to act as (typically) 'hostess' for corporate functions. Partners now more frequently have their own career, and expect to work in the new country (see Chapter 15).

- The expatriate population is now better educated than it used to be. Increasing demands for expatriates to deliver value during assignments, linked to the use of expatriate assignments for developmental purposes for high-potentials, have resulted in an expatriate population made up substantially of well-educated individuals, with degrees or MBAs.

- Changes have occurred in employee expectations that international assignments will lead to career progression, in line with changes in the psychological contract. Research suggests that managers increasingly view an international assignment as enhancing their careers (Tung, 1998), even if that may not be with their current employer (Jokinen *et al*, 2008). Emerging notions of 'internal' or 'boundary-less' careers (Arthur and Rousseau, 1996; Parker and Inkson, 1999) suggest that managers value an international assignment for the opportunity it brings for skill acquisition, personal development and career enhancement, even though it may not help them advance within their company. Many expatriates now find their own way to another country rather than being sent by their organisation (Suutari *et al*, 2000; Suutari and Brewster, 2003; Banai and Harry, 2004). This trend has major implications for organisational policy and practice in terms of repatriation and career management.

- The increasing development of new communications technology – and new transport options – means that many, though not all, of the advantages of using expatriates can be achieved by other means: short-term assignments and frequent flying (Welch and Worm, 2006) and virtual teamworking (Zimmerman and Sparrow, 2008) (see Chapter 15).

Figure 41 The global assignment cycle

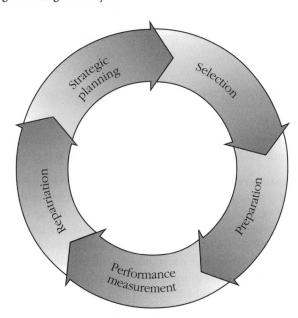

Source: Brewster *et al* (2003) *International Human Resource Management*

In order to address some of the ways that organisations are attempting to manage their expatriate workforce, Figure 41 shows the 'cycle of expatriation'.

The complexities of managing this cycle have been the focus of sustained academic research over many years. Despite this focus, key challenges still remain under each of the cycle components. The whole of the global assignment cycle has to be managed effectively. Expatriate failure in the usually defined sense – the premature return home of an expatriate manager – is rare (Harzing, 1995). Some US literature has claimed very high failure rates, and it does seem that expatriate failure may be a less significant issue for European MNCs (Brewster, 1991; Scullion, 1994; Suutari and Brewster, 1998; PriceWaterhouseCoopers, 2000). However, the cases that occur are invariably traumatic for the individual and the organisation. And perhaps more serious are the many more numerous cases of poor performance. Preventing or minimising these will involve HRM specialists in work on:

- planning
- selection (recruitment)
- preparation
- adjustment
- rewards
- performance measurement – and, finally,
- repatriation.

REFLECTIVE ACTIVITY

In what circumstances might ethnocentric staffing be valuable, and why?

And when should it be avoided?

STRATEGIC PLANNING

Discussions of overall orientation to internationalisation and its impact on staffing practices provide the context for the more detailed formulation of strategic operational goals and their link to international assignments.

Bonache and Fernandez (1999) addressed the question 'What relationship exists between the MNC's international strategy and the expatriate selection policy?' According to their resource-based view, competitive advantage can occur only in situations of heterogeneity (resources are unevenly distributed and deployed across firms) and immobility (they cannot be transferred easily from one firm to another). A sustainable competitive advantage is achieved when firms implement a value-creating strategy that is grounded in resources that are valuable, rare, imperfectly imitable and non-substitutable. In an international context, resources that provide the company with a competitive advantage in the firm's home country are also useful in other countries.

Now look back once more at the advantages and disadvantages of ethnocentric staffing as listed in Table 18.

THEORY AND PRACTICE

KEY FRAMEWORK

Four categories of subsidiary

In line with the resource-based view of the firm, it is the transfer of intangible resources – in particular, knowledge – which is most important to the firm both in value and as a basis for competitive advantage. Depending on the extent to which subsidiaries develop these dimensions of internationalisation, Bonache and Fernandez (1999) classified them in four categories:

- *Implementor* subsidiaries apply the resources developed in the headquarters or other units of the organisation to a specific geographic area. Skills knowledge transfer is expected to be a critical reason for using expatriation here due to the high need for tacit knowledge transfer.

- *Autonomous units* are much less dependent on the human and organisational resources existing in the rest of the company's international network. They therefore will have little use for expatriates for knowledge transfer and co-ordination, and would tend to use local country nationals in key positions.

- *Learning units* acquire and develop new resources that may later be exported to other parts of the organisation. The dominant pattern of international transfer will therefore be one of managers from these units to another country.

- Finally, *globally integrated units* develop new expertise but also use the resources generated in other subsidiaries or in the headquarters. Expatriates are used for knowledge transfer, but also for co-ordination.

Research reveals an extensive list of possible strategic reasons for MNCs using international assignments (see checklist in the *Key framework* below).

THEORY AND PRACTICE

KEY FRAMEWORK

Strategic targets addressed by an international assignment:

- to improve business performance
- to foster the parent corporate culture in the subsidiary, or share cultural views: to develop the 'corporate glue' that holds international organisations together
- to break down barriers between the parent company and subsidiaries
- to solve technical problems
- to develop top talent and future leaders of the company
- to open new international markets
- to handle politically sensitive business
- to control business improvement initiatives
- to improve the trust/commitment of the subsidiary

- to reduce risks

- to train host-national employees in order to improve individual skills

- to improve team skills

- to implement knowledge practices – eg development, sharing, codification, combination, transfer and mapping of the organisation's knowledge

- to develop, share, and transfer best practices

- to improve business relationships

- to develop networking processes at intra- and inter-organisational level

- to develop an international leadership with a global mindset

- to control financial results.

At this level, management has to answer a fundamental question: why do we need to send people on an international assignment to perform the strategic goals? Since expatriates are very expensive, an organisation has to clarify why it is sending them on an assignment. For an organisation they represent a high-cost investment. This cost should be justified against a set of pay-off benefits (see Chapter 15). The situation with regard to the use of expatriates as both a vanguard for international recruitment and as a form of 'corporate glue' has been changing quite rapidly in recent years. Rising costs and staff expectations and greater risks associated with certain locations mean that each assignment is increasingly viewed on the basis of a cost-benefit analysis. Many organisations are in the process of reconsidering the role of their internationally mobile employees (Sparrow, 2006c).

SELECTION (RECRUITMENT)

After planning, the next step in the cycle is identifying the right person for the post. For the organisation, we are generally discussing selection rather than recruitment because in most cases the candidates are already employed by the organisation (but note that Suutari and Brewster (2003) found a substantial proportion of people working outside their own country had made their own way there). These appointments normally fall into the category of transfers or promotions and are often linked with prior identification of potential (particularly in the case of developmental assignments). External recruitment tends to be limited to very specific skills (deep-sea drilling, logistics, etc) and to difficult-to-fill assignments in unpopular or dangerous countries.

How best should we think about the selection of people for international roles inside organisations? Morley and Heraty (2004; p634) point out that:

There is an emerging recognition that international assignees may impact the bottom-line performance of MNEs, and thus, as Dowling and Welch

(2004) observe, finding and nurturing the human resources required to implement an international strategy is of critical importance.

REFLECTIVE ACTIVITY

While/after reading the following sections, answer the questions below:

● Can the competencies that become important for international management be developed?

● Are some competencies so complex, rare on the ground or time-consuming to build that the real issue is to select and motivate a small elite of managers?

● Can we identify a clear hierarchy of international management skills, from the most basic, to higher levels of performance and sophistication, or must we be left with endless lists of desirable characteristics with assumed relevance?

● Do internal resourcing systems realistically make such graded and calibrated decisions about managers?

● Are line managers just happy to find candidates who are half-competent but are willing and mobile?

The consensus view from HRM practitioners is that it is possible (if not actually practical to try to put into practice) to specify a set of competencies for international assignments, and that these can be used to assist the selection of some people in some jobs. However, there are very different views about the practicality of using them to select international managers.

Sparrow (1999) reported two competing resourcing philosophies: one view, the clinical risk assessment approach, finds favour with HRM professionals who argue that there are limits to the use of personal competencies as a selection criterion for international employees. The reasons for unsuccessful international management assignments often go beyond problems of the managers' cultural adaptability, maturity, and stability to include issues such as the adaptability of the partner, dual-career difficulties, national attitudes to mobility, and pay arrangements. Scullion (with Starkey (2000), and Collings and Saillion, 2006) has argued that the pool of potential expatriates is reducing (although it may be that this is only true in certain cases and in ethnocentric organisations). They cite NCR as an example of an organisation that pursues the strategy of designing the assignment to match the skills of the manager, rather than the other way round.

The second, more traditional psychometric approach, argues that there is an identifiable set of competencies that are associated with success and that these can be used to predict effective performers in international roles (see Chapter 15 for a review of this work). It is generally accepted that certain factors have to be given more attention when operating internationally (such as openness to experience, tolerance of ambiguity, extroversion, the ability to generate and inspire trust in others, and proactive information-seeking). Research in many countries finds that despite this, technical competence is seen as the number one criterion.

SELECTION CRITERIA: THE THEORY

The literature on the criteria used for expatriate manager selection also has a tendency towards prescription and a heavy North American bias. We discussed some of the assumptions and competing perspectives about the desirability of selecting people against individual characteristics for successful international working in Chapter 8. In the context of selecting expatriates, sometimes theoretical lists of competencies for international managers can look amusing. One book on cross-cultural management (Harris and Moran, 1996) cites 68 dimensions of competency, of which 21 are perceived as 'most desirable'. Staff with these competencies should probably be chief executive officer rather than expatriates! Yamazaki and Kayes (2004) reviewed the expatriate literature and analysis of the skills necessary for cross-cultural learning and identified 73 skills that clustered into 10 high-level competencies! Others (eg Phillips, 1992) suggest that there is not much difference between the competencies required for an international manager and those required for a domestic manager. Most studies dealing with the skills needed for expatriates have focused on lists of criteria, competencies and personal characteristics that should be assessed. In terms of characteristics to be considered, an amalgam of recent studies (see Aycan, 1997; Pucik, 1998; Yamazaki and Kayes, 2004; and Stroh *et al,* 2005) reveals the characteristics listed in the *Key framework* below.

THEORY AND PRACTICE

KEY FRAMEWORK

Characteristics of the successful expatriate manager

Professional and technical competence and experience on the job:

- Experience in the company
- Technical knowledge of the business
- Previous overseas experience
- Managerial talent
- Overall experience and education.

Relational ability 1 – Personality traits and relational abilities:

- Communicative ability and interpersonal skills
- Maturity and emotional stability
- Tolerance for ambiguity in personal relations, unfamiliar situations/new experiences
- Behavioural and attitudinal flexibility: willingness to acquire new patterns
- Respect for the culture of the host country
- Adaptability and flexibility in a new environment.

Relational ability 2 – Perceptual dimensions and life strategies:

- Information-seeking skills: listening and observation

- Modelling capacities: drawing upon observational learning to acquire knowledge, attitudes, values, emotional proclivities and competences
- Non-judgemental frameworks
- Non-evaluative in interpreting the behaviour of host-country nationals.

Self-maintenance factors

- Ability to substitute traditional reinforcements with other activities
- Stress-reduction techniques
- Self-maintenance, confidence in own ability to perform specific behaviours (self-efficacy).

Leadership and motivational factors:

- Relationship development and personal influencing skills
- Willingness to communicate
- Action and initiative skills
- Belief in the mission
- Interest in overseas experience
- Congruence with the career path.

Cultural awareness:

- Cultural robustness: understanding of the differences between countries
- Host-country language skills and translation of concepts, ideas and thoughts in verbal form
- Understanding non-verbal communication.

Family situation:

- Stability of the family situation
- Spouse and family's adaptability and supportiveness.

Certainly global leaders must possess some very specific skills and competencies simply because the roles that they perform are complex: '[Global leaders] have to possess a complex amalgamation of technical, functional, cultural, social and political competencies to navigate successfully the intricacies of changing cross-border responsibilities' (Harvey and Novicevic, 2004; p1173). There have been many attempts to distil the key criteria from the more extensive lists. However, it may be the case that expatriates from some countries are more successful than others, either because of their cultural similarity with the host country (Gong, 2003) or because some cultures (for example, those with a higher tolerance of uncertainty (see Chapters 2 and 3) make better expatriates. There are two main findings from the empirical research into selection practices amongst MNCs. The first is that expatriates are primarily selected on the basis of their technical competence (see, for example, Tung, 1981, 1982; Zeira and Banai, 1984, 1985; Harris, 1999). Companies' perception of international selection as a high-risk operation leads to a tendency to place emphasis in recruitment on technical and managerial qualifications, to ensure that the job can be done competently (Miller, 1972; Antal and Izraeli, 1993). Put another way, expatriates who are not at least competent in the job they are performing are really going to struggle to bring any other competences into play. The second finding is that there is an underlying assumption of the universal nature of managerial skills, as first identified by Baker and Ivancevich (1971).

THE ASSUMPTIONS ABOUT THE SKILLS NEEDED BY INTERNATIONAL MANAGERS FOR ADJUSTMENT

CASE STUDIES

Mendenhall *et al* (2002) explain that the assumptions we make about the skills needed by international managers can be traced back to four theoretical models:

- *Learning models* – These assume that the skills and competencies that international employees need have to do with learning new skills and techniques of adaptation in coping with the impact of the 'other' culture. The major task facing expatriates is to adjust their social skills such that they can learn the salient characteristics of the new environment in terms of new roles, rules and norms of social interaction. Cross-cultural training is generally designed on the basis of this assumption.

- *Stress-coping models* – These assume that feelings of anxiety, confusion and disruption associated with culture shock are akin to individual stress reactions under conditions of uncertainty, information overload and loss of control. Role theory argues that competing assignment demands make role conflicts unavoidable and it is this that impacts on effectiveness. Stress management (coping strategies), rather than stress avoidance, is necessary in order for expatriates to engage in necessary engagement behaviours. International employees have to draw from a wide range of such

strategies to manage problems, although there may not be congruence between what is necessary to manage stress and what is required for effective management of the assignment.

- *Developmental models* – These assume that there are a series of phases of adjustment that an international employee has to go through (for example, contact, disintegration, reintegration, autonomy and independence) that reflect progressive stages of cultural awareness. Individuals undertake adaptive activities only when environmental challenges threaten their internal equilibrium. Processes of periodic (rather than linear) disintegration, regrouping/ regeneration then higher maturation (progressive inter-cultural sensitivity often also associated with global leadership competence) are an inevitable consequence of exposure to other cultures. In a rare qualitative study of returned expatriate stories, researchers adapted the metaphor of heroic adventures to note the importance of personal transformations that accompany adjustment processes.

- *Personality-based models* – These assume that such development can in part be predicted by a set of generalisable attitudes and traits, such as adaptation, cross-cultural and partnership skills or personality variables that are associated with model cross-cultural collaborators. The importance of these prerequisites depends on the nature of the position and task variables, organisational characteristics and the host country. Empirical support is, however, still weak, and again there may be contradictions between what is required for interaction adjustment and work adjustment. Moreover, as found in a study of German international employees assigned to work in Japan and the USA, each country presented different problems and conflicts for the employees and therefore required differential personality-related coping strategies.

SELECTION CRITERIA: THE PRACTICE

In practice, most expatriates are not selected on the basis of such criteria. One factor is the selection process. Research into expatriate selection practice (see Mendenhall and Oddou, 1985; Dowling *et al*, 1994) highlights the predominance of informal selection processes – what Harris and Brewster (1999b) called the 'coffee-machine system' – which leads to selection from a small pool known to senior managers, to potentially discriminatory outcomes and to some serious failures. Lack of attention to developing formal expatriate selection systems can be extremely costly to an organisation. Many leading-edge organisations, however, have recently been employing more sophisticated procedures. One such approach is outlined by Sparrow (1999). This consists of a cultural adaptability assessment developed by Kaisen Consulting. The assessment is focused on helping employees understand the personal qualities required to work overseas and the implications of an international assignment for themselves and their families. It also draws attention to the mechanisms that can assist them in coping with their new environment. The approach concentrates on identifying the psychological adaptations that have to take place on an international assignment. One potential drawback with such an approach is the reluctance on the part of an employee to be completely honest about family problems when the assignment is seen to be critical to progression. Issues of political and social capital also have relevance to this kind of 'risk assessment' approach to international resourcing.

PREPARATION

One of the key ways in which organisations can support individuals undertaking international assignments is through the provision of pre-departure preparation, which can include training and other forms such as briefings, visits and shadowing. Expatriates are very positive about the value of training programmes (Ehnert and Brewster, 2008; Harris and Brewster, 1999a; Waxin and Panaccio, 2005). However, the latest consultancy surveys continue to find that formal cross-cultural training is given in only around a fifth of all organisations – even though most expatriates want it. A major problem is that the length of time between the decision to go and leaving for the new country is often very short.

Cross-cultural training has long been advocated as a means of facilitating effective interactions (Brislin, 1986). Tung's (1981) framework for selecting cross-cultural training methods has two main dimensions: degree of interaction required in the host culture, and the similarity between the expatriate's home culture and the host culture. Mendenhall and Oddou (1985) developed this framework to include the degree of integration and level of rigour required, and translated this into the needed duration of time for each type of training programme. The framework consisted of three levels: information-giving approaches (eg factual briefing and awareness training), affective approaches (eg culture assimilator training, critical incidents and role-plays) and immersion approaches (eg assessment centres, field experience and simulations).

Mendenhall himself (Mendenhall *et al*, 1995), however, points out that this model does not specify how the level of rigour is determined and refers only to cross-cultural training. A framework developed by Black and Mendenhall (1989), based on social learning theory, suggested a decision-tree model which logically links and integrates the variables of culture novelty, required degree of interaction with host nationals, job novelty and training rigour.

 REFLECTIVE ACTIVITY

Check out your own organisation, or one that you know:

● What forms of pre-departure training does it offer?

After reviewing existing approaches to pre-departure preparation, Harris and Brewster (1999a) argued that organisations should take a more holistic approach to pre-departure preparation for expatriates. The authors suggested an integrative framework that takes into account job variables at the home- and host-country level, including the nature of the international operation, the size of the home-country organisation, the host-country location, the objective of the assignment, the nature of the job and the level of organisational support, together with individual variables in terms of the expatriate profile and partner considerations (see Figure 42). These antecedents are considered alongside an assessment of the individual's existing level of competency before deciding on an appropriate preparation scenario.

Figure 42 Integrative framework for pre-departure preparation

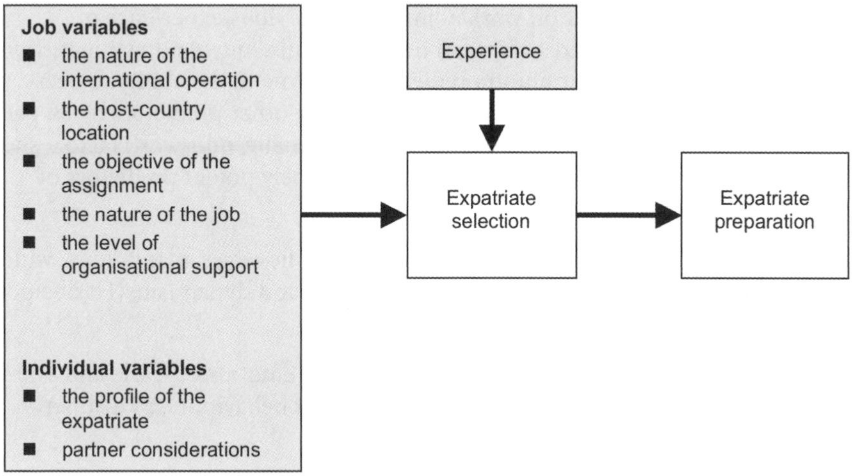

Job variables

- the nature of the international operation
- the host-country location
- the objective of the assignment
- the nature of the job
- the level of organisational support

Individual variables

- the profile of the expatriate
- partner considerations

Experience

Expatriate selection

Expatriate preparation

Source: Harris and Brewster (1999a; p236)

ADJUSTMENT

Once selected and prepared, a key issue concerns the ability of the expatriates – and their families – to adjust to their new environment. But note, too, that adjustment may not be entirely one-way: one of the roles of expatriates is often to introduce new practices into the subsidiary organisation – local employees will have to adjust, to some extent, to the ways of the expatriate and perhaps to the new practices they are bringing in (Brewster, 1993, 1995).

The prevalent adjustment model describes linear causal relationships between antecedents and three, narrowly conceived and one-dimensional, adjustment outcomes: interaction adjustment, general adjustment, and work adjustment. These categories are an artificial construct from the adjustment measure used (Black and Stephens, 1989) and are not comprehensive or, more critically, analytical or discrete. Further, the model excludes feedback loops to account for the real-life dynamics of expatriate adjustment. Thus, it does not reflect the complexities of expatriate adjustment (Haslberger, 2005). Finally, the model addresses adjustment only on one level – that of the individual expatriate. Recent research indicates that about three quarters of expatriates are accompanied by at least one family member (Dickmann *et al*, 2006) so that family adjustment becomes important too (Haslberger and Brewster, 2008).

Work based on the Black and Stephens (1989) model has been very productive. Hechanova *et al* (2003) examined the research that had been conducted on that model until then and found that adjustment affected strain, job satisfaction, organisational commitment, intention to leave and work performance. A more recent study of such research showed the centrality, criticality and complexity of adjustment and strongly supported the impact that it has on job satisfaction, withdrawal cognitions and performance (Bhaskar-Shrinivas *et al,* 2005). Language skills helped international managers engage in rewarding interpersonal exchanges but had no impact on work adjustment. Previous experience of international assignments had a minimal impact on subsequent adjustment. Two individual factors were important in predicting adjustment: the ability to be a 'self-starter', and relational skills – the latter exceeding other predictors by 30 per cent in terms of explaining variance in adjustment. Finally, non-work factors such as culture novelty and spouse adjustment were extremely potent predictors of successful overseas adjustment.

The weaknesses of the Black and Stephens model are, however, manifold. A wider model of adjustment, covering 'dimensions, domains and dynamism' (Haslberger and Brewster, 2009) fits reality better.

The *dimensions* of adjustment include cognitions and emotions (Searle and Ward, 1990; Ward *et al,* 1998; Ward and Kennedy, 1999) and behaviours, as distinct outcome components (Kim, 1988).

KEY FRAMEWORK

THEORY AND PRACTICE

The variety of factors that determine adjustment

These fall into four main groups:

- Factors to do with the individual include self-efficacy, relational and perception skills, flexibility, a desire to adjust, tolerance of ambiguity, leadership qualities, interpersonal skills and self-confidence, cultural empathy, emotional stability (Hiltrop and Janssens, 1990; Coyle, 1992; Collins, 1995), language ability and previous international experience (Black and Stephens, 1989; Black and Gregersen, 1991).

- Non-work factors include, particularly, the family situation. Crossover effects exist between expatriate and spouse adjustment (eg Takeuchi *et al,* 2002). An inability of the spouse and children to adapt to the cultural environment is a common source of difficulty (Moore and Punnett, 1994; Collins, 1995; Jones, 1997). If a spouse or family member is undergoing severe culture shock or experiencing difficulty in making the cross-cultural adjustment, the morale and performance of the expatriate may be affected adversely (Torbiörn, 1997). Children may also be very resistant to moving due to the educational and social disruption it may cause. A positive family situation is likely to enhance the expatriate's cross-cultural adjustment and increase the chances of a successful assignment (Punnett and Ricks, 1992; Collins, 1995).

- Organisational factors have been classified by Black *et al* (1991) as organisation culture novelty (how different the subsidiary is from the expatriate's previous experience), social support (whether the organisational culture encourages support from others) and logistical help (housing, payment of school tuition, practical information about shopping, etc). McCaughey and Bruning (2005) review evidence on expatriate satisfaction and a range of important outcomes such as assignment completion. They look at how three sorts of support strategies impact on satisfaction (and adjustment): pre-assignment support strategies (such as career planning and development, training in deficits in knowledge, skills and abilities, partner/family involvement); assignment support strategies (such as using mentors and partner employment counselling); and repatriation support strategies (utilisation of knowledge, skills and abilities learned on assignment). Mendenhall *et al* (1995), however, warn that too many 'buffers' may reduce the learning that the expatriate gets from the experience.

● Job factors which affect adjustment include role novelty, role clarity, role discretion, role conflict and role overload.

The *domains* within which adjustment occurs vary too. Analyses from the migration literature (Navas *et al*, 2005, 2007) identify a number of different domains in which adjustment has to take place:

● systems of public order, reflecting rules of conduct such as registration requirements, traffic laws, etc

● work

● economics, including consumption of goods and services

● social relations

● family relations

● ideology, including culture, religion, etc.

In broad terms, these are easier to adjust to at the top of the list (driving on the correct side of the road, carrying appropriate documentation), more difficult as one reaches the domains at the bottom – families may have to behave differently in public, but in private will often go back to their own ways. And it is unlikely that expatriates, usually only in the country for a limited time, would change their deep-seated beliefs or their religion.

Adjustment, crucially, is a *dynamic process*. It is likely that cognition (understanding) will improve in a more or less straight line over time, and so might behaviours, but feelings are likely to go through a roller-coaster of ups and downs as different experiences happen. Equally, the expatriate might adjust to systems of public order and to work fairly quickly but need more to adjust to social relationships (Haslberger and Brewster, 2009). The expatriate may find it difficult to perceive and learn appropriate behaviours, thus increasing the period of time required for adjustment. Glanz (2003) has examined how sensemaking – the use of rational thought to re-analyse and bring order to confusion and surprise – can be engendered through the use of narratives about the expatriate experience. This perspective shows that expatriate experience is not simply an incremental development towards adjustment but involves periods in which previous learning becomes overturned and revelations occur at an accelerated pace.

REFLECTIVE ACTIVITY

Take any one of the factors itemised above and ask yourself:

● What might the individual – and what might his or her employer – do to make adjustment less of a problem?

THE REWARD PACKAGE

Managing compensation and benefits for international assignments has traditionally been one of the core functions of the IHR manager (Bonache, 2006; Suutari and Tornikoski, 2001). The high costs of assignments mean that attention is focused on developing more cost-effective systems which will still provide an incentive to move. Key determinants of the type of system to be employed include (Evans *et al*, 2002; p131):

● cost-efficiency – making sure that the plan delivers the intended benefits in the most cost-effective manner (including tax consequences)

● equity issues – making sure that the plan is equitable irrespective of the assignment location or nationality of the expatriate

● system maintenance – making sure that the plan is relatively transparent and easy to administer.

CASE STUDIES

DEVELOPMENTS IN INTERNATIONAL REWARD AND RECOGNITION

There is increasing focus on how expatriates perform and add value across global networks inside the organisation. The study by Perkins (2006; p26) found that rewards strategists at Boots, BT, Cable and Wireless, Cadbury-Schweppes, Citigroup, Diageo and Shell are reappraising the basis on which expatriation has to be managed, 'integrating organisational networks around common governance principles'. This brings tensions into the relationships between expatriates and local employees, and renewed attention to reward comparability factors. Package design is moving towards generically composed frameworks that can be flexed to ensure a fair reflection of the mobility pressures. Organisations are exerting more

control over the reward–effort bargain by standardising aspects of their rewards systems. Motivating talented employees to undertake assignments in an environment of regionalised political tensions continues to require idiosyncratic reward solutions, but there are moves to eliminate personal deals, increase transparency and knowledge about the assignment, and encourage ownership amongst local line managers. A philosophy of 'value creation' is being exported across operations (a 'one organisation – one global reward system' strategy), reducing the difference between rewards systems designed purely for expatriates and those that are designed to manage an internationally mobile set of talented managers. There is a process of directional convergence, not final convergence, in rewards policies. 62 per cent of rewards specialists claimed that rewards systems were still adapted to local context, but 78 per cent would prefer a globally integrated approach, and 84 per cent wanted to integrate the rewards approach with global strategy. MNCs are combining tools and techniques across the whole HRM process and applying them to all populations of internationally mobile managers. Unilever combined the talent management, organisational effectiveness, learning and reward functions in order to help its international managers better understand how they add value. The balance between what the business wants and what is fair to employees is increasingly reflecting the underlying reason for mobility and estimate of business value, which varies according to factors such as skills shortages, project logics, employee-initiated or career development motivations.

Table 19 provides a summary of the current approaches to expatriate compensation systems.

Table 19 A summary of expatriate compensation schemes

Compensation system	For whom most appropriate	Advantages	Disadvantages
Negotiation	Special situations Organisation with few expatriates	Conceptually simple	Breaks down with increasing number of expatriates
Localisation	Permanent transfers and long-term assignments Entry-level expatriates	Simple to administer Equity with local nationals	Expatriates usually come from economic conditions different from those experienced by local nationals
Headquarters-based balance-sheet	Many nationalities of expatriates working together	No nationality discrimination Simple administration	High compensation costs Difficult to repatriate TCNs
Home-country-based balance-sheet	Several nationalities of expatriates on out-and-back-home assignments	Low compensation costs Simple to repatriate TCNs	Discrimination by nationality Highly complex administration Lack of conceptual purity
Lump-sum approaches	Consistently short assignments (less than three years), followed by repatriation	Resembles domestic compensation practices Does not intrude on expatriate finances	Exchange rate variation makes this unworkable except for short assignments

Compensation system	For whom most appropriate	Advantages	Disadvantages
International pay structures	Senior executives of all nationalities	Tax- and cost-effective Expatriates and local nationals may be on the same compensation plan	Inhibits mobility for lower levels of expatriates Lack of consistency among locations
Cafeteria approaches	Senior executives	Tax- and cost-effective	To be effective, options needed for each country Difficult to use with lower levels of expatriates
Regional plans	Large numbers of expatriates mobile within region(s)	Less costly than global uniformity Can be tailored to regional requirements	Multiple plans to administer Discrimination between regionalists and globalists
Multiple programmes	Many expatriates on different types of assignments	Can tailor compensation programs to different types of expatriates Possible lower compensation costs	Difficulty of establishing and maintaining categories Discrimination by category Highly complex administration

Source: Evans *et al* (2002; p132)

One of the most popular methods is the 'balance-sheet' approach. This is designed to maintain standards of living for expatriates, irrespective of their assignment location. Under this approach, expatriates are kept on the home pay system, while allowances and differentials are used to maintain home equity for items such as goods and services, housing and income tax. The idea is that the expatriate should neither gain nor lose, thus encouraging mobility. The system is administratively simple.

 REFLECTIVE ACTIVITY

What are the potential disadvantages of the balance-sheet approach for:

● the individual?

● the organisation?

Alternatives to the balance-sheet approach include a 'global' compensation structure in which national origin or home has no impact. This type of scheme is more often applied to senior executives who are regarded as truly global employees. However, such systems are fraught with standard-of-living issues, not to mention complexities of tax and pension planning.

Expatriate compensation is becoming more problematic as the profile of the typical expatriate becomes more diverse. Packages based on the traditional white male with a trailing spouse and children may be completely inappropriate for a woman from the Indian subcontinent who leaves her children at home. In addition, the role of the compensation package as a key motivator for international mobility may well differ, depending on the life-stage and/or career intentions of the assignee. The trend towards rationalisation of expatriate compensation and benefits packages, linked with increasing numbers of dual-career couples, makes the decision whether to accept an international assignment or not a much more complex one.

A developing trend in Europe is for companies to treat the whole of the EU and its related partners in EFTA as 'one country' – no work permits are required, there is a right to residence in every country, medical help is available everywhere, etc. Moving people within the EU means providing the same sort of support that a transfer within one country would attract, but no 'expatriate' allowances.

PERFORMANCE MEASUREMENT

Expatriates are amongst the most expensive people that an organisation employs, yet it is surprising how little is known about the assessment of their performance and contribution. Of course, it involves a complex range of issues, and research to date suggests that rigorous performance appraisal systems for expatriates are far from universal (Brewster, 1991; Schuler *et al*, 1991; Fenwick *et al*, 1999). The assessment of expatriate performance requires an understanding of the variables that influence an expatriate's success or failure in a foreign assignment.

An objective appraisal of expatriate performance is likely to be highly complex. This is because the general difficulties of performance measurement are compounded in the case of expatriates by the HQ's lack of knowledge of the local situation.

The already problematic relationship is further complicated by the necessity of reconciling the tension between the need for universal appraisal standards with specific objectives in local units. It is also important to recognise that more time may be needed to achieve results in markets which enjoy little supporting infrastructure from the parent company (Schuler *et al*, 1991).

 REFLECTIVE ACTIVITY

What techniques might an organisation use to assess the performance of an expatriate?

MNCs are aware that there are no easy answers here and tend to use a variety of methods. Thus they may combine formal performance appraisal with visits from HQ; visits back to HQ; an assessment of results in the area under the expatriate's command; reports; emails – in short, anything that will help them make a judgement. Formal appraisal systems for expatriates may either be local (with the value of cultural sensitivity and local knowledge, but with little comparability between results from different parts of the world) or be worldwide, with the opposite advantages and disadvantages.

REPATRIATION

The final element in the global assignment cycle is the repatriation phase. The relationship between the foreign assignment and the future human resource needs of the organisation has become more important with an increasing focus on the need to develop international/global mindsets (Osland *et al*, 2006) and the role of expatriates as mechanisms of knowledge transfer (Bonache and Brewster, 2001a). In this respect, evidence of major problems with repatriation for multinational companies is worrying evidence of inadequate HRM. Surveys suggest that 10 to 25 per cent of expatriates leave their company within 12 months of repatriation (Black, 1992; Black and Gregersen, 1991; Solomon, 1995), a figure which is notably higher than for equivalent non-expatriates (Black and Gregersen, 1991), and that between a quarter and a third of repatriates leave their firms within two years of returning (Suutari and Brewster, 2000). Since nearly half the companies did not keep records of the career outcomes of repatriates, the true figure is likely to be higher. In a sample of Finnish expatriates, even amongst those who stayed with the same employer well over half had seriously considered leaving (Suutari and Brewster, 2003). About one-third of the repatriate group studied by Suutari and Brewster (2003) had changed their employer. From those, one-third had done so while they were still abroad. The timing indicates that they had changed employer earlier than the average repatriation job negotiations started.

The problem has been emphasised in recent years, particularly in Europe, because the expansion of foreign operations has taken place coincident with a rationalisation of HQ operations. In the leaner HQ operations of today's world there are few spaces for expatriates to 'fill in' while the organisation seeks for a more permanent position for them. A majority of organisations nowadays do not provide post-assignment guarantees (BGRS 2010, GMAC 2008). From the repatriate perspective, other problems associated with re-integrating into the home country are: loss of status, loss of autonomy, loss of career direction, and a feeling that international experience is undervalued by the company (Johnston, 1991). Alongside these there will also be a loss of income and life style, and family readjustment problems.

A critical issue in repatriation is the management of expectations (Stroh *et al*, 1998; Welch, 1998). Work-related expectations of repatriates can include: job position after repatriation, standard of living, improved longer-term career prospects, opportunities to utilise skills acquired while abroad, and support and interest from supervisors and colleagues in the home country. There are few empirical studies concerning the expectations of repatriates. The ones that have been reported note generally high expectations. Most expatriates expect the return to enhance their career prospects and their return to be exciting and/or challenging (Suutari and Brewster, 2003). Often it is not. Research on the careers of CEOs in the USA and Europe (Hamori and Koyuncu, 2011) found that – at least for those at the very top – international experience was a negative influence on careers: better to stay in the political spider's web of headquarters if you want to make it that far.

For most expatriates, the experience is hugely positive and of great value in their careers. Often, however, this value is obtained for a company other than the one that paid for the international experience. This is a substantial loss for the company, made worse by the fact that these individuals rarely change their careers radically: they are more likely to go and work for competitors than move into an entirely different industry. This is not great HRM.

Together, these findings suggest that organisations should devote more attention to their handling of repatriation, and that it should be part of the overall planning of the international assignment. Examples of best practice in this area include:

- pre-departure career discussions
- a named contact person at the home-country organisation
- a mentor at the host location
- re-entry counselling
- family repatriation programmes
- employee debriefings
- succession planning.

In any international company, effective handling of all stages of an international assignment is critical to ensuring the full utilisation and development of human resources. Mishandling of returning expatriates means that a good deal of critical knowledge is lost to the organisation.

THE INDIVIDUAL PERSPECTIVE: CAREERS

So far, we have examined all these issues from the point of the organisation – our book is about IHRM. However, it is also the case that expatriation can be considered from an individual perspective. Research has only recently begun into why people go on expatriate assignments (Dickmann et al, 2006), the relationships between expatriates and locals (Toh and DeNisi, 2007) and the effects of expatriate assignments on careers (Cappellen and Janssens, 2005; Larsen, 2004; Stahl and Cerdin, 2004; Suutari, 2003). There is some recognition in the literature that expatriation is for most people a very exciting and enjoyable experience. Much of the careers research, however, focuses around the notion of career capital – the fact that expatriation is one of the strongest learning experiences that anyone can have (they learn all about themselves, their relationships, their ability to cope, a new country, a different view of the world, etc). In the process they tend to build three types of career capital: know-how (competencies: the ability to understand the way things work and to see how they work differently in different situations), know-whom (relationships: the network of contacts and people that the individual can relate with), and know-why (motivation: a deeper understanding of what is important in their life and their career anchors (Jokinen *et al*, 2008).

The next chapter explores this issue further, and also examines the issues related to other kinds of international working.

KEY LEARNING POINTS

- The international aspect adds many difficulties in addition to those involved in managing staff in one country, and those difficulties occur at each point of what we have called the 'global assignment cycle'.

- This is likely to be an ever-growing part of the work of HRM departments.

- However, changes at both organisational and individual level are causing a fundamental rethink of international staffing policies.

- There have been major changes in terms of the profiles of individuals undertaking international assignments and their expectations; more people from outside the headquarters country; more women; more 'dual-career couples'.

- The expatriate population is also now better educated and changes have occurred in employee expectations of international assignments.

- In newer affiliates there is a clear correlation between the use of expatriates and organisational success; and if it is a larger subsidiary, having more expatriates also correlates with success.

- Because expatriates are almost invariably amongst the most expensive people for companies to employ, and because they are usually in important positions, the necessity of taking a strategic view of the use and management of expatriates is obvious.

- The whole of the global assignment cycle has to be managed effectively: strategic planning, selection, preparation, performance measurement and repatriation.

- It is possible (if not actually practical to try to put into practice) to specify a set of competencies for international assignments, and to use these to assist the selection of some people in some jobs, but there are very different views about the practicality of using them to select international managers. The 'coffee-machine system' is ever-present.

- Organisations should take a more holistic approach to pre-departure preparation for expatriates.

- The ability of the expatriates – and their families – to adjust to their new environment may be problematic, but adjustment has to be two-way.

- Adjustment has to take place to: systems of public order, reflecting rules of conduct such as registration requirements, traffic laws, etc; work; economics, including consumption of goods and services; social relations; family relations; and to ideology, including culture and religion.

- Expatriate compensation is becoming more problematic as the profile of the typical expatriate becomes more diverse. One of the most popular methods for rewarding expatriates is the 'balance-sheet' approach but 'global' compensation structures in which national origin or home has no impact are also used.

- Surprisingly little is known about the assessment of the performance and contribution of expatriates.

- Evidence of major problems with repatriation for multinational companies provides worrying evidence of inadequate HRM: expansion of foreign operations has taken place coincident with a rationalisation of HQ operations in many geographies.

- Looking at expatriation from the individual and not just organisational view is important: why people go on expatriate assignments; the relationships between expatriates and locals; and the effects of expatriate assignments on careers.

EXPLORE FURTHER

Expatriation is an expensive process: what are the reasons that cause companies to continue to use it?

In light of the ease with which we can communicate internationally through electronic means, and the increasing ease of air transport, is it likely that there will be fewer expatriates in the future? Give reasons for your answer.

Compare the advantages for companies and individuals of using permanent, career expatriates who go from country to country as opposed to single-assignment expatriates.

What would be the best and most cost-effective form of pre-departure training and development for an expatriate?

Why should a company be worried about expatriates leaving them at the end of an assignment? What should they do to minimise the possibility?

Stroh, L. K., Black, J. S., Mendenhall, M. E. and Gregersen, H. B. (2005) *International Assignments: An integration of strategy, research and practice*, London, Lawrence Erlbaum.

Jokinen, T., Brewster, C. and Suutari, V. (2008) 'Career capital during international work experiences: contrasting self-initiated expatriate experiences and assigned expatriation', *International Journal of Human Resource Management*, 19 (6): 981–1000

www.eca-international.com

www.cipd.co.uk/global

For expatriates themselves there are a large number of potential websites available to help: they should just type 'expatriate' into their search engine.

CHAPTER 15

Managing Diversity in International Forms of Working

LEARNING OUTCOMES

When they have read this chapter, students will:

- be familiar with the various forms of international working and be able to assess the pros and cons for international enterprises of using them

- appreciate the issues involved in measuring the value of international assignments

- be able to evaluate the strengths and weaknesses of various forms of diversity initiatives in international organisations

- be able to recommend ways of increasing the number of women in international management

- be able to explain how organisations operating internationally can manage the mix of international working and assignees

- understand the problems of assessing performance and outline ways in which such enterprises might manage these issues in practice

- recognise the challenges in managing international management teams.

INTRODUCTION

In order to become truly global in orientation, organisations need to ensure that they maximise their human resources wherever they are located. As we have seen in the preceding chapters, achieving this entails a clear understanding of a wide range of cultural and institutional factors that impact the development of a truly diverse workforce and management cadre. Here we examine in more detail the variety of ways that international enterprises can provide international experience for their employees and discuss some of the HRM policies and practices associated with each type. Within that we explore diversity management initiatives which aim to capitalise on the diversity in a firm's workforce (including such characteristics as race, ethnicity, national origin, gender, age and disability).

Finally, we consider how internationally operating organisations can manage the mix of these forms of international experience, and how they assess whether or not they are working effectively.

The range of formats and the types of people that multinational enterprises use for international work is growing ever wider. We start by assessing the range of formats, and then look at the range of people.

GLOBAL SKILLS SUPPLY STRATEGIES

Organisations now have to develop global skills supply strategies. The study of global staffing has traditionally concentrated on the need to resource key positions within multinational enterprises (MNEs) and top management team positions at HQ and subsidiary locations. However, the definition of the 'international employee' inside organisations continues to expand (Briscoe and Schuler, 2004; p223):

> The tradition of referring to all international employees as expatriates – or even international assignees – falls short of the need for international HR practitioners to understand the options available … and fit them to evolving international business strategies.

REFLECTIVE ACTIVITY

What factors have led to the increase in demand for more flexible forms of international management?

The changing structure and role of IHRM functions means that these functions and their HRM business partners now have to help their organisations manage a very wide range of options associated with global sourcing (Hustad and Munkvold, 2005). This increased demand for new forms of international mobility is due to a number of factors (Salt and Millar, 2006):

- the need for skilled expatriates to help build new international markets (Findlay *et al*, 2000).

- the growing importance of temporary and short-term access to specialised talent in sending countries to assist the execution of overseas projects (Minbaeva and Michailova, 2004; Hocking *et al*, 2004).

- the growing need for highly mobile elites of management to perform boundary-spanning roles to help build social networks and facilitate the exchange of knowledge (Tushman and Scanlan, 2005).

Moreover, the opportunity for broader resourcing strategies has increased markedly in certain labour markets because these labour markets have themselves become globalised (Ward, 2004). For example, considerable attention has been given to the globalisation of healthcare labour markets (Aiken *et al*, 2004; Clark *et al*, 2006).

Globalisation is also leading to new relationships between a number of corporate functions and the development of many hybrid professionals capable of using the tools and techniques of each function (Sparrow *et al*, 2004). A number of tools and techniques strongly influenced by marketing, corporate communications and IT thinking have become part of the mainstream armoury of HRM functions when dealing with international recruitment. This convergence of thinking has brought the language of employee value propositions, employer branding, corporate social responsibility, market mapping and recruiting ahead of the curve into the mix of HRM activity in this area. The challenge now is to try to manage these approaches on a global scale. An issue for many recruitment and selection functions in many organisations is that they have not yet 'internalised' this influence of global markets into their structures and strategies. Many believe that they will increasingly have to do so (Harvey *et al*, 2000; p382):

> What is needed is a global management staffing strategy that enables global consistency among various managerial pools and the foreign subsidiaries.

The correct balance of standardisation versus differentiation is hard to achieve. Harvey *et al* (2000) argue that organisations need to integrate a transcultural emphasis into their global staffing systems. Often it is the local in-country HRM Business Partner who has to manage these tensions (Sparrow, 2007).

INTERNATIONALISING THE SOURCING PROCESS IN ORGANISATIONS

Organisations can use the development of an increasingly multicultural workforce to the advantage of an internationalisation strategy. However, as the Barclaycard International case study below shows, the sorts of HRM issues that have to be managed in relation to recruitment as the internationalisation process proceeds are also quite complex (Sparrow, 2007).

BARCLAYCARD INTERNATIONAL: RECRUITMENT IN THE CONTEXT OF AN INTERNATIONALISATION STRATEGY

CASE STUDIES

Barclaycard was the UK's first credit card, and as one of the largest global credit card businesses now has a rapid growth strategy. Outside the UK, it operates in the USA, Germany, Spain, Greece, Italy, Portugal, Ireland, Sweden, Norway, France, Asia-Pacific and across Africa. A strategy to become as meaningful a contributor to the group

by 2013 as Barclaycard UK currently is has witnessed alliances with Standard Bank of South Africa, acquisition of Juniper Financial Corporation (rebranded as Barclays USA) and a series of in-country launches. It employed 3,000 staff, with 15 per cent based in the UK. To enable expansion, Barclaycard International built a platform of people management processes (processes, structures and frameworks) to bring stability, governance and control. Challenges varied across countries but always included ensuring rigour and consistency across operations in very different cultures, business markets and labour markets. Primary agenda items for the HRM team in 2006 were international resourcing, international mobility, talent acquisition and development of global policies and frameworks. Resourcing, then transferring, capability globally, either within an existing business or during start-up and building of a local business, necessitated a range of preferred recruitment suppliers and the building of networks across them to transfer learning about the management of different types of supplier and agency, the assessment of their true global capability, and the availability of skills in each labour market. Intranets exchanged vacancy information between Hamburg, Zaragoza and Dublin. A new International Resourcing Business Partner role acted as a support mechanism for HRM Business Partners and business leaders to facilitate the acquisition of top talent through negotiation of global preferred supplier arrangements for headhunters and research institutions, through the development of an employee value proposition and employment brand across countries, advice on global versus local process, sources of best practice, and through appropriate geographical diversity in the use of international talent.

Barclaycard's call centre in Dublin acted as a central platform and nursery for future international expansion. It grew from 10 to 360 people between 1997 and 2006. Initially intended to support non-UK operations, it grew to serve eight countries including the Republic of Ireland, Italy, Spain, France, Germany, Portugal, Greece, and Botswana. Dublin was chosen because of the nature of the role, the employee base, and the City's labour market. The recruitment population was well-qualified, with intentions to stay in country for around 12 to 18 months. Employees spoke (and

were hired for) their mother tongue in the markets they served, requiring principles of cross-cultural management to be applied to a single internal labour market. The acquisition of Banco Zaragozano enabled a new contact centre in Spain: 35 employees moved from Dublin to Spain to help transfer practices. HRM Business Partners dealt with setting up legal entities to transfer employees, deciding the best mix of local recruitment, the use of local job centres, assessing funding support, and understanding the implications and ramifications of local employment law and sector agreements. New country operations oversaw other start-up operations (Portugal and Italy were initially resourced under the guidance of the Spanish HRM partner). Considerable insight into country capability resided at HRM partner level. A 'framework for growth' was established to replicate in-country moves and transfer learning. Many aspects of recruitment and selection could be 'cut and pasted' across operations (procedures, training plans, interview and induction processes, job standards) whereas others had to be dealt with flexibly (for example, criteria-based interviewing and diversity practices). Dublin acted as a nursery (providing people to facilitate international expansion).

Rapid global expansion required the deployment of skills and experience in a multitude of countries at short notice, not always achievable quickly through local recruitment. A new international mobility framework reduced the cost and complexity of expatriating individuals by securing talented employees on global contracts with a premium for global mobility but only 'light' expatriation benefits. Assignments were designed by HRM Business Partners and International Assignments Services (IAS) teams located within key global regions. Two initiatives supported a global mindset: awareness-building amongst the senior leadership community through workshops on the cultures of current and potential labour markets, and cross-cultural training interventions linked to a global induction programme. Talent management tools and techniques supported international resourcing through successive application to top leadership roles, senior cross-Barclays role potential, top 450 leadership potential, and finally, a broad business talent population. Succession planning and talent identification processes were integrated with long-term incentives tied to identified capabilities. The top 10 per cent within internal expertise fields were identified on a global basis. Rather than wait until Barclaycard International was in- or near-market, people were recruited for target markets ('resourcing ahead of the curve') with investments made in forward market mapping (using research agencies and headhunters to map a wider range of geographical labour markets, and researching people working in target roles). Global policies and frameworks operated on an exception basis (even if culturally uncomfortable, explicit guidance and global

protocols governed activity unless it was illegal to do so). The aim was to ensure that consistency, rigour, global governance and risk management and control monitoring processes were aligned with institutional requirements such as Sarbanes-Oxley in areas such as pre-employment screening policy.

Questions

Is there a clear sequence of HRM issues that have been managed during the internationalisation process?

As an organisation globalises, what decisions have to be made as to which HRM processes will be managed at a global level and co-ordinated in-country?

What is the role of local business partners in relation to recruitment and selection as the activity develops?

OTHER FORMS OF INTERNATIONAL WORKING

The nature of international work is fragmenting – there are many ways in which organisations might now source and use what can be termed international employees. The traditional expatriate, or long-term, assignment discussed in the previous chapter, is by no means dead. In fact, despite predictions during the economic crisis that began in 2008 that the use of these expensive types of assignments would decline as organisations found cheaper ways to work internationally, they appear to continue to be growing. However, organisations also use a variety of other types of assignment to fulfil international working obligations, and these appear to be growing even faster. Amongst these, some of the key ones are short-term or project assignments; international commuting; frequent flying; and working in international teams or 'home-based international working'! The first few forms have been called 'new' (Peltonen, 2001) or 'alternative' or 'emerging alternatives' (Collings et al, 2007), but they have in fact been used for a long time, although improved travel arrangements have made them easier. The final forms are more recent, created and sustained by more communications technology.

ALTERNATIVE FORMS OF INTERNATIONAL WORKING

Short-term assignments – An assignment with a specified duration, usually between one and 12 months (Collings *et al*, 2007). Usually such assignments are for less than six months because in many countries this means that the assignee can continue to be paid from home, and tax and social security issues do not arise. The family may accompany the employee, but normally they do not. Many of these assignments are project-based with clear and limited targets, and the contract ends when the targets have been met.

International commuters – Employees who commute to a place of work in another country, usually on a weekly or bi-weekly basis, while the family remains at home or in a nearby country. These are often used for less safe countries but are also common in Europe where borders are less restrictive and people can travel easily.

Frequent flyers – Employees who undertake frequent international business trips, spending just one or a few days in each location, but do not relocate at all. Often used by salespeople who sell externally and by senior managers to ensure social relationships within the organisation.

Remote international working – This is where an individual or a team of people has responsibility for work in another country or across the organisation but do it from their home location, relying on email, social networking, telephone calls and video-conferencing to achieve their objectives.

One of the main reasons for organisations to adopt alternative methods of international working is to avoid some of the problems with expatriation outlined in Chapter 14, particularly the cost. Some methods such as short-term expatriation, however, are mainly used because they simply fit the work requirement better. But none of these alternatives to expatriation is without problems of its own, for both organisations and the individuals concerned.

Critical problems for *short-term assignments* are:

- For individuals:
  - the work–life balance issues, which include social and family separation
  - long working hours on a project: because they are usually under severe time constraints and staying in a hotel or compound, many project workers prefer to put in long hours. This may not always be the most efficient way to work.
- For organisations:
  - that controlling the number of employees on such arrangements is often difficult because their numbers are linked to specific projects which are controlled by the line management
  - handling the complaints about variations within the organisation caused by the type of project rather than reflecting the individuals involved
  - that short-term assignees may fail to develop good relationships with local colleagues and customers (Tahvanainen *et al*, 2006).

For *international commuter assignments* the main problems are:

- For individuals:
  - the issue of 'burnout': like the short-term assignments but on a longer-term

basis, commuters spend extra time at work and, in addition, a lot of time travelling

- maintaining a balance between work in one country, and home life in another

- dealing effectively with cultural issues in a foreign setting (very few organisations provide cross-cultural training for employees on these types of assignments) and the image created in the host country when, on every chance that the commuter gets, he or she rushes away from that location.

- For organisations:

  - that it is often difficult to strike a balance between pressing the commuter to be available in the office for more days and recognising that he or she has to get home.

Frequent flyers are often more difficult to handle – major problems include:

- For individuals:

  - that there are again work–life balance issues. Paradoxically, these employees may spend less time at home than, say, short-term assignees or international commuters

  - that there is a limit to how long employees can successfully operate when they live 'out of a suitcase'. Burn-out is common (Collings *et al*, 2007).

- For organisations:

  - that many companies are unable to identify frequent flyers within their workforce because the budgets are often under the control of line managers

  - an absence of a policy for this type of the international assignments (CReME, 2000; PWC, 2000)

  - a concern with cost-effectiveness. How valuable can someone be who flies into a situation that they do not understand in detail, takes responsibility and makes decisions (otherwise why send them?), sometimes cutting across authority lines within the host organisation, and then leaves others to cope with the fall-out from their decisions?

Remote international working has expanded as the technology, particularly tele-conferencing and video-conferencing, has developed from the original clunky systems to the much more user-friendly versions now available. It avoids many of the problems noted above but raises others:

- For individuals:

  - that these individuals have to work outside the comfort of their home culture (Spreitzer *et al*, 1997), but without the expatriate experience learning how to manage across cultures, in most instances without training or education in cross-cultural skills (see previous chapter), is difficult. And remote international workers often have to work with a wide range of different cultures simultaneously – what seems appropriate for one person may not be for another of those involved in the interaction

– that taking responsibility for or sharing responsibility with others that you may physically meet only very rarely is not always a comfortable situation

– that an expatriate's adjustment when placed within an international team is not influenced solely by his or her own competencies (Zimmermann and Sparrow, 2008). Instead, the power balance between team members is likely to have a major influence on the course of adjustment. Depending on the distribution of the nationality of headquarters, leadership, and the customer interface, the expatriate will have more or less power to demand changes from the other side, and to achieve them through teaching and control.

For organisations:

– that those concerned with the early identification of international management potential often argue that many of the lessons learned about the recruitment of expatriates (see previous chapter) can be generalised to people working in other international contexts

– that selecting the right people to make up a multi-cultural team can also be problematic

– that team training can be important but costly. Organisations such as Ciba-Geigy insist that in all remote international teams the members meet face-to-face, for business and socialising, before remote working commences, so that they 'know who they are working with'

– that alternative forms of international working do not provide a complete solution to the problems arising from long-term assignments. Findings from current studies reinforce the need for careful attention to the possible implications of adopting alternative forms of international working.

TYPES OF INTERNATIONAL EMPLOYEES

The format of international working is changing, but so too is the profile of individuals doing international work and the way that they get into it. The traditional long-term expatriate was very often white or at least from one of the developed countries, was male, was an experienced practitioner, and was selected and sent by his ethnocentric employer. Increasingly, international employees come from all parts of the world, are female, are well-educated and have used their own initiative to get the post.

DIVERSITY MANAGEMENT PROGRAMMES

Despite a prevalence of diversity programmes in the USA, and anti-discrimination programmes in the EU, it is unclear how much this type of approach has been taken up in organisations in other parts of the world (Klarsfeld *et al*, 2011).

THEORY AND PRACTICE

KEY FRAMEWORK

Common features of diversity programmes in the USA

These include:

- a broad definition of diversity, often known as *universal inclusion*. This is a broader definition than employment discrimination legal compliance and can encompass any personal characteristics that affect employees' workplace treatment or productivity.

- a *business case* motivation for diversity initiatives. Typical objectives include being an employer of choice, attracting and retaining talent, developing high-potential employees, increasing productivity, and keeping up with competitors.

- diversity *administrative structures*, which may include a small, specialist consulting group at headquarters, either reporting directly to a senior executive or located in the firm's human resources department; diversity councils at corporate and local levels; and affinity groups (eg women or ethnic minority networks) to link and represent employees who are members of specific demographic groups. Short training programmes are a key feature of the diversity approach.

- integration of the organisation's diversity initiatives into organisational change programmes.

In countries other than the USA, patterns are different and there are acceptable approaches to dealing differently with employees of, for example, different genders (as in the Arab countries, for example), or different ethnic groups (as in India and Malaysia, where some ethic groups are privileged) that would not be acceptable in other countries.

In IHRM contexts, a key debate is the extent to which diversity programmes should be standardised across subsidiaries. In principle, the organisational structure of a multinational enterprise's diversity management activities should support the one the firm has adopted for its overall activities. This would assume that an organisation adopting an ethnocentric or geocentric approach would have more or less standardised programmes across the world. However, this area is particularly influenced by local institutions and culture, which may render company-wide programmes inappropriate. Many organisations therefore allow a considerable degree of autonomy to their subsidiaries in developing their own diversity programmes, often providing expert assistance from headquarters if needed.

INTERNATIONALISING DIVERSITY MANAGEMENT IN A US-BASED TELECOM COMPANY

Telco (not the company's real name) adopts a 'multi-local' approach in all aspects of internationalisation. Internationalising diversity is therefore driven from the bottom rather than by the top. Each international facility is responsible for developing, designing, implementing and funding its own diversity management work. The role of the corporate headquarters is an advisory one, communicating the corporate-wide diversity message and responding to requests for assistance.

The experience of Telco in running a multi-domestic diversity approach has highlighted both the strengths and weaknesses of such a system. Making local staff responsible for shaping diversity activities was seen to have the following positive benefits:

● harnessing the energy of managers who feel personally involved in the outcomes

● unleashing considerable creativity and commitment

● resulting in activities well targeted towards issues of local relevance.

On the negative side, localised efforts were seen to be problematic due to:

● lack of time to invest in diversity initiatives on an ongoing basis

● lack of training and expertise in diversity management on the part of local managers, which led to 'reinventing the wheel' on occasions

● the fact that initiatives were limited to training interventions because of managers' lack of resources and authority to explore system-wide diversity problems embedded in HR systems.

Question

What steps would you take to implement a global diversity strategy, taking into account the issue raised in the case above?

WOMEN IN INTERNATIONAL MANAGEMENT

The development of a global mindset – the goal of many transnational organisations – can only be achieved through exposure to diversity. It is hardly likely that a homogeneous group of managers will develop a global mindset unless the composition of the group is changed to reflect the diversity within the organisation and potentially within its client base. Many aspiring global organisations strive to develop a broad international cadre of managers amongst their most promising junior and middle management employees who are expected to feed into the most senior positions in the company. International management assignments constitute a vital component of the development of a geocentric mindset amongst this body of managers. Adler and Bartholomew (1992; p18) stressed the importance of international assignments to developing a 'global firm':

> Foreign assignments become a core component of the organisational and career development process. … Foreign assignments are used … to enhance individual and organizational learning in all parts of the system.

Despite this increase in demand for international assignees, the numbers of women in such positions is increasing only slowly, although there is evidence that it is higher in multinationals from the Nordic countries (Suutari and Brewster, 2003). This situation might slowly be improving. For example, a GMAC survey (GMAC 2008) suggests that with regard to global mobility more than a quarter of expatriates are now women (up from 10 per cent in 1994). Although exact numbers have to be taken with a pinch of salt – consultant surveys tend to cover just larger and more sophisticated companies – the trend seems to be clear.

The still low incidence of women on international assignments is puzzling when one looks at research into the criteria for effective international managers. Here, as noted in Chapter 14, the emphasis is on interpersonal, intuitive and co-operative styles of management as the key skills for working internationally. These same skills have long been argued to be typical of a 'female' style of management (Fondas, 1997; Marshall, 1984; Rosener, 1990; Sharma, 1990; Vinnicombe, 1987). Why, therefore, do organisations continue to under-use such a valuable source of diversity and a potentially powerful aid towards developing a truly global mindset? Adler (1984a, 1984b, 1984c, 1986, 1987) argued that there were 'myths' at work: women do not want to be international managers; foreigners' prejudice against women renders them ineffective, even when they are sent; and companies don't like to send women abroad. Her research found that the first and second myths were wrong; but the third was accurate.

Caligiuri and Cascio (1998) developed a four-factor model for predicting the success of female global assignees. The four antecedents in the model are: personality traits, organisational support, family support, and host nationals' attitudes towards female expatriates. Organisation support is defined in the model in terms of cross-cultural and gender-specific training for women on assignments and projecting female expatriate managers as being most suitable and highly qualified for the job to local nationals. The model does not, however, include the role of organisational selection systems for international assignments as a critical variable in organisational support.

Harris (1999) examined the impact of organisational selection systems for international assignments on the participation rates of women. She drew on the wider research into discrimination in selection to assess the extent to which differing types of selection system would influence ideas about 'fit'. From a sociological perspective, selection is seen as a *social* process, to be used by those in power within the organisation as a means of determining the continuing form of the organisation by recruiting and promoting only those individuals who most closely conform to organisational norms. Individuals would therefore be judged more on the basis of their acceptability than their suitability (Jewson and Mason, 1986).

Social psychological studies explore the role of individual values in perpetuating discrimination in selection through the use of schema and stereotyping (see, for example, Futoran and Wyer, 1986; Heilman 1983). Such studies suggest that individual selectors will develop schema of 'ideal job-holders' and will use them as a yardstick against which all prospective candidates are measured during the process of selection. In groups where there is a dominance of one gender, job-holder schema are likely to be gender-typed. In addition, the less distinct the information concerning the vacancy and/or the candidate, the more likely selectors are to use schema and stereotypes.

Harris's research with UK-based MNCs revealed the existence of four typologies of selection systems for international manager positions. These were constituted in two dimensions. The first related to the extent to which organisations operated open or closed selection systems for international management assignments. An 'open' system is one in which all vacancies are advertised and anyone with appropriate qualifications and experience may apply, and candidates are interviewed with greater or lesser degrees of formalised testing. Selection decisions are taken by consensus amongst selectors. In contrast, a 'closed' system is one in which selectors at corporate headquarters nominate 'suitable' candidates to line managers who have the option of accepting or rejecting them. In this situation there may be only one manager involved in the selection process at head office. The candidate is informed only once agreement about acceptability has been reached between head office personnel and the line manager. The interview in this process consists of a negotiation about the terms and conditions of the assignment.

The second dimension related to the extent to which the process was a 'formal' or an 'informal' process. Within a 'formal' system, selection criteria are made explicit, with objective debate amongst selectors as to which candidate most closely matches the criteria. An 'informal' system consists of selectors using subjective and often unstated criteria for assessment with minimal systematic evaluation. Four possible variations of selection systems were therefore identified:

- open/formal

Table 20 A typology of international manager selection systems

	Formal	Informal
Open	Clearly defined criteria Clearly defined measures Training for selectors Open advertising vacancy (internal/external) Panel discussions	Less defined criteria Less defined measures Limited training for selectors No panel discussions Open advertising of vacancy Recommendations
Closed	Clearly defined criteria Clearly defined measures Training for selectors Panel discussions Nominations only (networking/reputation)	Selectors' individual preferences determine criteria and measures No panel discussions Nominations only (networking/reputation)

- closed/formal
- open/informal, and
- closed/informal (see Table 20).

The implications of these variations in selection systems for international assignments in relation to women's participation are:

- *An open/formal system* would see greater clarity and consistency in thinking about international managers and a greater link with formal criteria. This system was seen to provide the greatest opportunities for women to be selected for international manager positions.

- *A closed/formal system* was seen to be similar to an open/formal system. However, the lack of personal contact with the candidate and the fact that the field of potential applicants is determined by the selector/s with the attendant risk of omission of suitable candidates, may permit individual preferences by selectors to influence nominating individuals.

- *An open/informal system* would decrease clarity and consistency and linkage with formal criteria, and was therefore seen to provide less opportunity for women to enter international management positions, because selection decisions would be more subjective.

- *A closed/informal system* was perceived as the worst situation for equality of opportunity in this area, combining as it does the potential for subjectivity on the part of the selectors and a lack of access on the part of potential candidates.

Case study investigations, carried out as part of this research, indicated that the type of selection system in use for international assignments clearly affected the number of women in international organisations. In organisations with roughly equal numbers of men and women at entry and junior management levels and operating in similar overseas environments, the main differentiating factor in participation rates for male and female expatriates was the type of international selection system in operation.

REFLECTIVE ACTIVITY

From your own experience:

- What do you feel are the key barriers to women gaining international assignments in your own organisation?
- What recommendations would you make to increase the number of women on international assignments?

Harris (1999) recommended the following key actions for organisations wishing to foster diversity in their expatriate management population. It should be noted that although these recommendations refer to women, they are equally valid in relation to ethnic or other groups that are currently not seen as the norm in the international employee population.

- Organisations need to become more strategic in their planning for international assignments in order to prevent ad hoc and informal placements that may replicate an existing expatriate profile and prevent the adoption of alternative approaches.

- A sophisticated approach to the determination of criteria for effective international managers should be adopted. Competencies should be developed and debated in as wide and diverse a forum as possible.

- Selection processes for international management assignments should be monitored to ensure that access is not unfairly restricted to specific sections of employees. This includes auditing career development systems leading up to international assignments for potential unintended bias.

- Selection skills training for all employees involved in selection for international assignments should be implemented. This training should include raising awareness of the advantages of using diverse groups of employees on international assignments and should challenge existing stereotypes relating to women and other non-traditional groups.

- Full support should be provided for alternative arrangements for the domestic aspect of international assignments that might influence the perception of accessibility amongst people with non-traditional domestic arrangements.

DUAL-CAREER COUPLES

The issue of dual-career couples is becoming increasingly common and an increasing source of concern to organisations sending individuals on international assignments. Assumptions about the problems associated with sending a woman abroad if she is in a dual-career couple have in the past caused organisations to use this as a reason for not selecting potential female expatriates (Adler, 1984c). There is evidence, however, that male managers are now often less prepared to make sacrifices that might harm their domestic lifestyles (Forster, 1992; Scase and Goffee, 1989). As a result, organisations can no longer expect to supply their expanding global management requirements from male managers alone. The issues surrounding dual-career couples will remain a significant part of the decision over whether or not to send an employee on an international assignment. However, organisations will have to look for solutions to the dual-career issue for *both* genders, not just for male employees.

How organisations handle dual-career issues is currently the focus of considerable attention. Surveys indicate a wide divergence of practice amongst organisations in this area. One survey (GMAC GRS/Windham International, 2000) reported that 51 per cent of the larger organisations that were surveyed provide education assistance for the partner, and 46 per cent establish partner networks. One company quoted in the report stated that:

> We have a $5,000 partner allowance if the spouse [sic] is working prior to the assignment. It is up to $2,500 if the spouse is not working. There

is job-search assistance in host and home locations up to $5,000 and a dislocation payment.

In contrast, other consultancy surveys find that taking into account the loss of a partner's income is rare, and many provide no assistance for partners at all.

THE IMPLICATIONS OF INTERNATIONAL WORKING ON WORK–LIFE BALANCE

We introduced the topic of work–life balance in Chapter 7. In the context of international working and international assignments, dual-career issues have been used as a key constraint to women accessing international management positions. Research into dual-career couples undertaking long-term assignments highlights the need to take into account both partners' willingness to relocate in order to ensure a successful assignment (Harvey, 1995, 1996, 1997; Linehan and Walsh, 2000). However, a broader concern for international organisations, and for their employees, is the impact of international working on work–life balance. This book has underlined the importance of international assignments to organisations working across national borders in order to build global competence and integration. It has also shown evidence of failure in some long-term assignments. It is important to realise, however, that success in long-term assignments is not just a function of the individual but also of the partner and family. Families have only occasionally been seen as a focus of research (Haslberger and Brewster, 2008). The disruption caused by geographical relocations has also been seen to create tremendous disruption in the lives of all family members (Munton, 1990; Noe and Barbar, 1993; Guzzo *et al*, 1994). Work–life issues are amongst the most cited problems associated with international working patterns for both those in relationships and single employees (CReMe, 2000; Fenwick, 2001; Suutari, 2003).

Over the last two decades, the need to acknowledge the influence of work factors on family satisfaction and non-work factors on job satisfaction has become a dominant theme in the organisational behaviour and human resource management literature.

In line with spillover theory (Aldous, 1969; Crouter, 1984; Piotrkowski, 1979), however, most studies are now based on the assumption of a reciprocal relationship between the two types of work–family conflict: work-interference-with-family conflict, and family-interference-with-work conflict. Not only does the adjustment of one partner spill over from one aspect of their lives into others, but there will be an interaction (cross-over) between them (see Figure 43). With other family members (children, parents) this relationship becomes even more complex. Thus effective adjustment in one area can affect adjustment in others, and the effective adjustment of one will also affect the others – and the links run both ways, so an expatriate happy in their work (or unhappy) will bring that well-adjusted (or ill-adjusted) feeling to their family. The nature of the family's adjustment will also impact on the expatriate at work.

Although work–family balance has been the focus of a great deal of organisational, governmental and academic interest, it has remained a predominantly domestic-based issue. Work–family conflict is, however, likely to increase in international working scenarios, which may involve the physical relocation of the entire family. In such cases, the boundaries between work and home become blurred due to the involvement of the whole family (Harvey, 1985). For dual-career couples, the partner's career may be disrupted and his or her sense of worth and identity may suffer (Harvey, 1997). The children's education may also be interrupted (Fukuda and Chu, 1994) and their social networks destroyed, which may affect their feelings of security and well-being. In short, in international assignments, family life becomes more significant because the whole family is uprooted. Even in the case of short-term assignments and international commuting assignments, where the family may not physically relocate, the additional stressors of the individual's living away from home have been seen to exacerbate work–family conflict (CReMe, 2000; Fenwick, 2001; Peltonen, 2001).

Figure 43 Spillover versus crossover

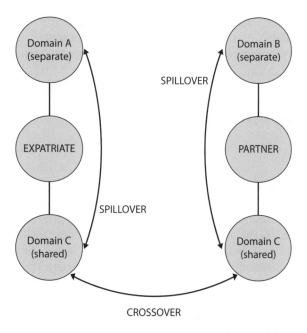

 REFLECTIVE ACTIVITY

What can organisations do to ensure a good work–life balance for employees and their families while on international assignments?

MEASURING THE VALUE OF INTERNATIONAL ASSIGNMENTS

The need for a more strategic and detailed approach to managing international working from both the organisational and individual perspective has been highlighted in this chapter and previously in Chapter 14. Ideally, the financial and non-financial costs should be less than the financial and non-financial benefits of the assignment to the organisations (McNulty and Tharenou, 2004). It is increasingly believed that MNCs are under ever-greater pressure to ensure that such assignments pay their way (Benito *et al*, 2005; Brewster *et al*, 2005; Perkins, 2006). However, despite the importance of international assignments, MNCs are not yet able to fully evaluate the benefits associated with their use. Far less than a fifth even try to apply any kind of return-on-investment measures (Johnson, 2005). Thus, although some organisations have a clear outline of the international assignments' costs, very few, if any, have anything but a vague or unclear picture of the related return on investment. The need to develop a methodology to measure the value of international assignments is currently the focus of many consultancies operating in the area of IHRM.

Under this approach, the international assignment is seen as a value-generation process, which contributes to the company's business performance improvement (Schiuma *et al*, 2003). As already noted in the previous chapter, international assignees are usually sent abroad for one of five main strategic reasons:

- professional development
- knowledge transfer
- transfer of scarce skills
- control
- co-ordination.

Each of these strategic reasons can add value to the organisation in terms of either financial value or knowledge value. Financial value refers to the overall assets of the organisation which can be easily expressed in monetary terms. Knowledge value, on the other hand, includes all the company's intangible assets. This could include stakeholder relationships as well as tacit rules and procedures, corporate culture, etc. In order for managers to be able to measure the value of each assignment, they must be able to identify where each assignment objective will be adding most value. Professional development, for instance, will probably be contributing to increasing the value of the organisation's human capital.

Table 21 points out the direct links that exist between the value driver categories and the value areas of an organisation.

Professional development provides direct value within the human resource area. In fact, it is mainly aimed to develop the competence and attitude of the assignee undertaking the assignment.

Knowledge transfer can provide direct value within the stakeholder relationship, human resource, internal business process and intangible infrastructure area.

Table 21 A matrix of the direct value-added contribution of an international assignment's value drivers to the value areas of a company

	Financial value	Stakeholder relationship	Human resources	International business processes	Virtual infrastructure
Professional development			📄		
Knowledge transfer		📄	📄	📄	📄
Fulfilment of scarce skills		📄		📄	
Coordination		📄		📄	📄
Control	📄	📄		📄	📄

Within the stakeholder area, knowledge transfer can generate value, for example, in terms of the improvement of relationships with the regulator by transferring to them the organisational cultural approaches to business management – eg in respect of the tax, socio-cultural, and environment regulations. Knowledge transfer provides value within the area of human resource in the form of employee competence. Value in the area of internal business processes can be generated by transferring knowledge in the form of procedures and standards to improve operation process performance. Finally, knowledge transfer can involve disseminating organisational culture and management philosophy providing value within the intangible infrastructure area.

Provision of scarce skills provides direct value within the stakeholder relationship and internal business processes. In fact, an assignment aiming to fill skills gaps can produce value in the area of stakeholder relationships, in terms of improvement of the management relationships with the stakeholders of the company, and in the area of internal business process, allowing an improvement in process performance by putting in place specialised people.

Co-ordination provides direct value within the stakeholder relationship, internal business processes and intangible infrastructure areas. For example, it contributes to improving the communication processes between the organisation and its stakeholders; it allows better integration of the operations on a global base by sharing information and targets; it supports the organisation in developing a culture on a global base.

Control can generate direct value within the financial value, stakeholder relationship, internal business processes and intangible infrastructure area. In fact, the assignment as a control mechanism can provide value within the financial area by constraining local financial practices; within the stakeholder relationship it can contribute to maintaining good relationships by checking that subsidiaries behave consistently within the local norms and regulations; it can generate value within the internal business area by the definition of standards against which the operation processes have to be executed; finally, within the intangible infrastructure area value it can provide value by shaping the local management philosophy.

A key concern with this type of methodology is that the definition of the metrics requires considerable time and effort on the part of managers. A major issue for organisations will be whether these metrics can be operationalised and over what timescale. If, for example, the organisation is using international working to develop a cadre of knowledgeable and internationally minded executives, at what point are the measures applied? It remains to be seen whether organisations will adopt the discipline of developing metrics in an area that is noticeable for its lack of sophistication in planning and measurement.

THE MULTI-CULTURAL TEAM

Looking at the different assumptions that we make about the skills and competencies that are needed by global leaders, one could be forgiven for saying, 'But surely, this is only important for large organisations that employ a small cadre of internationally mobile managers and expatriates? What about organisations that might simply source international employees from and in different parts of the world? Do they need to recruit for the sorts of competencies discussed here?' If we look at what we know about the use of international employees, the answer is probably 'Yes'. Organisations rely upon cross-cultural skills and at surprisingly low levels in the hierarchy. Salas *et al* (2008; p115) note that:

> The United States has often been referred to as a melting pot, consisting of individuals from numerous cultures, backgrounds and religions. With the expansion [by the late 1990s] of over 10,000 companies worldwide to global markets, a multicultural workforce is inevitable … To add further complexity, organisations' use of teams as a means of improving organisational outcomes is increasing. The likelihood of multicultural teams (ie two or more individuals from at least two different national cultures who must work interdependently to reach the team's goals) being developed in organisations is therefore greater than ever.

The use of teams, even within highly individualist countries such as the US, has become accepted as a key means of coping with the highly complex and dynamic nature of work in the twenty-first century. Why do internationalisation strategies require managers increasingly to work through multinational team networks?

WHY DO INTERNATIONALISATION STRATEGIES RELY ON TEAMS?

There are three main reasons:

- Organisations are pursuing strategies of localisation, attempting to reduce their reliance on expatriates in their traditional co-ordination and control role.

- Strategies that rely on rapid internationalisation through international joint venturing, strategic partnership arrangements and global start-ups place international managers into team and work contexts in which they may have less position-power but a heightened need to ensure that their organisation learns from the partnership.

- As organisations globalise their operations, the requirement for international working is pushed lower down the hierarchy.

It is essential for HRM professionals to develop policies and practices that support the use of teams. This includes selecting team players, rewarding on the basis of teamwork, and developing mentoring and coaching behaviours for potential leaders.

For international organisations, there are a number of benefits of working in transnational teams (Schneider and Barsoux, 1997). They can encourage cohesiveness amongst national and functional units. They are very useful in creating lateral networks to improve communication and information flow between subsidiaries and HQ, and among subsidiaries (Ghoshal *et al*, 1994). They provide opportunities for team members to understand international issues better and to note the interdependencies between units. They also provide opportunities for team members to learn how to function more effectively within different cultures with suppliers, customers or employees. Finally, they can help foster knowledge transfer and organisational learning.

Evans *et al* (2002) view cross-boundary teams as the basic unit of the global economy and argue that strategic decisions in global organisations are complex. They say that the best way to achieve sound decisions is often through a transnational team of managers and specialists whose talents have been carefully blended. Transnational teams therefore contribute to what they term 'glue technology'. This describes the underlying process technology used in co-ordinating mechanisms within international organisations. Under this perspective, the foundation of most mechanisms of co-ordination is relationships between people.

Cross-boundary teams can take many shapes and forms – they may (for example) be part of an international supply chain in a major pharmaceutical company, or a cross-national team of consultants put together to deliver a business solution for a global services company, or an international relief team working for a not-for-profit organisation.

REFLECTIVE ACTIVITY

From our earlier discussions of cross-cultural differences,

● What would you see to be the pros and cons of forming a team with individuals from the USA, Germany, Japan and Brazil?

● What process recommendations would you make to ensure effective functioning of the team?

Research suggests that multi-cultural teams tend to be either very high-performing or very low-performing (Shapiro *et al*, 2002). Figure 44 shows the relative productivity of a series of four- to six-member problem-solving teams. Culturally diverse teams tend to become either the most or the least effective, whereas single-culture teams tend to be average.

Figure 44 The relative productivity of cross-cultural and single-culture teams

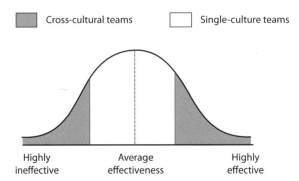

Adler (1997) argues that the difference between highly productive and less productive teams lies in how they manage their diversity, not in the fact that they include diversity. According to Adler, a multi-cultural team's productivity depends on its task, stage of development and the ways in which its diversity is managed (see Table 22).

Table 22 Managing diversity effectively

	Effective	**Ineffective**
Task	Innovative	Routing
	Divergence (earlier)	Convergence (later)
	Differences recognised	Differences ignored
Stage	Members selected for task-related abilities	Member selected on basis of ethnicity
	Mutual respect	Ethnocentrism
Conditions	Equal power	Culturalism dominance
	Superordinate goal	Individual goals
	External feedback	No feedback (complete autonomy)

Source: Adler (1997; p139)

In terms of task, multicultural or diverse teams are seen to perform better than homogeneous teams in situations where innovative ideas/solutions are required. Most of the major consulting companies create international and cross-functional teams to deliver competitive leading-edge solutions for multinational clients. In contrast, a team working on the standardised assembly of electronic components will require individuals with the same standard of manual dexterity.

A team also progresses through various stages, defined by Adler as:

- entry
- work
- action.

At the *entry* stage a team must develop cohesiveness. This involves members beginning to know and to trust each other. Creativity is essential at the *work* stage, when the team has to devise ways of defining its objectives, gathering and analysing information and assessing alternative plans of action. Convergence is needed at the final *action* stage, when agreement on a final solution is required. Diversity can be seen to hinder both the first and final stages, but be extremely beneficial at the middle stage (see Table 23).

Table 23 **Managing diversity, based on the team's stage of development**

Stage	Process	Diversity makes the process ...	The process is based on ...
Entry: initial team formation	Trust-building (developing cohesion)	more difficult	using similarities and understanding differences
Work: problem description and analysis	Ideation (creating ideas)	easier	using differences
Action: decision-making and implementation	Consensus-building (agreeing and acting)	more difficult	recognising and creating similarities

Source: Adler (1997; p140) reproduced with permission

KEY COMPETENCIES FOR MULTI-CULTURAL TEAMS

CASE STUDIES

MUTUAL ADJUSTMENT WITHIN INTERNATIONAL TEAMS IN GERMAN MNCS

Cross-border research regarding what occurs when two diverse groups begin interacting is an example of what Sackmann and Phillips (2004) call the intercultural interaction perspective. Study of international teams often shows the need for accelerated processes of cultural bridging. Cross-cultural interactions are an integral part of the functioning of such teams. Zimmermann and Sparrow (2008) studied 116 participants over a one-year period in 11 bi-national teams within German MNCs: two German-British teams, five German-Indian, two German-Japanese, and two German-Austrian teams. The study showed the importance of *mutual adjustment processes* (multiple interactions between team members of several different nationalities) across all combinations in order to overcome the difficulties associated with differences regarding work practices and communication styles. Such mutual adjustment achieved better relational and work outcomes. Five internal adjustment components (strategies) were identified: communication,

change of views, evaluation of differences, negotiation, and teaching and control. These highlight the cognitive, affective, and behavioural skills that become important for international managers when working through international team structures. External factors were also important. The nationality of headquarters impacted on the way team members changed both work practices and communication styles. Three elements were important: organisational culture and regulations guided work practices across the countries; globally standardised practices and structures designed at headquarters to co-ordinate team activities across nations; and headquarter membership within teams allowing for greater access to information. The organisations' globalisation and localisation strategies also set the ground for the degree of influence that the nationality of headquarters, the nationality of leadership, and the external customer had on the direction of adjustment within teams.

REFLECTIVE ACTIVITY

What international differences in work practices and interaction styles do you think are most likely to cause difficulties that require international teams to mutually adjust?

How do you think mutual adjustment takes place?

Members of international teams have to understand what the required behaviour is, why it is considered desirable, at whom it is aimed, where it is most often to be seen, and how that behaviour is delivered (Sparrow, 2006c). Although individuals with cultural intelligence are important, it is also the quality of cross-cultural communication at team level that determines the effectiveness of multi-cultural teams (Kealey and Protheroe, 1996; Gudykunst, 1998; Matveev and Nelson, 2004). Table 24 shows the specification of cross-cultural communication competence that can be applied both to individual and also to team interactions.

Table 24 Cross-cultural communication competencies

Interpersonal skills	Team effectiveness	Cultural uncertainty	Cultural empathy
Ability to acknowledge differences in communication and interaction styles Ability to deal with misunderstandings Being comfortable when communicating with foreign nationals Being aware of own cultural conditioning Having basic knowledge about the country, the culture, and the language of team members	Ability to understand and define team goals, roles and norms Ability to give and receive constructive feedback Ability to discuss and solve problems Ability to deal with conflict situations Ability to display respect for other team members Displaying a participatory leadership style Ability to work co-operatively with others	Ability to deal with cultural uncertainty Ability to display patience Tolerance of ambiguity and uncertainty due to cultural differences Being open to cultural differences Ability to exercise flexibility	Ability to see and understand the world from others' cultural perspectives Exhibiting a spirit of inquiry about other cultures, values, beliefs and communication patterns Ability to appreciate dissimilar working styles Ability to accept different ways of doing things Non-judgemental stance toward the ways things are done in other situations

Source: Matveev and Nelson (2004)

STRATEGIES FOR MANAGING MULTI-CULTURAL TEAMS

Multi-cultural teams do not differ from mono-cultural teams in terms of basic team dynamics – typically they will go through four stages of development, often dubbed forming (Adler's 'entry' stage), storming (Adler's 'work' stage), norming and performing (Adler's 'action' stage). They will also have to consider composition issues such as the resources allocated to the team, membership profile, numbers, etc. And they will have to address how to run the team. Core team dynamics studies should identify both task and process issues relating to effective team performance. The same is true for multi-cultural groups, but given the complexity of different cultural perspectives, assumptions about the nature of task and process issues ought to be questioned by all team members in order to achieve a 'common reality' and from there to establish common ground rules for the development of the team.

A comprehensive list of the issues to be addressed in both task and process aspects of managing multi-cultural teams is presented by Schneider and Barsoux – see Table 25.

Table 25 Task and process issues to be addressed in multi-cultural teams

Task strategies	Process strategies
• What is the purpose, process, and timing of meetings? • To what extent does the mission need to be made clear and explicit? • Is it more important to achieve cost targets, or are cost overruns OK given time/quality targets? • What does 'on time' mean? • What is the priority of time? • What are the importance and priority of deadlines? • Is it more important to achieve time deadlines, or to delay for higher quality? • What do we do about missed commitments? • To what extent does the agenda need to be clearly structured and followed? • To what extent do the rules of the game need to be spelled out? • To what extent do roles and responsibilities need to be formalised and written? • Who needs to attend, and when? • What is the role of the leader? Of team members? • How will the tasks be divided up and then integrated? • What work can be done together or apart? • What technologies can be used (video-conferencing, email)? • What is an effective presentation? • What is needed to be convincing: facts and figures, philosophy, feelings? • How will information be passed? To whom? When? Formally or informally? Within the team or outside? • How, where and when do we make decisions? Consensus, majority rule, compromise?	• How will we manage relationships – dive right into business or take time to socialise? • To what extent will we socialise together, and when? • What is trust, and how is it earned? • How will we address people? First or last name? Titles? • How formal or informal will we be? • What language(s) will we use? • How will differences in language fluency be managed? • To what extent does participation reflect potential contributions? • Who dominates? • Who listens to whom? • Who talks to whom? • How are interruptions managed? • How is conflict managed? Forcing, accommodating, avoiding, collaborating, compromising? • How is negotiation viewed? Win/lose, or win/win? • How is feedback provided? Face to face, third-party, direct?

Source: Schneider and Barsoux (1997; p186)

The checklist of communication competencies shown in Table 24 illustrates the potential for conflict on even the most basic team management issues. Teams incorporating diverse nationalities tend to ignore differences at the start-up stages of the teams and to focus on similarities (ie young, well-educated, professional). With depressing regularity, team dynamic problems surface later, when the pressure of work kicks in. Complaints of non-inclusion from those from high-context, neutral cultures are greeted with shocked surprise by UK and US members who view their time- and task-focused approach, combined with an assertive manner, as the 'right' approach to teamwork. The introduction of inter-cultural awareness sessions, combined with discussion around team-building issues for multi-cultural teams (perhaps using selected questions from Schneider and Barsoux's task and process strategy checklist), leads to a significant decrease in complaints and more effective teams.

KEY LEARNING POINTS

- Diversity in an international workforce is a major advantage – and a major concern for internationally operating organisations.

- The role of women in international management should be addressed: their low participation rates are to some extent a function of the home-country selection.

- International working can have a significant effect on work–life balance.

- Organisations need to measure the value of international assignments, including diversity considerations, but this is not easy and in practice multiple methods are adopted in most organisations.

LEARNING QUESTIONS

1 What are the advantages for international organisations in ensuring a diverse workforce?

2 If diversity is seen to be a critical factor of competitive advantage for international organisations, why is the expatriate population still largely white and male?

3 Suggest practical steps an organisation can take to alleviate work–family issues for international assignments.

4 Is it possible to create metrics to measure the value of international assignments? Suggest critical success factors for implementation.

EXPLORE FURTHER

Adler, N. J. (1997) *International Dimensions of Organisational Behavior*, 3rd edition, Cincinnati, Ohio, South Western Publishing.

Caligiuri, P. M. and Cascio, W. (1998) 'Can we send her there? Maximising the success of western women on global assignments', *Journal of World Business*, 33 (4): 394–416.

Klarsfeld, A., Combs, G. W., Susaeta, L. and Belizon, M. J. (2011) 'International perspectives on diversity and equal treatment policies and practices', in C. Brewster and W. Mayrhofer (eds) *Handbook of Comparative Human Resource Management*, Cheltenham, Edward Elgar.

Zimmermann, A. and Sparrow, P. R. (2008) 'Mutual adjustment processes in international teams: lessons for the study of expatriation', *International Studies of Management and Organization*, 37 (3): 65–88.

CHAPTER 16

Globalising HRM

LEARNING OUTCOMES

When they have read this chapter, students will:

- understand the challenges involved in balancing global integration and local responsiveness in IHRM

- be able to apply a three-box HR delivery model to the IHRM context

- identify the key integration activities engaged in by the IHRM function

- be able to determine the key elements of a talent management strategy

- explain why MNCs attempt to create global employer brands

- appreciate the role of knowledge management and knowledge transfer between international operations

- understand the issues involved in building organisational capability through global expertise networks

- be able to debate the role of IHR professionals as guardians of national culture.

INTRODUCTION

This chapter takes a strategic view of some of the developments in IHRM that are occurring as a result of decisions being made about the function and the scope and scale of its activities. It examines how, as organisations implement global operations, the IHRM function can help facilitate this.

The IHRM function has to help its organisation manage the consequences of several strategic initiatives. This might be global business process redesign, the pursuit of a global centre of excellence strategy or the global redistribution and relocation of work that this often entails. The HRM personnel have to help their organisation absorb acquired businesses from what might previously have been competitor businesses. They become involved in the merging of existing operations on a global scale and the staffing of strategic integration teams. They must manage attempts to develop and harmonise core HRM processes within these merged businesses, and also manage growth through the process of acquisition whereby new country operations are often built around the purchase of a series of national teams. The rapid start-up of international operations brings with it the requirement to provide insights into the organisational development needs of new operations as they mature through different stages of the business life cycle. In many international operations the capabilities are changing rapidly as many skills become obsolete very quickly and as changes in the organisational structure and design expose managers to more complex roles. This often requires a general up-skilling of local operations.

In order to help free up time for the function to engage in these sorts of activities, it has to capitalise on technology while at the same time ensuring that local social and cultural insights are duly considered when it is imperative to do so. A particular problem in that area occurs when IT is being used to centralise and 'transactionalise' HRM processes (e-HRM), or to create shared services, on a global basis. In order to make these sorts of judgements IHRM functions have to understand the changes being wrought in the HRM service supply chain as the need for several intermediary service providers is being reduced, and as web-based HRM provision is leading to greater individualisation of HRM across international operations. Often these international operations have very different levels of 'HRM sophistication'. Partly as a consequence, IHRM professionals have to learn how to operate through formal or informal global HRM networks and how to act as knowledge brokers across international operations.

In truth, there are often quite marked identity issues faced by IHRM professionals. Operating through global networks and transferring knowledge across international operations mean that they have to learn how to avoid automatically pursuing a one-best-way philosophy (whether for HRM solutions or indeed in terms of general management activity). As organisations become less ethnocentric and knowledge and ideas about best practice flow from both the centre to the operations and vice versa, it is not uncommon for IHRM professionals at all levels of the organisation to feel that their ideas are being overridden by those of other nationalities or business systems. Whereas within a domestic HRM setting offering advice on best practice might seem to be an appropriate solution and a service that has to be delivered by the HRM function, IHRM specialists cannot be experts in the context of all the countries they cover and have to work with other 'domestic experts'. Moreover, IHRM professionals have to experience and endure frequent changes in the level of decentralisation/ centralisation across their constituent international businesses, making it very difficult to establish with authority where their power lies.

As the process of optimisation and standardisation of HRM processes takes place in many organisations, facilitated by the e-enablement of HRM systems and procedures on a regional, and in some cases global, scale, new systems are being put in place. Organisations often invent these systems at different paces and within different parts of their business. A critical aspect of creating effective IHRM strategies, therefore, is the ability to judge the extent to which an organisation should implement similar practices across the world or adapt them to suit local conditions – the 'global versus local' debate. There is a new 'line in the sand' being drawn between standardised or optimised global processes and local HRM practices. This key challenge requires a high level of strategic thinking on the part of IHRM professionals. While scanning the world for best practice, they need to ensure that the policies and practices they implement are appropriate to the unique nature of their international operations. IHRM professionals have also to act as the guardians or caretakers of national difference.

A number of protagonists of the importance of the IHRM function argue that a series of generic international management issues involved in globalisation inevitably create a search for optimal HRM practice. Globalisation of itself brings the HRM function closer to the strategic core of the business and also leads to considerable changes in the content of HRM (Pucik, 1992). It has been argued that a major determinant of success or failure in international business is the effective management of human resources internationally (Stroh and Caligiuri, 1998). Indeed, many organisations underestimate the complex nature of HRM problems involved in managing increasingly international operations (Dowling et al, 1999).

THE PURSUIT OF GLOBAL OPERATIONS AND DESIGNS

Although, of course, many organisations, especially in the electronics arena, are now 'born global', the traditional and evolutionary progression of most MNCs through international, multinational, global and transnational/network/ heterarchy is well understood, and is generally discussed in the context of the trade-off between global integration and local responsiveness – two concepts that we examine a little later in the chapter. However, MNCs have increasingly dispersed activities. As we saw in Chapter 13, they have relied on specialised and often network-based structures to co-ordinate these activities.

The corporate headquarters typically adjusts its level of co-ordination and control to reflect the role of the subsidiary and the strategic importance of its mandate (Bartlett and Ghoshal, 1989). Organisations are, however, composed of many diverse, interdependent work groups, such as new product development teams and manufacturing planning teams, all of which have unique decision domains, and which develop unique perspectives in response to different tasks, goals and environments. Although managers can act autonomously within each of these decision domains, they are affected by each other's actions. Consequently, mechanisms of integration (and the underlying organisational capability to manage these integration mechanisms effectively) are needed, above and beyond the simple summation of the different perspectives that exist within the organisation.

As MNCs change their organisation design in response to the need to build more global capability, as part of their natural development they often establish dedicated organisational forms to facilitate this. Starting around a decade ago, one of the designs that has become an important feature of MNCs is the creation of centres of excellence (COEs) on a global basis (Frost *et al*, 2002; p1016):

> A growing body of anecdotal evidence suggests that the COE phenomenon is increasing amongst the world's major MNEs, at the same time that this evidence also suggests that many firms are struggling with the managerial issues involved.

COEs are organisational units that embody a set of organisational capabilities. These capabilities must be explicitly recognised as an important source of value creation (Frost *et al*, 2002). There needs also to be a strategic remit, such as the intention to leverage or disseminate these capabilities to other parts of the firm. At the subsidiary level, COEs tend to be established as a consequence of a long and slow internationalisation process within the organisation, or as a deliberate part of organisation design where HQ managers decide to grant autonomy to units that have also been given a specific strategic mandate. Increasingly small teams or units *within* either subsidiaries or central functions take a lead COE role in one area, and other units take the lead in different areas of capability. Although the leadership of a COE might be vested in a physical location, the centre itself may be virtual, spread across networks of teams in different geographies.

 REFLECTIVE ACTIVITY

What activities, processes and capabilities might constitute a COE, and how should such units be mandated?

What has to happen in terms of the 'capability building investments' that are needed? Is it possible to specify capabilities such as decision-making autonomy, requisite levels of connectivity to other sources of competence inside the organisation, leadership and processes of knowledge management?

To what extent do institutional factors preclude or support the long-term survival and contribution of COEs?

In many cases, experts argue that COEs need to be quite loosely tied into the organisation and co-ordinated with other units if they are to help search for new knowledge and augment the capability of the MNC (Hansen *et al*, 1999; Kuemmerle, 1999).

Understanding and building globally distributed COEs into viable operations has become a significant challenge. Holm and Pedersen (2000) found that they must be more than just specialised in their own knowledge. They have to be able to maintain one or several critical fields of knowledge that have a long-term impact on the development of activity in the other subsidiaries and units of the MNC.

Sparrow *et al* (2004) examined the challenges created for IHRM functions when they have to assist the organisation in globalising its operations this way.

THEORY AND PRACTICE

KEY FRAMEWORK

Roles for IHRM professionals in the development of global centres of excellence

Sparrow *et al* (2004) identified three ways in which the IHRM function can help to relocate centres of excellence around the MNC on a global basis:

- managing the international relocation of staff as organisations move these centres of excellence nearer to the global centre of gravity of their core customers; as organisations reconfigure their core competencies on a global scale by moving manufacturing, research and development or logistics operations closer to the best national infrastructures in terms of education or transport facilities; or as organisations set up new centres as part of international ventures or as a result of mergers

- advising on the best HRM strategies to co-ordinate and control such activities

- understanding the centres of excellence that can be created within their own activities, and building networks of HRM experts within these areas of competence on a global basis.

Supporting a global business insourcing strategy requires significant management of change activity within the new location. Paradoxically, this can sometimes bring with it the need to 'relocalise' some aspects of HRM.

CASE STUDIES

OFFSHORING BUSINESS TO INDIA, THAILAND AND CHINA IN REUTERS

Sparrow and Brewster (2011) examined the IHRM role in managing offshoring in Reuters to its Indian, Thai and Chinese captive sites. This created its own range of HRM policy decisions and activities. These had to be layered into the overall globalisation strategy. Setting up new offshore activities required:

- aggressively recruiting and building up centres

- hiring in, and later 'creating', managers with the relevant capabilities

- supporting downsizing in other parts of the business

- knowledge-sharing

- knowledge transfer

- pursuing a broad learning and development support effort

- redefining roles to change the conditioning and nature of key job roles

- extending career paths

- managing the 'entrepreneurship' challenge: creating new businesses in the context of large existing businesses

- making decisions about the level of flexibility in HRM process standardisation: creating what was called 'HRM lite'

These led to some 'reverse pressures' and a need to relocalise HRM practices in some areas.

REFLECTING GLOBAL OPERATIONS IN IHRM

MNCs still face the challenge of, on the one hand, providing some degree of consistency (through either standardisation or optimisation) of practices around the world so that their operations use the same HRM tools and techniques, and, on the other hand, maintaining locally responsive and differentiated approaches (Ryan *et al*, 2003; p85):

> There is a great deal of resistance to designing and implementing global systems and policies because 'people are different', 'laws are different' and 'labour markets are different'. Because the complexity of designing and implementing effective HR systems on an international scale cannot be denied, there are many areas in which HR professionals have shied away from going global, preferring instead to implement local or regional solutions. However, ... as more organisations begin to operate on a global (or at least multinational) scale, the need for HR systems that can be used across multiple countries continues to grow.

Historically, considerable energy has been spent translating central initiatives into what works within different countries. Now, however, there is a much stronger focus on cross-country and cross-business border implementation issues. HRM is moving towards a world where it has to satisfy line-of-business – and not just country – needs, and this is beginning to shift the way that HRM professionals think about problems (Sparrow *et al*, 2004).

In this section we examine two key debates in how best IHRM functions can reflect global operations in their own activities:

- managing the balance between global integration and local differentiation in HRM practices
- adopting a global HRM delivery model.

THE BALANCE BETWEEN GLOBAL INTEGRATION AND LOCAL RESPONSIVENESS

It is widely accepted that one of the key issues in the practice of IHRM is the need to manage the dual pressures of global integration and local responsiveness (Brewster *et al*, 2008; Evans *et al*, 2002; Rosenzweig, 2005). The bottom-line question cited by Scullion and Starkey (2000) and originally asked by Foss (1997; p314) is:

What is it that the corporate HQ can do that cannot be done by financial markets or the business units, acting as independent market contractors?

These studies have shown that foreign subsidiaries' HRM practices reveal some similarities with, but also differences from, both local practices and parents' practices, depending on particular contexts (see Farndale *et al*, 2008; Farndale and Paauwe, 2007) . They are typically based on diverse theoretical perspectives (see Chapter 13) on social capital, trust, knowledge management and procedural justice. As a stream of research, it highlights the importance of intra-organisational factors, rather than solely emphasising external factors such as national institutional and cultural factors.

Sparrow and Brewster (2011) have analysed how MNCs attempt to manage these processes of migration, often initially towards regional HRM service centres, with an aspiration of eventually moving towards global ones. The IHRM function had to understand which of its processes really have to be different – should remain localised – and which ones must be made core to all countries, globally integrated.

THEORY AND PRACTICE

KEY FRAMEWORK

Learning from examining HRM function globalisation processes

The IHRM function has to work through the structural and organisation design issues that changes in the organisation's business model have invoked. It needs to analyse what decisions on the business model, sourcing and shoring mean for the retained HRM organisation.

The global HRM function has to structure itself and design its service offerings in a way that enables it to support these wider business changes, but then also to apply the learning from this to the decisions it makes about its own operations. HRM specialists have to understand the new globally executed business models that have become possible.

For the HRM department, facilitating global sourcing and shoring options creates a significant change agenda for the function and often a separate and counter force for relocalisation.

Although the HRM strategy may be designed on a global basis to ensure a focusing on key deliverables, this often just sets an overall framework. On a regional basis, attention shifts to what is unique in the local environment.

Source: Sparrow and Brewster (2011)

CASE STUDIES

PRAGMATIC ROUTES TO GLOBALISATION: REUTERS

Reuters is an MNC in the high-technology information industry, issuing financial information and more general news to the financial sector and to news organisations. By 2008 it had grown, and continued to grow, through acquisitions. With revenues of over £2.5 billion it employed around 17,000 staff in over 100 countries and had nearly 200 in-country sites and establishments. There were three regional headquarters: in Europe, the Middle East and Africa (Switzerland), the Americas (the USA), and Asia-Pacific (Singapore). It operated through business divisions, a series of geographical sales and service channels and shared resources operations.

The change management processes were owned by the business and supported by HRM, so were positioned and embedded in the cycle of business activities, forming part of an annual HRM 'roadmap'. The global/local divide was driven by the following prerogatives:

- High-level strategy was set globally.

- HRM Business Partners worked with leadership teams globally

and nationally to develop a talent pipeline in the right context for their needs.

- Some central initiatives (eg reverse mentoring for senior leaders) were replicated locally as required.

- Accountability was taken by the line, and overall ownership held by the group leadership team.

- Regional councils took responsibility for leading initiatives that resonated with local needs.

Support and budget was given to local employee groups to encourage mutual support of activities. The organisation needed global consistency – it could not afford the information provided to vary depending upon source. It had structured its business model to reflect this globalised reality and invested heavily in a globally applicable management information system with a strong e-HRM component. Every manager and every employee was given access to the HRM information they needed from the website. The global HRM function was given information on all aspects of HRM around the business, wherever located.

The organisational domain within MNCs is always contested – it is characterised by 'actors' who have competing rationalities, coming as they do from multiple institutional contexts – contexts that may be influenced by transnational, home- and host-national institutions (Geppert *et al,* 2006). This contested nature of the MNC makes the task of attaining global integration and local responsiveness problematic. In turn, corporate actors have to act with nuanced sensibilities, informed by a deep understanding of the underlying dynamics behind the hidden and potentially contradictory forces that are involved in striking the balance between global integration and local responsiveness.

A significant amount of research on the HRM of MNCs has examined the degree of global integration or local responsiveness in subsidiary HRM practices by assessing whether a particular HRM practice or configuration of HRM practices resemble local practices, parent firm's practices or a hybrid of the two, and attempted to identify the contextual determinants of the balance (Brewster *et al*, 2008; Rosenzweig, 2006; Björkman, 2006). This research examines the patterns of adaptation of particular HRM practices within the context of dual pressures, as well as the external factors that influence those adaptation patterns.

However, Edwards *et al* (2007) argue that a large proportion of the research is deterministic. The main focus is on external factors, such as the influences of home country, parent company, host country and other MNCs. As shown in their case study of the UK subsidiary of US MNCs, even with the institutional pressures of the American business system, there remained a space for choice and negotiation by the UK actors. Research has therefore failed to consider the role and importance of strategic actors. Similarly, Björkman and colleagues (see Björkman, 2006; Björkman and Lervik, 2007; Björkman *et al,* 2009; Mäkelä *et al,* 2009) argue that the current literature does not provide sufficient insight regarding the intra-organisational factors that matter in the management of this dual pressure of global integration and local responsiveness, again arguing that we understate the factors at play when seen from the point of view of important corporate actors.

Chung *et al* (2012) have investigated the intra-organisational factors that corporate HRM actors perceive as being a key in shifting the balance of dual forces in the direction they desire, using two Korean MNCs.

CASE STUDIES

KOREAN MNCS: PROBLEMS IN TRANSFERRING THEIR BEST HRM PRACTICE TO SUBSIDIARIES

Chung *et al* (2012) studied two Korean MNCs, both global players in their respective industries, automotives and electronics, with significant global market shares and organisational spread. Their overseas operations included manufacturing plants, sales and marketing offices, service centres, R&D centres and design centres. Both had been transitioning their HRM function from a multi-domestic state to a transnational state but faced serious resistance from their subsidiaries and hence considerable tensions inside the organisation. Two salient themes emerged. HRM professionals in both companies acknowledged that the needs of global integration and local responsiveness are not an either/

or choice; rather, they see that both are mandatory requirements that need to be sought simultaneously. However, there was a perceived lack of a strong sense of legitimacy, the 'liability of country of origin' issue (Chang, Mellahi and Wilkinson, 2009). As MNCs from a non-dominant economy, transferring their home country's HRM practices to their subsidiaries was difficult. It would be inappropriate to impose what they called 'Korean-style HRM practices', which could be mostly characterised as the seniority-based HRM system traditionally used in Korean firms, to subsidiaries. Adopting so-called global best practices would be the better solution. This drove them to search for external sources of legitimacy such as 'ready-legitimised' global best practices. In both organisations, their US subsidiaries initially showed negative responses to the global HRM frameworks. That the practices were staunchly resisted by the subsidiaries in a country that could largely be seen as the origin of such practices presented an interesting irony.

In this process, key corporate actors came to recognise the importance of a number of enabling mechanisms, notably a range of cognitive, social and procedural factors, in managing the duality of international HRM and in helping to ensure that the integration mechanisms being pursued were actually effective.

THEORY AND PRACTICE

KEY FRAMEWORK

We introduced the integration-responsiveness continuum in Chapter 13. Factors inside organisations linked to finding the appropriate balance between global integration and local responsiveness

Chung *et al* (2012) sort the intra-organisational factors into three broad categories:

- *Actor-related factors* – Because managing the dual pressures in an MNC is, to a large degree, related with a learning and knowledge-sharing process among different parties in the MNC context, actors' capacity for complexity may be an important factor in managing the duality of HRM in MNCs. In organisational trust research, the competence of important actors in a particular area as perceived by their counterparts has been shown to provide a basis of trust, which is also important in the contested contexts of MNCs.

- *Relational factors* – The growing interest in applying social capital theory to HRM in general, and to HRM within MNCs in particular (Björkman *et al*, 2009; Sparrow *et al,* 2009; Taylor, 2007), shows that the social ties and the characteristics of relationships between managers are important factors in knowledge-sharing within MNCs. The particular factors typically considered important are social interaction ties, trustworthy relationships and shared cognitions. These constitute social capital between corporate and local actors.

- *Procedural factors* – The perceived fairness of decision-making processes affects the attitudes and behaviour of managers, particularly in respect of greater acceptance of decisions and collaborative actions (Kim and Mauborgne, 2005). Björkman and Lervik (2007) draw attention to the involvement of multiple actors in the decision-making process and the application of change management skills.

ADOPTING A GLOBAL HRM DELIVERY MODEL

The development of what has become called the three-box model – outlined in Chapter 12 – is having a significant impact on IHRM functions. In combination with the other changes – e-enablement, centres of excellence, outsourcing and offshoring – it is being used to provide the template for a global HRM delivery model. It is moving the focus of the IHRM function away from managing a global set of managers towards becoming a function that can operate a series of value-adding HRM processes within the business internationally. As with many HRM innovations, elements of this model (DeFidelto and Slater, 2001; p281)

> have followed the Gulf Stream ... drifting in from the USA and hitting the UK first, then crossing the Benelux countries ... and Germany and France and proceeding finally to southern Europe.

To date there does not appear to be a common path to the internationalisation of shared-service models. Many organisations have chosen to create regional centres as part of a single international organisation structure. The constraints tend to be around those HRM services that are affected by employment law, employee relations, works councils, procedures governing dismissal and setting up an employment contract – all more country-focused activities. There are cultural differences affecting shared-service models and the e-enablement of HRM. There are institutional constraints – for example, around issues such as data protection. Additionally, the holding and processing of personal data in EU countries invokes requirements to gain consent from employees and is associated with different restrictions in different countries (data-listing religion and ethnic origin is forbidden for German and Italian companies, for example).

THE IMPACT OF A THREE-BOX DELIVERY MODEL ON THE IHRM FUNCTION

The adoption of this model creates a number of pressures, requiring MNCs to:

- consider the cost efficiencies of delivering HRM services across different geographical areas

- identify the new HRM co-ordination needs as organisations continue to move away from line-of-country reporting arrangements towards global lines of business

- provide the systems necessary to support strategy on a global basis

- understand which HRM processes really have be different, and which ones are core to all countries

- manage a process of migration towards regional and then global HRM service centres

- cope with problems of information deficiency where country-based systems do not provide the information needed to support a global line of business

- manage deficiencies in their own manpower, where headcount savings mean that there is not a good match between HRM professionals in each area and the functional data that is needed.

Progress in globalising HRM service delivery is being made in three areas (Sparrow and Brewster, 2006):

- technology (commonality of underlying systems and databases)

- process streamlining (optimisation of processes)

- sourcing (making decisions about the possible centralisation or outsourcing of some areas of activity).

Developing a global HRM and technology strategy and implementation plan covers everything from the information management of data to global appraisal systems, compensation and benefits management, to a knowledge base with a single global Internet feel and look, and to a knowledge management system. However, effective technology-based solutions are to a large extent dependent on the level of process streamlining.

In Chapter 12 we examined HRM departments in a comparative context and outlined the mechanics of a three-box HRM model. Of course, for a number of MNCs influenced by this way of thinking about HRM structures, the challenge becomes one of making the model work across multiple geographies.

REFLECTIVE ACTIVITY

Some MNCs find it a challenge to adopt a standardised delivery model for their HRM services. This activity gets you to think about some of the challenges in relation to a model often associated with the work of Ulrich outlined in Chapter 12. Imagine that an organisation has chosen to adopt this type of structure at a corporate level. This would have very significant implications at a local – or country – level. It would also require significant changes in the skills and capabilities of local HRM professionals. It would additionally impact on the way that important international HRM responsibilities, such as the management of international mobility, might be organised. As a reminder:

● The first box represents the more transactional aspects of activity, which may be delivered from service centres or processing hubs, in multiple geographical locations, or outsourced to third-party providers.

● The second box illustrates an embedded HRM business partner (HRBP) structure.

● The third box describes more added-value and specialist centres of excellence or functional support.

Choose a particular country, and some of the major international organisations within it. For those organisations, consider the following questions:

● In the light of the rise of service centres in HRM operating models, which aspects of the international mobility work stream might fall into this category, and which other HRM or global service activities might it encompass?

● Outsourcing scenarios can involve the movement of responsibilities across countries of relatively narrow bands of activity, such as support for immigration or school-search activity, through to the entire expatriation process, or indeed the advent of multi-tower outsourcing scenarios where the organisation seeks to include finance and information systems (IS) activities alongside HRM transactional activities. What would each scenario mean in the organisation?

● We discussed expatriation in Chapter 14. In the context of international HRM, an Ulrich operating model for HRM raises the question of what is the most appropriate relationship and split of responsibilities between central international mobility specialists,and in-country or in-business division HRM partners over specific aspects of the international assignment life cycle (the HRM decisions needed through from the selection of expatriates, their preparation, training and development, to the management of performance while on assignment, their repatriation and career development)? What should this split be? Who should manage which responsibilities for international managers?

- Should the international mobility (or any associated expatriation activity) become a centre of excellence in its own right, or should it report via another such centre, such as talent management?

THE INTEGRATION MECHANISMS PROVIDED BY THE CORPORATE CENTRE

Martin and Beaumont (2001) point out that the corporate centre still generally attempts to shape the strategic direction and strategic change programmes of international subsidiaries by acting either directly as an explicit source of innovation in the pursuit of global cost advantage, local differentiation or knowledge transfer amongst subsidiaries, or indirectly by openly or tacitly structuring an agenda for acceptable HRM change strategies or innovations in subsidiaries. These change programmes are often designed to:

- modify the culture of subsidiaries through vision and values programmes (Buller and McEvoy, 1999)
- introduce new or reformed central or normative control over HRM policies (Legge, 1995)
- transfer 'best' organisational practice through international benchmarking exercises (Martin and Beaumont, 1998; Kostova, 1999).

However, such programmes are often criticised for having culture-laden or ethical assumptions (Cray and Mallory, 1998; Woodall and Winstanley, 2000). The problems of cross-border transfer of ideas across multiple countries and layers of management are considerable. We need much better insight into how IHRM functions manage the events, activities and emotions in their organisation that usually embed or hinder HR change initiatives (Martin and Beaumont, 2001).

Drawing upon the work of Kostova (Kostova, 1999; Kostova and Roth, 2002) on HRM practice transfer, Martin and Beaumont (2001) developed a process model of strategic HRM change in MNCs involving MNC-internal factors that influence the transfer of HRM practices from headquarters to foreign units. They identified four different adoption patterns, referred to as ideal types, or archetypes, of foreign subsidiary adoption based upon different combinations of high versus low levels of implementation and internalisation:

- true believers
- ritualists
- non-conformists
- dissidents.

They discuss how human, social and organisational capital (see Chapter 13) explains the outcomes and different adoption patterns. In particular, they tease out three different types of social capital (structural, relational and cognitive) that become important, and two different forms of organisational capital, in an attempt to inspire researchers to conduct further conceptual and empirical research on this topic.

Ghoshal and Gratton (2002) point to a number of important integration activities at corporate level (see *Key framework*).

THEORY AND PRACTICE

KEY FRAMEWORK

Methods of integration

The corporate centre has the ability to manage the process of integration. This process has four critical components:

- *Operational integration through standardised technology* – Portals can provide a common front for employees and help integrate the HRM function around a common employee brand, as is the case, for example, in BP

- *Intellectual integration through the creation of a shared knowledge base* – By creating an emphasis on creating, sharing and exchanging knowledge both within and beyond the HRM community, corporate HRM functions can ensure that the intellectual capital of the function is rapidly codified and shared across constituent HRM functions

- *Social integration through the creation of collective bonds of performance* – This is where the function develops a clear sense of what it wants to achieve and how it wants to achieve it

- *Emotional integration through a sense of shared identity and meaning* – This concerns the mobilisation of hearts and minds behind change processes.

In practice, then, global HRM revolves around the ability of the organisation to find a concept that has 'relevance' to managers across several countries – despite the fact that they have different values embedded in different national cultures and despite the reality that these global themes may end up being operationalised with some local adaptation. The corporate strategy is usually expressed through performance management systems applied globally that measure and manage a balanced series of outcomes that must be achieved.

However, organisations also use some *superordinate themes* to provide a degree of consistency in their people management worldwide and as an attempt to socialise employee behaviour and action.

The most common superordinate themes in the process of globalising HRM, which we now examine, are:

- talent management and strategic workforce planning, where an integrated set of corporate initiatives are aimed at improving the calibre, availability and flexible utilisation of exceptionally capable (high-potential) employees who can have a disproportionate impact on organisational performance (Scullion and Starkey, 2000; Smilansky, 2004; Scullion and Collings, 2006). These are usually reflected in a series of organisational capabilities or competencies that once specified are integrated into career development and/or performance management systems (Sparrow, 1997)

- corporate and global brands, whereby organisations think about their external brand image and corporate reputation, and the ways in which their employees identify with and actively support the brand (Harris and de Chernatony, 2001; Davies *et al*, 2003; Martin and Hetrick, 2006)

- global knowledge management strategies, and the adoption of global expertise networks, built around core strategic competences that are considered to differentiate the firm and lead to its competitive advantage.

Each of these brings its own challenges when managed on the global stage and is considered in turn.

TALENT MANAGEMENT

The first main integration role for IHRM professionals that we discuss is the contribution that they can make to the management of talent on a global basis. We considered the issue of expatriate management in Chapter 14 and noted that talent management on a global basis is a far broader concept than plotting a series of international assignments for young high-potentials. Scullion and Starkey (2000; p1065) concluded that there is a

> growing recognition that the success of international business depends most importantly on the quality of top executive talent and how effectively these critical resources are managed and developed.

In practice, talent markets still operate in very national ways and even global organisations can find that their relative positioning varies markedly from one country to another. Those organisations that are consistently in the top ten tend to maintain local recruitment strategies, but they combine this local strategy with more global transfer of information and best practices. This is because the talent itself has become more mobile and organisations are therefore having to co-ordinate the way they manage it on a global basis. Competition also has become more generic – global organisations do not just compete with the best local employers but also with each other. For example, Shell used to estimate that only 5 per cent of graduates even from the top business schools have the potential for country chairmanship roles (Sparrow *et al*, 2004).

Talent management processes can bring a degree of consistency to international resourcing decisions. A strong corporate culture can make the use of talent management approaches and harmonised activities across countries easier. Many talent management systems have an underlying focus on a series of core values that are strongly reflective of the corporate and industry culture, and therefore more easily seen as being universal (Scullion and Collings, 2006).

The purpose of a successful talent management system is to attract, retain, develop and utilise employees in ways that create (Smilansky, 2004):

- sustainable commercial competitiveness through the alignment of employee competence, behaviours and intellectual energy with business activity
- higher levels of focused innovation
- improved staff engagement and commitment
- lower loss rates of knowledge and experience
- lower external resourcing costs.

When global lines of business are introduced, there is a more immediate relationship between the IHRM professional and the global leadership teams within major business functions or markets. Many organisations conduct various 'calibrations' of talent on a global basis in order to plan business development. International organisations want to know who their top people are and what the key roles are within the business that they need these people for. They want to know how they can develop people, get them to key positions, and build succession cover for these key positions. They have to develop a much deeper level of understanding about the links between the business agenda and the capabilities of the most talented people in the organisation, and also understand the potential for mobility around these people (Sparrow *et al*, 2004).

In recent years a new multi-disciplinary area of enquiry has emerged called global talent management (GTM). It has become a topical issue both for research and practice as competition between employers has become more generic and the importance placed on *global* talent, and the related supply and demand pressures, has shifted from the country level to the regional and global levels. These pressures have the potential to impact on the role of HRM in MNCs (Scullion and Starkey, 2000; Novicevic and Harvey, 2001; Sparrow *et al*, 2004; Ashton and Morton, 2005; Collings and Mellahi, 2009; Tarique and Schuler, 2010; Scullion and Collings, 2011; Farndale *et al*, 2010).

A decade ago studies began emphasising the key role of corporate HRM in GTM for the *top* talent across the company (Novicevic and Harvey, 2001; Scullion and Brewster, 2001). These studies found that for European firms shortages of international management talent were a significant constraint on the successful implementation of global strategies, a shortage of leadership talent in particular being a major obstacle faced by firms as they sought to operate on a global scale. The extent to which organisations can effectively manage their talent in this way often fails to live up to the hype (Cappelli, 2008).

Scullion, Sparrow and Farndale have examined the implications of this rise in global talent management for corporate HRM functions (Farndale *et al*, 2010; Sparrow *et al*, 2011; and Scullion *et al*, 2011). They note that there are of course a number of different philosophies evident in discussion of talent management – even within a single country. It may be considered the management of only the top elites in an organisation, or everybody might be deemed to be 'talent'. It may be considered to deal with either critical people or critical roles. In terms of practices, systems may be designed internally or externally, they may or may not have links to performance management or rewards, they may be focused on distinctions between performance versus potential, practices might be linked to more strategic issues such as organisational capabilities, strategic workforce planning or employer branding, and finally, the remit of the system may be domestic or global. Generally, such systems define talent in terms of the key positions within an organisation, rather than as the 'stars' who will fill these positions. GTM must therefore:

- focus on developing a global talent pool of people and appropriate flows of people to both fill these critical positions and enable their successful operation through the building of the necessary organisational capabilities

- involve the creation of a differentiated set of HRM practices to support the people filling the key positions through this combination of role, people and capability means, and

- enable the delivery of performance and organisational capabilities in the appropriate geographies.

This conceptualisation creates three new opportunities for the study of GTM:

- both a top-down (management-controlled approach to moving talent around the firm) and a bottom-up (self-initiated, culture-driven flow of talent through key positions) perspective on the impact of GTM on the corporate HRM role (Farndale *et al*, 2010)

- an expansion of the territory that might legitimately be considered part of a GTM system into marketing-driven concerns such as market-mapping and employer branding (Sparrow, 2007)

- an opportunity for HRM to redefine and demonstrate its contribution to international business strategy.

It is argued that regardless of the ups and downs in the international business cycle, there is a war for talent taking place (Cappelli, 2008; Michaels *et al*, 2001). Marketing strategies quickly become outdated and the pecking order of the most desired employees changes quickly. In order to attract and retain the best talent anywhere in the world, an organisation must have a strong and positive employer brand. Many international organisations therefore put considerable effort into developing an 'employee value proposition' (EVP) by identifying the most important features of working for them (Michaels *et al*, 2001) – here, HRM policy is influenced by marketing thinking. Employee value propositions are generally used to drive attraction and retention behaviour. The organisation is asking, 'Why should you buy my product or service – why would a highly talented person want to work in my organisation?' The EVP conveys a clear statement of some of the more explicit obligations that the organisation commits to.

In theory, EVPs should be aligned to each major unit within the organisation. However, most international organisations work hard to create a positive and more global brand for potential recruits. A key challenge for international organisations is therefore the extent to which it is possible to create such global EVPs. This entails offering a compelling value proposition to the employees of the organisation, and to understand and then to market the brand that the organisation represents across global labour markets that all have different values and different perceptions. The challenge for global organisations is to decide what the overriding message is of who they are and what they stand for.

As the world gets smaller, global organisations need to make sure that the way in which they are perceived as a company is similar wherever they go. What do their consumers want from them? What do current employees think? This involves constantly reselling to employees the proposition that their organisation is the place they should work. The challenge is to understand what makes a really good person want to stay with them globally. The answer affects the development of people, which is a key driver of retention, and finally impinges on how the organisation recruits. It affects how the organisation approaches the media, how it conducts its investor relations, how it designs compensation and benefits, and how it designs performance management systems – ie it informs all policies and procedures. These messages cannot be aspirational – they have to be grounded in what the organisation really offers and what potential employees really want. The processes must back up what the organisation says it is. The key messages to potential employees also must make sense in all the organisation's markets worldwide. The organisation has to pick out which messages it can match and where it is able to give out a message that can be fulfilled.

Sparrow *et al* (2004) noted a number of common responses to talent management in global organisations:

- researching into 'consumer insights' with current and potential employees, sister companies, external agencies, and benchmarking with external companies
- managing the 'talent pipeline' – trying to recruit 'ahead of the curve' instead of the more traditional vacancy-based recruitment
- communicating an awareness in graduate schools and businesses to get the people they are looking for
- developing internal talent pools around the world
- creating skilled and competent teams of assessors in different areas of the world
- managing recruitment suppliers on a global basis, introducing speed, cost and quality controls, establishing master contracts to co-ordinate the messages conveyed and the use of preferred partners, ensuring audit trails to protect against legal issues associated with global diversity
- e-enabling jobs notice boards, redesigning websites to convey important messages about the employer brand.

REFLECTIVE ACTIVITY

It can often be assumed that many talent management practices are the preserve of large multinationals. However, charities face similar issues of having to compete for a small number of talented people. For example, when a crisis arises, will that expert in dysentry work for Save the Children or for Oxfam? Although of course the financial resources that might be devoted to talent management strategies are more constrained, the practices and experiences of not-for-profit organisations in the international management area are very similar to those of large private sector firms.

Imagine you are the IHRM director of an international charity.

● What are the talent management issues that you believe you would have to deal with?

● What would be the key elements of your talent management strategy, and what would you need employees to do to 'make it happen'?

STRATEGIC WORKFORCE PLANNING

Strategic workforce planning (SWP) approaches are generally seen as a subset of talent management, although in terms of the HRM structure and reporting relationships, this is not always the case. In practice, organisations tend to set up networks of global experts, or special task forces, to undertake the work, because the results of a strategic workforce plan will have implications for several central functions such as international mobility, rewards and resourcing, those HRM professionals in-the-business (HRM business partners) and local HRM operations (HRM-in-the-country).

DEVELOPING AN ASIA TALENT PLAN AT ASTRAZENECA

CASE STUDIES

AstraZeneca is a leading global pharmaceutical company which by 2008 employed 67,000 people worldwide, 55 per cent in Europe, 30 per cent in America and 15 per cent in the rest of the world. In 2008 the HRM function undertook a project to 'develop an Asia talent plan', strengthening the talent pipeline for key leadership roles in the country and then more broadly developing a strategic workforce plan to identify the pipeline of skills and capabilities needed to support the business plan.

The first element involved the need to create robust and customised career plans for local employees, identify gaps in the internal leadership pipeline and document investment cases four years forward. An Asia Talent Pool

was created on the basis of reviews of performance track and talent data (assessments of potential). The career plan analysis identified key experiences still needed: navigating the global organisation, leadership skills demonstrated in working with other cultures and managing delivery through a global matrix organisation, management skills, professional skills in areas such as strategic marketing skills, business development and licensing, and language skills. A blend of local career development, short-term international moves but also long-term assignments designed around learning needs was selected. The international assignment process was redesigned around shared accountability for planning the assignment between host and home line managers, shifting to a primary objective of assignments being used for individual development with provision of local mentors rather than filling local skills gaps, and return roles planned before the outward assignment started.

The second element was the development of a forward Asian talent plan – looking three to five years out – and scoped around three geographical priorities: Japan, China and India (with follow-on plans created for Korea and Thailand). Each market created unique talent challenges – Japan is the second-largest pharmaceuticals market in the world and needs constant resourcing, China is an area of growth, India represents a strong market for scientific talent. AstraZeneca looked at competitor

practice – for example, Shell with its scenario-planning mentality was known to have developed plans for what would happen to talent should the Soviet Union have collapsed before it actually did. The planning process required the development of clarity around the mid- to long-term business strategy, reviews of current workforce data around demographics, hiring patterns, turnover and movement, establishing and reviewing external labour market data and trends, projecting future capability profiles, replacement costs, defining workforce optimisation plans around projected business volumes, staffing needs and alternative staffing models.

In many instances, SWP initiatives are also triggered by changes in the global supply of skills (see Chapter 15) or by the pressures created by demographic shifts.

THE JAPANESE RESPONSE TO DEPENDENCE ON CHINESE LABOUR AND MIGRATION

CASE STUDIES

Demographic trends are producing a shrinking workforce in Japan, and coupled with declining domestic spending this has increased demand in Japan for low-skilled workers in factories. China is also now Japan's largest trading partner, accounting for a quarter of Japanese exports. This creates an incentive for Japanese firms to make more effort to adapt to local customs and demands. The Japan International Training Co-operation Organisation was set up by five government ministries to oversee a skills transfer programme. Guest workers reportedly undertake high levels of overtime – mortality rates from heart disease and stress-related ailments amongst 20- to 30-year-old Chinese trainees is twice that of Japanese youth of the same

age (*Economist*, 2010a). Data from the Immigration Bureau of the Justice Ministry suggests that the number of Chinese trainees working in Japan has increased from 30,000 in 2002 to 80,000 in 2008, falling back to 60,000 in 2009 during the economic downturn. At the other end of the labour supply chain, subsidiaries of Toyota, Honda, Mitsumi Electric and Nippon Sheet Glass experienced industrial unrest amongst their suppliers in China in 2010. As China begins to shift from being the world's workshop to building a domestic consumer bas, wage demands have increased. Wages in foreign-owned factories have been rising by 10 to 15 per cent a year in 2010 (*Economist*, 2010b). The Japanese business lobby Keidanren argues that Japanese firms have been hit by these changes more because they have historically used Chinese operations mainly for inexpensive parts and labour-intensive assembly, but recently have been moving to higher-value work with more skilled staff. Their just-in-time production system leaves them vulnerable to disruption. In comparison with many other foreign-owned operations, decisions on pay are also not made at plant level but centrally, and dependent on a consensus-style system. The response has been threefold: higher pay (Honda increased wages by up to 24 per cent in China); higher promotion levels for local managers (Komatsu set a goal of having Chinese managers to lead all 16 of local subsidiaries by 2012); and moving more labour-intensive work to Vietnam, Thailand and Cambodia (the garment manufacturer Uniqlo is reducing its proportion of Chinese-made garments from 90 per cent to 65 per cent between 2013 and 2015).

EMPLOYER BRANDING

The second main integration role for IHRM professionals that we discuss is the contribution that they can make to the management of an employer brand on an international basis. Sparrow *et al* (2004) argue that the topics of employer branding and talent management are intimately linked for most global organisations. International organisations are concerned with their 'talent pipeline'. This means that they have to develop a much deeper level of understanding about the links between the business agenda and the capabilities of the most talented people in the organisation, and also understand the potential for mobility around these people. When they conduct such a calibration of talent on a global basis, they have to ask what this suggests for the planned business development. In short, when global lines of business are introduced, there is a more immediate relationship between the IHRM professional and the global leadership teams within major business functions or markets.

Not all international organisations seek global branding: banks, for example, have the choice of looking like a major interational operation with international branding, or retaining subsidaries they have taken over in a country with the local branding with the intention of selling themselves as 'local and close to the customer'. But the management of employer brands internationally is an important challenge for many large international organisations. Employer branding – the image of the organisation as seen through the eyes of *external* stakeholders – represents an extension of brand management and is another development whereby HRM thinking has been influenced by that of the marketing function. Building or defending the corporate brand or reputation has become a major concern in many industries. Employer branding requires consistency and uniformity in delivering the brand identity by all *internal* stakeholders, including employees. However, currently, we still know little about the links between HRM and marketing in the brand management process, despite increasing awareness that the HRM function is now becoming involved in this work on an international scale.

For global organisations, however, the challenge is how best to create an *authentic and legitimate* brand (Martin and Hetrick, 2006). We can all think of marketing material that serves to put people off, either through its blandness or its rhetoric. The need for authenticity involves constantly reselling an accurate and sustainable message.

CASE STUDIES

EMPLOYER BRAND AND LOCALISATION IN CHINA

In most national markets consultancies run surveys on along the lines of 'best employer' as perceived by graduates. By way of example, UNIVERSUM, active in this field, published data from over 58,000 students from mainland China in 90 universities (UNIVERSUM, 2011). Graduates are also flooding on to Asia's job market from local universities, and Asians with degrees from Western ones are returning home (*Economist*, 2011a). From 2003 to 2011 roughly 325,000 Chinese returned home after studying overseas – more than three times as many as in the entire two decades before. In addition to this positive change in talent supply, international organisations are looking for ready-made (business and political relationships) and people committed to staying in the countries. In 2008 Singapore granted 156,900 work visas to foreigners and less than half that number of jobs went to residents. Now the numbers are roughly equal.

Managing the employee value proposition in each overseas market becomes very important. In China, after leading the engineering ranking since 2008, China Mobile is no longer the most attractive employer among engineering students. China Mobile lost its number one position to SGCC. In the business ranking, China Mobile moved down to third, behind the Bank of China and Procter & Gamble. By way of example, HSBC is ninth, Apple 12th, Google 18th and Unilever 35th. The differences in employer brand image between Chinese organisations that are international employers and state-owned companies are also huge. State-owned companies are highly associated with secure employment and good work–life balance, whereas international companies are very much associated with an international career, challenging and varied work, and attractive and innovative products. For Chinese female students, having an international career is more important than it is for male students, and this means a desire to live and work overseas for a period.

Martin and Hetrick (2009) examine employer branding as an international co-ordination strategy within IHRM. IHRM researchers see a trend among MNCs to use employer branding as an important tool for:

- creating a sense of 'corporateness' among often decentralised operations
- differentiating themselves in overseas labour markets.

That we do still know little about the links between HRM and marketing in the brand management process Martin and Hetrick (2009) feel is surprising, in that employer branding is being adopted as a means of reconciling a key tension faced by MNCs – balancing the needs for corporate integration, control and legitimacy on the one hand with local differentiation, autonomy and initiative on the other. Those authors develop a simplified model of the branding process, theorising key variables (such as corporate and organisational identity), reviewing the evidence as to whether it works in international context. Despite many supposed attractions to the practice, they highlight the challenges of facing unreceptive contexts for change (where MNC subsidiaries in different countries hold markedly different and somewhat negative views about the corporate headquarters' leadership, HRM and people management policies). Company image and positioning is difficult to manage internationally because cultural brands rely on corporate stories being seen as locally authentic and charismatically appealing to employees in settings which may be marked by large cultural and institutional distances between headquarters and subsidiaries.

Sparrow (2007) found that as organisations deal with employer branding issues on an international basis, the issues develop through a clear sequence over time. Initially, attention is given to 'stabilising' key people management processes across different geographical operations (making sure that recruitment, performance management, communication activities and so forth operate to the same levels of professionalisam). Once this has been done, decisions can then be made about the 'look and consistency' of the employer brand. Basic considerations include:

- creating the same physical brand – for example, the logo and literature – drawing upon the business strategy and the reasons it provides as to why the organisation is now operating in a particular international labour market

- sharing a common mission, vision and set of stated values: attention is given to communicating these consistently through the various programmes and media

- setting minimum HRM standards and conditions to shape the nature of employee engagement

- examining how the pay strategy and associated benchmarks define the calibre of applicants

- understanding how this helps to bring consistency to the employee experience in terms of competencies and leadership capability.

It should be clear from the above that managing the employer brand across international operations as a way of bringing some consistency into HRM requires 'judgements' to be made about the capability of the international HR operations to manage such a sophisticated task.

 REFLECTIVE ACTIVITY

In the light of what you know about IHRM now that you are in the last chapter, how easy do you think it is to manage a global employer brand? What issues would an IHRM professional expect to have to manage? To answer this, analyse the HRM activities of an organisation (yours, perhaps) across a series of countries, and answer the following questions:

- How important is it that the performance management and development processes are made the same across all the countries as early as possible? What sorts of adjustments to these processes will inevitably have to be made for local cultural and legal reasons?

- How much does the organisation's international operations vary in terms of their adherence to standards and procedures in the area of recruitment? Is there a need to set minimum standards for the conduct of HRM before you can create a consistent brand?

- What input is needed from in-country HRM partners to a branding strategy intended to work across countries, and what central supervision is necessary?

- Does pay strategy in different countries define the calibre of applicants that can be attracted? If you attract a different calibre of manager across countries because of this, does it matter? Does it impact on the way that employees will 'experience' the brand?

- Do you have similar 'employee engagement' data across the organisation's operations? If scores differ, does this reflect different national values, or different business models being applied, or different levels of professional line management?

GLOBAL KNOWLEDGE MANAGEMENT STRATEGIES AND MANAGEMENT THROUGH GLOBAL NETWORKS

The third and final integration activity for IHRM functions that we discuss here is the development of intellectual integration through the creation of shared knowledge bases. In a competitive marketplace, the act of integrating disparate sources of knowledge within the bounds of the organisation has become a source of advantage (Grant, 1996). For IHRM professionals there is capability-building agenda that is often more concerned with the up-skilling of a business function, and with spending more time engaging with the leadership teams of these functions.

There has been considerable attention paid to the issue of knowledge management in recent years. Sparrow (2006c) outlined five main forms of global knowledge management, or integration mechanisms, that are currently dominating the actions of organisations:

- organisational designs, such as the use of centres of excellence (discussed earlier)

- managing systems and technology-driven approaches to global knowledge management systems

- capitalising on expatriate advice networks (see Chapter 14)

- co-ordinating international management teams (see Chapter 15)

- developing communities of practice (COPs) or global expertise networks.

We concentrate here on the role of knowledge management in the work of IHRM managers. Global networking is one of the ways that the IHRM function can help build this capability across international operations. Parkhe *et al* (2006; p560) state that:

Networks are reshaping the global business architecture ... the ubiquity of networks and networking at the industry, firm, group, and individual levels has attracted significant research attention.

Historically, global information, insight into local conditions and best practice have all tended to be shared through the process of IHRM professionals just talking to each other – getting groups of people together within the organisation to facilitate some transfer of learning. Networks have then always been important within IHRM. However, they are now considered to play a critical role. Sparrow and Brewster (2006) argue that network- and project-based structures have had a significant impact on the conduct and quality of IHRM interventions and on the career trajectories of HRM professionals. However, there is little clarity about the extent to which these networks can be local as well as global, external as well as internal.

What is clear is that there is considerable 'social capital' within these communities (see Chapter 13). Mäkelä *et al* (2009) have examined the level of human and social capital that different archetypes of subsidiary staffing are associated with, and how this influences the management of knowledge stocks and flows within the MNC. They identified four subsidiary staffing archetypes:

- *local-internal* – may carry a dual role in both exploiting existing knowledge stocks in their local markets and transferring market knowledge to the headquarters, through the co-existence of a high level of market knowledge and external social capital combined with at least some degree of MNC-specific knowledge and social capital

- *local-external* – can play a valuable role in the exploration of new non-redundant knowledge

- *global-internal* – serves a key function in transferring knowledge and best practices from the headquarters to the subsidiaries

- *global-external* – only has limited human- and social-capital related advantages.

They suggest that each type can be used for different knowledge-related purposes within the organisation.

Tregaskis *et al* (2005) conducted interviews in six firms describing the function, structure and processes typically associated with IHRM networks. These networks can be run through top-down or more collaborative remits and operate through leadership, project or special-event team structures. They serve a range of functions including policy development and implementation, information capture, exploitation of knowledge, sharing of best practice, achieving political buy-in and socialisation of members. Face-to-face contact is important in the process of relationship- and reputation-building but is often supplemented by virtual working as a way of signalling more global cultures. The level of localisation is generally driven by the politics of acquisition, size, expertise and level of resistance in subsidiaries. HRM leadership through networks can facilitate more collaborative solutions, but this depends on the strategic capability of the function, board-level support and strength of IHRM networks. The social ties that the HRM specialists can develop across the globe and the extent and value of those ties become important elements of the armoury of the IHRM specialist (Sparrow *et al*, 2009).

REFLECTIVE ACTIVITY

What difficulties might organisations face in building IHRM networks?

How might these be overcome?

Global networks serve several important purposes (Sparrow *et al,* 2004):

- providing a forum to encourage innovation and growth throughout the business, and a vehicle to get the right people onto the right teams in order to make this happen

- encouraging HR professionals and line managers to think beyond their 'own patch'

- creating a situation whereby membership of the network provides advantages in terms of better-quality implementation for both the line managers and the HRM professionals

- getting stakeholders (the senior HRM community, presidents in businesses) to buy in to business changes

- forcing the business agenda in forums outside the networks in subtle ways based on shared insight within the network.

THE ROLE OF GLOBAL HRM NETWORKS

- to provide and enable value-added and cost-effective global, regional, and local solutions in a series of core HR processes

- to identify customer-driven pan-national issues

- to design solutions to meet specific customer needs and support the corporate people management strategy

- to demonstrate to customers that global connectivity adds value by sharing knowledge and expertise

- to ensure that knowledge and intellectual property that resides within HRM 'silos' is made freely available to all of the organisation.

REFLECTIVE ACTIVITY

Take the example of an organisation that you know:

- How would you rate it in terms of its support for global networking?

Compare your conclusions with those of colleagues.

KEY LEARNING POINTS

- As organisations operate more internationally, the HRM function becomes the gatekeeper of both national institutional and cultural differences, advising on which processes can be standardised and which must remain localised.

- The HRM function also becomes a knowledge agent that transfers ideas across businesses, functions and geographical boundaries within the global firm.

- The processes and capabilities for becoming a strategic partner for the business are: the achievement of board-level representation, the ability to fully understand the business, the need for excellent analytical and planning skills, the ability to measure the effectiveness of HRM interventions.

- However, being a strategic partner for the business is not the same thing for HRM professionals working in domestically based organisations as for their colleagues working in international organisations: a much more strategic role awaits the global HRM function. This brings with it the need for additional knowledge and abilities on the part of HRM professionals.

- The added value of the HRM function in an international organisation lies in its ability to manage the delicate balance between overall co-ordinated systems and sensitivity to local needs, including cultural differences, in a way that aligns with both business needs and senior management philosophy.

- As the process of optimisation and standardisation of HRM processes takes place in many organisations, facilitated by the e-enablement of HRM systems and procedures on a regional, and in some cases global, scale, new systems are being put in place.

- The IHRM function has to work through the structural and organisation design issues that changes in the organisation's business model have invoked, and has to structure itself and design its service offerings in a way that enables it to support these wider business changes

- IHRM research has examined the degree of global integration or local responsiveness in subsidiary HRM practices by assessing whether a particular HRM practice or configuration of HRM practices resemble local practices, parent firm's practices or a hybrid of the two, and attempted to identify the contextual determinants of the balance.

- The organisational domain within MNCs is always contested – it is characterised by 'actors' who have competing rationalities, coming as they do from multiple institutional contexts – contexts that may be influenced by transnational, home- and host-national institutions.

- Progress in globalising HRM service delivery is being made in three areas: technology (commonality of underlying systems and databases); process streamlining (optimisation of processes); and sourcing (making decisions about the possible centralisation or outsourcing of some areas of activity).

- The most common superordinate themes in the process of globalising HRM are: talent management and strategic workforce planning, corporate and global brands, and global knowledge management strategies.

- A distinction is emerging between IHRM and global HRM.

- Traditionally, IHRM has been about managing an international workforce – the expatriates, frequent commuters, cross-cultural team members and specialists involved in international knowledge transfer.

- Global HRM revolves around the ability of the organisation to find a concept that has 'relevance' to managers across several countries. It is not just simply about covering these staff around the world. It concerns managing IHRM activities through the application of global rule-sets to HRM processes.

LEARNING QUESTIONS

1 What are the implications for IHRM departments of the vogue for outsourcing HRM activities?

2 Identify the effects of thinking about resource capability as the key to competitive success for an IHRM department.

3 What would be the HRM effects of creating a centre of excellence at the British headquarters of an MNC? How might these change if it was decided that the centre should be located in Hong Kong?

4 How might the concepts of HRM centres of excellence and of outsourcing HRM be connected?

5 To what extent is there still a role for the corporate HRM function in IHRM?

6 Is it possible to create an employee value proposition on a global scale?

7 What types of knowledge do global HRM expertise networks need to transfer?

8 What will be the impact of working through networks on the careers of IHRM professionals?

9 Who will act as the guardians of national culture if not the IHRM function? Does this role still matter?

EXPLORE FURTHER

Sparrow, P. R., Brewster, C. J. and Harris, H. (2004) *Globalizing HR*, London, Routledge. This is the original bool on Globalising HR.

Sparrow, P. R., Brewster, C. J., Budhwar, P. and De Cieri, H. (2012) *The Globalization of Human Resource Management*, London, Routledge. This is the successor book to the above.

Useful articles on some of the component HR strategies are:

Björkman, I. and Lervik, J. E. (2007) 'Transferring HR practices within multinational corporations', *Human Resource Management Journal*, 17: 320–335.

Edwards, T., Colling, T. and Ferner, A. (2007) 'Conceptual approaches to the transfer of employment practices in multinational companies: an integrated approach', *Human Resource Management Journal*, 17: 201–217.

Farndale, E., Scullion, H. and Sparrow, P. R. (2010) 'The role of the corporate HR function in global talent management', *Journal of World Business*, 45 (2): 161–168.

Frost, A., Birkinshaw, J. M. and Prescott, C. E. (2002) 'Centers of excellence in multinational corporations', *Strategic Management Journal*, 23 (11): 997–1018.

Mäkelä, K., Björkman, I. and Ehrnrooth,

M. (2009) 'MNC subsidiary staffing architecture: building human and social capital within the organization', *International Journal of Human Resource Management*, 20 (6): 1273–1290.

Tarique, I. and Schuler, R. (2010) 'Global talent management: literature review, integrative framework, and suggestions for further research', *Journal of World Business*, 45: 122–133.

References

Abramovsky, L., Griffith, R. and Sako, M. (2005) *Offshoring: Myth and Reality*, London, Advanced Institute of Management Research.

Adams, J. S. (1963) Towards an understanding of inequity. *The Journal of Abnormal and Social Psychology*, Vol 67(5), pp422–436.

Adams, K. (1991) 'Externalisation vs specialisation: what is happening to personnel?', *Human Resource Management Journal*, 1 (4): 40–54.

Adler, N. J. (1984a) 'Women in international management: where are they?', *California Management Review*, 26 (4): 78–89.

Adler, N. J. (1984b) 'Women do not want international careers: and other myths about international management', *Organizational Dynamics*, 19 (3): 79–85.

Adler, N. J. (1984c) 'Expecting international success: female managers overseas', *Columbia Journal of World Business*, 19 (3): 79–85.

Adler, N. J. (1986) *International Dimensions Of Organizational Behaviour*, 1st edition, Boston, MA, PWS–Kent.

Adler, N. J. (1987) 'Women as androgynous managers: a conceptualisation of the potential for American women in international management', *International Journal of Intercultural Relations*, 3: 407–436.

Adler, N. J. (1993) 'Competitive frontiers: women managers in the Triad', *International Studies of Management and Organizations*, 23: 3–23.

Adler, N. J. (1997) *International Dimensions of Organisational Behavior*, 3rd edition, Cincinnati, Ohio, South Western Publishing (a part of Cengage Learning, Inc).

Adler, N. J. and Bartholomew S. (1992) 'Managing globally competent people', *Academy of Management Executive*, 6 (3): 52–65.

Adler, N. J. and Ghadar, F. (1990) 'International strategy from the perspective of people and culture: the North American context', in A. Rugman (ed.) *Research in Global Strategic Management*, Vol.1, Greenwood, CT, JAI Press.

Adsit, D. J., London, M., Crom, S. and Jones, D. (1997) 'Cross-cultural differences in upward ratings in a multinational company', *International Journal of Human Resource Management*, 8: 385–401.

Aguinis, H. (2007) *Performance Management*, 2nd edition, Upper Saddle River, NJ, Pearson/Prentice Hall.

Aiken, L. H., Buchan, J., Sochalski, J., Nichols, B. and Powell, M. (2004) 'Trends in international nurse migration', *Health Affairs*, 23 (3): 69–78.

Ajzen, I. (1985) 'From intentions to actions: a theory of planned behaviour', in J. Kuhl and J. Beckman (eds) *Action Control: From cognition to behaviour*, New York, Springer-Verlag, pp 11–39.

Al-Ali, J. (2008) 'Emiratisation: drawing UAE nationals into their surging economy', *International Journal of Sociology and Social Policy*, 28 (9/10): 365–379.

Al-Enzi, A. (2002) 'Kuwait's employment policy: its formulation, implications and challenges', *International Journal of Public Administration*, 25 (7): 885–900.

Al-Hamadi, A. B. and Budhwar, P. S. (2006) 'Human resource management in Oman'.in P. S.

Budhwar and K. Mellahi (eds) *Managing Human Resources in the Middle East*, London, Routledge, pp40–56.

Al-Hamadi, A. B., Budhwar, P. S. and Shipton, H. (2007) 'Management of human resources in Oman', *International Journal of Human Resource Management*, 18 (1): 100–113.

Albert, M. (1991) *Capitalisme Contre Capitalisme*, Paris, Seuil.

Aldous, J. (1969) 'Occupational characteristics and males' role performance in the family', *Journal of Marriage and Family*, 31: 707–712.

Alewell, D., Hauff, S., Thommes, K. and Weiland, K. (2009) 'Triggers of HR outsourcing decisions – an empirical analysis of German firms', *International Journal of Human Resource Management*, 20 (7): 1599–1617.

Ali, A. J. (1999) 'The evolution of work ethic and management thought: an Islamic view', in H. Kao, D. Sinha and B. Wilpert (eds) *Management and Cultural Values*, New Delhi, Sage, pp197–212.

Ali, A. J. (2011) 'Talent management in the Middle East', in H. Scullion and D. G. Collings (eds) *Global Talent Management*, London, Routledge, pp155–177.

Ali, A. J. and Al-Kazemi, A. (2006) 'Human resource management in Kuwait', in P. S. Budhwar and K. Mellahi (eds) *Managing Human Resources in the Middle East*, London, Routledge, pp79–96.

Amable, B. (2003) *The Diversity of Modern Capitalism*, Oxford, Oxford University Press.

Andersen, S. K. and Mailand, M. (2005) 'The Danish Flexicurity Model: The Role of the Collective Bargaining System', Faos Working paper, Copenhagen, Faos.

Andreason, A. W. and Kinneer, K. D. (2005) 'Repatriation adjustment problems and the successful reintegration of expatriates and their families', *The Journal of Behavioral and Applied Management*, 6: 109–126.

Angwin, D. and Vaara, E. (2005) '"Connectivity" in merging organizations: beyond traditional cultural perspectives', *Organization Studies*, 26 (10): 1445–1453.

Antal, A. and Izraeli, D. (1993) 'Women managers from a global perspective: women managers in their international homelands and as expatriates', in E. Fagenson (ed.) *Women in Management: Trends, issues and challenges in management diversity – Women and Work*, Vol.4., Newbury Park, CA, Sage.

Antoni, C., Bergen, A., Baeten, X., Verbruggen, A., Leuven, V., Emans, B., Hulkko, K., Vartiainen, M., Kessler, I. and Neu, E. (2005) *Wage And Working Conditions In The European Union – Project No. 0261: Final Report,* European Foundation for the Improvement of Living and Working Conditions, Luxembourg, Office for Official Publication of the European Community.

Antoni, C. H., Baeten, X., Emans, B. J. M. and Kira, M. (2007) *Shaping pay in Europe: a stakeholder approach.* Oxford. P.I.E. Peter Lang.

Aparicio-Valverde, M. and Soler, C. (1996) 'Flexibility in Spain', in *Cranet-E Working Time and Contract Flexibility,*Report prepared for the European Commission, Directorate-General V. Centre for European HRM, Cranfield University.

Appelbaum, E., Bailey, T., Berg, P. and Kalleberg, A. L. (2000) *Manufacturing Advantage: Why high-performance work systems pay off*, Ithaca, NY, Cornell University Press.

Argyris, C. (1964) *Integrating the Individual and the Organisation*, New York, Wiley.

Armstrong, M. (1999) *A Handbook of Human Resource Management Practice*, London, Kogan Page.

Armstrong, M. (2000) *Performance Management Practice: Key practices and practical guidelines*, London, Kogan Page.

Armstrong, M. (2006) *Employee Reward*, 3rd Edition, London, CIPD.

Armstrong, M. and Baron, A. (1998) *Performance Management: The new realities*, CIPD, London.

Arrowsmith, J., Marginson, P. and Sisson, K. (2003) 'Externalisation and internalisation in Europe: variation in the role of large companies', *Industrielle Beziehungen*, 10 (3): 363–392.

Arthur, L. (2002) *Work-Life Balance: Towards an agenda for policy learning between Britain and Germany*, Anglo-German Foundation for the Study of Industrial Society.

Arthur, W. and Rousseau, D. M. (1996) *Boundaryless Careers*, Oxford, Blackwell.

Ashkenas, R., Ulrich, D., Jick, T. and Kerr, S. (1995) *The Boundaryless Organization*, San Francisco, CA, Jossey-Bass.

Ashkanasy, N. M., Trevor-Roberts, E. and Earnshaw, L. (2002) 'The Anglo cluster: legacy of the British Empire', *Journal of World Business*, 37: 28–39.

Ashton, C. and Morton, L. (2005) 'Managing talent for competitive advantage', *Strategic HR Review*, 4 (5): 28–31.

Ashton, D. and Felstead, D. (2001) 'From training to lifelong learning: the birth of the knowledge society?' in J. Storey (ed.) *HRM: A critical text*, London, Thomson Learning.

Atkinson, J. (1984) 'Manpower strategies for flexible organisations', *Personnel Management*, 16 (8): 32–35.

Atkinson, J. and Meager, N. (1986) 'Is flexibility just a flash in the pan?', *Personnel Management*, 18 (9): 26–29.

Atwater L., Waldman D., Ostroff, C. C. and Johnson K. M. (2005) 'Self–other agreement: comparing relationship with performance in the US and Europe', *International Journal of Selection and Assessment*, 13: 25–40.

Avery, G., Donnenberg, G. and Hilb, M. (1999) 'Challenges for management development in the German-speaking nations for the twenty-first century', *Journal of Management Development*, 18 (1): 18.

Awasthi V. N., Chow C. W. and Wu A. (2001) 'Cross-cultural differences in the behavioral consequences of imposing performance evaluation and reward systems: and experimental investigation', *International Journal of Accounting*, 36: 291–309.

Aycan, Z. (1997) 'Expatriate adjustment as a multifaceted phenomenon: individual and organisational level predictors', *International Journal of Human Resource Management*, 8 (4): 434–456.

Aycan, Z. (2005) 'The interplay between cultural and institutional/structural contingencies in human resource management practices', *International Journal of Human Resource Management*, 16 (7): 1083–1119.

Aycan, Z. (2006) 'Human resource management in Turkey', in P. S. Budhwar and K. Mellahi (eds) *Managing Human Resources in the Middle East*, London, Routledge, pp160–180.

Aycan, Z., Al-Hamadi, A. B., Davis, A. and Budhwar, P. (2007) 'Cultural orientations and preferences for HRM policies and practices: the case of Oman', *International Journal of Human Resource Management*, 18 (1): 11–32.

Aycan, Z., Kanungo, R.N., Mendonca, M., Yu, K., Deller, J., Stahl G. and Khursid, A. (2000) 'Impact of culture on human resource management practices: a 10-country comparison', *Applied Psychology: An International Review*, 49 (1): 192–221.

Bach, S. (2000) 'From performance appraisal to performance management', in S. Bach and K. Sisson (eds) *Personnel Management*, 3rd edition, Oxford, Blackwell.

Bacon, N. and Storey, J. (1993) 'Individualization of the employment relationship and the implications for trade unions', *Employee Relations*, 15 (1): 5–17.

Baglioni, G. (1990) 'Industrial relations in Europe in the 1980s', in G. Baglioni and C. Crouch (eds) *European Industrial Relations: The challenge of flexibility*, Newsbury Park, CA, Sage.

Bai, X. and Bennington, L. (2005) 'Performance appraisal in the Chinese state-owned coal industry', *International Journal of Business Performance Management*, 7 (3): 275–287.

Baird, L., Meshoulam, I. and DeGive, G. (1983) 'Meshing human resources planning with strategic business planning: a model approach', *Personnel*, 60 (5): 14–25.

Baker, J. and Ivancevich, J. (1971) 'The assignment of American executives abroad: systematic, haphazard or chaotic?', *California Management Review*, 13 (3): 39–44.

Baldry, C. (1994) 'Convergence in Europe: a matter of perspective', *Industrial Relations Journal*, 25 (2): 96–109.

Banai, M. and Harry, W. (2004) 'Boundaryless global careers', *International Studies of Management and Organization*, 34 (3): 96–120.

Banal-Estañol, A. and Seldeslachts, J. (2005) 'Merger failures', CIG Working Papers, SP II 2005–09, *Wissenschaftszentrum Berlin (WZB)*, Research Unit, Competition and Innovation (CIG).

Banal-Estañol, A. and Seldeslachts, J. (2009) 'Merger failures', Economics Working Papers 1192, Department of Economics and Business, Universitat Pompeu Fabra.

Bandura, A. (2002) 'Social cognitive theory in cultural context', *Applied Psychology: An International Review*, 51 (2): 269–90.

Barbash, J. (1987) 'Like nature, industrial relations abhors a vacuum: the case of the union-free strategy', *Industrial Relations*, 42 (1): 168–178.

Barber, A. E. (1998) *Recruiting Employees*, London, Sage.

Barkema, H. G. and Gomez-Mejia, L. R. (1998) 'Managerial compensation and firm performance: a general research framework', *Academy of Management Journal*, 41: 135–145.

Barnes, D. and Todd, F. (1977) *Communication and Learning in Small Groups*, London, Routledge & Kegan Paul.

Barney, J. B. (1991) 'Firm resources and sustained competitive advantage', *Journal of Management*, 17: 99–120.

Barney, J. B. (1997) *Gaining and Sustaining Competitive Advantage*, Reading, MA, Addison-Wesley.

Bartlett, C. A. and Ghoshal, S. (1986) 'Tap your subsidiaries for global reach', *Harvard Business Review*, 4 (6): 87–94.

Bartlett, C. A. and Ghoshal, S. (1987) 'Managing across borders: new strategic requirements', *Sloan Management Review*, 28 (Summer): 7–17.

Bartlett, C. A. and Ghoshal, S. (1989) *Managing Across Borders: The transnational solution*, Boston, MA, Harvard Business School Press.

Baruel, K. (1996) 'Spain in the context of European human resource management', in T. Clarke (ed.) *European Human Resource Management*, Oxford, Blackwell, pp93–117.

Barzantny, C. and Festing, M. (2008) 'Performance management in France and Germany', in A. Varma, P. S. Budhwar and A.S. DeNisi (eds) *Performance Management Systems: A global perspective*, London, Routledge.

Bassanini, A., Nunziata, L. and Venn, D. (2008) *Job Protection Legislation and Productivity Growth in OECD Countries*, IZA Discussion Paper No.3555, Paris, Institute for the Study of Labour.

Beatty, R. and Schneider. C. (1997) 'New HR roles to impact organizational performance: from partners to players', *Human Resource Management*, 36: 29–37.

Beaverstock, J. (2004) 'Managing across borders: knowledge management and expatriation in professional service legal firms', *Journal of Economic Geography*, 4 (2): 157–179.

Bebchuk, L. and Roe, M. (1999) 'A theory of path dependence of corporate ownership and governance', *Stanford Law Review*, 52: 127–170.

Becker, B. and Gerhart, B. (1996) 'The impact of human resource practices on organisational performance: progress and prospects', *Academy of Management Journal*, 39: 779–801.

Becker, B., Huselid, M., Pickus, P. and Spratt, M. (1997) 'HR as a source of shareholder value: research and recommendations', *Human Resource Management*, 36 (1): 39–47.

Bell, J., McNaughton, R., Young, S. and Crick, D. (2003) 'Towards an integrative model of small firm internationalisation', *Journal of International Entrepreneurship*, 1: 339–362.

Bender, K. A. and Elliott, R. F. (2003) *Decentralised Pay Setting. A study of the outcomes of collective bargaining reform in the civil service in Australia, Sweden and the UK*, Aldershot, Ashgate Publishing.

Benito, C. R. G., Tomassen, S., Bonache, J. and Pla-Barber, J. (2005) 'A transaction cost analysis of staffing decisions in multi-national operations', *Scandinavian Journal of Management*, 21: 101–126.

Bennett, N., Ketchen, D. and Schultz, E. (1998) 'An examination of factors associated with the integration of human resource management and strategic decision-making', *Human Resource Management*, 37: 3–16.

Bennett, R. (1997) *European Business*, London, Pitman.

Bento, R. and Ferreira, L. (1992) 'Incentive pay and organisational culture', in W. Bruns (ed.) *Performance Measurement, Evaluation, and Incentives*, Boston, MA, Harvard Business School Press.

Berger, P. L. and Luckman, T. (1967) *The Social Construction of Reality*, Garden City, NY, Doubleday.

Berggren, C. (1993) 'Lean production: the end of history?', *Work, Employment and Society*, 7 (2): 163–188.

Berggren, C. (1994) *The Volvo Experience: Alternatives to lean production in the auto industry*, London, Sage.

Berrell, M., Wrathall, J. and Wright, P. M. (2001) 'A model for Chinese management education: adapting the case study method to transfer management knowledge', *Journal of Cross Cultural Management*, 8 (1): 28–66.

Berry, J. W. (1966) 'Temne and Eskimo perceptual skills', *Journal of Personality and Social Psychology*, 7: 415–418.

Bevan, S. (1996) *Who cares? Business benefits of carer-friendly employment policies*, Brighton, Institute for Employment Studies.

BGRS (2010) *Global Relocation Trends Survey 2010*, London, Brookfield Global Relocation Services.

Bhaskar-Shrinivas, P., Harrison, D. A., Shaffer, M. A. and Luk, D. M. (2005) 'Input-based and time-based models of international adjustment: meta-analytic evidence and theoretical extensions', *Academy of Management Journal*, 48 (2): 257–281.

Bielenski, H., Alaluf, M., Atkinson, J., Bellini, R., Castillo, J. J., Donati, P., Graverson, G., Huygen, F. and Wickham J. (1992) *New Forms of Work and Activity: A survey of experiences at establishment level in eight European countries*, Dublin, European Foundation for the Improvement of Working and Living Conditions, Working Papers.

Birkinshaw, J. M. and Morrison, A. J. (1995) 'Configurations of strategy and structure in subsidiaries of multinational corporations', *Journal of International Business Studies*, 4: 729–753.

Biron, M., Farndale, E. and Paauwe, J. (2011) 'Performance management effectiveness: lessons from world-leading firms', *International Journal of Human Resource Management*, 22 (6): 1294–1311.

Björkman, I. (2006) 'International human resource management research and institutional theory', in G. Stahl and I. Björkman (eds) *Handbook of research in International HRM*, Cheltenham, UK, Edward Elgar, pp463–474.

Björkman, I. and Furu, P. (2000) 'Determinants of variable pay for top managers of foreign subsidiaries in Finland', *International Journal of Human Resource Management*, 11 (4): 698–713.

Björkman, I. and Lervik, J. E. (2007) 'Transferring HR practices within multinational corporations', *Human Resource Management Journal*, 17: 320–335.

Björkman, I. and Lu, Y. (1999) 'The management of human resources in Chinese-Western ventures', *Journal of World Business*, 34: 306–324

Björkman, I. and Lu, Y. (2001) 'Institutionalization and bargaining power explanations of HRM practices in international joint ventures – the case of Chinese-Western joint ventures', *Organization Studies*, 22 (3): 491–512.

Björkman, I., Barner-Rasmussen, W., Ehrnrooth, M., and Mäkelä, K. (2009) 'Performance management across borders', in P. R. Sparrow (ed.) *Handbook of International Human Resource Management*, Chichester, John Wiley & Sons.

Björkman, I., Fey, C. F. and Park, H. J. (2007) 'Institutional theory and MNC subsidiary HRM practices: evidence from a three-country study', *Journal of International Business Studies*, 38: 430–446.

Black, J. S. (1992) 'Coming home: the relationship of expatriate expectations with repatriation adjustment and work performance', *Human Relations*, 45 (2): 177–192.

Black, J. S. and Gregersen, H. B. (1991) 'Antecedents to cross-cultural adjustment for expatriates in Pacific Rim assignments', *Human Relations*, 44: 497–515.

Black, J. S. and Mendenhall, M. E. (1989) 'A practical but theory-based framework for selecting cross-cultural training methods', *Human Resource Management*, 28: 511–539.

Black, J. S. and Stephens, G. K. (1989) 'The influence of the spouse on American expatriate adjustment in overseas assignments', *Journal of Management*, 15: 529–544.

Black, J. S., Mendenhall, M. E. and Oddou, G. (1991) 'Toward a comprehensive model of international adjustment: an integration of multiple theoretical perspectives', *Academy of Management Review*, 16: 291–317.

Black, J. S., Morrison, A. and Gregersen H. (1999) *Global Explorers: The next generation of leaders*, New York, Routledge.

Blake, R. and Mouton, J. (1976) *Consultation*, Reading, Mass., Addison-Wesley.

Blanchflower, D. and Freeman, R. (1990) *Going Different Ways: Unionism in the US and other advanced OECD countries*, Centre for Economic Performance Discussion Paper 5, LSE, London.

Blanchflower, D. and Freeman, R. (1992) 'Unionism in the United States and other advanced OECD countries', *Industrial Relations*, 31 (1): 56–80.

Bloom, M. and Milkovich, G. T. (1999) 'A SHRM perspective on international compensation', in P. M. Wright, L. D. Dyer, J. W. Boudreau and G. T. Milkovich (eds) *Strategic Human Resources Management in the Twenty-First Century*, Stamford, CT, JAI Press.

Bloom, M.B., Milkovich, G.T., and Mitra, A. (2003) 'International compensation: learning from how managers respond to variations in local host contexts', *International Journal of Human Resource Management*, 14(8): 1350–1367.

Bloom, N., Kretschmer, T. and Van Reenan, J. (2009) 'Work-life balance, management practices and productivity', in Freeman, R. B. and Shaw, K. L. (eds) *International Differences in the Business Practices and Productivity of Firms*, Chicago, University of Chicago Press.

Blyton, P. (1992) 'Flexible times? Recent developments in temporal flexibility', *Industrial Relations Journal*, 23 (1): 26–36

Blyton, P. and Turnbull P. (1992) *Reassessing Human Resource Management*, London, Sage Publications.

Blyton, P. and Turnbull, P. (2004) *Dynamics of Employee Relations*, 2nd/3rd edition, London, Macmillan.

Boisot, M. and Xing, G. L. (1991) 'The nature of managerial work in China', in N. Campbell, S. R. F. Plasschaert and D. H. Brown (eds) *Advances in Chinese Industrial Studies*: Volume 2, *The Changing Nature of Management in China*, London, JAI Press.

Bolkestein, F. (1999) 'The Dutch model: the high road that leads out of the Low Countries', *The Economist*, 22 May, 75–76.

Bolle, P. (1997) 'Part-time work: solution or trap?', *International Labour Review*, 136 (4): 1–18.

Bolton, P. and Dewatripont, M. (1994) 'The firm as a communication network', *Quarterly Journal of Economics*, 109 (4): 809–840.

Bonache, J. (2006) 'The compensation of expatriates: a review and a future research agenda', in G. Stahl and I. Björkman (eds) *Handbook of research in International HRM,* Cheltenham, UK, Edward Elgar, pp158–175.

Bonache, J. and Brewster, C. J. (2001a) 'Knowledge transfer and the management of expatriation', *Thunderbird International Business Review*, 43 (1): 145–168.

Bonache, J. and Brewster, C. J. (2001b) 'Expatriation: a developing research agenda', *Thunderbird International Business Review*, 43 (1): 3–20.

Bonache, J. and Fernandez, Z. (1999) 'Multinational companies: a resource based approach', in C. Brewster and H. Harris (eds) *International Human Resource Management, Contemporary Issues in Europe*, London, Routledge.

Bonache, J., Brewster, C. J. and Suutari, V. (2007) 'International mobility and careers: editorial', special edition *International Studies in Management and Organization.*

Bond, S., Hyman, J., Summers, J. and Wise, S. (2002) *Family-Friendly Working? Putting policy into practice*, York, Joseph Rowntree Foundation.

Bondarouk, T. and Ruël, H. (2009) 'Structuring the IT-enabled transformation of HR: an HRM frames analysis in an international company', in P. R. Sparrow (ed.) *Handbook of International HR Research: Integrating people, process and context*, Oxford, Blackwell, pp271–292.

Bondarouk, T., Ruël, H., Guiderdoni-Jourdain, K. and Oiry, E (2009) (eds) *Handbook of Research on E-Transformation and Human Resource Management Technologies: Organizational outcomes and challenges*, New York, Hershey.

Borgonjon, J. and Vanhonacker, W. R (1992) 'Modernizing China's managers', *China Business Review*, 19 (5): 12.

Boselie, P., Dietz, G. and Boon, C. (2005) 'Commonalities and contradictions in research on human resource management and performance.' *Human Resource Management Journal*, 15, 3, 67–94.

Boselie, P., Farndale, E. and Paauwe, J. (2011) 'Performance management', in C. J. Brewster and W. Mayrhofer (eds) *Handbook of Research in Comparative Human Resource Management*, Cheltenham, Edward Elgar Publishing.

Bouquet, C. and Birkinshaw, J. (2008) 'Weight versus voice: how foreign subsidiaries gain attention from corporate headquarters', *Academy of Management Journal*, 51 (3): 577–601.

Bourdieu, P. and Wacquant, L. J. D. (1992) *An Invitation to Reflexive Sociology*, Chicago, IL, University of Chicago Press.

Bourguignon, A (1998) 'L'évaluation de la performance: un instrument de gestion éclaté', *Rapport de recherché, ESSEC-CR-DR – 98 –042.*

Bournois, F,. Chauchat. J. H. and Rousillon. S. (1994) 'Training and management development in Europe', in Brewster, C. and Hegewisch. A. (eds) *Policy and Practice in European Human Resource Management*, London, Routledge, pp122–138.

Boxall, P. (1993) 'The significance of human resource management: a reconsideration of the evidence', *International Journal of Human Resource Management*, (3): 645–664.

Boxall, P. (1995) 'Building the theory of comparative HRM', *Human Resource Management Journal*, 5 (5): 5–17.

Boxall, P. and Purcell, J. (2011) Strategy and Human Resource Management – Management, Work and Organisations, 3rd edition, Basingstoke, Palgrave Macmillan.

Boyer, R. (2005) 'How and why capitalisms differ', *Economy and Society*, 34 (4): 509–557.

Boyer, R. (2006) 'How do institutions cohere and change?', in G. Wood and P. James (eds) *Institutions and Working Life*, Oxford, Oxford University Press, pp13–61.

Boyer, R. and Hollingsworth, J. R. (1997) 'From national embeddedness to spatial and institutional nestedness', in J. R. Hollingsworth and R. Boyer (eds) *Contemporary Capitalism: The embeddedness of institutions*, Cambridge and New York, Cambridge University Press.

Bozionelos, N. and Wang, L. (2007) 'An investigation on the attitudes of Chinese workers towards individually-based performance-related reward systems', *International Journal of Human Resource Management*, 18 (2): 284–302.

Brady, D. (2002) 'Rethinking the ratrace', *Business Week*, 26 August: 142–143.

Brandl, J. and Pohler, D. (2010) 'The human resource department's role and conditions that affect its development: explanations from Austrian CEOs', *Human Resource Management*, 49: 1025–1046.

Branine, M. (1996) 'Observations on training and management development in the People's Republic of China', *Personnel Review*, 25 (1): 25.

Branine, M. (2005) 'Cross-cultural training of managers: an evaluation of a management development programme for Chinese managers', *Journal of Management Development*, 24 (5/6): 459.

Branine, M. (2006) 'Human resource management in Algeria', in P. S. Budhwar and K. Mellahi (eds) *Managing Human Resources in the Middle East*, London, Routledge, pp250–272.

Braun, W., Sparrow, P. R., Brewster, C. J. and Harris, H. (2003) *Stepstone Case Study: Building global HR capability*, Manchester, Manchester Business School.

Bretz, R. D., Malkovich, G. T. and Read, W. (1992) 'The current state of performance appraisal research and practice: concerns, directions and implications', *Journal of Management*, 18 (2): 321–353.

Brewer, M. B., Dull, V. and Lui, L. (1981) 'Perceptions of the elderly: stereotypes as prototypes', *Journal of Personality and Social Psychology,* 41: 656–670.

Brewster, C. J. (1991) *The Management of Expatriates*, London, Kogan Page.

Brewster, C. J. (1994) 'Human resource management in Europe: reflection of, or challenge to, the American concept', in P. Kirkbride (ed.) *Human Resource Management In Europe: Perspectives for the 1990s*, London, Routledge, pp56–89.

Brewster, C. J. (1995) 'Towards a European model of human resource management', *Journal of International Business Studies*, 26, 1–22.

Brewster, C. J. (1998) 'Flexible working in Europe: extent, growth and challenge for HRM', in P. Sparrow and M. Marchington (eds) *HRM: The New Agenda*, Pitman, London.

Brewster, C. J. (1999) 'Different paradigms in strategic HRM: questions raised by comparative research', in P. M. Wright, L. D. Dyer, J. W. Boudreau and G. T. Milkovich (eds) *Research in Personnel and Human Resource Management*, Stamford, CT, JAI Press.

Brewster, C. J. (2004) 'European perspectives on human resource management', *Human Resource Management Review*, 14 (4): 365–382.

Brewster, C. J. (2006) 'Comparing HRM across countries', in G. Stahl and I. Björkman (eds) *Handbook of Research in International HRM*, Cheltenham, UK, Edward Elgar, pp68–90.

Brewster, C. J. and Larsen, H. H. (1992) 'Human resource management in Europe: evidence from ten countries', *International Journal of Human Resource Management*, 3 (3): 409–434.

Brewster, C. J. and Larsen, H. H. (2000a) *Human Resource Management in Northern Europe*, Oxford, Blackwell.

Brewster, C. J. and Larsen, H. H. (2000b) 'Flexibility in HRM', in C. J. Brewster and H. H. Larsen (eds) *Human Resource Management in Northern Europe*, Oxford, Blackwell.

Brewster, C. J., Larsen, H. H. and Mayrhofer, W. (2000) 'Human Resource Management: a strategic approach?' In Brewster, C. and Larsen, H. H. (eds) *Human Resource Management in Northern Europe*, Oxford: Blackwells.

Brewster, C. J. and Lee, S. (2006) 'HRM in not-for-profit international organisatizations: different, but also alike', in H. H. Larsen and W. Mayrhofer (eds) *European Human Resource Management*, London, Routledge, pp131–148.

Brewster, C. J. and Mayne, L. (1994) *The Changing Relationship Between Personnel and the Line: The European dimension*, Report to the Institute of Personnel and Development, Wimbledon.

Brewster, C. J. and Mayrhofer, W. (eds) (2011) *A Handbook of Comparative Human Resource Management*, Cheltenham, Edward Elgar.

Brewster, C. J. and Soderstrom, M. (1994) 'Human resources and line management', in C. J. Brewster and A. Hegewisch (eds) *Policy and Practice in European Human Resource Management*, London, Routledge.

Brewster, C. J. and Tregaskis, O. (2001) 'Adaptive, reactive and inclusive organisational approaches to workforce flexibility in Europe', *Comportamento Organizacional e Gestão*, 7 (2): 209–232.

Brewster, C. J. and Tregaskis, O. (2002) 'Convergence or divergence of contingent employment practices? Evidence of the role of MNCs in Europe', in W. Cooke (ed.) *Multinational Companies and Transnational Workplace Issues*, New York, Greenwood Publishing.

Brewster, C. J., Larsen, H. H. and Mayrhofer, W. (1997) 'Integration and assignment: a paradox in human resource management', *Journal of International Management*, 3 (1): 1–23.

Brewster, C. J., Mayrhofer, W. and Morley, M. (eds) (2004) *Trends in Human Resource Management in Europe: Convergence or divergence*, London, Butterworth-Heinemann.

Brewster, C. J., Sparrow, P. R. and Dickmann, M. (2007) (eds) *International Human Resource Management: Contemporary issues in Europe*, London, Routledge.

Brewster, C. J., Sparrow, P. R. and Harris, H. (2003) *International Human Resource Management*, 1st edition, London, CIPD.

Brewster, C. J., Sparrow, P. R. and Harris, H. (2005) 'Towards a new model of globalizing HRM', *International Journal of Human Resource Management*, 16 (6): 953–974.

Brewster, C. J., Sparrow, P. R. and Vernon, G. (2007) *International Human Resource Management*, 2nd edition, London, Chartered Institute of Personnel and Development.

Brewster, C. J., Tregaskis, O., Hegewisch, A. and Mayne, L. (1996) 'Comparative research in human resource management: a review and an example', *International Journal of Human Resource Management*, 7 (3): 585–604.

Brewster, C. J., Wood, G. and Brookes, M. (2006a) 'Varieties of capitalism and varieties of firms', in G. Wood and P. James (eds) *Institutions, Production and Working Life*, Oxford, Oxford University Press.

Brewster, C. J., Wood, G. and Brookes, M. (2008) 'Similarity, isomorphism or duality: recent survey evidence on the HRM policies of multinational corporations', *British Journal of Management*, 19 (4): 320–342.

Brewster, C. J., Wood, G., Brookes, M. and van Ommeren, J. (2006b) 'What determines the size of the HR function? A cross-national analysis', *Human Resource Management*, 45 (1): 3–21.

Brewster, C. J., Wood, G., Croucher, C. and Brookes, M. (2007a) 'Are works councils and joint consultative committees a threat to trade unions? A comparative analysis', *Economic and Industrial Democracy*, 28 (1): 53–81.

Brewster, C. J., Wood, G., Croucher, C. and Brookes, M. (2007b) 'Collective and individual voice: convergence in Europe?', *International Journal of Human Resource Management*, 18 (7): 1246–1262.

Brewster, C., Wood, G., Van Ommeren, J. and Brookes, M. (2006) 'The determinants of HR size', *Human Resource Management* (US), 45, 1: 3–21.

Brewster, C. J., Mayne, L., Tregaskis, O., Parsons, D., Atterbury, S., Hegewisch, A., Soler, C., Aparicio-Valverde, M., Picq, T., Weber, T., Kabst, R., Waglund, M. and Lindstrom, K. (1996) *Working Time and Contract Flexibility*, Report prepared for the European Commission, Directorate-General V, Centre for European HRM, Cranfield University.

Briscoe, D. and Schuler, R. S. (2004) *International Human Resource Management*, 2nd edition, New York, Routledge.

Brislin, R. W. (1986) 'The working and translation of research instruments', in W. J. Lonner and J. W. Berry (eds) *Field Methods in Cross-Cultural Research*, Beverly Hills, Sage Publications, pp137–164.

Brislin, R. W., Worthley, R. and Macnab, B. (2006) 'Cultural intelligence: understanding behaviors that serve people's goals', *Group and Organization Management*, 31 (1): 40–55.

Brookes, M., Brewster, C. J., and Wood, G. (2005) 'Social relations, firms and societies: a study in institutional embeddedness', *International Sociology*, 20 (4): 403–426.

Brookfield Global Relocation Services (2010) *2010 Global Relocation Trends Survey Report,* Technical report, http://www.brookfieldgrs.com/insights_ideas/trends.asp.

Brown, D. (1999) 'States of pay', *People Management*, 5 (23): 52–55.

Brunstein, I. (1995) *Human Resource Management in Western Europe*, Berlin, Walter de Gruyter.

Brutus, S., Derayeh, M., Fletcher, C., Bailey, C., Velasquez, P., Shi. K, Simon, C. and Labath, V. (2006) 'Internationalization of multi-source feedback systems: a six-country exploratory analysis of 360-degree feedback', *International Journal of Human Resource Management,* 17 (11): 1888–1906.

Bryson, A., Forth, J. and Kirby, S. (2005) 'High-involvement management practices, trade union representation and workplace performance in Britain', *Scottish Journal of Political Economy*, 52 (3): 451–491.

Buckley, F., Monks, K. and Sinnott, A. (1997) *Communication Enhancement: A process dividend for the organisation and the HRM department?*, Dublin, Dublin City University Business School.

Buckley, P. and Muccielli, J. (1997) *Multinational Firms and International Relocation*, Cheltenham, Edward Elgar.

Buckley, P. J. and Ghauri, P. N. (2004) 'Globalisation, economic geography and the strategy of multinational enterprises', *Journal of International Business Studies*, 35 (2): 81–98.

Budhwar, P. S. (2004) (ed.) *Managing Human Resources in Asia-Pacific*, London, Routledge.

Budhwar, P. S. and Cooke, F. L. (2009) 'HR offshoring and outsourcing: research issues for IHRM', in P. R. Sparrow (ed.) *Handbook of International HR Research: Integrating people, process and context*, Oxford, Blackwell, pp341–362.

Budhwar, P. S. and Mellahi, K. (2006) (eds) *Managing Human Resources in the Middle East*, London, Routledge.

Budhwar, P. S and Sparrow, P. R. (2003) 'An integrative framework for understanding cross-national human resource management practices', *Human Resource Management Review*, 12: 377–403.

Buechtemann, C. F. and Verdier, E. (1998) 'Education and training regimes: macro-institutional evidence', *Revue d'économie politique*, 108 (3): 291–320.

Buller, P. F. and McEvoy, G. M. (1999) 'Creating and sustaining ethical capability in the multinational corporation', in R. S. Schuler and S. E. Jackson (eds) *Strategic Human Resource Management*, Oxford, Blackwell.

Burt, R. S. (2000) 'The network structure of social capital'. in B. M. Staw and R. I. Sutton (eds) *Research in Organizational Behavior: An annual series of analytical essays and critical reviews*, Volume 22, New York: JAI Press.

Caldwell, R. (2008) 'HR business partner competency models: re-contextualising effectiveness', *Human Resource Management Journal*, 18 (3): 275–294.

Caligiuri, P. M. and Cascio, W. (1998) 'Can we send her there? Maximising the success of western women on global assignments', *Journal of World Business*, 33 (4): 394–416.

Caligiuri, P. M. and Tung, R. L. (1998) 'Are masculine cultures female-friendly? Male and female expatriates' success in countries differing in work value orientations', Paper presented at the International Congress of the International Association for Cross-Cultural Psychology: The Silver Jubilee Congress, Bellingham, WA.

Caligiuri, P. M., Hyland, M., Joshi, A. and Bross, A. (1998) 'A theoretical framework for examining the relationship between family adjustment and expatriate adjustment to working in the host country', *Journal of Applied Psychology*, 83 (4): 598–614.

Callaghan, G. and Thompson, P. (*2001)* 'Edwards revisited: technical control and call centres', *Economic and Industrial Democracy*, 22 (1): 13–37.

Cameron A., Greg, J. and Bamber, N. T. (2006) 'Fast-food work: are McJobs satisfying?', *Employee Relations*, 28 (5): 402–420.

Campbell, D. (1995) *Learning Consultation: A systematic framework*, London, Karnac Books.

Cannell, M. and Wood, S. (1992) *Incentive Pay: Impact and evolution*. London, IPM/NEDO

Cappellen, T. and Janssens, T. (2005) 'Career paths of global managers: towards future research', *Journal of World Business*, 40: 348–360.

Cappelli, P. (2008) *Talent on Demand*, Boston, MA, Harvard University Press.

Carpenter, S. (2000) 'Effects of cultural tightness and collectivism on self-concept and causal attributions', *Cross-Cultural Research*, 34: 38–56.

Cartwright, S. (2005) 'Mergers and acquisitions: an update and appraisal', *International Review of Industrial and Organizational Psychology*, 20: 1–38.

Cascio W. F. (2006) 'Global performance management systems', in G. Stahl and I. Björkman (eds) *Handbook of Research in International HRM*, Cheltenham, UK, Edward Elgar, pp176–196.

Cascio W. F. and Serapio M. G. (1991) 'Human resource systems in an international alliance: the undoing of a done deal', *Organizational Dynamics*, 19: 63–74.

Cascio, E., Clark, D. and Gordon, N. (2008) 'Education and the age profile of literacy into adulthood', *Journal of Economic Perspectives*, 22 (3): 47.

Cashman, E. M. and McElroy, J. C. (1991) 'Evaluating the HR function', *HR Magazine*, January: 70–73.

Caves, R. E. (1982) *Multinational Enterprise and Economic Analysis*, Cambridge, Cambridge University Press.

Caves, R. E. (1996) *Multinational Enterprise and Economic Analysis*, Cambridge, Cambridge University Press.

Cavusgil, S. T. (1994) 'From the editor in chief', *Journal of International Marketing,* 2 (3): 4–6.

Cavusgil, S. T. and Knight, G. (2009) *Born Global Firms: A new international enterprise*, New York, Business Expert Press.

Centre for Policy and Business Analysis (2008) *Job Mobility in the European Union: Optimising its social and economic benefits*, European Commission, Directorate General for Employment, Social Affairs and Equal Opportunities.

Chakrabarty, S. (2006) 'Making sense of the sourcing and shoring maze: various outsourcing and offshoring alternatives", in H. S. Kehal and V. A. Singh (eds) *Outsourcing and Offshoring in the 21st Century: A socio-economic perspective*, London, Idea Group, pp18–53.

Chan, A. and Lui, S. (2004) 'HRM in Hong Kong', in P. S. Budhwar (ed.) *Managing Human Resources in Asia*, London, Routledge, pp75–91.

Chandola, T., Martikainen, P., Bartley, M., Lahelma, E., Marmot, M., Nasermoaddeli, A. and

Kagamimori, S. (2004) 'Does conflict between home and work explain the effect of multiple roles on mental health? A comparative study of Finland, Japan and the UK', *International Journal of Epidemiology*, 33 (4): 884–893.

Chang, Y. Y., Mellahi, K., and Wilkinson, A. (2009) 'Control of subsidiaries of MNCs from emerging economies in developed countries: the case of Taiwanese MNCs in the UK', *The International Journal of Human Resource Management*, 20: 75–95.

Chartered Institute of Personnel and Development (2001) *Working Time Regulations: Have they made a difference?*, London, Chartered Institute of Personnel and Development.

Chen, T.-J., Chen, H. and Ku, Y.-H. (2004) 'Foreign direct investment and local linkages', *Journal of International Business Studies*, 35 (4): 320–333.

Chiang F. F. T. and Birch, T. A. (2007) 'Examining the perceived causes of successful employee performance: an East-West comparison', *International Journal of Human Resource Management*, 18 (2): 232–248.

Child, J. (1981) 'Culture, contingency and capitalism in the cross-national study of organisations', in B. M. Staw and L. L. Cummings (eds) *Research in Organizational Behavior*, Volume 3, Greenwich, CT, JAI Press, pp303–356.

Chung, C., Bozkurt, O. and Sparrow, P. R. (2012) 'Managing the duality of IHRM: unravelling the strategy and perceptions of key actors in South Korean MNCs', *International Journal of Human Resource Management*, in press.

CIA *World Factbook*, freely available at: www.cia.gov/library/publications/the-world-factbook.

CIPD (2002) *Globalising HR*. London, Chartered Institute of Personnel and Development.

CIPD (2005a) *HR Outsourcing: The key decisions*, London, Chartered Institute of Personnel and Development.

CIPD (2005b) *People Management and Technology: Progress and potential*, Survey Report, London, Chartered Institute of Personnel and Development.

Clark, P. F., Stewart, J. B. and Clark, D. A. (2006) 'The globalisation of the labour market for health-care professionals', *International Labour Review*, 145 (1/2): 37–64.

Clarke, S. (2005) 'Post-socialist trade unions: China and Russia', *Industrial Relations Journal*, 36: 2–18.

Claus, L and Briscoe, D. (2009) 'Employee performance management across borders: a review of relevant academic literature', *International Journal of Management Review*, 11 (2): 175–196.

Claus, L. and Hand, M. L. (2009) 'Customization decisions regarding performance management', *International Journal of Cross Cultural Management*, 9 (2): 237–258.

Cohen, W. M. and Levinthal, D. A. (1990) 'Absorptive capacity: a new perspective on learning and innovations', *Administrative Science Quarterly*, 35: 128–152.

Collinge, C. (2001) 'Self organization of society by scale', in B. Jessop (ed.) *Regulation Theory and the Crisis of Capitalism*, Volume 4 – *Development and Extensions*, London, Edward Elgar.

Collings, D. G. and Mellahi, K. (2009) 'Strategic talent management: a review and research agenda', *Human Resource Management Review*, 19: 304–313.

Collings, D. G., Scullion, H. and Morley, M. J. (2007) 'Changing patterns of global staffing in the multinational enterprise: challenges to the conventional expatriate assignments and emerging alternatives', *Journal of World Business*, 42: 198–213.

Collings, D. G., and Scullion, H. (2006). Approaches to international staffing. In H. Scullion. and D. J. Collings (Eds) *Global staffing*, London: Routledge.

Collins, S. (1995) *Expatriation: A moving experience*, Dublin, Michael Smurfitt Graduate School of Business.

Conference Board (1992) *Recruiting and Selecting International Managers*, Report No 998, New York, The Conference Board.

Conner, K. and Prahalad, C. K. (1996) 'A resource-based theory of the firm: knowledge versus opportunism', *Organization Science*, 7 (5): 477–501.

Conrad, P. and Pieper, R. (1990) 'HRM in the Federal Republic of Germany', in R. Pieper (ed.) *Human Resource Management: An International Comparison*, Berlin, Walter de Gruyter.

Cook, M. (1999) *Personnel Selection: Adding value through people*. Chichester, John Wiley.

Cooke, F. L. (2001) 'Equal opportunities? The role of legislation and public policies in women's employment in China', *Journal of Women in Management Review*, 16 (7): 334–348.

Cooke, F. L. (2005) *HRM, Work and Employment in China*, London, Routledge.

Cooke, F. L. (2006) 'Modeling and HR shared services center: experience of an MNC in the United Kingdom', *Human Resource Management*, 45: 211–228.

Cooke, F. L. (2008) 'Performance management in China', in A. Varma, P. S. Budhwar and A. S. DeNisi (eds) *Performance Management Systems: A global perspective*, London, Routledge.

Costigan, R. D., Iter, S. S., Insinga, R. C., Kranas, G., Berman, J. J. and Kureshov, V. A. (2005) 'An examination of the relationship of a Western performance-management process to key workplace behaviours in transition economies', *Canadian Journal of Administrative Science*, 22 (3): 255–267.

Coulson Thomas, C. (1990) *Professional Development of and for the Board*, London, Institute of Directors.

Coulson Thomas, C. and Wakeham, A. (1991) *The Effective Board: Current practice, myths and realities*, London, Institute of Directors.

Coupland, N., Giles, H. and Wienmann, J. (1991) *Miscommunication and Problematic Talk*, Newbury Park, CA, Sage.

Coviello, N. E. and Munro, H. J. (1997) 'Network relationships and the internationalisation process of small software firms', *International Business Review*, 6 (2): 1–26.

Coyle, W. (1992) *International Relocation*, Oxford, Butterworth-Heinemann.

Coyle-Shapiro, Jacqueline A-M. (2002) *Changing employee attitudes: the independent effects of TQM. and profit sharing on continuous improvement orientation. Journal of Applied Behavioral Science*, 38 (1): 57–77.

Cranet (2006) *Cranet Survey on Comparative Human Resource Management: International Executive Report 2005*, Cranfield, Cranfield University.

Cray, D. and Mallory, G. R. (1998) *Making Sense of Managing Culture*, London, Thomson Business Press.

CRELL (Centre for Research into Life-long Learning) (2005) Based on EU-SILC data.

CReMe (2000) *New Forms of International Working*, Executive Report, UK, Cranfield School of Management.

Crouch, C. (2005a) 'Models of capitalism', *New Political Economy*, 10 (4): 439–456.

Crouch, C. (2005b) 'Three meanings of complementarity', *Socio-Economic Review*, 3(2): 359–363.

Crouch, C., Finegold, D. and Sako, M. (1999) *Are Skills the Answer? The political economy of skill creation in advanced industrial countries*, Oxford, Oxford University Press.

Crouch, C., Schroeder, M. and Voelzkow, H. (2009) 'Regional and sectoral varieties of capitalism', *Economy and Society*, 38 (4): 654–678.

Croucher, R. and Brewster, C. J. (1998) 'Flexible working practices and the trade unions', *Employee Relations*, 20 (5): 443–452.

Croucher, R., Gooderham, P. and Parry, P. (2006) 'The influences on direct communication in British and Danish firms', *European Journal of Industrial Relations*, 12 (3): 267–286.

Crouter, A. (1984) 'Spillover from family to work: the neglected side of the work-family interface', *Human Relations*, 37: 425–442.

Crozier, M. (1964) *The Bureaucratic Phenomenon*, London, Tavistock.

Cunningham, I. and Hyman, J. (1995) 'Transforming the HRM vision into reality', *Employee Relations*, 17 (8): 5–15.

D'Art, D. and Turner, T. (2004) 'Profit-sharing, firm performance and union influence in selected European countries', *Personnel Review*, 33 (3): 335–350.

Daft, R. and Macintosh, N. (1981) 'A tentative exploration into the amount and equivocality of information processing in organisational work units', *Administrative Science Quarterly*, 26 (2): 207–224.

Davies, G., Chun, R., Da Silva, R. V. and Roper, S. (2003) *Corporate Reputation and Competitiveness*, London, Routledge.

De Cieri, H. and Dowling, P. J. (1999) *Strategic HRM in Multinational Enterprises: Theoretical and empirical developments*, Greenwich, CT, JAI Press Inc.

De Cieri, H. and Kramar, R. (2003) *Human Resource Management In Australia: Strategy, People, Performance*, Sydney, McGraw-Hill.

De Cieri, H., Wolfram Cox, J. and Fenwick, M. (2007). 'A review of international human resource management: integration, interrogation, imitation', *International Journal of Management Reviews*, 9 (4): 281–302.

De Grip, A., Hoevenberg, J. and Willems, E. (1997) 'Atypical employment in the European Union', *International Labor Review*, 136 (1): 49–72.

De Vries, M. F. R. and Florent-Treacy, E. (2002) 'Global leadership from A to Z: creating high commitment organizations', *Organizational Dynamics*, 30 (4): 295–309.

Deeg, R. (2005) 'Complementary and institutional change: how useful a concept?', *Social Science Research Centre*, Vol. 21, Discussion Paper, Berlin, SP II.

Deeg, R. (2009) 'The rise of internal capitalist diversity? Changing patterns of finance and corporate governance in Europe', *Economy and Society*, 38 (3): 552–579.

DeFidelto, C. and Slater, I. (2001) 'Web-based HR in an international setting', in A. J. Walker (ed.) *Web-Based Human Resources: The technologies that are transforming HR*, London, McGraw-Hill.

DeFrank, R. S., Konopaske, R. and Ivancevich, J. M. (2000) 'Executive travel stress: perils of the road warrior', *Academy of the Management Executive*, 14 (2): 58–71.

Delbridge, R., Hauptmier, M. and Sen Gupta, S. (2011) *Beyond the Enterprise: Broadening the Horizons of International HRM* (forthcoming), Human Relations, 64, 4: 483–505.

Delmestri, G. and Walgenbach, P. (2009) 'Interference among conflicting institutions and technical-economic conditions: the adoption of the assessment center in French, German, Italian, UK, and US multinational firms', *International Journal of Human Resource Management*, 20 (4): 885–911.

Delsen, L. (1991) 'Atypical employment relations and government policy in Europe', *Labor*, 5 (3): 123–149.

Den Hartog, D. N, Boselie, P and Paauwe, J. (2004) 'Performance management: a model and research agenda', *Applied Psychology: An International Review*, 53 (4): 556–569.

DeNisi, A. S. (2000) 'Performance appraisal and performance management: a multilevel analysis', in S. Kozlowski and K. J. Klein (eds) *Multilevel Theory, Research and Methods in Organization*, San Francisco, Jossey-Bass.

DeNisi, A. S. and Pritchard, R. D. (2006) 'Performance appraisal, performance management and improving individual performance: a motivational framework', *Management and Organization Review*, 2 (2): 253–277.

DeNisi, A. S, Varma, A. and Budhwar, P. S. (2008) 'Performance management around the globe: what have we learned?', in A. Varma, P. S. Budhar and A. S. DeNisi (eds) *Performance Management Systems: A global perspective*, London, Routledge.

Denny, K. J., Harmon, C. P. and O'Sullivan, V. (2004) *Education, Earnings and Skills: A multi-country comparison*, WP04/08, The Institute of Fiscal Studies, Dublin.

Dentsu Institute (2001) *Value Changes with Globalization: The fifth comparative analysis of global values*, Dentsu Institute for Human Studies, www.dci.dentsu.co .

Devoe, S. E. and Iyengar, S. S. (2004) 'Managers' theories of subordinates: a cross-cultural examination of manager perceptions of motivation and appraisal of performance', *Organizational Behavior and Human Decision Processes*, 93: 47–61.

Dewettinck, K. (2008) 'Employee performance management systems in Belgian organizations: purpose, contextual dependence and effectiveness', *European Journal of International Management*, 2(2):192–207.

Dickmann, M. (1999) *Balancing Global, Parent and Local Influences: International human resource management of German multinational companies*, PhD thesis, University of London.

Dickmann, M. and Müller-Camen, M. (2006) 'A typology of international human resource management strategies and processes', *International Journal of Human Resource Management*, 17 (4): 580–601.

Dickmann, M., Brewster, C. J. and Sparrow, P. R. (2008) (eds) *International Human Resource Management: A European perspective*, London, Routledge.

Dickmann, M., Doherty, N. and Brewster, C. J. (2006) 'Why do they go? Individual and corporate perspectives on the factors influencing the decision to accept an international assignment', *International Journal of Human Resource Management*, 19 (4): 731–751.

DiMaggio, P. J. and Powell, W. W. (1983) 'The iron cage revisited: Institutional isomorphism and collective rationality in organizational fields', *American Sociological Review*, 48 (2): 147–160.

Dipboye, R. L. and Johnson, S. K. (2008) 'The clash between "best practices" for selection and national culture', in D. L. Stone and E. F. Stone-Romero (eds) *The Influence of Culture on Human Resource Management Processes and Practices*, New York, Lawrence Erlbaum, pp53–84.

Doellgast, V. (2010) 'Collective voice under decentralized bargaining: a comparative study of work reorganization in US and German call centres', *British Journal of Industrial Relations*, 48 (2): 375–399.

Doh, J. P., Stumpf, S. A., Tymon, W. and Haid, M. (2008) 'How to manage talent in fast-moving labor markets: some findings from India', *MIT Sloan Management Review*, 50 (1): 6–7.

Dore, R. (2000) *Stock Market Capitalism: Welfare capitalism*, Cambridge, Cambridge University Press.

Dowling, P. J. and Welch, D. (2004) *International Human Resource Management: Managing people in a multinational context*, 4th edition, London, Thomson Learning.

Dowling, P. J., Engle Sr., A. D. and Festing, M. (2008) *International Dimensions of Human Resource Management*, 5th edition, London, Thomson.

Dowling, P. J., Schuler, R. S. and Welch, D. (1994) *International Dimensions of Human Resource Management*, 2nd edition, California, Wadsworth.

Dowling, P. J., Welch, D. E., and Schuler, R. S. (1999). *International Human Resource Management*. Cincinnati, OH: South-Western.

Doz, Y., Santos, J. and Williamson, P. (2001) *From Global to Metanational: How companies win in the knowledge economy*, Cambridge, MA, Harvard Business School.

Due, J., Madsen, J. S. and Jensen, C. S. (1991) 'The social dimension: convergence or diversification of IR in the Single European Market?', *Industrial Relations Journal*, 22 (2): 85–102.

Dunkel, T., Le Mouillour, I. and Teichler, U. (2006) *Vocational Education and Training and Higher Education: Final Report*, INCHER-Kassel.

Dunnett, M. D. (1993) 'My hammer or your hammer?', *Human Resource Management,* 32: 373–384.

Dutton, J., Dukerich, J. and Harquail, C. (1994) 'Organizational images and membership commitment', *Administrative Science Quarterly*, 39 (2): 239–263.

Dyer, L. and Kochan, T. (1995) 'Is there a new HRM? Contemporary evidence and future directions', in B. Downie, P. Kumar and M. L. Coates (eds) *Managing Human Resources in the 1990s and Beyond: Is the workplace being transformed?*, Kingston, Ontario, Industrial Relations Centre Press, Queen's University.

Earley, P. C. and Ang, S. (2003) *Cultural Intelligence: Individual interactions across cultures*, Stanford, CA, Stanford University Press.

Earley, P. C. and Mosakowski, E. (2002) 'Linking cultures and behaviour in organizations: suggestions for theory development and research methodology', in F. Dansereau and F J. Yammarino (eds) *Research in Multi-level Issues*. Volume 1: *The Many Faces of Multi-Level Issues*, San Francisco, Elsevier Science.

Earley, P. C. and Mosakowski, E. (2004) 'Cultural intelligence', *Harvard Business Review*, 82 (10): 139–146.

Earley, P. C. and Stubbledine, P. (1989) 'Intercultural assessment of performance feedback', *Group and Organization Studies,* 14: 161–181.

Easterby-Smith, M., Malina, D. and Yuan, L. (1995) 'How culture-sensitive is HRM? A comparative analysis of practice in Chinese and UK companies', *International Journal of Human Resource Management*, 6 (1): 31–59.

Eccles, E. G, (1991) 'The performance management manifesto', *Harvard Business Review*, January-February: 131–137.

Economist (1999) 'A survey of Germany: the Berlin Republic', *The Economist,* 350 (8105): 10.

Economist (2000a) 'The world's view of multinationals', *The Economist*, 354 (8155): 21–22.

Economist (2000b) 'Special report: a survey of globalisation and tax', *The Economist*, 354 (8155): 1–18.

Economist (2006) 'Travelling more lightly', *The Economist*, 379 (8483): 99–101.

Economist (2009a) 'Spanish companies in Latin America: a good bet', *The Economist,* 393 (8634): 69.

Economist (2009b) 'Domestic outsourcing in India: bittersweet synergy', *The Economist,* 393 (8654): 80–81.

Economist (2009c) 'Getting it together at last: arrivals and departures in Brazil, *The Economist,* 393 (8657): Special report: 3.

Economist (2009d) 'Secret sauce: China's rapid growth, *The Economist*, 393 (8657): 98.

Economist (2010a) 'The Chinese in Japan: department stores and sweat shops', *The Economist*, 396 (8690): 58.

Economist (2010b) Japanese firms in China: culture shock. *The Economist*, 396 (8690): 68.

Economist (2011a) 'Asia's talent market: locals first. Employment in Asian firms is booming – but for locals, not Western expats', *The Economist*, 398 (8731).

Economist (2011b) 'The French community in London: Paris-on-Thames', *The Economist*, 398 (8722): 73–74.

Economist (2011c) 'Financial careers: go East young man', *The Economist*, 399 (8729): 79–80.

Economist (2011d) 'The Chinese in Africa: trying to pull together', *The Economist,* 399 (8730): 74–76.

Economist (2011e) 'Decline of the working man: America's jobless men', *The Economist,* 399 (8731): 72.

Economist (2011f) 'Multinational manufacturers: moving back to America', *The Economist,* 399 (8733): 73–74.

Edwards, T. and Ferner, A. (2004) 'Multinationals, reverse diffusion and national business systems', *Management International Review,* 1: 49–79.

Edwards, T. and Rees, C. (2008) *International Human Resource Management: Globalisation, national systems and multinational companies,* London, Financial Times/Prentice Hall.

Edwards, T., Colling, T. and Ferner, A. (2007) 'Conceptual approaches to the transfer of employment practices in multinational companies: an integrated approach', *Human Resource Management Journal,* 17: 201–217.

Edwards, A., Almond, P., Clark, I., Colling, T. and Ferner, A. (2005) 'Reverse diffusion in US multinationals: barriers from the American business system', *Journal of Management Studies,* 42 (6): 1261–1286.

EFILWC *see* European Foundation for the Improvement of Living and Working Conditions

Egelhoff, W. G. (1991) 'Information-processing theory and the multinational enterprise', *Journal International Business Studies,* 22 (3): 341–369.

Ehnert, I. and Brewster, C. J. (2008)'An integrative framework for expatriate preparation and training', in C. J. Brewster, P. R. Sparrow and M. Dickmann (eds) *International Human Resource Management: Contemporary issues in Europe,* 2nd edition, London, Routledge.

EIRO (2002) *Industrial Relations in the EU Member States and Candidate Countries,* Dublin, Foundation for the Improvement of Living and Working Conditions.

EIU (1994) *Country Report: Spain,* London, Economic Intelligence Unit.

Elvira, M. M. and Davila, A. (2005) *Managing Human Resources in Latin America,* London, Routledge.

Emery, F. and Thorsrud, E. (1969) *Form and Content in Industrial Democracy,* London, Tavistock.

Erdogan, B. (2002) 'Antecedents and consequences of justice perceptions in performance appraisals', *Human Resource Management Review,* 12 (4): 555–578.

Erez, M. and Gati, E. (2004) 'A dynamic, multi-level model of culture: from the micro level of the individual to the macro level of a global culture', *Applied Psychology: An International Review,* 53 (4): 583–598.

Eshigi, G. (1985) 'Nationality bias and performance evaluations in multinational corporations', *National Academy of Management Proceedings,* 93–97.

Esping-Andersen, G. (1999) *Social Foundations of Post-Industrial Economies,* Oxford, OUP.

Espino-Rodríguez, T. F. and Padrón-Robaina, V. (2006) 'A review of outsourcing from the resource-based view of the firm', *International Journal of Management Reviews,* 8 (1): 49–70.

Esteves-Abe, M., Iversen, T. and Soskice, D. (2001) 'Social protection and the formation of skills: a reinterpretation of the welfare state', in P. A. Hall and D. Soskice (eds)*Varieties of Capitalism: The institutional foundations of comparative advantage,* Oxford, Oxford University Press.

European Foundation for the Improvement of Living and Working Conditions (2009) *Working Conditions in the European Union: Work organization,* EFILWC, Luxemburg.

European Industrial Relations Dictionary (2010) www.eurofound.europa.eu/areas/industrialrelations/dictionary

Eurostat (2002) *Continuing Vocational Training Survey.*

Evans, P., Pucik, V. and Barsoux, J.-L. (2002) *The Global Challenge: Frameworks for International Human Resource Management,* New York, McGraw-Hill/Irwin.

Evans, P., Pucik, V. and Björkman, I. (2010) *The Global Challenge: International human resource management*, Boston, MA, McGraw-Hill.

Eyraud, F., Marsden, D. W. and Silvestre, J. J. (1990) 'Internal and occupational labour markets in Britain and France', *International Labour Review*, 129 (4): 501–517.

Farndale, E and Paauwe, J. (2005) 'The role of corporate HR functions in MNCs: the interplay between corporate, regional/national and plant level', Working Paper 05–10, Cornell University (http//www.cornell.edu/depts./cahrs/downloads/PDFs/Working Papers/WP05–10.pdf).

Farndale, E. (2005) 'HR department professionalism: a comparison between the UK and other European countries', *International Journal of Human Resource Management*, 16 (5): 660–675.

Farndale, E. and Brewster, C. J. (1999) 'Regionalism in human resource management', *Journal of Professional HRM*, 15: April.

Farndale, E. and Brewster, C. J. (2005) 'In search of legitimacy: national professional associations and the professionalism of HR practitioners', *Human Resource Management Journal*, 15 (3): 33–48.

Farndale, E. and Paauwe, J. (2007) 'Uncovering competitive and institutional drivers of HRM practices in multi-national corporations', *Human Resource Management Journal*, 17 (4): 355–375.

Farndale, E., Brewster, C. J. and Poutsma, E. (2008) 'Co-ordinated vs liberal market HRM: the impact of institutionalisation on multinational firms', *International Journal of Human Resource Management*, 19 (11): 2004–2023.

Farndale, E., Paauwe, J., Morris, S. S., Stahl, G. K., Stiles, P., Trevor, J. and Wright, P. M. (2010) 'Context-bound configurations of corporate HR functions in multinational corporations around the globe', *Human Resource Management*, 49 (1): 45–66.

Farndale, E., Scullion, H. and Sparrow, P. R. (2010) 'The role of the corporate HR function in global talent management', *Journal of World Business*, 45 (2): 161–168.

Fenwick, M. (2001) 'Emerging forms of international working: evidence from Australia', Paper at the Academy of Management Conference, Washington.

Fenwick, M. S., De Cieri, H. and Welch, D. E. (1999) 'Cultural and bureaucratic control in MNEs: the role of expatriate performance management', *Management International Review*, 39 (3): 107–124.

Ferner, A. and Hyman, R. (1992) *Industrial Relations in the New Europe*, Oxford, Blackwell.

Ferner, A. and Quintanilla, J. (1998) 'Multinational, national business systems and HRM: the enduring influence of national identity or a process of "Anglo-Saxonization"?', *International Journal of Human Resource Management*, 9 (4): 710–731.

Ferner, A. and Varul, M. Z. (2000) 'Internationalisation and the personnel function in German multi-nationals', *Human Resource Management Journal*, 10 (3): 79–96.

Festing, M., Knappert, L., Dowling, P. J. and Engle, A. D. (2010) 'Country specific profiles in global performance management: a contribution to balancing global standardization and local adaptation in MNEs', Paper presented at the 11th International Human Resource Management Conference, Birmingham.

Filella, J. and Hegewisch, A. (1994) 'European experiments with pay and benefits policies', in C. J. Brewster and A. Hegewisch (eds) *Policy and Practice in European Human Resource Management*, London, Routledge.

Filella, J. and Soler, C. (1992) 'Spain', in C. J. Brewster, A. Hegewisch, L. Holden and T. Lockhart (eds) *The European Human Resource Management Guide*, London, Academic Press.

Filipczak, B. (1995) 'Obfuscation resounding: corporate communication in America', *Training*, 32 (7): 29–37.

Findlay, A. M., Li, F. L. N., Jowett, A. J. and Skeldon, R. (2000) Skilled international migration and the global city: a study of expatriates in Hong Kong. *Applied Geography*, 20 (3): 277–304.

Fiol, C. (1995) 'Corporate communications: comparing executives' private and public statements', *Academy of Management Journal*, 38 (2): 522–537.

Fischer, R., Ferreira, M. C., Assmar, M. L., Redford, P. and Harb, C. (2005) 'Organisational behaviour across cultures: theoretical and methodological issues for developing multi-level frameworks involving culture', *International Journal of Cross Cultural Management*, 5 (1): 27–48.

Fletcher, C. (2001) 'Performance appraisal and management: the developing research agenda', *Journal of Occupational and Organizational Psychology*, 74: 473–487.

Fletcher, C. and Perry, E. L. (2001) 'Performance appraisal and feedback: a consideration of national culture and a review of contemporary research and future trends', in N. Anderson, D. S. Ones, K. Sinangil and C. Viswesvaran (eds) *Handbook of Industrial Work and Organizational Psychology*, Thousand Oaks, CA, Sage Publications.

Fletcher, C. and Williams, (1992) 'The route to performance management', *Personnel Management*, 24 (10): 47–51.

Florkowski, G. W. and Fogel, D. S. (1995) 'Perceived host ethnocentrism as a determinant of expatriate adjustment and organizational commitment', Paper presented at the National Academy of Management Meeting, Vancouver, Canada.

Florkowski, G. W. and Olivas-Lujan, M. R. (2011) 'The diffusion of human resource information technology innovations in US and non-US firms', *Personnel Review* (in press).

Folger, J. and Poole, M. (1984) *Working Through Conflict: A communication perspective*, Glenview, IL, Scott, Foresman.

Folger, R., Konovsoy, M. A. and Cropanzano, R. (1992) 'A due process metaphor for performance appraisal', in B. M. Staw and L. L. Cummings (eds) *Research in Organisational Behaviour*, Volume 14, Greenwich, CT, JAI Press, pp129–177.

Fombrun, C., Tichy, N. M. and Devanna, M. A. (eds) (1984). *Strategic human resource management.* New York: Wiley.

Fondas, N. (1997) 'Feminization unveiled: management qualities in contemporary writings', *Academy of Management Review*, 22 (1): 257–282.

Forster, N. (1992) 'International managers and mobile families: the professional and personal dynamics of trans-national career pathing and job mobility in the 1990s', *International Journal of Human Resource Management*, 3 (3): 605–624.

Foss, N. J. and Pedersen, T. (2002) 'Transferring knowledge in MNCs: the role of sources of subsidiary knowledge and organizational context', *Journal of International Management*, 8: 1–19.

Foss, N. J. and Pedersen, T. (2004) 'Organizing knowledge processes in the multinational corporation: an introduction', *Journal of International Business Studies*, 35 (5): 340–349.

Franck, E. and Opitz, C. (2007) 'The singularity of the German doctorate as a signal for managerial talent: causes, consequences and future developments', *Management Revue*, 18 (2): 220–241.

Frank, C., Lundmark, A. and Vejbrink, K. (1990) *Personalfunktionen i Statsförvaltningen*, Uppsala, IPF.

Freedman, A. (1986) 'Jobs: insecurity at all levels', *Across the Board*, 23 (1): 4–5.

Freedman, A. (1991) *The Changing Human Resources Function*, New York, The Conference Board.

Freeman, M. A. and Bordia, P. (2001) 'Assessing alternative models of individualism and collectivism: a confirmatory factor analysis', *European Journal of Personality*, 15: 105–121.

Friedman, B.A. (2007) 'Globalization implications for human resource management roles', *Employment Responsibilities and Rights Journal*, 19: 157–171.

Frink, D. D. and Klimoski, R. J. (1998) 'Toward a theory of accountability in organizations and human resource management', *Research in Personnel and Human Resources Management*, 16: 1–51.

Frost, A., Birkinshaw, J. M. and Prescott, C. E. (2002) 'Centers of excellence in multinational corporations', *Strategic Management Journal*, 23 (11): 997–1018.

Fukuda, J. K. and Chu, P. (1994) 'Wrestling with expatriate family problems: Japanese experience in East Asia', *International Studies of Management and Organization*, Volume 24.

Fulcher, J. (1991) *Labour Movements, Employers and the State: Conflict and co-operation in Britain and Sweden,* Oxford, Clarendon Press.

Futoran, G. C. and Wyer, R. S. (1986) 'The effects of traits and gender stereotypes on occupational suitability judgements and the recall of judgement-relevant information', *Journal of Experimental Social Psychology*, 22: 475–503.

Gabrielsson, M., Kirpalani, V. H. M., Dimistratos, P., Solberg, A. and Zucchella, A. (2008) 'Born-global: propositions to help advance the theory', *International Business Review*, 17 (4): 385–401.

Galbraith, J. R. (1987) 'Organization design', in J. Lorsch (ed.) *Handbook of Organization Behavior*, Englewood Cliffs, NJ, Prentice Hall.

Gallie, D. (2003) 'The quality of working life: is Scandinavia different?', *European Sociological Review*, 19: 61–79.

Gamble, J. (2003) 'Transferring HR practices from the UK to China: the limits and potential for convergence', *International Journal of HRM,* 14 (3): 369–387.

Gamble, J., Morris, J. and Wilkinson, B. (2004) 'Mass production is alive and well: the future of work and organization in East Asia', *Journal of Human Resource Management*, 15 (2): 397–409.

Garavan, T., Costine, P., Heraty, N. and Morley, M. (1995) 'Human resource management: a stakeholder perspective', *Journal of European Industrial Training*, 19 (10): 1–45.

Garrison-Jenn, N. (1998) *The Global 200 Executive Recruiters*, San Francisco, Jossey-Bass.

Gelade, G. A. and Young, S. (2005) 'Test of a service profit chain model in the retail banking sector', *Journal of Occupational and Organizational Psychology*, 78 (1): 1–22.

Gelfand, M. J., Nishii, L. H. and Raver, J. L. (2006) 'On the nature and importance of cultural tightness-looseness', *Journal of Applied Psychology*, 91 (6): 1225–1244.

Gennard, J. and Kelly, J. (1997) 'The unimportance of labels: the diffusion of the personnel/HRM function', *Industrial Relations Journal*, 28 (1): 27–42.

Geoghegan, T. (2010) *Were You Born on the Wrong Continent? How the European model can help you get a life*, London, The New Press.

Geppert, M., Matten, D. and Walgenbach, P. (2006) 'Transnational institution building and the multinational corporation: an emerging field of research', *Human Relations*, 59: 1451–1465.

Gerhart, B. (2008) 'Cross cultural management research: assumptions, evidence and suggested directions', *International Journal of Cross Cultural Management*, 8 (3): 259–274.

Gerhart, B. and Fang, M. (2005) 'National culture and human resource management: assumptions, and evidence', *International Journal of Human Resource Management*, 16: 975–990.

Ghemawat, P. (2007) *Redefining Global Strategy*, Boston, Harvard Business School Press.

Ghosh, P. and Geetika, (2007) 'Recruitment strategies: exploring the dimensions in the Indian software industry', *Asian Journal of Management Cases*, 4 (1): 5–25.

Ghoshal, S. (1987) 'Global strategy: an organizing framework', *Strategic Management Journal*, 8: 425–440.

Ghoshal, S. and Gratton, L. (2002) 'Integrating the enterprise', *Sloan Management Review*, 44 (1): 31–38.

Ghoshal, S., Korine, H. and Szulanski, G. (1994) 'Interunit communications in multinational corporations', *Management Science*, 40 (1): 96–110.

Giacobbe-Miller, J. K., Miller, D. J., Zhang, W. and Victorov, V. I. (2003) 'Country and organisational-level adaptation to foreign workplace ideologies: a comparative study of distributive justice values in China, Russia and the United States', *Journal of International Business Studies*, 34: 389–406.

Gill, J. (1996) 'Communication: is it really that simple? An analysis of a communication exercise in a case study situation', *Personnel Review*, 25 (5): 23–37.

Glanz, L. (2003) 'Expatriate stories: a vehicle of professional development abroad?', *Journal of Managerial Psychology*, 18 (3): 259–274.

GMAC (2000) *Global Relocation Trends 2000 Survey Report*, New York, GMAC/Windham.

GMAC (2008) *Global Relocation Trends: 2008 Survey Report*, Woodridge, IL, GMAC Global Relocation Services.

Godard, J. (2004) 'A critical assessment of the high-performance paradigm', *British Journal of Industrial Relations*, 42 (2): 349–378.

Goergen, M., Brewster, C. J. and Wood, G. (2009a) 'Corporate governance and training', *Journal of Industrial Relations*, 51 (4): 461–489.

Goergen, M., Brewster, C. J. and Wood, G. (2009b) 'Corporate governance regimes and employment relations in Europe', *Relations Industrielles/Industrial Relations*, 64 (4): 620–640.

Goetschy, J. (1998) 'France: the limits of reform', in A. Ferner and R. Hyman (eds) *Changing Industrial Relations in Europe*, Oxford, Basil Blackwell.

Gold, M. and Hall, M. (1990) *Legal Regulation and the Practice of Employee Participation in the European Community*, European Foundation for the Improvement of Living and Working Conditions paper EF/WP/90/40/EN, Dublin, EFILWC.

Gomez-Mejia, I. and Welbourne, T. (1991) 'Compensation strategies in a global context', *Human Resource Planning*, 14 (1): 29–42.

Gomez, C. and Sanchez, J. I. (2005) 'Managing HR to build social capital in Latin America within MNCs', in M. M. Elvira and A. Davila (eds) *Managing Human Resources in Latin America*, London, Routledge, pp57–74.

Gong, Y. (2003) 'Subsidiary staffing in multinational enterprises: agency, resources and performance', *Academy of Management Journal*, 46: 728–739.

Gooderham, P. N. and Nordhaug, O. (2010) 'One European model of HRM?Cranet empirical contributions', *Human Resource Management Review*, 21 (1): 27–36.

Gooderham, P. N., Nordhaug, O. and Ringdal, K. (1999) 'Institutional and rational determinants of organizational practices: human resource management in European firms', *Administrative Science Quarterly*, 44: 507–531.

Goodhart, D. (1994) *The Reshaping of the German Social Market*, London, Institute of Public Policy Research.

Gordon, D. (1996) *Fat and Mean*, New York, Free Press.

Graen, G. B. and Hui, C. (1999) 'Transcultural global leadership in the 21st century: challenges and implications for development' in W. Mobley, M. J. Gessner and V. Arnold (eds) *Advances in Global Leadership*. Stamford, CT, JAI Press

Grant, E. (2008) 'How to retain talent in India', *MIT Sloan Management Review*, 50 (1): 6–7.

Grant, R. M. (1996) 'Prospering in dynamically-competitive environments: organizational capability as knowledge integration', *Organization Science*, 7 (4): 375–387.

Grant, R. M. (1996a) 'Toward a knowledge-based theory of the firm', *Strategic Management Journal*, 17 (S2): 109–122.

Grant, R. M. (1996b) 'Prospering in dynamically-competitive environments: organizational capability as knowledge integration', *Organization Science,* 7 (4): 375–387.

Gratton, L. (2005) 'Managing integration through cooperation', *Human Resource Management*, 44 (2): 151–158.

Grugulis, I. and Stoyanova, D. (2006) 'Skills and performance', Economic and Social Research Council SKOPE Issue Paper 9, Swindon, ESRC.

Grund, C. (2005) 'The wage policy of firms: comparative evidence for the US and Germany from personnel records', *International Journal of Human Resource Management*, 16: 104–119.

Gudykunst, W. B. (1998) 'Applying anxiety/uncertainty management theory to intercultural adjustment training', *International Journal of Intercultural Relations*, 22: 227–250.

Guest, D. (1987) 'Human resource management and industrial relations', *Journal of Management Studies*, 24 (3): 503–522.

Guest, D. (1992) 'Right enough to be dangerously wrong: an analysis of *In Search of Excellence*', in G. Salaman (ed.) *Human Resource Strategies*, London, Sage Publications.

Guest, D. (1997) 'HRM and performance', *International Journal of Human Resource Management*, 8 (3): 265–276.

Gueutal, H. G. and Falbe, C. (2005) 'eHR: trends in delivery methods', in H. G. Gueutal and D. L. Stone (eds) *The Brave New World of eHR: Human resources in the digital age*, San Francisco, Jossey-Bass, pp190–225.

Gueutal, H. G. and Stone, D. L (eds) (2005) *The Brave New World of eHR: Human resources in the digital age*, San Francisco, Jossey-Bass.

Gunnigle, P., Heraty, N. and Morley M. (2006) *Human Resource Management in Ireland*, 3rd edition, Dublin, Gill & Macmillan.

Guzzo, R. A., Noonan, K. A. and Elron, E. (1994) 'Expatriate managers and the psychological contract', *Journal of Applied Psychology*, 79: 617–626.

Hackman, J. R., Oldham, G., Janson, R. and Purdy, K. (1982) 'A new strategy for job enrichment', in H. L. Tosi and W. C. Hamner (eds) *Organizational Behaviour and Management: A contingency approach*, New York. John Wiley & Sons, pp423–441.

Hagen, I. M. (2010) 'Board level representation – still an unused resource?', Paper for the IIRA European Congress, Copenhagen.

Hall, E. T. (1959) *The Silent Language*, New York, Anchor Books.

Hall, E. T. (1976) *Beyond Culture*. New York, Doubleday.

Hall, E. T. (2000) 'Context and meaning', in L. A. Samovar and R. E. Porter (eds) *Intercultural Communication: A reader*, 9th edition, Belmont, California, Wadsworth Publishing.

Hall, P. A. and Soskice, D. (2001) 'An introduction to varieties of capitalism', in P. A. Hall and D. Soskice (eds) *Varieties of Capitalism: The institutional foundations of competitive advantage*, Oxford, Oxford University Press, pp1–68.

Hamel, G. (2000) *Leading the Revolution*, Boston, MA, Harvard Business School Press.

Hamel, G. and Prahalad, C. K. (1985) 'Do you really have a global strategy?', *Harvard Business Review*, July/August, 139–148.

Hamori, M. and Koyuncu, B. (2011) 'Career advancement in large organisations in Europe and the United States: do international assignments add value?', *International Journal of Human Resource Management*, 22 (4): 843–862.

Hampden-Turner, C. and Trompenaars, F. (2006) 'Cultural intelligence: is such a capacity credible?', *Group and Organization Management*, 31 (1): 56–63.

Hannon, J. M., Huang, I.-C. and Jaw, B.-S. (1995) 'International human resource strategy and its determinants: the case of subsidiaries in Taiwan', *Journal of International Business Studies*, 26: 531–554.

Hansen, M. T., Nohria, N. and Tierney, T. (1999) 'What is your strategy for managing knowledge?', *Harvard Business Review*, 77 (2): 106–116.

Harris, F. and de Chernatony, L. (2001) 'Corporate branding and corporate brand performance', *European Marketing Journal*, 35 (3/4): 441–456.

Harris, H. (1995) 'Women's role in international management', in A. W. K. Harzing and J. van Ruysseveldt (eds) *International Human Resource Management*, London, Sage.

Harris, H. (1999) 'Women in international management: why are they not selected?', in C. J. Brewster and H. Harris (eds) *International HRM: Contemporary issues in Europe*, London, Routledge.

Harris, H. and Brewster, C. J. (1999a) 'A framework for pre-departure preparation', in C. J. Brewster and H. Harris (eds) *International HRM: Contemporary issues in Europe*, London, Routledge.

Harris, H. and Brewster, C. J. (1999b) 'The coffee-machine system: how international selection really works', *International Journal of Human Resource Management*, 10 (2): 488–500.

Harris, H., Brewster, C. J. and Sparrow, P. R. (2001) *Globalisation and HR: A literature review*, London, CIPD.

Harris, M., Van Hoye, G. and Lievens, F. (2003) 'Privacy and attitudes towards internet-based selection systems: a cross-cultural comparison', *International Journal of Selection and Assessment*, 11 (2/3): 230–236.

Harris, P. R. and Moran, R. T. (1996) *Managing Cultural Differences*, 2nd edition, Houston, Texas, Gulf.

Harris, R., Sumner, R. and Rainey, L. (2005) *Student Traffic: Two-way movement between vocational education and training and higher education*, Centre for Research in Education, Equity and Work, University of South Australia, Australian National Training Authority.

Harry, W. (2007) 'Employment creation and localization: the crucial human resource issue for the GCC', *International Journal of Human Resource Management*, 18 (1): 132–146.

Harvard Business Review (2003) 'Perspectives: in search of global leaders', *Harvard Business Review*, August: 38–45.

Harvey, M. (1985) 'The expat family: an overlooked variable in international assignments', *Columbia Journal of World Business*, Spring, 84–92.

Harvey, M. (1995) 'The impact of dual-career families on international relocations', *Human Resources Management Review*, 5 (3): 223–244.

Harvey, M. (1996) 'Addressing the dual-career expatriation dilemma in international relocation', *Human Resource Planning*, 19 (4): 18–40.

Harvey, M. (1997) 'Dual career expatriates: expectations, adjustment and aatisfaction with international relocation', *Journal of International Business Studies*, 28 (3): 627–657.

Harvey, M. and Novicevic, M. M. (2004) 'The development of political skill and political capital by global leaders through global assignments', *International Journal of Human Resource Management*, 15 (7): 1173–1188.

Harvey, M., Novicevic, M. M., and Speier, C. (2000) 'Strategic Global Human Resource Management: The Role of Inpatriate Managers', *Human Resource Management Review*, 10 (2): 153–175.

Harzing, A. W. K. (1995) 'The persistent myth of high expatriate failure rate', *International Journal of Human Resource Management*, 6 (2): 457–475.

Harzing, A. W. K. and Ruysseveldt, J. V. (1995) *International Human Resource Management*, London, Sage.

Haslberger, A. (2005) 'The complexities of expatriate adaptation', *Human Resource Management Review*, 15: 160–180.

Haslberger, A. and Brewster, C. J. (2008) 'The expatriate family – an international perspective', *Journal of Managerial Psychology*, 23 (3): 324–346.

Haslberger, A. and Brewster, C. J. (2009) 'Capital gains: expatriate adjustment and the psychological contract in international careers', *Human Resource Management*, 48 (3): 379–397.

Hayden, A. and Edwards, T. (2001) 'The erosion of the country of origin effect: a case study of a Swedish multinational company', *Relations Industrielles*, 56 (1): 116–140.

Hechanova, R., Beehr, T. A. and Christiansen, N. D. (2003) 'Antecedents and consequences of employees' adjustment to overseas assignment: a meta-analytical review', *Applied Psychology: An International Review*, 52 (2): 213–236.

Hedlund, G. (1986) 'The hypermodern MNC – a heterarchy?', *Human Resource Management*, 25 (1): 9–35.

Hedlund, G. (1990) *Personalfragor i Tredje Vägen*, Uppsala, IPF.

Hedlund, G. and Kverneland, A. (1985) 'Are strategies for foreign markets changing? The case of Swedish investment in Japan', *International Studies of Management and Organization*, 15 (2): 41–59.

Heenan, D. A. and Perlmutter, H. V. (1979) *Multinational Organizational Development: A social architectural approach*, Reading, MA, Addison-Wesley.

Heery, E. (2000) 'Trade unions and the management of reward', in G. White and J. Druker (eds) *Reward Management: A critical text*, London, Routledge.

Hees, M. (1995) 'Belgium', in I. Brunstein (ed.) *Human Resource Management in Western Europe*, Berlin, Walter De Gruyter.

Heffernan, M., Flood, P. C. and Liu, W. (2011) 'High performance work systems international evidence of the impact on firms and employees', in A.-W. Harzing and A. Pinnington (eds) *International Human Resource Management*, London, Sage.

Heilman, M. (1983) 'Sex bias in work settings: the lack of fit model', *Research in Organizational Behaviour*, 5: 269–298.

Hempel P. S. (2001) 'Differences between Chinese and Western managerial views of performance', *Personnel Review*, 30: 303–226.

Heskett, J. (2006) 'What's to be done about performance reviews?', *Harvard Business School Working Knowledge*, November.

Higginbottom, K. (2001) 'Flexible working policy rings in rewards for BT', *People Management*, 27 September, p11.

Hiltrop, J.-M. and Janssens, M. (1990) 'Expatriation: challenges and recommendations', *European Management Journal*, March, 19–27.

Hippler, T. (2008). Book review of Handbook of Research in International Human Resource Management. *Journal of International Management*, 14: 89–92.

Hjalager, A.-M. (2003) 'Virtually working: traditional and emerging institutional frameworks for the contingent workforce', *International Journal of Manpower*, 24 (2): 187–207.

Hocking, J. B., Brown, M. E., and Harzing, A.-W. (2007) Balancing global and local strategic contexts: expatriate knowledge transfer, applications and learning within a transnational organization. *Human Resource Management,* 46 (4): 513–533.

Hoecklin, L. (1994) *Managing Cultural Differences*, Harlow, Addison-Wesley Longman.

Hofstede, G. (1980) *Culture's Consequences: International differences in work-related values*, London, Sage Publications.

Hofstede, G. (1991) *Cultures and Organizations: Software of the mind*, London, McGraw-Hill.

Hofstede, G. (1993) 'Cultural constraints in management theories', *Academy of Management Executive,* 7 (1): 81–93.

Hofstede, G (1995) 'Multilevel research of human systems: flowers, bouquets and gardens', *Human Systems Research*, 14: 207–217.

Hofstede, G. (1998) 'Think locally, act globally: Cultural constraints in personnel management', *Management International Review*, 38(2): 7–26.

Hofstede, G. (2001) *Culture's Consequences*, 2nd edition, London, Thousand Oaks.

Holden, L. (1997) 'Human resource management in Europe', in I. Beardwell and L. Holden (eds) *Human Resource Management: A contemporary perspective*, London, Pitman Publishing.

Holden, L. and Livian, Y. (1993) 'Does strategic training policy exist? Some evidence from ten European countries', in A. Hegewisch and C. J. Brewster (eds) *European Developments in HRM*, London, Kogan Page.

Hollingsworth, J. R. (2006) 'Advancing our understanding of capitalism with Niels Bohr's thinking about complementarity', in G. T. Wood and P. James (eds) *Institutions, Production and Working Life*, Oxford, Oxford University Press.

Hollingsworth, J. R. and Boyer, R. (1997) 'Coordination of economic actors and social systems of production', in J. R. Hollingsworth and R. Boyer (eds) *Contemporary Capitalism: The embeddedness of institutions*, Cambridge, Cambridge University Press.

Holm, U. I. F. and Pedersen, T. (2000) *The Emergence And Impact Of MNC Centre Of Excellence*. London: Macmillan Press.

Holt Larsen, H. and Brewster, C. J. (2003) Line management responsibility for HRM: what is happening in Europe? *Employee Relations*, 25 (3): 228–244.

Holtbrügge, D. and Enßlinger, B. (2009) 'Initiating forces and success factors of born global firms', *European Journal of International Management*, 3 (2): 232–260.

Hoogendoorn, J. and Brewster, C. J. (1992) 'Human resource aspects: decentralization and devolution', *Personnel Review*, 21 (1): 4–11.

Hou, W. C. (2010) 'Developing Asia's corporate leadership: challenges and moving forward', in D. Ulrich (ed.) *Leadership in Asia: Challenges and opportunities*, Singapore, Ministry of Manpower, pp40–80.

House, R. J., Javidan, M., Hanges, P. and Dorfman, P. (2002) 'Understanding cultures and implicit leadership theories across the globe: an introduction to project GLOBE', *Journal of World Business*, 37: 3–10.

House, R. J., Hanges, P. J., Javidan, M., Dorfman, P. W. and Gupta, V. (2004) *Culture, Leadership and Organization, The GLOBE Study of 62 Societies*, Thousand Oaks, CA, Sage.

Hudson, R. (2006) 'The production of institutional complementarity? The case of North-East England', in G. Wood, and P. James (eds) *Institutions and Working Life*, Oxford, Oxford University Press.

Huo, Y. P., Huang, H. J. and Napier, N. K. (2002) 'Divergence or convergence: a cross-national comparison of personnel selection systems', *Human Resource Management*, 41 (1): 31–44.

Huselid, M. (1995) 'The impact of human resource management practices on turnover, productivity and corporate financial performance', *Academy of Management Journal*, 38: 635–672.

Hustad, E. and Munkvold, B. E. (2005) IT-supported Competence Management: a case study at Ericsson. *Knowledge Management*, Spring, 78–88.

Hutchinson, S. and Brewster, C. J. (1995) (eds) *Personnel and the Line: Developing the new relationship*, Report to the CIPD, Wimbledon.

Hutchinson, S. and Wood S. (1995) 'The UK experience', in S. Hutchinson and C. J. Brewster (eds) *Personnel and the Line: Developing the new relationship*, Report to the CIPD, Wimbledon.

Hyman, R. (1987) 'Strategy or structure? Capital, labour and control', *Work, Employment and Society*, 1 (1): 25–55.

Hyman, R. (1994) 'Industrial relations in Western Europe: an era of ambiguity?', *Industrial Relations*, 33 (1): 1–24.

Hyman, R. (2001) *Understanding European Trade Unionism: Between market, class and society*, London, Sage.

Hyman, R. and Ferner, A. (eds) (1994) *New Frontiers in European Industrial Relations*, Oxford, Blackwell.

Ilsøe, A. (2007) 'Decentralisering i et flexicurity-perspektiv – på vej mod et opdelt arbejdsmarked', *Theme Issue of Tidskrift for Arbejdsliv*, 4, November.

Ilsøe, A., Madsen, J. S, and Due, J. (2007) 'Impacts of decentralisation – erosion or renewal? The decisive link between workplace representation and company size in German and Danish industrial relations', *Industrielle Beziehungen*, Jahrgang 14, Heft 3: 201–222.

Immervoll, H. (2007) 'Minimum wages, minimum labour costs and the tax treatment of low-wage employment', OECD Social, Employment and Migration Working Paper No.46, Paris, OECD.

Income Data Services (1993) *Training and Development*, London, IPD.

Inkpen, A. and Ramaswamy, K. (2006) *Global Strategy: Creating and sustaining advantage across borders*, New York, Oxford University Press.

IPC (1987) *Joint Consultation in Practice: A study of procedures and actions*, Dublin, Irish Productivity Centre.

IRS Employment Trends (1991) 'Devolving personnel management at the AA and Prudential Corporation', *IRS Employment Trends*, 479: 4–9.

Jackson, G. (2005a) 'Employee representation in the board compared', *Industrielle Beziehungen*, 12 (3): 1–28.

Jackson, G. (2005b) *Reforming Stakeholder Models: Comparing Germany and Japan*, London, DTI Eco.

Jackson, G. (2009) 'The Japanese firm and its diversity', *Economy and Society*, 38 (3): 605–628.

Jackson, G. and Deeg, R. (2006) 'How many varieties of capitalism? Comparing the comparative institutional analyses of capitalist diversity', *MPfIG Discussion Paper 06/2* (http//:ssrn.com/abstract+896384).

Jackson, G. and Deeg, R. (2008) 'Comparing capitalisms: understanding institutional diversity and its implications for international business', *Journal of International Business Studies*, 39: 540–561.

Jackson, S. E. and Schuler, R. S. (1995) 'Understanding human resource management in the context of organizations and their environments', *Annual Review of Psychology*, 46 (1): 237–265.

Jackson, S. E., Hitt, M. A. and DeNisi, A. S. (2003) 'Managing human resources for knowledge-based competition: new research directions', in S. E. Jackson, M. A. Hitt and A .S. DeNisi (eds) *Managing Knowledge for Sustained Competitive Advantage: Designing strategies for effective human resource management*, San Francisco, CA, Jossey-Bass.

Jacoby, S. (1997) *Modern Manors*, Princeton, NJ, Princeton University Press.

Janis, I. (1982) *Groupthink: Psychological Studies in Policy Decisions and Fiascos*, Boston, MA, Houghton Mifflin.

Janssens, M. and Brett, J. M. (2006) 'Cultural intelligence in global teams: a fusion model of collaboration', *Group and Organisation Management*, 31 (1): 124–153.

Jelinek, M. and Adler, N. J. (1988) 'Women: world-class managers for global competition', *Academy of Management Executive*, 2 (1): 11–19.

Jessop, B. (2001) 'Series preface', in B. Jessop (ed.) *The Parisian Regulation School: Regulation theory and the crisis of capitalism*, Volume 1, London, Edward Elgar, ppix-xxiii.

Jewson, N. and Mason, D. (1986) 'Modes of discrimination in the recruitment process: formalization, fairness and efficiency', *Sociology*, 20 (1): 43–63.

Ji, L. and Karakowsky, L. (2001) 'Do we see eye-to-eye? Implications of cultural differences for cross-cultural management research and practices', *Journal of Psychology*, 135: 501–518.

Johanson, J. and Vahlne, J. E. (1977) 'The internationalisation process of the firm: a model of knowledge development and increasing foreign market commitments', *Journal of International Business Studies*, 8 (1): 23–32.

Johanson, J. and Vahlne, J. E. (2009) 'The Uppsala internationalisation process model revisited: from liability of foreignness to liability of outsidership', *Journal of International Business Studies*, 40 (9): 1411–1431.

Johnson, L. (2005) 'Measuring international assignment return on investment', *Compensation and Benefits Review*, 37 (2): 50–54.

Johnston, J. (1991) 'An empirical study of repatriation of managers in UK multinationals', *Human Resource Management Journal*, 1 (4): 102–108.

Jokinen, T. Brewster, C. J. and Suutari, V. (2008) 'Career capital during international work experiences: contrasting self-initiated expatriate experiences and assigned expatriation'. *International Journal of Human Resource Management*, 19 (6): 981–1000.

Jones, B. (1997) 'Getting ahead in Switzerland', *Management Review*, 86 (6): 58–61.

Kalmi, P., Pendleton, A. and Poutsma, E. (2005) 'Financial participation and performance in Europe', *Human Resource Management Journal*, 15 (4): 54–67.

Kamoche, K., Debrah, Y., Horwitz, F. and Nkombo, M. G. (2004) *Managing Human Resources in Africa*, London, Routledge.

Kane, P. (1996) 'Two-way communication fosters greater commitment', *HR Magazine*, 41 (10): 50–54.

Kang, S., Morris, S. and Snell, S. (2007) 'Relational archetypes, organizational learning, and value creation: extending the human resource architecture', *Academy of Management Review*, 32 (1): 234–256.

Kaplan, R. S. and Norton, D. P. (1996) 'Using the balanced scorecard as a strategic management system', *Harvard Business Review*, 74 (1): 75–85.

Karagozoglu, N. and Lindell, M. (1998) 'Internationalization of small and medium-sized technology-based firms: an exploratory study', *Journal of Small Business Management*, 36 (1): 44–59.

Karasek, R. and Theorell, T. (1990) *Healthy Work: Stress, productivity and the reconstruction of working life*, New York, Basic Books.

Katz, H. and Darbishire, O. (2000) *Converging Divergences: Worldwide changes in employment systems*, New York, Cornell University Press.

Kealey, D. J. and Protheroe, D. R. (1996) 'The effectiveness of cross-cultural training for expatriates: an assessment of the literature on the issue', *International Journal of Intercultural Relations*, 20 (2): 141–165.

Keenoy, T. (1990) 'HRM: a case of the wolf in sheep's clothing', *Personnel Review*, 19 (2): 3–9.

Kelly, J.M (2002) 'Why we should take performance measurement of faith (facts being hard to come by and not terribly important)', *Public Performance and Management Review*, 25 (4): 372–380.

Kessler, I. (2007) 'Reward choices: strategy and equity', in Storey, J. (ed.) *Human Resource Management: A critical text*, 3rd edition, London, Thomson.

Kessler, I., Undy, R. and Heron, P. (2004) 'Employee perspectives on communication and consultation', *International Journal of Human Resource Management*, 15 (3): 512–532.

Kettley. P. and Reilly, P. (2003) *An Introduction to e-HR*, Report 398, Brighton, Institute of Employment Studies.

Kidger, P. J. (1991) 'The emergence of international human resource management', *International Journal of Human Resource Management*, 2 (2): 149–163.

Kim, D.-O. (2006) 'Industrial relations in Asia: old regimes and new orders', in M. Morley, P. Gunnigle and D. Collings (eds) *Global Industrial Relations*, London, Routledge.

Kim, K., Park, J-H. and Prescott, J. E. (2003) 'The global integration of business functions: a study of multinational businesses in integrated global industries', *Journal of International Business Studies*, 34: 327–344.

Kim, S. and Wright, P. M. (2010) 'Putting SHRM in context: a contextualized model of high commitment work systems and its implications in China', *Management and Organization Review*, 7 (1): 153–174.

Kim, W. C. and Mauborgne, R. (2005) 'Procedural justice theory and the multinational corporation', in S. Ghoshal and D. E. Westney (eds) *Organization Theory and the Multinational Corporation*, New York, St. Martin's Press.

Kim, Y. Y. (1988) *Communication and Cross-Cultural Adaptation*, Clevedon, England/Philadelphia, PA, Multilingual Matters.

Kittler, M. G., Rygl, D., Mackinnon, A. (2011) 'Beyond culture or beyond control? Reviewing the use of Hall's high-/low-context concept', *International Journal of Cross-Cultural Management*, 11 (1): 63–82.

Kjellberg, A. (1992) 'Sweden: can the model survive?' In Ferner, A. and R. Hyman (eds.) *Industrial relations in the new Europe*, Blackwell, Oxford.

Kjellberg, A. (1998) 'Sweden: restoring the model?', in A. Ferner and R. Hyman (eds.) *Changing Industrial Relations in Europe*, Oxford, Basil Blackwell.

Klarsfeld, A., Combs, G. W., Susaeta, L. and Belizon, M. J. (2011) 'International perspectives on diversity and equal treatment policies and practices', in C. Brewster and W. Mayrhofer (eds) *Handbook of Comparative Human Resource Management*, Cheltenham, Edward Elgar.

Klarsfeld, A., Combs, G. M., Susaeta, L. and Belizon, M.-J. (2011) 'Comparing diversity management and equal treatment policies across countries', *ARAANZ Conference*, Auckland, 7 février - 8 février.

Kluckhohn F. F. and Strodtbeck F. L. (1961) *Variations in Value Orientations*, New York, Row, Peterson & Co.

Knight, G. A. and Cavusgil, S. T. (1996) 'The born global firm: a challenge to traditional internationalization theory', *Advances in International Marketing*, 8: 11–26.

Knight, G. A. and Cavusgil, S. T. (2004) 'Innovation, organizational capabilities, and the born-global firm', *Journal of International Business Studies*, 35 (2): 124–141.

Knudsen, H. (1995) *Employee Participation in Europe*, London, Sage.

Koch, M. J. and McGrath, R. G. (1996) 'Improving labor productivity: human resource management policies do matter', *Strategic Management Journal*, 17: 335–354.

Kochan, T., Katz, H. and McKersie, R. (1986) *The Transformation of American Industrial Relations*, New York, Basic Books.

Kogut, B. and Singh, H. (1988) 'The effect of national culture on the choice of entry mode', *Journal of International Business Studies*, 19: 411–432.

Kohn, A. (1998) 'Challenging behaviourist dogma: myths about money and motivation', *Compensation and Benefits Review*, March–April: 27–33.

Koslowsky, M., Sagie, A., and Stashevsky, S. (2002) 'Introduction: cultural relativism and universalism in organizational behaviours', *International Journal of Cross Cultural Management*, 2 (2): 131–135.

Kostova, T. (1999) 'Transnational transfer of strategic organizational practices: a contextual perspective', *Academy of Management Review*, 24 (2): 308–324.

Kostova, T. and Roth, K. (2002) 'Adoption of an organizational practice by subsidiaries of multinational corporations: institutional and relational effects', *Academy of Management Journal*, 45 (1): 215–233.

Kostova, T. and Roth, K. (2003) 'Social capital in multinational corporations and micro-macro model of its formation', *Academy of Management Journal*, 28 (2): 297–317.

Koubek, J. (2009) 'Managing human resources in the Czech Republic', in M. J. Morley, N. Heraty and S. Michailova (eds) *Managing Human Resources in Central and Eastern Europe*, London, Routledge, pp132–157.

Kovach, R. C. (1995) 'Matching assumptions to environment in the transfer of management practices: performance appraisal in Hungary', *International Studies of Management and Organization*, 24 (4): 83–99.

Kruse, D. L. (1993) Profit-sharing: does it make a difference? Kalamazoo, MI. W. E. Upjohn.

Kuemmerle, W. (1999) 'Building effective R&D capabilities abroad', *Harvard Business Review*, March–April, 61–69.

Kunda, Z. and Thagard, P. F. (1996) 'Forming impressions from stereotypes, traits and behaviors: a parallel-constraint-satisfaction theory', *Psychological Review*, 103: 284–308

Kurdelbusch, A. (2002) 'Variable pay in Germany', *European Journal of Industrial Relations*, 8 (3): 325.

Kuvaas, B. (2003) Employee ownership and affective organizational commitment. *Scandinavian Journal of Management*, 19: 193–212.

Kuvaas, B. (2007) 'Different relationships between perceptions of developmental performance appraisal and work performance', *Personnel Review*, 36 (3): 378–397.

Lado, A. and Wilson, M. (1994) 'Human resource systems and sustained competitive advantage: a competency-based perspective', *Academy of Management Review*, 19: 699–727.

Lam, A. (1994) 'The utilisation of human resources: a comparative study of British and Japanese engineers in electronics industries', *Human Resource Management Journal*, 4 (3): 22–40.

Lam, S. S. K., Schaubroeck, J. and Aryee, S. (2002) 'Relationship between organisational justice and employee work outcomes: a cross-national study', *Journal of Organizational Behavior*, 23 (1): 1–12.

Lammers C. J. and Hickson, D. (eds) (1979) *Organizations Alike and Unlike*, London, Routledge & Kegan Paul.

Landrine, H. and Klonoff, E. A. (1992) 'Culture and health-related schemas: a review proposal for inter-disciplinary integration', *Health Psychology*, 11: 267–276.

Lane, C. (1989) *Management and Labour in Europe*, Aldershot, Edward Elgar.

Lane, C. (1992) 'European business systems: Britain and Germany compared', in R. Whitley (ed.) *European Business Systems*, London, Sage.

Lane, C. (1998) 'European companies between globalization and localization: a comparison of internationalization strategies of British and German MNCs'. *Economy and Society*, 27 (4): 462–485.

Larsen, H. H. (2004) 'Global career as dual dependency between the organisation and the individual', *Journal of Management Development*, 23 (9): 860–869.

Larsen, H. H. and Brewster, C. J. (2003) 'Line management responsibility for HRM: what's happening in Europe?', *Employee Relations*, 25 (3): 228–244.

Larsen, H. H. and Mayrhofer, W. (2006) *Managing Human Resources in Europe*, London, Routledge.

Larson, E. and King, J. (1996) 'The systematic distortion of information: an ongoing challenge to management', *Organizational Dynamics*, 24 (3): 49–63.

Laurent, A. (1983) 'The cultural diversity of Western conceptions of management', *International Studies of Management and Organization*, 13 (1,2): 75–96.

Laurent, A. (1986) 'The cross-cultural puzzle of international human resource management', *Human Resource Management*, 25 (1): 91–102.

Lawler, E. and Mohrman, S. (2003) *Creating a Strategic Human Resources Organization: An assessment of trends and new directions*, San Francisco, CA, Stanford University Press.

Lawler, E. E. (1990) *Strategic Pay*, San Francisco, Jossey-Bass.

Lawler, E. E., Boudreau, J. W. and Mohrman, S. A. (2006) *Achieving Strategic Excellence: An assessment of human resource organizations*, Stanford, CA, Stanford Business Press.

Lawrence, P. (1993) 'Management development in Europe: a study in cultural contrast', *Human Resource Management Journal*, 3 (1): 11–23.

Lawrence, P. and Edwards, V. (2000) *Management in Western Europe*, London, Macmillan.

Lawson, J. and Bourner, T. (1997) 'Developing communication within new workgroups', *Journal of Applied Management Studies*, 6 (2): 149–168.

Lazear, E. (2000) 'Performance pay and productivity.' *American Economic Review*, 90: 1346–1361.

Lazear, E. and Oyer, P. (2004) 'Internal and external labour markets', *Labour Economics*, 11: 527–554.

Lazear, E. and Shaw, K. (eds) (2008) *The Structure of Wages: An international comparison*, Chicago, NBER.

Lee, S., Peng, M. W. and Lee, K. (2008) 'From diversification premium to diversification discount during institutional transitions', *Journal of World Business*, 43: 47–65.

Legge, K. (1989) 'Human resource management: a critical analysis', in J. Storey (ed.) *New Perspectives on Human Resource Management*, London, Routledge.

Legge, K. (1995) 'HRM: rhetoric, reality and hidden agendas', in J. Storey (ed.) *Human Resource Management: A critical text*, London, Routledge.

Leney, T. (2005) *Achieving the Lisbon Goal: The contribution of VET*, London, Lisbon-to-Copenhagen-to-Maastricht Consortium Partners.

Lengnick-Hall, C. A. and Lengnick-Hall, M. L. (2006) 'HR, ERP and knowledge management for competitive advantage', *Human Resource Management*, 45: 179–194.

Lengnick-Hall, M. L. and Lengnick-Hall, C. A. (2005) 'International human resource management research and social network/social capital theory', in G. Stahl and I.Björkman (eds) *Handbook of Research in International HRM*, Cheltenham, UK, Edward Elgar, pp475–487.

Lepak, D. and Snell, S. (1999) 'The human resource architecture: towards a theory of human capital allocation and development', *Academy of Management Executive:* 24: 1–31.

Lilja, K. (1998) 'Finland: continuity and modest moves towards company-level corporatism', in A. Ferner and R. Hyman (eds) *Changing Industrial Relations in Europe*, Oxford, Basil Blackwell.

Lin, L.-H. and Ho, Y.-L. (2009) 'Confucian dynamism, culture and ethical changes in Chinese societies – a comparative study of China, Taiwan, and Hong Kong', *International Journal of Human Resource Management*, 20 (11): 2402–2417.

Lincoln, J. and Kalleberg, A. (1990) *Culture, Control and Commitment: A study of work organization in the United States and Japan*, Cambridge, Cambridge University Press.

Lindholm, N. (2000) 'National culture and performance management in MNC subsidiaries', *International Studies of Management and Organization*, 29: 45–66.

Linehan, M. and Walsh, J. S. (2000) 'Work–family conflict and the senior female international manager', *British Journal of Management*, 11 (Special Issue): 49–58.

Lippit, M. (1997) 'Say what you mean, mean what you say', *Journal of Business Strategy*, 18 (4): 17–21.

Locke, E. A. (1968) 'Toward a theory of task motivation and incentives', *Organizational Behavior and Human Performance*, 2 (3): 157–189.

Locke, E. A. and Latham, G. P. (1990) *A Theory of Goal Setting and Task Performance*, Englewood Cliffs, NJ, Prentice Hall.

London, M. and Smither J. W. (1995) 'Can multi-source feedback change perceptions of goal accomplishment, self-evaluations and performance related outcomes? Theory-based application and directions for research', *Personnel Psychology,* 48: 803–839.

Longnecker, C. O. (1997) 'Why managerial performance appraisals are ineffective: causes and lessons', *Career Development International,* 2 (5): 212–218.

Lowe, J. (1992) 'Locating the line: the front-line supervisor and human resource management', in P. Blyton and P. Turnbull (eds) *Reassessing Human Resource Management*, London, Sage Publications.

Lowe, K., Downes, M. and Kroek, K. (1999) 'The impact of gender and location on the willingness to accept overseas assignments', *International Journal of Human Resource Management*, 10 (2): 223–234.

Lowe, K., Milliman, J., De Cieri, H. and Dowling, P. (2002) 'International compensation practices: a ten country comparative analysis', *Human Resource Management*, 41: 45–66.

Lu, Y. and Björkman, I. (1997) 'HRM practices in China-Western joint ventures: MNC standardization versus localization', *International Journal of Human Resource Management*, 8: 614–627.

Lu, Y., Tao, Z. and Wang, Y. (2009) *Union Effects on Performance and Employment Relations: Evidence from China*, Mimeo, University of Hong Kong, August.

Mabey, C. and Ramirez, M. (2004) *Developing Managers: A European perspective*, London, Chartered Management Institute.

Mabey, C. and Ramirez, M. (2011) 'Comparing national approaches to management development', in C. J. Brewster and W. Mayrhofer (eds) *A Handbook of Comparative HRM*, Cheltenham, Edward Elgar.

Mackay, L. and Torrington, D. (1986) *The Changing Nature of Personnel Management*, London, Institute of Personnel Management.

Mailand, M. (2009) 'Denmark: flexicurity and industrial relations'. Dublin, IE, Eurofound, http://www.eurofound.europa.eu/eiro/studies/tn0803038s/dk0803039q.htm

Mäkelä, K. (2007) 'Knowledge sharing through expatriate relationships: a social capital perspective', *International Studies of Management and Organisation*, 37: 108–125.

Mäkelä, K., Björkman, I. and Ehrnrooth, M. (2009) 'MNC subsidiary staffing architecture: building human and social capital within the organization', *International Journal of Human Resource Management*, 20 (6): 1273–1290.

Makhija, M. V., Kim, K. and Williamson, S. D. (1997) 'Measuring globalization of industries using a national industry approach: empirical evidence across five countries and over time', *Journal of International Business Studies*, 28 (4): 679–710.

Malbright, T. (1995) 'Globalization of an ethnographic firm', *Strategic Management Journal*, 16: 119–141.

Malhotra, N. and Hinings, C. R. (2010) 'An organizational model for understanding internationalisation processes', *Journal of International Business Studies*, 41: 330–349.

Marchington, M., Goodman, J., Wilkinson, A. and Ackers, P. (1992) *New Developments in Employee Involvement*, Research Series, No 2, Sheffield, Employment Department.

Marginson, P., Sisson, K. and Arrowsmith, J. (2003) 'Between decentralisation and Europeanisation: sectoral bargaining in four countries and two sectors', *European Journal of Industrial Relations*, 9 (2): 163–187.

Markus H. R. and Kitayama S. (1998) 'The cultural psychology of personality', *Journal of Cross-Cultural Psychology*, 29 (1): 63–87.

Marr, B. and Schiuma, G. (2001) 'Measuring and managing intellectual capital and knowledge assets in new economy organisations', in M. Bourne (ed.) *Handbook of Performance Measurement*, London, Gee.

Marsden, D. (1995) 'Deregulation or cooperation? The future of Europe's labour markets?', *Labour*, Special Issue, S67–S91.

Marsden, D. (1999) *A theory of employment systems*. OUP: Oxford.

Marsden, D. and Belfield, R. (2005) 'Unions and performance related pay.' In Fernie, S. and D.Metcalf (eds.) *Trade unions: resurgence or demise?* Routledge: London.

Marshall, J. (1984) *Women Managers: Travellers in a male world*, London, Wiley.

Martin, G. (2005) *Technology and People Management: Transforming the function of HR and the HR function*, London, Chartered Institute of Personnel and Development.

Martin, G. and Beaumont, P. B. (1998) 'HRM and the diffusion of best practice', *International Journal of Human Resource Management*, 9 (4): 671–695.

Martin, G. and Beaumont, P. B. (2001) 'Transforming multinational enterprises: towards a process model of strategic human resource management change', *International Journal of Human Resource Management*, 12 (8): 1234–1250.

Martin, G. and Hetrick, S. (2006) *Corporate Reputations, Branding and people management*, Oxford, Butterworth-Heinemann.

Martin, G. and Hetrick, S. (2009) 'Employer branding and corporate reputation management in an international context', in P. R. Sparrow (ed.) *Handbook of International Human Resource Management: Integrating people, process and context*, Chichester, Wiley, pp293–320.

Martin, G., Reddington, M. and Alexander, H., eds. (2008) *Technology, Outsourcing. and Transforming HR*. Series: Advanced HR practitioner series. Elsevier/Butterworth Heinemann, Oxford.

Martin, X. and Salomon, R. (2003) 'Knowledge transfer capacity and its implications for the theory of the multinational corporation', *Journal of International Business Studies*, 34: 356–373.

Mashood, N., Verhoeven, H., Chansarkar, B. (2009) 'Emiratisation, Omanisation and Saudisation – common causes: common solutions?', *Proceedings of the Tenth International Business Research Conference*, Crowne Plaza Hotel, Dubai, 16–17 April.

Matlay, H. (1997) 'The paradox of training in the small business sector of the British economy', *Journal of Vocational Education and Training*, 49 (4): 573–589.

Matsumoto, D. (1994) *People: Psychology from a cultural perspective*, Pacific Grove, CA, Brooks-Cole.

Matveev, A. V. and Nelson, P. E. (2004) 'Cross cultural communication competence and multicultural team performance: perceptions of American and Russian managers', *International Journal of Cross Cultural Management*, 4 (2): 253–270.

Maurice, M., Sellier, F. and Silvestre, J.-J. (1986) *The Social Foundations of Industrial Power: A comparison of France and Germany*, Cambridge, MA, MIT Press.

Mayhew, C. and Quinlan, M. (2002) 'Fordism in the fast food industry', *Sociology of Health and Illness*, 24 (3): 261–284.

Mayrhofer, W. and Brewster, C. J. (1996) 'In praise of ethnocentricity: expatriate policies in European multinationals', *International Executive*, 38 (6): 749–778.

Mayrhofer, W. and Brewster, C. J. (2005) 'European human resource management: researching developments over time', *Management Revue*, 16 (1): 36–62.

Mayrhofer, W., Brewster, C. J., Morley, M. and Gunnigle, P. (2000) 'Communication, consultation and the HRM debate', in C. J. Brewster, W. Mayrhofer and M. Morley (eds) *New Challenges for European Human Resource Management*, Basingstoke, Macmillan.

Mayrhofer, W., Brewster, C. J., Morley, M. and Ledolter, J. (2011a) 'Hearing a different drummer? Evidence of convergence in European HRM', *Human Resource Management Review,* 21 (1): 50–67.

Mayrhofer, W., M. Morley, C. Brewster, (2004) Convergence, Stasis, or Divergence?, in Brewster, C., Mayrhofer, W. and Morley, M. (Eds.), *European Human Resource Management: Evidence of Convergence?*, Oxford: Butterworth-Heinemann, pp415-437.

Mayrhofer, W., Sparrow, P. R and Brewster, C. J. (2011b) 'European human resource management: a contextualised stakeholder perspective', in C. J. Brewster and W. Mayrhofer (eds) *A Handbook of Comparative Human Resource Management*, Cheltenham, Edward Elgar.

Mayrhofer, W., Sparrow, P. R. and Zimmermann, A. (2008) 'Modern forms of international working', in C. J. Brewster, P. R. Sparrow and M. Dickmann (eds) *International Human Resource Management*, London, Routledge.

McCaughey, D. and Bruning, N. S. (2005) 'Enhancing opportunities for expatriate job satisfaction: HR strategies for foreign assignment success', *Human Resource Planning*, 28 (4): 21–29.

McGregor, D. (1960) *The Nature of Human Enterprise*, New York, McGraw-Hill.

McIntosh, S. and Vignoles, A. (2000) *Measuring and Assessing the Impact of Basic Skills on Labour*, CEE Discussion Papers 0003, London, LSE.

McKinsey and Co. (1993) *Emerging Exporters: Australia's high value-added manufacturing exporters*, Melbourne, McKinsey and Company and the Australian Manufacturing Council.

McNulty Y .M. and Tharenou, P. (2004) 'Expatriate returns on investment', *International Studies of Management and Organization*, 34 (3): 68–95.

McPhail, R. and Fisher, R. (2008) 'It's more than wages: analysis of the impact of internal labour markets on the quality of jobs', *International Journal of Human Resource Management*, 19: 3.

Meindl, J. R., Cheng, Y. K. and Jun, L. (1990) 'Distributive justice in the workplace: preliminary data on managerial preferences in the PRC', in B. B. Shaw, J. E. Beck, G. R. Ferris and K. M. Rowland (eds) *Research in Personnel and Human Resource Management*, Supplement 2, New York, JAI Press.

Mellahi, K. and Wood, G. (2006) 'HRM in Malaysia', in P. S. Budhwar (ed.) *Managing Human Resources In Asia-Pacific*, London, Routledge, pp201–220.

Mendenhall, M. E. and Oddou, G. (1985) 'The dimensions of expatriate acculturation: a review', *Academy of Management Review*, 10: 39–47.

Mendenhall, M. E., Kühlmann T. M. and Stahl, G. D. (eds) (2001) *Developing Global Business Leaders*, Westport, Quorum.

Mendenhall, M. E., Kühlmann, T. M., Stahl, G. D. and Osland, J. S. (2002) 'Employee development and expatriate assignents', in M. J. Gannon and K. L. Newman (eds) *Handbook of Cross-Cultural Management*, London, Blackwell.

Mendenhall, M. E., Punnett, B. J. and Ricks, D. (1995) *Global Management*, Cambridge, MA, Blackwell.

Mendonca M. and Kanungo R. N. (1996) 'Impact of culture on performance', *International Journal of Manpower*, 17: 65–69.

Menon. S. T. (2004) 'Culture's consequences for 21st-century research and practice', *International Journal of Cross Cultural Management*, 4 (2): 135–140.

Metcalf, D. (2004) 'Unions and productivity, financial performance and investment: international evidence', in J. Addison and C. Schnabel (eds) *International Handbook of Trade Unions*, Northampton, MA, Edward Elgar, pp118–171.

Metcalf, D. and Li, J. (2006) 'Chinese unions: an Alice in Wonderland dream world', *Advances In Industrial and Labor Relations,*15: 213–268.

Meyer, J. W. and Rowan, B. (1977) 'Institutional organizations: formal structure as myth and ceremony', *American Journal of Sociology*, 83: 340–363.

Michaels, E., Handfield-Jones, H. and Axelrod, B. (2001) *The War for Talent*, Boston, MA, Harvard Business School Press.

Miguelez, F. and Prieto, C. (1991) *Las Relaciones Laborales en España* (Industrial Relations in Spain), Madrid, Siglo Veintiuno.

Miles, R. and Snow C. (1986) 'Designing strategic human resource systems', *Organizational Dynamics*, 12 (2): 36–52.

Miles, E., Patrick, S. and King, W. (1996) 'Job level as a systematic variable in predicting the relationship between supervisory communication and job satisfaction', *Journal of Occupational and Organizational Psychology*, 69 (3): 277–293.

Miller, E. (1972) 'The selection decision for an international assignment: a study of the decision-makers behaviour', *Journal of International Business Studies*, 3: 49–65.

Miller, J. S., Hom, P. W. and Gomez-Mejia, L. R. (2001) 'The high cost of low wages: does Maquiladora compensation reduce turnover?', *Journal of International Business Studies*, 32 (3): 585–595.

Milliman, J. S., Nason, S., Gallaher, E. House, P., von Glinow, M. A. and Lowe K. B. (1998). *The impact of national culture on human resource management practices: the case of performance appraisal.* Advances in International Comparative Management 12: 157–183.

Milliman, J., Nason, S., Zhu, C. and De Cieri, H. (2002) 'An exploratory assessment of the purposes of performance appraisals in North and Central America and the Pacific Rim', *Human Resource Management*, 41 (1): 87–102.

Minbaeva, D. B. and Michailova, S. (2004) Knowledge transfer and expatriation in multinational corporations: the role of disseminative capacity. *Employee Relations*, 26 (6): 663–679.

Minbaeva, D., Pedersen, T., Björkman, I., Fey, C. F. and Park, H. J. (2003) 'MNC knowledge transfer, subsidiary absorptive capacity, and HRM', *Journal of International Business Studies*, 34: 586–599.

Mintzberg, H. (1975) 'The managers' job: folklore and fact', *Harvard Business Review*, July–Aug, 49–61.

Mintzberg, H. (1978) 'Patterns in strategy formation', *Management Science*, 24: 934–948.

Mintzberg, H., Jorgensen, J., Dougherty, D. and Westley, F. (1996) 'Some surprising things about collaboration: knowing how people connect makes it work better', *Organizational Dynamics*, 25 (1): 60–72.

Monge, P. and Eisenberg, E. (1987) 'Emergent communication networks', in F. Jablin, L. Putnam, K. Roberts and L. Porter (eds) *Handbook of Organizational Communication: An interdisciplinary perspective*, Newbury Park, CA, Sage.

Moore, S. and Punnett, J. (1994) 'Expatriates and their spouses: a pilot study in the Limerick region and directions for future research', *Irish Business and Administration Research*, 15: 178–184.

Morgan, G. (2007) 'National business systems research: process and prospects', *Scandinavian Journal of Management*, 23: 127–145.

Morishima, M. (1995) 'Strategic diversification of HRM in Japan', in P. M. Wright, L. D. Dyer, J. W. Boudreau and G. T. Milkovich (eds) *Strategic Human Resources Management in the Twenty-First Century*, Stamford, CT, JAI Press.

Morishima, M. and Feuille, P. (2000) 'Effects of the use of contingent workers on regular status workers: a Japan-US comparison', Paper presented at the IIRA conference, Tokyo, Japan.

Morley, M. and Heraty, N. (2004) 'International assignments and global careers', *Thunderbird International Business Review*, 46 (6): 633–646.

Morley, M., Brewster, C. J., Gunnigle, P. and Mayrhofer, W. (1996) 'Evaluating change in European industrial relations: research evidence on trends at organisational level', *International Journal of Human Resource Management*, 7 (3): 640–656.

Morley, M., Brewster, C. J., Gunnigle, P. and Mayrhofer, W. (2000) 'Evaluating change in European industrial relations: research evidence on trends at organisational level', in C. J. Brewster, W. Mayrhofer and M. Morley (eds) *New Challenges for European Human Resource Management*, Basingstoke, Macmillan.

Morley, M., Mayrhofer, W. and Brewster, C. J. (2000) 'Communications in northern Europe', in C. J. Brewster and H. H. Larsen (eds) *Human Resource Management in Northern Europe*, Oxford, Blackwell.

Morris M. W. and Peng, K. (1994) 'Culture and cause: American and Chinese attribution for social and physical events', *Journal of Personality and Social Psychology*, 67: 6–16.

Morris, M. W. and Leung, K. (2000) 'Justice for all? Progress in research on cultural variation in the psychology of distributive and procedural justice', *Applied Psychology: An International Review*, 49 (1): 100–132.

Morris, S. S., Snell, S. A. and Wright, P. M. (2005) 'A resource-based view of international human resources: towards a framework of integrative and creative capabilities', in G. Stahl and I. Björkman (eds) *Handbook of Research in International HRM,* Cheltenham, UK, Edward Elgar, pp433–448.

Morrison, A. J. (2000) 'Developing a global leadership model', *Human Resource Management*, Summer/Fall, 39 (2/3): 117–131.

Mosco, V. (1996) *The Political Economy of Communication: Rethinking and renewal*, Thousand Oaks, CA, Sage Publications.

Mowery, D. C., Oxley, J. E. and Silverman, B. S. (1996) 'Strategic alliances and interfirm knowledge transfer', *Strategic Management Journal*, 17: 77–99.

Muchinsky, P. M (1997) *Psychology Applied to Work: An introduction to industrial and organisational psychology*, Pacific Grove, CA, Brooks/Cole Publishing Company.

Mulder, M. (1960) 'Communication structure, decision structure and group performance', *Sociometry*, 23 (1): 1–14.

Muller, M. (1997) 'Institutional resilience in a changing world economy? The case of the German banking and chemical industries', *British Journal of Industrial Relations*, 35 (4): 609–626.

Munton, A. G. (1990) 'Job relocation, stress and the family', *Journal of Organizational Behavior*, 11: 401–406.

Murphy-Berman, V. and Berman, J. J. (2002) 'Cross-cultural differences in perceptions of distributive justice: a comparison of Hong Kong and Indonesia', *Journal of Cross-Cultural Psychology*, 33 (2): 157–170.

Murphy, K. R and Cleveland, J. N. (1995) *Understanding Performance Appraisal: social, organizational and goal-based perspectives*, Thousand Oaks, CA, Sage.

Murphy, K. R. and DeNisi, A. (2008) 'A model of the appraisal process', in A. Varma, P. S. Budhwar and A. DeNisi (eds) *Performance Management Systems A global perspective*, London, Routledge, pp81–96.

Murtha, T. P., Lenway, S. A. and Bagozzi, R. P. (1998) 'Global mind-sets and cognitive shift in a complex multinational corporation', *Strategic Management Journal*, 19: 97–114.

Nahapiet, J. and Ghoshal, S. (1998) 'Social capital, intellectual capital and the organizational advantage', *Academy of Management Review*, 23: 242–266.

Nakane, C. (1972) *Japanese Society*, Berkeley, University of California Press.

Navas, M., Garcia, M. C., Sánchez, J., Rojas, A. J., Pumares, P., and Fernández, J. S. (2005) 'Relative acculturation extended model (RAEM): new contributions with regard to the study of acculturation', *International Journal of Intercultural Relations*, 29: 21–37.

Navas, M., Rojas, A. J., García, M. and Pumares, P. (2007) 'Acculturation strategies and attitudes according to the relative acculturation extended model (RAEM): the perspectives of natives versus immigrants', *International Journal of Intercultural Relations*, 31: 67–86.

Neelankavil, J. P. (2000) 'Determinants of managerial performance: a cross-cultural comparison of the perceptions of middle-level managers in four countries', *Journal of International Business Studies*, 31 (1): 121–140.

Ng, K.-Y. and Earley, P. C. (2006) 'Old constructs, new frontiers', *Group and Organization Management*, 31 (1): 4–19.

Ng, S. H. and Warner, M. (1998) *China Trade Unions and Management*, London, Macmillan.

Nikandrou, I., Aspospori, E., Panayotopoulou, L., Stavrou, E. and Papalexandris, N. (2008) 'Training and firm performance in Europe: the impact of national and organizational characteristics', *International Journal of Human Resource Management*, 19 (11): 2057–2078.

Nikandrou, I., Aspospori, E. and Papalexandris, N. (2005) 'Changes in HRM in Europe: a longitudinal comparative study among 18 European countries', *Journal of European Industrial Training*, 2 (7): 541–560.

Noe, R. A. and Barbar, A. E. (1993) 'Willingness to accept mobility opportunities: destination makes a difference', *Journal of Organizational Behavior*, 14: 159–175.

Nohria, N. and Ghoshal, S. (1997) *The Differentiated Network: Organizing multinational corporations for value creation*, San Francisco, CA, Jossey-Bass.

Novicevic, M. M. and Harvey, M. (2001) 'The changing role of the corporate HR function in global organizations of the twenty-first century', *International Journal of Human Resource Management*, 12: 1251–1268.

Nyambegera, S., Sparrow, P. R. and Daniels, K. (2000) 'The impact of cultural value orientations on individual HRM preferences in developing countries: lessons from Kenyan organizations', *International Journal of Human Resource Management*, 11 (4): 639–663.

O'Brien, L. (2001) 'Unions seek big break in bank holiday drive', *People Management*, 13 September, p12.

O'Mahoney, M. and de Boer, W. (2002) *Britain's Relative Productivity Performance: Updates to 1999*, Final Report to the DTI, London, National Institute for Economic and Social Research.

OECD (1996) *Employment Outlook*. Paris, OECD.

OECD (1998) 'Making the most of the minimum: statutory minimum wages, employment and poverty', *Employment Outlook*, Paris, OECD.

OECD (2001) *Knowledge and Skills for Life: First results from PISA 2000*, Paris, OECD.

OECD (2002) *Education At A Glance*, Glossary, Paris, OECD.

OECD (2006) *Organizational Learning and Value Creation: Extending the human resource*, Education at a Glance, Paris, OECD.

Office for National Statistics (1999) *Social Trends*, London, Office for National Statistics.

Ohmae, K. (1990) *The Borderless World*, New York: HarperCollins.

Ohmae, K. (1996) *The End of the Nation State*, Cambridge, MA, Free Press.

Organization Resources Counselors (1998) *North American Survey of International Assignment Policies and Practices*, New York, ORC.

Organization Resources Counselors (2000) *Worldwide Survey of International Assignment Policies and Practices*, London and New York, ORC.

Osegowitsch, T. and Sammartino, A. (2008) 'Reassessing home-regionalisation', *Journal of International Business Studies*, 39: 184–196.

Osland, J., Bird, A., Mendenhall, M. E. and Osland, A. (2006) 'Developing global leadership and global mindsets: a review', in G. Stahl and I. Björkman (eds) *Handbook of Research in International HRM*, Cheltenham, UK, Edward Elgar, pp197–222.

Osterman, P. (1987) 'Choice of employment systems in internal labour markets', *Industrial Relations*, 26: 1.

Ostroff, C. and Bowen, D. E. (2000) 'Moving HR to a higher level: HR practices and organisational effectiveness', in J. K. Klein and S. W. J. Kozlowski (eds) *Multilevel Theory, Research and Methods in Organizations: Foundations, extensions and new directions*, San Francisco, Jossey-Bass.

Ouchi, W. (1981) *Theory Z*, New York, Addison-Wesley.

Paauwe, J. (1995) 'Personnel management without personnel managers: varying degrees of outsourcing the personnel function', in P. Flood, M. Gannon and J. Paauwe (eds) *Managing Without Traditional Methods*, Wokingham, Addison-Wesley.

Paauwe, J. (2004) *HRM and Performance: Achieving long-term viability*, Oxford, OUP.

Paik, Y., Vance, C. and Stage, H. D. (2000) 'A test of assumed cluster homogeneity for performance appraisal in four South-East Asian countries', *International Journal of Human Resource Management*, 11: 736–750.

Papalexandris, N. and Panayotopoulou, L. (2004) 'Exploring the mutual interaction of societal culture and HRM practices', *Employee Relations*, 26 (5): 495–509.

Paradella, M., Saez, F., Sanroma, E. and Torres, C. (2002) *La Formación Continua en las Empresas Españoles y el Papel de las Universidades*, Madrid, Civitas.

Parker, B. (1998) *Globalization and Business Practice: Managing across boundaries*, London, Sage.

Parkhe, A., Wasserman, S. and Ralston, D. A. (2006) 'New frontiers in network theory development', *Academy of Management Review*, 31 (3): 560–568.

Patrickson, M. and Sutiyono, W. (2006) 'HRM in Australia', in P. S. Budhwar (ed.) *Managing Human Resources in Asia-Pacific*, London, Routledge, pp239–252.

Pekkarinen, T. and Vartiainen, J. (2006). 'Gender differences in promotion on a job ladder: evidence from Finnish metalworkers.' *Industrial and Labor Relations Review*, 59 (2): 285–301.

Pelto, P. (1968) 'The difference between "tight" and "loose" societies', *Transaction*, 5: 37–40.

Peltonen, T. (2001) *New Forms of International Work: An international survey study – Results of the Finnish survey*, University of Oulu, Finland.

Peltonen, T. (2006) 'Critical theoretical perspectives on international human resource management', in G. Stahl and I. Björkman (eds) *Handbook of Research in International Human Resource Management*, Cheltenham, Edward Elgar, pp523–535.

Pendleton, A., Poutsma, E., Brewster, C. J. and van Ommeren, J. (2001) 'Employee share ownership and profit-sharing in the European Union', European Foundation for the Improvement of Living and Working Conditions, Dublin.

Pendleton, A., Poutsma, E., Brewster, C. J. and van Ommeren, J. (2002) 'Employee share ownership and profit-sharing in the European Union: incidence, characteristics, and representation', *Transfer*, 8 (1): 47–62.

Pendleton, A., Poutsma, E., van Ommeren, J. and Brewster, C. (2000) *Financial Participation in Europe: An investigation of profit sharing and employee share ownership*, Dublin, European Foundation for the Improvement of Living and Working Conditions.

Peng, M. W. (2006) *Global Strategy*, Cincinatti, OH, South-Western Thomson.

Peng, M. W. and Khory, T. (2008) 'Unbundling the institution-based view of international business strategy', in A. Rugman (ed.) *Oxford Handbook of International Business*, Oxford, Oxford University Press.

Peng, M. W. and Pleggenkuhle-Miles, E. G. (2009) 'Current debates in global strategy', *International Journal of Management Reviews*, 11 (1): 51–68.

Peng, M. W., Wang, D. Y. I. and Jiang, Y. (2008) 'An institution-based view of international business strategy: a focus on emerging economies', *Journal of International Business Studies*, 39: 920–936.

Penrose, E. T. (1959) *The Theory of Growth of the Firm*, London, Basil Blackwell.

Perkins, S. (2006) *International Reward and Recognition*, London, Chartered Institute of Personnel and Development.

Perlmutter H. V. (1969) 'The tortuous evolution of the multinational corporation', *Columbia Journal of World Business*, 1: 9–18.

Peteraf, M. A. (1993) 'The cornerstones of competitive advantage: a resource-based view', *Strategic Management Journal*, 14 (3): 179–191.

Pettit, J. (1997) 'Team communication: it's in the cards', *Training and Development*, 51 (1): 12–16.

Pfeffer, J. (1994) *Competitive Advantage Through People*, Boston, MA, Harvard University Press.

Pfeffer, J. (1998) 'Six dangerous myths about pay', *Harvard Business Review*, May-June, 109–119.

Pfeffer, J. and Salancik, G. (1978) *The External Control of Organizations: A resource dependence perspective*, New York, Harper & Row.

Phillips, N. (1992) 'Cross cultural training', *Journal of European Industrial Training*, 17 (2): 3–11.

Phillips, N. and Brown, J. (1993) 'Analysing communication in and around organisations: a critical hermeneutic approach', *Academy of Management Journal*, 36 (6): 1547–1577.

Pieper, R. (ed) (1990) *Human Resource Management: An international comparison*, Berlin, Walter de Gruyter.

Piotrkowski, C. (1979) *Work and the Family System*, New York, Free Press.

Plews, T. J. (1988) 'Labor force data in the next century', *Monthly Labour Review*, 113 (4): 3–8.

Polivk, A. E. and Nardone, T. (1989) 'The definition of contingent work', *Monthly Labour Review*, 112: 9–16.

Pollitt, C. (2006) 'Performance management in practice: a comparative study of executive agencies', *Journal of Public Administration Research and Theory*, 16 (1): 25–44.

Pollitt, D. (2009) 'Recruitment goes into overdrive as InterContinental Hotels battles for talent', *Training and Management Development Methods*, 23 (1): 509–551.

Poole, M. (1986) *Industrial Relations: Origins and patterns of national diversity*, London, Routledge & Kegan Paul.

Poole, M. (1990) 'Editorial: Human resource management in an international perspective', *International Journal of Human Resource Management*, 1 (1): 1–15.

Porter, L. W and Lawler, E. E (1968) *Managing Attitudes and Performance*, Homewood, IL, Irwin.

Porter, M. E. (1990) *The Competitive Advantage of Nations*, London, Macmillan.

Powell, W. and DiMaggio, P. (1991) *The New Institutionalism in Organizational Analysis*, Chicago, University of Chicago Press.

Prahalad, C. K. and Doz, Y. (1987) *The Multinational Mission: Balancing local demands and global vision*, New York, Free Press.

Prais, S. J. (1995) *Productivity, Education and Training: An international perspective*, Cambridge, Cambridge University Press.

PriceWaterhouse Coopers (2000) *International Assignments: European policy and practice 1999/2000*, London, PWC.

Pucik, V. (1992) 'Globalization and human resource management', in V. Pucik, N. Tichy and C. K. Barnett (eds) *Globalizing Management*, New York, Wiley.

Pucik, V. (1998) 'Selecting and developing the global versus the expatriate manager: a review of the state of the art', *Human Resource Planning*, 21 (4): 40–54.

Pudelko, M. and Harzing, A.-W. (2007) 'Country-of-origin, localization, or dominance effect? An empirical investigation of HRM practices in foreign subsidiaries', *Human Resource Management*, 46 (4): 535–559.

Pulakos, E. D, Mueller-Hanson, R. A and O'Leary, R. S. (2008) 'Performance management in the United States', in A. Varma, P. S. Budhwar and A. DeNisi (eds) *Performance Management Systems: A global perspective*, London, Routledge, pp97–114.

Punnett, B. J. and Ricks D. A. (1992) *International Business*, Boston, MA, PWS–Kent.

Punnett, B. J., Crocker, O. and Stevens, M. A. (1992) 'The challenge for women expatriates and spouses: some empirical evidence', *International Journal of Human Resource Management*, 3 (3): 585–592.

Purcell, J. (1995) 'Corporate strategy and its links to human resource management', in J. Storey (ed.) *Human Resource Management: A critical text*, London, Routledge.

Purcell, J. and Ahlstrand, B. (1994) *Human Resource Management in the Multi-Divisional Firm*, Oxford, Oxford University Press.

Rao, P. (2009) 'The role of national culture on Mexican staffing practices', *Employee Relations*, 31 (3): 295–311.

Rasmussen, E. S., Tage, K. M. and Felicitas, E. (2001) 'The founding of the born global company in Denmark and Australia: sensemaking and networking', *Asia Pacific Journal of Marketing and Logistics*, 13 (3): 75–107.

Reddington, M., Williamson, M. and Withers, M. (2005) *Transforming HR: Creating value through people*, Oxford, Elsevier, Butterworth-Heinemann.

Reed, M. (1996) 'Organizational theorizing: a historically contested terrain', in S. R. Clegg, C. Hardy and W. R. Nord (eds) *Handbook of Organization Studies*, London, Sage.

Rees, B. and Brewster, C. J. (1995) 'Supporting equality: patriarchy at work in Europe', *Personnel Review*, 24 (1): 19–40.

Rees, C. J., Mamman, A. and Bin Braik, A. (2007) 'Emiratization as a strategic HRM change initiative: case study evidence from UAE petroleum company', *International Journal of Human Resource Management*, 18 (1): 33–53.

Regalia, I. and Regini, M. (1998) 'Italy: the dual character of industrial relations', in A. Ferner and R. Hyman (eds) *Changing Industrial Relations in Europe*, Oxford, Basil Blackwell.

Rehder, R. R. (1994) 'Saturn, Uddevalla and the Japanese lean systems: paradoxical prototypes for the twenty-first century', *International Journal of Human Resource Management*, 5 (1): 1–31.

Reid, M. A., Barrington, H. and Brown, M. (2004) *HRD: Beyond training interventions*, London, Chartered Institute of Personnel and Development.

Reilly, P. (2000) 'HR shared services and the realignment of HR', *Institute of Employment Studies Report 368*, Brighton, IES.

Reynolds, C. and Bennett, R. (1991) 'The career couple challenge', *Personnel Journal*, 70 (3): 46–50.

Richbell, S., Brookes, M., Wood, G. and Brewster, C. (2011) 'Non-standard working time: An international and comparative analysis', *International Journal of Human Resource Management*, 22 (4): 944–961.

Rigby, M., Smith, R. and Brewster, C. J. (2004) 'The changing impact and strength of the labour movement in Europe', in M. Harcourt and G. Wood (eds) *Trade Unions and Democracy: Strategies and perspectives*, Manchester, Manchester University Press.

Riusala, K. and Smale. A. (2007) 'Predicting stickiness factors in the international transfer of knowledge through expatriates', *International Studies in Management and Organization*, 37 (3): 16–43.

Roos, J., Roos, G., Dragonetti, N. C. and Edvinsson, L. (1997) *Intellectual Capital: Navigating in the new business landscape*, London, Macmillan.

Rose, M. J. (1991) 'Comparing forms of comparative analysis', *Political Studies*, 3: 446–462.

Rosener, J. (1990) 'Ways women lead', *Harvard Business Review*, 68 (6): 119–125.

Rosenzweig, P. M. (2005) 'The dual logics behind international human resource management: pressures for global integration and local responsiveness', in G. Stahl and I. Björkman (eds) *Handbook of Research in International HRM*, Cheltenham, UK, Edward Elgar, pp36–48.

Rosenzweig, P. M. and Nohria, N. (1994) 'Influences on human resource management practices in multinational corporations', *Journal of International Business Studies*, 25 (2): 229–251.

Rotchford, N. L (2002) 'Performance management', in J. W. Hedge and E. D. Pulakos (eds) *Implementing Organizational Interventions*, San Francisco: Jossey-Bass, pp167–197.

Rowley, C. and Bae, J. (2003) 'Culture and management in South Korea', in M. Warner (ed.) *Culture and Management in Asia*, London, Curzon Press, pp187–209.

Rowley, C. and Bae, J. (2004) 'HRM in South Korea', in P. S. Budhwar (ed.) *Managing Human Resources in Asia*, London, Routledge, pp35–60.

Royle, T. (2000) *Working for McDonald's in Europe: The unequal struggle?* London, Routledge.

Royle, T. (2004) Low road convergence? The significance of sectoral factors in understanding MNC cross-border behaviour: the case of the Spanish and German quick food service sectors. *European Journal of Industrial Relations*, 10 (1): 51–71.

Rubery, J. and Fagan, C. (1993) 'Occupational segregation of women and men in the European Community', *Social Europe*, Supplement 3.

Rubery, J. and Grimshaw, D. (2003) *The Organisation of Employment: An international perspective*, Basingstoke, Palgrave Macmillan.

Rubery, J., Fagan, C., Almond, P. and Parker, J. (1996) *Trends and Prospects for Women's Employment in the 1990s*, Report for the DGV of European Commission, Manchester, UMIST.

Rueda, D. and Pontusson, J. (2000) 'Wage inequality and varieties of capitalism', *World Politics*, 52: 350–383.

Rugman, A. M. and Verbeke, A. (2004) 'A perspective on regional and global strategies of multinational enterprises', *Journal of International Business Studies*, 35: 3–18.

Rugman, A. M. and Verbeke, A. (2008) 'The theory and practice of regional strategy: a response to Osegowitsch and Sammartino', *Journal of International Business Studies*, 39: 326–332.

Rugman, A. M., D'Cruz, J. R. and Verbeke, A. (1995) 'Internationalisation and de-internationalisation: Will business networks replace multinationals?', in G. Boyd (ed.) *Competitive and Co-operative Macromanagement*, Aldershot, Edward Elgar, pp107–129.

Ruzic, F. (2006) 'New ethics for e-business offshore outsourcing', in H. S. Kehal and V. A. Singh (eds) *Outsourcing and Offshoring in the 21st Century: A socio-economic perspective*, London, Idea Group, pp87–121.

Ryan, A. M., McFarland, L., Baron, H. and Page, R. (1999) 'An international look at selection practices: nation and culture as explanations for variability in practice', *Personnel Psychology*, 52: 359–391.

Ryan, A. M., Wiechmann, D. and Hemingway, M. (2003) 'Designing and implementing global staffing systems: Part II. Best practices', *Human Resource Management*, 42 (1): 85–94.

Rynes, S. L. (1991) 'Recruitment, job choice, and post-hire consequences. A call for new research directions', in M. D. Dunnette and L. M. Hough (eds) *Handbook of Industrial and Organizational Psychology*, 2nd edition, Palo Alto, CA, Consulting Psychologists Press, pp399–444.

Sackmann, S. A. and Phillips, M. E. (2004) 'Contextual influences on culture research: shifting assumptions for new workplace realities', *International Journal of Cross Cultural Management*, 4 (3): 370–390.

Sahlberg. P, (2007) 'Secondary education in OECD countries: common challenges, differing solutions', European Training Foundation, presented at the Seminário Internacional sobre Ensino Médio Diversificado, Brasilia, Brazil, 17 September.

Salaman, G. (ed.) (1991) *Human Resource Management Strategies*, Milton Keynes, The Open University.

Salas, E., Wilson, K. A. and Lyons, R. (2008) 'Designing and delivering training for multicultural interactions in organisations', in D. L. Stone and E. F. Stone-Romero (eds) *The Influence of Culture on Human Resource Management Processes and Practices*, New York, Psychology Press, pp115–134.

Salt, J. and Millar, J. (2006) 'International migration in interesting times: the case of the UK', *People and Place*, 14 (2): 14–25.

Satherley, P., Lawes, E. and Sok, S. (2008) *The Adult Literacy and Life Skills (ALL) Survey: Overview and international comparisons*, Wellington, Ministry of Education.

Scase, R. and Goffee, R. (1989) 'Women in management: towards a research agenda', Paper for the Third Annual Meeting of the British Academy of Management.

Schein, E. H. (1978) *Career Dynamics: Matching individual and organisational needs*, Boston, MA, Addison-Wesley.

Schein, E. H. (1985) *Organisational Culture and Leadership*, San Francisco, Jossey-Bass.

Schiuma, G., Harris, H. and Bourne, M. (2003) 'Assessing the value of international assignments', *Report for Centre for Business Performance/Centre for Research into the Management of Expatriation*, Cranfield, Cranfield School of Management.

Schmidt, F. L and Hunter J. E. (1998) 'The validity and utility of selection methods in personnel psychology: practical and theoretical implications of 85 years of research findings', *Psychological Bulletin*, 124 (2): 262–274.

Schneider, B. R. and Soskice, D. (2009) 'Inequality in developed countries and Latin America: coordinated, liberal and hierarchical systems', *Economy and Society*, 38 (1): 17–52.

Schneider, S. and Barsoux, J.-L. (1997) 'The multicultural team', in S. Schneider and J.-L. Barsoux (eds) *Managing Across Cultures*, Hemel Hempstead, Prentice Hall.

Scholtes, P. R (1993) 'Total quality or performance appraisal: choose one', *National Productivity Review*, 12 (3): 349–364.

Schuler, R. S. (1990) 'Repositioning the human resource function: transformation or demise?', *Academy of Management Executive*, 4 (3): 49–60.

Schuler, R. S., Budhwar, P. S. and Florkowski, G. W. (2002) 'International human resource management: review and critique', *International Journal of Management Reviews*, 4 (1): 41.

Schuler, R. S., Sparrow, P. R. and Budhwar, P. S. (2009). Preface: Major Works in International Human Resource Management. In P. S. Budhwar, R. S. Schuler. and P. R. Sparrow (eds.) *Major works in international human resource management. Volume 1. International HRM*. London: Sage Publications, ppxxiii–xxviii.

Schuler, R. S. and Jackson, P. (1987) 'Linking competitive strategy and human resource management practices', *Academy of Management Executive*, 3 (1): 207–219.

Schuler, R. S. and Rogovsky, N. (1998) 'Understanding compensation practice variations across firms: the impact of national culture', *Journal of International Business Studies*, 29 (1): 159–177.

Schuler, R. S., Budhwar, P. S. and Florkowski, G. W. (2002) 'International human resource management: review and critique', *International Journal of Management Reviews*, 4 (1): 41.

Schuler, R. S., Dowling, P. J. and De Cieri, H. (1993) 'An integrative framework of strategic international human resource management', *Journal of Management*, 19 (2): 419–459.

Schuler, R. S., Fulkerson, J. R. and Dowling, P. J. (1991) 'Strategic performance measurement and management in multinational corporations', *Human Resource Management*, 30: 365–392.

Schwartz, S. H. (1992) 'Universals in the content and structure of values: theoretical advances and empirical tests in 20 countries', in M. P. Zanna (ed.) *Advances in Experimental Social Psychology*, Volume 25, New York, Academic Press.

Schwartz, S. H. (1994) 'Beyond individualism/collectivism: new cultural dimensions of values', in U. Kim, H. C. Triandis, C. Kagitcibasi, S. C. Choi and G. Yoon (eds) *Individualism and Collectivism*, London, Sage Publications.

Schwartz, S. H. (1999) 'A theory of cultural values and some implications for work', *Applied Psychology: An International Review*, 48 (1): 23–47.

Schwartz, S. H. and Bardi, A. (2001) 'Value hierarchies across cultures: taking a similarity perspective', *Journal of Cross-Cultural Psychology*, 32 (3): 268–290.

Scott Myers, M. (1991) *Every Employee a Manager: More meaningful work through job enrichment*, New York, McGraw-Hill.

Scullion, H. (1994) 'Creating international managers: recruitment and development issues', in P. Kirkbride (ed.) *Human Resource Management in Europe*, London, Routledge.

Scullion, H. (2005) 'International HRM: an introduction', in H. Scullion and M. Linehan (eds) *International Human Resource Management: A critical text*, Basingstoke, Palgrave Macmillan, pp3–21.

Scullion, H. and Brewster, C. J. (2001) 'Managing expatriates: messages from Europe', *Journal of World Business*, 36: 346–365.

Scullion, H. and Collings, D. G. (eds) (2006) *Global Staffing*, London, Routledge.

Scullion, H. and Collings, D. G. (eds) (2011) *Global Talent Management*, London, Routledge.

Scullion, H. and Starkey, K. (2000) 'In search of the changing role of the corporate human resource function in the international firm', *International Journal of Human Resource Management*, 11 (6): 1061–1081.

Scullion, H., Sparrow, P. R. and Farndale, E. (2011) 'Global talent management: new challenges for the corporate HR function in the global recession', *Zarzadzanie Zasobami Ludzkimi*, in press.

Searle, W. and Ward, C. (1990) 'The prediction of psychological and sociocultural adjustment during cross-cultural transitions', *International Journal of Intercultural Relations*, 14: 449–464.

Sekiguchi, T., Bebenroth, R. and Li, D (2011) 'Nationality background of MNC affiliates' top management and affiliate performance in Japan: knowledge-based and upper echelons perspectives', *International Journal of Human Resource Management*, 22 (5): 999–1016.

Seneviratna, C. and Turton, S. (2001) 'Dependents' day', *People Management*, 7 (24): 38–40.

Shapiro, D. L., Furst, S. A., Spreitzer, G. M. and Von Glinow, M. A. (2002) 'Transnational teams in the electronic age: are team identity and high performance at risk?', *Journal of Organizational Behavior*, 23: 455–467.

Sharma, S. (1990) 'Psychology of women in management: a distinct feminine leadership', *Equal Opportunities International*, 9 (2): 13–18.

Sharma, T., Budhwar, P. S. and Varma, A. (2008). Performance management in India, in *performance management systems: A global perspective* (edited by A. Varma, P. S. Budhwar. and A. DeNisi). Routledge L UK, pp180–192.

Shenton, G. (1996) 'Management education in Europe: diversity and integration', in M. Lee, H. Letiche and R. Crawshaw (eds) *Management Education in the New Europe*, London, International Thomson Publishing Inc, pp32–47.

Shipper, F., Hoffman, R. C. and Rotondo, D. (2004) 'Does the 360 feedback process create actionable knowledge equally across cultures?', *Proceedings of the Academy of Management*, New Orleans, LA, AOM.

Shleifer, A. and Vishny, R. (1997) 'A survey of corporate governance', *Journal of Finance*, 52: 737–783.

Shrivastava, S. and Shaw, J. B. (2004) 'Liberating HR through technology', *Human Resource Management*, 42 (3): 201–222.

Singh, R. (1992) 'Human resource management: a sceptical look', in B. Towers (ed.) *Handbook of Human Resource Management*, Oxford, Blackwell.

Sinha, J. B. P. (1990) *Work Culture in the Indian Context*, New Delhi, Sage.

Sisson, K. (1995) 'The personnel function', in J. Storey (ed.) *Human Resource Management: A critical text*, London, Routledge.

Sisson, K. (1997) *New Forms of Work Organisation: Can Europe realise its potential? Results of a survey of direct employee participation in Europe*, Dublin, European Foundation for the Improvement of Living and Working Conditions.

Sisson, K. (2001) 'Human resource management and the personnel function: a case of partial impact?', in J. Storey (ed.) *Human Resource Management: A critical text*, 2nd edition, London, Thomson Learning.

Sisson, K. (2006) 'International employee representation – a case of industrial relations systems following the market?', in T. Edwards and C. Rees (eds) *International Human Resource Management: Globalization, national systems and multinational companies*, Harlow, Prentice Hall, pp242–261.

Smilansky, J. (2004) *The Systematic Management of Executive Talent*, Wimbledon, CIPD.

Smith, C. (1992) 'Dual careers, dual loyalties', *Asian Pacific Journal of Human Resources*, 30 (4): 19–30.

Smith, C. and Meiksins, P. (1995) 'System, society and dominance effects in cross-national organisational analysis', *Work, Employment and Society*, 9: 241–268.

Smith, P. (2010) 'The right leaders in place in Asia … the right future leaders in the pipeline', in D. Ulrich (ed.) *Leadership in Asia: Challenges and opportunities*, Singapore, Ministry of Manpower Singapore.

Smith, P. C and Goddard, M. (2002) 'Performance management and operational research: a marriage made in heaven?', *Journal of the Operational Research Society*, 53: 247–255.

Smyth, J. (1995) 'Harvesting the office grapevine: internal communication', *People Management*, 1 (18): 24–28.

Snape, E., Thompson, D., Yan, F. K. and Redman, T. (1998) 'Performance appraisal and culture: practice and attitudes in Hong Kong and Great Britain', *International Journal of Human Resource Management*, 9 (5): 841–861.

Snape, R. (1999) 'Legal regulation of employment', in G. Hollinshead, P. Nicholls, and S. Tailby (eds) *Employee Relations*, London, *Financial Times*/Pitman.

Snell, S. A., Stueber, D. and Lepak, D. P. (2001) 'Virtual HR departments: getting out of the middle', in R. L. Henan and D. B. Greenberger (eds) *Human Resource Management in Virtual Organizations*, London, Information Age Publishing, pp81–102.

Society of Human Resource Management (2001) *How Is a Diversity Initiative Different from My Affirmative Action Plan?*, Report 23 July, New York, SHRM.

Södergren, B. (1992) *Decentralisering, Förändring i Företag och Arbetsliv*, Stockholm, Stockholm School of Economics.

Solomon, C. M. (1995) 'Repatriation: up, down or out?', *Personnel Journal*, April, 74 (1): 28–37.

Sonnentag, S. and Frese, M. (2002) 'Perspectives on performance', in S. Sonnentag (ed.) *Psychological Management of Individual Performance*, London, Wiley.

Sparks, K., Cooper, C. L., Fried, Y. and Shirom, A. (1997) 'The effects of hours of work on health: a meta-analytic review', *Journal of Occupational and Organizational Psychology*, 70, 391–408.

Sparrow, P. R. (1995) 'Towards a dynamic and comparative model of European human resource management: an extended review', *International Journal of Human Resource Management*, 6 (4): 935–953.

Sparrow, P. R. (1996) 'Careers and the psychological contract: understanding the European context' *European Journal of Work and Organizational Psychology*, 5 (4): 479–500.

Sparrow, P. R. (1997) Organisational competencies: creating a strategic behavioural framework for selection and assessment. In N. Anderson and P. Herriot (eds) *International Handbook of selection and assessment*, Chichester: John Wiley. pp343–368.

Sparrow, P. R. (1999) 'International recruitment, selection and assessment: whose route map will you follow?', in P. Joynt and B. Morton (eds) *The Global HR Manager: Creating the seamless organisation*, London, IPD.

Sparrow, P. R. (2000) 'International reward management', in G. White and J. Druker (eds) *Reward Management: A critical text*, London, Routledge.

Sparrow, P. R. (2006a) 'International management: some key challenges for industrial and organizational psychology', in G. Hodgkinson and J. K. Ford (eds) *International Review of Industrial and Organizational Psychology*, Volume 21, Chichester, Wiley.

Sparrow, P. R. (2006b) 'Knowledge management in global organisations', in G. Stahl and I. Björkman (eds) *Handbook of Research in International HRM*, Cheltenham, UK, Edward Elgar, pp113–140.

Sparrow, P. R. (2006c) *International Recruitment, Selection and Assessment*, London, Chartered Institute of Personnel and Development.

Sparrow, P. R. (2007) 'Globalisation of HR at function level: four case studies of the international recruitment, selection and assessment process', *International Journal of Human Resource Management*, 18 (5): 144–166.

Sparrow, P. R. (2008) 'Performance management in the UK', in A. Varma, P. S. Budhwar and A. DeNisi (eds) *Performance Management Systems: A global perspective*, London, Routledge, p131–146.

Sparrow, P. R. (2009). Integrating people, process. and context issues in the field of IHRM. In P. R. Sparrow (ed.) *Handbook of International Human resource Management: Integrating People, Process. and Context.* London: Wiley. pp 3–40.

Sparrow, P. R. (2011) 'Comparative analysis of employment contracts', in C. J. Brewster and W. Mayrhofer (eds) *Handbook of Research in Comparative Human Resource Management*, London, Edward Elgar Publishing.

Sparrow, P. R. and Braun, W. (2007) 'HR strategy theory in international context', in R. S. Schuler and S. E. Jackson (eds) *Strategic Human Resource Management*, London, Blackwell.

Sparrow, P. R. and Braun, W. (2008) 'HR sourcing and shoring: strategies, drivers, success factors and implications for HR', in M. Dickmann, C. J. Brewster and P. R. Sparrow (eds) *International Human Resource Management: A European perspective*, London, Routledge, pp39–66.

Sparrow, P. R. and Brewster, C. J. (2006) 'Globalizing HRM: the growing revolution in managing employees internationally', in C. L. Cooper and R. Burke (eds) *The Human Resources Revolution: Research and practice*, London, Elsevier.

Sparrow, P. R. and Brewster, C. J. (2011) 'Reuters: HRM in international perspective', in A. Dundon and A. Wilkinson (eds) *Case Studies in People Management, Strategy and Innovation*, Sydney, Tilde University Press.

Sparrow, P. R. and Cooper, C. L. (2003) *The Employment Relationship: Challenges facing HR*, London, Butterworth-Heinemann.

Sparrow, P. R. and Hiltrop, J. M. (1994) *European Human Resource Management in Transition*, London, Prentice Hall.

Sparrow, P. R. and Hiltrop, J. M. (1997) 'Redefining the field of European human resource management: a battle between national mindsets and forces of business transition', *Human Resource Management*, 36 (2): 1–19.

Sparrow, P. R. and Wu, P. C. (1998) 'How much do national value orientations really matter? Predicting HRM preferences of Taiwanese employees', *Employee Relations: The International Journal*, 20 (1): 26–56.

Sparrow, P. R., Brewster, C. J. and Harris, H. (2004) *Globalizing HRM*, London, Routledge.

Sparrow, P. R., Brewster, C. J. and Lightart, P. (2009) 'Globalising human resource management: examining the role of networks', in P. R. Sparrow (ed.) *Handbook of International Human Resource Management: Integrating people, process and context*, London, Wiley, pp361–385.

Sparrow, P. R., Hird, M., Hesketh, A. and Cooper, C. (eds) (2010) *Leading HR*, London, Palgrave Macmillan.

Sparrow, P. R., Schuler, R. S. and Budhwar, P. S. (2009) 'Introduction: cross cultural human resource management', in P. S. Budhwar, R. S. Schuler and P. R. Sparrow (eds) *Major Works in International Human Resource Management*, Volume 3: *Cross-Cultural HRM*, London, Sage Publications, ppvii–xviii.

Sparrow, P. R., Scullion, H. and Farndale, E. (2011) 'Global talent management: new roles for the corporate HR function', in H. Scullion and D. Collings (eds) *Global Talent Management*, London, Routledge, pp39–55.

Spreitzer, G. M., McCall, M. W. and Mahoney, J. D. (1997) 'Early identification of international executive potential', *Journal of Applied Psychology*, 82 (1): 6–29.

Stahl, G. K. and Björkman, I. (2006) (eds) *Handbook of Research in International Human Resource Management*, Cheltenham, Edward Elgar.

Stahl, G. K. and Cerdin, J. (2004) 'Global careers in French and German multinational corporations', *Journal of Management Development*, 23 (9): 885–902.

Stavrou, E., Brewster, C. J. and Charalambous, C. (2010) 'Human resource management and firm performance in Europe through the lens of business systems: best fit, best practice or both?', *International Journal of Human Resource Management*, 21 (7): 933–962.

Stavrou, E. T. and Brewster, C. J. (2005) 'The configurational approach to linking strategic human resource management bundles with business performance: myth or reality?', *Management Revue*, 16 (2): 186–201.

Staw, B. M. (1980) 'Rationality and justification in organizational life', in B. Staw and L. L. Cummings (eds) *Research in Organizational Behaviour: A regional review*, Volume 2, Greenwich, CT, JAI Press, pp45–80.

Steel, G. (1997) 'Global leadership in a mature multinational enterprise', *Academy of Management Symposium on Global Leadership in the 21st Century*, Boston, MA, AOM.

Steinberg, R. (1998) 'No, it couldn't happen here', *Management Review*, 87 (8): 68–73.

Steiner, D. D. and Gilliland, S. W. (2001) 'Procedural justice in personnel selection: international and cross-cultural perspectives', *International Journal of Selection and Assessment*, 9 (1/2): 124–137.

Sternberg, R. J. and Grigorenko, E. L. (2006) 'Cultural intelligence and successful intelligence', *Group and Organization Management*, 31 (1): 27–39.

Stiglitz, J. (2003) *The Roaring Nineties*, London, Penguin.

Stiles, P. and Trevor, J. (2006) 'The human resource department: roles, coordination and influence', in G. Stahl and I. Björkman (eds) *Handbook of Research in International HRM*, Cheltenham, UK, Edward Elgar, pp49–67.

Stokke, T. A. (2008) 'The anatomy of two-tier bargaining models', *European Journal of Industrial Relations*, 14 (March)**.**

Stone, D. L., Isenhour, L. and Lukaszewski, K. M. (2008) 'A model of the influence of cultural values on job application intentions and behaviors', in D. L. Stone and E. F. Stone-Romero (eds) *The Influence of Culture on Human Resource Management Processes and Practices*, New York, Lawrence Erlbaum, pp25–52.

Storey, J. (ed.) (1992) *New Developments in Human Resource Management*, Oxford, Blackwell.

Storey, J. (ed.) (1995) *Human Resource Management: A critical text*, London, Routledge.

Storey, J. (2007) *Human Resource Management: A critical text*, London, Routledge.

Storey, J. and Sisson, K. (1993) *Managing Human Resources and Industrial Relations*, Buckingham, Open University Press.

Strauss, G. and Hanson, M. (1997) 'Review article: American anti-management theories of organization: a critique of paradigm proliferation', *Human Relations*, 50: 1426–1429.

Streeck, W. (1992) *Social Institutions and Economic Performance*, Sage, London.

Streeck, W. (1993) 'National diversity, regime competition and institutional deadlock: problems in forming a European industrial relations system', *Journal of Public Policy*, 12: 301–330.

Streeck, W. (2005) 'Rejoinder: on terminology, functionalism, (historical) institutionalism and liberalization', *Socio-Economic Review*, 5: 577–587.

Streeck, W. (1997) 'German capitalism: does it exist, can it survive?' In C. Crouch and W. Streeck (eds.) *The political economy of modern capitalism: mapping convergence and diversity*. London, Sage.

Streeck, W. and Thelen, K. (2005) (eds) *Beyond Continuity: Institutional change in advanced political economies*, Oxford, Oxford University Press.

Stroh, L. and Caligiuri, P. M. (1998) 'Increasing global competitiveness through effective people management', *Journal of World Business*, 33 (1): 1–16.

Stroh, L. K., Black, J. S., Mendenhall, M. E. and Gregersen, H. B. (2005) *International Assignments: An integration of strategy, research and practice*, London, Lawrence Erlbaum.

Stroh, L. K., Gregerson, H. B. and Black, J. S. (1998) 'Closing the gap: expectations versus reality among expatriates', *Journal of World Business*, 33 (2): 111–124.

Sullivan, D. (1994) 'Measuring the Degree of Internationalization of a Firm.' *Journal of International Business Studies* 25, 325–342.

Sullivan, J. J., Suzuki, T. and Kondo, Y. (1986) 'Managerial perceptions of performance', *Journal of Cross-Cultural Psychology*, 17: 379–398.

Sundaram, A. K. and Black, J. S. (1992) 'The environment and internal organization of multinational enterprises', *Academy of Management Review*, 17: 729–757.

Suutari, V. (2003) 'Global managers: career orientation, career tracks, life-style implications, and career commitment', *Journal of Managerial Psychology*, 18 (3): 185–207.

Suutari, V. and Brewster, C. J. (1998) 'The adaptation of expatriates in Europe: evidence from Finnish companies', *Personnel Review*, 27 (2): 89–103.

Suutari, V. and Brewster, C. J. (2000) 'Making their own way: international experience through self-initiated foreign assignments', *Journal of World Business*, 35 (4): 417–436.

Suutari, V. and Brewster, C. J. (2003) 'Repatriation: empirical evidence from a longitudinal study of careers and expectations among Finnish expatriates', *International Journal of Human Resource Management*, 14 (7): 1132–1151.

Suutari, V. and Tornikoski, C. (2001) 'The challenge of expatriate compensation: the source of satisfaction and dissatisfaction among expatriates', *International Journal of Human Resource Management*, 12 (3): 1–16.

Swenson, P. (1989) *Fair Shares: Unions, pay and politics in Sweden and Germany*, London, Adamantine.

Szulanski, G. (1996) 'Exploring internal stickiness: impediments to the transfer of best practice within the firm', *Strategic Management Journal*, 17: 27–43.

Tahvanainen, M., Worm, V. and Welch, D. (2005) 'Implications of short-term international assignments', *European Management Journal*, 23 (6): 663–673.

Takeuchi, R., Tesluk, P. E., Yun, S. and Lepak, D. P. (2005) 'An integrative view of international experience', *Academy of Management Journal*, 48: 85–100.

Tallman, S. and Fladmoe-Lindquist, K. (2002) 'Internationalization, globalization and capability-based strategy', *California Management Review*, 45 (1): 116–135.

Tang, T. L. P., Tang, D. S. H., Tang, C. S. Y. and Dozier, T. S. (1998) 'CEO pay, pay differentials and pay-performance linkage', *Journal of Compensation and Benefits*, 14 (3): 41–46.

Tarique, I. and Schuler, R. (2010) 'Global talent management: literature review, integrative framework, and suggestions for further research', *Journal of World Business*, 45: 122–133.

Tata, J., Fu, P. P. and Wu, R. (2003) 'An examination of procedural justice principles in China and the US', *Asia-Pacific Journal of Management*, 20 (2): 205–215.

Tayeb, M. H. (1988) *Organizations and National Culture*. London, Sage Publications.

Tayeb, M. H. (1996) *The Management of a Multicultural Workforce*, Chichester, John Wiley & Sons.

Taylor, P., Mulvey, G. and Hyman, J. (2002) 'Work organization, control and the experience of work in call centres', *Work, Employment and Society*, 16 (1): 133–150.

Taylor, R. (2002) *The Future of Work-Life Balance*, Swindon, Economic and Social Research Council, p17.

Taylor, S. (2007) 'Creating social capital in MNCs: the international human resource management challenge', *Human Resource Management Journal*, 17: 336–354.

Taylor, S., Beechler, S. and Napier, N. (1996) 'Towards an integrative model of strategic international human resource management', *Academy of Management Review*, 21 (4): 959–965.

Tessaring, M. and Wannan, J. (2004) *Vocational Education and Training – Key to the Future*, Thessaloniki, Cedefop.

Tetlock, P. E. (2002) 'Social functionalist frameworks for judgement and choice: intuitive politicians, theologians, and prosecutors', *Psychological Review*, 109: 451–471.

Thelen, K. (2004) *How Institutions Evolve: The political economy of skills in Germany, Britain, the United States and Japan*, Cambridge, Cambridge University Press.

Thelen, K. (2007) 'Contemporary challenges to the German vocational training system', *Regulation and Governance*, 1: 247–260.

Thierry, H. (1998) 'Compensating work', in P. J. D. Drenth, H. Thierry and C. J. de Wolff (eds) *Handbook of Work and Organisational Psychology*, Volume 4: *Organisational Psychology*, Brighton, Psychology Press.

Thomas, D. C. (2006) 'Domain and development of cultural intelligence', *Group and Organization Management*, 31 (1): 78–99.

Thomas, D. C., Elron, E., Stahl, G., Ekelund, B., Ravlin, E., Cerdin, J.-L., Poelmans, S., Brislin, R., Pekerti, A., Aycan, Z., Maznevski, M., Au, K and Lazarova, M. B. (2008) 'Cultural intelligence: domain and assessment', *International Journal of Cross Cultural Management*, 8 (2): 123–143.

Thomson, A., Mabey, C., Storey, J., Gray, C. and Iles, P. (2001) *Changing Patterns of Management Development*, Oxford, Blackwell.

Thorn, W. (2009) 'International adult literacy and basic skills surveys in the OECD region', *OECD Education Working Papers*, No. 26, Paris, OECD Publishing.

Thornton, G. C. and Krause, D. E. (2009) 'Selection versus development assessment centers: an international survey of design, execution, and evaluation', *International Journal of Human Resource Management*, 20 (2): 478–498.

Thorpe, R and Holloway, J. (2008) *Performance Management: Multidisciplinary perspectives*, Basingstoke, Palgrave.

Tichy, N., Fombrun, C. J. and Devanna, M. A. (1982) 'Strategic human resource management', *Sloan Management Review*, 23 (2): 47–60.

Toh, S. M. and DeNisi, A. S. (2007) 'Host country nationals as socializing agents: a social identity approach', *Journal of Organizational Behavior*, 28: 281–301.

Torbiörn, I. (1997) 'Staffing for international operations', *Human Resource Management Journal*, 7 (3): 42–53.

Tornow, W. W. (1993) 'Perceptions or reality: is multi-perspective measurement a means or an end?', *Human Resource Management*, 32: 221–230.

Torrington, D. (1989) 'Human resource management and the personnel function', in J. Storey (ed.) *New Perspectives on Human Resource Management*, London, Routledge.

Tregaskis, O. (1997) 'The role of national context and HR strategy in shaping training and development in French and UK organizations', *Organization Studies*, 18 (5): 839.

Tregaskis, O. and Brewster, C. J. (2006) 'Converging or diverging? A comparative analysis of trends in contingent employment practice in Europe over a decade', *Journal of International Business Studies*, 37 (1): 111–126.

Tregaskis, O. and Heraty, N. (2011) 'Human resource development: national embeddedness', in C. J. Brewster and W. Mayrhofer (eds) *A Handbook oOf Comparative HRM*, Cheltenham, Edward Elgar.

Tregaskis, O., Atterbury, S. and Mahoney, C. (2003) 'International survey methodology: experiences from the Cranet network', in C. J. Brewster, W. Mayrhofer and M. Morley (eds) *European Human Resource Management: Evidence of convergence?*, London, Butterworth-Heinemann.

Tregaskis, O., Glover, L. and Ferner, A. (2005) *International HR Networks in Multinational Companies*, London, CIPD.

Tregaskis, O., Heraty, N. and Morley, M. (2001) 'HRD in multinationals: the global local mix', *Human Resource Management Journal*, 11 (2): 34–56.

Trends International (2001) 'Foreign investment: Belgium favourite', *Trends International*, Belgium, April, 3: 42.

Triandis, H. C. (1989) *Culture and Social Behavior*, New York, McGraw-Hill.

Triandis, H. C. (2006) 'Cultural intelligence in organizations', *Group and Organization Management*, 31 (1): 20–26.

Triandis, H. C. and Wasti, S. A. (2008) 'Culture', in D. L. Stone and E. F. Stone-Romero (eds) *The Influence of Culture on Human Resource Management Processes and Practices*, New York, Psychology Press, pp1–24.

Trompenaars, F. (1993) *Riding the Waves of Culture: Understanding cultural diversity in business*, London, Economist Books.

Trompenaars, F. and Hampden-Turner, C. (1997) *Riding the Waves of Culture: Understanding cultural diversity in business*, 2nd edition, London, Nicholas Brealey Publishing.

Tsai, W. (2000) 'Social capital, strategic relatedness and the formation of intra-organizational linkages', *Strategic Management Journal*, 21: 925–939.

Tsai, W. (2002) 'Social structure of "coopetition" within a multi-unit organization: coordination, competition, and intraorganizational knowledge sharing', *Organization Science*, 13: 179–190.

Tsai, W. and Ghoshal, S. (1998) 'Social capital and value creation: the role of intrafirm networks', *Academy of Management Journal*, 41: 464–476.

Tsang, E. W. K. (1994) 'Human resource management problems in Sino-Foreign joint ventures', *International Journal of Manpower*, 15 (9): 4–22.

Tsang, E. (2001) 'Managerial learning in foreign-invested enterprises of China', *Management International Review*, 41 (1): 29.

Tung, R. L. (1981) 'Selection and training of personnel for overseas assignments', *Columbia Journal of World Business*, 16 (1): 68–78.

Tung, R. L. (1982) 'Selection and training procedures of US, European and Japanese multinationals', *California Management Review*, 25 (1): 57–71.

Tung, R. L. (1984) 'Human resource planning in Japanese multinationals: a model for U.S firms?', *Journal of International Business Studies*, 15 (2): 139–149.

Tung, R. L. (1986) 'Corporate Executives. and their Families in China: The Need for Cross-Cultural Understanding in Business', *Columbia Journal of World Business,* Summer, 51–56.

Tung, R. L. (1988) *The New Expatriates: Managing Human Resources Abroad.* Cambridge, Mass.: Ballinger Publisher.

Tung, R. L. (1996) 'Corporate executives and their families in China: the need for cross-cultural understanding in business', *Columbia Journal of World Business*, 21 (1): 21–26.

Turner, T. and Morley, M. (1995) *Industrial Relations and the New Order: Case studies in conflict and co-operation*, Dublin, Oak Tree Press.

Tüselmann, H.-J. (1999) 'Standort Deutschland: German direct foreign investment – exodus of German industry and export of jobs', *Journal of World Business*, 33 (3): 295–313.

Tushman, M. L., and Scanlan, T. J. (2005). 'Boundary spanning individuals: their role in information transfer and their antecedents', *Academy of Management Journal*, 24 (2): 289–305.

Tushman, M. L. and Nadler, D. A. (1978) 'Information processing as an integrating concept in organizational design', *Academy of Management Review*, 3: 613–624.

Tyson, S. (1995) *Human Resource Strategy: Towards a general theory of human resource management*, London, Pitman.

UIS (2006) *Participation in Formal Technical and Vocational Education and Training Programmes Worldwide: An initial statistical study*, Bonn, UNESCO/UNEVOC International Centre for Technical and Vocational Education and Training.

Ulrich, D. (1987) 'Organisational capability as competitive advantage: human resource professionals as strategic partners', *Human Resource Planning*, 10: 169–184.

Ulrich, D. (1989) 'Tie the corporate knot: gaining complete customer commitment', *Sloan Management Review*, Summer: 19–28.

Ulrich, D. (1997) *Human Resource Champions: The next agenda for adding value to HR practices*, Boston, MA, Harvard Business School Press.

Ulrich, D. (2000) 'From eBusiness to eHR', *Human Resource Planning*, 20 (3): 12–21.

Ulrich, D. and Brockbank, W. (2005) 'Role call', *People Management*, 16 June: 24–28.

Ulrich, D. and Lake, D. (1990) *Organization Capability: Competing from the inside out*, New York, Wiley.

Ulrich, D., Brockbank, W., Johnson, D., Younger, J. and Sandholtz, K. (2008) *HR Competencies: Mastery at the intersection of people and business*, London, Society for Human Resource Management.

UNCTAD (2007) *The Universe of the Largest Transnational Corporations*, New York, United Nations.

UNIVERSUM (2011) 'China's ideal employers 2011', http://www.universumglobal.com/IDEAL-Employer-Rankings/The-National-Editions/China [accessed 17 May 2011].

US Department of Labor (1993) *High Performance Work Practices and Firm Performance*, Washington DC, US Government Printing Office.

Vaill, P. (1989) *Managing as a Performing Art: New ideas for a world of chaotic change*, San Francisco, Jossey-Bass.

Vaiman, V. and Holden, N. (2011) 'Talent management in Central and Eastern Europe', in H. Scullion and D. G. Collings (eds) *Global Talent Management*, London, Routledge, pp178–193.

Vallance S. (1995) 'Perfomance appraisal in Singapore, Thailand and the Philippines: a cultural perspective', *Australian Journal of Public Administration*, 58: 78–95.

Van de Vijver, F. J. R. (2002) 'Cross-cultural assessment: value for money?', *Applied Psychology: An International Review*, 51 (4): 545–566.

Van de Vijver, F. J. R. and Leung, K. (1997) *Methods and Data Collection for Cross-Cultural Research*, Newbury Park, CA, Sage.

Van de Vliert, E., Shi, K., Sanders, K., Wang, Y. and Huang, X. (2004) 'Chinese and Dutch interpretations of supervisory feedback', *Journal of Cross-Cultural Psychology*, 35 (4): 417–435.

van het Kaar, R. and Grünell, M. (2001) 'Variable pay in Europe', *European Industrial Relations Observatory*, April: www.eiro.eurofound.ie/2001/04/study/TN0104201S.html .

Van Vianen, A. E. M. (2000) 'Person-organization fit: The match between newcomers' and recruiters' perceptions for organizational cultures', *Personnel Psychology*, 53: 113–149.

Varma, A., Budhwar, P. S. and DeNisi, A. (eds) (2008) *Performance Management Systems: A global perspective*, Abingdon, Routledge.

Verma, A. and Zhiming, Y. (1995) 'The changing face of HRM in China: opportunities, problems, and strategies', in A. Verma, T. Kochan and R. Lansbury (eds) *Employment Relations in the Growing Asian Economies*, London, Routledge.

Vernon, G. (2003) 'Comparative occupational classifications, managerial hierarchies and work organisation', *Employee Relations*, 25 (4): 389–404.

Vernon, G. (2005) 'International pay and reward', in P. Edwards and C. Rees (eds) *International Human Resource Management*, London, FT/Prentice Hall.

Vernon, G. (2006a) 'Does density matter? The significance of comparative historical variation in unionisation', *European Journal of Industrial Relations*, 12 (2; March): 189–209.

Vernon, G. (2006b) 'The potential of management dominated work organisation: the critical case of Japan', *Economic and Industrial Democracy*, 27 (3): 399–424.

Vernon, G. (2010) 'International pay and reward', in P. Edwards and C. Rees (eds) *International Human Resource Management*, 2nd edition, London, FT/Prentice Hall.

Vernon, G. (2011) 'Still accounting for difference?', *Economic and Industrial Democracy*, in press.

Vernon, G. and Brewster, C. J. (2009) 'Collective employee voice and the strategic integration of HR: international evidence', www.buseco.monash.edu.au/mgt/research/.../brewster-seminar-paper.pdf.

Vernon, G. and Rogers, M. (2009) 'Union organization and productivity growth', IREU, Athens.

Vernon, G. and Rogers, M. (2009) 'Where do unions add value? Union structure, collective bargaining and manufacturing productivity growth in the OECD, Mimeo, http://users.ox.ac.uk/~manc0346/ Unions and productivityVernon Rogers2009.pdf

Vernon, G., Andersson, R., Baeten, X. and Neu, E. (2007) 'Unions, employers' associations and the joint regulation of reward in Europe', in C. Antoni, X. Baeten, B. Emans and M. Kira (eds) *Shaping Pay in Europe: A stakeholder approach*, Brussels, Peter Lang (for Uppsala University).

Vinnicombe, S. (1987) 'What exactly are the differences in male and female working styles?', *Women in Management Review*, 3 (1): 13–22.

Visser, J. and Hemerijck, A. (1997) *A Dutch Miracle*, Amsterdam, Amsterdam University Press.

von Glinow, M. A., Drost, E. and Teagarden, M. (2002) 'Convergence of IHRM practices: lessons learned from a globally distributed consortium of theory and practice', *Human Resource Management*, 41: 123–141.

Vroom, V. J. (1964) *Work and Motivation*, New York, John Wiley & Sons.

Wachter, H. and Stangelhofer, K. (1995) 'Germany', in I. Brunstein (ed.) *Human Resource Management in Western Europe*, Berlin, Walter De Gruyter.

Wadhwa, V. (2008) 'A disciple becomes the guru: should United States learn from India?', *Harvard International Review*, 30 (3): 72–75.

Waechter, H. and Muller-Camen, M. (2002) 'Co-determination and strategic integration in German firms', *Human Resource Management Journal*, 12 (3): 76–87.

Wall, D. and Wood, S. (2003) *The Romance of HRM and Business Performance, and the Case for Big Science*, Mimeo, Institute of Work Psychology, University of Sheffield.

Ward, C. and Kennedy, A. (1999) 'The measurement of sociocultural adaptation', *International Journal of Intercultural Relations*, 23: 659–677.

Ward, C., Okura, Y., Kennedy, A. and Kojima, T. (1998) 'The U-curve on trial: a longitudinal study of psychological and sociocultural adjustment during cross-cultural transition', *International Journal of Intercultural Relations*, 11 (22): 277–291.

Ward, K. (2004) 'Going global? Internationalization and diversification in the temporary staffing industry', *Journal of Economic Geography*, 4: 251–273.

Warner, M. (1994) 'Japanese culture, Western management', *Organization Studies*, 15 (July): 509–533.

Warner, M. (1996) 'The long march of Chinese management education', *Chinese Quarterly*, 106: 326–342.

Waxin M. F. and Panaccio A. J. (2005) 'Cross-cultural training to facilitate expatriate adjustment: it works!', *Personnel Review*, 34, (1): 51–67.

Wederspahn, G. M. (2000) *Intercultural Services: A worldwide buyer's guide and sourcebook*, Houston, Gulf Publishing Company.

Weerawardena, J., Mort, G. S., Liesch, P. W. and Knight G. (2007) 'Conceptualizing accelerated internationalization in the born global firm: a dynamic capabilities perspective', *Journal of World Business*, 42 (3): 294–306.

Weick, K. E. (1989) 'Theorizing about organizational communication', in F. Jablin, L. Putnam and K. Roberts (eds) *Handbook of Organisational Communication: An interdisciplinary perspective*, Newbury Park, CA., Sage, pp97–122.

Weiss, D. (1988) *La Fonction Ressources Humaines*, Paris, Editions d'Organisation.

Welch, D. and Worm, V. (2006) 'International business travellers: a challenge for IHRM', in G. Stahl and I. Björkman (eds) *Handbook of Research in International HRM*, Cheltenham, UK, Edward Elgar, pp283–301.

Werner, S. (2002). Recent developments in international management research: a review of 20 top management journals, *Journal of Management* 28 (3): 277–305.

Werner, S. (2007) *Managing Human Resources in North America*, London, Routledge.

Wernerfelt, B. (1984) 'A resource-based view of the firm', *Strategic Management Journal*, 5 (2): 171–180.

Westney, D. E. (1993) 'Institutional theory and the multinational corporation', in S. Ghoshal and D.

E. Westney (eds) *Organization Theory and the Multinational Corporation*, New York, St. Martin's Press.

Westwood, R. I. and Leung, S. M. (1994) 'The female expatriate manager experience: coping with gender and culture', *International Studies of Management and Organization*, 24: 64–85.

White, G., Luk, V., Druker, J. and Chiu, R. (1996) 'Paying their way: a comparison of managerial reward systems in London and Hong Kong banking industries', *Asia-Pacific Journal of Human Resources*, 36 (1): 54–71.

Whitener, E. M. (2001) 'Do high commitment human resource practices affect employee commitment?', *Journal of Management*, 27: 515–535.

Whitley, R. D. (1992) (ed.) *European Business Systems: Firms and markets in their national contexts*, London, Sage Publications.

Whitley, R. D. (1999) *Divergent Capitalisms: The social structuring and change of business systems*, Oxford,: Oxford University Press.

Wibbeke, E. S. (2009) *Global Business Leadership*, Oxford, Elsevier.

Wilkins, S. (2001) 'International briefing 9: Training and development in the United Arab Emirates', *International Journal of Human Resource Management*, 5 (2): 153–165.

Williams, R. (2002) *Managing Employee Performance: Design and implementation in organizations*, Thomson, London.

Williamson, O. E., Wachter, M. L. and Harris, J. E. (1975) 'Understanding the employment relation: the analysis of idiosyncratic exchange', *Bell Journal of Economics*, 6: 250–277.

Willman, P. A. and Bryson, R. G. (2003) *Why Do Voice Regimes Differ?* Mimeo.

Winch, G. M., Clifton, N. and Millar, C. (2000) 'Organization and management in an Anglo-French consortium: the case of the Transmanche-link', *Journal of Management Studies*, 37 (5): 663–685.

Wong, C.-S., Wong, Y.-T., Hui, C. and Law, K. S. (2001) 'The significant role of Chinese employees' organizational commitment: implications for managing employees in Chinese societies', *Journal of World Business*, 36 (3): 326–340.

Wood, G., and Frynas, G. (2006) 'The institutional basis of economic failure: anatomy of the segmented business system', *Socio-Economic Review*, 4 (2): 239–277.

Wood, G., Psychogios, A., Szamosi, L. T. and Collings, D. G (2011) 'Institutional perspectives on comparative HRM', in C. J. Brewster and W. Mayrhofer (eds) *A Handbook of Comparative HRM*, Edward Elgar, Cheltenham (in press).

Wood, G. T. and Brewster, C. J. (eds) (2007) *Industrial Relations in Africa*, Basingstoke, Palgrave.

Wood, G. T., Croucher, C., Brewster, C. J., Collings, G. C. and Brooks, M. (2009) 'Varieties of firm: complementarity and bounded diversity', *Journal of Economic Issues*, 43 (1): 241–260.

Wood, S. (1999) 'Family-friendly management: testing the various perspectives', *National Institute for Economic Research*, Number 168, 2 April: 99–116.

Woodall, J. (2005) 'International management development', in T. Edwards and C. Rees (eds) *International Human Resource Management: Globalization, national systems and multinational companies*, Harlow, FT/Prentice Hall.

Woodall, J. and Winstanley, D. (2000) 'Winning hearts and minds: ethical issues in human resource development', in D. Winstanley and J. Woodall (eds) *Ethical Issues in Contemporary Human Resource Management*, Basingstoke, Macmillan.

Woodhams, C, Xian, H. and Lupton, B. (2009) 'Furthering equal opportunity in China: sex discrimination and gender segregation in Chinese labour markets', *International Journal of Human Resource Management*, 20 (10): 2084–2019.

Work USA (2004) *Work USA*, New York, Towers Watson.

Workforce Management (2008) 'Tiered mentoring at Infosys', *Workforce Management Online*, June: http://www.workforce.com/section/11/feature/25/59/06/255910.html [accessed 11 January 2011].

Worm, V. (2001) 'HRD for localisation: European MNCs in China', in J. B. Kidd and F.-J. Richter (eds) *Advances in HRM in Asia*, Basingstoke, Palgrave.

Wright, P. M. and McMahan, G. C. (1992) 'Theoretical perspectives for strategic human resource management', *Journal of Management*, 18 (2): 295–320.

Wright, P. M. and Nishii, L. H. (2011) 'Strategic HRM and organizational behavior: integrating multiple levels of analysis', in D. E. Guest, J. Paauwe and P. M. Wright (eds) *Human Resource Management and Performance: Progress and prospects*, Oxford, UK, Blackwell Publishing.

Wright, P. M. and Snell, S. A. (1991) 'Toward an integrative view of strategic human resource management', *Human Resource Management Review*, 1: 203–225.

Wright, P. M., Dunford, B. B. and Snell, S. A. (2001) 'Human resources and the resource-based view of the firm', *Journal of Management*, 27: 701–721.

Wright, P. M., McMahan, G. C. and McWilliams, A. (1994) 'Human resources as a source of sustained competitive advantage: a resource-based perspective', *International Journal of Human Resource Management*, 5: 301–326.

Yamazaki, Y. and Kayes, C. (2004) 'An experiential approach to cross-cultural learning: A review and integration of competencies for successful expatriate adaptation', *Academy of Management Learning and Education*, 5 (4): 362–379.

Yi Lu, Tao, Z. and Wang, Y. (2009) *Union Effects on Performance and Employment Relations: Evidence from China*, Mimeo, August.

Yip, G. S. (1992) *Total Global Strategy*, Englewood Cliffs, NJ, Prentice-Hall.

Zander, U. and Kogut. B (1995) 'Knowledge and the speed of the transfer and imitation of organisational capabilities: an empirical test', *Organizational Science*, 6 (1): 76–92.

Zanko, M. (ed.) (2002) *The Handbook of HRM Policies and Practices in Asia-Pacific Economies*, Cheltenham, Edward Elgar.

Zeira, Y. and Banai, M. (1984) 'Selection of expatriate managers in MNEs: the lost environment point of view', *International Studies of Management and Organisation*, 15 (1): 33–51.

Zeira, Y. and Banai, M. (1985) 'Present and desired methods of selecting expatriate managers for international assignments', *Personnel Review*, 13 (3): 29–35.

Zhang, M., Edwards, T. and Edwards, C. (2005) 'Internationalisation and developing countries: the case of China', in T. Edwards and C. Rees (eds) *International Human Resource Management: Globalization, national systems and multinational companies*, Harlow, FT/Prentice Hall.

Zimmermann, A. and Sparrow, P. R. (2008) 'Mutual adjustment processes in international teams: lessons for the study of expatriation', *International Studies of Management and Organization*, 37 (3): 65–88.

Zwick, T. (2004) 'Employee participation and productivity', *Labour Economics*, 11 (6): 715–740.

Index

University of
South Wales
Prifysgol
De Cymru

Library Services